Second Edition

American
Social Welfare
Policy

A Pluralist Approach

Howard Jacob Karger
Louisiana State University

David Stoesz
San Diego State University

Longman

American Social Welfare Policy: A Pluralist Approach, Second Edition

Copyright © 1994, 1990, by Longman Publishing Group.
All right reserved.
No part of this publication may be reproduced,
stored in a retrieval system, or transmitted
in any form or by any means, electronic, mechanical,
photocopying, recording, or otherwise,
without the prior permission of the publisher.

Longman, 10 Bank Street, White Plains, N.Y. 10606

Associated companies:
Longman Group Ltd., London
Longman Cheshire Pty., Melbourne
Longman Paul Pty., Auckland
Copp Clark Pitman, Toronto

Senior acquisitions editor: David M. Shapiro
Development editor: Susan Alkana
Production editor: Linda W. Witzling
Cover design and illustration: Susan J. Moore
Text art: Fine Line, Inc.
Production supervisor: Richard Bretan

Library of Congress Cataloging-in-Publication Data

Karger, Howard Jacob
    American social welfare policy : a pluralist approach / Howard
Jacob Karger and David Stoesz.—2nd ed.
       p.   cm.
   Includes index.
   ISBN 0-8013-1170-5
   1. Public welfare—United States. 2. United States—Social
policy. 3. Welfare state. I. Stoesz, David. II. Title.
HV95.K354   1993
361.973—dc20   93-2172
                                     CIP

6 7 8 9 10-MA-9796

Contents

CHAPTER 11   THE AMERICAN HEALTH CARE SYSTEM   279

CHAPTER 12   MENTAL HEALTH AND SUBSTANCE ABUSE POLICY   313

Preface

In starting to think about the second edition of *American Social Welfare Policy*, we were initially struck by how little had changed on the domestic front since we began the first edition in 1987. President Bush had continued the policies of Ronald Reagan, albeit with less flair and theatricality. A domestic agenda was conspicuous only by its absence. As a result, the tear in the nation's social fabric began to resemble a shredded rag. Race relations deteriorated as, in 1992, Los Angeles burned for the first time in 25 years. The fire was beginning to spread to other cities, and it was only by quick and brutal force that the storm of rage was finally subdued. In its wake lay more than 50 dead. Through a combination of neglect and recession, poverty grew to its highest level since the mid-1960s. Homelessness, its corollary, also grew rapidly even though experts still can't agree on how many individuals and families are actually without homes. On the other hand, in 1992, a Democrat was elected president of the United States for the first time in 12 years. Moreover, new and exciting ideas about Individual Development Accounts, National Service programs, and welfare reform crept into the social agenda. On reflection, we realized that things had in fact changed in the five years since we began the first edition of the book.

In the American welfare state, a wide gulf separates social welfare policy from social work practice. It is common for students entering the human service professions to focus on intervention with clients around discrete problems, or "direct" practice. Occasionally, students understand that their professional careers will lead to responsibilities of an administrative nature, but rarely do they express and interest in social policy. Over the years welfare institutions have come to reflect these preferences. The result is not without considerable cost to welfare professionals, who find themselves having to work by—and frequently around—social policies that have little consonance with the needs of the practitioner or client.

When institutional practices are so out of line with human requirements, momentum builds to change social programs. This seems to have taken two forms in relation to social welfare in the United States. On the one hand, many human service professionals have left the traditional settings of welfare practice—the voluntary and governmental sectors—in favor of new settings—the corporate sector and private practice. On the other hand, pressure to reform government welfare programs has grown, as evidenced by the increasing number of "welfare reform" proposals introduced in Congress.

These proposals are of particular interest because much of the welfare reform legislation penalizes disenfranchised populations—women, racial minorities, the aged, children, the handicapped—who have been a traditional concern of welfare professionals. As a result, much of what we understand to be social welfare in America is in flux, yet welfare professionals are exerting little influence in redefining this important social institution.

The failure of welfare professionals to act effectively in the area of social welfare policy is troubling. It is difficult to imagine changes in health policy or legal policy that did not involve the collaboration of physicians or attorneys. Yet social workers have not played a prominent role in welfare policy for some time. Such was not always the case. Mary Richmond proved instrumental in the Charity Organization Society* movement, Jane Addams became a heroine through her work in the settlement movement, and Harry Hopkins championed programs pioneered by the New Deal. More recently, Wilbur Cohen engineered important parts of the programs that comprised the War on Poverty. But few social workers of national prominence have emerged since the Great Society programs of the 1960s.

*(COS)

Fortunately, this omission is being addressed, albeit in somewhat haphazard fashion. The National Association of Social Workers (NASW) has mobilized a political action committee and has recently established a policy institute to press for social welfare policies congruent with NASW priorities. In 1984, Barbara Mikulski, a social worker from Maryland, was elected to the United States Senate, joining Ron Dellums, a representative from California, and "Ed" Towns, a representative from New York, as the only congresspersons who are social workers. It remains to be seen whether the large mass of welfare professionals will become accustomed to thinking about social welfare policy. We hope so. This book reflects our belief that social welfare policy has an immediate and profound effect on the work of welfare professionals, and our conviction is that welfare programs could be made more humane and better respond to the needs of the people they serve if these professionals were more actively engaged in setting social policy.

In trying to bridge this gap, we have adopted a "pluralist approach" to social welfare policy. In doing so, we have organized the book around the primary sectors that have evolved in American social welfare: the voluntary sector, the governmental sector, and, more recently, both the corporate sector and private practice. These sectors have addressed the problems that presented themselves at different periods in our national life. Today, these sectors of American social welfare coexist, reflecting a diversity that is as characteristic of American pluralism as they are sometimes maddening to the student of welfare policy analysis.

The rationale for our approach is straightforward. First, social welfare encompasses, in the American experience, a complicated arrangement of policies and programs. A pluralist approach helps sort out the major institutional actors and introduces a measure of order to what might otherwise appear institutional anarchy. Second, many welfare professionals (and, for that matter, nonprofessionals) begin their careers in agencies of the voluntary sector. Unfortunately, these agencies are not always given the credit they deserve. In our judgment, the voluntary sector is an integral component of social welfare in the United States, even if it relates to policy with a small *p*. Our emphasis on the voluntary sector is based on the belief that as public policy shifts, more of the welfare burden will be transferred from the government to the private sector. Third, a proprietary, corporate sector has rapidly emerged during the last two decades, providing a substantial volume of services and a corresponding number of employment opportunities for human service professionals. Failure to recognize the importance of this sector is tantamount to ignoring what is probably the most important development in social welfare since the War on Poverty, and possibly even since the New Deal. Finally, many social workers have found private practice, independent of the organizational restraints associated with the voluntary, governmental, and corporate sectors, an attractive method of service delivery. The popularity of private practice among human service professionals justifies its inclusion in any discussion of social welfare policy. Through an examination of these sectors we hope to acquaint students with the central structures and processes now shaping American social welfare.

Throughout this book we have attempted to use the most current data and statistics available. Where possible, we have used statistics from 1991 and later. However, the ambivalence with which federal agencies under the Reagan and Bush administrations collected data together with the budgetary punishment meted out over the last decade to federal data-gathering agencies have taken their toll. In some cases, the newest data available dated from 1989. In other cases, the most reliable data we could find came from the studies done in the early and middle 1980s.

In order to facilitate the comprehension of material, we have used Part One to focus on the basic concepts underlying social policy analysis. This segment also includes a historical survey of social welfare in the United States and a discussion of the values, social forces, and theoretical assumptions that affect the creation, operation, and implementation of social policies. In much of this we have borrowed heavily from economics as well as from political and social theory. Because of the disparity between the intentions of policymakers and the program realities facing welfare professionals, we have examined in a critical manner the legislative, judicial, and administrative processes that influence the design and implementation of social welfare policy. A special focus is placed on the interactional effects of social policies and programs on such vulnerable groups as the aged, minorities, women, homosexuals, and the poor, as well as on children and families. This segment

of the book also provides students with a framework for understanding the complex nature of American social welfare. Throughout the book, essential social policy terms are referenced to a glossary located at the end of the book. With the basic conceptual tools at hand, students will find the descriptive material of Parts Two and Three, dealing with voluntary, governmental, corporate, and private practice, less overwhelming. Familiarity with these analytic concepts will also help students to better understand the preliminary welfare reform proposals we make in Chapter 18. Lastly, in this edition we have included a chapter on the American welfare state in international perspective. Written by James Midgley, a well-known authority in the field of international social policy and the dean of Louisiana State University's School of Social Work, this chapter was added in the recognition that the American welfare state exists within a continuum of other welfare states. Moreover, this chapter is a tacit acknowledgment that we can learn from the experiences, successes, and mistakes of other nations. We wish to thank Dean Midgley for taking his valuable time to write a chapter for this book.

Because of our emphasis on institutional transformation, we have included developments that we believe are likely to become more prominent in the future, among them privatization, the role of the global economy in the welfare state, unionization in social work, and the restructuring of American welfare. By including such developments we of course risk being out of date because current policies and events can change swiftly. Should this occur, we beg the reader's forgiveness. Such is the price of aiming for relevance.

We have also tried to balance theory with program detail. However, we have omitted some of the details of program specifications that appear in other treatments of welfare policy. In doing so, we are less concerned with program detail—which practitioners become acquainted with during their first day on the job—than we are with defining the themes around which welfare policy is constructed. Given political developments since the mid-1970s, we believe that this corrects an error on the part of many liberal analysts. Specifically, while preoccupied with program intricacies, many welfare professionals have found, much to their chagrin, that ideologies of the political right have in the past commanded public attention, attained high public office, and then used that power effectively to alter the rules of the game, in the process executing punishing cuts in social programs. If welfare professionals are to redirect social welfare policy to liberal goals, they will have temporarily to abandon questions of program "puzzle solving" and return to defining the paradigm of social programs.[1] In other words, social workers need to play more than the notes—they also need to play the music.

Social work students often ask why they are required to study social policy. Many have entered social work to help people and thus they believe their sole concern is with the provision of direct services. As experienced social workers, we recognize the distance between social welfare policy and direct practice, and we have come to appreciate the difficulties that clients and practitioners often encounter because of social welfare policy. Accordingly, we insist that direct service is inextricably linked to policy. Clients exist in a given society and are continually influenced by the larger social forces affecting that society. The more disenfranchised the clients, the more exposed they are to the maelstrom of social forces swirling about them. Social workers help clients not only by working with them individually but by protecting the collective interests of vulnerable populations— children, the aged, racial and ethnic minorities, the handicapped, and the poor, among others. There are many ways of helping, and social workers must try to learn them all.

One of the major goals we had in writing this book was to encourage students to think critically about social policy. We hope that students and instructors will critique and even argue about the ideas they find here. For us, that is part of the joy of policy analysis. Unfortunately, the student of policy analysis will soon find that few things are carved in stone and that there are many gray areas. Although sometimes frustrating, these gray areas can provide an exciting challenge. Because social policy is not rigid in its methods, it demands creative ideas and solutions. The very openness of policy requires that each student come up with his or her own answers for the major social policy questions of our times.

American Social Welfare Policy is the product of two authors, both of the same mind. Over the years we have collaborated on so many assignments that it is sometimes unclear who originated what. The interaction that has led us this far is what scholarship is all about, and we have found it immensely gratifying. There is a strange convention in publishing about junior and senior authors. In this regard, we note that the listing of the authors on the title page and cover is alphabetical. Both authors contributed equally, and neither was more senior than the other in the preparation of this book.

We offer special thanks to Steve McMurty and Thomas Watts for their thorough and systematic critique of the original manuscript of the first edition. Thanks also to Larry Litterst, a good friend and a fine economist. His thorough critique of economic principles helped strengthen the book, especially in areas where his advice was heeded. Our deep appreciation goes to Stephen J. Boland, computer wizard, Paul Michaelewicz, data cruncher, Debbie Dycaico, "sleuth" reader, and Lucinda Roginske and Suzanne Cooper, table and glossary compilers, for their assistance in assembling technical materials. We also extend our appreciation to Michael Kelly for his generosity in sharing high tech equipment and to Karen Stout, Mary Ann Reitmeir, Joanne Mermelstein, Paul Sundet, and Roland Meinert, as well as other people too numerous to mention. To our associates at policyAmerica, a nonprofit research group established in 1985 to develop innovations in social welfare policy, we owe a special thanks. This band of intellectual guerrillas not only critiqued parts of the first edition but also convinced us that thinking about social welfare policy and dancing to zydeco music were not mutually exclusive.

We also extend our deep-felt appreciation to our colleagues at Longman. As former senior editor, David Estrin showed his confidence in us by accepting the idea for this book on principle and without formalities. The manner in which he directed this publication was a model for editorial coordination. Victoria Mifsud, former editorial assistant, helped keep the book on track by efficiently handling our requests and the details involved in the preparation of the manuscript.

For the second edition we owe special thanks to David Shapiro, senior editor; Susan Alkana, development editor; Owen Lancer, editorial assistant; and Linda Witzling, production editor, for putting this book on the fast track to and through production. Their shepherding of the second edition allowed us to be more contemporary and more relevant than is usually possible in a textbook. We also owe thanks to the reviewers who helped us to fashion a better book through their ideas and suggestions. These reviewers include:

Patrick Leung, University of Houston
Thomas D. Watts, University of Texas at Arlington

Matthew J. Tuohey, Azusa Pacific University
Catherine Havens, University of Connecticut
Sharon M. Keigher, University of Wisconsin-Milwaukee
Nancy Gewirtz, Rhode Island College
Douglas K. Chung, Grand Valley State College
Jean Howard, Illinois State University
Doman Lum, California State University-Sacramento
Barbara Kail, University of Texas at Arlington

A warm thanks goes to Suzanne Tidwell for help in library research. The students who sat through our policy classes also deserve special credit for their patience, insight, and ideas.

H.J.K.

A special debt is owned to Connie for doing more than her share of everyday work and for her patience in putting up with me. An apology goes to Aaron and Shaulie for having to put up with a moody and often distracted daddy. Shaulie, "I am finally finished with the chapter."

NOTE

1. See Thomas Kuhn, *The Structure of Scientific Revolutions* (Chicago: University of Chicago Press, 1956).

PART ONE

American Social Welfare Policy

CHAPTER 1

Social Policy and the American Welfare State

This chapter will provide an overview of the American welfare state. In particular, it will examine various definitions of social welfare policy, the relationship between social policy and social problems, and the value system that drives American social welfare. In addition, this chapter will examine the effects of ideology on the U.S. welfare state, including the important role of neoconservatism and neoliberalism in shaping welfare policy. As part of examining the influence of ideology on social welfare, the chapter will explore the political economy of American welfare, including the role played by various economic schools of thought such as the Keynesians, supply-side theorists, and socialists. It will then examine the place of pluralism in American social welfare policy, including the influence of established interests in shaping welfare policy. Lastly, this chapter will explore the relationship between social work, politics, and advocacy organizations.

American social welfare is in transition. Since the Social Security Act of 1935, advocates of the unfortunate have held that federal social programs were the best way to help the disadvantaged. Now, after a half-century of experimentation with the "welfare state," a discernible shift has occurred. The conservatism of American culture—so evident in the Reagan

and Bush presidencies—has left private institutions to shoulder more of the welfare burden. Meanwhile, during the same period, many social programs were reduced or eliminated as federal and state governments struggled to prop up shaky budgets. For proponents of social justice, the suggestion that the private sector should assume more responsibility for welfare represents a retreat from hard-won governmental social legislation that for many years has provided essential benefits to millions of Americans—children, the aged, racial minorities, veterans, farmers, the poor, women, certain ethnic groups, and the handicapped. Justifiably, these groups fear the loss of basic goods and services during the transition in American social welfare. While a Clinton presidency may reassure those who have borne the brunt of budget cuts, it remains to be seen whether sufficient resources will be available to restore the American welfare state to its pre-1980s vitality. Pundits who followed the 1992 presidential campaign noted Clinton's clear rejection of the liberal preference for federal intervention in social problems in favor of a "third way," distinct from both liberalism and conservatism. The new Democratic administration thus adds more momentum to the transition away from federal hegemony in welfare policy in favor of a respect for the many institutions necessary to address the nation's social problems.

Thus, pluralism is an essential feature of American social welfare. As is true of other institutions, such as education, private institutions in social welfare exist alongside those of the public sector. American social welfare has a noble tradition of voluntary groups of citizens taking the initiative to solve local problems. Today, private voluntary groups are providing important services to patients with Acquired Immune Deficiency Syndrome (AIDS), the homeless, and refugees. Although voluntary activities represent the historical contribution by the private sector to American social welfare, a more recent development within the private sector raises fundamental questions for the future provision of human services. Social welfare has become big business. During the last 25 years the number of human service corporations—for-profit firms providing social welfare through the marketplace—has increased dramatically. Human service corporations are prominent in long-term nursing care, health maintenance, child day care, psychiatric and substance abuse services, even corrections. For many welfare professionals, this proprietary provision of human services is troubling because it occurs at a time when government has reduced its commitment to social programs. Yet human service corporations are likely to be prominent players in the shaping of the nation's social welfare policies. So long as American culture is open, democratic, and capitalistic, groups will be free to establish social welfare services in the private sector, both as nonprofit agencies and as for-profit corporations.

The pluralism of American social welfare, in which the voluntary, governmental, and corporate sectors coexist, poses important questions for social welfare policy. To what extent can voluntary groups assume responsibility for public welfare when their fiscal resources are limited? For which groups, if any, should government divest itself of responsibility? Can human service corporations be induced to care for poor and multiproblem clients while continuing to generate profits? Equally important, how can welfare professionals shape coherent social welfare policies given the fragmentation that is inherent in such pluralism? Clearly, the answers to these questions have much to say about how social welfare programs are perceived by human service professionals, their clients, and the taxpayers who continue to subsidize social programs.

The multitude of questions posed by the transition of American social welfare is in itself daunting. Indeed, the interaction of ideological, political, social, and economic factors has exacerbated the problem to the extent that the idea of "the welfare mess" has become a fixture in contemporary folklore. Yet past advocates of social justice such as Jane Addams, Whitney Young, Jr., and Wilbur Cohen, to name just a few, interpreted the inadequacy of social provision and the confusion of their times as an opportunity to further social justice. It remains for another generation of welfare professionals to demonstrate the same imagination, perseverance, and courage to advance social welfare in the years ahead. Those accepting this challenge will need to be familiar with the various meanings of social welfare policy, differing political and economic explanations for social welfare, and the various interest groups that have emerged within American social welfare.

DEFINITIONS OF SOCIAL WELFARE POLICY

Social welfare policy is a subset of social policy, which may be defined as the formal and consistent ordering of human affairs. Beyond this, social welfare policy is influenced to a large extent by the context in which benefits are provided to people. For example, social welfare policy is often associated with governmental programs that are mandated by legislation, as in the case of Aid to Families with Dependent Children

(AFDC). In the instance of AFDC, social welfare policy consists of the rules by which the state apportions benefits to an economically disadvantaged population by taxing citizens who are better off. Benefits provided through governmental social welfare policy are generally of two types: cash benefits and in-kind benefits. Cash benefits are further divided into social insurance and public assistance grants.

In-kind benefits (meaning benefits that are provided instead of cash) include a variety of social services (family, mental health, and child welfare) and vouchers (such as Food Stamps and Medicaid). While this classification of social welfare policy is complicated, it reflects a common theme, the redistribution of resources from those who are well off to those who are comparatively disadvantaged. This redistributional aspect of social welfare policy is typical of those who view social welfare as a function of the state. Richard Titmuss, for example, has defined social services as "a series of collective interventions that contribute to the general welfare by assigning claims from one set of people who are said to produce or earn the national income to another set of people who may merit compassion and charity."[1] This form of governmental social welfare policy is often referred to as "public" policy because it is the result of decisions reached through a process that involves a legislature which is representative of the entire population.

But social welfare is also provided by entities that are nongovernmental, in which case social welfare policy is not a manifestation of public policy but, rather, of "private" policy. For example, a nonprofit agency that has only limited resources but is beset by an increased demand for its services may establish a waiting list as agency policy. As other agencies in similar circumstances adopt the same strategy for rationing services, clients begin to pile up on waiting lists. Eventually, some clients are denied services because private agencies have established these waiting lists. In this case, the policies of independent private agencies have a significant effect on the welfare of clients. Or consider the practice of "dumping," a policy of private health care providers by which uninsured patients are abruptly transferred to public hospitals even though they are suffering from traumatic injuries. In some instances, patients have died as a result of a policy that is essentially a private social welfare policy.

Because American social welfare has been shaped to a great extent by policies of the government and nonprofit agencies, a good deal of confusion has arisen with the emergence of for-profit firms that provide human services. Traditionally, the distinction between the "public" and "private" sectors was marked by the boundary between governmental and nonprofit agencies. However, for-profit firms are also "private" in that they are nongovernmental entities; but they differ from the traditional private voluntary agencies, which are run on a not-for-profit basis. Consequently, it is important to distinguish within private social welfare between policies of for-profit organizations and policies of nonprofit organizations. A logical way to redraw the social welfare map is to adopt the following usage: Governmental social welfare policy refers to decisions established by the state; voluntary social welfare policy refers to decisions reached by nonprofit agencies; and corporate social welfare policy refers to decisions by for-profit firms. Whether it is the product of governmental, voluntary, or corporate institutions, welfare policy is concerned with allocating goods, services, and opportunities in order to enhance social functioning. Thus, in actual application, social welfare policy usually regulates the provision of benefits to people for the purpose of meeting basic life needs, such as employment, income, food, housing, health care, and relationships.[2]

A final point of clarification is necessary to describe the context of social welfare policy. With the change in name from the federal Department of Health, Education and Welfare to the Department of Health and Human Services, the term "*human services*" has become prevalent. For all practical purposes, human services refer to welfare programs administered by the federal government and by nonprofit and for-profit agencies, so that the terms are interchangeable. Because of the stigma associated with the word "*welfare*," some analysts prefer the term *human services* to describe social welfare. For those concerned about guilt by association, *human services* provides some distance from the negative connotations of *welfare*.

SOCIAL PROBLEMS AND SOCIAL WELFARE POLICY

Social problems often provide the rationale for social welfare policy. The massive social and economic dislocation caused by the Great Depression provided the justification for the first generation of federal welfare legislation. As part of the New Deal, the Social Security Act of 1935 addressed the problems of a family's loss of income due to retirement, unemployment, disability, and widowhood. The second generation of federal welfare legislation was passed during the period of the Civil Rights movement. The War on Poverty, usually marked by the enactment of the Economic Opportunity Act of 1964, addressed problems of poverty and discrimination through a wide range of programs. The 1970s and 1980s saw no new welfare initiatives on the scale of the New Deal or the War on Poverty, but social problems continued to serve as the justification for social welfare programs. Problems of child abuse, substance abuse, AIDS, and welfare dependency led to comparatively limited social welfare policies to remedy these problems. Probably the greatest single challenge facing Bill Clinton will be mobilizing the nation's resources to mount an effective domestic policy response to ever increasing social problems.

The relationship between social problems and social welfare policy is not simple, however. Not all social problems generate social welfare policies. Millions of undocumented workers and their families are in need of social welfare services, yet the United States has no coherent policy for addressing their needs. While many European countries have "guest worker" policies, the closest the United States has come to recognizing the needs of foreign workers is the Immigration Reform and Control Act of 1986, which established strict requirements for obtaining legal residence status—a provision that covered only a minority of alien workers and that expired by 1988.

In other instances, social welfare policies exist but are funded at such inadequate levels that they are ineffectual. The Child Abuse Prevention and Treatment Act of 1974, for example, introduced standards that should have contended with the problem of child abuse, yet underbudgeting left Child Protective Service (CPS) workers in a catch-22 situation. The act required that CPS workers investigate complaints of child abuse shortly after receiving them, yet agencies had inadequate staff resources to deal with the skyrocketing number of complaints. Caught in a resources crunch, CPS workers were unable to properly investigate allegations of abuse, and thus many children were seriously injured or died as a result of abusive adults. Eventually, the Supreme Court agreed to determine whether governments were liable for the poor performance of CPS workers in cases where abused children received injuries after being placed under the care of child welfare personnel. As this example might suggest, social welfare policies sometimes aggravate social problems. For decades, states authorized mental hospitals to warehouse the mentally disturbed, a practice that further handicapped mental patients. To replace state mental hospitals, the federal Community Mental Health Centers (CMHC) Act of 1963 authorized the creation of community-based facilities. This reform proved short-lived and was subverted by a lack of support for CMHCs. Now, with a substantial number of the homeless having been hospitalized for mental illness in the past, the

CMHC Act is associated with a worsening of care for the seriously mentally ill. Thus, what was once seen as mental health care reform seems actually to have exacerbated a social problem.

As the relationship between social problems and social welfare policy suggests, social welfare is not merely an expression of social altruism; it contributes to the maintenance, indeed the survival, of society. In this respect, social welfare policy can be instrumental in helping to hold together a society that tends to fracture along social, political, and economic stress lines. Social welfare policy can thus be useful in enforcing social control, especially as a proxy for other coercive forms of societal control, such as law enforcement and the courts.[3] In having a minimum of their basic needs provided, the disadvantaged are less inclined to revolt against the unequal distribution of resources. A population that has nothing to lose is highly volatile, as the 1992 Los Angeles riot amply demonstrated. Social welfare policies also subsidize the marketplace. Public social welfare benefits often supplement wages that are so low that people could not survive on them alone. Such wage supplements in effect subsidize employers who would otherwise have to their raise wage levels. Social welfare also supports important industries, such as agriculture, housing, and health care. Indeed, if social welfare benefits were eliminated, a substantial segment of American business would collapse. In addition, social welfare redistributes income from one segment of the population to another, allowing the disadvantaged essential income and services. Without such social benefits, fundamental questions would arise about the moral, spiritual, and ethical quality of American society. Moreover, social welfare policies relieve the social and economic dislocations caused by the uneven nature of economic development. Finally, social welfare policies are a means for rectifying past injustices. For example, affirmative action is intended to remedy historical racist and sexist practices that have denied African Americans and women access to economic opportunities and positions of power.

VALUES WITHIN SOCIAL WELFARE POLICY

If social welfare policy were simply a matter of social engineering, arriving at objectives and methods of producing optimal societal functioning would be relatively easy. But social welfare policies are not created in a vacuum; they are shaped by a set of social and personal values that reflect the preferences of those in decision-making capacities. According to veteran policy analyst David Gil, "choices in social welfare policy are heavily influenced by the dominant beliefs, values, ideologies, customs, and traditions of the cultural and political elites recruited mainly from among the more powerful and privileged strata."[4] Yet even if social welfare policies were established through a more representative process, the odds are high that the result would not be straightforward. Charles Prigmore and Charles Atherton list no fewer than fifteen values that influence social welfare policy: achievement and success, activity and work, public morality, humanitarian concerns, efficiency and practicality, material comfort, equality, freedom, external conformity, science and secular rationality, nationalism and patriotism, democracy and self-determination, individualism, racism and group superiority, and belief in progress.[5]

How these values are played out in the world of social welfare is the domain of the policy analyst. Despite the best of intentions, social welfare policy is not always based on a rational set of assumptions and reliable research. One view of social policy is that for it to be worthwhile it should leave no one worse off and at least one person better off, at least as that person judges his or her wants. In the real world of policy that is rarely the case. More often, the policy game is played as a zero-sum game, where some people are advantaged at the expense of others. When value-laden stereotypes about welfare "cheats," insensitive bureaucrats, and "greedy" professionals are added to the script, social welfare policy begins to resemble a morality play. In fact, some analysts believe that the value dimension is the most important element in determining social welfare policy. Alfred Kahn, for example, believes that major social policy changes are made in relation to values, not through the careful consideration of effectiveness of alternative policies.[6]

Of course, there are serious consequences when social welfare policy is determined to a high degree by values. Since 1980, social welfare policy has been shaped largely by values that emphasize individualism, self-sufficiency, and work. Since the disadvantaged were expected to be more independent, supports from government social programs were cut significantly. While these reductions in social programs saved substantial sums in the short run, they were predicated on assumptions that were not well founded. Most of the beneficiaries of social programs that fell to the budget ax were children. Eventually, cuts in social programs are likely to lead to greater expenditures as the generation of children who went without essential services begins to require programs to remedy problems associated with poor maternal and infant health care, poverty, illiteracy, and family disorganization, among others. As Silvia Ann Hewlett has poignantly observed, "although the United States ranks No. 2 worldwide in per capita income, this country does not even make it into the top ten on any significant indicator of child welfare."[7]

AMERICAN IDEOLOGIES

Ideology is the framework of commonly held beliefs through which we view the world. In other words, ideology is a set of assumptions about how the world works: what has value, what is worth living and dying for, what is good and true, and what is right. For the most part,

these assumptions are rarely examined and are simply assumed to be true, a priori. When widely held ideological beliefs are questioned, society often reacts with strong sanctions. The core of ideological tenets around which society is organized exists as a collective social consciousness that defines the world for its members. All societies reproduce themselves, in part, through reproducing ideology. In this way each generation accepts the basic ideological suppositions of the preceding generation.

In the United States the primary ideologies are liberalism and conservatism. One need only watch a political campaign to appreciate the historical significance of these ideological traditions: Democrats invoke the names of liberal presidents, such as Franklin Delano Roosevelt or John F. Kennedy, when they wish to trace the source of their ideas; Republicans can go back further, citing Abraham Lincoln. That ideology is associated with political parties—Democrats tending to be liberal, Republicans conservative—does not mean that there is no overlap. Nor does it mean that ideologies are fixed. Yet these ideological orientations have significant implications for social welfare policy.

Many welfare professionals had built their careers around a vision of an American welfare state that was European in origin.[8] Social workers in the United States have tended to adhere to a liberal philosophy toward welfare which assumed that a system of national programs would be deployed as a greater portion of the citizenry demanded a variety of services and benefits through governmental social programs. The implicit vision behind the expansion of the government-driven welfare state was the European model, especially the Scandinavian variant in which health care, housing, income benefits, and employment opportunities were available more equitably throughout the population than in any other region in the world.[9] It was this example that led the English social scientist Richard Titmuss to hope that the welfare state, as an instrument of government, would eventually lead to a "welfare world."[10] Ultimately, governmental programs, which were the basis of the welfare state, were treated by most welfare philosophers as synonymous with social welfare.

This convention was followed in the United States as well. For American welfare philosophers, government programs designed to ameliorate the caprices of capitalism were both desirable and inevitable. In their classic *Industrial Society and Social Welfare,* Harold Wilensky and Charles Lebeaux suggested that "under continuing industrialization all institutions will be oriented toward and evaluated in terms of social welfare aims. The 'welfare state' will become the 'welfare society,' and both will be more reality than epithet."[11] Accordingly, from the New Deal through the War on Poverty, the notion that government should be the primary institution for promoting social welfare was a persistent theme among American welfare philosophers.[12]

These explanations of the emergence of social welfare in American society were experienced by welfare professionals who took jobs with governmental agencies or with voluntary sector agencies that were heavily dependent on governmental contracts. In fact, the combination of a government bureaucracy and casework agency became so prevalent that Wilensky and Lebeaux concluded, "virtually all welfare service is dispensed through social agencies . . . and virtually all social workers operate through such agencies."[13] For most social welfare professionals, the welfare state was not a philosophical abstraction; it was the basis of livelihood.

Yet the promise of the American welfare state eventually to expand so as to provide the degree of protection typical of the European model was compromised by the ambivalence of many Americans toward centralized government. "The emphasis consistently has been on the local, the pluralistic, the voluntary, and the business-like over the national, the universal, the legally entitled, and the governmental," observed policy analyst Marc Bendick.

Given such a consistent pattern of anti-government bias in the American response style, it is unfortunate that much of American social policy has looked to Europe for models of both specific programs and general approaches. Reflecting political, social, economic, and intellectual circumstances very different from those in the United States, most European nations have evolved an approach to social welfare services that is strongly state-centered. . . . When presented explicitly to the American public, the European welfare state approach has won few adherents outside of academic circles.[14]

Given the pluralism of American society, it was perhaps inevitable that questions about the dominant role of government in social welfare would emerge.

This intrinsic problem of the American welfare state—distrust of centralized government—was exacerbated by the desertion of New Deal allies. Staunch defenders of social programs—Democratic politicians such as George McGovern, Hubert Humphrey, and Daniel Patrick Moynihan—have either retired, died, or changed their ideological allegiance. Even liberal holdouts have had second thoughts about the traditional formulations of American social welfare. Speaking to the Women's National Democratic Club, Senator Edward Kennedy—"the last of the liberal lions"— questioned the basis of American social policy: "We now stand between two Americas, the one we have known and the one toward which we are heading. The New Deal will live in American history forever as a supreme example of government responsiveness to the times. But it is no answer to the problems of today."[15] All but confirming that the New Deal was dead, Harvard University academician Michael Sandel stated that as early as "the 1970s the New Deal agenda had become obsolete."[16] During the 1980s public ambivalence about social programs was exploited by the Reagan administration, placing liberals on the defensive. Having conceded the middle ground in the public policy debate, liberals were in a poor position to press for additional programs that would benefit vulnerable populations that remained unprotected by the "reluctant" American welfare state.[17] Cuts in social welfare programs executed by the Reagan administration were met with an ineffectual response, and the prospect of increasing welfare—even among leaders of the Democratic party, the traditional defenders of the welfare state—was jettisoned.

Meanwhile, the conservative critique of the welfare state gained plausibility, if only because it was repeated so frequently. Conservatives maintained that high taxation and government regulation of business served as disincentives to investment, while individual claims on social insurance and public welfare grants discouraged work. Together, critics of social policies alleged, these factors led to a decline in economic growth and an increase in the expectations of beneficiaries of welfare programs. For conservatives, the only way to correct the irrationality of government social programs was to smash them completely. Charles Murray, in his much-celebrated *Losing Ground*, suggested that

> the proposed program, our final and most ambitious thought experiment, consists of scrapping the entire federal welfare and income support structure for working-aged persons, including AFDC, Medicaid, Food Stamps, Unemployment Insurance, Worker's Compensation, subsidized housing, disability insurance, and the rest. It would leave the working-aged person with no recourse whatsoever except the job market, family members, friends, and public or private locally funded services. It is the Alexandrian solution: cut the knot, for there is no way to untie it.[18]

During the last decade, important variations on the basic American ideological conventions have appeared in the forms of neoliberalism and neoconservatism.

Neoconservatism

Prior to the 1970s, conservative thought held that business activity and government programs were essentially independent of one another. Accordingly, conservatives seemed content merely to snipe at welfare programs, reserving their attention for areas more in line with traditional conservative concerns: the economy, defense, and foreign affairs. By the mid-1970s, however, younger conservative intellectuals recognized that this classically conservative stance vis-à-vis social welfare was no longer tenable: Welfare had become too important to be dismissed so lightly. Consequently, a neoconservative formulation[19] emerged that sought to contain the growth in governmental welfare programs while at the same time transferring as much welfare responsibility as possible from government to the private sector. Explicit in this was an unqualified antagonism to government intrusion in social affairs. Government programs were faulted for a breakdown in the mutual obligation between groups, the lack of attention to efficiencies and incentives in the way programs were operated and benefits awarded, the induced dependency of beneficiaries on programs, and the growth of the welfare industry and its special interest groups, particularly professional associations.[20]

The Hoover Institution of Stanford, California, proved instrumental in shaping the neoconservative position on welfare. "There is no inherent reason that Americans should look to government for those goods and services that can be individually acquired," argued Hoover's Alvin Rabushka, who listed four strategies for reforming welfare: (1) letting users pay; (2) contracting for services; (3) funding mandated services through the state; and (4) emphasizing private substitution.[21] Martin Anderson, a Hoover senior fellow and subsequent domestic policy adviser to the Reagan administration, elaborated the neoconservative position on welfare in terms of the need to:

Reaffirm the need-only philosophical approach to welfare and state it as explicit national policy.

Increase efforts to eliminate fraud.

Establish and enforce a fair, clear, work requirement.

Remove inappropriate beneficiaries from the welfare rolls.

Enforce support of dependents by those who have the responsibility and are shirking it.

Improve the efficiency and effectiveness of welfare administration.

Shift more responsibility from the federal government to state and local governments and private institutions.[22]

Complementing the work of the Hoover analysts, the American Enterprise Institute (AEI) commissioned Peter Berger, a sociologist, and Richard John Neuhaus, a theologian, to prepare a theoretical analysis of American society. Berger and Neuhaus's *To Empower People: The Role of Mediating Structures in Public Policy* identified the fundamental problem confronting American culture as the growth of megastructures (i.e., big government, big business, big labor, and professional bureaucracies) and the corresponding diminution in the value of the individual. The route to empowerment of people, then, was to revitalize "mediating structures," among them, the neighborhood, family, church, and voluntary associations.[23] In a subsequent analysis, an AEI scholar transferred the corporation from a megastructure to a mediating structure, thus leaving the basic institutions of liberal social reform—government, the professions, and labor—as the sources of mass alienation.[24]

Based on these preliminary works, conservative scholars began to develop plausible proposals for welfare reform. With the election of Ronald Reagan, a hoary and worn rhetoric about counterproductive welfare programs suddenly gave way to some relatively sophisticated thinking about social policy. In place of spouting

clichés about welfare cheats, parochial bureaucrats, and bleeding-heart social workers, neoconservatives made serious proposals in the areas of workfare, community development, and child welfare. In a short period, the liberal hegemony in social welfare was confronted by a group of scholars who held a vastly different vision of American social welfare.

A handful of works served as beachheads for the conservative assault on the liberal welfare state. George Gilder's *Wealth and Poverty* argued that beneficent welfare programs represented a "moral hazard," insulating people against risks essential to capitalism and thus contributing to dependency. Instead of welfare, Gilder concluded, "In order to succeed, the poor need most of all the spur of their poverty."[25] Martin Anderson contended that the poverty-line figure should include the cash equivalent of in-kind benefits—Food Stamps, Medicaid, and housing vouchers—and that doing this would effectively lower the poverty rate by 40 percent. "The war on poverty has been won," Anderson proclaimed, "except for perhaps a few mopping-up operations."[26] Meanwhile, AEI prepared *Meeting Human Needs,* an anthology detailing how the private sector could shoulder more of the public welfare burden.[27] Subsequently, neoconservatives seemed to relish making proposals to reform welfare; no policy institute from the right of the ideological spectrum had proven its mettle unless it too produced a plan to clean up "the welfare mess." The Heritage Foundation featured *Out of the Poverty Trap: A Conservative Strategy for Welfare Reform* by Stuart Butler and Anna Kondratas.[28] AEI countered with *The New Consensus on Family and Welfare,* the product of a distinguished panel of neoconservative scholars directed by Michael Novak.[29] Not to be outdone, the Free Congress Research and Education Foundation proposed reforming welfare through "cultural conservatism," that is, by reinforcing "traditional values: delayed gratification, work and saving, commitment to family and to the next generation, education and training, self-improvement, and rejection of crime, drugs, and casual sex."[30] As a collection, these works provided conservatives with a potent critique of liberal governmental welfare programs. Unlike classical conservatives of an earlier generation who simply refused to deal with welfare policy questions, neoconservatives not only did their homework on social welfare policy but began to prepare serious proposals for welfare reform.

Neoliberalism

Smarting from the defeat of Jimmy Carter and the loss of the Senate to the Republican party in 1980, many liberal Democrats began to re-evaluate their party's traditional position on domestic policy. This reexamination, christened "neoliberalism" by Charles Peters to differentiate the new ideology from both old-style liberalism and neoconservatism, attracted a small following in the early 1980s. With the resounding defeat of Walter Mondale, a candidate who symbolized liberal social policy, neoliberalism moved to stage center of Democratic party politics. The defeat of Michael Dukakis underlined the need for Democrats to reformulate their positions on domestic policy. By the late 1980s, several leading Democrats were identified as neoliberal. Moreover, the movement rapidly influenced social policy proposals advanced by the Democratic party. Randall Rothenberg charted the influence of neoliberalism on the Democratic domestic policy platform as early as 1982:

> The party's June 1982 midterm convention in Philadelphia did not endorse a large-scale federal jobs program, in spite of more than 9 million unemployed. It did not re-propose national health insurance, even though medical costs were still soaring. It did not submit yet again a plan for a guaranteed annual income, although the American welfare system was still not operating efficiently.[31]

In place of the usual liberal proposals calling for an expansion of government effort, neoliberal proposals have tended to support reducing governmental costs while encouraging business to assume more responsibility for the welfare of the population. For example, Charles Peters, editor of the *Washington Monthly,* advocated means-testing welfare programs. In defense of neoliberalism, Peters explained: "We still believe in liberty and justice and a fair chance for all, in mercy for the afflicted, and help for the down and out . . . but we no longer automatically favor unions and big government or oppose the military and big business." In reviewing income maintenance programs like social security, welfare, veterans' pensions, and unemployment compensation, Peters outlined the neoliberal position:

> We want to eliminate duplication and apply a means-test to these programs. As a practical matter the country can't afford to spend money on people who don't need it . . . as liberal idealists, we don't think the well-off should be getting money from these programs anyway—every cent we can afford should go to helping those in real need. Social Security for those totally dependent on it is miserably inadequate, as is welfare in many states.[32]

Economist Robert Reich for his part, advocated investments in "human capital" and thought that these should be adapted to productivity. Restructuring human capital investment, or, in other words, reforming the current welfare apparatus, involved a thorough retooling of virtually every program. Writing in 1983, he anticipated that a significant part of the present welfare system would be replaced by government grants to businesses that agreed to hire the chronically unemployed and made these further predictions:

> Other social services—health care, social security, day care, disability benefits, unemployment benefits, relocation assis-

tance—will become part of the process of structural adjustment. Public funds now spent directly on these services will instead be made available to businesses, according to the number of people they agree to hire. Government bureaucracies that now administer these programs to individuals will be supplanted, to a large extent, by companies that administer them to their employees. Companies, rather than state and local governments, will be the agents and intermediaries through which such assistance is provided.[33]

Predictably, neoconservatism and neoliberalism were joined in a volatile debate during much of the 1980s. Liberals chastised neoconservatives for having sold out the legitimate needs of the disadvantaged. Conservatives entered the argument, questioning the motives of the "neocons" while sniping at their archenemies the liberals through a cynical definition that gained currency during the decade: "A neoconservative is a liberal who has been mugged by reality." Eventually, the defection of neoconservatives from the ranks of liberalism led many social program advocates to reconsider their adherence to liberal precepts. The success of neoconservatives in domestic policy innovation suggested that welfare policy advocates should move closer to the ideological center if they were to be taken seriously in matters of welfare policy. The failed presidential candidacies of Walter Mondale and Michael Dukakis provoked leaders within the Democratic party to establish the Democratic Leadership Council (DLC) for the purpose of moving liberals toward the ideological mainstream. Emboldened, neoliberals castigated adherents of unconditional, federal social entitlements as paleoliberals, leading to an ideological split within the Democratic party. This debate was settled convincingly in 1992 with the triumph of the Clinton-Gore presidential ticket. Bill Clinton as governor of Arkansas and Al Gore as senator from Tennessee had both been founding members of the DLC; their neoliberal credentials were impeccable.

IDEOLOGY AND SOCIAL WELFARE

Ideology influences social welfare in two important ways. First, the basic American ideologies, liberalism and conservatism, hold vastly different views of social welfare. Liberals have tended to view government as the only institution capable of bringing a measure of social justice to the millions of Americans who cannot participate in the social mainstream because of societal obstacles such as racism, poverty, and sexism, among others. As a result, liberals have favored government social welfare programs. Conservatives, by contrast, prefer that individuals and families meet their welfare needs by participating in the marketplace, primarily through work. According to conservatives, government has only a minimal and temporary role, as a "safety net," in ensuring the social welfare of citizens. Accordingly, conservatives have preferred private sector approaches to social welfare, while advocating smaller government social welfare programs. These ideological trends influence social welfare directly when adherents of one ideological orientation hold a majority in decision-making bodies, such as the state or national legislature. From the mid-1930s to the mid-1970s, government social programs expanded because to a great extent liberal Democrats controlled Congress. In 1980, further growth of government social programs was abruptly halted when conservative Republicans won control of both the White House and the Senate. During his administration, George Bush effectively used his veto power to check virtually every initiative in social policy. With control of the Congress and the White House once again in the hands of Democrats as of the 1992 election, the conventional wisdom suggests a much more favorable climate for social welfare proposals.

Second, ideology shapes social welfare during periods of social and economic instability. The steady continuity of American history has been shattered intermittently when certain oppressed groups have asserted their rights in the face of mainstream norms. Too easily forgotten, perhaps, are the egregious conditions that provided justification for the militancy displayed by workers before the New Deal, by women during the struggle for suffrage, and by African Americans fighting for their basic civil rights. Periods of social unrest strain the capacity of conventional ideologies to explain social problems and offer solutions. Sometimes social unrest is met with force, as during the period of the great strikes of 1877. In other instances, as in the Great Depression, social unrest is met with the expansion of social welfare programs. Frances Fox Piven and Richard Cloward have attributed the cyclical nature of social welfare programs to periods of social unrest.

> Relief arrangements are ancillary to economic arrangements. Their chief function is to regulate labor, and they do that in two general ways. First, when mass unemployment leads to outbreaks of turmoil, relief programs are ordinarily initiated or expanded to absorb or control enough of the unemployed to restore order; then, as turbulence subsides, the relief system contracts, expelling those who are needed to populate the labor markets.[34]

From a radical perspective, Louis Althusser has described two functions of ideology as the Ideological State Apparatus (ISA), a set of ideological means that includes education, the print media, the family, television, and tradition; and the Repressive State Apparatus (RSA), which includes the courts, police, jails, and so on.[35] In most stable societies the ISA is sufficient to ensure order, stability, and the reproduction of ideological "stories." Through the family, the media, religion, and so forth, most people become convinced that a given society is far better than radically different social models. When the ISA breaks down and social instability results, the RSA becomes activated. For example, one need only look to Iraq, Cuba, North Korea, and South Africa to see the power of the RSA. Virtually all societies have powerful RSA apparatuses that lurk just below the surface.

The RSA is a trigger mechanism that is usually activated when a group or individual refuses to act in accordance with generally held social norms. Should a powerful insurgency movement arise in the United States, as it did in the late 1960s and early 1970s, it is possible that the omnipresent repressive state apparatuses would again be activated. In fact, many groups, including the American Indian Movement (AIM) and the once popular Black Panthers, have found that the RSA was—and, in the case of AIM, still is—directed against them. Continual—and often illegal—covert operations of the Federal Bureau of Investigation against groups perceived to be a threat to American security attest to the presence of a powerful RSA in the United States.

In the American political-economy, the ISA and RSA can be understood in the context of the tension between liberal and conservative paradigms. While Americans are assured of their political rights through a Constitution that delineates a representative democracy, they have no corresponding document to guarantee their economic "rights." For adherents of a capitalistic market economy, such a document would be undesirable, because it would allow government to interfere in the operations of a free market. In the absence of any guaranteed economic rights, large numbers of Americans have found that the economy is not responsive to their needs and that the political system is the only vehicle through which to seek redress. But because access to the political system often presupposes wealth and status, it is a less than optimal method for achieving social justice for many citizens. The political-economy of the United States thus increases the likelihood that disruptions in the social order will occur. Social welfare programs are one method of compensating for deficiencies in the American political-economy by appeasing dissident groups. This role of social welfare is well established within the ISA; both political parties recognize the importance of social programs in American culture. When advocates of the disadvantaged are unable to seek necessary concessions through manipulating the ISA, they occasionally resort to tactics that deliberately provoke the RSA. For example, in the 1960s the civil rights movement gained much public sympathy when the national news broadcast film clips of police dogs turned loose on freedom marchers. Savvy proponents of social welfare initiatives, then, often demonstrate a willingness to use both the ISA and the RSA to advance their ends.

THE POLITICAL-ECONOMY OF AMERICAN SOCIAL WELFARE

The term *political-economy* refers to the interaction of political and economic institutions in a society. The political-economy of the United States has been labeled "democratic-capitalist," reflecting an open, representative form of government coexisting with a market economy. As noted, this interaction of political and economic institutions is frequently irregular, and social welfare functions to make the society more stable. The main function of social welfare is to modify the play of market forces and to ameliorate the social and economic inequities that the market generates.[36] In order to accomplish that end, two sets of activities are necessary: state provision of social services (benefits of cash and in-kind services) and state regulation of private activities to alter (but not necessarily improve) the lives of citizens. In short, social welfare bolsters ideology by helping to remedy the problems associated with economic dislocation, thereby allowing a society to remain in a state of more or less controlled balance.

An understanding of the political-economy is important because of the breadth of social welfare and because of the intense disagreement as to the most desirable way to enhance the general welfare. Federal expenditures for health and welfare claim approximately 50 percent of the federal budget, more than any other category, including defense.[37] In 1991, major social welfare expenditures by the federal government totaled about $635 billion, or close to 11 percent of the gross national product.[38] Yet, despite such enormous expenditures, there is no common understanding of how the American political-economy *does* work or of how it *should* work. Instead, several competing schools of thought purport to explain not only how the political-economy functions but also the best way that it should be deployed to solve new problems. The stakes are clearly high in that major institutions—government, corporations, organized labor, social programs—stand to lose or gain greatly once one school of thought has gained the public's confidence. Invariably, any given explanation of the political-economy will benefit some institutions more than others. Since social welfare is advantaged or disadvantaged according to which school of political-economy holds sway at any given moment, social welfare policy analysts pay close attention to the most important schools of thought.

Keynesian Economics

John Maynard Keynes was the intellectual progenitor of the welfare state, and all welfare societies are built on Keynesian economics. Sometimes called "demand" or "consumer-side" economics, Keynesian economics emerged from a model developed in 1936 by Keynes in *The General Theory of Employment, Interest and Money*. Keynes took the classical model of economic analysis (self-regulating markets, perfect competition, the laws of supply and demand, etc.) and added the insight that macroeconomic stabilization by government is necessary to keep the economic clock operating smoothly.[39] Keynes rejected the classical laissez-faire idea that because a perfectly competitive economy tended automatically toward a balance of full employment, the government should not interfere with the process. Keynes observed that, instead of a self-correcting economy that pulled itself out of recessions easily, the modern economy was quite recession-prone and the attainment of full employment was problematic. Periodic volatile economic situations during which unemployment peaked were primarily caused by an instability in investment expenditures. The government could stabilize, that is, correct, recessionary or inflationary trends by increasing or decreasing total spending on output. This could be accomplished by the government increasing or decreasing taxes, thereby increasing or decreasing consumption, as well as by the transfer of public goods or services. For Keynes, the "good" government was an activist government in economic matters, especially when the economy got out of a full employment mode. Keynesians hypothesize that social welfare expenditures are investments in human capital which ultimately increase the national wealth and thereby boost everyone's net income.

Supply-Side Economics

Supply-side economics is a school of political and economic thought that gained considerable currency during the 1980s. Although some supply-siders would prefer to think of it as pure economics, it contains enough political implications (both covert and overt) to qualify as a political as well as an economic theory. Popularized by ardent supporters such as Jack Kemp and, later, Ronald Reagan, supply-side economics provided the major rationale for the cuts in federal social programs executed during the Reagan administration. Supply-side economics stresses the concept of a self-regulating economy and posits an economic system based on "perfect competition." Transactions in the economy are likened to those that occur in simple marketplaces; the rationality of supply and demand serves to provide the market with a "general equilibrium" that characterizes the entire economy.[40] This model emphasizes the efficiency of markets and focuses on the supplier (hence the term *supply-side economics*).

Supply-side adherents maintain that large social welfare programs—including unemployment benefits and public service jobs—are detrimental to the society in two ways. First, government social programs erode the work ethic by supporting those who do not work. Second, public sector social welfare programs divert money away from the private sector because they are funded by taxes—diverted income that could otherwise be invested in capital formation. Supply-siders also believe that when government alters the patterns of rewards to favor work over leisure, and investment over consumption, it fosters the expansion of real economic demand. Supporters of supply-side economics believe that economic growth helps everyone because overall prosperity creates more jobs, income, and goods, and that these eventually filter down to the poor. Investment is the key to prosperity for supply-siders; it is the raw material that fuels the economic machine, and without it the economy is frozen. It is this investment in capital that creates the economic growth which results in more jobs, income, and goods. Accordingly, supply-siders favor tax breaks for the wealthy. The more disposable after-tax income that is available, the greater the amount that will be freed up for investment. High taxes are therefore an impediment to economic progress because they channel money away from "private" investment into "public" investment.

Despite its popularity during the early years of the Reagan administration, supply-siders fell out of favor when it became clear that massive tax cuts for the wealthy and corporations did not result in increased capital formation and economic activity. Rather, the wealthy spent their tax savings on luxury items, and corporations used their tax rebates to purchase other companies in a merger mania that took even

Wall Street by surprise. Many corporations took advantage of temporary tax savings to transfer their operations abroad, further reducing the supply of higher-paying industrial jobs in the United States. For these and other reasons, the budget deficit during the Reagan administration grew at an unprecedented rate (from about $50 billion a year in the Carter term to $352 billion a year in 1992).[41] This contradiction was explained away by a belief that sound economic growth would result in a larger tax base, which would then yield more federal taxes without a tax increase. Critics of supply-side economics complained that the only "trickle-down" would be in the form of massive debt.

Socialism

Socialism differs from both Keynesian and supply-side theories. In fact, these schools, as different as they are, have more in common with each other than with any radical, leftist perspective. According to Jeffry Galper, one of social work's most articulate proponents of a radical perspective, socialists see social problems as a logical consequence of an unjust society.[42] Galper and other left-wing theorists maintain that it is the failure of capitalism which has led to political movements that have pressured institutions to respond with increased social welfare services. For socialists, social welfare is an ingenious arrangement on the part of business to get the public to assume the costs incurred by the social and economic dislocations attributable to capitalism.

Social welfare, then, serves both the needs of people and the needs of capitalist expansion and production. According to socialists, social welfare expenditures "socialize" the costs of capitalist production; in other words, they make public the costs of private enterprise. In the final analysis, social welfare programs do respond to human needs, but they do so in a way that supports an unjust economic system which continues to generate problems requiring social programs.

Socialists believe that real social welfare is structural and can only be accomplished through a redistribution of resources. In a just society—where all goods, resources, and opportunities were made available to everyone—all but the most specific forms of welfare (health care, rehabilitation, counseling, and so forth) would be unnecessary. In the context of a radical framework, poverty is inextricably linked to structural inequality. Therefore, people need welfare because they are exploited and denied access to resources. In an unjust society, welfare functions as a substitute, albeit a puny one, for social justice.

Radicals maintain that social welfare programs function like "junk food" for the impoverished: They provide just enough subsistence to discourage revolution, but not enough to make a real difference in the lives of the poor. Within the radical framework, social welfare is seen as a form of social control. In place of liberal social welfare reforms, the radical vision requires that the entire system—social, political, and, especially, economic—undergo a major overhaul. In short, the radical position is that real welfare reform—including a complete redistribution of goods, income, and services—can occur only in the context of a socialist system.

Other Schools of Thought

While the Keynesian, supply-side, and socialist schools represent the major themes of political and economic thought in the United States, they do not reflect all of them. As our discussion of the three major schools illustrates, ideas on the best way to address questions of the political-economy change over time. Some of the newer schools of thought deserve attention because they may become prominent in the future. One school of thought that is having an impact on American social welfare is the *traditionalist* school. Having a Christian religious orientation to social policy, and exemplified by evangelical groups such as the Moral Majority, traditionists emphasize the moral relationship between politics and religion. According to traditionalists, God's laws must be translated into politics and "higher laws" must become the laws of the state. Because this group presumes the United States to be, for all practical purposes, a Christian nation, the separation of church and state is seen as unnatural. Apart from its belief in a strong military defense, this group emphasizes the Christian value of hard work and proposes little welfare, except for the most needy. Traditionalists have been highly critical of governmental social programs, which they associate with a liberal social philosophy (secular humanism), a philosophy which in their opinion has eroded traditional social institutions, particularly the family and the church. Lightning-rod issues for traditionalists have been abortion, prohibition of prayer in school, affirmative action, and school integration—all of which are associated by them with the increasing liberalism of society. Traditionalists have been among the most severe critics of governmental social programs.

Another perspective can be found among _libertarians_. This relatively small but increasingly influential group believes in virtually no government regulation. Libertarians hold that the smaller government is, the better, since government invariably grows at the expense of individual freedom. Libertarians believe that the only proper role for government is to provide a police force and a military. Moreover, the only weapons that the military should possess are defensive. Libertarians are highly critical of taxation, recognizing that government is dependent on tax revenues. Aside from advocating minimal taxation earmarked for military and police activities, libertarians oppose the income tax. Because of their emphasis on individual freedom, and therefore individual responsibility, libertarians advocate the decriminalization of narcotics. Government should intercede in social affairs only when the behavior of an individual threatens the safety of another. The libertarian critique of social welfare is based on the belief that the state should not be involved in social and economic activities save in very limited and extreme circumstances.

The _self-reliance_ school offers a newly emerging perspective that is gaining adherents in economically distressed areas of the United States as well as in Third World countries.[43] This school maintains that industrial economic models are irrelevant to the economic needs of poor communities and are often damaging to the spiritual life of their peoples.[44] Adherents of self-reliance repudiate Western economic philosophies that stress economic growth and the idea that the quality of life can be measured by the material acquisitions of citizens. These economists stress a balanced economy based on the real needs of people, production designed for internal consumption rather than export, productive technologies that are congruent with the culture and background of the population, the use of appropriate and manageable technologies, and a small-scale and decentralized form of economic organization.[45] Simply put, proponents of self-reliance postulate that more is less and less is more. The objective of self-reliance is the creation of a no-poverty society in which economic life is organized around issues of subsistence rather than trade and economic expansion. Accepting a world of finite resources and inherent limitations to economic growth, proponents argue that the true question of social and economic development is not what people think they want or need but what people must have for survival. The self-reliance school accepts the need for social welfare programs to ameliorate the social and economic dislocations caused by industrialization, but it prefers low-technology and local solutions to social problems. This contrasts with the conventional meaning of the welfare state, which describes a set of programs on a national scale, administered by large bureaucracies through sophisticated management systems.

Lastly, the _public choice_ school has become more prominent among conservative analysts, particularly as faith has ebbed in the supply-side school. The public choice school was not widely known beyond academic circles until its major proponent, James Buchanan, was awarded the Nobel Prize for economics in 1986. According to this school, a political economy with a large number of interest groups tends to generate budget deficits. As a result, government must be vigilant and very selective about making concessions to interest groups or their demands will eventually destabilize the economy. Briefly, the public choice model states that there are strong incentives for interest groups to make demands on government in that the concessions flow directly to the group while the costs of these concessions are spread among all taxpayers. Initial concessions lead to demands for further concessions, which are likely to be forthcoming so long as the interest group is vociferous in its demands. Under such an incentive system, different interests are also encouraged to band together to make demands since there is no reason for an interest group to oppose the demands of others. But while demands for goods and services increase, revenues tend to decrease. This is because interest groups resist paying taxes directed toward them specifically and because no interest group has much individual incentive to support general taxes. The result of such a scenario is predictable: Irresistible demands for government benefits accompanied by declining revenues lead to government borrowing to finance programs, which results in large budget deficits.[46] While the public choice school is critical of the demands posed by any interest group, it has been adopted by conservatives to explain the gradual expansion of government social programs. As a result, adherents of public choice theory view social welfare as a series of concessions to disadvantaged groups that could be endless, eventually bankrupting the government. On the other hand, it is just as logical to apply public choice analysis to interest groups related to the defense industry that make similar demands on government while not paying corresponding taxes. Despite such contradictions in its analysis, the public choice

school is likely to be more influential in shaping future social welfare policy by calling for further reductions in public expenditures for social programs.

PLURALISM IN AMERICAN SOCIAL WELFARE

Consistent with the pluralism of thought evident in the various schools of political-economy, social welfare in the United States is characterized by a high degree of diversity. American social welfare is not a monolithic, highly centralized, and well-coordinated system of programs. Rather, a great variety of organizations provide a wide range of benefits and services to different client populations. The vast array of social welfare organizations contributes to what is commonly called "the welfare mess." As the phrase suggests, different programs serving different groups through still different procedures have become part of an impenetrable tangle of institutional red tape that often functions poorly for administrators, human service professionals, and their clients.

The complexity of social welfare can be attributed to several cultural influences, some of which are peculiar to the American experience. The U.S. Constitution outlines a federal system of government through which the states vest certain functions in the national government. Although the states have assumed primary responsibility for social welfare through much of the history of the United States, this changed with the New Deal of Franklin Delano Roosevelt, which ushered in a raft of federal programs. Over subsequent decades, federal social welfare initiatives took on a dominant role in the nation's social welfare effort. Still, states continued to manage important social welfare programs, such as mental health and social services. Over time, then, the relationship between the federal government and the states has changed. From the New Deal of the 1930s through the Great Society of the 1960s, federal welfare programs expanded, forming the American version of the "welfare state." During the 1980s, however, the Reagan administration sought to return more of the responsibility for welfare to the states, a process called *devolution*.[47]

A second confounding element can be attributed to the relatively open character of American society. Often called the "melting pot," the national culture is a protean brew of groups that have immigrated to the United States, and then competed with each other to become an established part of national life.[48] An enormous influx of Europeans during the last century has given way to waves of Hispanics and Asians entering the United States a century later.[49] Historically, social welfare programs have played an important part in the acculturation of these groups. At the same time, many ethnic groups bring with them their own fraternal and community associations, which not only provide welfare benefits to members of the community but also serve to maintain its norms. Other groups that have exerted important influences on American social welfare are African Americans, the aged, women, and Native Americans. The very pluralism of American society—a diverse collection of peoples, each with somewhat different needs—contributes to the complexity in social welfare.

The American economic system is another reason why social welfare is complex. With some important exceptions, the economy of the United States is predominantly capitalist, with most goods and services being owned, produced, and distributed through the marketplace. In a capitalist economy, people are expected to meet their basic needs through the marketplace, and they ordinarily do this through participation in the labor market. When groups are unable to participate fully in the labor market because, like the aged or the handicapped, they are unable to work or because, like women and African Americans historically, they do not earn enough as a result of discrimination, "social" programs are deployed to support these groups. These

programs take various forms. Many are governmental programs that are mandated by legislation. Private sector programs often complement those of the public sector. Within the private sector, two organizational forms are common—nonprofit organizations and for-profit corporations. Sometimes public and both forms of private sector organizations coexist, approximate to one another.[50] For instance, in many communities, family planning services are provided by the public health department, a governmental agency; by Planned Parenthood, a private, nonprofit agency; and by a private, for-profit health maintenance organization.

Finally, various religious organizations have influenced social welfare. This is most clearly seen in the range of sectarian agencies that appear in most American cities: Jewish Family Services, Lutheran Social Services, Catholic Charities, and the Salvation Army, among others. Because of the American tradition of the separation of church and state, these nongovernmental agencies are vehicles for providing services to groups that would not otherwise get them because government does not support religious activities or because corporations do not find them profitable. However, this is not to say that there is no relationship between the government and sectarian agencies. During the 1970s, the federal government experimented with contracting out some services to the private sector, and sectarian agencies frequently competed for these contracts. Today, many sectarian agencies receive federal funds for particular services they provide to the public. A more recent illustration of the influence of religion on social welfare has been the religious right, which has sought to curtail the reproductive rights of adults through opposing federal funding of family planning programs and abortion services.

The pluralism of American culture is of increasing interest to social welfare policy analysts as the influence of the federal government in social policy diminishes. With reductions in many federal social programs and calls for the private sector to assume more responsibility for welfare, the prospect of molding the diverse entities involved in American social welfare into one unified whole under the auspices of a central authority—the federal government—seems remote. This vision is often implicit in the proposals of advocates for nationalized programs that ensure basic goods and services such as food, housing, education, health, and income to all as a right of citizenship. While programs of this nature have been integral to the welfare states of northern Europe for decades, there is a serious question as to how plausible they are for the United States, which already has so much complexity built into its social welfare system.[51]

Questions about the correct role of the federal government in social welfare reached controversial proportions by the late 1980s. Proponents of a strong federal role conceded that the American welfare state was, by European standards, incomplete. For these analysts, the "reluctant welfare state"[52] or the "semi-welfare state"[53] required further elaboration through social programs in primary areas of need—income, health, and employment. The principle that social welfare should be a "national effort on behalf of those in need," noted Robert Reich, has been central to American social welfare for a half-century. According to Reich, "The theme permeated Roosevelt's New Deal, Truman's Fair Deal, Johnson's Great Society: America is a single, national community, bound by a common ideal of equal opportunity, and generosity toward the less fortunate. E Pluribus Unum."[54] To proponents of more state intervention in social welfare, the advocates of nongovernmental initiatives represented the abandonment of the most effective method for assuring protection of vulnerable populations. "Conservatives," some observed, "continually assert that many social services in the public sector can be transferred to the voluntary sector."[55]

Advocates of more nongovernmental activity in social welfare trace their argument to the colonial era in America. Daniel Boorstin, former Librarian of Congress, has written passionately about the unique role played by voluntary organizations in the United States. Boorstin maintains that voluntary organizations "have many unique characteristics and a spirit all their own." Voluntary organizations are no less than "monuments to what in the Old World was familiar neither as private charity nor as governmental munificence. They are monuments to community. They originate in the community, depend on the community, are developed by the community, serve the community, and rise or fall with the community."[56]

But can the problems of a postindustrial America be addressed adequately without massive federal social programs? Daniel Patrick Moynihan, an authority in Congress on welfare, claims that there is no choice but to begin thinking about new ways to solve social problems. According to Moynihan, *"The issues of social policy the United States faces today have no European counterpart nor any European model of a viable solution. They are American problems, and we Americans are going to have to think them through by ourselves."*[57] To the extent that Moynihan is correct, future welfare initiatives are increasingly likely to reflect the diversity of American social welfare.

INTEREST GROUPS WITHIN SOCIAL WELFARE

Differences on how best to promote the general welfare also exist within the social welfare community. Considering the scope of social welfare in a postindustrial society, the divisive influences attributable to our national culture, and the ideologies that frequently guide social policy, it is not surprising that human service professionals should have varying ideas about the best way to address human needs. One theory posits that four such groups can be identified within American social welfare: traditional providers, welfare bureaucrats, clinical entrepreneurs, and human service executives.[58] Because these groups have become integrated into the nation's political-economy, they are termed *structural interests*.

Traditional Providers

Traditional providers are both professionals and laypersons who seek to maintain and enhance traditional relations, values, and structures in their communities. Traditional providers hold an organismic conception of social welfare, seeing it tightly interwoven with other community institutions. According to traditional providers, voluntary nonprofit agencies offer the advantages of neighborliness, a reaffirmation of community values, a concern for community as opposed to personal gain, and freedom to alter programming so as to conform to changes in local priorities. Their base of influence consists of the private, nonprofit agencies, often referred to as the voluntary sector.

Much of the heritage of social welfare can be traced to this interest (e.g., Mary Richmond of the Charity Organization Society movement, and Jane Addams of the Settlement House movement). Charity Organization Societies and settlement houses were transformed by two influences: the need for scientifically based treatment techniques and the socialization of charity. Together, these factors functioned as an anchor for the social casework agencies in American industrial society. The agency provided the grist for scientific casework that was instrumental in the emergence of the social work profession. The new schools of social work, in turn, relied on casework agencies for internship training, a substantial portion of a professional's education. Once graduated, many professionals elected to work in the voluntary sector, ensuring agencies of a steady supply of personnel.

Voluntary agencies routinized philanthropic contributions by socializing charity. Beginning with Denver's Associated Charities in 1887, the concept of a community appeal spread so rapidly that by the 1920s over 200 cities had community chests. The needs of workers for effective treatment techniques and the economic imperatives for organizational survival functioned together to standardize the social agency. Perhaps the best description of the casework agency is found in the Milford Conference Report of 1923, *Social Casework: Generic and Specific,* which comprehensively outlined the organization through which professional caseworkers delivered services.[59] By the 1940s, the social casework agency had become a predominant form of service delivery. Today, much social service provision exists in the form of United Way-subsidized sectarian and nonsectarian agencies, whose member groups collected $2.4 billion in 1986.[60]

Welfare Bureaucrats

Welfare bureaucrats are public functionaries who maintain the welfare state in much the same form in which it was conceived during the New Deal. "Their ideology," according to Robert Alford, "stresses a rational, efficient, cost-conscious, coordinated . . . delivery system."[61] They view government intervention vis-à-vis social problems as legitimate and necessary, considering the apparent lack of concern by the private sector and local government. Moreover, they contend that government intervention is more effective because authority is centralized, guidelines are standardized, and benefits are allocated according to principles of equity and equality.

The influence of welfare bureaucrats grew as a result of the Social Security Act of 1935. To a limited extent, the larger community chests "exerted a pressure toward rationalization of the professional welfare machinery,"[62] but this did not diminish the effect of the federal welfare bureaucracy, which soon eclipsed the authority of traditional providers. Actually, a unilinear evolution between these interests could have occurred had Harry Hopkins, head of the Federal Emergency Relief Administration, not prohibited states from turning federal welfare funds over to private agencies.[63] Denied the resources to significantly address the massive social problems caused by the Great Depression, private agencies lapsed into a secondary role while federal and state agencies ascended in importance. An array of welfare legislation followed the Social Security Act, including the Housing Act of 1937, the G.I. Bill of 1944, the Community Mental Health Centers Act of 1963, the Civil Rights Act of 1964, the Food Stamp Act of 1964, the Economic Opportunity Act of 1964, the Elementary and Secondary Education Act of 1965, the Medicare and Medicaid Acts of 1965, Supplemental Security Income in 1974, Title XX of the Social Security Act of 1975, and the Full Employment Act of 1978.

The flourishing of bureaucratic rationality concomitant with this legislative activity represented the institutionalization of liberal thought, which sought to control the caprice of the market, ensure a measure of equality among widely divergent economic classes, and establish the administrative apparatus that would ensure the continuity of these principles. Confronted with a rapidly industrializing society lacking basic programs for ameliorating social and economic catastrophes, progressives perceived the state as a vehicle for social reform. Their solutions focused on "coordinating fragmented services, instituting planning, and extending public funding."[64] Implicit in the methods advocated by welfare bureaucrats is an expectation, if not an assumption, that the social welfare administration should be centralized, that eligibility for benefits should be universalized, and that social welfare should be firmly anchored in the institutional fabric of society.

The influence of welfare bureaucrats had been curtailed by the mid-1980s. The Reagan administration all but capped the growth of social programs, expenditures of which as a percent of the gross domestic product (GDP) fell from 12.4 in 1983 to 11.3 in 1991.[65] Even Democrats who had smarted from election losses in 1980, 1984, and 1988 began to voice a preference for private sector solutions to social problems. Still, the volume of resources and the number of people dependent on public welfare assure welfare bureaucrats of a dominant and continuing role in the near future.

Clinical Entrepreneurs

Clinical entrepreneurs are professional service providers, chiefly social workers, psychologists, and physicians, who work for themselves instead of being salaried employees. Important to clinical entrepreneurs is the establishment of a professional monopoly, the evolution of which represents a concern on the part of practitioners that their occupational activity not be subject to political interference from the state or the ignorance of the lay public. In the United States, the professions found that a market economy was conducive to occupational success. In the most fundamental sense, private practice reconciles the professionals' desire for autonomy with the imperatives of a market economy. The transition from entrepreneur to professional monopolist is a matter of obtaining legislation restricting practice to those duly licensed by the state. "Professionalism provides a way of preserving monopolistic control over services without the risks of competition."[66] As an extension of the entrepreneurial model of service delivery, professional monopoly offers privacy in practice, freedom to valuate one's worth through setting fees, and the security ensured by membership in the professional monopoly.

The social worker as clinical entrepreneur is a relatively recent phenomenon, and the National Association of Social Workers (NASW) did not officially sanction this form of service delivery until 1964. Prior to that, privately practicing social workers identified themselves as psychotherapists and lay analysts. Typically, they relied on referrals from physicians and psychiatrists and, after World War II, they began to establish "flourishing and lucrative" practices.[67] By the 1970s, private practice in social work was developing as an important form of service delivery, although analysts disagreed about the number of social workers engaged in independent practice. In 1975, NASW estimated that from 10,000 to 20,000 social workers were engaged in private practice. By 1983, Dr. Robert Barker, author of *Social Work in Private Practice* and a column on private practice in *NASW News,* speculated that about 30,000 social workers, or 32 percent of all social workers, engaged in private practice on a full- or part-time basis.[68] By 1985, a large portion of psychotherapy was being done by social workers, and the *New York Times* noted that "growing numbers of social workers are treating more affluent, private clients, thus moving into the traditional preserve of the elite psychiatrists and clinical psychologists."[69] Yet, in the early 1990s, NASW reported that only about 15,000 of its members—11.1 percent—were in solo or partnership practice as private practitioners.[70]

Clinical entrepreneurs are an emerging interest in social welfare. Continued growth of this group is likely for several reasons. Through local and state chapters, NASW has been effective in expanding the scope of its professional monopoly. In 1983, 31 states had passed legislation regulating the practice of social work; by 1992, all 50 states regulated social work practice. At the same time, professional groups have lobbied for vendorship privileges that allow them more regular income through insurance held by clients. Finally, large numbers of students entering graduate schools of social work do so with the expressed intent of setting up a private practice.[71] Thus, clinical entrepreneurs are likely to become a more influential interest group in the future.

Human Service Executives

Human service executives share an important characteristic with clinical entrepreneurs: Both represent ways of organizing service delivery in the context of the market. However, in some important ways they differ. Unlike clinical entrepreneurs, human service executives are salaried employees of proprietary firms and, as such, have less autonomy. As administrators or chief executive officers of large corporations, human service executives advance market strategies for promoting social welfare. Welfare bureaucrats emphasize the planning and regulatory functions of the state, whereas human service executives favor the rationality of the marketplace in allocating resources and evaluating programs. In the present circumstances, human service executives advocate market reform of the welfare state—the domain of welfare bureaucrats—and thus are in a position to challenge this interest.

For-profit firms became prominent in American social welfare during the 1960s, when Medicaid and Medicare funds were paid to proprietary nursing homes and hospitals.[72] Since then, human service executives have been rapidly creating independent, for-profit human service corporations that provide an extensive range of nationwide services. Human service corporations have established prominent, if not dominant, positions in several human service markets, including nursing home care, hospital management, health maintenance, child care, home care, and corrections. In 1981, 34 human service corporations reported annual revenues above $10 million; by 1985, the number of firms had increased to 66. Several corporations reported revenues higher than the total contributions to the United Way of America.[73]

As the proprietary sector expands to dominate different human service markets, oligopolies emerge and a fundamental change occurs. No longer passively dependent on government appropriations, proprietary firms are in a strong position to shape the very markets they serve, influencing not only consumer demand but governmental policy as well. It is this capacity to determine or control a market that qualitatively distinguishes corporate welfare from the earlier form of business involvement in social welfare, that is, philanthropic contributions to nonprofit agencies of the voluntary sector. For these reasons, human service executives are well positioned to influence welfare bureaucrats.

The structural interests just described can be located in relation to two variables: span of

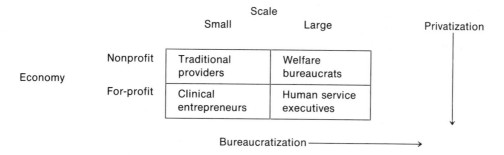

Figure 1.1. Dynamics of Structural Interests. (SOURCE: David Stoesz, "A Theory of Social Welfare," *Social Work* 34, no. 2 [March 1989]: 106.)

influence and type of economy. As Figure 1.1 indicates, power shifts as a result of significant social influences: privatization and bureaucratization. The consequences of these forces will be evident in subsequent chapters of this book.

Marginal Interests

Social welfare in America is populated by numerous groups that have *not* become as symbiotically attached to the social structure as have the structural interests described. These marginal interest groups usually represent special populations that have been ignored, excluded, or oppressed by mainstream society. The number of these groups reflects the capacity of American culture to maintain its equilibrium while excluding many groups from full social participation. A partial list of marginal interest groups includes African Americans, women, Native Americans, homosexuals, residents of rural areas, and Hispanic Americans. These groups are of great interest to welfare professionals because of their concern for social justice. Within the context of democratic capitalism, transforming marginal interests into structural interests remains extraordinarily difficult.

The marginal status of many groups relates to the nature of the social welfare industry. In American culture, groups excluded from the mainstream are expected to gather their resources and identify leaders who will mount programs to serve their particular group. Al-

though this expectation is congruent with traditional values, such as self-sufficiency and community solidarity, that approach does not ensure success. The voluntary sector may be able to accommodate only a limited number of marginal interests because of financial restraints, or it may be unresponsive to groups that violate traditional community norms.

In a democratic polity, marginal groups can make claims on the social order by seeking benefits through governmental programs, but to do so presents other problems. Government programs are likely to be managed by welfare bureaucrats, who have their own understanding of what is best for the marginal interest. For a marginal group to get benefits through government programs, its claim must be interpreted, programmed, and monitored by agents of the welfare state, who have a welfare ideology that differs from that of oppressed groups. The result is likely to be a program that is more consonant with the ideology of the welfare bureaucrats than with that of the marginal group.

Because of these obstacles, members of marginal groups have powerful incentives to work within existing structures. Their success in this regard has been mixed. As a result of affirmative action, African-American males have been able to secure positions within the welfare bureaucracy in relatively significant numbers and are now well established among welfare bureaucrats. White women, however, have found independent practice more desirable and are represented more among clinical entrepreneurs. Despite such changes, many marginal groups continue to struggle against a welfare industry that is controlled by structural interests indifferent to minority concerns. The structural interest of human service executives, for example, remains a bastion of white patriarchy.

PLURALISM AND RECENT INITIATIVES IN SOCIAL WELFARE

The complexity of American social welfare helps account for changes in welfare policies and programs. Since 1980, for example, a convergence of social, political, and economic forces has led to a reappraisal of welfare in the United States. Both liberal and conservative scholars have questioned the dominance of government programs in welfare provision. At the same time, a firestorm of fundamentalism swept across the nation, attracting the allegiance of groups associated with evangelicalism. The "traditionalist movement" flexed its muscles through the elections of Ronald Reagan and George Bush, the installation of a Republican Senate during the early 1980s, and an effective grass-roots mobilization that challenged government policies on issues that ranged from the family to affirmative action. Current social policy initiatives that can be traced to conservative influences include:

- The designation of Enterprise Zones through which incentives would be offered to businesses in exchange for locating in distressed areas and employing poor workers.
- Expanding the Earned Income Tax Credit, a negative income tax, through which the working poor are mailed payments by the Internal Revenue Service to make up for low income.[74]
- Incorporating "reciprocity" in public assistance programs, such as requiring

mothers on AFDC to work, obtain immunizations for their children, and send them to school.

By the mid-1980s, social conservatism had begun to influence leaders of the Democratic party, a traditional supporter of government welfare programs. In order to reestablish credibility in an increasingly conservative political climate, liberals distanced themselves from the large-scale government welfare programs with which Democrats had been associated since the New Deal. In their place, they called for a reliance on personal responsibility, work, and thrift. These values have assumed primary importance in the domestic agenda of the Clinton presidency. Current social policy initiatives being promoted by liberals include:

- Creating Individual Development Accounts, tax-exempt deposits through which the government matches individual contributions for specific purposes such as: finishing college, buying a home, establishing a business, or supplementing a pension.
- Emphasizing "civic liberalism" in social policy by engineering class-mixing situations, such as a National Service Corps (approved by Congress in 1993).
- Extending the idea of child support enforcement to ensure a minimum benefit for all children from broken homes.

How these initiatives will be sorted out by a Democratic Congress and the administration of President Clinton will make the mid-1990s an unpredictable yet exciting period in American social welfare. Conservative public sentiment toward social welfare will serve as a backdrop for the debate on the future of welfare policy.[75] The conservative legacy for social welfare from the 1980s will continue to limit the range of the welfare policy discussion. With the possible exception of healthcare, the classic trinity of liberal welfare reform—full employment, a guaranteed income, and a national health care system—is unlikely to be part of the public debate.

The structural interests within social welfare have keenly felt the conservative shift. Having braced themselves against repeated blows to social programs during the 1980s, welfare bureaucrats are unlikely to feel any relief in the near future in view of the extraordinary fiscal problems troubling both federal and state government. As more of the responsibility for welfare is shifted to private institutions, the voluntary sector has been called upon to expand its programs. At the same time, the voluntary sector has struggled to maintain programming despite diminishing support from government, not to mention reductions in voluntary contributions associated with a nagging recession. Meanwhile, programs run by corporate human service executives have prospered, as have clinical entrepreneurs. The consequences of the conservative movement in social policy have been felt most acutely by marginal groups. Government programs that benefited African Americans, women, and the poor have been severely cut, leaving these groups more vulnerable. As the end of the century approaches, welfare professionals face a formidable challenge: How can basic goods and services be brought to vulnerable populations within a context of such complexity and uncertainty?

The Budget Deficit

Perhaps the most important legacy left by the Reagan and Bush administrations is fiscal rather than ideological. Skillfully brought to the foreground by Ross Perot's presidential bid in 1992, the current budget deficit promises to be a more potent force in driving social welfare policy than either conservative ideology or mainstream American values.

The budget problem can be understood as comprising three separate deficits. The first is a massive fiscal deficit that soaks up private savings and leaves a shortage of capital available for private investment in new plants, equip-

ment, and other items. As a result, this deficit makes the economy less productive and less competitive internationally. The second deficit is a shortage of public (governmental) investment in areas that would make the economy more productive in the future, including investments in infrastructure, education and training, research and development, and preventative health and education programs for children. For example, capital expenditures grew at a rate of 1.6 percent from 1969 to 1977; during the Reagan years they plummeted to 0.9 percent per year, or less than half the rate of overall growth.[76] The last is a social deficit that is reflected in the neglect of various domestic needs, which has contributed to high rates of poverty among children and others.[77]

At first glance, the budget deficit numbers are frightening and confusing. In 1991 the total national debt was roughly $4 trillion dollars, or almost four-fifths of the $5.68 trillion gross domestic product (GDP) for that year (see Table 1.1). This is equivalent to someone having a debt totaling four-fifths of his or her yearly income. However, to understand the relationship between the budget deficit and social welfare spending, it is important to first separate hyperbole from fact. In 1991 the federal government collected $1.05 trillion in revenues; the total federal outlay was $1.32 trillion. After adjustments, this translated into a $268-billion federal budget deficit for that year. However, this deficit was on top of a $220-billion deficit in 1990, a $153-billion deficit in 1989, and a $155-billion deficit in 1988. As a result, the cumulative federal debt was almost $4 trillion by 1991. By comparison, the budget deficit in 1978 was only $59 billion, and the cumulative federal debt was $776 billion.[78]

To make sense out of the budget deficit, it must be placed in historical perspective. Situating the budget deficit in this context provides both good and bad news. For example, while the total federal debt currently totals a very high 64 percent of the GDP, the federal debt was equal to 71.5 percent of the GDP in 1955, 65

TABLE 1.1. The Federal Budget Deficit: Revenues, Outlays, Deficits, and the GDP (In billions of dollars)

Year	Revenues	Outlays	Deficit	Gross Deficit	GDP	Gross Deficit as Percent of GDP
1970	192	196	2	381	1,010	38.6
1971	187	210	23	408	1,097	38.8
1972	207	231	23	436	1,207	38.0
1973	231	246	14	466	1,350	36.5
1974	263	269	6	484	1,459	34.5
1975	279	332	53	542	1,586	35.9
1976	298	372	74	629	1,768	37.3
1977	356	409	54	706	1,974	36.8
1978	400	459	59	777	2,233	36.0
1979	463	504	40	829	2,489	34.1
1980	517	591	74	909	2,708	34.4
1981	599	678	79	994	3,031	33.5
1982	618	746	128	1,137	3,150	36.4
1983	600	808	208	1,371	3,405	41.3
1984	666	852	185	1,564	3,777	42.3
1985	734	946	212	1,817	4,039	45.8
1986	769	990	221	2,120	4,269	50.2
1987	854	1,004	150	2,346	4,540	52.7
1988	909	1,064	155	2,601	4,900	54.1
1989	991	1,144	154	2,868	5,244	55.5
1990	1,031	1,251	220	3,206	5,514	58.7
1991	1,054	1,323	269	3,600	5,672	64.0

SOURCE: Compiled from tables in the Committee on Ways and Means, U.S. House of Representatives, *Overview of Entitlement Programs, 1992 Green Book* (Washington, D.C.: U.S. Government Printing Office, 1992), Table 1, p. 1584; Table 33, p. 1795; Table 35, p. 1797; and Table 39, p. 1801.

percent in 1956, 62 percent in 1957, and 50 percent in 1964. Even during the period of high social spending between 1965 and 1970, the federal debt declined in relationship to the GDP. By 1981 the federal debt was reduced to 33.5 percent of the GDP before it started its upward climb again in 1982. Moreover, federal outlays as a percentage of the GDP remained relatively constant between 1962 and 1991, hovering between 19 and 23.5 percent for those three decades.[79] Thus, contrary to conventional wisdom the federal debt has been proportionately higher in previous years and, more important, it has also been reduced in the past. The federal debt

(at least as a percentage of the GDP) does not always spiral upward.

Despite some cause for optimism, the federal debt remains a serious problem. For example, when Richard Nixon took office in 1969 the federal government ran a $3-billion surplus. When Jimmy Carter took office in 1977 the deficit was $54 billion. It rose to $79 billion by the time Ronald Reagan assumed the presidency. During the eight years of the Reagan presidency the yearly federal deficit nearly doubled to $152.5 billion. The Bush presidency saw the deficit nearly double again, this time to $300 billion. By the time Bill Clinton was elected to office the budget deficit was over $300 billion a year with a combined federal deficit of well over $4.3 trillion.[80]

The federal deficit can be understood in other ways. For example, although the GDP has generally risen, the percentage of the total debt as a percentage of the GDP soared throughout the 1980s and early 1990s. In 1981 the gross federal deficit equaled 33.5 percent of the GDP; by 1991 that number had risen to 64 percent. Moreover, while the federal deficit equaled 1.7 percent of the GDP in 1979, by 1991 it had risen to 4.8 percent. By 1991 the debt held by the public totaled 47.8 percent of the GDP, the highest number since 1962.[81] Furthermore, the interest alone on the federal debt was almost $200 billion in 1991, which made it the third-largest single expenditure in the federal budget.

The *real* federal debt is masked by other variables, including the funds being borrowed from the surplus in the Social Security (OASDI) fund. For example, the *official* budget deficit in 1992 was $368 billion. However, if the money borrowed from the OASDI surplus (see the discussion of Social Security in Chapter 10) is factored in, that debt increases to $421 billion. In 1991 alone, the OASDI trust fund generated a surplus of $53.5 billion, which was on top of a $58.2 billion surplus in 1990.[82] When the OASDI fund is depleted in 2045, however, the federal government will have to cash in the IOUs it is holding to maintain the Social Security system. At that point, the *real* federal budget deficit will surface.

Despite the increase in governmental spending, the revenue base has remained relatively constant in some cases and has declined in others. For example, federal income taxes as a percentage of the GDP remained relatively stable between 1962 and 1991, hovering between 8.2 and 8.3 percent. On the other hand, corporate taxes as a percentage of the GDP declined from a high of 4.3 percent in 1967 to 1.7 percent in 1991. In effect, while public spending increased, total revenues as a percentage of the GDP remained relatively constant (from 17.8 to 20 percent) between 1962 and 1991.[83] Thus, the major strategy for funding the public sector has focused on increasing economic growth rather than on increasing revenues through higher levels of taxation. While this strategy has worked in periods of rapid economic growth, in other periods, for example, the recession of the late 1980s and early 1990s, it led to higher deficits.

Most budget deficit proposals presented in the 1980s and early 1990s sought to reduce the budget deficit in ways that would aggravate both the investment and the social deficit. One such example is the 1992 balanced budget amendment that was defeated by only nine votes in the U.S. House of Representatives and is scheduled to be reintroduced in 1993. This amendment would require a balanced budget by 1999, a goal that would necessitate deep budget cuts. Under a balanced budget act, governmental expenditures must match revenues. Where expenditures are greater than revenues, either more revenues must be raised or spending cuts must be enacted. In effect, the balanced budget amendment would deny the federal government the possibility of borrowing to finance all expenditures, including investments with long-term payoffs. Moreover, a balanced budget amendment would reverse the current economic strategy by requiring larger spending cuts or revenue increases in years of slow growth rather than in economically robust years. In addition, this amendment would make it harder to raise revenues than to cut programs, because any bill to raise revenues would have to be approved by the majority of the *full membership* of each house, whereas bills to cut programs would require only a majority of those *present* and *voting*.[84]

Severe budgetary problems also exist in many states. In 1991, 28 states instituted spending cuts or revenue increases to avoid deficits.[85] According to the National Conference of State Legislatures, state deficits totaled $30 billion in 1992.[86] Moreover, 35 states that had enacted balanced budgets for 1992 faced deficits as revenues lagged behind projections, expenditures were higher than predicted, or a combination of both occurred. In 1993, a large number of states again faced budget shortfalls.[87] These revenue shortfalls were exacerbated because the majority of states operate under balanced budget acts that prohibit deficit spending. In many of those states, arcane amendments were added to these acts that made it extremely difficult to raise additional taxes. For example, some states require a two-thirds vote of the legislature to raise taxes and other states mandate that tax increases must be enacted only through a special session of the legislature.

The 1993 budget deficit proposal offered by the Clinton administration attempted to chart a different course. First, the budget proposed to make substantial reductions in lower-priority spending areas, particularly where spending goes for consumption rather than investment. Second, Clinton proposed raising new revenues through tax increases, most of which would have been borne by those earning over $100,000 a year. Under Clinton's budget, two out of every three dollars saved from spending cuts and revenue increases would have been used for deficit reduction, while the third dollar would be earmarked for new investment to improve prospects for long-term economic growth. The Clinton administration argued that this budget plan would lower the federal deficit to $206 billion by FY 1997. However, the budget deficit was expected to rise to $241 billion in FY 1998 because of exploding health care costs.[88] In 1993 Congress approved a watered-down version of this budget.

In the end, the long-term effect of any governmental debt is based on how and where that deficit is spent. Specifically, if the bulk of the budget deficit is spent on physical and human capital improvements (e.g., roads, new schools, telecommunications, job training programs, etc.), then society can look forward to reaping long-term rewards in the form of future economic growth. But if the debt is spent entirely on entitlement programs and domestic consumption, then the long-term benefits of the debt are spurious. Regardless of the political administration, the federal debt will influence the funding of existing social programs and the creation of new ones well into the next century.

SOCIAL WORK, POLITICS, AND ADVOCACY ORGANIZATIONS

The formulation of social welfare policy in the United States is a complicated and often arduous process. Much of this can be attributed to the nature of American culture—to the competing interests that contribute to a pluralistic society, to the federal system of government that authorizes decision making on several levels at once, to the public and private bureaucracies that serve large numbers of consumers, to economic and technological developments that lead to specialization. Under these circumstances, the prospect of changing social welfare policy toward preconceived ends that improve the circumstances of disadvantaged groups can be a daunting task. Regrettably, few welfare professionals consider social policy an enterprise worthy of undertaking. Most social workers prefer direct service activity, where they have little opportunity for direct involvement in social welfare policy. Some social workers have attained important positions in federal and state human service bureaucracies and are much closer to the policy process. Unfortunately, these managers are often administering welfare policies that have been made by legislatures and that do not necessarily represent either clients or human service professionals. Perhaps most troubling, the involvement of social workers in the formulation of social policy has been diminishing in recent years. In a provocative statement, June Hopps, dean of the Boston College School of Social Work and former editor-in-chief of *Social Work,* acknowledged that "since the late 1960s and early 1970s, the [social work] profession has experienced a dramatic loss of influence in the arenas where policy is shaped and administered."[89]

If one indicator of good social policy is the correspondence between the policy and the social reality of its intended beneficiaries, then social welfare policy should be enhanced by the input of social workers. However, social workers have left much of the decision making about social welfare to professionals from other disciplines. "There are increasing numbers of non-social workers, including psychologists and urban planners," observed Eleanor Brilliant, "taking what might have been social work jobs in service delivery and policy analysis."[90] The consequences of welfare professionals opting to leave social policy in the hands of others are important. For direct service workers, it can mean having to apply eligibility standards or procedures that, while logical in some respects, make little sense in the social context of many clients. For the public, it may mean a gradual disenchantment with social programs that do not seem to work. While the causes of the retrenchment affecting social programs since the late 1970s are complex, it is worth noting that public dissatisfaction with social programs has escalated as welfare professionals have retreated from active involvement in social welfare policy.

For welfare professionals to reassert their voice in the formulation and execution of social policy will take concerted effort. Individual leadership is a necessary, but no longer sufficient, precondition for achieving this objective. Essential to the undertaking is the ability to understand and manipulate complex organizations and programs. In fact, this skill may be the most critical for welfare professionals to acquire if they are to advance social justice, for it addresses a question central to the postindustrial era. During the Industrial Revolution, Karl Marx suggested that the central question was "Who controls the means of production?" A mature industrial order and the expansion of civil bureaucracy led Max Weber to ask, "Who controls the means of administration?" The evolution of a postindustrial order where primary economic activity occurs in a service sector de-pendent on processed information raises another question: "Who controls the means of analysis?" If social workers are to shape social policy as effectively as they have in the past, they will have to learn to control the means of analysis. This means conducting research on social problems, surveying public opinion about welfare programs, analyzing existing social policy for opportunities to enhance welfare provision, and winning elected office in order to make decisions about proposed social welfare policies.

Advocacy Organizations and the New Welfare Institutes

In order to be successful in an increasingly complex political climate, social reformers must be able to take advantage of sophisticated advocacy methods. In social work, the organization that provides assistance to candidates is PACE, "the political arm of the National Association of Social Workers." PACE uses a variety of tactics to "expand social workers' activity in politics," including voter registration, support in political campaigns, and analysis of incumbents' voting records.[91] In 1986, PACE donated $110,000 to candidates running for national office; and 39 NASW chapters supported candidates for state and local office.[92] According to Toby Weismiller, NASW staff director for political affairs, PACE encourages social workers to view holding public office as a practice option. In her summary of the 1986 election, Weismiller noted that social workers who have "learned how to solve problems by working within the community" can use this to great political advantage,[93] as did Barbara Mikulski.

While PACE attempts to influence social welfare policy by sponsoring candidates for public office, other organizations focus on the policy process itself. Policy analysis organizations have been instrumental in shaping social policy from as early as the New Deal period. Subsequently, policy institutes have had liberal or conservative labels ascribed to them, with the liberal organizations achieving dominance

RETRENCHMENT - REDUCTION, CURTAILMENT

up until the late 1970s, when conservative institutes began gaining popularity. The failure of government social programs to expand during the Carter presidency, followed by the profoundly negative impact of the Reagan and Bush administrations, led social reformers to look to the traditional policy institutes—the Brookings Institution and the Urban Institute—for leadership. But the inability of these organizations to shape the debate on American social welfare policy compelled increasingly impatient reformers to establish a new group of policy analysis organizations.

Children's Defense Fund. Begun by Marian Wright Edelman in 1974, the Children's Defense Fund (CDF) sought to address the health, educational, and income needs of the nation's children.[94] By the mid-1980s, CDF had become a major voice in children's policy and had successfully advocated programs at the federal and state levels. CDF helped pass the Child Health Assurance Program in 1984, which expanded Medicaid eligibility to poor pregnant women and to children. Following the federal devolution of social programs to the states, CDF deployed field offices in five states and provided services to groups in many more. Notably, CDF has not winced at championing groups that have benefited least by welfare programs. Recently, CDF established the Adolescent Pregnancy Prevention project, an imaginative initiative relying on local groups to identify resources for teens.

In less than a decade, the CDF budget had grown to more than $4 million, and its staff to more than 70. Contributions have been received from important foundations, and support secured from influential persons, including Hillary Rodham Clinton. In addition to distributing educational packets to poor mothers, CDF regularly sends editorial packets to 200 newspapers across the nation. CDF also prints eye-catching posters and a number of publications for public education purposes. Its annual *The State of America's Children* is an authoritative compendium of issues and programs concerning children.

Independent Sector. In 1978, former Secretary of Health, Education and Welfare John Gardner and philanthropic executive Brian O'Connell merged the Coalition of National Voluntary Organizations and the National Council on Philanthropy to enhance the capacity of the nonprofit sector to deal with social problems. An organizing committee comprised of Gardner, O'Connell, John Filer (CEO of Aetna Insurance Company and chairperson of the Commission on Private Philanthropy and Public Needs) and Richard Lyman (president of the Rockefeller Foundation) chartered Independent Sector (IS) in 1980 to further voluntary sector activities. By 1986, IS had cultivated a board of directors numbering 40, which represented influential corporations and nonprofit organizations. From the dues of its 650 institutional members and from contributions, IS boasted a budget exceeding $4.5 million in 1986.[95]

IS quickly became an influential voice for the nonprofit sector, occupying a suite of executive offices in Washington, D.C. In addition to annual seminars on policies affecting nonprofit organizations, IS has sponsored seminal studies of the contributions of nonprofit organizations to the national culture. In an effort to extend the scope of its activities, IS has helped establish research centers in major universities, such as the Mandel Center for Nonprofit Management at Case Western Reserve University.[96]

The Center on Budget and Policy Priorities. Established in 1981 by Robert Greenstein, former administrator of the Food and Nutrition Service in the Agriculture Department, the Center on Budget and Policy Priorities (CBPP) has fought to defend social programs for low-income people against budget cuts. With a modest staff, CBPP distributes its analyses to congressional staffs, the media, and grass-roots organizations. Despite its small size, CBPP provided much of the program analysis to refute arguments presented by officials of the Reagan administration to cut means-tested social programs. Significantly, CBPP and CDF have developed a close working relationship. CBPP regularly provides data to CDF on the health and income status of children, and Greenstein is a regular contributor to CDF reports.[97]

The National Center for Social Policy and Practice. Still in the early stages of its development, the National Center for Social Policy and Practice (NCSPP) originated with the National Association of Social Workers (NASW). In launching NCSPP, NASW sought an institute that would serve as an advocate for a more just and equitable society through analyses of social problems, policy, and social work practice. Toward that end, NASW commenced a capital campaign to raise $10 million, and began a series of symposia designed to inform human service professionals about NCSPP and solicit their financial support. In the fall of 1986, Karen Orloff Kaplan, a clinical social worker with expertise in health policy and extensive legislative experience, was named director of NCSPP. Among the projects begun by NCSPP are a survey of benefits for employees of corporations that cover catastrophic illness and long-term care, an AIDS ethics forum, and a policy statement on welfare reform. Located near Washington, D.C., NCSPP is potentially well-positioned to influence social welfare policy.[98]

Social Work's Impact on Social Welfare Policy

The capacity of social workers to reassert their role in social welfare policy depends on the willingness of individuals to consider public office as a setting for social work practice and the ability of the new policy institutes to prepare sophisticated policy analyses. Despite the openness of the American political system, only the naive would ignore the very real obstacles to progressive social reform. Corporate contributions to candidates for federal office, $38.9 million in 1983 and 1984,[99] far exceeded the NASW-PACE effort. Without a strong economic base, new candidates for national office are unlikely to be successful in elections where massive campaign war chests are a prerequisite for office. The development of the new policy institutes is an encouraging sign, but even the more prominent of these—CDF and IS—are operating on budgets half the size of the more established policy organizations.

Political Practice. Although many welfare professionals began their careers advocating for social welfare policy, then assuming administrative positions managing social programs, others used elected office to advance social reform. The first woman elected to the House of Representatives was Jeannette Rankin, who won a seat in 1916 running as a Republican in Montana. As a social worker who had studied under Frances Perkins, Rankin voted for early social welfare legislation and against military expansion. More recently, social workers in political practice have included Maryann Mahaffey, a member of the Detroit City Council, and Ruth Messinger, a member of the New York City Council. Other social workers became mayors of major American cities. Sidney Barthelemy earned his Master of Social Work degree and directed the New Orleans City Welfare Department. In 1974, Barthelemy became the first African American elected to the Louisiana State Senate since Reconstruction. After serving on the New Orleans City Council, he was elected mayor in 1986.[100]

By the late 1980s, three social workers had attained national office. Ronald Dellums, a Marine Corps veteran, earned his Master of Social Work degree, then served on the Berkeley (California) City Council from 1967 to 1971, when he was elected to Congress. Since then he has proposed an alternative military budget based on arms reduction, fought for greater employment opportunities for minorities, and sought services for the homeless. Dellums is perhaps best known for his proposed National Health Service Act, "the most comprehensive health care legislation ever introduced in Congress."[101]

Barbara Mikulski received her Master of Social Work degree in 1965 and then served on the Baltimore City Council and in the United States House of Representatives. In 1986, Mikulski became the first Democratic woman to be elected to the United States Senate in her own right. Through appointments to the powerful Appropriations Committee and the Labor and Human Resources Committee, Mikulski is well positioned to advocate programs in health and human services.[102]

Edolphus "Ed" Towns received his Master of Social Work degree in 1973. Elected as the Democratic state committeeman and then the first African-American deputy borough president in Brooklyn's history, Towns was elected to serve as the representative of the 11th Congressional District of New York in 1982, with 90 percent of the vote. Towns's appointments to committees overseeing government operations, public works, and narcotics directly address the primary concerns of his inner-city constituents.[103]

Perhaps the best indicator of social work's future influence on social policy appears at the local level. Social workers have lobbied successfully on behalf of nonprofit agencies facing threats to their tax-exempt status,[104] encouraged students to engage in election campaigns and to become more knowledgeable about politics,[105] and managed a campaign for the election of a state senator.[106] In each of these instances, social workers were gaining experience that is essential to political involvement at higher levels.

A good example of what social workers can accomplish at the local level can be found in Tim Dee, the alderman from St. Louis's Seventeenth Ward from 1977 to 1987. Early in his tenure as alderman, Dee documented that the Seventeenth Ward had lost about one-third of its population during the 1970s, a demographic hemorrhage he attributed to the absence of employment opportunities in this inner-city political district. Using a little-known state law that provided for the creation of enterprise zones, Dee created legislation establishing the Seventeenth Ward as an enterprise zone which allowed businesses tax abatement and other advantages if they located in Dee's ward. The strategy paid off. In a few years following the creation of the enterprise zone in September 1983, the Seventeenth Ward boasted some 15 new businesses and 1,200 new jobs, and Dee's enterprise zone was noted as one of the 10 best nationally. But Dee was not content to allow his district to be manipulated by businesses seeking concessions from local government as a justification for their relocation. In order to make the enterprise zone responsive to the needs of local residents, Dee built into the enabling legislation an intriguing provision that established an enterprise zone commission, representing business and residents, to oversee the economic development of the area. It is difficult to imagine a better example of a social worker using the local political process to improve the conditions of so many disadvantaged people than Tim Dee's innovative work as an alderman in St. Louis.[107]

Social workers disinclined to engage in high-visibility activities such as campaigning for public office could make their imprint on politics through "constituent services." Writing of new developments in Congress, Pulitzer Prize-winning journalist Hedrick Smith observed that members of Congress are increasingly relying on constituent services in place of pork barrel projects as domestic expenditures dry up. Using a term familiar to most social workers, politicians call constituent services "casework"—which includes having your staff track down missing Social Security checks, inquire about sons and husbands in the armed services, help veterans get medical care, pursue applications for small-business loans."[108] The importance of political casework has been noted by political scientists who attribute up to 5 percent of the vote to such activities, a significant amount in close elections. David Himes of the National Republican Congressional Committee claimed that "our surveys have shown that constituency service—especially in the House—is more important than issues."[109]

The cultivation of practice skills in the political arena at the local level offers perhaps the most promise for social workers to regain influence in social welfare policy. Such activity can be undertaken by virtually any professional interested in the opportunity. On a volunteer basis, social workers would find few politicians willing to turn down their professional assistance in the provision of constituent services. With experience, enterprising social workers might find that political practice can be remunerative, providing that they possess the skills—such as conducting surveys, maintaining data banks of contributors, organizing public meetings, and keeping current on legislation important to constituents—needed by elected officials. From another perspective, however, the prospect of political practice should be taken seriously indeed. If social workers are sincere about making essential resources available to their clients—a responsibility stated in the *NASW Code of Ethics*—then some form of political practice is a professional obligation. "To do less," noted Maryann Mahaffey, "to avoid the political action necessary to provide these resources, is to fail to live up to the profession's code of ethical practice."[110]

DISCUSSION QUESTIONS

1. According to the authors, American social welfare is undergoing a transition. Which ideologies, schools of political economy, and interest groups within social welfare stand to gain most from this transition?

2. Ideology tends to parallel schools of political economy. From a sample of current social welfare issues—health care, long-term care of the aged, substance abuse, as examples—how would traditional conservatives and liberals address these problems?
   How would neoconservatives and neoliberals diverge from traditional conservatives and liberals in their proposals?

3. Welfare pluralism suggests that there are multiple definitions of welfare according to the different interest groups within social welfare. How would the various structural interests address current issues, such as abortion, the provision of adequate pay and benefits to poor workers, and ensuring that women have opportunities comparable to those of men?

4. If the structural interests in American welfare tend to exclude marginal groups, how could social policy be changed to better include these groups? What would be the likely reaction of the different structural interests to proposals for wideranging reforms?

5. The concept of structural interests suggests that institutions tend to reinforce the status quo. How does the social work program at your school reinforce structural interests? Which ones? What could your social work program do to provide more opportunities to marginal interests?

6. What are the pros and cons of the mixed welfare economy? Does the mixed welfare economy enhance or detract from the chances of disenfranchised groups receiving high quality social services? Why?

7. Which of the scenarios for the future welfare state presented in this chapter (the mixed welfare economy, the corporate welfare state, and dual welfare systems) stand the best chance of being realized? Why?

NOTES

1. Richard Titmuss, *Essays on the Welfare State* (Boston: Beacon Press, 1963), p. 16.

2. Education would, logically, be included here, except that in the American experience it has been treated separately.

3. Frances Fox Piven and Richard Cloward, *Regulating the Poor* (New York: Vintage, 1971).

4. David Gil, *Unraveling Social Policy* (Boston: Schenkman, 1981), p. 32.

5. Charles Prigmore and Charles Atherton, *Social Welfare Policy* (Lexington, Mass.: D.C. Heath, 1979), pp. 25–31.

6. Alfred Kahn, *Social Policy and Social Services* (New York: Random House, 1979).

7. Silvia Ann Hewlett, *When the Bough Breaks* (New York: Basic Books, 1991), p. 12.

8. Daniel Patrick Moynihan, *Came the Revolution* (New York: Harcourt Brace Jovanovich, 1988), p. 291.

9. R. Erikson, E. Hansen, S. Ringen, and H. Uusitalo, *The Scandinavian Model* (Armonk, N.Y.: M. E. Sharpe, 1987).

10. Richard Titmuss, *Commitment to Welfare* (New York: Pantheon, 1968), p. 127.

11. Harold Wilensky and Charles Lebeaux, *Industrial Society and Social Welfare* (New York: Free Press, 1965), p. 147.

12. Mimi Abramovitz, "The Privatization of the Welfare State," *Social Work* 31 (July-August 1986): pp. 257–64.

13. Wilensky and Lebeaux, *Industrial Society and Social Welfare*, p. 231.

14. Marc Bendick, *Privatizing the Delivery of Social Welfare Service* (Washington, D.C.: National Conference on Social Welfare, 1985), pp. 1, 6.

15. Quoted in David Broder, "Reagan's Policies Are Standard for Would-Be Successors," *Omaha World-Herald*, January 24, 1988, p. A-25.

16. Michael Sandel, "Democrats and Community," *The New Republic* (January 22, 1988), p. 21.

17. Bruce Jansson, *The Reluctant Welfare State* (Belmont, Calif.: Wadsworth, 1988).

18. Charles Murray, *Losing Ground* (New York: Basic Books, 1984), pp. 227–28.

19. See Peter Steinfels, *The Neoconservatives* (New York: Simon and Schuster, 1979).

20. Interview with Stuart Butler, Director of Domestic Policy at the Heritage Foundation, October 4, 1984.

21. Alvin Rabushka, "Tax and Spending Limits," in Peter Duignan and Alvin Rabushka (eds.), *The United States in the 1980s* (Stanford, Calif.: Hoover Institution, 1980), pp. 104–106.

22. Martin Anderson, "Welfare Reform," in Peter Duignan and Alvin Rabushka (eds.), *The United States in the 1980s*, pp. 171–76.

23. Peter Berger and John Neuhaus, *To Empower People* (Washington, D.C.: American Enterprise Institute, 1977).

24. Michael Novak, *Toward a Theology of the Corporation* (Washington, D.C.: American Enterprise Institute, 1981), p. 5.

25. George Gilder, *Wealth and Poverty* (New York: Basic Books, 1981), p. 118.

26. Anderson, "Welfare Reform," p. 145.

27. Jack Meyer (ed.), *Meeting Human Needs* (Washington, D.C.: American Enterprise Institute, 1983).

28. Stuart Butler and Anna Kondratas, *Out of the Poverty Trap: A Conservative Strategy for Welfare Reform* (New York: The Free Press, 1987).

29. Michael Novak, *The New Consensus on Family and Welfare* (Washington, D.C.: American Enterprise Institute, 1987).

30. William Lind and William Marshner, *Cultural Conservatism: Toward a New National Agenda* (Washington, D.C.: Free Congress Research and Education Foundation, 1987), p. 83.

31. Randall Rothenberg, *The Neoliberals* (New York: Simon and Schuster, 1984), pp. 244–45.

32. Charles Peters, "A New Politics," *Public Welfare* 41, no. 2 (Spring 1983): 34, 36.

33. Robert Reich, *The Next American Frontier* (New York: Times Books, 1983), p. 248.

34. Piven and Cloward, *Regulating the Poor*, pp. 3–4.

35. Louis Althusser, *Lenin and Other Essays* (London: N.B. Books, 1974).

36. Claus Offe, *Contradictions of the Welfare State* (Cambridge, Mass.: The MIT Press, 1984).

37. Diana DiNitto and Thomas Dye, *Social Welfare: Politics and Public Policy* (Englewood Cliffs, N.J.: Prentice-Hall, 1987), p. 25.

38. Committee on Ways and Means, U.S. House of Representatives, *Overview of Entitlement Programs, 1992 Green Book* (Washington, D.C.: U.S. Government Printing Office, 1992), p. 1799.

39. John Maynard Keynes, *The General Theory of Employment, Interest and Money* (London: Macmillan, 1936).

40. Robert Kuttner, "The Poverty of Economics," *The Atlantic Monthly*, February 1985, p. 74.

41. Congressional Budget Office, *The Economic and Budget Outlook: Fiscal Years 1993–1997* (Washington, D.C.: Congressional Budget Office, 1992), p. 28.

42. Jeffry Galper, "Introduction of Radical Theory and Practice in Social Work Education: Social Policy." Mimeographed paper, Michigan State University School of Social Work, ca. 1978.

43. Bruce Stokes, *Helping Ourselves: Local Solutions to Global Problems* (New York: W. W. Norton, 1981).

44. Sugata Dasgupta, "Towards a No-Poverty Society," *Social Development Issues* 12 (Winter 1983): 85–93.

45. Some of these economic principles were addressed by E. F. Schumacher, in *Small Is Beautiful* (New York: Harper and Row, 1973).

46. *Privatization: Toward More Effective Government* (Washington, D.C.: U.S. Government Printing Office, 1988), pp. 233–34.

47. Domestic Policy Council, *Up from Dependency* (Washington, D.C.: White House Domestic Policy Council, December 1986).

48. For a classic description of the assimilation phenomenon, see Nathan Glazer and Daniel Patrick Moynihan, *Beyond the Melting Pot* (Cambridge, Mass.: MIT Press, 1970).

49. Thomas Muller et al., *The Fourth Wave* (Washington, D.C.: Urban Institute, 1985).

50. The three auspices of social welfare in the United States have been termed the "mixed economy of welfare." See Sheila Kamerman, "The New Mixed Economy of Welfare," *Social Work* 28 (January-February 1983): 43–50.

51. Marc Bendick, *Privatizing the Delivery of Social Welfare Service* (Washington, D.C.: National Conference on Social Welfare, 1985).

52. Bruce Jansson, *The Reluctant Welfare State* (Belmont, Calif.: Wadsworth, 1988).

53. Michael Katz, *In the Shadow of the Poorhouse* (New York: Basic Books, 1986).

54. Robert Reich, *Tales of a New America* (New York: Vintage, 1987), p. 11.

55. Robert Schilling, Steven Schinke, and Richard Weatherly, "Service Trends in a Conservative Era: Social Workers Rediscover the Past," *Social Work* 33 (January-February 1988): 7.

56. Daniel Boorstin, *Hidden History* (New York: Harper and Row, 1987), p. 194.

57. Original emphasis, Daniel Patrick Moynihan, *Came the Revolution* (New York: Harcourt Brace Jovanovich, 1988), p. 291.

58. David Stoesz, "A Structural Interest Theory of Social Welfare," *Social Development Issues* 10 (Winter 1985): 73–85.

59. National Association of Social Workers, *Social Casework: Generic and Specific* (Silver Spring, Md.: NASW, 1974).

60. As per conversation with United Way of America staff, Washington, D.C., April 15, 1986.

61. Robert Alford, *Health Care Politics* (Chicago: University of Chicago Press, 1975), p. 204.

62. Roy Lubove, *The Professional Altruist* (New York: Atheneum, 1969), p. 197.

63. Walter Trattner, *From Poor Law to Welfare State* (New York: Macmillan, 1974), p. 237; and "The First Days of Social Security," *Public Welfare* 43 (Fall 1985): 112–19.

64. Alford, *Health Care Politics*, p. 2.

65. Congressional Budget Office, *The Economic and Budget Outlook*, p. 123.

66. Ibid., p. 199.

67. Trattner, *From Poor Law to Welfare State*, p. 250.

68. Robert Barker, "Private Practice Primer for Social Work," *NASW News*, October 1983, p. 13.

69. D. Goleman, "Social Workers Vault Into a Leading Role in Psychotherapy," *New York Times*, April 3, 1985, p. C-1.

70. Per conversation with NASW staff, November 16, 1992.

71. Maryann Mahaffey, "Fulfilling the Promise," *Proceedings*, Fifth Annual Association of Baccalaureate Program Directors Conference, Kansas City, 1987.

72. Donald Light, "Corporate Medicine for Profit," *Scientific American* 255 (December 1986): 81–89.

73. David Stoesz, "Human Service Corporations and the Welfare State," *Society/Transaction* 26 (Fall 1989): 321–32.

74. The EITC can be considered a "conservative" policy because it is tied to labor force participation instead of being based solely on need.

75. For further details, see David Stoesz, "The Functional Conception of Social Welfare," *Social Work* 34 (March 1989): 86–91.

76. Robert Kuttner, *The End of Laissez-faire* (New York: Alfred A. Knopf, 1991), p. 275.

77. Robert Greenstein and Paul Leonard, *A New Direction: The Clinton Budget and Economic Plan* (Washington, D.C.: Center on Budget and Policy Priorities, March 1993), p. 1.

78. U.S. House of Representatives, *1992 Green Book*, pp. 1795–1801.

79. Ibid.

80. Greenstein and Leonard, *A New Direction*, p. 2.

81. U.S. House of Representatives, *1992 Green Book*, pp. 1795–1801.

82. Ibid.

83. Ibid.

84. Greenstein and Leonard, *A New Direction,* pp. 1, 5.

85. Isaac Shapiro and Robert Greenstein, *A Painless Recession* (Washington, D.C.: Center on Budget and Policy Priorities, February 1991), p. ix.

86. Isaac Shapiro, Mark Sheft, Julie Strawn, Laura Summer, Robert Greenstein, and Steven D. Gold, *The States and the Poor: How Budget Decisions in 1991 Affected Low-Income People* (Washington, D.C.: Center on Budget and Policy Priorities, December 1991), p. vii.

87. Iris Lav and Steven Gold, *The States and the Poor* (Washington, D.C.: Center on Budget and Policy Priorities, 1993), p. vii.

88. Greenstein and Leonard, *A New Direction*, p. 4.

89. June Hopps, "Reclaiming Leadership," *Social Work* 31 (September-October 1986): 323.

90. Eleanor Brilliant, "Social Work Leadership: A Missing Ingredient?" *Social Work* 31 (September-October 1986): 328.

91. Interview with Toby Weismiller, NASW, Washington, D.C., January 11, 1988.

92. National Association of Social Workers, *Annual Report 1987* (Washington, D.C.: NASW, 1987), p. 23.

93. Interview, Weissmiller, January 11, 1988.

94. For details on CDF, see Joanna Biggar, "The Protector," *The Washington Post Magazine* (May 18, 1986), p. C-4; and *The Children's Defense Fund Annual Report 1984–85* (Washington, D.C.: Children's Defense Fund, 1985).

95. "CONVO: Background Information and Initial Statements by John Gardner and Brian O'Connell" (Washington, D.C.: Independent Sector, n.d.); Annual Report 1986 (Washington, D.C.: Independent Sector, 1986).

96. Brian O'Connell, *Philanthropy in Action* (New York: Foundation Center, 1987), pp. 103–104.

97. Information on CBPP was obtained from an interview with David Kahan at CBPP on March 12. 1984.

98. Interview with Karen Orloff Kaplan on January 11, 1988, at NCSPP; *National Association of Social Workers, Annual Report 1987* (Silver Spring, Md.: NASW, 1987), p. 18.

99. Steven Lydenberg, *Rating America's Corporate Conscience* (Reading, Mass.: Addison-Wesley, 1986), p. 39.

100. "Biographical Profile," courtesy of the Office of the Mayor, New Orleans, n.d.

101. "Biographical Sketch," courtesy of Congressman Dellums's Office, n.d.

102. "Biographical Sketch," courtesy of Senator Mikulski's Office, n.d.

103. "Congressman Ed Towns," courtesy of the Congressman's Office, n.d.

104. Elliot Pagliaccio and Burton Gummer, "Casework and Congress: A Lobbying Strategy," *Social Casework* 69 (March 1988): 321–30.

105. Grafton Hull, "Joining Together: A Faculty-Student Experience in Political Campaigning," *Journal of Social Work Education* 23 (Fall 1987): 116–23.

106. William Whittaker and Jan Flory-Baker, "Ragtag Social Workers Take on the Good Old Boys and Elect a State Senator," in Maryann Mahaffey and John Hanks (eds.), *Practical Politics: Social Work and Political Responsibility* (Silver Spring, Md.: National Association of Social Workers, 1982).

107. Telephone interview with Tim Dee, March 20, 1988.

108. Hedrick Smith, *The Power Game* (New York: Random House, 1988), p. 124.

109. Ibid., p. 152.

110. Mahaffey and Hanks, *Practical Politics* (see chap. 10, "Political Action in Social Work"), p. 284.

CHAPTER 2

A Framework for Social Policy Analysis

This chapter examines one of the major tools used by the policy researcher—a structured framework for policy analysis—as well as the common components of such policy frameworks. We also propose our own model for policy analysis.

The previous chapter examined how ideology, economic theories, and interest groups influence the social welfare state, and the role that concepts such as social justice and equity play in the formation of social welfare policy. A policy framework—in other words, a systematic means for examining a specific social welfare policy or a series of policies—is one means for evaluating the congruence of a policy with the mission and goals of the social welfare state. Policy frameworks also assess whether key social welfare values (e.g., social justice, redistribution, equity) are incorporated within a given policy. Moreover, policy frameworks are useful in determining whether a policy fits within the theoretical guidelines of social welfare activities, and whether a policy is consistent with established social welfare foundations, that is, with the historical precedents that guide social welfare initiatives. For example, let us consider the proposal that AIDS testing should be made mandatory for everyone and that those found to be AIDS-positive should be quarantined. The

use of a policy framework would show that this proposal represents a clear break with the general drift of late twentieth-century social policy and, moreover, that it repudiates general social welfare values that stress self-determination, justice, equity, and compassion. In addition, a systematic analysis would show that this policy is not feasible—economically, politically, or socially.

Apart from examining a given policy, an analytic framework is also useful for comparing existing policies. For example, comparing the mental health policies of Missouri with those of Massachusetts and Minnesota would yield valuable information for all three states. A comparative analysis of the health systems of the United States, Canada, and Sweden would also provide useful information for decision makers. Lastly, analytic frameworks can be used to evaluate competing policies. Given alternative policies, the analytic framework could be used to help the analyst make a recommendation as to which policy would most effectively solve a problem or remedy a need.

Social welfare policies and programs are complex phenomena. For example, it is easy to propose a social policy such as mandatory drug testing for all federal employees. On the surface, th policy may appear simple: Drug users are discovered by the tests and are then forced to seek treatment. On closer scrutiny, however, the hidden issues appear more problematic. Is it constitutional to require drug treatment if a positive result is found? Is occasional use of marijuana sufficient grounds for mandatory drug treatment? Because it is a legal substance, tests do not measure the appearance of alcohol. Is alcohol therefore less debilitating than marijuana? Can the policy of mandatory drug testing be misused by supervisors to harass employees? Will the policy produce the intended results? Although these questions must be addressed, without a way to systematically analyze the effects of an intended policy, decisions become arbitrary and may produce side effects worse than the original problem.

All well-designed policy frameworks are characterized by eight key elements:

1. Policy frameworks attempt to *systematically* analyze a social policy or program.
2. Policy frameworks reflect an understanding that social policy is not created in a vacuum but is, rather, context-sensitive and that policy options usually contain a set of competing priorities.
3. Policy frameworks employ rational methods of inquiry and analysis. The evidence used for the analysis of a policy is derived from scientific inquiry, and all data must be collected from reliable and legitimate sources. Furthermore, the data should be interpreted and analyzed as objectively as possible.
4. Although open to interpretation, the analytic method is explicit, and all succeeding analysts should be able to approximate the same conclusion.
5. The objectives of policy analysis reflect a commitment to deriving the largest possible social benefit at the least possible social cost. Thus, a good social policy is one that benefits at least one person (as that person perceives his or her own best self-interest) while at the same time hurting no

one. In the real world of finite resources—and of proliferating claims upon them—that goal is rarely achieved. Nevertheless, analysts should strive to realize that aim.
6. Policy frameworks should take into account the unintended consequences of a particular policy or program.
7. Policy frameworks examine a particular policy in the context of alternatives, that is, alternative social policies or alternative uses of the resources allocated to a given policy.
8. Policy frameworks examine the potential impact of a policy (or series of policies) on other social policies, social problems, and the public.

In the end, the analysis of social policy—often through utilizing a policy framework—provides decision makers and the general public with information, an understanding of the possible ramifications of the policy on the target problem as well as on other problems and policies, and a series of alternative policies that could be more effective in dealing with the problem. Untoward costs and injuries are more likely to result when a systematic framework for policy analysis is not used.

History is replete with examples of well-intentioned policies that proved to be catastrophic. For example, the prohibition of alcohol from 1919 to 1932 was enacted by the U.S. Congress in order to cut down on crime, familial instability, unemployment, and many other social problems. Proponents of Prohibition, including many social workers, touted the end of alcohol as a major step forward in the social evolution of the United States. However, when Prohibition was repealed 13 years later, most of the original supporters did not vigorously argue for its continuance. Despite the hopes of its backers, Prohibition did not decrease crime and familial instability or encourage social order; instead, Prohibition encouraged the growth of an organized crime industry that fed the ongoing taste of Americans for alcohol. Instead of eliminating an alcohol-related night life, Prohibition fostered the growth of illegal but well-attended speakeasies. Even many supporters conceded that alcohol was almost as abundant as before Prohibition. Had a systematic policy analysis of Prohibition been undertaken, good policy analysts might have demonstrated the futility of the measure. However, social policy is often driven by politics, and rarely, if ever, systematically analyzed. Policy analysis often occurs only after a bill or policy is enacted, and analysts are occasionally asked to perform an autopsy to determine why a specific bill or policy failed.

The purpose of a policy framework is to provide the analyst with a model—a set of questions—for systematically analyzing a policy.[1] As such, the choice of a framework must fit the requirements of the project as well as those of the analyst. Every existing policy framework can either be fine-tuned or substantially modified. In fact, the best policy framework may result from a synthesis of existing models. In short, a policy framework is simply a set of questions that is systematically asked of a past, present, or future policy to determine its desirability.

A PROPOSED MODEL
FOR POLICY ANALYSIS

The policy analyst is expected to evaluate a policy and make recommendations. In order to succeed in this charge, the analyst must accept his or her own values while, at the same time, basing the analysis on objective criteria. The policy framework that we propose here is divided into four sections: (1) the historical background of the policy, (2) the description of the problem that necessitated the policy, (3) the description of the policy, and (4) the policy analysis.

Policy Framework

The Historical Background of the Policy. Understanding the historical antecedents of a particular policy is important to the policy analyst for two reasons: The analyst needs to know the historic problems that led to the creation of the policy, and he or she needs to know the historical background of the policy under consideration. Questions that are addressed should include: What historical problems led to the creation of the policy? How important have these problems been historically? How was the problem previously handled? What is the historical background of the policy? When did the policy originate? How has the original policy changed over time? And what is the legislative history of the policy (e.g., what similar issues have been discussed and debated in the House and the Senate)? In addition, the policy analyst must examine similar policies that were adopted in the past and how they fared.

Apart from providing continuity, a historical analysis helps to curb the tendency of decision makers to reinvent the wheel. Policies that were previously unsuccessful may continue to be so, or the analyst may come to realize that historical circumstances have changed, thus creating a climate in which a previously failed policy might now be viable. In addition, a historical analysis helps the analyst to understand the forces that were previously mobilized to support or oppose a given policy. In short, a historical analysis locates a particular policy within a historical fabric, thus helping to explicate the often evolutionary nature of a specific social policy or series of policies.

Description of the Problem That Necessitated the Policy. The second major step in analyzing a policy addresses the problem(s) that led to the creation of the policy. In order to assess the ability of a policy to successfully remediate a social problem, the analyst must understand the parameters of the problem. Furthermore, the analyst must be familiar with the nature, scope, and magnitude of the problem and with the populations affected by the problem. In this way, the policy analyst is able to discern early the appropriateness of the policy for tackling the problem it is expected to remedy. Specific questions that the policy analyst might ask include: What is the nature of the problem? How widespread is the problem? How many people are affected by the problem? Who is affected and how? What are the causes of the problem? How will the policy help to address the problem?

③ *Description of the Policy.*   The next step in this policy framework is the description of the policy. This section requires a detailed explanation of the policy, including a description of: (1) the way the policy is intended to work; (2) the resources or opportunities the policy is expected to provide (i.e., power, cash, economic opportunity, in-kind services, status redistribution, goods and services, and so forth); (3) who will be covered by the policy and how (e.g., universal versus selective entitlement, means testing, and so forth); (4) how the policy will be implemented, including means for coordination; (5) the intended short- and long-term goals and outcomes of the policy; (6) the administrative auspices under which the policy will be lodged, including the roles of the private sector and of local, state, and federal governments in the development and implementation of the policy; (7) the funding mechanism for the policy, including long- and short-term funding commitments; (8) the agencies or organizations that have overall responsibility for overseeing, evaluating, and coordinating the policy; (9) the criteria, formal or informal, that will be used, to determine the effectiveness of the policy and its appropriateness; (10) the length of time the policy is expected to be in existence—for example, is it a ''Sunset law'' (a law designed to end at a certain date)? and (11) the knowledge base or scientific grounding on which the policy rests.

④ *Policy Analysis.*   In this section, the policy analyst goes beyond a simple description of the policy and engages in a *systematic analysis* of the policy (the heart of any good policy analysis).

Policy Goals. The goals of the policy are the criteria by which all else is measured. Oftentimes the goals of a policy are not overtly stated,

and the analyst must tease out or conjecture as to what the overall goals of the policy are. The following questions may help to explicate the goals of a particular policy.

- Are the goals of the policy legal?
- Are the goals of the policy just and democratic?
- Do the goals of the policy contribute to greater social equality?
- Do the goals of the policy positively affect the redistribution of income, resources, rights, entitlements, rewards, opportunities, and status?
- Do the goals of the policy contribute to a better quality of life for the target population? Will the goals adversely affect the quality of life of the target group?
- Does the policy contribute to positive social relations between the target population and the overall society?
- Are the goals of the policy consistent with the values of professional social work (i.e., self-determination, client rights, self-realization, and so forth)?

Other, perhaps more difficult questions should also be asked. Analysts must understand the value premises of the policy as well as the ideological assumptions underlying it. To this end, several questions should be asked: What are the hidden ideological suppositions contained within the policy? How is the target population viewed in the context of the policy? What social vision, if any, does the policy contain? Does the policy encourage the continuation of the status quo or does it represent a radical departure? Who are the major beneficiaries of the policy—the target population or some other group? In whose best interest is the policy? Is the policy designed to foster real social change or merely to placate a potentially insurgent group? Uncovering the hidden ideological dimensions of a policy is often the most difficult task for the policy analyst.

Feasibility. Despite the good intentions of a prospective policy, its goals must be achievable for it to be successfully implemented. American history is littered with good policies that were simply not viable at the time they were proposed. For example, during the middle 1930s (at the height of the Great Depression), a California physician named Francis Townsend proposed that all citizens over the age of 65 be given a flat governmental pension of $200 per month. Although in more prosperous times this proposal might have been given at least a cursory hearing, in the midst of one of the greatest depressions in American history policymakers summarily dismissed the proposal as not viable. The overall feasibility of a policy is based on three factors: political feasibility, economic feasibility, and administrative feasibility.

Political Feasibility of a Policy

The political feasibility of a particular policy is always a judgment call. In order to evaluate a policy, the analyst must assess which groups will oppose and which groups will support a particular policy, as well as estimate the constituency and power base of each group. In American politics, however, the size of the constituency base and its relative power are sometimes unrelated. For example, despite its relatively small numbers, the American Medical Association (AMA) is a powerful lobby in American politics. Conversely, although more than 30 million people in the United States are poor, their political clout at this point is negligible. Thus, the analyst must carefully weigh the political salience of each side in the policy struggle.

The political viability of a policy is always subject to the public's perception of its feasibility. In other words, for a policy to be feasible, it must be _perceived_ as being feasible by the public. For example, although some observers maintain that a sizable portion, if not the majority, of the public would like to see some form of National Health Insurance (NHI), none exists. In part, an NHI plan has not been enacted because the public believes that it cannot happen, and in part, because of the power of the medical lobby, particularly the AMA and the insurance lobby. Therefore, the United States lacks NHI not because the public rejects it, but because it believes that it cannot occur. Thus is born a public myth around what is possible and impossible. Many good policy options are not enacted because of the public mythology surrounding what is feasible.

To assess the political feasibility of a policy, the analyst must also examine the public sentiment toward it. Is a large segment of the public concerned about the policy? Do people feel that they will be directly affected by the policy? Does the policy address a problem that is considered to be a major political issue? Does the policy threaten fundamental social values? Is the policy compatible with the present social and political climate? What is the general public sentiment toward the policy? What is the possibility that either side will be able to marshal public sentiment for or against the policy? The answers to these questions help the policy analyst determine the political feasibility of the policy.

The politics of political feasibility also encompass a smaller, but no less important, dimension. In order to do a thorough assessment, the analyst must understand the relationship between the policy and external factors in agencies and institutions. For example, which social welfare agencies, institutions, or organizations support or oppose the policy? What is the relative strength of each group? How strong is their support or opposition to the policy? What are the major federal, state, or local agencies affected by this policy? How are they affected? The world of social policy is heavily political, with some governmental and private social welfare agencies having political power that is on a par with that of elected decision makers. These groups often coalesce around issues, problems, or policies that directly affect them, and through their lobbying strength they have the ability to defeat legislation. In cases where they cannot defeat a policy outright, these administrative institutions can choose to implement a policy in such a way as to ensure its failure. The analyst must therefore take into account whether these administrative organs support or oppose a proposed or existing social policy.

Economic Feasibility of a Policy

Many, if not most, social policies require some form of direct or indirect funding. In assessing the economic feasibility of a policy, the analyst must ask several hard questions: What is the minimum level of funding required for the successful implementation of the policy? Does adequate funding for the policy currently exist? If not, what is the public sentiment toward reallocating resources for the policy? Is the funding called for by the policy adequate? What are the future funding needs of the policy likely to be?

Given the magnitude of the current federal deficit (around $4.2 trillion in late 1992), it appears unlikely that new social policy initiatives requiring large revenues will be successful. Perhaps new policy legislation necessitating additional revenues will be based on the reallocation of existing resources (budget-neutral policies) rather than on new revenue sources, a situation that may result in taking money away from one program to fund another. (This is referred to in Congress as "paygo" funding.) The inherent danger in this approach is that by thinning out fiscal resources among many programs none will be adequately funded. The analyst must therefore decide whether a new policy initiative should be recommended regardless of the funding prospects. The positive and negative aspects of this decision are complex. If a new policy is recommended, despite insufficient resources, the chances of its failure are greater. However, if a policy is not recommended, the possibility exists that adequate fiscal resources might be allocated in the future. Many policy analysts lean toward incremental approaches, thus tending to recommend policies in the hope that suitable funding will become available in the future.

Administrative Feasibility of a Policy

The analyst must also be concerned with the administrative viability of the policy. Whatever the potential value of the policy, responsible administrative agencies must be capable of effectively implementing it. In other words, administrative and supervisory agencies must possess the personnel, resources, skills, and expertise needed to effectively implement the policy. If the requisite personnel are lacking, agencies must have the fiscal resources to hire qualified employees. In addition, directors and supervisors must be sympathetic to the goals of the policy, have the expertise and skill necessary to implement or oversee the policy, and possess an understanding of the fundamental objectives of the policy initiative.

Effectiveness. Effectiveness refers to the likelihood that the policy can meet its stated objectives. In short, is the policy likely to accomplish what its creators intended? The answer to this question encompasses several further questions: Is the policy broad enough to accomplish its stated goals? Will the benefits of the policy reach the target group? Are the side effects of the policy likely to cause other social problems? What ramifications does the policy have for the nontarget sector (e.g., higher taxes, reduced opportunity, diminished freedom, fewer resources, and so forth)?

An important question facing policy analysts involves the nature and extent of the unintended consequences of a policy. Virtually all policies have certain consequences that are unforeseen. An example of the unforeseeable consequences of a social policy can be seen in the case of methadone, a drug legally administered to addicts as a substitute for heroin. When introduced in the 1960s, methadone was thought to be a safe way to wean addicts away from heroin. By the mid-1970s, however, health experts realized that methadone was almost as addictive as heroin and that some addicts were selling their methadone as a street drug. Despite this outcome, some addicts were able to withdraw from heroin and, in hindsight, the methadone program was probably a positive development. Because policy analysts cannot see into the future, they make their recommendations on the basis of available data. Nevertheless, an attempt must be made to predict possible adverse future consequences.

Efficiency and Alternative Policies.   These refer to the cost-effectiveness of the proposed policy compared to that of alternative policies, no policy, or the present policy. Social policy always involves a trade-off. Even in the best of economic times, societal resources are always inadequate compared to the breadth of human need. For example, virtually everyone could benefit from some form of social welfare allocation, whether it be counseling services, food stamps, or free health care. But because resources are finite, society must choose the primary beneficiaries of its social allocations. Publicly financed services are often awarded on the basis of two criteria: (1) the severity of the problem, with services going to those who most require the allocation; and (2) means, with services provided to those who can least afford them. As a result of finite resources, the adequate funding of one policy often means denying or curbing allocations to another. This is the essential trade-off in social welfare policy. When analysts evaluate a policy, they must be cognizant that promoting one policy means that needs in other areas may go unmet. Thus, a primary question remains: Is this policy important enough to justify the expenditure of scarce resources? And are there other areas where resources could be better used?

The policy analyst is also concerned with the cost-effectiveness of a given policy compared to the cost-effectiveness of alternative policies. Given the additional expenditure of money, will the new policy provide results that are better than either the present policy or no policy at all? Is it advantageous to enlarge or modify the present policy as opposed to creating a new one? Can an alternative policy provide better results at lower cost? What alternative policies could be created that would achieve the same results? How do these alternative policies compare with each other and with the proposed policy? These questions must be answered in any thorough policy analysis.

In conclusion, the policy analyst must address several key questions: Is the proposed policy workable and desirable? What, if any, modifications should be made in the policy? Does the policy represent a wise use of resources? Are there alternative policies that would be preferable? How feasible is the implementation of the policy? What barriers, if any, are there to the full implementation of the policy? These questions represent the core of policy analysis.

ANALYZING A SOCIAL POLICY

There are two major hurdles in policy analysis. The first is focusing on a manageable social policy, and the second is finding or generating information relevant to it.

One of the most difficult tasks in analyzing a social policy is the choice of the actual policy. In order to do a careful policy analysis, the analyst must choose a policy that is both discrete and specific. For example, it would be difficult, if not impossible, to do an exhaustive analysis of child welfare policy in the United States. For one thing, the United States does not have *one* specific child welfare policy. The American policy on child welfare is composed of myriad programs that constitute a patchwork quilt of social policies. Given the limitations of time and resources, the question then becomes *which* policy will be analyzed. Second, the differences in child welfare policies on the national versus the state or community levels makes such a policy analysis even more daunting. Thus, defining and narrowing down a specific and manageable social policy constitutes one of the most formidable tasks in policy analysis.

A second task involves locating relevant information on a specific social policy. In general, there are seven major avenues for finding information on a specific policy.

First, policy analysts may choose to generate their own data through conducting primary research, including surveys, opinion polls, experimental research, longitudinal studies, and so forth. Although this method can yield a rich body of information, the time and cost constraints may prove an impossible obstacle. Moreover, the same research may already exist in other places, in which case the replication of the effort would be unwarranted.

Second, governmental or agency records are often an important source of relevant data on a specific policy. These records can include archives, memos, and the minutes of the meetings of boards of directors, governmental officials, and staff. This research method can also include an examination of policy manuals, departmental records, and minutes of public meetings.

A third avenue for policy research involves use of the records and published minutes of legislative bodies and committees. On the federal level, this includes the *Congressional Record* and the minutes of the various House and Senate committees and subcommittees. All state legislatures have similar record-keeping procedures, and most of these legislative records can be found in regional or university libraries.

A fourth source of information is found in governmental publications. For example, the U.S. Government Printing Office maintains catalogues of all government documents published. Other documents include the Census Bureau's population studies (many of which are updated annually), publications of the Departments of Labor, Commerce, Housing, and Health and Human Services, and the Green Book (a yearly publication containing the most comprehensive information available on social programs and participants). Many of these publications can be found in regional and university libraries.

A fifth source of policy-relevant information is provided by think tanks, advocacy organizations, and professional associations. All think tanks (many of which also function as advocacy organizations) employ research staff who evaluate and analyze social policies. Examples of these think tanks include the Brookings Institute, the American Enterprise Institute, the Heritage Foundation, the Hoover Institute, the Urban Institute, the Center for Budget and Policy Priorities, the Reason Foundation, the Hudson Foundation, the Progressive Policy Institute, the Economic Policy Institute, the Independent Sector, and NASW's National Center for Policy and Practice, to name a few. Because most, if not all, of these think tanks are affiliated with a particular political ideology, their evaluation of data and their policy recommendations should be viewed critically.

Many national advocacy organizations retain research staff and publish reports that may be helpful to the policy analyst. Some of these organizations are the Urban League, the NAACP, the Children's Defense Fund, the National Farm Organization, and the National Organization for Women. Many professional associations, like the American Medical Association, the American Public Welfare Association, and the American Psychological Association, also publish policy-relevant information. A listing of these organizations can be found in any major library.

A sixth procedure used by policy analysts is to consult professional journals, books, and monographs. Articles or books on specific policy areas can be found in various places, including the *Social Science Index*, the subject headings in card catalogues, in on-line library systems, and in electronic data bases, which are becoming increasingly common in the larger professional associations. Electronic data bases are also becoming common commercial ventures.

Seventh and last, policy-relevant information may be gathered from interviews with principals in the policy process, advocates, recipients of services, and government officials. Personal interviews may be useful in determining the background of the issue, in assessing the opposition to a particular policy, or in gauging the public reaction to a policy. Taken together, these sources can be a gold mine for the policy analyst.

THE INCOMPLETENESS OF POLICY ANALYSIS

The choice of a framework for policy analysis is dependent upon a number of considerations, including: (1) the kind of problem or policy that must be analyzed; (2) the available resources of the policy analyst, including time, money, staff, facilities, and the availability of data; (3) the requirements of the decision maker requesting the analysis; and (4) the time frame in which the analysis must be completed.

No policy analysis is ever complete. Because it is impossible to discover *all* of the data (data are essentially infinite) and to ask *all* of the possible questions, policy analysis is never either complete or perfect. Policy analysis is always an approximation of the ideal and, as such, decisions are always made on the basis of in-

complete data. How incomplete the data are and how close an approximation of a rational decision is provided to decision makers will depend on the skills of the analyst, the available resources, and the time allotted for the project.

Despite its reliance on an analytic framework, social policy analysis in the real world is to some degree always subjective. Because policy is analyzed by human beings who are only human, it is always done through the lens of the analyst's value system, ideological beliefs, and particular understanding of the goals and purposes of social welfare. Subjectivity may be seen in the omission (conscious or otherwise) of facts or questions or in the relative weight given to one variable at the expense of others. Subjectivity may also be expressed by asking the wrong questions of the policy, evaluating it on the basis of expectations that it cannot meet, and by expecting it to tackle a problem that it was not designed to address. Lastly, political pressure may be put on the policy analyst to come up with recommendations that are acceptable to a certain interest group. Regardless of the causes of subjectivity, policy analysis is always an approximation of the ideal, in effect an informed hunch as to the effects of a policy or a set of policies.

DISCUSSION QUESTIONS

1. What are the main advantages of using a systematic framework for social policy analysis? Describe the benefits of using such a framework. What, if any, are the potential drawbacks?
2. Although by definition the *unintended* consequences of a social policy are unpredictable, what specifically can a policy analyst do to minimize the risks of a policy producing harmful and unintended consequences? Describe a recent social policy that has produced unintended consequences that were either positive or harmful.
3. Is it possible to neutralize a policy researcher's personal values when conducting a policy analysis? If so, describe ways in which this can be done.

4. What specific components could be added to the proposed policy framework presented in this chapter? Which of the components provided in this framework are the most important and why?
5. Are most social policies analyzed thoroughly and rationally? If not, why not? Describe the factors that stand in the way of a systematic and rational analysis of social policy in American society. How much value do decision makers place on social policy research before reaching a decision?
6. Because any analysis of social policy is by nature incomplete, should decision makers therefore not rely heavily on policy studies? What alternatives, if any, can be used in lieu of a thorough and systematic policy analysis?

NOTE

1. Many social policy writers, including Elizabeth Huttman, *Introduction to Social Policy* (New York: McGraw-Hill, 1981); Neil Gilbert and Harry Specht, *Dimensions of Social Welfare Policy,* 2nd ed. (Englewood Cliffs, N.J.: Prentice-Hall, 1986); Gail Marker, ''Guidelines for Analysis of a Social Welfare Program,'' in John E. Tropman et al. (eds.), *Strategic Perspectives on Social Policy* (New York: Pergamon Press, 1976); David Gil, *Unraveling Social Policy* (Boston: Schenkman, 1981); and Charles Prigmore and Charles Atherton, *Social Welfare Policy* (New York: D. C. Heath, 1979), have developed excellent policy frameworks.

CHAPTER 3

The Origins of the American Social Welfare State

The American social welfare state did not emerge out of nowhere. To grasp its complexity, the student of social welfare policy must understand the historical foundations on which it has been built. This chapter examines the historical antecedents of the American social welfare state, taking the reader from its distant roots in the English Poor Laws to the more recent developments that mark the emergence of the modern social welfare state.

THE ENGLISH POOR LAWS

The English Poor Laws in many ways functioned as an early model for American social welfare. Early social welfare relief in England was considered a private and church matter. For example, individual benefactors took responsibility for building almshouses, hospitals, and even bridges and roads. Despite private philanthropy, the main burden for the poor rested on the shoulders of the Church. Most European governments, including that of England, assumed little responsibility for the care of the poor. This situation would change, however, with the emergence of industrialization and its stark realities.

As a result of rapid industrialization and the transformation of farmland into more profitable pasture areas for sheep—a transformation that was necessary to feed the hungry wool mills of England—the ensuing urban migration of displaced and impoverished peasants produced untoward social consequences, including begging and vagrancy. In 1349, after the Black Death had drastically reduced the population of England, King Edward III created the Statute of Labourers, which fixed maximum wages, placed travel restrictions on unemployed persons, forced the jobless to work for any employer willing to hire them, and outlawed giving alms to the able-bodied.[1] In 1531 the English Parliament outlawed begging for the able-bodied. Although repressive, the act also instructed local officials to seek out the worthy poor and to assign them areas where they could beg.[2]

The passage of the Act for the Punishment of Sturdy Vagabonds and Beggars in 1536—the Poor Law—further mandated the English government to take limited responsibility for the poor. Although this act increased the punishment for begging, it also ordered officials to obtain resources—through voluntary church donations—to care for the poor, the sick, the lame, and the aged. In addition, the statute required local officials to find work for the able-bodied and to arrange for the apprenticeship of poor children aged five to fourteen. In 1572 the English Parliament enacted yet another poor law, this time requiring local officials to implement a mandatory tax for the provision of economic relief to the poor.[3]

In 1601 the English government established the Elizabethan Poor Laws. These laws were developed primarily to control those poor who were unable to obtain employment in the new industrial sector and who, because of that, might become disruptive. Taxes were levied to finance the law, but the rules were, by our standards, harsh. Again a primary theme of the law was to distinguish the "deserving" from the "undeserving" poor. The worthy poor were the lame, the blind, orphaned children, and those who were unemployed through no fault of their own. The unworthy poor were vagrants, drunkards, and those considered slothful. The Elizabethan Poor Laws, which with minor modifications were to stand for 250 years, contained positive and repressive features. For example, parents with means were legally responsible for supporting their children and grandchildren. Children were responsible for supporting their parents and grandparents. On the repressive side, the unworthy poor were sent to workhouses and forced to do menial work for the minimum necessities of life. Poor people who refused to work could be sent to jail or, in some cases, executed. In addition, the English Poor Laws established the principle of "less eligibility," the idea that welfare will be less than the lowest prevailing wage.

In essence, these laws established the responsibility of the English government to provide relief to the needy. Furthermore, the laws decreed that the needy had a legal right to receive governmental assistance. In order to define the boundaries of government help, the law distinguished among three classes of dependents and proposed remediative measures: Needy children were given apprenticeships, the able-bodied were given work, and the worthy poor were provided either indoor (institutional) or outdoor (home) relief. Lastly, the law or-

dered local governments to assume responsibility for the needy.[4] The English Poor Laws formed the basis for statutes that were enacted in both colonial and postcolonial America.[5]

THE POOR IN COLONIAL AMERICA

Many aspects of the Elizabethan welfare system were adopted by the American colonists. Like its English corollary, the parish, the colonial town was responsible for its residents. Up to about 1700, when almshouses began to appear, cases of pauperism were handled on an individual basis in town meetings. When the number of poverty cases increased as a result of indentured servants and abandoned children, the English system of overseers was introduced.

Most settlers in colonial America were poor.[6] However, unlike their European ancestors, they were not destitute. Therefore, despite the poverty in colonial America, pauperism was not widespread. According to Robert Morris, less than 1 percent of American colonists received help from outside sources.[7]

In smaller towns unable to support an almshouse, it was not uncommon for the town council to auction off the poor to neighboring farmers, apprentice out children, place the poor in private homes at public expense, or send them to privately operated almshouses. Settlers believed that children should be part of a family unit and thus the practice of indenture became widespread. However, by the end of the colonial period, the locus of responsibility for the poor began to shift from the town to the province.[8]

While the settlers had compassion for indigent townspeople, they showed considerably less compassion for destitute strangers. As the numbers of poor increased, some communities enacted laws of settlement. Residency requirements were strictly enforced through the policies of "warning out" or "passing on." The former term meant that newcomers were urged to move on if they appeared to be indigent. Passing on meant returning the transient poor to their former counties of residence. In addition to these "warning out" practices, some colonies established residency requirements to determine eligibility for public assistance. The "fit" poor in colonial America were treated harshly. Idleness was regarded as a vice and the able-bodied loafer was either indentured, expelled from town, whipped, or jailed. By the eighteenth century the able-bodied unemployed were placed in workhouses or almshouses.[9]

By the early 1800s the process for helping the poor had changed radically. The quasi-benevolence of the town council was replaced by a reliance on workhouses. In some areas, the use of outdoor relief was all but abandoned in favor of institutional care. Moreover, it was not until the mid-1800s that the national government conceded even limited responsibility for the poor. Local government activities were based on a belief that poverty was a consequence of moral weakness, a theory linked to Puritan values and hence more prevalent in the New England than in the Middle Atlantic states, and thus demanded reeducation and an economical system of relief.[10]

SOCIAL WELFARE IN THE CIVIL WAR ERA

Historically, the federal government's role in providing relief has been a contentious issue. This question was to be advanced by the reform activities of Dorothea Dix, a name that has become synonymous with the movement for the humane care of the mentally ill. As a result of volunteering as a Sunday school teacher for an insane asylum in 1841, Dix went through a form of emotional conversion. Appalled by the conditions she saw at the asylum, Dix committed herself to fighting for reform in the care of the mentally ill.

The majority of mentally ill people in the 1840s were placed in public mental institutions, jails, or almshouses. Their treatment was often brutal and consisted of beatings, being chained, or being sequestered in cages or pens. Dix decided that neither private philanthropy nor local action could remedy the problem. For Dix, the solution to caring for the insane lay in state and federal intervention.

After having successfully lobbied for state action, Dix decided that, because of the large expenditures required, federal intervention was necessary. With the support of well-known clergymen, prominent citizens, newspapermen, and public and private organizations, a bill was passed in 1854 by both houses of Congress that provided federal support for the mentally ill. Unfortunately, President Franklin Pierce vetoed the bill, claiming that, "If Congress has the power to make provisions for the indigent insane . . . it has the same power for the indigent who are not insane . . . I cannot find any authority in the Constitution for making the Federal Government the great almoner of public charity throughout the United States."[11] Pierce's veto was in large part based on his belief in states' rights, but, more important, for the next 75 years his veto provided the rationale for the federal government's refusal to provide social welfare services.[12]

The Civil War ushered in a new period for relief activities. Families who had lost a breadwinner or who had a breadwinner return from the war permanently disabled could not be blamed for their misfortunes. As a response to the hardship created by the Civil War, localities passed laws that raised funds for the sick and needy and, in some instances, for the founding of homes for disabled soldiers.

Other welfare issues during the Civil War included the disease and filth rampant in army camps and hospitals and the shortage of trained medical personnel. In an effort to remedy this situation, a group of citizens (composed mainly of women) in 1861 organized the U.S. Sanitary Commission, the first important national public health group. Functioning as a quasi-governmental body, the Commission was financed and directed by the private voluntary sector. Working initially in the area of preventive health education, the Commission eventually became involved in a variety of direct and indirect ways of serving the needs of soldiers.[13]

FED FUNDED

Another social welfare institution that emerged from the Civil War was the Freedmen's Bureau. By the close of the war, political leaders realized that the emancipation of millions of slaves would create serious social problems. Former slaves having no occupational training, land, or jobs would require assistance. In 1865, therefore, Congress established the Bureau of Refugees, Freedmen, and Abandoned Lands. The Freedmen's Bureau, as it was commonly called, was responsible for directing a program of temporary relief for the duration of the war and one year afterward. After a bitter struggle, Congress extended the Freedmen's Bureau for an additional six years.

The Bureau, under General Oliver Howard, performed a variety of services designed to help African Americans make the transition from slavery to freedom. For example, the Bureau served as an emergency relief center that distributed 22 million rations to needy Southerners. The Bureau also functioned as an African-American employment agency, a settlement agency, a health center that employed doctors and operated hospitals, an educational agency that encouraged the funding of African-American colleges and provided financial aid, and, finally, as a legal agency that maintained courts in which civil and criminal cases involving African Americans were heard. The Freedmen's Bureau set a crucial precedent for federal involvement in a variety of human services. In 1872 the Bureau was dissolved by Congress.[14]

INDUSTRIALIZATION AND THE VOLUNTARY SECTOR

Private efforts to enhance the welfare of the community have been a prominent part of social welfare throughout the history of the United States. During his travels through the young na-

tion early in the nineteenth century, Alexis de Tocqueville commented on the proclivity of Americans to band together voluntarily to solve the problems besetting their communities:

> Americans of all ages, all conditions, and all dispositions, constantly form associations. They have not only commercial and manufacturing companies, in which all take part, but associations of a thousand other kinds—religious, moral, serious, futile, extensive or restrictive, enormous and diminutive. The Americans make associations to give entertainments, to found establishments for education, to build inns, to construct churches, to diffuse books, to send missionaries to the antipodes; and in this manner they found hospitals, prisons, and schools. If it be proposed to advance some truth, or to foster some feeling of encouragement of a great example, they form a society. Wherever, at the head of some new undertaking, you see the Government of France, or a man of rank in England, in the United States you will be sure to find an association.[15]

Reliance on voluntary associations to solve problems corresponded with the nature of the community in that era. Prior to industrialization, most people lived in communities with an array of institutions that afforded a high degree of self-sufficiency. Survival necessitated a degree of solidarity, or interdependence, that was taken as a law of nature. Cohesiveness of this kind can still be found among certain religious sects, such as the Amish, which manage human needs through the voluntary impulses of members, who see good deeds as a normal extension of their daily activities.

With industrialization, however, this method of managing welfare proved inadequate for most groups, and special entities were designated to provide for social welfare.[16] The fact that institutions specializing in welfare would emerge at this time is related to the spreading industrialization of America and to the subsequent social dislocation that resulted in the relocation of millions of families. From 1890 to 1920, 22 million immigrants came to the United States. At the same time, the American people became more urban. Seventy-five percent of foreign immigrants lived in the cities; and, during the decade following 1920, 6 million people moved from farms to cities.[17]

Life in late nineteenth-century America was hard. The dream of milk and honey that motivated many immigrants to leave their homelands became, for many, a nightmare. The streets of American cities were not paved with gold; instead, they were overcrowded, rampant with disease and crime, and economically destitute. Many tenement houses in the larger cities contained neither windows nor indoor plumbing. Tuberculosis was widespread and, among some groups, infant mortality ran as high as 50 percent. Scant medical care existed for the poor; there was no public education, and insanity and prostitution rates among immigrants were high.[18] The industrial and economic prospects were equally bleak. Factory conditions were abominable: Workers were expected to labor six or seven days a week (often on Sunday), and 18-hour days were not unusual, especially in summer.[19] Factories were poorly lit and unsanitary, easily turned into fire traps, and offered almost no job security. Moreover, homework (taking piecework home, usually for assembly by whole families in one- or two-room tenements) was common. Women were forced to work night shifts and then take care of their homes and children by day.[20] No special protective legislation for women existed until the early 1900s, and child labor was legal. According to Richard Hofstadter, industrial accidents affected one out of 10 to 12 workers, and employees had neither worker's compensation nor disability insurance.[21] When these conditions are added to the fact that every 15 or 20 years there was another depression, it is obvious that the lot of the immigrant and of most working-class Americans was very hard. The extent of their suffering is evident in a modern scholar's description of New York City during the period:

> With the shift of population from the grange to the tenement house came a degree of over expansion and under management that brought large cities to the crisis point: sanitation and health were plainly inadequate; there was a constant fear of rioting and crime; the police used their night sticks against the people they were sworn to protect. Fed by immigrants streaming through Castle Garden and, after 1891, Ellis Island, New York's East Side was the end point of all cities. With over 500 people for each acre, nearly five times the average for the rest of Manhattan, the Tenth Ward was the most densely settled area in the world, and its ghetto was larger than Warsaw's. It was "the suicide ward" and "the typhus ward," and the breeding place of the "white plague" of tuberculosis, epidemics of all kinds, crime, pauperism, alcoholism, sweated labor, hopelessness, and a frightful mortality rate.[22]

Faced with this dilemma, a growing middle class struggled to explain and cope with the mounting social debris in American cities. There was an urgency to this task. Through the germ theory, medical science had identified the cause of many contagious diseases but had yet to develop preventive vaccines or cures. Thus, it was no accident that Charles Loring Brace, a pioneer of child welfare, entitled his book *The Dangerous Classes of New York*. Moreover, graft and corruption became rife as urban immigrants competed for scarce food, housing, and jobs, eking out a marginal existence in squalid city tenements. Eventually, political machines emerged that converted city governments into fiefdoms of patronage. In an exposé of graft in New York City, Jacob Riis, a muckraking journalist, alleged that the political machine of Boss Tweed's Tammany Hall was nothing more than "a band of political cutthroats." Not particularly surprising, Riis noted that Tweed was the product of a Fourth Ward tenement.[23] Yet, even when muckrakers uncovered abuses and railed against them in banner headlines, political bosses were so confident of the indispensability of ''the machine'' that they responded to accusations with defiance. For example, upon hearing of an exposé by Lincoln Steffens, George Washington Plunkett, a Tammany Hall crony, quipped: ''Steffens means well but, like all reformers, he don't know how to make distinctions. He can't see no difference between honest graft and dishonest graft and, consequently, he gets things all mixed up.''[24]

Social Darwinism

Many people looked to the developing social sciences for guidance in redefining social policy. There, prominent scholars drew lessons from the natural sciences that could be used for purposes of social engineering. Borrowing from biology, some American proponents of the new science of sociology applied the idea of natural selection to social affairs.

Social Darwinism was a bastard outgrowth of Charles Darwin's theory of evolution as described in his 1859 classic, *The Origin of Species.*[25] Social theorists such as Herbert Spencer and America's William Graham Sumner reasoned that if Darwin's laws of evolution determined the origin and development of species, then they might also be applied to understanding the laws of society.[26]

Applying Darwin's rules to society and then adapting laissez-faire principles of economics to sociology led to a problematic set of assumptions. For one, if the ''survival of the fittest'' (a term coined by Spencer) was a law governing the lower species, then it must also govern the higher species. Since subsidizing the poor allowed them to survive, this circumvented the law of nature. And because the poor reproduced more rapidly than the middle classes, society was thus subsidizing its own demise.* Social Darwinists believed essentially that the poor would eventually overrun society and bring down the general level of civilization.

Second, if as Darwin maintained, competition for resources was the law of life, then the poor are impoverished because they cannot compete. Conversely, the economic elite are entitled to their spoils because of their ''fitness'' and competitive abilities. In any case, by subsidizing the poor, thus allowing them to reproduce, society artificially alters the laws of nature, and, in doing so, weakens the human gene pool.

Finally, Social Darwinists believed that, although unfortunate, the poor must pay the price demanded by nature and be allowed to die out. According to the Social Darwinists, social welfare thwarts nature's plan of evolutionary progress toward higher forms of social life. Speaking for many intellectuals, the British theorist Herbert Spencer drew this conclusion:

> It seems hard that widows and orphans should be left to struggle for life or death. Nevertheless, when regarded not separately but in connexion with the interests of universal humanity, these harsh fatalities are seen to be full of beneficence—the same beneficence which brings to early graves the children of diseased parents, and singles out the intemperate and the debilitated as the victims of an epidemic.[27]

While some thinkers promoted the harsh strictures of Social Darwinism, and socialists saw poverty as a manifestation of an unjust class society, Christianity provided yet another answer.

Religion and Social Welfare

Religion and social welfare in nineteenth-century America were inextricably linked. Almost all forms of relief emanated from church groups, and all major denominations had some mechanism for providing social welfare.[28] For example, as early as 1880 there were 500 private,

* EXCLUDING HUMAN CAPACITY FOR MORAL CONSCIOUSNESS

church-related social welfare organizations in New York City alone, with the largest network for social services provided by Protestant churches.

Poverty was seen as a "moral failing in the context of orthodox Protestant theology. Martin Luther viewed work as a responsibility to God. Furthermore, work conferred dignity and was a "calling" by God. In Luther's view, a person served God by doing the work of his vocation. Therefore, those who are able-bodied and yet unemployed are sinners. John Calvin took Luther's argument one step further by claiming that work carried out the will of God and, as such, would ultimately help to create God's kingdom on earth. According to both Luther and Calvin, God-fearing people must work regardless of their wage or type of employment.[29]

Because the command to work came from God, economic success was seen as a sign of favor. Poverty, therefore, was also a sign of God's will. This Protestant ethic fueled the creation of a work-oriented society and provided a religious foundation for the indifference of the elite classes toward the poor. In addition, by adding a religious dimension to poverty, conservative Protestantism more sharply focused the distinction between the worthy and the unworthy poor.[30]

Conservative theologians used a religious framework to connect poverty and improvidence: People were poor because they engaged in drinking, slothfulness, licentious behavior, and gambling. Some critics have argued that despite the social welfare services provided by the churches, in the final analysis Protestant theology was basically opposed to social welfare.[31]

It was thought that in order to reclaim providence the poor must be taught to live a moral and self-disciplined life. While early religious social workers clung tenaciously to their desire to teach the moral life, they also understood the need to provide material assistance.[32] The major emphasis of the early social worker, however, was more often on spiritual guidance than on material aid.

The relief assistance provided by these evangelical social workers was often linked to harsh criteria. For example, it was not uncommon for social workers to appraise the worth of the family's possessions and then instruct them to sell off everything in order to qualify for relief. Nor was it uncommon for social workers to deny relief because they felt that the poor family was intemperate and not sufficiently contrite. And if the family refused to accept moral guidance, it could be deemed ineligible for relief. Despite the fact that these social workers dispensed relief, they were basically opposed to the concept of it. They believed that distributing relief was imprudent, because a reliance on charity would weaken the moral fabric of the poor and provide a disincentive for work.

The reign of conservative Protestant theology was not without opposition. In the late nineteenth and early twentieth century, a movement known as the Social Gospel emerged. Composed of theologians concerned with the abuses created by industrialization and the excesses of capitalism, Social Gospelists such as Josiah Strong, Graham Taylor, and others believed that the church should recapture the militant spirit of Christ by taking on the issues of social justice and poverty. The critique posed by the Social Gospelists called for fair play and simple justice for the worker.[33]

Proponents of the Social Gospel movement maintained that churches wrongfully stressed spirituality rather than morality.[34] The condemnation of classical economics, business ethics, and the lawlessness of the plutocracy was centered on a moral rather than a spiritual plane. For the Social Gospelists, social reformation could not occur without a regeneration of character.[35] Although the movement contained degrees of radicalism, all Social Gospelists were moved by a sense of social crisis, and all believed in the necessity of a Christian solution.[36] The legacy of the Social Gospel movement is evident in the current rise of Liberation Theology, a grass-roots movement of progressive theologians that is gaining strength in many

Latin American and African nations. In any case, the combination of Social Darwinism and Christian charity suffused the organizations that assumed a major share of the responsibility for social welfare during the industrial era—Charity Organization Societies and Settlement Houses.

Charity Organization Societies

First evident in the 1870s, Charity Organization Societies (COSs) had offices in most American cities by 1900.[37] With the exception of meager state-sponsored indoor and outdoor relief, the COS movement was a major provider of care to the destitute. COSs varied in their structures and methods. In general, they coordinated relief giving by operating community-wide registration bureaus, providing direct relief, and "educating" both the upper and lower classes as to their mutual obligations.

The work of the COS was carried out by a committee of volunteers and agency representatives who examined "cases" of needy applicants and decided on a course of action. The agent of the COS was the "friendly visitor," whose task was to conduct an investigation of the circumstances surrounding the "cases" and to instruct the poor in ways of better managing their lives. Friendly visitors, drawn from the upper classes, often held a morally superior attitude toward their clientele, and their intervention in the lives of the poor was interpreted by some observers as a form of social control[38] as well as a means of providing assistance. In any case, the charity provided by these organizations was often less than generous. Leaders of the movement drew an important lesson from Social Darwinism in believing that beneficent charity was counterproductive because it contributed to sloth and dependency. Josephine Shaw Lowell, president of the New York Charity Organization Society, believed that charity should be dispensed "only when starvation was imminent."[39]

To be sure, it was difficult for friendly visitors to maintain a sense of Christian duty in the midst of immoral behavior. In such instances, when some wretched soul seemed beyond instruction and charity, more radical measures were in order. Charles Loring Brace, head of the New York Children's Aid Society, described his approach to dealing with a German mother who worked as a "swill-gatherer" in "Dutch Hill":

On the eastern side of the city, in the neighborhood of Fortieth Street, is a village of squatters, which enjoys the title of "Dutch Hill." The inhabitants are not, however, "Dutch," but mainly poor Irish, who have taken temporary possession of unused sites on a hill, and have erected shanties which serve at once for pig-pens, hen-coops, bedrooms, and living-rooms. They enjoy the privilege of squatters in having no rent to pay; but they are exposed to the penalty of being at any moment turned out from their dens, and losing land and house at once. . . . The village is filled with snarling dogs, which aid in drawing the swill or coal carts, for the children are mainly employed in collecting swill and picking coals through the streets.

[An] old rag-picker I remember whose shanty was a sight to behold; all the odds and ends of a great city seemed piled up in it—bones, broken dishes, rags, bits of furniture, cinders, old tin, useless lamps, decaying vegetables, ribbons, cloths, legless chairs, and carrion, all mixed together, and heaped up nearly to the ceiling, leaving hardly room for a bed on the floor where the woman and her two children slept. Yet all these [children] were marvels of health and vigor, far surpassing most children I know in the comfortable classes. The woman was German, and after years of effort could never be induced to do anything for the education of her children, until finally I put the police on their track as vagrants, and they were safely housed in the "Juvenile Asylum."[40]

And what happened to the children who had been placed in the "Juvenile Asylum"? Brace's solution was as ingenious as it was compatible with the tenets of Social Darwinism and Christian charity. The Children's Aid Society transported between 50,000 and 100,000 "orphans" westward by train, where they were placed with farm families.[41] The advertisement in Figure 3.1, posted in McPherson, Kansas, provides some detail on the procedures devised by Brace and his associates.

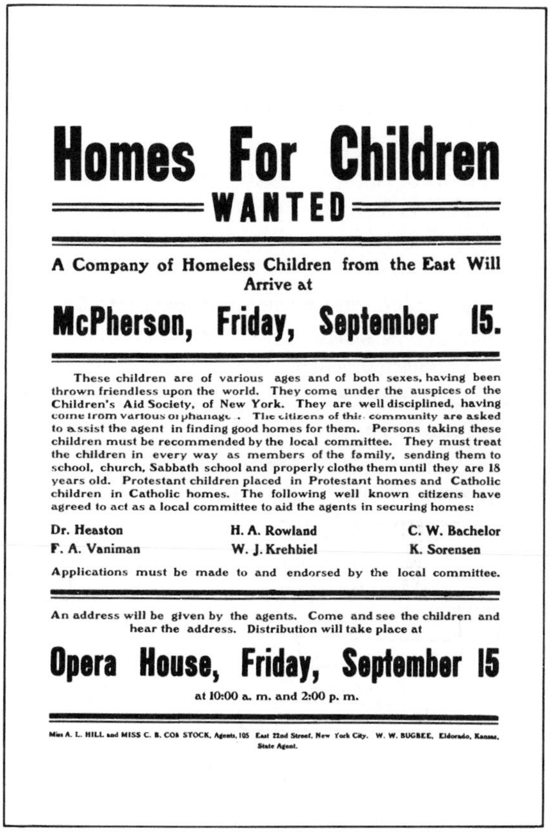

Homes For Children

WANTED

A Company of Homeless Children from the East Will Arrive at

McPherson, Friday, September 15.

These children are of various ages and of both sexes, having been thrown friendless upon the world. They come under the auspices of the Children's Aid Society, of New York. They are well disciplined, having come from various orphanage . The citizens of this community are asked to assist the agent in finding good homes for them. Persons taking these children must be recommended by the local committee. They must treat the children in every way as members of the family, sending them to school, church, Sabbath school and properly clothe them until they are 18 years old. Protestant children placed in Protestant homes and Catholic children in Catholic homes. The following well known citizens have agreed to act as a local committee to aid the agents in securing homes:

Dr. Heaston	H. A. Rowland	C. W. Bachelor
F. A. Vaniman	W. J. Krehbiel	K. Sorensen

Applications must be made to and endorsed by the local committee.

An address will be given by the agents. Come and see the children and hear the address. Distribution will take place at

Opera House, Friday, September 15

at 10:00 a. m. and 2:00 p. m.

Miss A. L. HILL and MISS C. B. COMSTOCK, Agents, 105 East 22nd Street, New York City. W. W. BUGBEE, Eldorado, Kansas, State Agent.

Figure 3.1. Handbills promoted the orphan trains. This one is for McPherson, KS, in 1911. (SOURCE: Reprinted from Martha Nelson Vogt and Christina Vogt, *Searching for Home* [Martha Nelson Vogt and Christina Vogt, 1062 Edison N. W., Grand Rapids, Michigan, 1979].)

Settlement Houses

The settlement house movement, which began in the 1880s and emerged in most of the big cities over the next two decades, was also a response to the urban conditions of the times. Settlement houses were primarily set up in immigrant neighborhoods by wealthy people, college students, unattached women, teachers, doctors, and lawyers, who themselves moved into the slums as residents. Rather than simply engaging in friendly visiting, the upper- and middle-class settlement leaders tried to bridge class differences and to develop a less patronizing form of charity. Rather than coordinate existing charities as had the COSs, they sought to help the people in the neighborhoods to organize themselves. Because they actually lived in the same neighborhoods as the impoverished immigrants, settlement workers could provide fresh and reliable knowledge about the social and economic conditions of American cities.

Jane Addams established Hull House in 1889. She approached the project—and the Chicago ethnic community in which it was based—with a sense of Christian Socialism that was derived from a "rather strenuous moral purgation"[42] rather than a sense of noblesse oblige. The cofounder of Hull House, Ellen Gates Starr described the values of the settlement house worker.

> After we had been here long enough and people see that we don't catch diseases and that vicious people do not destroy us or our property . . . we have well founded reason to believe that there are at least half a dozen girls in the city who will be glad to come and stay a while and learn to know the people and understand them and their ways of life; to give out of their culture and leisure and overindulgence and to receive the culture that comes from self-denial and poverty and failure which these people have always known.[43]

By 1915 this altruism was shared by enough settlement workers that over 300 settlements had been established, and most of the larger American cities could boast at least one or more settlement houses.[44]

While providing individual services to the poor, the larger settlements were essentially reform-oriented. These reforms were achieved not only by organizing the poor to press for change but also by using interest groups formed by elite citizens, as well as by the formation of national alliances. Settlement-pioneered reforms included tuberculosis prevention, the establishment of well-baby clinics, the implementation of housing codes, the construction of outdoor playgrounds, the enactment of child labor and industrial safety legislation, and the promotion of some of the first studies of the urban black in America, such as W. E. B. Du Bois's *The Philadelphia Negro.* Many of the leaders of the New Deal had worked in settlements. For example, alumnae of Hull House included Edith Abbott, drafter of the Social Security Act; her sister, Grace Abbott, and Julia Lathrop, who became directors of the U.S. Children's Bureau; and Frances Perkins, Secretary of Labor and the first woman to be appointed to a cabinet post.[45]

African-American Associations

If the conditions of immigrants were difficult, those of African Americans were even more trying. In the absence of government programs, African Americans had to rely on private sources of welfare, even though many of these voluntary agencies frequently discriminated against them. Consequently, a number of fraternal and benefit associations emerged within the African-American community, such as the Knights of Tabor, the Knights of Pythias, the Ancient Sons of Israel, and the Grand United Order of True Reformers.[46] These organizations, many of them indigenous to the African-American community, were instrumental in binding the fabric of a community that suffered from continual distress compounded by limited resources. As an example, consider some of the constitutional provisions of one health and burial society:

Sec. 1.   This society shall be known as the Sons and Daughters of Zion.

Sec. 2.   The object of this society shall be to care for its sick and bury its dead members and all moneys paid therein shall be expended for same. By a two-thirds vote, however, of all the active members, money may be expended for other purposes.

Sec. 5.   The monthly fee of all members in Sons and Daughters of Zion shall be 25 cents.

Sec. 17.   The Society shall not employ more than three doctors, who shall be elected annually, and shall purchase all medicine from one drug store.

Sec. 18.   The burial expenses shall in no case exceed $25.00, and in all cases the hearse shall be used in conveying the body to the cemetery.

Rule 19.   The chairman of the sick and burial committee shall summon as many male members as are necessary to dig a grave. In his absence the male messenger shall discharge this duty. Members who fail to assist in digging a grave after having been appointed, and who don't get anyone in their place, shall pay a fine of 75 cents or be suspended for six months.

Rule 26.   The society shall not be responsible for the following bills: Bills caused from accident or death in disreputable places, self-abuse among men as diseases brought on by lewd habits, women confined, accident or death from stealing or anything dishonorable.[47]

Before government played a prominent role

in guaranteeing the basic rights of citizens, important events in the history of African Americans were often connected with voluntary associations that arose within the African American community. Talladega College, the first distinguished liberal arts college serving rural African Americans, had its origin in a carpenter shop where David White, Sr., a freedman, and Leonard Johnson, "a black man who had in some way acquired the rudiments of learning," began a school.[48] Morehouse College, the alma mater of Martin Luther King, Jr., began in 1867 as a night school in the Springfield Baptist Church of Augusta, Georgia.[49] When it appeared that the industrial education approach of Booker T. Washington would not guarantee African Americans full citizenship, W. E. B. Du Bois galvanized a group of reformers, among them social workers such as Ida B. Wells, Mary White Covington, and Jane Addams, into the Niagara Movement. Marshaling support through meetings at centers of abolitionist sentiment, the Niagara Movement became the National Association for the Advancement of Colored People. Meanwhile, a concern for economic justice led George Edmund Haynes, a Columbia University graduate student, to write *The Negro at Work in New York City*. The attention attracted by this study contributed to the formation in 1911 of the National Urban League on Urban Conditions. Using philanthropic assistance from foundations, the League established a program for social work training that "made possible the education of many of America's most distinguished social work leaders in the next generation."[50]

Prior to World War I, social welfare in the United States consisted almost exclusively of private agencies voluntarily established by groups for the purpose of enhancing the public welfare. Indeed, many of the community agencies with which most Americans are familiar were established at this time, as shown in the following list of the founding dates of selected organizations:

YMCA

1851—Young Men's Christian Association

YWCA

1858—Young Women's Christian Association
1880—Salvation Army
1881—American Red Cross
1896—Volunteers of America
1902—Goodwill Industries
1907—Boys' Clubs of America
1910—Boy Scouts of America
1910—Catholic Charities
1911—Family Service Association of America
1912—Girl Scouts of America

The Social Casework Agency

Charity Organization Societies and Settlement Houses served as models for the delivery of social welfare services in the voluntary sector organizations that emerged during the Progressive Era. Similar in many respects, these organizations evolved to form the social casework agency. Both were of modest size in terms of staff, both were located in the communities of the clientele they served, both served a predominantly poor population, and both relied on contributions from a variety of sources—private donations, the Community Chest, and foundations.[51] Typically, workers in these agencies were female volunteers. COS techniques for investigation were refined, their aim being the identification of a "social diagnosis" as the basis for case intervention.[52] Subsequently, these activities, along with the community-oriented work of the settlement reformers, gave birth to the profession of social work.

Despite the efforts of these early women social workers, their professional status was not highly esteemed or even recognized. At the time, the caricature of the journalist H. L. Mencken was perhaps typical of public sentiment:

The social worker, judging by her own pretensions, helps to preserve multitudes of persons who would perish if left to themselves. Thus her work is clearly dysgenic and anti-social. For every victim of sheer misfortune that she restores to self-sustaining and social usefulness, she must keep alive scores of misfits and incompetents who can never, for all her help, pull their weight in the boat. Such persons can do nothing more valuable than dying.[53]

As predominant service delivery forms, COSs and Settlements were transformed by two influences: the need for scientifically based treatment techniques, and the socialization of charity. Together, these factors contributed to the emergence of the social casework agency. COSs and Settlements had provided meaningful activity for upper- and middle-class women who found it necessary to ground their work in treatment techniques that were derived from science. This necessity had been driven home in 1915 during the National Conference of Charities and Correction, when Abraham Flexner, a renowned authority on professional graduate education, was asked to address the question of whether social work was a profession. Much to the disappointment of the audience, Flexner judged that social work lacked all the requirements of a profession, particularly a scientifically derived knowledge base that was transmittable.[54] Subsequently, the Milford Conference Report of 1923 underscored the importance of a scientific base for social work knowledge.

> The future growth of social casework is in large measure dependent upon its developing a scientific character. Its scientific character will be the result of a scientific attitude in social caseworkers towards their own problems, and as part of increasingly scientific adaptations from the subject matter of other sciences.[55]

Scientific social work served the manifest function of improving the effectiveness of social work practice, and thereby increased the status of the new profession. At the same time, it served a latent function. Describing the social worker's client in scientific terms functioned to elevate the image of the client from one of an inept wretch to one characterized by specific afflictions that were mutable.

At the same time, the funding of COSs, Settlements, and other service organizations had proven undependable because of the competition among agencies for donors' funds and the fact that these gifts were dependent on a largesse that fluctuated with an unstable economy. The solution to this problem emerged in the form of a collective approach to philanthropic giving. As early as 1887, Denver's Associated Charities had pioneered the concept whereby a group of agencies appealed to the conscience of the community for operating funds. By the 1920s, more than 200 cities had adopted community chests, thus reducing the need for the independent agency to curry favors on its own.[56] The socialization of charity provided agencies with a relatively steady income while demanding uniformity in operations. Uniformity was allied with efficiency, a guiding principle of the Progressive Era,[57] and this resulted in an organizational form that served to rationalize a previously haphazard array of social services.[58] Together, the needs of workers for effective treatment techniques and the economic imperatives for organizational survival functioned to standardize the social casework agency.

Perhaps the best description of the casework agency evolved from the Milford Conference of 1923, when 16 executives and board members from six national organizations drafted a document endorsing agency-based service delivery. The Milford Conference Report provided a comprehensive outline of the organization through which professional caseworkers delivered services. The social casework agency was located in a community and derived its objectives and purposes from it. The agency was governed by a board of directors that hired the agency director and met monthly to monitor agency affairs. Caseworkers functioned under supervision, thus combining the need for administrative and professional accountability. Most important, workers had a repertoire of over 25 methods—among them diagnosis, interviewing, prognosis, planning, treatment, and reeducation. Moreover, some or all of these methods were useful for countering a host of "deviations" from "normal social life," such as alcoholism, delinquency, family antagonisms, mental ill health, pauperism, and vagrancy. The social casework agency concept encompassed the fields of child welfare, family welfare, visitor teaching, medical social work, psychiatric social work, and probation work. They accomplished this charge within administrative procedures that were "in accordance with accepted business standards and practice, including audits of accounts at least annually by an accredited public accountant."[59]

This characterization of the social agency was prophetic and served as a model for human service delivery over the following decades. Child guidance clinics, probation departments, mental health clinics, family planning clinics, and public welfare offices resembled the casework agency envisaged by the Milford Conference Report. Despite differences in auspices and service mandate, the fundamental elements remained intact. The social casework agency provided a service delivery model through which the emerging profession of social work could apply its skills.

Economically, the social casework agency met the accountability requirements of different funding sources. In the case of private donations—corporate, individual, and foundation—the casework agency was managed by an executive officer and operated in accordance with established business practices. In the case of other charities—the Community Chest and United Way—the casework agency was under the guidance of a board of directors that upheld the best interests of the community. In the case of public (governmental) funding, the casework agency was administered on the basis of governmental regulations by the executive director who was part of the government bureaucracy. According to the needs of the professional social

work community and the fiscal requirements of philanthropic and governmental funding sources, the casework agency was perceived to be professionally managed and economically efficient. Through much of the twentieth century the social casework agency was a common setting for the provision of human services, reflecting the basic principles outlined in the Milford Conference of 1923.

The Progressive Movement

A reaction to the heartlessness that characterized a large segment of American society came in the form of the Progressive movement, a social movement that was popular from the early 1900s to World War I.

Progressive Era philosophy, intended to inject a measure of public credibility and Christian morality into social, political, and economic affairs, was a unique blend of social reform encompassing anti-big business attitudes, a belief that government should regulate the public good, a strong emphasis on ethics in business and personal life, a commitment to social justice, a concern for the "common man," a strong sense of paternalism and, not surprisingly, a tendency toward jingoism. Progressives believed that the state had a responsibility for protecting the interests of the public, especially people who were vulnerable. The Progressive Party, supported by the nation's most respected social workers, including Jane Addams, Lillian Wald, and Paul U. Kellogg, presented a presidential ticket in 1912.

Impressive governmental reforms were enacted during the Progressive period. For example, President Theodore Roosevelt made great strides in the areas of natural resource conservation and civil service reform and strengthened the power of the Interstate Commerce Commission. President Woodrow Wilson's administration enacted major reforms in the areas of tariffs and banking and curbed monopolistic practices through the Clayton Antitrust Act of 1914. Other reforms enacted during Wilson's administration included better credit facilities and agricultural education for farmers, better working conditions in the Merchant Marine, a worker's compensation law for all federal civil service employees, the establishment of the eight-hour day for all workers on interstate railroads, a law excluding the products of child labor from interstate commerce, and federal aid to states for highway construction.[60]

Progressive reformers also experienced limited successes in protecting the rights of working women. By 1912, a total of 11 states had legislated a floor under which women's wages could not fall. In 1919, Massachusetts passed a bill that limited the maximum number of hours (for most classes of working women) to 44 per week. New York followed suit in 1919 with a 54-hour week for a limited number of women workers.[61] In addition to minimum wage and maximum hour legislation, many states enacted laws prohibiting night work for women in certain industries, as well as lifting restrictions regulating the maximum weight a woman could be required to handle.[62]

The advent of World War I helped diminish the liberal fervor that had characterized the Progressive Era of the late 1800s and early 1900s. In the wake of the disillusionment that followed the war, the mood of the country became conservative. Progressive ideas were treated skeptically in the 1920s; frequently the proponents of those ideas were accused of being "Bolsheviks." By 1924 the situation was even worse: Congress had curtailed immigration, the child labor amendment was all but defeated, political repression became common, many foreign radicals were deported as a result of the raids conducted by Attorney General A. Mitchell Palmer, the Ku Klux Klan was gaining strength, labor unrest exploded everywhere, and corruption in high places was rampant.[63] Americanization and intolerance became operational concepts, and even the settlement houses lost much of their sway during the conservative post-World War I era. Despite the suffrage movement, which gave women the right to vote, the 1920s represented an extremely conservative period in American history.

Although we think of the 1920s as a period of prosperity, more than one-third of the American population at this time lived in poverty.[64] Many of the reforms enacted during the Progressive Era of the early 1900s were rescinded in the "Roaring Twenties." By the late 1920s some states had enacted widows' pensions and workers' compensation laws, but most charity still occurred by way of private social service organizations.

THE GREAT DEPRESSION AND THE MODERN WELFARE STATE

In the election of 1928 Herbert Hoover ran for president against the Catholic and Democratic governor of New York State, Alfred E. Smith. Known as a militant prohibitionist and a strong humanitarian (because of his relief activities at the end of World War I), Hoover handily beat Smith, in the process winning the support of many social workers, including Jane Addams.[65]

In October 1929 the stock market crashed. A year later, 6 million men and women were walking the streets looking for work. By 1932, over 600,000 were jobless in Chicago, and a million in New York City. In Cleveland, 50 percent of workers were unemployed, in Akron 60 percent, and in Toledo 80 percent of the population was looking for work. Only three years after the crash, more than 100,000 workers were being fired in an average week.[66] By the early 1930s the gross national product (GNP)—the sum total of all the goods and services produced in the country—had dropped to a half of what it had been prior to the depression. The national income dropped from $81 billion in 1929 to $40 billion in 1932.[67] By 1932 manufacturing output had fallen to 54 percent of what it had been in 1929, a little less than the total production in 1913. In that same year the automobile industry was operating at only one-fifth of its 1929 capacity. Steel plants operated at only 12 percent of their potential and the output of pig iron was the lowest since 1896. In addition, factory wages shrank from $12 billion in 1929 to $7 billion in 1932. Unemployment reached a high of 24 percent and, for the first time, more people emigrated from America than migrated to it (in 1932, 35,329 people emigrated to America and 103,295 left). Even the birthrate was cut almost in half—from 30 births per thousand in 1929 to 18 births per thousand in 1940. By 1932, 20 million people were on the relief rolls.[68]

In search of work, or perhaps just motion, thousands of Americans aimlessly wandered the country. In 1929 the Missouri Pacific Railroad reported 13,745 migrants; in 1931, 186,028; and by 1932, between 1 and 2 million people were roaming the country.[69] The unemployed who chose to stay close to home often frequented the thousands of soup lines that sprang up across the country.

Relief under the Hoover administration proved wholly inadequate. Private charities and local governments soon exhausted their coffers. Relief payments, which in 1929 totaled $5 per week for an entire family, were cut to $2.39 in New York, and still less elsewhere. Dallas and Houston refused relief to all Hispanic-American and African-American families. Detroit slashed its relief rolls by one-third. New Orleans refused all new relief applicants, and St. Louis cut its relief rolls in half. Except for New York, Illinois, Pennsylvania, New Jersey, and Wisconsin, state governments did almost nothing to aid the victims of the Great Depression. More than 100 cities had no relief appropriations in 1932.[70]

Having seen little of the acclaimed prosperity of the 1920s, most farmers were devastated by the depression. American foreign trade declined from $10 billion in 1929 to $3 billion in 1932. Crop prices registered new lows: Wheat fell from $1.05 a bushel in 1929 to 39 cents in 1932, corn from 81 cents to 33 cents a bushel, cotton from 17 to 6 cents a pound, and tobacco from 19 to 10 cents a pound. As a result, gross farm income fell from nearly $12 billion in 1929 to only $5 billion in 1932.[71] Farmers responded

to these economic conditions with angry protests. From Pennsylvania to Nebraska, farmers banded together to prevent banks and insurance companies from foreclosing on mortgages. When sheriffs attempted to break up these actions, some farmers brandished pitchforks and hangman's nooses to make their point.

Herbert Hoover's response to the depression was, for the most part, inaction. Hoover opted to rely on the voluntary social welfare sector, justifying his position by the belief that federal relief would weaken the social and moral fiber of the society, impair the credit and solvency of the government, and delay the ability of the natural forces at work to restore the economy. Moreover, according to Hoover, federal relief was illegal and a violation of states' rights.[72]

The voluntary social welfare sector responded to the depression by organizing massive fund drives, but, because of the sheer scope of the problem, these proved ineffective. Although a large segment of the social work community and most voluntary social welfare agencies agreed with Hoover in his opposition to federal aid, by 1932 he was forced to propose an unemployment assistance program in which the federal government paid 80 percent of the costs. By the time Hoover was defeated by Franklin Delano Roosevelt (FDR) in the election of 1932, Hoovervilles (shantytowns sarcastically named in Hoover's honor) had sprung up in most large cities. Soup lines became a part of the urban landscape, economically motivated suicides were commonplace, and legendary robbers like Dillinger, Baby Face Nelson, and Bonnie Parker and Clyde Barrow were the rage.

When FDR assumed the presidency in 1933 he faced a country increasingly divided between right- and left-wing political factions, an industrial system experiencing convulsions in the form of violent labor strikes, a class society at the breaking point, and a banking system on the verge of collapse. As one of his first acts, FDR declared a ''bank holiday.'' While the banks were closed, FDR put in place the FDIC program (later called FSLIC), which guaranteed depositors that the federal government would insure their deposits (up to a certain dollar amount) if a member bank became insolvent. FDR's response to the depression involved a massive social experiment whose objectives were relief, recovery, and reform.[73] Despite the accusations made by his critics, FDR was not a socialist. The philosophy of the New Deal was neither socialistic nor Marxian. In the final analysis, FDR was not a proponent of radicalism, and his New Deal programs served to salvage capitalism. Faced with an economic system at the breaking point, Roosevelt plunged into relief activities to save capitalism. In that sense, FDR was the quintessential liberal capitalist.

Roosevelt's first task was to alleviate suffering and provide food, shelter, and clothing for the millions of unemployed workers. In 1933, Congress established the Federal Emergency Relief Administration (FERA), which distributed over $5.2 billion of emergency relief to states and local communities. In 1933, FDR initiated the National Recovery Act (NRA), which provided a comprehensive series of public works projects. Under the umbrella of the NRA, Congress instituted the Public Works Administration (later changed to the Works Progress Administration—WPA) to coordinate the system of public works. Workers employed by this make-work program built dams, bridges, and other important public structures. In 1935 the WPA was expanded to provide more employment through an emphasis on long-range projects that had a positive value for the country. WPA projects employed white- and blue-collar workers as well as unskilled laborers. The WPA ultimately cost about $11.3 billion, employed 3.2 million workers a month by 1938, and produced roads, public parks, airports, schools, post offices, and various other public buildings. In addition, the white-collar division of the WPA provided work opportunities through the Federal Writers' Project, the Federal Arts Project, and the Federal Theater Project.[74]

FDR created the Civilian Conservation Corps (CCC) and the National Youth Administration (NYA) to address the problem of unemployed youth. The purpose of the CCC was to employ poor youths (ages 17 to 23) to replant forests and to help conserve the soil. Apart from obtaining employment, the 2.5 million young men served by the CCC received a leisure-time educational program as well as vocational and academic training. The NYA, on the other hand, was designed for young adults who wanted to stay at home and for needy high school and college students. Begun in 1935, the NYA eventually provided part-time employment for over 1.7 million young people and assisted more than 1.8 million high school and college students.

Other experiments followed suit: In 1933, Congress established the Tennessee Valley Authority (TVA), a radical technological and social experiment that brought electricity to the South, helped control flooding, reclaimed land, improved river navigation, and produced nitrates; the Farm Security Administration (FSA) aided farmers and migratory workers by attempting to raise prices of farm goods; and in 1934, Congress established the Federal Housing Administration (FHA), an agency designed to provide insurance to lenders against losses on secured and unsecured loans for repairs and improvements, and on first mortgages for residential property. In addition, in 1937, Congress began a slum clearance and low-income housing program under the auspices of the WPA.[75]

In 1937, Congress passed the Fair Labor Standards Act (FLSA), which established a minimum wage (25 cents an hour) and a maximum work week (44 hours, and then time and a half for additional hours). The FLSA also abolished child labor for those under 16. In addition, the passage of the National Labor Relations Act (NLRA) gave private-sector workers the right to collectively bargain, organize, and strike.

The apogee of FDR's New Deal was the Social Security Act of 1935. This legislation included: (1) a national old-age insurance system; (2) federal grants to states for maternal and child welfare services, relief to dependent children

(ADC), vocational rehabilitation for the handicapped, medical care for crippled children, aid to the blind, and a plan to strengthen public health services; and (3) a federal-state unemployment system. Conspicuously omitted was a national health insurance plan, a policy that was included in virtually every other social security plan adopted by nations in the industrialized world. The Social Security Act of 1935 was clearly the most enduring of all FDR's programs.

Although the New Deal programs were important, some argue that they did not represent a real change of direction. Most of FDR's policies were based on past employment, and thus did not help the hard-core poor who had a meager work record, if any. FDR's policies had several long-range effects. Federal policy was used to make income more equal (through minimum wage laws, and establishment of the right of workers to strike and collectively bargain); and the New Deal programs, especially the Social security Act, established the framework for the modern social welfare state.

THE POST–WORLD WAR II WELFARE STATE

The end of World War II brought with it a repression similar to what had occurred after World War I. Progressive ideas were labeled as Communist-inspired, and the House Un-American Activities Committee hearings, chaired by Martin Dies, frightened away all but the most intrepid social reformers. Welfare programs also suffered. The antiwelfare reaction was so strong that some major newspapers published lists of welfare recipients in an attempt to shame them off the rolls. Virtually no new welfare programs were proposed, and the existing ones were in constant jeopardy. Many political leaders balked at the need for welfare programs, given the relatively healthy economy of the period.

The 1950s were marked by a kind of smugness. Americans believed that for the most part poverty had been eradicated, and even though small pockets of poverty remained, the age of affluence had arrived. The concept of a poverty-free America was ruptured by several social reformers, including Michael Harrington, whose book *The Other America: Poverty in the United States,* became a classic. Harrington and others maintained that American society encompassed a subculture of poverty. These poor were hidden from the middle classes but, like specters, haunted the cities, towns, and villages. This poor subculture was composed of African Americans, Native Americans, Mexican Americans, and whites.[76] Harrington and others were correct, because in 1959 about 22 percent of the nation lived below the poverty level.[77]

The relative quiet of the 1950s gave way to the quasi-revolutionary spirit of the 1960s. After John F. Kennedy was assassinated in 1963, President Lyndon Johnson exploited the sentiments of the nation and declared a "War on Poverty." This War on Poverty—whose name was later changed to the Great Society—comprised many social programs designed to cure poverty in America. Driven by massive urban riots in African-American communities during the middle and late 1960s, Johnson's programs were aimed at empowering poor communities to arrest poverty and increase economic opportunity within their own neighborhoods. Operating under the umbrella of the Office of Economic Opportunity (OEO), various programs were tried, including Volunteers in Service to America (VISTA), a domestic peace corps; Upward Bound, a program that encouraged poor and ghetto children to attend college; a Neighborhood Youth Corps for unemployed teenagers; Operation Head Start, a program that provided preschool training for lower-income children; special grants and loans to rural families and migrant workers; a comprehensive Community Action Program (CAP) designed to mobilize community resources; the Legal Services Corporation; the Model Cities Program; the Job Corps, a manpower program providing job training for disadvantaged youths from 16 to 21; and the Economic Development Act of 1965, which provided states with grants and loans for public works and technical assistance. The Economic Opportunity Act of 1964 (incorporated in 1973 under the Comprehensive Employment and Training Act, CETA) emphasized education and job training.

A key phrase in Johnson's Great Society program was "the maximum feasible participation of the poor," a concept that informed poor communities that they should invoke self-determination in their attempt to politically and economically empower themselves. The major thrust of Johnson's War on Poverty was fueled by the belief that job creation, education, and other incentives can alleviate poverty.

By 1968 the Great Society programs had become unpopular with the American public. Despite the huge amounts of money the Johnson administration spent on the poverty problem, critics claimed that the programs were ineffective. Several causes emerge as plausible explanations for this phenomenon. For one, Johnson was faced with a costly war in Vietnam at the same time that he was constructing his war on poverty. Although America was wealthy, it became increasingly clear that it could not afford to conduct two wars simultaneously. In addition, confusion in Washington, inexperienced personnel, delays in funding, corrupt local politicians, intransigent bureaucrats, and ineffective community leaders all contributed to massive problems in the programs. Despite the grim postmortem offered by subsequent scholars, however, during the Great Society period the number of people living below the poverty line was cut almost in half, from about 25 percent in the early 1960s to around 12 percent by 1969. Richard Nixon assumed the presidency in 1969 and promptly began to dismantle the Great Society. As one of his first moves, he curbed the power of the then-influential OEO. Determined to clean up the "welfare mess," Nixon in 1969 proposed another type of welfare reform—a guaranteed annual income for all poor

persons. Under Nixon's Family Assistance Plan (FAP), every unemployed family of four would receive $2,400 a year from the federal government. The working poor would be allowed a minimum of $1,600 per year until their earned income reached $4,000, after which the payments would be discontinued. In order to be eligible for assistance, the able-bodied—including women with children over three years of age—would be required to work or to be enrolled in a job-training program. The program was eventually to be turned over to the states.[78] Although parts of this plan were adopted, notably the Supplemental Security Income (SSI) program in 1972, for the most part the concept of a guaranteed income was rejected by Congress. The biggest problems with this plan involved what the minimum income should be and the forced work approach.

Between 1965 and 1975, America's national priorities, in terms of the money spent on them, were reversed: In 1965 defense expenditures accounted for 42 percent of the federal budget while social welfare expenditures accounted for only 25 percent; but by 1975 defense expenditures accounted for only 25 percent of the federal budget while social welfare outlays accounted for 43 percent. Social welfare is currently the major expenditure in the federal budget. Even in Ronald Reagan's conservative budget of 1986, characterized by large increases in defense spending, only 29 percent was so earmarked, while 41 percent was allocated to social welfare.[79]

Beginning with Reagan's election in 1980, the years of his presidency saw a reappraisal of the welfare state. Reagan's ideological stance assumed that (1) federal government expenditures for social welfare should be minimal, (2) only those who were "truly needy" should receive welfare, and (3) welfare should be provided only on a short-term basis. As a result of Reagan's position, the American social welfare state was marked, at best, by inattention. In terms of real dollars, benefits for those on public assistance fell precipitously. Uneven economic development accelerated during this same period: While some people found themselves better off, larger segments of American society experienced greater economic hardship. Homelessness grew at unprecedented rates for a nondepression period. Real income continued to fall as higher-paying industrial jobs were lost and replaced by jobs in a burgeoning but relatively low-paid service sector. At the same time, most redistributive mechanisms, including social welfare allocations, experienced cuts or freezes. This situation was complicated by enormous budget and trade deficits that further justified curtailing the welfare functions of the federal government.

The parsimonious policies of the Reagan years continued throughout the administration of President George Bush. Despite his call for "a thousand points of light," Bush's policies fostered a rise in the number of those in poverty and a buildup of extreme racial, economic, and social pressures. Moreover, these policies resulted in the dramatic growth of hungry Americans and in increased unemployment, homelessness, racially based incidents, and a 5 percent increase in the AFDC rolls from 1989 to 1991. Some argue that the lack of a coherent domestic policy climaxed in the bloody Los Angeles riots of spring 1992. Based on a platform of change, Bill Clinton was elected President of the United States on November 3, 1992.

SOCIAL WORK'S LEADERSHIP IN SOCIAL WELFARE

Although the history of the welfare state is clearly linked to the social and economic history of the United States, there are nevertheless important actors, many of them social workers, who also helped shaped the direction of social welfare.

Throughout the history of American social welfare, advocates of care for vulnerable populations have been instrumental in shaping social policies. If one looks beneath the surface of policy statements, one finds a rich and often exciting account of the skirmishes fought by advocates for social justice. In some respects, social policy innovations can be looked upon as individual and collective biography written in official language. In an age of mass populations, often manipulated by private and public megastructures, it is easy to forget how powerful some individuals have been in shaping American social welfare policy. Many of these leaders are known because they achieved national prominence; yet some of the more heroic acts to advance social justice were performed by individuals whose names are not widely recognized. Not to be forgotten in this regard is Michael Schwerner, a social worker, who was murdered while working in a voter registration drive in the South during the Civil Rights movement.[80]

Early social welfare leaders emerged during the Progressive Era, a period when educated and socially conscious men and women sought to create structures that would advance social justice in America. The settlement house gained a reputation as the locus for reform activity, leading one historian to conclude that "settlement workers during the Progressive Era were probably more committed to political action than any other group of welfare workers before or since."[81] From this group, Jane Addams quickly surfaced as a leader of national prominence. Through her settlement home, Hull House, she not only fought for improvements in care for slum dwellers in inner-city Chicago but also for international peace. Social work for Jane Addams *was* social reform. Instead of focusing solely on restoration and rehabilitation, Addams claimed that there was a superior role for the profession: "It must decide whether it is to remain behind in the area of caring for the victimized," she argued, "or whether to press ahead into the dangerous area of conflict where the struggle must be pressed to bring to pass an order of society with few victims."[82] In that struggle, Addams served nobly, receiving an honorary degree from Yale University and serving as president of the Women's International League for Peace and Freedom. In 1931, Jane Addams was awarded the Nobel Peace Prize, a suitable distinction for a social worker who once had herself appointed a garbage collector in order to improve sanitation in the slums around Hull House.

Hull House proved a remarkable institution, and some of its tenants made lasting and important contributions to the New Deal:

Edith Abbott, president of the National Conference of Social Welfare, Dean of the University of Chicago School of Social Service Administration, and participant in the drafting of the Social Security Act of 1935

Grace Abbott, organizer of the first White House Conference on Children, director of the U.S. Children's Bureau, and participant in the construction of the Social Security Act

Julia Lathrop, developer of the first juvenile court and of the first child mental health clinic in the United States, and the first director of the U.S. Children's Bureau

Florence Kelley, director of the National Consumer League, cofounder of the U.S. Children's Bureau, and a member of the National Child Labor Committee

Frances Perkins, director of the New York Council of Organizations for War Services, director of the Council on Immigrant Education, and the first Secretary of Labor.[83]

The activity around Hull House was never limited to those with a narrow view of reform. A regular participant in the settlement was John Dewey, in his time "America's most influential philosopher, educator, as well as one of the most outspoken champions of social reform."[84]

Settlement experiences crystallized the motivations of other reformers as well. Harry Hopkins, primary architect of the New Deal and of the social programs that comprised the Social Security Act, had resided in New York's Christadora House Settlement. Ida Bell Wells-Barnett led the Negro Fellowship League to establish a settlement house for African Americans in Chicago. And Lillian Wald, with Florence Kelley, a cofounder of the U.S. Children's Bureau, had earlier established New York's Henry Street Settlement, an institution that was to achieve distinction within the African-American community. Under the guidance of Mary White Ovington, a social worker, the first meetings of the National Association for the Advancement of Colored People were held at the Henry Street Settlement.[85]

Early social welfare leaders championed causes that improved the conditions of children and immigrants, but they did not always forsake African Americans. When it became apparent that Booker T. Washington's program of "industrial education" was unable to contend effectively with ubiquitous racial discrimination, social reformers—Jane Addams, Ida Bell Wells-Barnett, and John Dewey—joined W. E. B. Du Bois in the Niagara Movement. The early organizations spawned by the Niagara Movement were later consolidated into the National Urban League, with George Edmund Haynes, a social worker, as one of its co-directors. In 1910, Haynes had been the first African American to graduate from the New York School of Philanthropy, so it is not surprising that an important Urban League program was the provision of fellowships for African Americans to the school.[86] Later, during the height of the Civil Rights movement, the National Urban League, under the direction of social worker Whitney Young, Jr. collaborated in organizing the August 28, 1963, march on Washington, memorialized by Martin Luther King, Jr.'s ringing words, "I have a dream!"[87]

If the New Deal bore the imprint of social workers, the Great Society was similarly marked some 30 years later. Significantly, one leader of the War on Poverty was Wilbur Cohen, a social worker who had been the first employee of the Social Security Board created in 1935. Eventually, Cohen was to be credited with some 65 innovations in social welfare policy, but his crowning achievement was the passage of the Medicare and Medicaid Acts in 1965. The Secretary of Health, Education and Welfare during the Johnson administration, Cohen was arguably the nation's most decorated social worker, receiving 18 honorary degrees from American universities.[88] In the end, the history of social work has always been inextricably bound up with the history of the American welfare state, a condition that is likely to prevail well into the future.

DISCUSSION QUESTIONS

1. Many commentators argue that the English Poor Laws continue to form the basis of current social welfare policy in America. How are the English Poor Laws reflected in modern social welfare policy? Specifically, which current values or social welfare policies can be traced to the influence of the English Poor laws?

2. Are there any residual social welfare policy values that have persisted from colonial times to the present? Describe specific social welfare policies or values that have their origin in colonial times.

3. What lasting legacy, if any, did the Freedmen's Bureau have for contemporary U.S. policy toward African Americans? Describe any influence that the Freedmen's Bureau had on the U.S. welfare state in terms of specific policies and programs.

4. The concept of Social Darwinism clearly had a big following in the late 1800s. Is this concept dead today or does a modified form of it continue to exercise influence? If you answer yes, describe how this idea is expressed in terms of values or specific social welfare policies or programs.

5. Religion clearly played an important role in the development of professional social work, especially in the late 1800s and early 1900s. What role, if any, does religion currently play in the creation of social welfare policy? Specifically, are religious impulses an important factor in decisions relating to social programs and policies? If you agree, describe specific policies and programs that reflect religious influences.

6. Although the Charity Organization Societies and the Settlement Houses seemed to be at opposite poles, some commentators argue that there were strong similarities between the two. Describe the similarities, in terms of both values and approaches, between the two organizations.

7. The Progressive Era was an important period in American history. Describe the major contributions of the Progressive Era, in terms of its programs and policies, for the later American welfare state.

8. FDR is often thought of as the father of the American welfare state, and most policy analysts agree that his New Deal policies formed the basis for the current welfare system. What is the most enduring legacy of the New Deal and why?

9. Most pundits across the political spectrum agree that Ronald Reagan had a major impact on the American welfare state. His impact included both concrete fiscal cuts and new ideas about welfare. What, if any, permanent legacy was left by this president? Specifically, in what ways did Reagan help shape current values and attitudes toward social programs?

10. The history of American social welfare is marked by the formidable accomplishments of key leaders in social work. These include Jane Addams, Lillian Wald, the Abbott sisters, and Wilbur Cohen, among many others. In effect, these leaders dominated the field of social welfare for more than half a century. Some critics point out that there are no leaders on the social work scene today who have the stature of those mentioned. What do you believe are the reasons for this predicament?

NOTES

1. Robert Morris, *Rethinking Social Welfare* (New York: Longman, 1986), pp. 7–8.
2. Karl de Schweinitz, *England's Road to Social Security* (Philadelphia: University of Pennsylvania Press, 1943).
3. Ibid.
4. Ibid.
5. Walter Trattner, *From Poor Law to Welfare State* (New York: Free Press, 1974), p. 12.
6. David Rothman and Sheila Rothman, eds., *On Their Own: The Poor in Modern America* (Reading, Mass.: Addison-Wesley, 1972).
7. Morris, *Rethinking Social Welfare*, p. 143.
8. Nathan Edward Cohen, *Social Work in the American Tradition* (New York: Holt, Rinehart and Winston, 1958), pp. 23–24.
9. Trattner, *From Poor Law to Welfare State*, p. 17.
10. Morris, *Rethinking Social Welfare*, p. 153.
11. Quoted in Trattner, *From Poor Law to Welfare State*, p. 62.
12. Cohen, *Social Work in the American Tradition*, p. 36.
13. Trattner, *From Poor Law to Welfare State*, p. 63.
14. Ibid., p. 87.
15. Alexis de Tocqueville, *Democracy in America*, vol. 2 (New Rochelle, N.Y.: Arlington House, 1966), p. 114.
16. Ibid.
17. June Axinn and Herman Levin, *Social Welfare* (New York: Dodd, Mead, 1975), p. 129.
18. Robert Bremner, *From the Depths: The Discovery of Poverty in the United States* (New York: New York University Press, 1956).
19. David Montgomery, *Workers' Control in America* (Cambridge: Cambridge University Press, 1979).
20. Ibid.
21. Richard Hofstadter, *The Age of Reform* (New York: Vintage Books, 1955), p. 242.
22. Justin Kaplan, *Lincoln Steffens* (New York: Simon and Schuster, 1974), pp. 50–51.
23. Jacob Riis, *How the Other Half Lives* (New York: Charles Scribner and Sons, 1890), p. 15.
24. Kaplan, *Lincoln Steffens*, p. 51.
25. Charles Darwin, *On the Origin of Species by Means of Natural Selection* (London: John Murray, 1859).
26. See Herbert Spencer, *An Autobiography*, 2 vols. (New York: D. Appleton, 1904); William Graham Sumner, *Social Darwinism* (Englewood Cliffs, N.J.: Prentice-Hall, 1963); and Richard Hofstadter, *Social Darwinism in American Thought* (Boston: Beacon Press, 1959).
27. Spencer, *An Autobiography*, p. 186.
28. David Macarov, *The Design of Social Welfare* (New York: Holt, Rinehart and Winston, 1978).
29. Ibid.
30. Ibid.
31. Herbert G. Guttman, *Work, Culture and Society* (New York: Vintage Books, 1977).
32. Roy Lubove, *The Professional Altruist: The Emergence of Social Work as a Career, 1880–1930* (New York: Atheneum Books, 1975).
33. Charles Howard Hopkins, *The Rise of the Social Gospel in American Protestantism, 1865–1915* (New Haven: Yale University Press, 1940).
34. Ibid.
35. Henry F. May, *Protestant Churches in Industrial America* (New York: Octagon Books, 1963).
36. Howard Jacob Karger, *The Sentinels of Order: A Study of Social Control and the Minneapolis Settlement House Movement, 1915–1950* (Lanham, Md.: University Press of America, 1987).
37. Lubove, *The Professional Altruist*, pp. 1–21.
38. Ibid., p. 14.
39. Axinn and Levin, *Social Welfare*, p. 100.
40. Charles Loring Brace, *The Dangerous Classes of New York* (New York: Wynkoop and Hallenbeck, 1872), pp. 151–52.
41. Jean Quam, "Charles Loring Brace," *Encyclopedia of Social Work*, 18th ed. (Silver Spring, Md.: NASW, 1987), p. 916.
42. Hofstadter, *The Age of Reform*, p. 211.
43. Allen F. Davis, *American Heroine: The Life and Legend of Jane Addams* (New York: Oxford University Press, 1973), p. 57.
44. Ibid., p. 92.
45. *Encyclopedia of Social Work*, 18th ed., pp. 913–36.
46. John Hope Franklin, *From Slavery to Freedom* (New York: Knopf, 1979), p. 288.
47. *Constitution of the Sons and Daughters of Zion*, author's collection.

48. Addie Louise Joyner Butler, *The Distinctive Black College: Talladega, Tuskegee, and Morehouse* (Metuchen, N.J.: Scarecrow Press, 1977), pp. 17–18.
49. Ibid., p. 102.
50. Franklin, *From Slavery to Freedom*, pp. 318–321.
51. H. L. Weissman, "Settlements and Community Centers," *Encyclopedia of Social Work*, 18th ed., p. 21.
52. Mary Richmond, *Social Diagnosis* (New York: Russell Sage Foundation, 1917).
53. H. L. Mencken, *Minority Report* (New York: Knopf, 1956), p. 153.
54. Maryann Syers, "Abraham Flexner," *Encyclopedia of Social Work*, 18th ed., p. 923.
55. National Association of Social Workers, *Social Casework: Generic and Specific* (Washington, D.C.: NASW, 1974), p. 27.
56. Trattner, *From Poor Law to Welfare State*, pp. 221–22.
57. Larry Hirschhorn, "The Social Service Crisis and the New Subjectivity," (Berkeley, Calif.: University of California, Berkeley, Institute of Urban and Regional Development, December 1974).
58. Lubove, *The Professional Altruist*, pp. 172, 185.
59. National Association of Social Workers, *Social Casework*, pp. 16–50.
60. See Cohen, *Social Work in the American Tradition;* and William E. Leuchtenburg, *The Perils of Prosperity, 1914–32* (Chicago: University of Chicago Press, 1958).
61. Clarke A. Chambers, *Seedtime of Reform: American Social Service and Social Action, 1918–1933* (Ann Arbor, Mich.: University of Michigan Press, 1967), p. 118.
62. Hofstadter, *Age of Reform*.
63. See Karger, *The Sentinels of Order*, and Chambers, *Seedtime of Reform*.
64. Chambers, *Seedtime of Reform*, p. 211.
65. Ibid., p. 219.
66. Leuchtenburg, *Perils of Prosperity*, p. 247.
67. Cohen, *Social Work in the American Tradition*, p. 161.
68. Ibid., p. 162.
69. Leuchtenburg, *Perils of Prosperity*, p. 254.
70. Ibid., pp. 252–53.
71. Ibid., p. 248.
72. Trattner, *From Poor Law to Welfare State*, p. 230.
73. Cohen, *Social Work in the American Tradition*, p. 169.
74. Ibid.
75. Ibid.
76. Michael Harrington, *The Other America: Poverty in the United States* (New York: Penguin Books, 1962).
77. Robert Morris, *Social Policy of the American Welfare State* (New York: Longman, 1985), p. 63.
78. Trattner, *From Poor Law to Welfare State*.
79. Diane M. DiNitto and Thomas R. Dye, *Social Welfare: Politics and Public Policy* (Englewood Cliffs, N.J.: Prentice-Hall, 1987), p. 56.
80. Maryann Mahaffey, "Political Action in Social Work," *Encyclopedia of Social Work*, 18th ed., p. 290.
81. Allen Davis, "Settlement Workers in Politics, 1890–1914," in Maryann Mahaffey and John Hanks, eds., *Practical Politics: Social Work and Political Responsibility* (Silver Spring, Md.: National Association of Social Workers, 1982), p. 32.
82. Davis, *American Heroine*, p. 292.
83. Biographical information from *Encyclopedia of Social Work*, 18th ed.
84. Richard Bernstein, "John Dewey," *Encyclopedia of Philosophy*, vol. II, Paul Edwards, ed. (New York: Macmillan and The Free Press, 1967), p. 380.
85. Mahaffey, "Political Action in Social Work," p. 286.
86. Franklin, *From Slavery to Freedom*, pp. 319–21.
87. Ibid., pp. 471–72.
88. Charles Schottland, "Wilbur Joseph Cohen: Some Recollections," *Social Work* 32, no. 5 (September-October 1987): 371–72.

CHAPTER 4

The Making of
Governmental Policy

This chapter describes the process by which governmental policy is made, examines the influence of various social groups on the policy process, and explores the phases of the policy process with particular attention focused on the role of key organizations. The public policy process is important because many social welfare policies are established by government, and decisions by federal and state agencies have a direct bearing on the administration and funding of social welfare programs that assist millions of Americans.

In an open, democratic society, it is desirable that public policy reflect the interests of all citizens to the greatest extent possible. For a variety of reasons, however, this ideal is not realized in the making of governmental policy. Although many Americans have the right to participate in the establishment of public policy, they often fail to do so. Governmental policy may be perceived as being too far removed from the daily activities of citizens, or too complicated, to warrant the type of coordinated and persistent efforts necessary to alter it. Moreover, many Americans with a direct interest in governmental policy are not in a position to shape it, as in the case of children and the emotionally impaired, who must rely on others to speak on their behalf. Consequently, governmental policy does not necessarily reflect the interests—or, for our purposes, the welfare—of the public even though it is intended to do so. The discrepancy between what is constitutionally prescribed in making public policy and the way decisions are actually made leads to two quite different understandings of the policy process. For welfare professionals concerned with instituting change in social welfare, a technical understanding of how policy is made is essential. It is equally important for them to recognize that the policy process is skewed to favor powerful officials and interests rather than the interests of the uninfluential. Because social workers and their clients tend to be comparatively powerless, a critical analysis of the policy process is all the more important.

TECHNICAL ASPECTS
OF THE POLICY PROCESS

A brief vignette illustrates what command of the legislative process can mean in making public policy. Toward the end of the 1970s, a reception was held in Washington, D.C., for veterans of the VISTA (Volunteers in Service to America) program. Organizers had not anticipated the attendance of the senior senator from New York,

Jacob Javits; but when the senator asked for a moment to offer a few remarks, what had been joviality and chatter quickly subsided into respectful silence. Although Senator Javits had just announced his retirement from politics, he was widely respected as a liberal Republican and as one who had no peer when it came to negotiating proposals through Congress. In a frail voice, Senator Javits stated his reasons for supporting the VISTA program over the years, despite the opposition of many of his conservative colleagues. VISTA reminded him, he recalled, of the Settlement House that he attended as a youth. "And that Settlement House was very important to me as I grew up," the senator said. "It was the place where I learned some of the most significant skills I was to need as an adult." Senator Javits paused so that the audience would focus on his childhood lessons.

"The first thing I learned was how to take a bath," he said, and the audience chuckled at this admission from such a powerful man. "The second thing I learned was how to play basketball," he went on, and the audience laughed heartily at the thought of this diminutive man on a basketball court. "The third thing I learned," and the senator paused again, "was parliamentary procedure." And the audience accepted the veracity of this statement with nodding heads and a validating murmur.

In the United States, public policy is made through a deliberative process that involves the two bodies of elected officials that comprise a legislature. This applies both to the federal government and to the states, with the singular exception of Nebraska, which has only one deliberative body, that is, a unicameral legislature.

The concern of a legislator is first developed into a legislative proposal and usually printed in the *Congressional Record*. Because legislators have a party affiliation and a constituency, their proposals tend to reflect these priorities. Usually, several legislators will prepare proposals that are important to similar constituencies, which ensures that all sides of an issue are aired. Through a subtle interaction of ideas,

the media, and legislative leadership, one proposal—usually a synthesis of several—is presented as a policy alternative. Other legislators are asked to sign on as co-sponsors and the measure is officially introduced. After it is assigned to the appropriate committee, hearings are held, and the committee convenes to "mark up" the legislation so that it incorporates the concerns of committee members who have heard the public testimony. Under propitious circumstances, the legislation is forwarded to the full body of the chamber which must approve it. While being approved by the full body of one chamber, a similar bill is often introduced in the other chamber, where it begins a parallel process. Differences in the legislation approved by each chamber are ironed out in a conference committee. The proposed legislation becomes law after it is signed by the chief executive, or by a two-thirds vote of each legislative chamber if the executive vetoes the bill. This process is always tortuous and usually unsuccessful. The eventual enactment of legislation under these conditions is a true testament to legislative leadership. A third branch of government, the judiciary, assesses legal challenges to existing legislation. In the upper levels of the judiciary, members are usually appointed by the chief executive, and they can hold their posts for life. The primary features of the policy process of the federal government are illustrated in Figure 4.1.

There are several critical junctures in a proposal's tortuous passage into legislation—or oblivion. First, most of the details in any proposal are worked out at the committee or subcommittee level. Differences—an inevitability in virtually every bill—are negotiated and reconciled at a "mark-up" session, during which committee members and staff write their changes onto the draft. This stage offers an important opportunity to inject minor, and sometimes major, changes into the substance of the bill or to alter the intent of the bill's originator(s). Second, the viability of a proposal depends to a large extent on the numbers and weight of the witnesses who testify as to its mer-

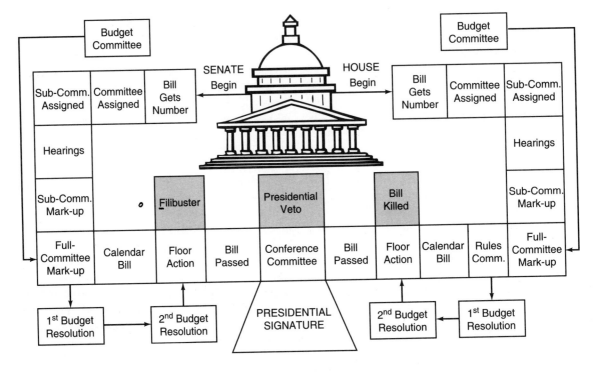

Figure 4.1. The Steps Necessary in Getting a Legislative Proposal Enacted into Law

its at subcommittee and committee hearings. Obviously, public testimony will work to the advantage of well-financed interests that can afford to pay lobbyists to do this professionally, while advocates of the disadvantaged must rely on volunteers. Nevertheless, the public testimony stage is an important opportunity to clarify "for the record" the position that welfare professionals may take on a given proposal. Third, budget considerations figure heavily in the likelihood of a bill's passage. The federal deficit coupled with the unwillingness of elected officials to raise taxes increases the likelihood that legislation will be underfunded or even passed with no additional funding whatsoever. Innovative revenue "enhancers," such as earmarked taxes or user fees, can make a proposal more acceptable during periods of fiscal belt-tightening. The policy process, then, is not necessarily intended to facilitate the passage of a

proposal into law. During the last 20 years, of some 20,000 bills presented to Congress only 10 percent were reported out of committee and only 5 percent became law.[1]

Beyond this general outline of the public policy process, multiple variations exist depending on historical circumstances. In the federal government, all proposals related to taxation must originate in the House of Representatives, a provision the founders of the nation included in the Constitution in order to locate revenue retrieval in the legislative body most representative of the people. Appointments to key executive posts, such as cabinet secretaries, ambassadors, and judges must be ratified through the advice and consent of the Senate, a body less responsive to popular sentiment. States exhibit countless variations within the general outline of the tripartite balance of powers format. California, for example, has experienced budget gridlock because the state government has been unable to raise sufficient revenue to keep up with mandated expenditures. Since the imposition of Proposition 13 in 1978, a two-thirds majority of the legislature is required not only to raise taxes but also to establish the state budget; this is far beyond the simple majority required in other states. Under these conditions, a small number of recalcitrant representatives can easily block the budget process. As these examples suggest, understanding the intricacies of the policy process is an essential step toward mastering public policy.

A few final points regarding the technical aspects of the policy process warrant mention. The decision-making process itself is defined by *Robert's Rules of Order*,[2] a text that lays out in detail the rules for democratic deliberation. Although *Robert's Rules* can appear obtuse, its value should not be underappreciated. As the vignette of Senator Javits shows, those who have mastered "the means of deliberation" are one step ahead of the rest of the crowd in seeing their ideas become public policy. Social activists who are optimistic that their proposal is working its way steadily through the legislative minefield may find their hopes exploded by an adroit procedural move on the part of an opponent who sidetracks a bill until the next legislative session. Elaborate rules of decision making, compounded by the traditions of deliberative bodies, may dissuade public citizens from participating more fully in the democratic process. Yet there are means public policy novices can employ to become better acquainted with the ways in which elected officials go about the public's business. Citizen advocate organizations, particularly the League of Women Voters and Common Cause, can be helpful in explaining how public policy is made. Finally, Congress and the legislatures of the larger states employ staff members as technical experts to aid them in decision making. Legislative staff are frequently the experts most versed in an area of legislative activity simply because they work through policy proposals on a regular basis. Staff reports

researched as part of committee deliberations can be valuable in that they often provide the most up-to-date data on particular programs or issues. A good example of this is the "Green Book" used by the U.S. House Ways and Means Committee in its consideration of social programs. Begun in the early 1980s to help committee members comprehend the vast number of programs under their jurisdiction—Social Security, Medicare, Medicaid, AFDC, SSI, and Unemployment Compensation, among others—the volume, *Background Material and Data on Programs within the Jurisdiction of the Committee on Ways and Means*, became essential reading for social program analysts. Because of its convoluted title, the volume became known by its standard-issue green paper cover, hence the "Green Book." Fortunately, its popularity led to a (merciful) shortening of its title to *Overview of Entitlement Programs*.[3]

A CRITICAL ANALYSIS OF THE POLICY PROCESS

Experience and sophistication notwithstanding, the public policy process often proves frustrating for social activists. Despite the most urgent of needs, the best of intentions, and the most strategic of proposals, the social welfare program output deriving from the legislative process often appears far short of what is required. Yet to conclude from this that public policy simply does not work would be an overstatement. A critical approach to public policy helps explain some of the limitations of the technical approach, and offers directions on how to make the legislative process a more effective strategy for those concerned with furthering social justice.

From a critical perspective, the policy process consists of a series of discrete decisions, each heavily conditioned by money and connections—in other words, by "power." The extent to which governmental policy reflects the concerns of one group of citizens while neglecting those of others is ultimately a question of power and influence. Power is derived from several sources and these have attracted the attention of philosophers over the centuries. Plato questioned the organization and execution of the civil authority of the state. Machiavelli focused on the limits of discretionary authority exercised by leaders of the state. During the Enlightenment, the social contract philosophers—Hobbes, Locke, and Rousseau—considered the moral obligations of the state toward its citizens. Later, as the Industrial Revolution proceeded unchecked, Karl Marx attributed inequities in influence to control over the means of production, or capital. Subsequently, as governmental authority expanded to ameliorate the economic and social dislocation brought on by industrial capitalism, Max Weber identified bureaucratic administrators as a pivotal group. As the postindustrial era unfolded, such social critics as Marshall McLuhan and Alvin Toffler emphasized how information can be processed and used as a source of power and influence.

From these general speculations about social organization, other writers have turned to more specific aspects of social policy as subjects of inquiry. Several schools of thought have emerged. According to the elitist orientation, individuals representing central institutions control social policy in order to maintain a status quo that advantages themselves and, in the process, excludes marginal groups. In contrast, a pluralist orientation assumes that social policy in a democratic polity is the sum total of trade-offs among different interest groups, all of which have an equal opportunity to participate. At another level altogether, incrementalists have suggested that the more important questions about social policy are the product of bit-by-bit additions to the public social infrastructure. Finally, a rationalist orientation has used the methods of social science to determine by objective standards to what extent policy changes approximate optimal values. As might be expected in the investigation of any phenomenon as complex as social policy, a comprehensive explana-

tion is likely to incorporate elements of more than one school of thought.

Somewhat separate from the inquiries into social policy just noted, there are also more specific analyses of social welfare policy. In these investigations, three orientations have become prominent. According to the evolutionary perspective, welfare policy reflects steady progress toward a desirable condition of human welfare for all. Most liberal analysts who have promoted the welfare state as an ideal have adopted an evolutionary perspective. Believers in the evolutionary perspective expect that the national government will progressively expand social programs until, eventually, the basic needs of the entire population are guaranteed as rights of citizenship. References to welfare state philosophy appear in many chapters of this book.

More commonly used in the American context is the systems approach. Adherents of social systems assume that welfare consists of basic institutions and processes that are related and changed to suit environmental conditions. In vogue during the 1960s and 1970s, when social programs were expanding, this approach commanded less credibility when many public programs were thrown into chaos as a result of budget cuts during the 1980s. What had once been coordinated service delivery systems suddenly became disordered and fragmented clusters of agencies struggling for survival.

Finally, a conflict perspective has emphasized the differences between organized groups that compete for social resources, one opportunity for this being the competition for public resources offered through social programs. The conflict perspective has a range of applications, some of which appear contradictory. Conflict theory has been used, variously, to explain economic competition within a capitalist market, political jockeying in a democratic polity, and riots by the oppressed. Again, any inclusive understanding of social welfare policy will respect the contribution of each of these orientations.

In order to illustrate how general orientations to social policy and specific explanations of welfare policy apply to social welfare, consider this question: What is the nature of governmental decision making? Questions of governmental decision making often focus on two aspects: the degree of change in policy represented by a decision, and the rationality of the decision. Governmental policies vary in the extent to which they depart from the status quo. Although it can be argued that, in the final analysis, there are no new ideas, there *are* new governmental policies that have enormous implications for certain groups. Few could dispute that the Social Security Act and the Civil Rights Act were radical departures from the status quo and substantially changed the circumstances of the aged and African Americans, respectively. On the other hand, such radical departures are dependent on a relatively unique set of circumstances, and occur rarely. As Charles Lindblom has observed, the great bulk of decision making is "incremental," representing only marginal improvements in social policy already in place.[4] From a rational perspective, Amitai Etzioni has suggested the concept of "mixed-scanning" to describe how decisions are reached. According to Etzioni, decision makers take a quick overview of a situation, weigh a range of alternatives—some incremental, some radical—and ultimately select the one that satisfies the most important factors impinging at the moment.[5] While significant changes in social policy are possible, they are infrequent. Most social policy changes consist of relatively minor technical adjustments in program administration and budgeting.

The rationality of a policy decision refers to how internally coherent or consistent it is and the extent to which it accomplishes its intended objectives. Paradoxically, most governmental policy is irrational when evaluated by these standards. Inevitably, public policy is elaborated to take into account the interests of the various groups that are concerned about its effects. It is not unusual for descriptions of governmental policy to require dozens of pages of text and for its various provisions to be contradictory. For example, the 98-page Immigration Reform and Control Act of 1986 reflected the concerns of three groups: undocumented residents, most of whom are Hispanic; truck farmers, who require migratory laborers to pick the crops; and the Immigration and Naturalization Service (INS), which regulates immigration to the United States.[6] Because the interests of these groups differed greatly, various provisions of the act appeared inconsistent at times. For example, in interpreting the act, the INS initially determined that children of families in which one parent failed to qualify for amnesty faced deportation, although single-parent families in which the parent qualified would be allowed to stay in the United States.[7] Hispanic groups were outraged at this interpretation because it encouraged families to break up in order to qualify for amnesty. Because of the importance of the family in Hispanic culture, this interpretation contributed to the reluctance of undocumented workers to apply for the amnesty program. Meanwhile, some truck farmers watched their crops go unharvested because migrant workers were not coming to the United States owing to the confusion over the provisions of the act.

Despite such irrationality, social policy does order human affairs and, to that extent, the logic of the policy is of great significance. There are two basic forms of rationality that justify social policy: bureaucratic rationality and market rationality.[8] Bureaucratic rationality refers to the ordering of social affairs by governmental agencies. Since Max Weber's work on the modern bureaucracy, this form of rationality has been central to governmental policy, and hence to the maintenance of the welfare state. According to bureaucratic rationality, civil servants can objectively define social problems, develop strategies to address them, and deploy programs in an equitable and nonpartisan manner. Bureaucratic rationality takes its authority from power vested in the state, and its bureaucracies have become predominant in social welfare at the federal (through the Department of Health and Human Services) and state levels. A characteristic of bureaucratic rationality is a reliance on social planning. Several social planning methods have been developed to anticipate future problems and deal with existing ones. Generally, these can be classified under two headings: technomethodological and sociopolitical. (1a) Technomethodological planning methods emphasize data bases from which projections about future program needs can be derived. Such methods place a premium on relatively sophisticated social research methods and work best with programs that can be quantified and routinized, as in the case of cash payments through the Social Security program. (1b) Sociopolitical approaches to planning are more interactive, involving groups likely to be affected by a program. Community development activities, for example, frequently feature planners bringing together neighborhood residents, businesspeople, and local officials to create a plan that is relevant to the needs of a particular area.[9] Regardless of planning method, it is important to recognize the power and influence that governmental agencies have assumed in social welfare policy, much of it by exercise of bureaucratic rationality.

(2) Market rationality refers to a reliance on the supply of and demand for goods and services as a method of ordering social affairs. While on the surface this may appear to be antithetical to the meaning of rationality, a high degree of social ordering in fact occurs within capitalism. Such organization is implicit in the very idea of a market, entailing a large number of prospective consumers that business seeks to exploit. In a modern market economy, the success of a business depends on the ability of managers to survey the market, merchandise goods and services, shape consumer preferences through advertising, and reduce competition by buying or outmaneuvering competitors. Of course, market rationality is not a panacea for providing social welfare because the marketplace is not particularly responsive to those who do not fully participate in it—such as racial minorities, women, children, the aged, and the handi-

capped. Yet market rationality cannot be dismissed as a rationale for delivering social welfare benefits. Some 132 million Americans get their health and welfare needs met through employer-provided benefits that are ultimately derived from the market.[10] Another example of the market providing social welfare benefits is the practice by governmental jurisdictions of contracting out particular human services to private sector businesses, usually with the rationale of reducing costs by taking advantage of efficiencies associated with the market.[11]

As a result of differences among policymakers between reliance on government and reliance on the market to ensure social welfare, acrimony frequently accompanies the policy process. If the United States has a serious problem of unemployment among adolescents and young adults, for example, what is the most effective policy response? Proponents of market rationality will prefer a market strategy that eliminates the minimum wage so that employers can hire more young workers for the same amount but at lower wage levels. Proponents of bureaucratic rationality will opt for a governmental public works program that assures constructive activities at an adequate wage. In the absence of definitive data on the most desirable course of action, decisions are often made on the basis of some loosely defined, intended outcome. And rationality—of a bureaucratic or market nature—often features prominently in establishing a policy that intends a particular outcome.

Now return to the earlier question: What is the nature of governmental decision making? An appreciation for the dynamic nature of public policy results in the incorporation of elements from several orientations. In certain instances, one orientation may appear clearly applicable, but alone it is incapable of explaining all the factors at play. An integration of orientations is called for, but it must be customized to specific events. While this may appear confusing, it is what makes social policy such a provocative and sometimes volatile area of study.

THE POLICY PROCESS

A critical analysis of the policy process highlights three elements: the social stratification of the society, the phases through which policy is formulated, and the organizational entities that have evolved as instrumental in the decision-making process. These will be described and charted in order to clarify how welfare policy is created in the American context.

Social Stratification

A variety of schemes have been presented to differentiate groups with influence from those lacking it. The most simple of these consists of a dual stratification, for instance, into capitalists and the proletariat, such as Marx used. A stratification common to Americans is in three parts: an upper class, a middle class, and a lower class. Placement of individuals in the appropriate class is usually made on the basis of income, education, and occupational status. This three-part stratification is limited in its capacity to explain very much about American social welfare, however. If asked, most Americans identify themselves as middle class, even if by objective criteria they belong to another class. Further, the designation *lower class* is not particularly informative about the social conditions of a large portion of the population about which welfare professionals are concerned.[12] Finally, the term *lower class* is pejorative, connoting a social station that has less value than others.

A more informative stratification was developed by social psychologist Dexter Dunphy, who identified six social groups.[13] Dunphy suggested that these groups differed according to several factors, the most important of which were wealth, internal solidarity, and the control over the environment. This stratification appears in Table 4.1.

As this social stratification illustrates, some groups—executives and organizers—are able to influence the environment, while other groups—erratics and apathetics—have virtually no influence. This has important implications for social welfare, since those who are of lower status tend to be the recipients of welfare benefits, which are the product of a social policy process in which they do not participate. The way in which these groups influence the social policy process will be discussed in greater detail.

With these clarifications in mind, the policy process can be divided into four stages: formulation, legislation, implementation, and evaluation. While these terms are somewhat self-explanatory, during the decision-making process different organizational entities exert their influence, making the process an uneven one that is frequently characterized by fits and starts. Organizations correspond to the stratification groups that figure prominently in their organizational activities and thereby in the policy process.

Formulation

Prior to the nineteenth century it would have been accurate to state that policy formulation began with the legislative phase. Clearly, this was intended by the drafters of the Constitution, but theirs was a largely agricultural society with comparatively little institutional specialization. With industrialization, many complexities were injected into the society and, in time, special institutions emerged to assist the legislature in evaluating social conditions and preparing policy options. Eventually, even constitutionally established bodies, such as Congress, lapsed into a reactive role, largely responsive to other entities that formulated policy.[14] Initially, institutions of higher education provided this technical intelligence to assist the legislative branch, and some still do. For example, the University of Wisconsin Institute for Research on Poverty provides analyses on important welfare policies.[15]

That legislators at the federal level, as well as those in the larger states, would rely on experts to assess social conditions and develop

TABLE 4.1. Social Stratification of the Population into Six Groups

Name of Group	Examples	Characteristics
Conservative groups (old wealth)	Upper elites, the independently wealthy, large stockholders	Ownership of resources is the main source of power; control over goals is very high, but control over means is through organizers.
Organizer groups (executives)	Top administrators in business, government, and the military	Organizational solidarity facilitates effective policy implementation; some control over goals and a high degree of control over means are enjoyed.
Cabal groups (professionals)	Middle-level managers, technical experts, private practitioners, community leaders	Environment encourages limited solidarity; control over means is high, and goal setting can be influenced if collective action is undertaken.
Strategic groups (organized workers)	Semiskilled workers, civic and political clubs, social action organizations	Environment encourages solidarity; groups have some control over the means by which goals are realized.
Erratic groups (working/ welfare poor)	Temporary and part-time workers earning minimum wage and who use welfare as a wage supplement	A subjugated position with no control over the environment; frustration is shared and irrational, and explosive behavior results.
Apathetic groups (underclass)	Unemployables and illiterates; disabled substance abusers; itinerants, drifters, and migrant workers	A subjugated position with no control over the environment; a sense of failure coupled with mobility reduces social interaction and leads to retreatism.

SOURCE: Dexter C. Dunphy, *The Primary Group: A Handbook for Analysis and Field Research,* © 1972, pp. 42–44. Reprinted by permission of Prentice-Hall, Inc. Englewood Cliffs, N.J.

policy options is not surprising given the fact that each legislator must attend to multiple committee and subcommittee assignments requiring expertise in particular matters, while at the same time contending with the general concerns of a large constituency. A typical day in the life of a legislator has been reconstructed by Charles Peters, a long-time Washington observer:

> The most striking feature of a congressman's life is its hectic jumble of votes, meetings, appointments, and visits from folks from back home who just drop by. From an 8 A.M. breakfast conference with a group of union leaders, a typical morning will take him to his office around 9, where the waiting room will be filled with people who want to see him. From 9 until 10:30 or so, he will try to give the impression that he is devoting his entire attention to a businessman from his state with a tax problem; to a delegation protesting their town's loss of air or rail service; to a constituent and his three children, who are in town for the day and want to say hello; and to a couple of staff members whose morale will collapse if they don't have five minutes alone to go over essential business with him. As he strives to project one-on-one sincerity to all these people, he is fielding phone calls at the rate of one every five minutes and

checking a press release that has to get out in time to make the afternoon papers in his district.

He leaves this madhouse to go to a committee meeting, accompanied by his legislative aide, who tries to brief him on the business before the committee meeting begins. The meeting started at 10, so he struggles to catch the thread of questioning, while a committee staff member whispers in his ear. And so the day continues.

The typical day . . . usually ends around 11:30 P.M., as the congressman leaves an embassy party, at which he has been hustling as if it were a key precinct on election eve. He is too tired to talk about any but the most trivial matters, too tired usually to do anything but fall into bed and go to sleep.[16]

As a result of competing demands, legislators pay somewhat less attention to the policy process than their public image, would have you believe, leaving much of the work to their staffs. Even then, public policy tends to get short shrift. Because reelection is a primary concern for legislators, their staffs are frequently assigned to solve the relatively minor problems presented by constituents. In fact, placating unhappy constituents has become so prominent a concern that one legislative observer notes that constituency services have become "more important than issues" for representatives.[17]

Gradually, institutions have begun to specialize in providing the social intelligence necessary for policy formulation. These policy institutes or "think tanks," as they are sometimes called, now wield substantial influence in the social policy process. Not unlike prestigious colleges, think tanks maintain multidisciplinary staffs of scholars who prepare position papers on a range of social issues. With multi-million dollar budgets and connections with national and state capitals, think tanks are well positioned to shape social policy. Generally, financial support is derived from wealthy individuals and corporations with a particular ideological inclination, a fact evidenced by the types of think tanks they support. Several prominent policy institutes are located on the ideological continuum in Figure 4.2.

Within policy institutes, prominent scholars, usually identified as senior fellows, hold endowed chairs, having often served in cabinet-level positions within the executive branch. When Republican administrations came into power, large numbers of senior fellows from conservative policy institutes assumed cabinet appointments, while their Democratic counterparts returned to liberal institutes, where senior chairs awaited them. For junior staff, an appointment in a think tank can provide invaluable experience in how the governmental policy process actually works. It is, however, important to recognize that think tanks are private, nongovernmental institutions that influence public policy.

Through much of this century, a first generation of largely liberal policy institutes, such as the Brookings Institution, contributed to the formulation of governmental welfare policy. Their role was essentially passive in that they provided technical expertise to legislators and governmental agencies upon request. By the

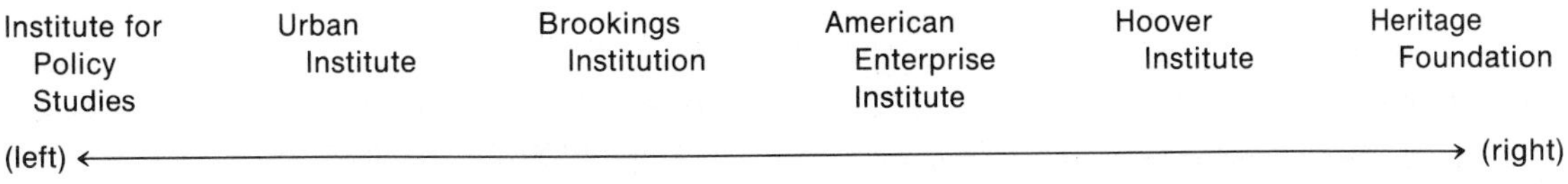

Institute for Policy Studies	Urban Institute	Brookings Institution	American Enterprise Institute	Hoover Institution	Heritage Foundation

(left) ←——————————————————————————————→ (right)

Figure 4.2. Place on the Ideological Continuum of Six Policy Institutes

mid-1970s, however, a second generation of conservative policy institutes, such as the American Enterprise Institute and the Heritage Foundation, moved aggressively forward to shape a public philosophy that was more consistent with their own values. The elections of Ronald Reagan and George Bush did much to further the influence of these organizations, and the works of scholars from these policy institutes became important to the implementation and continuation of the "Reagan revolution."[18] A third generation of policy institutes has emerged more recently to promote programs for the poor. The Children's Defense Fund, the Center on Budget and Policy Priorities, and the National Center on Policy and Practice (associated with NASW) are efforts to reassert the needs of the disadvantaged in social welfare policy.[19] The election of Bill Clinton to the presidency in 1992 brought to the forefront the Progressive Policy Institute, a think tank responsible for much of the policy research he used during the campaign, and later in establishing domestic policy.

Legislation

The legislative phase involves two primary groups: the legislature and special interest groups (often called advocacy groups in social welfare). The interaction of these groups is frequently intriguing, as Eric Redman's *The Dance of Legislation* portrays so well. Much public policy work is conducted by legislators who are appointed to committees and subcommittees on the basis of their particular interests. An important and often unappreciated component of the legislative phase is the role played by the staffs of committees and subcommittees. Legislative staffers are definitive experts in the subject area of a committee and are highly prized as lobbyists for special interest groups.[20] As a result of the increasing complexity of the policy process, the number of legislative staff has multiplied; 24,000 staff members now serve Congress, more than double the number a decade ago.[21] Committees

are the loci of testimony on issues, and legislative hearings provide an opportunity for official and sometimes the only input from the public on some matters. Accordingly, representatives of advocacy groups make it a point to testify before certain committees in order to ensure that their views are heard. At the federal level, the primary committees dealing with social welfare in 1992 are listed below.[22]

Senate

Finance Committee. Subcommittees: Health; Social Security; Family Policy
Agriculture, Nutrition and Forestry. Subcommittees: Nutrition; Investigations
Appropriations. Subcommittees: Labor; Human Services; Education
Labor and Human Resources. Subcommittees: Aging; Children; Family; Drugs and Alcoholism; Employment and Productivity; Handicapped; Labor
Special Aging

House of Representatives

Ways and Means. Subcommittees: Health; Public Assistance and Unemployment Compensation; Social Security
Education and Labor. Subcommittee: Human Resources
Appropriations. Subcommittees: Labor; Health and Human Service; Education
Aging
Children, Youth, and Families
Hunger

The procedure by which an idea becomes legislation was described earlier in this chapter in the discussion on technical aspects of the policy process. Throughout the process, advocacy groups attempt to shape the proposal so that it is more congruent with their interests. Large interest groups can exert almost continuous pressure on legislators by establishing political action committees (PACs). Through PACs, campaign contributions are funneled to candidates who reflect the priorities of the interest group—a legal exercise of influence that has increased dramatically over the past two decades. In 1974, 608 PACs contributed $8.5 million to congressional campaigns; but by 1986, 4,157 PACs were showing their muscle by donating $132.2 million. Most PACs are established by the corporate sector and reflect policy preferences that are relatively conservative.[23] Less well funded are the PACs established by labor and welfare advocacy groups. Regardless of ideological preference, most PACs hedge their bets by endorsing incumbents; over 90 percent of PAC contributions are given to members of Congress.[24] Anticipating a battle over the composition of a national health program, health care PACs were particularly active in funding the 1992 campaigns of officials, contributing $10 million. The largest contributions were made by PACs representing the American Medical Association ($677,969), the American Dental Association ($531,644), and the Independent Insurance Agents of America ($358,718). The largest recipient of health PAC money was Dan Rostenkowski ($162,498), chair of the House Ways and Means Committee, the committee that would have significant influence on the construction of a national health program.[25] In contrast to health PAC monies, welfare PACs are small. In conjunction with the National Association of Social Workers, Political Action for Candidate Election (PACE) makes contributions to candidates for national office who profess positions similar to those of the social work professional association. In 1984, PACE distributed over $250,000 to candidates for national office.[26]

Lest legislators become forgetful of the concerns of specific interest groups, many organizations hire career lobbyists to represent them. By 1987 some 23,011 lobbyists had registered, as required by law, to work the halls of Congress.[27] Limited by meager resources, social welfare advocacy groups usually rely on volunteer lobbyists. In addition to NASW, there are several advocacy groups within social welfare that have been instrumental in advanc-

ing legislation to assist vulnerable populations—among them, the National Conference on Social Welfare, the American Public Welfare Association, the Child Welfare League of America, the National Association for the Advancement of Colored People, the National Urban League, the National Assembly of Voluntary Health and Welfare Associations, the American Association of Retired Persons, and the National Organization for Women. Despite the number of welfare advocacy organizations and their successful record in evolving more comprehensive social legislation, changes in the policy process are making their work more difficult. Increases in the number of governmental agencies as well as in their staffs make it difficult to track policy developments and whatever changes there are in administrative procedures. Worse, the escalating cost of influencing social policy, evident in the number of paid lobbyists and the contributions lavished by PACs, is simply beyond the means of welfare advocacy organizations. As one Democratic candidate for the Senate lamented, "only the well-heeled have PACs—not the poor, the unemployed, the minorities or even most consumers."[28]

This is not to say that proponents of social justice are ineffectual. Despite their disadvantageous status, welfare advocacy groups were able to mobilize grass-roots support to beat back some of the more regressive proposals of the Reagan administration. In the early 1980s, for example, scholars from the conservative Cato Institute and the Heritage Foundation proposed cutting the Social Security program. They were trounced by an effective lobbying campaign mounted by the American Association of Retired Persons (AARP) under the leadership of the late octogenarian Congressman Claude Pepper. Unfortunately, other social welfare programs did not fare as well. At the same time that Social Security was spared budget cuts, social programs for the poor were reduced by significant margins. Among the newer advocacy organizations, the Children's Defense Fund stands to benefit significantly from the election of Bill

Clinton because First Lady Hillary Rodham Clinton is a former chair of its board of directors.

③ Implementation

Simply because a policy has been enacted does not necessarily mean it will be implemented. Often governmental policy fails to provide for adequate authority, personnel, or funding to accomplish its stated purpose. This is a chronic problem for social welfare programs. It is also possible that governmental policy will not be enforced even after it has been established. Many states have correctional and mental health institutions now operating under court supervision because judges have agreed with social advocates that these institutions are not in compliance with state or federal law. In another instance, full compliance with civil rights and affirmative action policies was not sought during the Reagan presidency because the Justice Department found these policies disagreeable.

Under the best of circumstances, implementation is problematic. In a book with a telling subtitle—*Implementation: How Great Expectations in Washington Are Dashed in Oakland: Or, Why It's Amazing that Federal Programs Work at All. This Being a Saga of the Economic Development Administration as Told by Two Sympathetic Observers Who Seek to Build Morals on a Foundation of Ruined Hopes*—authors Jeffrey Pressman and Aaron Wildavsky tell the story of an endeavor to reconstruct the inner city of Oakland, California. The Oakland Project was a collaborative effort involving the Economic Development Administration (EDA), city officials, and faculty of the University of California:

> Congress appropriated the necessary funds, the approval of city officials was obtained, and the program was announced to the public amidst the usual fanfare. Yet, years later, construction had been only partially completed, business loans had died entirely, and the results in terms of minority employment were meager and disappointing.[29]

Of the $23 million appropriated for the Oakland Project, only $3 million had been spent within the first three years—and that for an overpass to the coliseum and for architects' fees. Ironically, the project encountered no extraordinary obstacles. "If one is always looking for unusual circumstances and dramatic events," the authors concluded, "he cannot appreciate how difficult it is to make the ordinary happen."[30]

If implementation is trying in the normal course of events, it is that much more difficult given the disaffection of the public for governmental institutions. The episodic nature of public endorsement of governmental institutions has been studied by Albert O. Hirschman who investigated the relationship between "private interest and public action" in *Shifting Involvements*. According to Hirschman, public endorsement of governmental institutions is a fundamental problem for industrialized capitalist societies, which emphasize individual competitiveness while generating social and economic dislocations that require collective action. "Western societies," Hirschman observes, "appear to be condemned to long periods of privatization during which they live through an impoverished 'atrophy of public meanings,' followed by spasmodic outbursts of 'publicness' that are hardly likely to be constructive."[31] Disenchantment with governmental solutions to social problems makes public welfare programs vulnerable to their critics, leading to reductions in staff and fiscal support, often followed by an escalation in the social problem for which the social program was initially designed. Thus, the episodic nature of public support for programs designed to alleviate social problems further impedes effective implementation. A classic example of the cyclical nature of public policy appears in immigration legislation. In response to the estimated 12 million undocumented workers in the United States, the Immigration Reform and Control Act of 1986 allowed aliens who had been in the country before January 1, 1982, to apply for amnesty. Significantly, the amnesty provision was open for just one year, during which only half of the 4 million aliens thought eligible for amnesty applied. By the summer of 1988, hundreds of amnesty processing offices established by the Immigration and Naturalization Service (INS) were closed, not only leaving a large number of aliens ineligible for amnesty but also further contributing to the gradual buildup of the undocumented population. As the number of undocumented workers swells, Congress will once again be faced with the legalization problem and, in all likelihood, will authorize the INS to reopen the amnesty processing offices. To many welfare advocates, this opening and closing of immigration processing facilities is not only inhumane but also a foolish waste of administrative resources.

In some instances, public dissatisfaction with governmental programs has been exploited by astute politicians to virtually paralyze welfare activities. Richard Nixon attempted to cut welfare expenditures by impounding federal funds. Although the Supreme Court ruled this unconstitutional, the move effectively stymied programs for months. Taking a lesson from this, Ronald Reagan appointed cabinet-level officers who attempted to eliminate the very departments for which they had responsibility. In some instances, they reduced their department's influence by decimating programs through substantial reductions in funding and staff requests submitted to Congress. The politicization of the higher levels of government service represents a departure from a long-standing tradition. Until very recently, a high-level appointment in government service was viewed as a public service and an obligation owed the larger society for success in private life. This stewardship tradition acknowledged the validity of programs even though they might be personally distasteful, because they had been established through the legislative process. Under these circumstances, implementation was more feasible than it is when the executive branch has politicized the administration to such a degree that legislative intent is disregarded. Thus, appointed bureau heads have substantial influence over social policy through their control over the means by which programs are implemented.

Evaluation

The expansion of governmental welfare policies has spawned a veritable industry in program evaluation. Stung by the abuses of the executive branch during Watergate and the Vietnam War, Congress established additional oversight agencies to review federal programs.[32] As a result, multiple units within the executive and legislative branches of government have the evaluation of programs as their primary mission. At the federal level, the most important of these include the Government Accounting Office (GAO), the Office of Management and Budget (OMB), the Congressional Budget Office (CBO), and the Congressional Research Service (CRS). State governments have similar units. In addition, departments have evaluation units that monitor program activities for which they are responsible. Finally, federal and state levels of government commonly contract with nongovernmental organizations for evaluations of specific programs. As a result, many universities provide important research services to government. More recently, private consulting firms have entered the field, often hiring former government officials and capitalizing on their connections in order to secure research contracts. Of course, any politicization of the research process is frowned upon because it raises questions about the impartiality of the evaluation. Is a former government official willing to assess, rigorously and impartially, a program run by an agency in which he or she was employed in the past, or would like to be employed in the future? Questions about the validity of evaluation studies generated by the closeness between governmental agencies and research firms have become so common that the consulting firms located near the expressway surrounding Washington, D.C., are often referred to as "the beltway bandits."

Investigations by program evaluation organizations can be characterized as applied research (as opposed to "pure" research), the objective being to optimize program operations. As a result of this emphasis on the function of programs, evaluation studies frequently focus on waste, cost-effectiveness, and goal attainment. Owing to the contradictory objectives of many welfare policies, the constant readjustments in programs, and the limitations in the art of evaluation research, evaluations frequently conclude that any given program has mixed results. Rarely does a program evaluation provide a clear indication for future action. Often the results of program evaluations are used by critics and defenders alike either to dismantle or to advance a program. The very inconclusiveness of program evaluation contributes to the partisan use to which evaluation research can be put. It is not uncommon for decision makers to engage in statistical arguments that have a great influence on social welfare policy. Of the recent "stat wars," several relate directly to social welfare. One example is the question whether underemployed and discouraged workers should be included in the unemployment rate. Currently, the Department of Labor defines as unemployed only those who are out of work and looking for jobs, and considers part-time workers as employed. As a result, many African Americans, Hispanic Americans, young adults, and women are not considered unemployed even though advocates for these groups contend that they are not fully employed. Liberals argue that by including the underemployed and discouraged workers in the unemployment rate, it would become a more accurate measure of the employment experience of disadvantaged groups. Conservatives argue that the employment rate is not a good indicator of employment opportunity, citing the millions of undocumented workers who come to the United States every year illegally to take menial jobs. Further,

including underemployed and discouraged workers would increase the unemployment rate by as much as 50 percent, and would prove unacceptably expensive since extensions in the number of quarters for which workers are eligible for unemployment compensation are tied to the unemployment rate.

IMPLICATIONS FOR SOCIAL WELFARE

If the governmental decision-making process is somewhat irregular and irrational, it is also unrepresentative. As Figure 4.3 illustrates, groups in the upper levels of the social stratification populate the institutions through which policy is made. In the case of welfare policy, welfare beneficiaries must adjust to rules established by other social groups.

The primary players in the social policy game are organizers (executives) and cabals (professionals). Conservatives (old wealth) are able to opt out, leaving their social obligations in the hands of organizers. As one goes down the social stratification scale, the remaining groups have less influence on governmental policy. The interests of these groups are left in the hands of maverick professionals who work through advocacy organizations, although occasional unrest on the part of erratic (working/welfare poor) groups can result in increased welfare benefits. The difficulties that social program advocates can encounter in the policy process are evident in the attempt to legislate Urban Enterprise Zones (UEZs) in order to repair the extensive damage to South Central Los Angeles caused by the 1992 riot. Despite its being the worst civil disturbance in memory, the UEZ provisions of the 1992 Urban Aid Act amounted to a modest $2.5 billion for the creation of 50 enterprise zones. As the result of pressure by special business interests, unrelated tax concessions were added by the House and Senate, which increased appropriations to $28 billion,

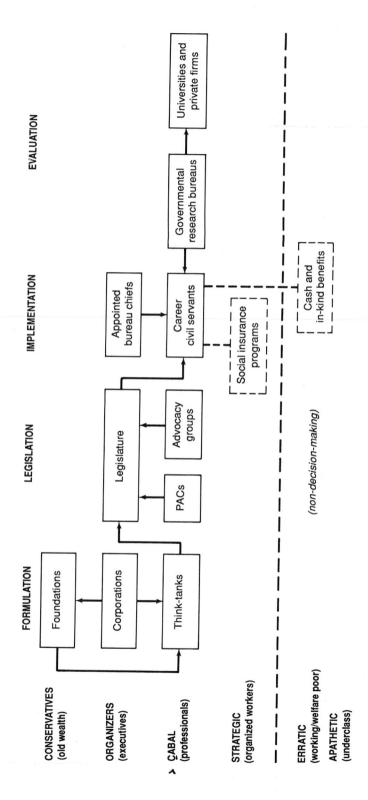

Figure 4.3. The Role Played by Six Social Levels in the Governmental Policy Process

87

an amount considered unacceptable by President Bush, who therefore vetoed the measure.[33]

The lack of influence on the part of lower socioeconomic groups in the social policy process is virtually built into governmental decision making. The term *nondecision making* has been coined to describe this phenomenon—the capacity to keep the interests of some groups off the decision-making agenda.[34] Nondecision making has a long history in the United States; generations of African Americans and women were legally excluded from decision making prior to emancipation and suffrage. More recent attempts to increase the influence of disadvantaged groups in decision making have not been well received. Perhaps the best-known example of this occurred during the War on Poverty when poor people were to be assured of "maximum feasible participation" in the Community Action Program (CAP). Even though this was interpreted to mean that one-third of the members of CAP boards of directors must be poor people—a seemingly reasonable expectation—the militancy of poor people in some cities at the time led to utter chaos in many CAPs. As a result of pressure from mayors and other officials, this requirement was rescinded in order to make CAPs more compliant.[35] Since then, the representation of lower socioeconomic groups in decision making has been limited, for all practical purposes, to an advisory capacity, if it is incorporated at all.

The governmental policy process also poses problems for administrators and practitioners. Policies frequently reflect assumptions about the human condition that may seem reasonable to the upper socioeconomic groups that make them but bear little resemblance to the reality of the lower socioeconomic groups that are supposed to be beneficiaries. For example, child support enforcement policy assumes that fathers of children on the AFDC program have the kind of regular, well-paying jobs that would allow them to meet the amounts of their court orders, when often their jobs are intermittent and low-wage. Consequently, support payments to children who are dependent on welfare have been relatively disappointing. To cite another example, workfare programs assume that youths want to complete their education and gain meaningful employment, when their socialization often tells them that school and work are irrelevant and that having a child may be the most meaningful thing they can do. Subsequently, AFDC has provided financial support to poor teenaged mothers, a benefit that many conservatives claim has actually induced girls to become pregnant.

It is not surprising, then, that welfare programs are not well received by many of the people who depend on them. Instead of being grateful, beneficiaries are frequently resentful. In turn, upper-income taxpayers find this ingratitude offensive and are inclined to make programs more punitive. Ironically, beneficiaries of welfare programs tend to respond to punitive policies with indifference and defiance because, for many of them, welfare programs have never been particularly helpful. The perception that welfare programs are only minimally helpful is occasionally validated when, due to exceptional circumstances, someone from an upper socioeconomic group falls into the social safety net and suddenly appreciates the importance of welfare programs for daily survival.

Not all welfare programs are perceived in such a negative light. Generally, programs that benefit persons solidly in the working class fare better. The social insurance programs, such as Social Security, Unemployment Compensation, and Medicare, are usually regarded more highly by beneficiaries. Of course, the insurance programs require people to first pay into the program in order to claim benefits later, so they are designed to be different from the means-tested programs intended for the poor.

A particular consequence of governmental policy-making falls on the shoulders of welfare professionals. "Workers on the front lines of the welfare state find themselves in a corrupted world of service," wrote Michael Lipsky in his award-winning *Street-Level Bureaucracy*. According to Lipsky, "Workers find that the best way to keep demand within manageable proportions is to deliver a consistently inaccessible or inferior product."[36] In response to the irrelevance often characteristic of governmental welfare policies, personnel in public welfare offices consequently deny benefits to people who are eligible for them, a process labeled "bureaucratic disentitlement."[37] It should come as no surprise, then, that public welfare programs mandated by governmental policy have acquired an undesirable reputation within the professional community. The executive director of the California chapter of NASW candidly stated that "Public social services are being abandoned by MSW social workers. It seems to be employment of last resort."[38] Another veteran observer was even more graphic: "To work in a public agency today is to work in a bureaucratic hell."[39] Within the context of public welfare it is not surprising to find that burnout has become pervasive among welfare professionals. The inadequacy of public welfare policies for both beneficiaries and professionals is an unfortunate consequence of the governmental policy process as it is currently structured.

Making the public policy process more representative is a primary concern of welfare advocates. Since the civil rights movement, African Americans and the poor have recognized the power of the ballot, and voter registration has become an important strategy for advancing the influence of these groups. Following this strategy, the Center for Participation in Democracy set as its goal the registration of 1 million voters in California prior to the 1988 national election.[40] The registration of Hispanic Americans in the Southwest has been the mission of the Southwest Voter Research Institute, founded by the late Willie Velasquez.

Under the visionary leadership of Velasquez, Latino voter registration grew steadily, reflected in an increase in the number of Chicano elected officials. Fifteen years of voter registration campaigning by the Institute contributed to a doubling of the number of Hispanic elected officials in the Southwest.[41] The most visible example of the political empowerment of people usually excluded from the decision-making process was Jesse Jackson's 1988 campaign to be the presidential nominee of the Democratic party. Expanding on the grass-roots political base built during his 1984 bid for the nomination, Jackson's 1988 Rainbow Coalition demonstrated the support he commanded from a wide spectrum of disenfranchised Americans. Thus, mobilization of the working- and welfare-poor, as Velasquez and Jackson have shown, can make the policy process more representative. Working to make public policy more democratic in origin is a continuous struggle and one that is supported by welfare advocacy organizations.

DISCUSSION QUESTIONS

1. Using a critical approach to welfare policy, select a social welfare program and identify the primary interests that are involved in its creation. To what extent do clients of the program influence the program? To what extent do social workers influence the program? Are there assumptions built ino the program that are inconsistent with the assumptions of the clients or social workers who are involved in it? To what extent have classism, racism, sexism, and ageism influenced health and human service programs of interest to you?

2. Politicians elected to the U.S. Congress can be reached through the Capitol Switchboard: (202) 224–3121. Contact your elected representative and one of your two senators and determine which health and human service committee assignments they have. Do your representatives have committee assignments that could make them influential on issues important to you? Do your representatives have position statements available to constituents about specific social programs?

3. Politicians elected to your state legislature have

responsibilities similar to those who are elected to Congress. Identify your state representatives. Do they have assignments on health and human service committees? Do they have position statements they could send to you on health and human service issues?

4. Select a legislative proposal in a health and human service area of concern to you and follow it through the national or state legislature. Which committees and interest groups supported or fought the proposed legislation? How was the bill changed to make it more acceptable to special interests? Have local interests, such as a major newspaper, endorsed or objected to the proposed legislation? Why?

5. Does your state chapter of the National Association of Social Workers make legislation a high priority for the professional community? What are the legislative priorities for the state NASW chapter? How is that reflected in the resources allocated? How would you prioritize health and human services in your community?

6. If nondecision making leaves many clients of social programs impotent in the public policy process, how could they be made more influential? How could the local professional community assist in empowering beneficiaries of social programs? What could you do?

NOTES

1. U.S. Congress, *U.S. Congress Handbook 1992* (McLean, Va.: Barbara Pullen, 1992), p. 184.
2. *Robert's Rules of Order* is available from several publishers.
3. The latest annual edition of *Overview of Entitlement Programs* can be obtained through the Government Printing Office in Washington, D.C.
4. Charles Lindblom and David Braybrooke, *Strategy of Decision* (New York: The Free Press, 1970).
5. Amitai Etzioni, *The Active Society* (New York: The Free Press, 1968), pp. 282–88.
6. U.S. Congress, "Conference Report on Immigration Reform and Control Act of 1986," *Congressional Record* (October 14, 1986), pp. H10068–95.
7. "An INS Recipe for Family Separation," *The San Diego Tribune,* October 24, 1987, p. B-3.
8. For a description of these forms of rationality, see Robert Alford, "Health Care Politics," *Politics and Society* 2 (Winter 1972): 127–64.
9. Neil Gilbert and Harry Specht, *Dimensions of Social Welfare Policy* (Englewood Cliffs, N.J.: Prentice-Hall, 1986), pp. 206–210.
10. "Nuking Employee Benefits," *Wall Street Journal,* August 29, 1988, p. 16.
11. For example, see Harry Hatry, *A Review of Private Approaches for Delivery of Public Services* (Washington, D.C.: Urban Institute, 1983).
12. Even Marx, who used a two-part classification, conceded the existence of a "lumpen-proletariat," although he did little to develop the concept.

13. Dexter Dunphy, *The Primary Group* (New York: Appleton-Century-Crofts, 1972), pp. 42–44.
14. Charles Peters, *How Washington Really Works,* rev. ed. (Reading, Mass.: Addison-Wesley, 1983), p. 112.
15. See, for example, Sheldon Danziger and Daniel Weinberg, *Fighting Poverty* (Cambridge, Mass.: Harvard University Press, 1986).
16. Peters, *How Washington Really Works,* pp. 101–102, 116.
17. Hedrick Smith, *The Power Game: How Washington Works* (New York: Random House, 1988), p. 152.
18. David Stoesz, "Policy Gambit: Conservative Think Tanks Take On the Welfare State," *Journal of Sociology and Social Welfare* 16 (1989): 8–16.
19. David Stoesz, "The New Welfare Policy Institutes." Unpublished manuscript, School of Social Work, San Diego State University, 1988.
20. Peters, *How Washington Really Works,* p. 114.
21. Smith, *The Power Game,* p. 24.
22. U.S. Congress, *The U.S. Congress Handbook 1987* (McLean, Va.: Barbara Pullen, 1987).
23. Smith, *The Power Game,* p. 252.
24. Charles Babcock, "At Least the PACs Still Love Those Incumbents in Congress," *Washington Post Weekly,* June 15–21, 1992, p. 32.
25. Dana Priest, "Health Care PACs Pay $10 million for 'Access,'" *Washington Post,* July 22, 1992, p. A–17.

26. Steve Burghardt, "Community-Based Social Action," *Encyclopedia of Social Work,* 18th ed. (Silver Spring, Md.: NASW, 1987), p. 297.
27. Smith, *The Power Game,* p. 238.
28. Ibid., p. 254.
29. Jeffrey Pressman and Aaron Wildavsky, *Implementation: How Great Expectations in Washington Are Dashed in Oakland* (Berkeley, Calif.: University of California Press, 1974), p. xii.
30. Ibid.
31. Albert O. Hirschman, *Shifting Involvements* (Princeton, N.J.: Princeton University Press, 1982), p. 132.
32. Peters, *How Washington Really Works,* p. 111.
33. Art Pine, "President Vetoes Urban Aid Measure," *Los Angeles Times,* November 5, 1992, p. A-4.
34. Peter Bachrach and Morton S. Baratz, *Power and Poverty* (New York: Oxford University Press, 1979), p. 7.
35. For a review of the CAP experience, see Daniel Patrick Moynihan, *Maximum Feasible Misunderstanding* (New York: Random House, 1973).
36. Quoted in Robert Kuttner, *The Economic Illusion* (Boston: Houghton Mifflin, 1984), p. 86.
37. Michael Lipsky, "Bureaucratic Disentitlement in Social Welfare Programs," *Social Service Review* 33, no. 4 (March 1984): 81–88.
38. Ellen Dunbar, "Future of Social Work," *NASW California News* 13, no. 18 (May 1987): 3.
39. Harris Chaiklin, "The New Homeless and Service Planning on a Professional Campus," University of Maryland, Chancellor's Colloquium, Baltimore, December 4, 1985, p. 7.
40. Sharon Griffin, "Voter-Registration Drive Well on Way to Goal," *San Diego Union,* September 3, 1988, p. A-10.
41. "Willie's Vision for Chicano Empowerment," *Southwest Voter Research Notes* 2, no. 3 (June 1988): 1.

CHAPTER 5

Social Stigma in the American Social Welfare State

Social stigma and poverty are inextricably linked in the fabric of American social welfare. As manifested in economic, social, and political discrimination, social stigma ultimately leads to poverty for most of its vulnerable victims and, in turn, results in income maintenance and poverty programs designed to address the effects of poverty. Realizing that social stigma encourages poverty, some policymakers have attempted to address this cycle of misery by attacking discrimination, one of its core components. In the end, these policymakers hope that by curtailing discriminatory practices and attitudes, vulnerable populations will be given equal opportunities for achievement and success, thereby reducing the need for expensive and often inadequate social welfare programs. This chapter probes discrimination that is based on race, gender, sexual orientation, disability, and age.

RACISM

Racism refers to the discrimination against and prejudicial treatment of a racially different minority group. This prejudicial treatment may take the form of differential hiring and firing practices, promotions, and resource allocations in health care and education, a two-tier structure in transportation systems, segregation in housing policies, discrimmatory behavior on the part of the judicial and law enforcement systems, and prejudicial images of the minority group in the media. A pattern of racial discrimination that is strongly entrenched in a society is called institutional racism.

Discrimination against African Americans

The results of individual and institutional racism manifest themselves most clearly as impoverishment. In 1990, African Americans comprised some 12 percent of the U.S. population (29.7 million). The African-American population is primarily urban, with more than 82 percent living in metropolitan areas. Almost 56 percent of African Americans live in the South; the remainder live in the Midwest (19.1 percent), the Northeast (16.5 percent), and the West (8.5 percent). Thirty-four percent of all African Americans live in only seven cities: New York, Los Angeles, Washington, D.C., Philadelphia, Baltimore, Chicago, and St. Louis. In 1988, 71 percent of all poor African-American children lived in central cities compared with 32.6 percent of poor white children.[1]

In recent years, many African Americans have not only improved their socioeconomic position but have done so at a relatively faster rate than comparable whites. The most noticeable gains have occurred in the areas of professional employment, incomes of two-earner families, higher education, and home ownership. For example, the number of African Americans in technical, professional, and managerial positions increased by 57 percent (from just under 1 million to over 1.5 million) from 1973 to 1982. By comparison, the number of whites in such positions increased by only 36 percent. In African-American households where couples were between the ages of 24 and 35, and where both the husband and wife were employed, the difference in annual income between African Americans and whites was less than $3,000, a significant improvement over earlier decades. The fraction of African-American families earning $25,000 a year or more (calculated in 1982 dollars) increased from 10.4 percent in 1960 to 24.5 percent in 1982. Furthermore, African Americans recorded a 47 percent increase in home ownership during the 1970s, compared to a 30 percent increase for whites.[2] Finally, African-American youngsters recorded a substantial gain in SAT scores from 1976 to 1989, earning 19 percent higher in verbal and 32 percent higher in math scores. By comparison, white students SAT scores dropped by 5 percent and 2 percent, respectively.[3] This gain may have contributed in part to the halving of the high school dropout rate for African Americans from 27.4 percent in 1968 to 13.2 percent in 1990, a rate very close to the 12.1 percent dropout rate for whites.[4] Despite this relative improvement, however, millions of African Americans did not progress during the last decade, but instead, experienced a significant erosion in their standard of living.

Discrimination against African Americans rears its head in all sectors of social, political, and economic life. Moreover, the effects of discrimination are evident when examining key socioeconomic indicators in the areas of poverty, housing, employment, family composition, health, education, crime, and welfare dependency.

Poverty is the area where the results of long-term discrimination against African Americans are the most visible. The poverty rate for African Americans was 25.1 percent in 1959; by 1990 it had risen to over 30 percent.[5] By the late 1980s the poverty rate for all Americans was 13.4 percent; for African Americans it was 31.7 percent.[6] In 1990, almost 45 percent of African-American children were poor, up from 40 percent in 1974. This figure compares unfavorably with the 1990 poverty rate for white children of about 16 percent.

The higher poverty rate for African Americans is also evident when disaggregating the data. For example, the poverty rate in 1990 for female-headed African-American families was 64.7 percent, compared with 45.9 percent for female-headed white families. In the same year the poverty rate for African-American families in which a male was present was 19.3 percent compared with 9.5 percent for similar white families.[7] This differential is even more marked when comparing poverty rates in nonmetropolitan (rural) and metropolitan areas. For example, the poverty rate for whites in nonmetropolitan areas was 13.7 percent compared with 44.1 percent for African Americans.[8] Thus, the differential between African-American and white poverty rates holds even when factoring in family composition and geographical differences.

Housing patterns also reflect the economic differential between African Americans and whites. Minority (African-American, Asian, and Native American) households are both poorer and more likely to be renters than white households. Minority households make up 41 percent of households with yearly incomes below $5,000, but only 13 percent of those with incomes above $50,000.[9] This factor encourages a home ownership rate of 43 percent for African Americans compared with 69 percent for whites.[10]

Some 29 percent of African-American households lived in severely or moderately deficient housing in 1989; by comparison, about 13 percent of poor white households lived in such conditions.[11] And, in 1989, 39 percent of African-American households spent at least 30 percent of their income for housing compared with 25 percent of white households doing so. Among poor African-American households, almost 54 percent paid 50 percent or more for housing.[12]

Employment is another area where discrimination is manifest. In 1989, the mean earnings for white men (employed full-time and year round) was $31,804; for equivalent African-American men it was $23,374.[13] This differential applied even when educational level was considered. For example, in 1989 the mean earnings for a white male who had completed 17-plus years of schooling was $44,396; for the equivalent African-American male it was $34,344 (see Table 5.1). While the mean earnings of that same white male increased by 10.5 percent from 1979 to 1989, it *decreased* for African-American males by 2.8 percent. Among *all* college graduates, only young African-American families were not economically better off in 1987 than they were in 1979.[14]

This differential in wages is even more marked when the percentage of employed men with low earnings is examined on the basis of educational level. In 1989, just over 12 percent of white males with 12 years of schooling were considered to have low earnings. For African-American males that figure was 25.5 percent.[15]

TABLE 5.1. 1989 Yearly Mean Income of African-American, Hispanic-American, and White Families by Educational Level

Years of Education	White	Black	Hispanic
0–8 years	$19,164	$13,800	$14,255
9–11 years	$19,780	$15,180	$15,413
12 years	$26,509	$19,020	$19,942
13–15 years	$31,116	$23,119	$24,811
16 years	$39,331	$28,287	$31,297
17 years plus	$44,396	$34,344	$36,863

SOURCE: Adapted from U.S. House of Representatives, *Overview of Entitlement Programs, 1992 Green Book* (Washington, D.C.: U.S. Government Printing Office, 1992), p. 598.

Moreover, 34 percent of African-American males earned poverty-level wages in 1987 (up from 18.4 percent in 1979), compared with 16.3 percent of white men.[16]

Perhaps the hardest hit during this period was the young African-American worker. While the average young worker aged 25 to 34 earned 7.2 percent less in 1987 than in 1979, the average African-American worker earned 21.6 percent less in that same period.[17] In short, the overall median African-American income in 1990 was about 59 percent of its white counterpart ($18,676 compared to $31,231).[18] African Americans earned less than whites irrespective of household composition, education, region, or religion.

Another indicator of economic distress is unemployment. From the mid-1950s until the late 1970s, the ratio of African-American to white unemployment stood at 2.0 (twice the white rate). However, beginning in the 1980s that ratio climbed to 2.5, despite the narrowing differences between the two groups in education, occupational mobility, and earnings. Although questions remain as to why this change occurred, one explanation is that as middle-class African Americans advanced, greater unemployment occurred among those with less education and skills. This explanation, however, does not address the large African-American/white unemployment differential among college-educated men, a disparity that is greater in central cities of the East and North, where 10.3 percent of college-educated African-American men are unemployed compared with only 3.9 percent of similar white men. According to Franklin Wilson, the cause of this discrepancy can be found in two factors: (1) the decline during the 1980s in the number of jobs traditionally filled by college-educated African-American men (e.g., public sector jobs dealing with affirmative action, social welfare, and criminal justice); and (2) the inability of educated African Americans to penetrate the professional/technical occupations that involve managerial or supervisory responsibilities, positions that usually have more security.[19]

Family composition is a powerful indicator of the effects of racism. Overall, a high percentage of births to *all* teenagers are to unmarried women. In 1989 births out of wedlock accounted for 93 percent of all births to females under age 15 and for 77 percent of all births to teenagers 15 to 17. Disaggregating the data shows that of teenagers aged 15 to 19, 56.5 percent of all white births and 91.7 percent of all African-American births were to unmarried teens.[20] In the 20- to 24-year-old age group, as many as 35 percent of all births are to unmarried women, with 25 percent of all white births and 70 percent of all African-American births occurring among unmarried mothers. This number represents a significant increase in the out-of-wedlock birth rate for African-American women, which soared from about 22 percent of all births in 1960 to almost 68 percent by 1989. The white rate also increased during the same period, going from 2 percent in 1960 to about 18.8 percent of all births in 1989. In 1989, this number translated into 457,480 out-of-wedlock births to African-American women and 593,911 out-of-wedlock births to white women. As a result, over 56 percent of all African-American families in 1990 were headed by single females as compared with 18.8 percent of white households.[21] Out-of-wedlock birth rates by race and decade are shown in Figure 5.1.

Out-of-wedlock births have grave economic consequences, especially considering that teenage mothers are now more likely to keep their children regardless of their income.[22] This decision translates into important economic realities. For example, teenage mothers are twice as likely to be poor as nonteen mothers, and a teenage mother earns only half the lifetime wage of a woman who waits until she is 20 to have her first child.[23] A strong correlation also exists between single, young mothers and high welfare dependency. In 1989, close to 32 percent of never-married adolescent mothers aged 15 to 19 received public welfare.[24] Of that number, the average time of welfare receipt was 9.33 years, and the number of recipients who reported welfare spells of 10 or more years was almost 40 percent.[25] Moreover, in 1989, teenage childbearing cost taxpayers almost $40 billion in AFDC, Food Stamps, and Medicaid charges.[26] While the absence of economic opportunities for young women may make childbirth and the welfare system seem more appealing than a dead-end, minimum-wage job, over 50 percent of African-American female-headed families fell below the poverty line in 1989, and more than half of all African-American children born in that year were poor.

Health is another important indicator of discrimination. For example, African Americans have one of the highest rates of infant mortality of any group in the United States, a rate that in 1989 equaled 17.7 deaths per 1,000 compared with 8.2 deaths per thousand for white women.[27] Had the African-American infant mortality rate been as low as the white rate over the past 50 years, more than 400,000 babies would have lived.

A major factor affecting infant mortality is low birth weight. Although the definitive cause is unknown, what is clear is that low birth weight (defined as less than 5.5 pounds) increases the chances of infant death during the first month by 40 times.[28] Also known is that low birth weight is often correlated with inadequate nutrition in mothers during pregnancy. Of the nearly 40,000 infant deaths each year, about 23,000 are estimated to result from low birth weight. In 1989, 7 percent of all babies were born at low birth weight; for African-American babies it was 13.2 percent, a percentage that was slightly higher than in 1987.[29] Moreover, less than half of all African-American children in 1985 had been fully immunized against measles, rubella, diphtheria, polio, and mumps.

African-American mothers are also four times more likely to die in childbirth than are white mothers.[30] Higher infant mortality and higher deaths in childbirth are often correlated with poor early prenatal care. In 1989, only 61.1 percent of African-American births were to women who had received early prenatal care.

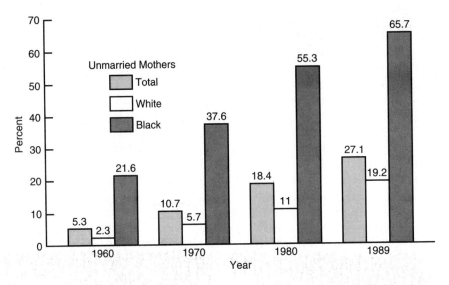

Figure 5.1. Percentage of Births to Unmarried Mothers, by Race for Selected Years. (SOURCE: Committee on Ways and Means, U.S. House of Representatives, *Overview of Entitlement Programs, 1992 Green Book* [Washington, D.C.: U.S. Government Printing Office, 1992], Chart 1, p. 1074.)

By comparison, almost 75 percent of white births were to women who had had such care. These variations are even sharper when the amount and frequency of care is considered. In 1988, 73.5 percent of babies were born to white mothers who had received care that began before the seventh month of pregnancy and included more than four visits; for African Americans the figure was only 50.7 percent.[31] The combination of these factors caused the African-American infant mortality rate to rank twenty-seventh internationally in 1989, behind such countries such as Hungary, Poland, and Cuba. Table 5.2[32] ranks countries according to their infant mortality rates.

The variation in health indicators between African Americans and whites goes beyond infant mortality. From age 1 until age 24, the African-American mortality rate is close to double that of whites, except in the area of suicide, where the African-American rate is almost half the white rate. This higher mortality follows African Americans throughout their lives, and the life expectancy of African Americans is 6.4 years less than it is for whites.[33] However, when environmental and economic variables are controlled, the effect of race on the African-American mortality rate is reduced by 75 percent.[34] In other words, the lower longevity of African Americans is based on poverty, not race.

Education is another indicator that illustrates the "diswelfare" of African Americans. Education is thought to be one of the most important variables in determining economic security. Despite the relatively high unemployment rate of college-educated African-American men, discussed earlier, those with college degrees were much less likely to have low earnings than those with only a high school education. In short, as a high school education alone becomes less valuable in the marketplace, only educational upgrading can protect men from large income losses. In fact, the incomes of college graduates rose from 20 percent above the earnings of high school graduates in the 1950s to about 40 to 50 percent higher than high school graduates' incomes by the mid-1970s. And, while the annual wage of a high school graduate

TABLE 5.2. International Infant Mortality Rates Ranked by Country, 1986–1988

Country	Rate*
Japan	5.0
Sweden	6.0
Finland	6.0
Switzerland	6.8
Netherlands	7.4
Canada	7.5
Hong Kong	7.5
France	7.9
Denmark	8.0
German F.R.	8.1
Norway	8.2
Singapore	8.3
U.S. (white)	8.7
Australia	8.8
Spain	9.2
England and Wales	9.3
Austria	9.4
Belgium	9.7
Italy	9.8
U.S.	10.1
New Zealand	10.7
Israel	10.8
Czechoslovakia	12.7
Portugal	14.4
Hungary	17.4
Poland	17.5
U.S. (black)	17.8
Yugoslavia	25.9

* Infant deaths per 1,000 births

SOURCE: U.S. House of Representatives, *Overview of Entitlement Programs: 1992 Green Book* (Washington, D.C.: U.S. Government Printing Office, 1992), p. 1119.

fell 8.6 percent from 1979 to 1987, the income of a college graduate rose by 9.2 percent.[35] Partly as a result of market conditions, African-American men have increased their schooling more than whites have since the mid-1970s.[36]

From 1968 to 1990, the white high school dropout rate remained relatively flat, falling from 14.7 to 12.0 percent. By contrast, the Afri-can-American dropout rate fell dramatically from 27.4 to 13.2 percent.[37] According to Lawrence Mishel and David Frankel, over 73 percent of African Americans completed high school in the 1980–1988 period, compared to 61 percent in the 1967–1973 period.[38] Although these figures may appear comforting, they also contain inconsistencies. For example, in 1988 only 58.4 percent of African Americans completed high school between ages 18 and 19, a figure that increased to 81.5 percent for the 20 to 21-year-old age group. Moreover, almost 29 percent of African-American students who entered ninth grade in 1984 failed to graduate from high school by 1988. These figures are exacerbated by a stagnant high school completion rate for African Americans, which rose only three percentage points in the past 20 years.[39]

The failure to complete high school is clearly correlated with poverty. According to the American Public Welfare Association, in 1989 nearly half of all female heads of families and 60 percent of parents receiving welfare in 36 of the previous 60 months did not finish high school.[40] Furthermore, an estimated 85 percent of juveniles appearing in court are functionally illiterate.[41]

While high school graduation rates have steadily, if slowly, improved among African Americans, college enrollment stagnated during the 1980s. Among 1989 high school graduates, about 60 percent of whites and 53 percent of African Americans entered college the following fall. Among 1980 high school graduates, however, only 10 percent of African Americans had completed their degree by 1986, compared with 20 percent of similar white college enrollees.[42] Moreover, while white college enrollment rates improved slightly from 1974 to 1988 (from 26 to 28.2 percent), African-American college enrollment was stuck between 20.4 and 20.5 percent. Also fewer minority college graduates have gone on to obtain advanced degrees. For example, in 1986–87, whites made up 80.8 percent of all undergraduates: They received 87.5 percent of the bachelor's degrees, 88.2 percent of the master's degrees, and 89.0 percent of all doctorates. By contrast, African Americans accounted for 9.4 percent of all undergraduates, but received only 5.9 percent of the bachelor's degrees, 5.3 percent of the master's degrees, and 3.9 percent of the doctorates.[43]

African-American college enrollment rates peaked in 1976. Much of that bubble was attributable to civil rights legislation and such variables as increased student aid. However, while overall financial aid decreased slightly between 1980 and 1989, public college costs for tuition and room and board (adjusted for inflation) rose from $3,838 in 1978–79 to $4,899 in 1987–88. Private college costs soared from $9,060 to $13,840 in the same period. The average financial aid award had so eroded by 1989 that it paid for less than 21 percent of the yearly costs of a private college and for only 60.6 percent of the costs of a public university.

Crime is another indicator of economic and social distress. Although African Americans constitute 12 percent of the population, they account for 30 percent of all arrests and for 51 percent of all violent crime arrests. Moreover, they are 8.5 times more likely than whites to go to prison.[44] Harvard economist Richard Freeman calculated that 35 percent of all African Americans aged 16 to 35 had been arrested in 1989.[45] In 1986, almost 47 percent of the inmates in state prisons were African American, four times their numerical representation in the population. According to the U.S. House Committee on Ways and Means, "Juveniles in public facilities are predominantly male, and disproportionately black, and four-fifths were 14 to 17 years old."[46] In fact, of the 56,000 juveniles held in public juvenile facilities, almost 34,000 were from minority groups. And of the 144 felons executed from 1977 to 1990, 40 percent were African American and another 5 percent Hispanic American.[47]

Perhaps one of the most startling statistics is the death rate for African Americans through homicide and legal intervention. In 1989, 101.8 African-American men in every 100,000 were killed through homicide or legal intervention. This compares with 11.5 per 100,000 white men. In effect, African-American men are almost 10 times more likely to die in this manner than white males. For African-American females the rate is 17.5 per 100,000, higher than the 11.5 death rate for white males and over four times higher than the death rate for white females.[48]

Welfare dependency is another indicator of racism. Although African Americans comprise only 12 percent of the U.S. population, they make up roughly 41 percent of all AFDC recipients, 35 percent of all food stamp recipients, 31 percent of Medicaid recipients, and 25 percent of SSI beneficiaries.[49]

Hispanic Americans and Poverty

Because of the large number of undocumented aliens coming from Central America and Mexico, the Hispanic-American population of the United States is difficult to measure accurately. Although some estimates of the number of undocumented workers in the United States (most of them from Spanish-speaking countries) are in the 12 million range, other researchers have estimated this population to be between 3 to 6 million.[50] Still other estimates suggest that by 1988 approximately 1.8 million illegal immigrants from Mexico and Central and South America were in the United States.[51] According to the Census Bureau, more than 20 million people of Spanish origin lived in the United States in 1989, or about 8.2 percent of the U.S. population. This number represented an increase of 67 percent from 1970 to 1989. The Hispanic-American population is highly concentrated geographically. For example, 65 percent of Hispanic Americans live in three states: California, Texas, and New York. Eighty-eight percent of all Hispanic Americans live in nine states, and 88 percent live in urban areas (a figure 13 percent higher than the national average).[52]

The poverty status of Hispanic Americans has worsened in the last two decades in relation to other groups, including African Americans.

For example, while the overall poverty rate for African Americans increased slightly from 1973 (31.4 percent) to 1990 (31.9 percent), the poverty rate for Hispanic Americans soared from 21.9 to 28.1 percent.[53] In 1979, 28 percent of Hispanic-American children were below the poverty line; by 1990 that number had risen to 38.4 percent. (That rate is well over twice the poverty rate of 15.9 percent for white children.) By 1990, some 2.8 million Hispanic-American children were living in poverty, the highest level ever recorded since the Census Bureau began keeping data on Hispanic Americans in 1973.[54] The high poverty rate for children is clearly correlated with the 47.5 percent of Hispanic-American female-headed families that fell below the poverty line in 1990, a number significantly higher than the 25.4 percent of white female-headed families in this category, and slightly above the 46.5 percent of African-American female-headed families in poverty.[55]

The median earnings of Hispanic-American males ($21,697) were also low, and in 1988 they were actually lower than those of African Americans ($23,374). (Almost the same wage differential existed between Hispanic-American and African-American women—$16,860 versus $17,811.) The loss of income for both Hispanic-American men and women represents a change from 1978, when they earned slightly more than African Americans.[56] More important, this translates into a loss of one-tenth of a percent in family income (adjusting for inflation in 1989 dollars) from 1973 to 1989, thus making Hispanic-American families the only minority group in the United States to have experienced a net loss of income in that period.[57] If current poverty trends continue, Hispanic Americans will replace African-Americans as the most impoverished group by the late 1990s.

Scott Barancik sums up the economic position of Hispanic Americans:

Hispanics account for a disproportionately large share of the American households with low incomes and a disproportionately small share of those with high incomes. Census Bureau data show that of all the households in the top income fifth in 1987, just over three percent were Hispanic. By contrast, nine percent of those in the bottom fifth were Hispanic, meaning that Hispanics were about three times as likely to be among the poorest fifth of U.S. households as among the wealthiest fifth.[58]

Although for statistical purposes the Hispanic-American population is often considered as a single group, the various subgroups among Hispanics have quite distinct social and historical backgrounds. For example, Cuban Americans living in Florida may have little in common historically and politically with Mexican Americans living in California, and Puerto Ricans living in New York may have little understanding of the culture of either Cuban Americans or Mexican Americans. These sociocultural differences are also reflected in the significant differences in incomes among these groups. For example, while the median Puerto Rican family income was $18,932 in 1988, it was $26,858 for Cuban Americans, $24,322 for Central and South Americans, and $21,025 for Mexican Americans.[59]

According to the Bureau of the Census, there were about 13 million Mexican Americans in the United States in 1989, a 100 percent increase over the 1970 census. Mexican Americans constitute about 63 percent of all Hispanic Americans in the United States and are the fastest growing of the Spanish-speaking subgroups. Moreover, the continuation of this rate of growth will place the Mexican-American population at about 17 million by the mid-1990s, and by the year 2000 it is expected to be the largest minority group in the United States.[60]

The poverty of Mexican Americans is correlated, at least in part, to deficits in educational attainment. Although Mexican Americans have made educational gains, in 1980 their median attendance in school was 9.8 years, the lowest of any Hispanic-American subgroup.[61] Moreover, they have the highest dropout rate in the United States. In 1980, over 62 percent of those between the ages of 25 and 64 had less than a high school education, and only 4.4 percent had some college.[62]

Migrant and seasonal farm workers, a group heavily composed of Mexican Americans, are among the most impoverished people in America. Working six to eight months a year, migrants travel in family groups, and virtually all family members—including children—work in the fields. Laboring under extremely difficult and hazardous conditions, migrants face dangers from both powerful pesticides and complicated farm equipment, thus making them highly vulnerable to health problems. For example, in 1985 the infant mortality rate for migrants was 25 percent higher than the national average; the death rate from influenza was 20 percent higher than in the general population; poor nutrition caused higher incidences of pre- and postnatal deaths; and parasitic infections affected 27 to 45 percent of migrant children.[63] Taken together, these health problems resulted in a life expectancy of only 49 years for migrant farm workers. Educational prospects for migrant children are equally bleak: 9 out of 10 migrant children never enter high school and, of those who do, only 3 out of 10 graduate.[64]

In the 1960s the deplorable conditions faced by farm workers led to the emergence of the United Farm Workers Association (UFW) in California, a movement led by the charismatic Cesar Chavez. Initiating a grape and lettuce boycott, the UFW was able to raise the wages of farm workers and lobby for protective legislation. However, despite the limited victories of the UFW, the plight of many migrant farm workers remains desperate at best.

Puerto Ricans constitute 12 percent of all Hispanics in the United States and less than 1 percent of the total U.S. population. In the past 25 years, Puerto Ricans have steadily lost ground in labor force participation, earnings of family heads, and poverty status. In 1988, Puerto Ricans had one of the lowest family incomes of any minority group in the United States—$18,932.[65] From 1960 to 1984, Puerto Rican family income dropped relative to other minority groups, and over 43 percent of all Puerto Rican families lived below the poverty line in 1984.[66]

At least some of the Hispanic-American poverty is attributable to the large numbers of illegal immigrants entering the United States and to the low-paying, menial jobs they work at. In 1986 Congress passed the Immigration Reform and Control Act (IRCA) (PL 99–603), which was in part an attempt to "legalize" immigrants already in the United States. According to Fariyal Ross-Sheriff, the three main objectives of IRCA were: (1) to decrease the number of illegal aliens currently living in the United States; (2) to regain control of U.S. national boundaries; and (3) to increase the number of legal or migrant farm and agricultural workers.[67]

IRCA is a mixed blessing for undocumented workers, most of whom are Hispanic Americans. For one thing, it includes an employer sanction provision that specifies imprisonment and fines of up to $10,000 per worker for employers who knowingly hire undocumented workers. In a controversial approach, the Immigration and Naturalization Service (INS) relies on employers to determine the legitimacy of each worker, thereby making it more risky to hire alien workers. Under the amnesty provision of the act, undocumented persons who could prove they entered the United States before 1982 were eligible to apply for temporary resident status. After 18 months they were permitted to apply for permanent resident status. Provided they had no criminal record, and did not apply for benefits from a federally subsidized welfare program for a period of five years, they were allowed to stay in the United States. After that, they were permitted to apply for citizenship. Therein lies the hitch. Forced to accept low-paying jobs because of language and educational deficits, these workers became banished to the netherworld of minimum-wage employment. These immigrants were thus forced to rely on family or nongovernmental aid, deprived of the welfare safety net guaranteed to most Americans.[68] The United States was effectively forcing prospective citizens to become second-class "citizens" in order to qualify for citizenship. By October 1988, 2 million people had applied for legalization, a number including the 1 million who had entered the country illegally before January 1, 1992, and the 510,000 agricultural workers who were in the country before 1986.[69]

Native Americans and Poverty

Oppression and exploitation are by no means limited to African Americans and Hispanic Americans. Native Americans, in some ways the most destitute group in the United States, experience the same intensity of oppression as do other disenfranchised populations. In 1989, Native Americans had the lowest per capita income of any ethnic group in the United States ($13,678), and 23.7 percent were living below the poverty line.[70]

The history of Native Americans is marked by hardship, deprivation, and gross injustice. Before the arrival of Christopher Columbus in the New World, the Indian population in the territorial United States was somewhere between 900,000 and 12 million.[71] As a result of the westward expansion of whites—and the wars and genocidal policies that ensued—the indigenous Indian population was dramatically reduced. By 1880 the census reported the existence of only 250,000 Indians.[72] Moreover, Native Americans were not granted citizenship until 1924, and New Mexico did not allow them to vote until 1940. Some Native Americans remained slaves until 1935.[73]

From 1970 to 1989, the Native American population increased from 574,000 to almost 2 million.[74] This population rise was due to a lower infant mortality rate, a high birthrate, and the fact that more individuals of mixed Indian descent were reporting their race as Indian. This last factor may be correlated with the resurgence of Native American pride that marked the period of the 1970s.

In 1980, about 25 percent of Native Americans (400,000) lived on 278 federal and state reservations. However, because of the federal policy of selling or leasing reservation land, only 49 percent of the inhabitants of reservations are Native Americans, the rest being non-Indian spouses, ranchers, merchants, teachers, doctors, and government employees. With the exception of the Navaho nation (containing more than 100,000 Indians), most reservations are small, having under 1,000 residents.[75] Sixty-three percent of all Native Americans live away from the reservations, and almost 600,000 live in urban areas. Thus, almost half the Native American population is now urban.

Native Americans often experience severe social and economic problems. For example, only 56 percent of Native American children graduate from high school, and it is estimated that about 38,000 Native American homes lack safe water and adequate sanitation. Moreover, 43 percent of Native Americans who live beyond infancy die before age 55, compared to just over 16 percent of the total population. Native Americans have a maternal death rate 20 percent higher than the national rate. Other health indicators for Native Americans are equally dismal. The Native American death rate for tuberculosis is six times that of the population as a whole; the death rate for chronic liver disease is four times the norm; for accidents, three times; for diabetes, influenza, and pneumonia, two times; and Native American suicide rates are twice the national average, with rates tending to be highest among young people. Moreover, Native Americans have the highest rate of alcoholism of any ethnic group in the United States.[76]

Caught in the paternalistic and authoritarian web of the Bureau of Indian Affairs (BIA), Native Americans struggle both for their identity and their survival. Having been robbed of their land, murdered indiscriminately by encroaching white settlers (as well as the U.S. Cavalry), and treated alternately as children and pests by the federal government, Native Americans were further oppressed by having their children removed from their homes by welfare officials. This widespread abuse by welfare workers, who evaluated Native American child-rearing practices as harsh in the context of white middle-class family values, was partially remedied by the Indian Child Welfare Act of 1978, which restored child-placement decisions to the individual tribes. As a result of this act, priority for the placement of Native American children was given to tribal members rather than white families. In an attempt to remedy historical injustices, the Indian Self-Determination Act of 1975 emphasized tribal self-government, self-sufficiency, and the establishment of independent health, education, and welfare services. Despite these limited gains, the plight of Native Americans serves as a reminder of the mistakes made by the United States both in its past and present policies toward disenfranchised minority groups.

Asian Americans

Asian Americans are quickly becoming one of the fastest-growing groups of immigrants in the United States. Of the 7.3 million Asian Americans in the country, 40 percent live in California.

Although there are considerable statistics available on the economic status of African and Hispanic Americans, there are no comparable data for Asian Americans. What we do know, however, is that unlike other oppressed minority groups, the poverty statistics for Asian Americans are mixed. For example, the most recent U.S. census data indicate that Asian-American poverty levels range from less than 5 percent for Japanese Americans to 35 percent for newly arrived Southeast Asian immigrants. These figures suggest that discrimination against Asian Americans does not always play itself out in the economic domain.

Asian Americans have been stigmatized in American society in a number of ways. Most dramatic was the internment of Japanese Americans in detention camps during World War II.

However, Asian Americans have also experienced more subtle forms of discrimination. For example, Asian Americans are often thought of as a "model minority." Because of this status, many take heat from the white majority as well as from other minorities. An example of this tension is evident in the hostility between Korean shopkeepers and inner-city African-American residents. Asian Americans have also been the victims of hate crimes, some motivated by the mudslinging that has been going on between Japan and the United States over recurrent trade problems. Specifically, the U.S. trade deficit with Japan and the resulting displacement of American blue-collar workers have often been blamed on all Asians. In addition, some Asian Americans complain that they are discriminated against in colleges and universities because of their superior academic performance.[77]

Asian Americans have also felt the backlash from mainstream Americans who are worried about the economic consequences of admitting non-European immigrants into American society. For example, groups such as the Federation for American Immigration Reform (FAIR) have promoted exclusionary messages in both national and international forums. For these groups, Asian immigration is a time bomb in terms of its negative effects on the U.S. economy and individual American workers. Moreover, this hostility is also rooted in the fear of losing an already vaguely defined American identity. In 1992, Republican presidential candidate Pat Buchanan made immigration policy a major plank in his bid for the nomination. According to Buchanan, "[One] reason that we are beset with conflict is that since 1965 a flood tide of immigration has rolled in from the Third World, legal and illegal, as our institutions of assimilation—public schools, popular culture, churches—disintegrated."[78] For their part, Asian Americans argue that immigrants are a productive sector of American society, one that puts in more than it takes out.

Facing this backlash, some Asian Americans are redoubling their efforts to become mainstream players in American society. As such, many Asian Americans want to be in the center of American society rather than on the margins as "hyphenated-Americans." They also want to bolster their clout in the political arena by helping to shape American policy.

Many Asian Americans point to the contributions to American society that can result from the input of Oriental cultural values. For example, Asian culture often includes a sense of frugality that leads to environmental consciousness, more consideration for the feelings of others, and a sense of balance between group and individual welfare. According to sociologist Tu Weiming, the less individualistic nature of Asians, their lower sense of self-interest, their less adversarial nature, and their less legalistic approach to society may have important applications for the United States.[79] In the end, the cross-fertilization of cultures is an important factor that has made America a strong and resilient society.

LEGAL ATTEMPTS TO REMEDY THE EFFECTS OF RACISM

A concerted attempt to eliminate racism is a relatively recent phenomenon. Although the Fourteenth Amendment of the Constitution guaranteed all citizens equal protection under the law, it was also used to perpetuate discrimination by forming the grounds for "separate but equal" treatment. In fact, complete segregation was condoned in the South until the middle of the twentieth century, and separate but (supposedly) equal public facilities characterized much of the social and economic activity of America. This extensive system of segregation included public transportation, schools, private economic activities, and even public drinking fountains. It was not until the mid-1950s that the U.S. Supreme Court overturned the *Plessy v. Ferguson* (1896) decision that had justified the separate but equal doctrine.

In 1954 the Supreme Court, in its landmark

decision on *Brown v. Board of Education of Topeka, Kansas,* ruled that "separate but equal" facilities in education were inherently unequal. The court ruled that separating the races was a way of denoting the inferiority of the African-American race. In addition, the court stated that segregation retarded the educational and mental development of African-American children. Although the Supreme Court ruled against officially sanctioned segregation in public schools, de facto segregation was not addressed until the *Swann v. Charlotte-Mecklenburg Board of Education* ruling of 1971. This ruling approved court-ordered busing to achieve racial integration of school districts that had a history of discrimination. In 1974 the Supreme Court flip-flopped by ruling in *Milliken v. Brady* that mandatory school busing across city-suburban boundaries to achieve integration was not required unless the segregation had resulted from an official action. In effect, this ruling allowed the continuation of de facto segregated schools in the white suburbs surrounding heavily black-populated inner cities. School busing designed to achieve integration continues to be a controversial issue.

The legal gains made by African Americans were won only through considerable, often bitter struggle. Up to the mid-1960s, Southern blacks enjoyed few rights, with total segregation enforced in almost all spheres of social, economic, political, and public activity. (Segregation in the North occurred through de facto or unofficial, rather than de jure, or legal, means, although the net effect was in many ways the same.) In 1955, Rosa Parks, too tired to stand in the "colored" section in the back of a bus in Montgomery, Alabama, sparked a nonviolent bus boycott led by Martin Luther King, Jr. Still another protest was begun when African-American students in North Carolina were refused service at an all-white lunch counter. The civil rights movement grew and resulted in widespread demonstrations (in Selma, Alabama, one march drew over 100,000 people), picket lines, sit-ins, and other forms of political protest.

Gaining international publicity, the protests attracted Northern religious leaders, students, and liberals—some of whom would lose their lives. By the time that Reverend Martin Luther King, Jr., was assassinated in 1968, many of the demands of the civil rights movement had been incorporated in the Civil Rights Act of 1964.

The Civil Rights Act of 1964 was the single most important reform act for racial equality since *Brown v. Board of Education*. In summary form, the act states that:

1. Voter registration is a legal right and must not be tampered with.
2. It is unlawful to discriminate or segregate persons on the grounds of race, color, religion, or national origin in any public accommodation, including hotels, motels, theaters, and other public places that offer to serve the public.
3. The attorney general shall undertake civil action on the part of any person who is denied access to a public accommodation. If the owner continues to discriminate, a court fine and imprisonment will result.
4. The attorney general is mandated to represent anyone who undertakes the desegregation of a public school.
5. Each federal department shall take action to end discrimination in all programs or activities receiving federal assistance.
6. It shall be unlawful for any employer or labor union with 25 or more persons to discriminate against an individual in any fashion because of their race, color, religion, national origin, or sex. An Equal Opportunity Commission shall be established to enforce this provision.

In 1968 an amendment to this act prohibited discrimination in housing. Paradoxically, Congress exempted itself from complying with the act until 1988.

The 1964 Civil Rights Act did not live up to its implicit promise. The balance of racial power did not shift, and, for the most part, African-Americans continued to be economically and politically disenfranchised. It soon became clear that other remedial methods were required, one of those being affirmative action, a set of policies designed to achieve equality in admissions and employment opportunities for minorities. Affirmative action tactics represent an aggressive step beyond the largely reactive stance taken by simple nondiscrimination policies. The intent of affirmative action is to right a historical wrong by aggressively recruiting minorities and other disenfranchised groups. In addition, the overall goal of affirmative action is to admit, hire, and promote women and minorities in direct proportion to their representation in the population. As such, rigorous affirmative action policies give preferential treatment to minority and female applicants and may include a quota system.

Critics of affirmative action charge that it violates the equal protection under the laws guaranteed in the Fourteenth Amendment and that it sets up a process of reverse discrimination. Moreover, these critics argue that rights inhere in individuals, not in groups. On three separate occasions, the U.S. Supreme Court upheld the opinions of affirmative action critics. In the Marco DeFunis, Jr., case, the Supreme Court ruled that Washington University Law School must admit DeFunis, who claimed that he was denied admission even though his grades and test scores were higher than those of African Americans who were accepted. In another case, the Supreme Court ruled that Alan Bakke was unfairly denied admission to the University of California-Davis Medical School. Bakke maintained that his qualifications were stronger than those of many of the minority candidates who were admitted. In 1984 the U.S. Supreme Court, in *Memphis Firefighters v. Stotts,* ruled that an employer may use bona fide seniority rules in laying off employees, even when those rules adversely affect the percentage of minority employees. The Court ruled that employers are permitted to use seniority rules governing layoffs when individual members of minority groups are not directly discriminated against. This ruling was a blow to affirmative action because it perpetuated the minority dilemma: Minorities are the last to be hired and the first to be fired.

At best, affirmative action policies were only passively enforced by the Justice Department under the Reagan and Bush administrations. The resistance of these administrations to enforcing affirmative action guidelines, and their relaxation of former federal initiatives, was based on the ideological assumption that these policies benefited minorities who were not victims of discrimination and disadvantaged whites who were innocent of any wrongdoing. Despite its power, the Justice Department had only limited success in promoting its argument and, in general, affirmative action initiatives have withstood attacks by critics.

Attacks on affirmative action have also come from liberal quarters. For example, William Julius Wilson, a progressive African-American sociologist, criticizes the ability of affirmative action strategies to help the most disadvantaged members of society:

Programs based solely on. . . [race-specific solutions] . . . are inadequate . . . to deal with the complex problems of race in America. . . . This is because the most disadvantaged members of racial minority groups, who suffer the cumulative effects of both race and class subjugation . . . are disproportionately represented amongst the segment of the general population that has been denied the resources to compete effectively in a free and open market.

On the other hand, the competitive resources developed by the *advantaged minority members* [original emphasis]—resources that flow directly from the family stability, schooling, income and peer groups that their parents have been able to provide—result in their benefiting disproportionately from policies that promote the rights of minority individuals by removing artificial barriers to valued positions. . . . .

Thus, if policies of preferential treatment . . . are developed in terms of racial group membership rather than real disadvantages suffered by individuals, then these policies will further improve the opportunities of the advantaged without necessarily addressing the problems of the truly disadvantaged such as the ghetto underclass.[80]

Wilson goes on to observe that:

Although present-day discrimination undoubtedly has contributed to the increasing social and economic woes of the ghetto underclass . . . these problems have been due far more to a complex web of other factors that include shifts in the American economy—which has produced extraordinary rates of black joblessness that have exacerbated other social problems in the inner city—the historic flow of immigrants, changes in the urban minority age structure, population changes in the central city, and the class transformation of the inner city.[81]

In short, Wilson maintains that, ''The problems of the truly disadvantaged may require *nonracial* [original emphasis] solutions such as full employment, balanced economic growth, and manpower training and education.''[82]

Despite *Brown v. the Board of Education,* the Civil Rights Act of 1964, and widespread affirmative action programs, the situation for most African Americans and other minorities has improved only marginally, if at all. And, as the preceding data suggest, the economic picture for minorities will remain bleak unless dramatic changes occur.

Discrimination based on race is not the only form discrimination takes in America. Gender discrimination represents a major obstacle to the social, political, and economic well-being of at least half of society.

SEXISM: HOW DO WE KNOW THAT IT EXISTS?

Sexism is a term that denotes the discriminatory and prejudicial treatment of women based solely on their gender. It is a problem that American society has wrestled with since the beginning of the republic. Moreover, sexism is widespread and permeates every aspect of social and political life in America. The fact that women's wages are considerably lower than those of men, and that they more often have to resort to public welfare programs, has led some scholars to coin the term *the feminization of poverty*. Advocates of this idea maintain that the feminization of poverty is evident if one examines the poverty demographics. For example, the number of female-headed households with children under 18 increased by almost 150 percent from 1970 to 1990; the poverty rate for female-headed households climbed to 34.6 percent in 1990.[83] Moreover, the number of poor families headed by women increased 54 percent by 1981, while at the same time the number of poor families headed by men dropped nearly 50 percent. The combined effects of the dual labor market, occupational segregation, and sex discrimination and racism have resulted in the 1988 median income for women being a scant $19,854 a year compared with $31,093 for men.[84] In any case, two out of three poor adults are women, and the economic status of families headed by women is declining.[85] Not surprisingly, the feminization of poverty has led to a high dependence of women on the welfare system. This pattern of dependency is illustrated by the huge increase in the welfare rolls from 1960 (3 million) to 1992 (13.5 million).[86]

The causes of this feminization of poverty are complex. When women are deserted or divorced, many have to find jobs immediately or go on welfare. Those who choose welfare are held in poverty by the low benefits, and those women who opt to work are kept in poverty by the low wages that tend to characterize service jobs, the most rapidly growing sector in the American labor market. These low-paying service jobs, such as servers in fast-food restaurants and sales clerks, make the paltry benefits of welfare seem attractive, because at least there are no child-care costs incurred if one stays at home.

When one examines the entrance of women into the marketplace, the door used most often is through the service and retail trades—involving clerical work, cleaning, food preparation or service, personal service work, auxiliary health service work, and so forth. These occupations are characterized by low pay, a low level of union organization, little status, meager work benefits, and limited prospects for job advancement. Many of these same service jobs were previously held by African Americans and other minorities. Thus, much of the increase of women in the work force has been in the secondary labor market, a marginal area of employment that provides few work benefits and little hope for economic betterment. When supporters of the status quo refer to the millions of jobs that were created in the 1980s, much of what they refer to has been in this secondary labor market, the underbelly of the work world. For example, of the 18.8 million jobs created between 1979 and 1989, 14.4 million were in retail trade and services (i.e., business, personal, and health services), the two lowest-paid sectors.[87]

The economics of low-paying service work are gloomy. For example, if a single mother[88] with two children chooses to avoid the stigma of welfare and finds work at the minimum wage, her prospects for economic survival are dismal. The conservative mock budget in Table 5.3 illustrates the dilemma of a single mother who finds full-time employment at $4.50 an hour (15 cents above the minimum wage).

Thus, work at minimum or close to minimum wage becomes infeasible, and the economic choices of the unskilled female head of a household are limited. Moreover, the National Commission on Children estimates that the typical family spends about $6,000 annually on expenses associated with raising a child.[89] This

TABLE 5.3. Monthly Budget for a Working Mother with One Child in School and One Infant in Day Care

Gross Monthly Income for Full-Time Work @ $4.50 per hour: $720.00

Expenses	
Day Care for 1 child	$427.00[1]
Rent	$450.00[2]
Health Care	$ 93.75[3]
Utilities	$ 60.00
Food	$235.00[4]
Clothing	$ 62.00
Transportation	$200.00[3]
Entertainment	$ 50.00
Sundry Items (e.g., soap, cleaners, repairs, sheets, blankets, etc.)	$100.00[3]
Total Approximate Cost	$1,677.75
Monthly Deficit between Income and Budget	− $957.75

[1] Child care costs are calculated according to 1990 rates and are based on the average of child care in four cities—Oakland, CA; Boulder, CO; Dallas, TX; and Orlando, FL. See Children's Defense Fund, *The State of America's Children* (Washington, D.C.: Children's Defense Fund, 1991), p. 43.

[2] Rent was calculated on the basis of the average of HUD-determined fair market rents in the lowest-cost metropolitan areas in a state. The average rent of all these states totaled $450.00 for 1989. See U.S. House of Representatives, Committee on Ways and Means, *Overview of Entitlement Programs, 1992 Green Book* (Washington, D.C.: U.S. Government Printing Office, 1992).

[3] This amount was based on figures provided in John E. Schwartz and Thomas J. Volgy, "A Cruel Hoax Upon the Poor," *The San Diego Union Tribune*, November 9, 1992, p. 5.

[4] The amount for food is based on the maximum Food Stamp allocation that this mother would receive in 1991 if she had no countable income.

would mean that, excluding a mother's personal expenses, having two children would require a minimum income of $12,000 per year. According to the National Commission on Children, "If a single mother with two children moved from welfare to a full-time, minimum wage job in 1991, her net income would increase by only about $50 per week."[90] Neither welfare nor low-income work provides single female-headed households with viable economic choices.

Single-mother families in the United States fare worse than do their counterparts in many European industrial nations. In a study of the relative economic well-being of single-mother families in eight nations, Yin-Ling Wong, Irwin Garfinkel, and Sara McLanahan found that compared with two-parent families, single mothers in the United States are in much worse financial shape. Of the eight countries surveyed, the United States ranked last on the list, surpassed by Canada, Australia, France, Germany, Norway, Sweden, and the United Kingdom.[91]

In some measure, welfare dependency is influenced by the refusal of fathers to pay child support. In 1989, single mothers received a total of $11 billion in child support. If all eligible women had child support awards tied to state guidelines, they would have been entitled to at least $30 billion. Thus, about $20 billion or more in child support goes unpaid each year.[92] Refusal to pay child support characterizes both poor and nonpoor fathers. One study found that 58 percent of nonpoor unwed fathers aged 19 to 56 reported paying child support, the average annual payment amounting to $2,492. Forty-two percent of these fathers, although not poor, reported paying no child support.[93]

These statistics are even starker when broken down. In 1989, almost 60 percent of children in single-parent families received no support from their absent parent. Of those custodial mothers eligible for child support, only 58 percent had court-ordered awards entitling them to such support in 1989. Among mothers who had court-ordered child support, only one in four received the full amount due from the absent father. The average amount paid in 1989 was $57 per week, or only $2,964 per year. Moreover, among mothers who had a child support court order in 1989, one in four received nothing. And fewer than 10 percent of fathers owing child support contributed $5,000 or more in 1989, even though about 90 percent of married fathers contributed earnings of at least $5,000 to total family income. In the end, single mothers who fail to receive child support are twice as likely to be poor as families who receive such support.[94]

The Family Support Act of 1988 significantly strengthened child support enforcement guidelines. First, the law contained major provisions for establishing paternity. This provision was important because paternity is currently established for fewer than half the children born to never-married parents in child support cases.[95] Second, the law required states to set uniform guidelines for child support awards and to withhold the wages of an absent parent for payment of child support on behalf of AFDC families who seek assistance from a state enforcement agency. Beginning in 1994, the act will require immediate wage withholding for payment of child support on behalf of *all* families. Some policy analysts, including Irwin Garfinkel and Harvard's David Ellwood, have suggested the creation of a Child Support Assurance program, consisting of three components: (1) setting child support as a percentage of an absent parent's income; (2) automatically deducting child support payments from income as is done with Social Security taxes; and (3) ensuring a minimum benefit to children if the absent parent defaults on payments.[96] These policy analysts argue that the poverty rate could be reduced by 8 to 10 percent, with a corresponding 12 to 20 percent reduction in welfare dependency.[97] As many as 16 million children living in single-parent families could benefit from this system.[98]

Inequities in public transfer programs also exacerbate the economic problems of low-income women. For example, Social Security and public assistance are often the only viable options for women, and about eight out of ten poor female-headed families rely on public cash transfers through public welfare programs.[99] Although median transfers to women are lower, they constitute a higher share of their total income, about one-third for female-headed households as compared with one-tenth for male-headed households. Moreover, Social Security is the only source of income for 60 percent of elderly women, and, in 1990, some 15 percent

of these women were in poverty compared with 8 percent of elderly men. Like other public transfer programs, Social Security is riddled with pitfalls. In large part, many problems with Social Security are based on the assumptions that all families are nuclear in character and that families with young children need more per capita income than aged couples or single individuals.

Some women have argued that Social Security has mistreated them and cite a number of reasons:

1. Because women's wages are lower than men's, their retirement benefits also tend to be lower.
2. Married female workers fare better on Social Security than those who are single. Individuals who have never worked can benefit from Social Security payments made by a spouse.
3. Couples in which one worker earned most of the wages may fare better than couples in which the husband and wife earned equal wages.
4. Homemakers are not covered on their own unless they held a job in the past. Widows do not qualify for benefits unless they are 60 years old or have a minor in the house.
5. Regardless of how long they were married, divorced women are entitled to only one-half of their ex-husband's benefits. If this partial payment is the only income of a divorced woman, it is usually inadequate. Furthermore, divorced women must have been married to the beneficiary of Social Security for at least 10 years to qualify for his benefits.
6. Because women are less likely to spend as much time in the work force as men—owing to child care responsibilities—their benefits are usually lower.[100]

As result of the Social Security Amendments of 1983, several sex-based qualifications were eliminated: Divorced persons were able to qualify for benefits at age 62 (even if the ex-spouse has not yet claimed benefits), and divorced husbands could claim benefits based on the earnings records of their ex-wives.[101] While these changes have been important, they have led to only a minor improvement in the system. Other reforms under discussion include an earnings-sharing option that would equally divide a couple's income between husband and wife (thereby eliminating the category of a primary wage earner and a dependent spouse) and a double-decker option in which everyone would be eligible for a basic benefit regardless of whether he or she contributed to the system (individuals who contributed to the paid labor force would receive a higher benefit).[102] These options are in the discussion phase, but with a $4.2 trillion federal budget deficit in 1992, their adoption seems unlikely in the near future.

Women and Work

Myths abound in attempts to explain why women consistently earn less than men. These myths include:[103]

Myth 1. A working mother's wages are not necessary to her family's survival, and her job is a secondary activity that usually ceases with marriage or childbirth.

Fact. Most families require two paychecks to maintain the same standard of living as their parents. Twenty percent of working mothers are heads of households; two out of three working mothers report that they cannot decrease their working hours because of economic need. In 1984, one-third of women who worked had a spouse who earned less than $15,000 per year.[104] Moreover, 18 percent of all working women bring home larger paychecks than their husbands do. Lastly, 66 percent of African-American women who work provide over half of the median family income of $37,787.

Myth 2. A working mother is unreliable because her family is her basic concern.

Fact. Although some working mothers choose the "mommy track," others are forced into it by a lack of quality and affordable day care. Moreover, 75 percent of mothers return to work within a year after childbirth. Even without family assistance programs, most working mothers continue to maintain employment.

Myth 3. Large numbers of working women leave the work force to return home to raise their children.

Fact. Statistics show that an opposite trend is occurring. In 1978, mothers of infants had a labor force participation rate of 35.7 percent; by 1988 it had risen to 50.8 percent. The slight drop in female participation in the work force in early 1991 was due mostly to the recession, and the choice of mothers to become full-time homemakers is the exception, not the rule.

Myth 4. The cost of providing benefits to assist working mothers with families is prohibitive. Small businesses cannot afford to provide benefits and services such as child care, maternity leave, and flextime. Even large businesses complain that such costs decrease their international competitiveness.

Fact. Family assistance programs raise productivity, increase worker loyalty, lower turnover, and curb absenteeism costs. The majority of employers in states with family leave laws report no change in costs owing to this legislation.[105]

To further dispel myths about working women, it is important to examine the characteristics of the female labor force. In 1990, nearly 40 percent of the 56.6 million workers in the United States were mothers, an increase of 4.4 million since 1980.[106] Women's labor force participation grew from 37.7 percent in 1960 to 55.3 percent in 1986, a rise that accounted for 60 percent of the total growth in the work force.[107] Almost 67 percent of mothers with children under 18 worked for pay in 1990, compared with 56.6 percent in 1980. When the figures are broken down, almost 50 percent of women with children under age 1 were in the labor force in 1990 (about 9.4 million working mothers of preschool children). Of the total female labor force, nearly 75 percent are married, and 81 percent of divorced women with children (2.6 million) under age 18 currently work.[108] The high labor force participation rates of women also extend to African Americans. Although African-American women are over three times more likely to be single heads of families than white women are, those with children under 18 are also more likely to be in the labor force (68.2 percent) than are their white counterparts (66.7 percent).[109]

There is a strong relationship between poverty and working mothers, especially single working mothers. For example, 43.6 percent of mothers living in poverty are in the work force. In 1989, the median income of a married couple with children ($39,969) was more than triple that of a single female-headed household with children ($12,062). Working women are almost twice as likely to earn the minimum wage or less than men are. Sixty-three percent of all workers earning the minimum wage or less are women, and 13 percent of working women earn the minimum wage as compared with 7.6 percent of men.[110]

Great disparities exist with regard to women and work. While women make up 40 percent of the total labor force, they hold 62 percent of the service industry jobs.[111] In 1989 women earned only 70 percent of what men did. Although there has been a decrease in the wage gap between men and women from 1975, when women earned 59 cents for every dollar earned by men, to 1989, when they earned 70 cents, about 25 percent of this reduction has occurred not because women are making more but because men are making less. As a result of declining employment in high-wage industries since 1973, full-time, year-round male earnings have dropped by 9.2 percent.[112]

Some of the income disparity between men and women can be traced to female occupational clusterings. Roughly half of all working women are employed in occupations where 80 percent of the other workers are women.[113] Moreover, in 1988 only 9 percent of women worked in occupations classified as nontraditional (i.e., where 75 percent of the employees are men). From 1983 to 1988 the greatest increase in women entering nontraditional jobs has taken place in the professional sphere. For example, from 1983 to 1988 the number of female attorneys increased from 15.3 to 19.4 percent; of female physicians, from 15.8 to 20 percent; of photographers, from 20.7 to 30.7 percent; and of managers in marketing and advertising, from 21.8 to 32 percent.[114] Nevertheless, women consistently earn less than men, both within and outside these clusterings. For example, female attorneys earn only 63 percent of what their male counterparts earn; female sales representatives earn between 62 and 72 cents of every dollar earned by a male in the same position; and female social workers earn only 73 cents for each dollar earned by a male social worker.[115] In short, when women work in the same occupations as men they usually earn less pay.

Although women are attending college at rates higher than men (by 1979 women outnumbered men, but not as full-time students), the average female college graduate fares worse. In 1980 the average female college graduate earned only 57.6 percent ($16,417) of a male college graduate's salary ($28,306). In fact, the average female college graduate earned only slightly more than a male with an eighth-grade education ($15,709). This discrepancy exists even for those with a graduate education. In 1980 women with five-plus years of college earned only 59 percent ($19,520) of the salary of males ($33,085) with a similar education. Moreover, women with five-plus years of college earn less than a male high school graduate.[116]

Many women face extraordinary challenges in finding and securing adequate employment for fair wages. Some of the obstacles faced by working women include the difficulty of finding good and affordable day care, the existence of limited family leave policies, inflexible working conditions, inadequate health insurance coverage, and problems of sexual harassment.

Day Care: A Barrier to Female Employment

A major barrier to female employment involves the problem of day care and of subsidized child-care leaves. For many working families child care has become a necessity. A 1982 Census Bureau survey found that 45 percent of single mothers would seek employment if affordable, quality child care were available. But infant and toddler care costs more than care for preschoolers does, and care provided in a center is more expensive than family day care. There are serious shortages of quality child care, and rates vary widely around the country. For example, the annual costs of an infant in day care ranges from around $4,000 a year in Dallas, Texas, to $11,000 a year in Boston, Massachusetts.[117] A single mother in Boston earning a minimum wage would have to spend 150 percent of her salary just to afford day care for one child!

Day care historically has been a service geared toward the working and middle classes. The first day-care center was begun in 1854 with the establishment of the Nursery for Children of Poor Women. The goal of this nursery was to prevent child neglect in the families of working mothers. An alternative model was a nursery school designed to address middle-class concerns. A group of faculty wives at the University of Chicago organized the first cooperative nursery in 1915, with the express purpose of providing middle-class women with a respite from child care.[118]

Federally funded day care grew rapidly because of the need for women to fill the industrial jobs vacated by men during World War II. However, when the men returned from the war, women were vigorously encouraged to leave their jobs and return to homemaking. Despite this discouragement, women continued to enter the work force in growing numbers from 1940 to 1971. In 1971 Congress passed the Comprehensive Child Care Act, later vetoed by Richard Nixon.

Title XX is the largest federal program for child-care services. As a result of the budget cuts enacted in the first three years of the Reagan administration, however, its funds were cut by 21 percent. Thirty-two states provided less care to poor children in 1983 than they had in 1981,[119] and those hurt most by these cutbacks were poor female-headed families. In 1990 the U.S. Congress passed legislation that was an important step in increasing the supply of child care and in expanding early childhood education. Through the Child Care and Development Block Grant and amendments to Title IV-A of the Social Security Act, Congress provided new funds to help families with child-care costs and to help states improve the quality and supply of child-care services.[120]

The lack of subsidized child-care leaves poses a major problem for American working women. Sheila Kammerman reported on a study of working mothers in five industrialized countries—Sweden, East and West Germany, Hungary, and France.[121] In all these countries, except for West Germany, a higher proportion of women were employed than in the United States. All nations, except the United States, provided a tax-free family allowance that ranged from $300 to $600 yearly. Guaranteed maternity leave (in Sweden the leave also pertained to fathers) ranged from fourteen weeks in West Germany to eight months in Sweden. Guaranteed maternity leave also included full pay in most places. No national guaranteed maternity leave exists at present in the United States.

The child-care system in the United States is two-tiered: Those with adequate incomes can afford to purchase first-rate child care or, if they desire, they can stay at home; those with low wages are at the mercy of the ebb and flow of political support for publicly supported day care.[122]

Other Obstacles to Women and Work

Apart from problems involving low wages and difficulties in securing child care, many working mothers also require a flexible family leave program. Although 30 states had some form of parental or medical leave law in the past, no such national statute existed until 1993. In 1992, President George Bush vetoed the Family and Medical Leave Act (FMLA) after it had passed the House and Senate for a second time. With the election of President Bill Clinton, the FMLA was rushed through Congress and was signed into law on February 5, 1993. The FMLA is designed to allow workers to receive unpaid leave for up to 12 weeks in the event of childbirth, adoption, or the serious illness of an immediate family member. Should a worker use the leave, he or she is guaranteed the same or a comparable job upon returning to work and continued health benefits. The FMLA applies to all firms with 50 or more employees. However, those who work in firms with under 50 employees are not protected by federal family leave legislation.

Another issue affecting working women is that of health insurance. Women working in traditionally female occupations (the largest share of working women) have the highest uninsured rate. More than 15 million women of childbearing age in the United States have no public or private medical coverage for maternity care, even though the average cost of having a baby is over $4,300. Half of all women earning $5.00 per hour or less are without health care, and divorced and separated women are twice as likely to be uninsured as married women. Of the 4 million births each year in the United States, 500,000 are not covered by any health care plan. About 5 million American women of reproductive age have private insurance policies that don't cover maternity care. Moreover, health insurance often does not cover important services for women's health, including family planning services, long-term care, reproductive care and elective abortions, and maternity care and childbirth.[123] If women are to participate even

more fully in the labor force, health care insurance obstacles must be overcome.

Another issue affecting women in the workplace is sexual harassment, an issue brought to the fore by Anita Hill in the 1990 Senate confirmation hearings of Supreme Court Justice Clarence Thomas. Sexual harassment is defined as unwelcome behaviors including jokes, teasing, remarks, questions, and deliberate touching; letters, telephone calls, or materials of a sexual nature; pressure for sexual favors; and sexual assault. Although sexual harassment is against the law (Title VII of the 1964 Civil Rights Act has been interpreted as prohibiting sexual harassment), it remains all too common in the workplace. Moreover, women in nontraditional jobs are at greater risk of sexual harassment.[124]

Finally, a major obstacle for many working women is the inflexibility of work. Because women often take on the major responsibility for child care, elder care, and home management, they often forego educational or training opportunities. In order for women workers to better balance family and work responsibilities, options such as flexible hours, job sharing, and part-time work with benefits need to be expanded.

Fighting Back: The Equal Rights Amendment and Comparable Worth

In 1920 the Nineteenth Amendment to the Constitution gave women the right to vote. That, however, did not seem to lessen their economic and social plight, and shortly after winning the vote the Women's Party proposed the first Equal Rights Amendment (ERA). Although at first glance it seemed a good idea, progressive social workers such as Jane Addams, Florence Kelley, and Julia Lathrop, among others, saw the ERA as endangering the hard-fought protection won for women workers. For example, reformers had successfully fought for a maximum weight limit on lifting for women workers, the establishment of maximum workday laws in many states, and mandatory work breaks.

These social workers saw the ERA as having the potential to eradicate protective legislation for women workers. Moreover, these reformers saw the ERA as mainly benefiting middle-class professional women at the expense of poor, working-class women. Many female trade unionists continued to oppose the ERA well into the 1970s.

In 1972, Congress passed the ERA and set a 1979 date for state ratification. When the ERA had not been ratified by 1978, Congress extended the deadline to June 30, 1982. Despite the endorsement of 450 organizations representing 50 million members, opponents of the ERA were able to defeat the amendment in 1982, just three states short of the 38 required for ratification.

Cutting through the controversy surrounding the ERA, the act reads as follows: "Equality of rights under the law shall not be denied or abridged by the United States or any other State on account of sex. . . . The Congress shall have the power to enforce, by appropriate legislation, the provisions of this article. . . . This amendment shall take effect two years after the date of ratification."[125]

Contrary to the myths surrounding it, the ERA would not have nullified all laws distinguishing on the basis of sex; instead, it would have required that men and women be treated equally. Most alimony, child support, and custody laws would not have been invalidated, although laws giving preference to one sex would have been struck down. On the other hand, special restrictions on the property rights of married women would have been invalidated; married women would have been free to manage their own separate finances and property. Again, contrary to popular myth, the ERA would have affected public employment only; private employment practices would not have been changed. In the areas of military service and jury duty, women would have been subject to participation under the same conditions as men. Like men, women would have been eligible for the draft.[126]

Surrounded by fear and misinformation—much of it purposeful—the ERA became a symbolic struggle. Opponents feared what *might* happen if the ERA were passed. These fears—often couched in hyperbolic language—suggested that the passage of the ERA would result in men and women being forced to share the same bathrooms, in the drafting of women to serve on the front line, and in granting women the legal right to refuse to cook for their husbands. If not for the seriousness of the ERA, the dialogue and the subsequent intellectual gyrations could have made a lively slapstick comedy. More important, the struggle around the ERA was a conflict about the future of gender relations in America.

Another front on which sexism has been fought is the issue of comparable worth—the idea that workers should be paid equally when they do *different* types of work requiring the same level of skill, education, knowledge, training, responsibility, and effort. The desire to rectify incomes through comparable worth is based on the belief that the dual labor market has created a situation in which "women's work" (i.e, secretarial, teaching, social work, nursing, child care) is automatically less highly valued than traditionally male occupations.

An illustration of the debate around comparable worth is provided in Table 5.4, which compares the pay for jobs typically occupied by women with the pay for those usually held by men. Although a controversial notion, 20 states have already passed laws making comparable worth a requirement or goal of state employment. While in theory a good idea, comparable worth brings up a difficult question: What criteria do we use to determine that different jobs are comparable? Moreover, comparable worth has been rejected by some people on the grounds that the inherent economic cost is infeasible.

Legal protection for women workers is not a recent phenomenon. As early as the turn of the century, protective legislation restricted the amount of weight a woman was required to lift,

TABLE 5.4. Comparable Worth and Average Annual
Income, 1988

	1988 Average Annual Income
Secretary	$14,976
Mechanic/Repairer	$18,816
Child Care Worker	$ 8,592
Motor Vehicle Operator	$13,488
Textile Sewing Machine Operator	$ 9,168
Mail Carrier	$21,120
Data Entry Keyer	$14,304
Construction Worker	$16,080

SOURCE: This data is drawn from the National Commission on Working Women of Wider Opportunities for Women, "Women and Nontraditional Work," Washington, D.C., Wider Opportunities for Women, n.d., n.p.

mandated rest and lunch periods, prohibited hours of work beyond a specified number, regulated night work, and prohibited employment in particular occupations. In 1963, Congress passed the Equal Pay Act, which required employers to compensate male and female workers equally for performing the same job under the same conditions (not all jobs were covered by the bill). Another protective measure was Title VII of the Civil Rights Act of 1964, which prohibited sex discrimination in employment practices and provided the right of redress in the courts. In 1972, Presidential Executive Order 11375 mandated that employers practicing sexual discrimination be prohibited from receiving federal contracts. Title IX of the Educational Amendments of 1972 prohibited discrimination in educational institutions receiving federal funds. Finally, the Equal Credit Act of 1975 prohibited discrimination by lending institutions on the basis of sex or marital status.

Abortion and Women's Rights

Feminists often point to the abortion debate as another arena in which sexism is expressed. Specifically, pro-choice advocates argue that where abortion is concerned male legislators and judges have promulgated laws and regulations to control the behavior of women, in this case by denying them their reproductive freedom. They argue that the choice of an abortion is a personal matter involving only a woman and her conscience. Anti-abortion forces claim that because life begins at conception abortion is murder. Moreover, they point to the 1.5 million abortions performed each year (half of them performed on women aged 15 to 19) while at the same time the search for children available for adoption has become an almost insurmountable task. This argument becomes even more focused when abortion statistics are examined: in 1987, 59 percent of those having abortions were younger than 25; 65 percent of them were white; 58 percent had experienced no previous abortion; and 82 percent were unmarried.[127]

In 1973, Sarah Weddington, a young attorney from Austin, Texas, argued *Roe v. Wade* before the Supreme Court. Though her client had long since relinquished her child for adoption, Weddington argued that a state could not unduly burden a woman's right to choose an abortion by making regulations that prohibited her from carrying out that decision. The Court ruled in favor of Weddington, and abortion was legalized in the United States, thereby nullifying all state laws that made abortion illegal during the first trimester of pregnancy. (Before 1970, four states—New York, Alaska, Hawaii, and Washington—had already made abortion legal contingent upon the agreement of a physician.) Within a decade after *Roe v. Wade* was successfully argued, almost 500 bills were introduced in Congress, most of which sought to restrict abortions by promoting a constitutional amendment outlawing abortion, by transferring the power to regulate abortion decisions to the states, or by limiting federal funding of abortions.[128]

The abortion issue has been marked by Byzantine maneuvers and complex twists and turns. In 1977 the Hyde Amendment prohibited the federal government from paying for abortions except to preserve the mother's life. The 1980 Supreme Court decision in *Harris v. McRae* upheld the constitutionality of the Hyde Amendment. In 1977, the federal government lifted its ban on providing abortions for promptly reported cases of rape and incest and in cases where severe and long-lasting harm would be caused to a woman by childbirth. In 1981, the government again reversed its position, this time curbing federal funding of abortions except to save the life of the mother.[129] By 1990, federal funds paid for only *165* abortions, a dramatic drop from the almost 300,000 federally funded abortions in 1977.[130]

The major strategy of the anti-abortion movement has been to whittle away at *Roe v. Wade* by attempting to restrict abortions on the state level. For example, in Akron, Ohio, rules were promulgated that required a minor to receive parental consent for an abortion and that imposed a one-day moratorium on the time between when a woman signs the consent form and when the abortion is actually performed. In 1986, the Supreme Court struck down a Pennsylvania law designed to discourage women from obtaining abortions. Yet in a 1989 landmark decision, the Supreme Court upheld a Missouri law that prohibited public hospitals and public employees from performing an abortion (except to save the life of the mother), required physicians to determine whether a woman who is at least 20 weeks pregnant is carrying a fetus able to survive outside the womb, and declared that life starts at conception.[131] During the 1990–91 term, the Court in *Rust v. Sullivan* ruled that the United States can prohibit federally financed family planning programs from giving out abortion information. On January 22, 1993, President Bill Clinton's second day in office, he signed a bill overturning this "gag rule" and, in another blow to anti-abortion advocates, on the same day overturned the federal ban on using fetal tissue matter gained from abortions in scientific experiments.

Since 1973, the question of abortion has proved to be one of the most divisive issues in public life. Although nearly three out of four voters polled in national surveys believe that abortion should be legal, 56 percent oppose the use of federal money to fund abortions for women who cannot afford them.[132] Nevertheless, this highly charged issue has led to fire-bombings of abortion clinics, large demonstrations on both sides of the issue, and widespread civil protest. With the election of Bill Clinton, an openly pro-choice president, it is possible that the abortion issue will finally recede from the top of the public agenda.

The problems of women have been compounded by the lack of responsive political institutions. In 1985 women comprised only 14.8 percent of state legislators, 9.6 percent of the mayors of cities of 30,000 or more, 2 out of the 100 U.S. senators, and only 23 out of the 435 U.S. representatives.[133] Although by 1992 there were six women senators (including Carol Moseley-Braun, the first African-American woman elected to the U.S. Senate), these numbers were still not representative of the total number of women in the general population. In short, sexual discrimination appears to operate in all areas of social, political, and economic life.

GAYS AND LESBIANS: TWO POPULATIONS AT RISK

Without fear of contradiction, homosexuals can lay claim to being historically scorned. Forced to live in the "closet," gays and lesbians have been compelled to conceal their sexual preferences in order to survive in a hostile world. Often the objects of ridicule, homosexuals have been denied housing, denied employment, harassed on the job, and beaten, assaulted, and even killed because of their sexual preference. In many states homosexuality is still considered a criminal or felony offense, and in some of those states the police systematically raid homosexual bars and randomly arrest the patrons. In 24 states women risk prosecution for being in a lesbian relationship.[134] Twenty-five states have no legislation or ordinances to protect gays and lesbians from discrimination based on their sexual orientation.[135]

Represented in all occupations and socio-economic strata, gays and lesbians make up between one and 10 percent of the general population.[136] Despite their numbers, when gays and lesbians have decided to "come out of the closet" and demand equal rights under the law, the result has been mixed, although generally negative. During the 1970s, Miami gays tried to pass a civil rights amendment that would have prevented discrimination based on sexual preference. The referendum failed in Miami, and similar ones were defeated in St. Paul and other cities. In 1986, Houston voters defeated two gay rights proposals, one calling for an end to discrimination based on sexual preference in city employment practices, the other proposing to stop the city from maintaining sexual orientation data in city employment records.[137] In 1992, Colorado voters unexpectedly banned laws to protect gays and lesbians from discrimination; in Tampa, Florida, and in Portland, Maine, voters overturned city ordinances protecting gays and lesbians.[138]

While there have been decisive defeats in the battle for gay rights, there have also been significant victories. In a landmark vote in 1992, Oregonians rejected Ballot Measure Nine by 55 to 45 percent. This referendum would have branded gays and lesbians as "abnormal and perverse" and would have required schools to teach that homosexuality is wrong. The referendum would also have barred antidiscrimination protection for gays and lesbians.[139] Overall, 21 cities and counties have adopted comprehensive gay/lesbian rights policies[140]; and by 1984, 26 states had implemented decriminalization. Seven states prohibit discrimination in public employment, and some form of protection is provided for gays and lesbians in 51 municipalities and 12 counties nationwide.[141]

For almost 20 years the Supreme Court refused to hear cases concerning gay rights, but in 1985 it decided to hear the case of *Oklahoma City Board of Education v. the National Gay Task Force*. In this case the Supreme Court ruled that public school teachers cannot be forbidden to advocate homosexuality (e.g., by way of public demonstrations), but they can be prohibited from engaging in homosexual acts in public. In a major setback for gay rights, the Supreme Court in 1986 refused to strike down laws in Georgia and Texas that forbid homosexuals from engaging in similar types of activity. In 1988 the Supreme Court ruled that the Central Intelligence Agency could not dismiss a homosexual without a reason justifying the dismissal. On the other hand, the Supreme Court has refused to rule on whether homosexuals have equal protection under the Fourteenth Amendment of the U.S. Constitution, including the right to serve in the military.

The United States armed forces have not tolerated homosexuality in their ranks. In 1940, draft board physicians were ordered to screen out homosexuals on the basis of such characteristics as a man's lisp or a woman's deep voice. However, these instructions were often overlooked when World War II created a desperate need for soldiers. After the war, however, gay and lesbian military personnel were discharged and exclusionary policies were again enforced. A similar situation occurred during the Vietnam War; once the conflict ended, gays and lesbians were again persecuted and their careers terminated.[142] The policy of the U.S. armed forces that excludes gays and lesbians from military service reads as follows: "Homosexuality is incompatible with military service. The presence in the military environment of persons who engage in homosexual conduct or who, by their statements, demonstrate a propensity to engage in homosexual conduct, seriously impairs the accomplishment of the military mission."[143] Individuals who admit to homosexuality at the time of enlistment are rejected; if homosexuality comes to light later on, the individual is separated. Although more liberal policies were put into effect during the 1970s and 1980s, they were directed at the type of separation, not at the morality of the separation itself.[144]

One of the principal justifications for excluding gays and lesbians from military service has been their supposed vulnerability to blackmail by enemy agents threatening to expose their sexuality. The Defense Department has conducted at least three separate studies to justify this belief. None of these studies supported the exclusionary policy.[145] In fact, the Personnel Security Research and Education Center of the Defense Department conducted an examination of the homosexual exclusion policy and found no evidence that gays and lesbians disrupt any branch of the military; instead, it praised their dedication and superior performance.[146]

The policy of excluding homosexuals from the military has far-reaching consequences. First, it adversely affects the career prospects of multitudes of gays and lesbians. Second, people discharged from military service without an honorable discharge may find it difficult to secure employment, and may not be eligible to obtain many benefits associated with military service. Even an honorable discharge given on the grounds of homosexual conduct will carry with it grave and important consequences for the future of an ex-serviceman or ex-servicewoman. In any case, the discriminatory treatment of gays and lesbians in the military was continued under both the Reagan and Bush administrations.

One of the campaign promises of Bill Clinton was to end discrimination against homosexuals in the military. As one of his first official acts, President Clinton signed an order that prohibited military recruiters from inquiring about the sexual orientation of potential recruits. Shortly afterward, Clinton proposed wide-ranging reforms that would ensure equal rights for gays and lesbians serving in the military. Proponents of such a plan argued that discrimination against homosexuals in the military was no different from the discrimination practiced against African-American soldiers in World Wars I and II. For these activists, the discrimination against homsexuals in the military was a civil rights issue. On the other side,

critics argued that homosexuality was a life-style choice rather than a factor of birth, such as skin color. Facing criticism from the Joint Chiefs of Staff and many influential members of Congress, Clinton retreated from his earlier position and instead supported a "don't ask, don't tell" policy which prohibited the military from asking questions as long as a homosexual behaved discreetly.

Despite the decision of the American Psychiatric Association in 1973 to remove homosexuality from its official list of mental disorders, homophobia—the irrational fear of homosexuality—is a social phenomenon that has resulted in attempts to limit the civil rights and legal protection of gays and lesbians. Justifications for this attitude have been found in traditional religious dogma that treats homosexuality as a sin against God, and in psychological explanations that view homosexuality as a disease, as a symptom of an arrested developmental process or a fear of intimacy. Nevertheless, in the last 15 years the self-perception of gays and lesbians has undergone a dramatic change. Gays and lesbians have begun to identify themselves as members of an oppressed minority, similar in many ways to other oppressed minority groups. As they have become more visible, gays and lesbians have organized support groups, religious groups (Dignity [Roman Catholics], Integrity [Episcopalians], Mishpachat Am [Jews], and Lutherans Concerned [Lutherans]), social service organizations, subchapters of professional associations, and political action groups. The political power of gays and lesbians has grown to the point that in 1984 they succeeded in inserting a gay civil rights plank in the platform of the Democratic party.

The AIDS crisis gave rise to the increased expression of omnipresent homophobic attitudes. The early days of the epidemic saw suggestions for quarantining AIDS victims, renewed attempts at punishing homosexual behavior, increased job discrimination, and a generally hostile climate for both gays and lesbians. At the federal level, right-wing Senator

Jesse Helms (R-N.C.) successfully introduced a bill that prevented the Centers for Disease Control from using AIDS education funds in ways that could foster homosexuality. Although AIDS is still predominantly a disease affecting selected population groups—gay and bisexual men (58 percent) and intravenous drug users (23 percent)—the movement of AIDS into the heterosexual community (now 6 percent of victims) has fueled, among some people, a certain sympathy toward the gay population. But any positive change has come only after the reporting of more than 230,000 AIDS cases in the United States, resulting in over 152,000 deaths through June 1992.[147] Robert Walker describes the early days of the AIDS epidemic:

> This was the time, the early 1980s, when the AIDS epidemic and its costs might have been contained, but effectively raising the alarm entailed serious political risks in all the affected communities—the political, the religious, and the homosexual. Political leaders took their cue from President Reagan's deafening silence, and most national, state, and local public and private institutions dithered through the critical years.[148]

The AIDS crisis has had a devastating effect on the lives of gay men. There are few gays in larger cities who have not lost either a lover or many friends to the disease. This suffering, combined with AIDS education, has led to a galvanizing of the gay community that is unprecedented. Comprehensive medical and support services have been developed in several of the larger cities, and many members of the gay community are exercising increased caution in the choice of sexual partners and in the sexual act itself. As a result of these measures, there has been a decrease in the numbers of AIDS cases in some cities. Despite these advances, AIDS remains one of the most significant health problems facing both gay and heterosexual communities.

Gays and lesbians face discrimination in all social and economic areas. This discrimination is manifest in the absence of gay and lesbian rights in the areas of employment, public accommodations, housing, immigration and naturalization, insurance, custody and adoption, and zoning regulations (neighborhood covenants) that bar access to singles or nonrelated couples.[149] Moreover, social service agencies routinely refuse to allow foster care in gay or lesbian homes; insurance companies deny workers the right to cover same-sex spouses or lovers under health insurance; gays and lesbians are often refused the right to name a lover as next of kin in medical emergencies; and there are no laws to prohibit insurance companies from asking questions that could determine sexual preference (and thereby lead them to deny coverage to a gay or lesbian).

AGEISM

Ageism, or discrimination against older persons, is a significant problem in a consumer-oriented society that idolizes youth. Like other minority groups, the aged have a series of social and economic obstacles to overcome. For example, the aged in America are seldom revered or respected for their wisdom and experience. They do not occupy an elevated social position protected by tradition. Instead, once they have lost their earning potential, the aged are often perceived as a financial albatross around the neck of an economically productive society. A youth-oriented society that values consumption and economic productivity above all else, and in which people's worth is determined by their economic contribution, tends to isolate its older members and look upon them as an economic drain. Socially isolated in retirement communities, low-income housing, or other old-age ghettos, the aged become invisible.

Apart from social isolation, many of the elderly are also faced with absolute or near poverty. About 3.7 million elderly people fell below the poverty line in 1990, which translated into a poverty rate of 12.2 percent. Another 2.1 million were classified as "near poor," with incomes up to 125 percent of the poverty line. The aged groups hardest hit by poverty, not surprisingly, are minority group members. While 10 percent of elderly whites were poor in 1990, 34 percent of aged African Americans and 22 percent of elderly Hispanic Americans were below the poverty line. Older women also had twice the poverty rate of elderly men—15 and 8 percent, respectively. Moreover, an astounding 71 percent of elderly African-American women who lived alone in 1990 were poor. And, although inflation continued, the income of the elderly remained relatively stagnant in 1990 ($14,183 for males and $8,044 for females). This problem was exacerbated after 1991, when interest rates paid on certificates of deposit and savings accounts dropped to under 4 percent per annum, thereby curtailing the substantial investment income that many elderly had received in the early and mid-1980s.[150]

Owing to medical advances that enable older people to live longer, the population of elderly persons is growing dramatically. In 1900 the number of elderly (above age 65) in the United States stood at 3.1 million; by 1990 this figure had risen to 31.2 million. By 2030 it is expected to rise to 65.6 million, two and one-half times the number of elderly in 1980. But, as the numbers of elderly increase, their demands on society for housing, health, and recreational services also become more pronounced. The stresses put on the health care system by this increase in the elderly population are already significant. For example, in 1989 older people accounted for 33 percent of all hospital stays and 45 percent of all days of hospital care. The average stay for older people was 8.9 days compared with 5.3 days for persons under 65. The average length of stay for older people has increased 5.3 days since 1968 and 1.8 days since 1980. Moreover, while the elderly account for

about 12 percent of the population, they account for 36 percent of personal health care expenditures. These expenditures totaled $162 billion in 1991 and averaged more than $5,300 per year for each older person. Benefits from Medicare ($72 billion) and Medicaid ($20 billion) covered about 63 percent of those costs in 1987, compared with only 26 percent for persons under 65.[151]

The most obvious expression of ageism is seen in employment policies. The Age Discrimination in Employment Act (ADEA) of 1967 protects most workers from ages 40 to 69 from discrimination in hiring, job retention, and promotion. However, for most workers the protection of the ADEA stops when they reach age 70. Legislation to remove the "70" cap has consistently failed in Congress, as employer lobbies have persuasively argued that they require a free hand in personnel policies. Like race, gender, and sexual preference, age is a liability that makes older populations vulnerable to oppression and injustice.

Because the elderly vote in large numbers, their demands have been heard more clearly by politicians than those of African Americans and other minorities. In the 1960s, policymakers began to respond to the needs of the elderly and passed the Older Americans Act (OAA) of 1965. The objectives of the OAA include: (1) an adequate retirement income that corresponds to the general standard of living; (2) the achievement of good physical and mental health, regardless of economic status; (3) the provision of centrally located, adequate, and affordable housing; (4) the necessity of meaningful employment, with the elimination of age-specific and discriminatory employment practices; (5) the pursuit of meaningful activities in the area of civic, cultural, and recreational opportunities; and (6) adequate community services, including low-cost transportation and supported living arrangements.[152]

Despite the attempts made by the American Association of Retired Persons (AARP) and other advocacy groups, such as the Gray Panthers, problems still persist. Negative stereotypes of elderly persons continue to dominate the media, and the availability of long-term nursing care for the aged has reached crisis proportions. The elderly continue to the victimized by violence and abuse, and for many of the elderly, especially minorities, their economic well-being is precarious.

PEOPLE WITH DISABILITIES

People with disabilities represent still another group that experiences the effects of discrimination. About 8 to 17 percent of the population between the ages of 20 and 64 have disabilities that limit their ability to work, and about half that number are disabled to the point that either they cannot work or can work only irregularly.[153]

Disability is a difficult concept to define. The medical definition is based on the assumption that it is a chronic disease requiring various forms of treatment. Another definition derived from the medical model—also used as a basis for determining eligibility in the Social Security Disability Insurance program—sees people with disabilities as unable to work (or unable to work as frequently) in the same range of jobs as nondisabled people.[154] People with disabilities are thus viewed as inherently less productive than the able-bodied. A third model defines disability in terms of what people with disabilities cannot do, seeing the disabled in terms of their inability to perform certain functions expected of the able-bodied population. As William Roth maintains: "The functional limitation, economic, and medical models all define disability by what a person is not—the medical model as not healthy, the economic model as not productive, the functional limitation model as not capable."[155]

A newer definition—the psychosocial model—views disability as a socially defined category. In other words, people with disabilities constitute a minority group, and if the person with disabilities is poor, it is less a result of personal inadequacy than of a discriminatory society. This definition situates the problem of disability in the interaction between the disabled person and the social environment. Therefore, the adjustment to disability is not merely a personal problem but one requiring the adjustment of society to people with disabilities. This definition requires that society adjust its attitudes and remove the barriers it has placed in the way of self-fulfillment for people with disabilities—through, architecture and transportation systems designed for the able-bodied and subtle stereotypes that impugn the competence of people with disabilities. In part, this newer definition of disability was expressed in Section 504 of the Rehabilitation Act of 1973 (PL 93-112).

Although the range of disabilities is great, people with disabilities share a central experience rooted in stigmatization, discrimination, and oppression. Like other stigmatized groups, people with disabilities experience poverty and destitution in numbers proportionately larger than the general population. Perhaps not surprisingly, rates of disability are greatest among the aged, African Americans, the poor, and blue-collar workers.[156] Compared to the able-bodied, people with disabilities tend to be more frequently unemployed and underemployed and, as a consequence, often fall below the poverty line. Moreover, because disability is often correlated with poor education, age, and poverty, it is not surprising that African Americans are twice as likely to be disabled as whites (their representation is even greater in the fully disabled population) and that more women are disabled than men. The problems of low wages and unemployment are exacerbated because people with disabilities often need more medical and hospital care than others, are less likely to have health insurance, and spend three times more of their own money on medical care than do the able-bodied.[157]

Although discrimination continues to exist, major strides have been made in the integration of people with disabilities into the social mainstream. These advances have often resulted from organized political activity on the part of people with disabilities and their families. For example, an outgrowth of this political activity is Title V of the Rehabilitation Act of 1973, which mandates the following rules for all programs and facilities that receive federal funds:

1. Federal agencies must have affirmative action programs designed to hire and promote people with disabilities.
2. The Architectural and Transportation Barriers Compliance Board must enforce a 1968 rule mandating that all buildings constructed with federal funds—including buildings owned or leased by federal agencies—be accessible to people with disabilities.
3. All businesses, universities, and other institutions having contracts with the federal government must implement affirmative action programs targeted for people with disabilities.
4. Discrimination against people with disabilities is prohibited in all public and private institutions receiving federal assistance.[158]

Perhaps the greatest stride was made on July 26, 1990, when President George Bush signed the Americans with Disabilities Act (ADA) (PL 101-336) into law. This act is the most comprehensive piece of legislation for people with disabilities ever passed in the United States. The ADA lays a foundation of equality for people with disabilities, and it extends to the disabled civil rights similar to those now available on the basis of race, sex, color, national origin, and religion through the Civil Rights Act of 1964. For example, the ADA prohibits discrimination on the basis of disability in private sector employment, in state and local government activities, and in public accommodations and services, including transportation that is provided by both public and private entities. It also includes provisions for telecommunications relay services. While some policies of the ADA

were to go into effect immediately, others were to be phased in over several years.[159]

In particular, the ADA is divided into five titles and covers the following areas:

I. Employment
   A. Employers may not discriminate against an individual with a disability in hiring or promotion if the person is otherwise qualified for the job.
   B. Employers can ask about one's ability to perform a job, but cannot inquire if someone has a disability or subject a person to tests that tend to screen out people with disabilities.
   C. Employers will need to provide "reasonable accommodation" to employees with disabilities. This includes job restructuring and modification of equipment. Employers do not need to provide accommodations that impose an "undue hardship" on business operations.
   D. All employers with 25 or more employees must have complied by July 26, 1992; employers with 15 to 24 employees must comply by July 26, 1994.

II. Transportation
   A. New public transit buses and rail cars ordered after August 26, 1990, must be accessible to individuals with disabilities.
   B. Transit authorities must provide comparable paratransit or other special transportation services to individuals with disabilities who cannot use fixed bus services, unless an undue burden would result.
   C. Existing rail systems must have one accessible car per train by July 26, 1995.
   D. New bus and train stations must be accessible. Key stations in rapid, light, and commuter rail systems must have been made accessible by

July 26, 1993, with extensions up to 20 years for commuter rail (30 years for rapid and light rail). All existing Amtrak stations must be accessible by July 26, 2010.

III. Public Accommodations
  A. Private entities such as restaurants, hotels, and retail stores may not discriminate against individuals with disabilities effective January 26, 1992.
  B. Auxiliary aids and services must be provided to individuals with vision or hearing impairments or to other individuals with disabilities, unless an undue burden would result.
  C. Physical barriers in existing facilities must be removed, if removal is readily achievable. If not, alternative methods of providing services must be offered, if they are readily achievable. All new construction and alterations of facilities must be accessible.

IV. State and Local Government
  A. State and local governments may not discriminate against individuals with disabilities.
  B. All government facilities, services, and communications must be accessible, consistent with the requirements of Section 504 of the Rehabilitation Act of 1973.

V. **Telecommunications**
  A. Companies offering telephone service to the general public must offer telephone relay services to individuals who use telecommunications services for the deaf (TDD's) or similar devices.[160]

In spite of its large loopholes, the ADA represents an important step forward for people with disabilities.

Yet federal laws discouraging discrimination notwithstanding, prejudice against people with disabilities is still widespread. For example, most buildings still do not meet the needs of people with disabilities in terms of access, exits, rest rooms, parking lots, warning systems, and so forth. Many apartment complexes and stores continue to be built without recognition of the needs of people with disabilities. The struggle of disabled people for full integration is an ongoing social, political, and economic battle.

SOCIAL STIGMA AND OPPRESSION

The causes of discrimination in American society are complex and elusive. An impressive range of literature attempts to explicate the motives for discrimination. Broken down, these theories fit into three broad categories—psychological, normative-cultural, and economic.

Psychological interpretations attempt to explain discrimination in terms of intrapsychic variables.[161] A theory called the frustration-aggression hypothesis, formulated by J. Dollard, maintains that discrimination is a form of aggression that is activated when individual needs become frustrated.[162] According to Dollard, when people cannot direct their aggression at the real sources of their rage, they seek a substitute target. Thus, relatively weak minority groups become an easy and safe target for the aggression and frustration of stronger discontented groups. For example, poor whites have been one of the most racist groups in Southern society. Although exploited by the rigid economic and social class system of the old South, poor whites often focused their rage on African Americans, a group that was even weaker than they were. African Americans have thus served a twin function for poor whites: On the one hand, they formed a lower socioeconomic group that made poor whites feel better about their own standing; on the other, they functioned as a scapegoat for the frustrations of poor whites. Women, racial minorities, homosexuals, and other disenfranchised groups serve the same function for those on a slightly higher social rung.

The "authoritarian personality" theory,

developed by Theodore Adorno and other psychoanalytic authors, posited that discriminatory behavior is determined by personality traits that involve a reaction to authority.[163] Persons who exhibit the traits of irrationality, rigidity, conformity, xenophobia, and so forth, are more likely to discriminate against minorities than are people lacking those traits. Other authors, such as Wilhelm Reich, argued that discriminatory attitudes emanate from a sense of insecurity, self-hatred, deep-seated fears, and unresolved childhood needs and frustrations.[164]

The normative-cultural explanation suggests that individuals hold prejudicial attitudes because of their socialization. Through both overt and covert messages, a society teaches discrimination and rewards those who conform to prevailing attitudes and behaviors. Because societal pressures to conform to established norms are great, resistance to discriminatory practices becomes difficult.[165] For example, particular wrath in the old South was reserved for liberal whites who broke the norms regarding interaction with African Americans. It is perhaps axiomatic that societies are more tolerant of "outsiders" who break the norms than they are of "insiders" who betray them. In any case, this theory suggests that as the social and institutional norms which support discriminatory practices change, individual attitudes will follow suit.

The economic argument contends that dominant groups discriminate in order to maintain their economic and political advantages. This theory is grounded in the belief that relative group advantages are gained from discrimination. For example, male workers might discriminate against women because they perceive that they are encroaching on their employment prospects. In short, male workers fear that they might be replaced by a female worker who would be satisfied with lower wages. On the other hand, employers might uphold discriminatory attitudes because, as long as women workers are stigmatized, they will command a lower salary and thereby serve as a cheap pool of labor. In that sense, the increasing racial tensions in American society can be partly understood as a reaction to the job advancements made by African Americans, and the fears of whites that this may affect their promotions and even their jobs. Regardless of the causes of discrimination, the net effect is to transform disenfranchised groups into a lower class.

All forms of stigma, including those based on race, gender, sexual orientation, or age, are connected with oppression to form the complex mosaic of American society. Sexism, racism, homophobia, and other forms of discrimination are present, in large part, because of their economic usefulness. Industrialization requires a mobile labor force willing to relocate to the available employment. Perhaps inadvertently, discrimination has resulted in disenfranchised groups being forced to relocate (usually westward) in order to flee persecution based on ethnic, religious, or racial differences. Capitalism also requires a marginal and unskilled labor pool willing to take jobs refused by economically enfranchised groups. The use of stigma reduces the economic currency of whole populations and thus creates an underclass forced to take whatever jobs are available at whatever wages are offered. Furthermore, by threatening relatively well-paid workers with replacement by a stigmatized group, employers are able to force wage concessions. By manipulating stigmatized groups against each other, employers can keep wage demands in these groups relatively low. Moreover, because stigmatized groups are often employed in unstable jobs, they can be moved around as the economy requires. Paradoxically, the reduction in the economic currency of disenfranchised groups increases their value to the economic order.

In order for discrimination to maintain an air of legitimacy, it must have a moral, social, and theological underpinning. To that end, ultraconservatives have used the Bible to explain the inferiority of women, the "sin" of homosexuality, and the necessity of separating the races. To augment or replace biblical interpretations, spurious scientific explanations have been developed that are rooted in quasi-psychoanalytic theory, Social Darwinism, and pseudomedical "insights" concerning the attributes of stigmatized groups. For example, some people maintain that menstrual cycles cause severe mood swings that make women incapable of being in positions of power. Others believe that African Americans are descended from Ham and have thus committed biblical sins that justify discrimination. Some members of the Ku Klux Klan argue that African Americans are racially inferior on the basis of theories grounded in shaky anthropological research confirmed by even more dubious intelligence testing. Without the legitimation offered by moral, religious, social,

and "scientific" sources, discrimination is devoid of social validity and becomes mere exploitation.

Out of the insidious brew of prejudice comes oppression—the enforcement of discrimination and unequal power relationships. It is perhaps a truism that oppression flows from prejudice in the same way that opportunity flows from tolerance. Discrimination is a likely manifestation in a society that breeds an individualistic and competitive ethos, status fears among marginal groups, and the need for visible scapegoats on which to blame the alienating quality of life. In the final analysis, social stigma and discrimination promote poverty and destitution.

DISCUSSION QUESTIONS

1. The results of racism are manifested in a variety of ways, including outright discrimination, poverty, housing problems, high rates of under- and unemployment, wage differentials, family composition, inferior educational opportunities, crime statistics, and welfare dependency. Moreover, the relationship between racism and poverty is clear. What is less clear, however, are the causes of racism. Describe what you believe to be the primary causes of both individual and institutional racism. How are these causal factors nourished or condemned by society?

2. Over the past decade there has been a marked increase in the number of racially based incidents, especially against African Americans and Asian Americans. What are some of the reasons for the rise in such incidents?

3. Over the past three decades many legal attempts have been made to eradicate the effects of racism, including the 1964 Civil Rights Act and a number of Supreme Court rulings. Were these legal attempts successful? If not, why? Could anything have been done legally to eliminate the impact of racism? If yes, what?

4. It is generally acknowledged that sexism is a powerful and pervasive force throughout much

of society. Describe some of the most important ways that sexism is expressed in American society. What strategies, if any, should be adopted to lessen the impact of sexism in society?

5. Most women in American society are forced to work either to provide a second household income or as the family's primary wage earner. What are the major obstacles faced by working women?

6. Gays and lesbians face severe economic and social problems, even apart from the AIDS epidemic. What are some of the most important social, political, and economic hurdles faced by gays and lesbians in achieving full equality?

7. Being elderly in our society is in many ways a social handicap. Describe some key social, economic, and political indicators that illustrate this thesis.

8. It is generally agreed that people with disabilities face a difficult form of social stigma. What is the evidence, if any, to support this thesis?

9. The Americans with Disabilities Act (ADA) is often considered the most important piece of legislation affecting people with disabilities ever passed. Why do analysts consider the ADA such an important act? What are its loopholes, if any?

10. Reviewing the various causes of discrimination discussed in this chapter, describe what you believe to be the major cause of discrimination today. Why is this cause more important than others? Using this cause as a framework for understanding discrimination, state what can be done to ameliorate the effects of discrimination.

NOTES

1. Carrell Peterson Horton and Jessie Carney Smith, *Statistical Record of Black America* (Detroit: Gale Research, Inc., 1990), pp. 546, 289–90.
2. William Julius Wilson, *The Truly Disadvantaged: The Inner City, the Underclass, and Public Policy* (Chicago: The University of Chicago Press, 1987), p. 109.
3. Lawrence Mishel and David M. Frankel, *The State of Working America* (Armonk, N.Y.: M. E. Sharpe, Inc., 1991), p. 251.
4. U.S. House of Representatives, Committee on Ways and Means, *Overview of Entitlement Programs: 1992 Green Book* (Washington, D.C.: U.S. Government Printing Office, 1992), p. 1073.
5. Ibid., p. 1286.
6. Jon D. Haverman, Sheldon Danziger, and Robert D. Plotnick, "State Poverty Rates for Whites, Blacks, and Hispanics in the late 1980s," *Focus* 13, no. 1 (Spring 1991): 3.
7. U.S. House of Representatives, *1992 Green Book*, pp. 1167–70.
8. Center on Budget and Policy Priorities, *Poverty in Rural America* (Washington, D.C.: Center on Budget and Policy Priorities, April 1989), p. 27.
9. Joint Center for Housing Studies, *The State of the Nation's Housing, 1992* (Boston: Joint Center for Housing Studies, Harvard University, 1992), p. 33.
10. Cushing N. Dolbeare, *The Widening Gap* (Washington, D.C.: Low Income Housing Information Service, 1992), p. 11.
11. Center on Budget and Policy Priorities, *A Place to Call Home* (Washington, D.C.: Center on Budget and Policy Priorities, December 1991), p. xx.
12. Edward B. Lazere and Paul A. Leonard, *The Crisis in Housing for the Poor: A Special Report on Hispanics and Blacks* (Washington, D.C.: Center on Budget and Policy Priorities, 1989), p. 3.
13. U.S. House of Representatives, *1992 Green Book*, p. 590.
14. Mishel and Frankel, *The State of Working America*, p. 201.
15. U.S. House of Representatives, *1992 Green Book*, p. 598.
16. Mishel and Frankel, *The State of Working America*, p. 218.
17. Ibid., p. 213.
18. Center on Budget and Policy Priorities, *Two Million Americans Become Poor as Recession Hits and Wages and Incomes Decline* (Washington, D.C.: Center on Budget and Policy Priorities, September 21, 1991), p. 5.
19. Franklin D. Wilson, Marta Tienda, and Lawrence Wu, "Racial Equality in the Labor Market: Still an Elusive Goal?" Institute for Research on Poverty, Madison, Wis., 1992, Discussion Paper no. 968–92.
20. Children's Defense Fund, *The State of America's Children 1991* (Washington, D.C.: The Children's Defense Fund, 1991), p. 94.
21. U.S. House of Representatives, *1992 Green Book*, p. 1078.
22. "Teenaged Childbearing and Welfare Policy," *Focus* 10, no. 1 (Spring 1987): 16.
23. Michael Harrington, with the assistance of Robert Greenstein and Eleanor Holmes Norton, *Who Are the Poor?* (Washington, D.C.: Justice for All, 1987), p. 12.
24. U.S. House of Representatives, *1992 Green Book*, p. 695.
25. Ibid., p. 687.
26. Ibid., p. 1100.
27. Ibid.
28. Children's Defense Fund, *The State of America's Children*, p. 61.
29. Ibid.
30. Council on Interracial Books for Children, Inc., "Fact Sheets on Institutional Racism" (New York: Council on Interracial Books, November 1984).

31. Ibid., p. 63.

32. Ibid., p. 60.

33. U.S. House of Representatives, *1992 Green Book*, p. 247.

34. "Poverty and Mortality Rates," *Insights,* no. 3 (January 1991): 1.

35. Mishel and Frankel, *The State of Working America*, p. 219.

36. Gregory Acs and Sheldon Danziger, "Educational Attainment, Industrial Structure, and Male Earnings, 1973–1987," Institute for Research on Poverty, 1991, Discussion Paper no. 945–91.

37. The figures on high school dropout rates are highly variable, with ranges of several percentage points between low and high figures. For a discussion of these measurement problems, see Robert M. Hauser, "What Happens to Youth After High School?" *Focus* 13, no. 3 (Fall and Winter 1991): 1–13. See also U.S. House of Representatives, *1992 Green Book*, p. 1073.

38. Mishel and Frankel, *The State of Working America*, p. 253.

39. Children's Defense Fund, *The State of America's Children*, p. 76.

40. Ibid., p. 25.

41. Ibid., p. 92.

42. Ibid.

43. Mishel and Frankel, *The State of Working America*, p. 253.

44. Robert Elias, *The Politics of Victimization* (New York: Oxford University Press, 1986), p. 56.

45. Quoted in Jonathan Marshall, "Targeting the Drugs, Wounding the Cities," *Washington Post Weekly*, May 25–31, 1992, p. 23.

46. U.S. House of Representatives, *1992 Green Book*, p. 1136.

47. Leon Ginsberg, *Social Work Almanac* (Silver Spring, Md.: National Association of Social Workers Press, 1992), pp. 54–55.

48. U.S. House of Representatives, *1992 Green Book*, p. 1135.

49. Diana M. DiNitto, *Social Welfare: Politics and Public Policy* (Englewood Cliffs, N.J.: Prentice-Hall, Inc., 1991), p. 247.

50. L. Lowell, F. Bean, and R. De La Garza, "The Dilemmas of Undocumented Immigration: An Analysis of the 1984 Simpson-Mazzoli Vote," *Social Service Quarterly* 67 (1986): 118–26.

51. Fariyal Ross-Sheriff, "Displaced Populations," *Encyclopedia of Social Work, 18th Edition, 1990 Supplement* (Silver Spring, Md.: National Association of Social Workers, 1990), p. 85.

52. U.S. Bureau of the Census, *The Hispanic Population in the United States* (Washington, D.C.: U.S. Government Printing Office, March 1989).

53. U.S. House of Representatives, *1992 Green Book*, p. 1275.

54. Ibid., p. 1072.

55. Ibid.

56. Ibid., pp. 590–91.

57. Mishel and Frankel, *The State of Working America*, p. 16. It should be noted that although Hispanic-American family income dropped in that period, it was still over $3,000 more yearly than African-American family income.

58. Scott Barancik, *Falling Through the Gap: Hispanics and the Growing Income Disparity Between Rich and Poor* (Washington, D.C.: Center on Budget and Policy Priorities, 1990), p. 3.

59. Ibid., p. 25.

60. Guadalupe Gibson, "Mexican Americans," *Encyclopedia of Social Work,* 18th ed. (Silver Spring, Md.: NASW, 1987), p. 139.

61. Ibid., p. 140.

62. Marta Tienda, "Puerto Ricans and the Underclass Debate," *The Annals of the American Academy,* no. 501 (January 1989): 115.

63. V. A. Wilk, *The Occupational Health of Migrant and Seasonal Farmworkers in the United States* (Washington, D.C.: Farmworkers Justice Fund, 1985).

64. Juan Ramos and Celia Torres, "Migrant and Seasonal Farm Workers," *Encyclopedia of Social Work,* 18th ed. (Silver Spring, Md.: NASW, 1987), p. 151.

65. Barancik, *Falling Through the Gap*, p. 25.

66. Marta Tienda, "Race, Ethnicity and the Portrait of Inequality: Approaching the 1990s," *Sociological Spectrum,* no. 9 (1989): 32.

67. Ross-Sheriff, "Displaced Populations," p. 84.

68. David Stoesz, "What Amnesty Means to All of Us," *Newsday,* May 18, 1987, p. 77.

69. Immigration and Naturalization Service, *Report* (Washington, D.C.: U.S. Government Printing office, 1988).

70. Leon Ginsberg, "Selected Statistical Review," *Encyclopedia of Social Work, 18th Edition, 1990 Supplement* (Silver Spring, Md.: National Association of Social Workers, 1990), p. 280.

71. H. F. Dobyns, *Native American Historical Demography: A Critical Bibliography* (Bloomington, Ind.: Indiana University Press, 1976), p. 32.

72. H. E. Fey and D. McNickle, *Indians and Other Americans: Two Ways of Life Meet* (New York: Harper and Row, 1970), pp. 9–12.

73. DiNitto, *Social Welfare*, p. 257.

74. Evelyn Lance Blanchard, "American Indians and Alaska Natives," *Encyclopedia of Social Work,* 18th ed. (Silver Spring, Md.: NASW, 1987), p. 61.; Bureau of the Census, *1990 Census of Population and Housing Summary* (Washington, D.C.: U.S. Government Printing Office, 1990), p. 93.

75. Blanchard, p. 142.

76. Ibid., pp. 143–44.

77. Susumu Awanchara, "Hit by a Backlash," *Far Eastern Economic Review* 155, no. 2 (March 26, 1992): 30.

78. Quoted in ibid., p. 32.

79. Ibid.

80. Wilson, *The Truly Disadvantaged,* pp. 146–47.

81. Ibid., p. 62.

82. Ibid., p. 147.

83. U.S. House of Representatives, *1992 Green Book,* pp. 591–96.

84. Ibid., p. 590.

85. Ruth Sidel, *Women and Children Last* (New York: Harper, 1984).

86. National Commission on Children, *Poverty, Welfare and America's Families: A Hard Look* (Washington. D.C.: National Commission on Children, 1992), p. 3.

87. Mishel and Frankel, *The State of Working America*, p. 105.

88. While we have stressed single female-headed families here, it is important to acknowledge that single male-headed families are growing even more rapidly. From 1959 to 1989, single male-headed families grew from 350,000 to 1.4 million, compared with 7.4 million mother-only and 25.5 million two-parent households. From 1960 to 1990, the percentage of father-only households increased 300 percent. See Daniel R. Mayer and Steven Garasky, "Custodial Fathers: Myths, Realities, and Child Support Policy," Institute for Research on Poverty, Madison, Wis., August 1992, Discussion Paper no. 982–92, pp. 8–9.

89. National Commission on Children, "Poverty, Welfare and America's Families," p. 3.

90. National Commission on Children. *Beyond Rhetoric: A New Economic Agenda for Children and Families* (Washington, D.C.: National Commission on Children, 1991), p. 90.

91. Yin-Ling Irene Wong, Irwin Garfinkel, and Sara McLanahan, "Single-Mother Families in Eight Countries: Economic Status and Social Policy," Institute for Research on Social Policy, Madison, Wis., 1992, Discussion paper no. 970–92.

92. U.S. Department of Commerce, Bureau of the Census, *Current Population Reports*, ser. P-60, no. 173, *Child Support and Alimony, 1989* (Washington, D.C.: U.S. Government Printing Office, 1991), p. 5.

93. *Congressional Record*, Senate, 1987.

94. Bureau of the Census, *Child Support and Alimony, 1989*, p. 5.

95. U.S. Department of Health and Human Services, Administration for Children and Families, Office of Child Support Enforcement, *Child Support Enforcement: Fifteenth Annual Report to Congress, For the Period Ending September 30, 1990* (Washington, D.C.: National Child Support Enforcement Center, n.d.), pp. 15–16.

96. Irwin Garfinkel, "Bringing Fathers Back In: The Child Support Assurance Strategy," *The American Prospect*, Spring 1992; David Ellwood, "Child Support Enforcement and Insurance," Harvard University, Kennedy School of Government, March 1992.

97. Daniel Meyer, Irwin Garfinkel, Philip Robins, and Donald Oellerich, "The Costs and Effects of a National Child Support Assurance System," Institute for Research on Poverty, March 1991, Discussion Paper 940–91, p. 28.

98. Bureau of the Census, *Child Support and Alimony, 1989*, p. 1.

99. Winifred Bell, *Contemporary Social Welfare* (New York: Macmillan, 1983), p. 129.

100. Martha N. Ozawa, "Gender and Ethnicity in Social Security," *Conference Proceedings*, Nelson A. Rockefeller Institute of Government, State University of New York at Albany, November 1985, pp. 2–6.

101. Ibid.

102. "Women and Social Security," *Social Security Bulletin* 48, no. 2 (February 1985).

103. Most of the following section, unless otherwise noted, is based on information found in Wider Opportunities for Women, *Making Both Ends Meet* (Washington, D.C.: Wider Opportunities for Women, Inc., 1991), pp. 4–9.

104. Nina Totenberg, "Why Women Earn Less," *Parade,* June 10, 1984, p. 5.

105. Family assistance was one of the major thrusts of the Clinton campaign. It is also an issue that seems to cross racial and social class lines.

106. National Commission on Working Women of Wider Opportunities for Women, "Women, Work and Family: Working Mothers—Overview" (Washington, D.C.: Wider Opportunities for Women, n.d.), n.p.

107. Harrington, *Who Are the Poor?*, p. 7.

108. National Commission on Working Women of Wider Opportunities for Women, "Women, Work and Family: Working Mothers—Overview."

109. Ibid.

110. Ibid.

111. Harrington, *Who Are the Poor?*, p. 8.

112. Ibid.

113. Bell, *Contemporary Social Welfare*, p. 126.

114. National Commission on Working Women of Wider Opportunities for Women, "Women and Nontraditional Work," Washington, D.C., Wider Opportunities for Women, n.d., n.p.

115. Dinitto, *Social Welfare*, p. 237.

116. Nijole V. Benokraitis and Joe R. Feagin, *Modern Sexism: Blatant, Subtle, and Covert Discrimination* (Englewood Cliffs, N.J.: Prentice-Hall, 1986), p. 55.

117. Children's Defense Fund, *The State of America's Children*, p. 42.

118. Sidel, *Women and Children Last*, p. 121.

119. Ibid.

120. Children's Defense Fund, *The State of America's Children*, p. 37.

121. Sheila B. Kammerman, "Child Care and Family Benefits: Policies of Six Industrialized Countries," *Monthly Labor Review* 103 (November 1980): 23–28.

122. Sidel, *Women and Children Last*, p. 123.

123. National Commission on Working Women of Wider Opportunities for Women, "Women, Work and Health Insurance" (Washington, D.C.: Wider Opportunities for Women, n.d.), n.p.

124. National Commission on Working Women, "Women and Nontraditional Work."

125. Jim Harris, *The Complete Text of the Equal Rights Amendment* (New York: Ganis and Harris, 1980), p. 7.

126. "Fighting Discrimination," *The Legal Advisor,* Spring 1982, pp. 457–58.

127. S. K. Henshaw, L. M. Koonin, and J. C. Smith, "Characteristics of U.S. Women Having Abortions, 1987," *Family Planning Perspectives* 23 (March/April, 1991): 75–81.

128. Nanneska Magee, "Should the Federal Government Fund Abortions?: No." In Howard Jacob Karger and James Midgley, eds., *Controversial Issues in Social Policy* (New York: Allyn and Bacon, 1993).

129. DiNitto, *Social Welfare*, p. 241.

130. R. B. Gold and D. Daley, "Public Funding of Contraceptive, Sterilization and Abortion Services, Fiscal Year 1990," *Family Planning Perspectives* 23 (September/October 1991): 204–211.

131. DiNitto, *Social Welfare*, p. 241.

132. M. Clements, "Should Abortion Remain Legal?" *Parade,* May 17, 1992, pp. 4–5.

133. National Women's Political Caucus, *National Directory of Women Elected Officials, 1985* (Washington, D.C.: National Women's Political Caucus, 1985).

134. Natalie Jane Woodman, "Homosexuality: Lesbian Women," *Encyclopedia of Social Work,* 18th ed. (Silver Spring, Md.: NASW, 1987), p. 809.

135. Lambda Legal Defense and Education Fund, Inc., "Information Sheet" (New York: Lambda, 1991).

136. A. P. Bell and M. S. Weinberg, *Homosexualities: A Study of Diversity Among Men and Women* (New York: Simon and Schuster, 1978), p. 101.

137. DiNitto, *Social Welfare*, p. 109.

138. Kent Kilpatrick, "Oregon Voters Reject Stigmatizing Homosexuals," *The Advocate,* November 5, 1992, p. 2C.

139. Ibid.

140. National Gay and Lesbian Task Force, *Lesbian and Gay Civil Rights in the U.S.,* New York, 1992.

141. National Gay Task Force, *Legal Rights of Gays and Lesbians* (Washington, D.C., 1984).

142. Much of this section on the military and gays and lesbians was derived from Rivette Vullo, "Homosexuals in the Military," unpublished paper, School of Social Work, Louisiana State University, Baton Rouge, La., December 4, 1991. See also K. Dyer, ed., *Gays in Uniform: The Pentagon's Secret Reports* (Boston, Alyson Publications, 1990).

143. Ibid., p. xiv.

144. Joseph Harry, "Homosexual Men and Women Who Served Their Country," *Journal of Homosexuality* 10 (1984): 117–25.

145. Dyer, *Gays in Uniform*, p. xv.

146. Conrad K. Harper and Jane E. Booth, "End Military Intolerance," *The National Law Journal* 13 (1991): 17–18.

147. Center for Disease Control, *HIV/AIDS Surveillance*, Second Quarter Edition, Public Health Service Centers for Disease Control, Atlanta, Ga., July 1992, p. 8.

148. Robert Searles Walker, *AIDS: Today, Tomorrow* (New Jersey: Humanities Press, 1992), p. 119.

149. Norman Wyers, "Is Gay Rights Necessary for the Well-Being of Gays and Lesbians?" In Howard Jacob Karger and James Midgley, eds., *Controversial Issues in Social Welfare Policy* (New York: Allyn and Bacon, forthcoming, 1993).

150. American Association of Retired Persons, *A Profile of Older Americans, 1991* (Washington, D.C.: AARP, 1991).

151. Ibid.

152. L. D. Haber, "Trends and Demographic Studies on Programs for Disabled Persons," in L. G. Perlman and G. Austin, eds., *A Report of the Ninth Annual Mary E. Switzer Memorial Seminar* (Alexandria, Va.: 1985), pp. 27–29.

153. Ibid., pp. 35–37. See also Bell, *Contemporary Social Welfare*, p. 174.

154. William Roth, "Disabilities: Physical," *Encyclopedia of Social Work*, 18th ed. (Silver Spring, Md.: NASW, 1987), p. 86.

155. Ibid.

156. Haber, "Trends and Demographic Studies on Programs for the Disabled," p. 32.

157. Bell, *Contemporary Social Welfare*, p. 174.

158. DiNitto, *Social Welfare*, p. 104.

159. Administration on Developmental Disabilities, *Fact Sheet* (Washington, D.C.: Administration on Developmental Disabilities, n.d.).

160. Ibid.

161. Billy J. Tidwell, "Racial Discrimination and Inequality," *Encyclopedia of Social Work*, 18th ed. (Silver Spring, Md.: NASW, 1987), p. 450.

162. J. Dollard et al., *Frustration and Aggression* (New Haven: Yale University Press, 1939).

163. Theodore W. Adorno et al., *The Authoritarian Personality* (New York: Harper and Row, 1950).

164. Wilhelm Reich, *Listen Little Man* (Boston: Beacon Books, 1971).

165. Tidwell, "Racial Discrimination and Inequality," p. 450.

CHAPTER 6

Poverty in America

This chapter examines the characteristics of poverty in America. Particular attention is focused on the definition of terms and concepts used in the study of poverty, the examination of its demographic aspects, and the relationship between poverty and income distribution. This chapter also provides an overview of strategies developed to combat poverty.

Poverty is at once a complex and a simple phenomenon. It can be defined as deprivation and, in particular, as absolute and relative deprivation. Absolute poverty refers to an unequivocal standard necessary for survival (involving the caloric intake necessary for physical maintenance, shelter adequate for protection against the elements, and clothing that provides enough warmth). People who fall below that absolute standard of poverty are considered poor.

Relative poverty refers to the idea that deprivation is relative to the standard of living enjoyed by other members of society. Although their basic needs are met, a segment of the population may be considered poor when they possess fewer resources, opportunities, or goods than other societal members. For example, if most families in a society have two cars and a particular family can afford only one, they are relatively poor. Relative poverty (or deprivation) can be understood as inequality in the dis-

tribution of income, goods, or opportunities. Currently, little attention is focused on relative deprivation.

There are three general categories of poverty: (1) people making only the minimum wage (the working poor); (2) the unemployed; and (3) people who have an occupational disability or poor health (i.e., a deficit in human capital such as poor education or a low quality and quantity of training and skills).

Data from the Panel Study of Income Dynamics (PSID), a study conducted at the University of Michigan that followed 5,000 American families for 10 years (1969–1978), found that only 2 percent of its families were persistently poor—that is, poor throughout the entire period.[1] This finding suggests that poverty is a fluid rather than a static condition. The data show that as people gain (or lose) jobs, as marriages are created (or dissolved), or as offspring are born (or leave home), people are either pushed into or escape from poverty.

Further research on the PSID data conducted by Greg Duncan and his colleagues at the University of Michigan showed that most of the people who are poor in a given year have not been poor (and probably will not remain poor) for an extended period of time.[2] In fact, Duncan found that about one-third of the individuals who were poor in any given year escaped from poverty the following year, and that only about one-third of the poor families in any given year had been poor for at least eight of the preceding years. Duncan and his colleagues also discovered that family composition, and especially divorce or separation, was the leading cause of poverty. Conversely, spells of poverty were most often ended by family reconstitution (i.e., remarriage).

MEASURING POVERTY

Absolute deprivation in the United States is defined by a poverty line drawn at a given income level set by the Social Security Administration (SSA). The poverty line used by the federal government was developed in the mid-1960s, using data from the 1950s. Specifically, the poverty line was created by taking the cost of the least expensive food plan developed by the Department of Agriculture, The Economy Food Plan (which later became the Thrifty Food Plan), and multiplying that number by three. The rationale for that calculation was based on 1955 survey data showing that the average family spent about one-third of its budget on food.[3] Formally adopted by the SSA in 1969, the official measure provides a set of income cutoffs adjusted for

the size of the household, the number of minor children (those under age 18) in it, and the age of the household head. In order to ensure the same purchasing power each year, the SSA adjusts the poverty threshold by using the Consumer Price Index (CPI). Through use of the CPI, the SSA estimates the yearly cash income required by individuals and families to satisfy their basic survival needs (for food, clothing, shelter, and medical attention). This absolute figure is known as the poverty index or poverty line.

In 1992 the federal poverty index for a family of four was set at $14,463 per year.[4] Looking at the poverty line (for a family of four) over recent decades, in 1970 the poverty index was set at $3,968, in 1980 it rose to $8,414, and in 1990 it rose again, this time to $13,359[5] (see Table 6.1). For the most part, these increases do not represent a liberalization of the poverty index but instead are due almost solely to the effects of inflation. Moreover, poverty is assumed to be eliminated when the income of a family exceeds the poverty line, regardless of the changes occurring nationally in the average household income.

The poverty index is plagued with structural problems that make it the subject of controversy. For example, in recent years there has been a heated debate over the poverty count.

TABLE 6.1. Changes in Poverty Levels Based on Income and Family Size, 1970–1990

Family Size	Income, Selected Years				
	1970	1975	1980	1985	1990
1	$1,954	$2,724	$ 4,190	$ 5,250	$ 6,652
2	2,525	3,506	5,363	7,050	8,509
3	3,099	4,293	6,565	8,850	10,419
4	3,968	5,500	8,414	10,650	13,359
5	4,680	6,499	9,966	12,450	15,572
6	5,260	7,316	11,269	14,250	17,839
7	6,468	9,022	13,955	16,050	20,241

SOURCE: Compiled from U.S. Bureau of the Census, *Technical Paper 56*, series P–60, Nos. 134 and 149 (Washington, D.C.: U.S. Government Printing Office, 1992).

Households that fall under the poverty line because they do not have adequate income from private market sources are considered the pretransfer poor. However, after receiving Food Stamps, housing assistance, and Medicaid, many of these families are raised above the poverty line. Some conservative critics argue that the value of noncash benefits (e.g., Food Stamps, Medicaid, Medicare) should be counted as income. If those benefits were counted, fewer people would be classified as poor. These criticisms have some validity; Food Stamps do indeed raise the purchasing power of a family. However, placing a value on noncash benefits produces a new set of problems; for instance, at how much should the noncash benefits be evaluated? Some critics who favor placing a dollar value on noncash benefits (the "market value" approach) believe that these benefits should be valued highly. But under this approach, elderly persons with no cash income would be considered as living above the poverty line simply because they possessed a Medicare card (assumed to have greater monetary value than the poverty line figure).

Another problem with the poverty index occurs in relation to the dollar threshold. Liberal policy analysts argue that the federal poverty line is out of date. For example, since the 1950s the proportion of the U.S. household budget spent on food has declined, whereas during the same years the proportion of the family budget spent on health care, housing, and child care has increased. The American family currently spends less than one-fifth of its income on food. If the poverty line were to be revised using the Agriculture Department's least expensive food plan, but this time multiplying it by five rather than by three (to reflect current spending patterns), the poverty line would be significantly higher.[6] Moreover, the Thrifty Food Plan is based on an emergency diet and assumes the existence of an educated consumer able to discern nutritious and inexpensive foods. Obviously not every consumer is exemplary. The Nationwide Food Consumption Survey in 1977–78 indicated that fewer than one-tenth of the families spending an amount equivalent to the cost of the Thrifty Food Plan were able to purchase a diet that met the recommended dietary allowance for all major nutrients. Food cost data from 1981 indicated that the diets of low-income families cost 24 percent more than the amount allotted in the Thrifty Food Plan.[7] Finally, other critics argue that the federal poverty line, established more than 25 years ago, does not reflect current shifts in employment. For instance, 25 years ago relatively few mothers of young children worked outside the home; today, child care costs consume a substantial share of the budgets of low-income families.

The government's poverty line is also not adjusted for regional cost-of-living differences. In 1981 the Bureau of Labor Statistics (BLS) calculated the cost of three family budgets in 24 metropolitan and four nonmetropolitan regions. The lower family budget was 19 percent higher in the highest-cost metropolitan area (Seattle-Everett, Washington) than in the lowest-cost metropolitan area (Dallas). The BLS also found that on the whole the cost of living in metropolitan areas was 6 percent higher than it was in nonmetropolitan areas.[8] Indeed, one is hard-pressed to imagine that the costs of food and, especially, of housing would be similar in New York City and Houma, Louisiana.

In 1989 the Gallup Organization asked a nationally representative sample of Americans what they thought the poverty line should be for a family of four in their communities. According to the Gallup poll, the American public thought that the poverty line should be higher than it was: The average figure reported by respondents was $15,017 yearly, which was nearly $3,000, or 25 percent, higher than the government's poverty line for that year. If this poverty line had been adopted, the number of Americans in poverty would have increased from 32 to 45 million. Moreover, the poverty rate would have been 18 rather than 13.5 percent. Poverty for children would have gone from 19 to 26 percent, and for the elderly it would have risen from 12 to 23 percent.[9] If the public's poverty line were adopted, obviously the effect on governmental spending for welfare programs would be profound.

Recently, poverty analysts have begun to explore other ways of constructing the poverty line. One alternative method is to base the poverty line on an inflation-sensitive "market basket," which includes food, housing, clothing, medical care, child care, transportation, and other necessities. The contents of this market basket would be updated periodically, and material items could be added (or deleted) as they were transformed from luxuries into necessities. Despite the SSA's calculations, reason suggests that $14,463 is simply not sufficient for the survival of either an urban or a rural family of four, particularly if they are renters.

WHO MAKE UP THE POOR?

Before entering into a discussion of the theories and causes involved in the study of poverty, it is necessary to ask the question "Who is poor in America?" Table 6.2 describes some of the characteristics of the poor over a 30-year period. In 1991, more than 35.7 million Americans were poor, an increase of over 11 million above the 1978 figure of 24.5 million. The overall poverty rate in 1992 was 13.5 percent, which was higher than in any year of the 1970s, including the recession years of 1974 and 1975.[10] In short, one out of every seven Americans was poor in 1992.

Although poverty occurs across a wide spectrum, several groups are hit hardest. Not surprisingly, in absolute numbers, more whites than African Americans are poor. In 1991, of the 35.7 million poor people in America, roughly 17 million were white and 10.2 million were African American. In that same year, whites comprised almost 50 percent of the poor, African Americans, 29.5 percent, and Hispanic Americans, 17.2 percent.[11] In contrast to popular stereotypes, whites constitute the single largest group of poor people in every region of the country and in the vast majority of states. Even in America's metropolitan areas, there are four poor whites for every three poor African Americans. In fact, poverty rates are increasing faster for whites than for African Americans.[12] Nevertheless, African Americans are almost three times as likely to experience poverty as whites: The poverty rate for African Americans in 1991 was 32.7 percent compared with 11.3 percent for whites and 28.7 percent for Hispanic Americans.[13]

Perhaps the hardest hit of any group in America are single female-headed families. In 1990 the poverty rate for families in which a male was present was 6.9 percent; for female-headed households it was 45.3 percent. When disaggregated, the figures become even starker: For families headed by white women the poverty rate was 37.5 percent; for families headed by African-American and Hispanic-American women, the poverty rate was 44.5 and 51.2 percent, respectively.[14]

Children are among the main victims of poverty and are twice as likely to be poor as adults. In 1990 there were more than 13.4 million poor children in America (an increase of 3 million over 1979), or about 20.6 percent of all children under age 18. For children under age five the poverty rate was even higher (22.5 percent). In 1990, the poverty rate for African-American children reached the highest level ever recorded, 44.8 percent, an increase of 3.5 percent over 1979. In short, almost one out of every two African-American children is poor. For Hispanic-American children the poverty rate stood at 38.4 percent, up sharply from 28 percent just 11 years earlier.[15]

More children also fell deeper into poverty during the 1980s. In 1978, 34 percent of all poor families lived below 50 percent of the poverty line; by 1989, that number had risen to 41 percent.[16] The probability of children growing up poor is strongly correlated with family circumstances. The Census Bureau estimated that 61

TABLE 6.2. Persons below the Poverty Line, Selected Years and Characteristics, 1959–1990 (Number and percentage below poverty, in thousands)

Year	Overall	Aged	Children[1]	Individuals in Female-Headed Families[2]	Blacks	Hispanic[3] Origin	White
1990	33,585	3,658	14,431	12,578	9,837	6,006	22,326
Rate	13.5%	12.2%	20.6%	37.2%	31.9%	28.1%	10.7%
1986	32,370	3,477	12,876	11,944	8,983	5,117	22,183
Rate	13.6	12.4	20.5	38.3	31.3	27.3	11.0
1980	29,272	3,871	11,543	10,120	8,579	3,491	19,699
Rate	13.0	15.7	18.3	36.7	32.5	25.7	10.2
1978	24,497	3,233	9,931	9,269	7,626	2,607	16,259
Rate	11.4	14.0	15.9	35.6	30.6	21.6	8.7
1969	21,147	4,787	9,961	6,879	7,095	NA	16,659
Rate	12.1	25.3	14.0	38.2	32.2	NA	9.5
1959	39,490	5,481	17,552	7,014	9,927	NA	28,484
Rate	22.4	35.2	27.3	49.4	55.1	NA	18.1

[1] All children, including unrelated children.

[2] Does not include females living alone.

[3] People of Hispanic origin may be of any race; it is an overlapping category. (SOURCES: Compiled from Committee on Ways and Means, U.S. House of Representatives, *Overview of Entitlement Programs: 1992 Green Book* [Washington, D.C.: U.S. Government Printing Office, 1992], Tables 2 and 3, pp. 1274–1275.)

percent of the children born in 1987 will spend some part of their childhood in single-parent families, which are five times more likely to be poor than a two-parent family.[17]

Although the rate of child poverty is increasing in every racial and ethnic group, white children account for the greatest number of children added to the poverty rolls. In fact, poverty rates for white children rose more than 25 percent in the past decade, putting about 1.4 million more children into poverty.[18] In 1991, some 41.2 percent of the children living in poverty were white. And in 1991 more than half (55.4 percent) of poor married couples with children were white.[19]

One of the major causes of child poverty is the high cost of raising a child. According to the bipartisan National Commission on Children, the typical family spends about $6,000 a year to raise a child. To reduce child poverty and to relieve the pressure on middle-class families, the Commission recommended a flat $1,000 re-

fundable tax credit per each child. This proposal would function like the child allowances provided by most Western European nations, and for middle-class families it would be worth three times the current exemption. Because it would operate like a negative income tax, poor families would receive the tax credit regardless of whether they filed tax returns.[20]

In a bolder initiative, Elaine Kamarck and William Galston have proposed a new family policy. The cornerstone of this policy is the restoration of the child exemption allowance on federal taxes that has eroded since 1948. Kamarck and Galston propose raising the personal exemption to between $6,000 and $7,500 per young dependent, much closer to the actual cost of raising a child. Because this would entail huge costs—about $43 billion in 1990—the increase would be targeted in two ways. First, the increased exemption would be targeted at families with young preschool-age children, where the costs of day care substantially reduce a low-income parent's income. Second, the exemption would be reduced as family income increases. For families earning $64,000 a year or more (double the median income) only the present exemption would apply.[21]

At least on the surface, the poverty picture appears less bleak for the elderly, once the poorest group in America. In 1959 the poverty rate for those over 65 stood at 35.2 percent, in 1970 that number was reduced to 24.5 percent, and in 1973 it further decreased to 16.3 percent. Although financially better off, the elderly still had a poverty rate of 12.2 percent in 1990. Despite economic gains, almost 3.7 million elderly citizens still live in poverty, with another 2.1 million (about 7 percent of the elderly population) classified as "near poor." Moreover, elderly women experience a disproportionate share of poverty: In 1990, elderly women had a higher poverty rate (15 percent) than elderly men (8 percent). A further examination of the poverty data reveals that the elderly of color also experience a greater share of poverty. In 1990 the poverty rate for elderly African Americans was 34 percent and that for Hispanic Americans was 22 percent.[22]

The government's calculation as to the number of elderly people in poverty is at best spurious. At present, the poverty line is bifurcated into two classifications: families headed by persons under age 65, and families headed by persons 65 or older, the latter group having a lower poverty line. In 1988, the poverty line for a two-person family headed by someone 65 or older was $7,158, exactly $800 lower than the poverty line for younger two-person families. This lower poverty line is predicated on the belief that the elderly spend less on food and other expenses. Had the poverty line for the elderly been identical to that for the rest of the population, their poverty rate would have *exceeded* the rate for the population as a whole. Moreover, the number of elderly classified as poor would have risen by 25 percent.[23]

People living in rural areas were almost as likely to be poor as those living in America's central cities. In 1987, about 16.9 percent of rural people had income levels below the poverty line, a rate almost as high as the 18.6 percent poverty rate in central cities. Rural African Americans did worse than those living in central cities: 44 percent of rural African Americans were poor compared with 33.3 percent of African Americans who lived in central cities. For Hispanic Americans, the elderly, and single female-headed families, the poverty rates in rural areas were just as high as they were in central cities. Poverty rates for whites were also as high in rural areas as in central cities.[24]

The composition of the rural poor is different from that of their counterparts in central cities. For one thing, the proportion of the poor living in two-parent families (61.1 percent) is much greater than it is in central cities (41.7 percent). The rural poor are also more likely than the urban poor to have at least one family member who works. In addition, more family heads among the rural poor work full-time, year-round, than do metropolitan family heads. The rural poor are also somewhat more likely to be elderly than their urban counterparts.[25]

Perhaps the most striking poverty statistic involves hunger. The Harvard School of Public Health estimated that in 1985 some 20 million Americans were hungry. In 1992, Dr. Vincent Breglio, a national survey researcher, estimated that 30 million Americans now experience hunger. Estimates of hunger in America range from a low of 22.1 million to a high of 41.2 million.[26]

International Comparisons

Although it is difficult to compare U.S. poverty rates with those of other countries, an attempt has been made by an international team of researchers. Known as the Luxembourg Income Study (LIS), this team has undertaken an extensive study comparing poverty rates and income levels in several Western nations, including the United States, Australia, Canada, France, Germany, the Netherlands, Sweden, and the United Kingdom. The LIS defines as poor households with incomes below 40 percent of their country's median income (adjusted for family size), which produces a poverty line for the United States that is close to the official poverty threshold used by the Census Bureau.[27]

Predictably, the results of this study show that poverty rates in the United States are much higher than they are in the other countries. Even comparing poverty rates for whites only[28] (the lowest poverty group in terms of percentages) reveals startling results. For example, the poverty rate for whites in the United States is higher than the poverty rate for the total population of the other countries. The data also show that in every age group the poverty rate in the United States is significantly higher than it is for the other nations studied, with the gap being greatest for children and the elderly. For example, in 1986 the poverty rate for whites was 9.1 percent, which was nearly twice the poverty rate (4.8 percent) of the other countries. The poverty rate for white children in the United States was 13.2 percent in 1986, more than double the child poverty rate in the other nations. Even among the elderly, the poverty rate of 8.9 percent was nearly five times the average poverty rate (1.8 percent) of the other countries.[29] The poverty rate of *all* children in the United States also compares unfavorably with that of the other nations in the LIS study, with U.S. child poverty ranking ninth highest in the field of advanced industrialized countries included.[30]

Moreover, the United States scores badly on other social indicators as well. In infant mortality and mortality for children under age five, the United States ranks nineteenth worldwide; in the percentage of low birth-weight babies, twenty-eighth; in the percentage of one-year-old children fully immunized against polio, it ranks seventeenth (for nonwhite babies, the United States ranks fifty-sixth). Among industrial nations, the United States ranks fourteenth in spending on elementary and secondary education as a percentage of the gross domestic product; and it ranks nineteenth in the number of school-age children per teacher.[31]

THE SOCIAL AND ECONOMIC DEMOGRAPHICS OF POVERTY

The demographics of poverty show some interesting twists and turns. In 1962 about 20 percent of the population was poor; as a result of increases in the AFDC rolls, by 1969 that figure had dropped to 12.1 percent, and by 1979 it had dropped even further to 11 percent. For African Americans, especially African-American children, the progress made in the 1960s was dramatic. In 1959, 65.5 percent of all African-American children were poor, but by 1969 that number had dropped to 39.6 percent. By 1979 a reversal had set in, and by 1990 the poverty rate for African-American children was over 44 percent.

Overall poverty rates declined from 1965 to 1978. According to Sheldon Danziger, much of this decline occurred between 1965 and the mid-1970s, when real expenditures for cash and in-kind transfers outpaced the real increase in general household income, a development that would slow in the 1980s. From 1978 to 1982, the average cash transfer to a poor household declined by 5 percent; for nonaged women heading households, that decline was 10 percent.[32] From 1978 onward the poverty rate has generally increased. In 1984, as a consequence of Reagan's economic policies and large social welfare cuts, the poverty rate increased to 15.3 percent, then dropped to 14.4 percent in 1985. Except for 1982 and 1983, the current poverty rate of 13.5 percent is the highest since 1966.

The slight drop in the poverty level from 1982 to 1987 (from 15.2 percent to 13.4 percent) was especially disappointing because it came on the heels of a major reduction in unemployment (from a high of 11 percent in 1979 to 6 percent in 1987). Thus, even though unemployment dropped by 5 percent, the level of poverty was reduced only minimally. This phenomenon suggests that at least a portion of those who were economically displaced by the high unemployment of the late 1970s and early 1980s have either not reentered the work force or have reentered it at significantly reduced wages.

From 1979 to 1983 poverty rose at a steady rate. This period was marked by high inflation, high unemployment, and large budget cuts for social programs serving lower-income people. This situation was exacerbated by the fact that almost 40 percent of nonaged poor households received no income transfers, and even many of those who did receive transfers did not get enough to lift their families out of poverty.[33] Although there was a major economic recovery in the mid-1980s, the levels of poverty did not correspond with the increased affluence. For example, in 1976 and 1977—before the rise in poverty began—unemployment levels were at the same point as in 1984, yet the poverty rate was almost three percentage points lower. Those three percentage points translated into 6 million Americans. The paradox involving the economic recovery of the mid- and late 1980s and the elevated poverty levels can best be understood by examining income distribution trends.

Income Distribution and Inequality

In large part, poverty can be understood as inequality in the distribution of income. Table 6.3 illustrates this unequal distribution and how it

has grown in recent years. By examining the distribution of wealth in society, it becomes obvious why poverty rates have not declined and why social welfare programs have only managed to keep poverty relatively constant rather than alleviate it. One of the prime causes of income disparity has been the low-wage and salary structure characteristic of many American businesses, a phenomenon encouraged by federal tax and investment policies. Specifically, the economic policies of the Reagan and Bush administrations resulted in an acceleration of income inequalities in the 1980s.

The net effect of these economic policies has been to push the nation toward a two-tier society in which the top 4 percent make as much as the bottom half of all U.S. workers. As such, the economic gap between upper- and lower-income American families was wider in the early 1990s than at any time since the Census Bureau began collecting this data in 1947. When breaking the population down into fifths, the poorest fifth in 1988 received just 4.3 percent of the national after-tax income, while the upper fifth received 49.8 percent. The top two-fifths of the population (40 percent) received 71 percent of the national after-tax income, the highest ever

TABLE 6.3. Percentage Share of Aggregate Pre-Tax Family Income Received by Each Fifth of Families, and Family Income at Selected Levels, 1950–1988

	Percentage of Aggregate Income Received by					
	Lowest 5th	Second 5th	Middle 5th	Fourth 5th	Highest 5th	Top 5%
1988	4.3	9.8	15.1	21.4	49.8	25.2
1985	4.4	10.1	15.3	22.0	49.0	23.4
1980	5.4	11.4	16.2	22.6	44.9	19.7
1977	5.7	11.6	16.3	22.7	44.0	18.5
1970	5.4	12.2	17.6	23.8	40.9	15.6
1965	5.2	12.2	17.8	23.9	40.9	15.6
1960	4.8	12.2	17.8	24.0	41.3	15.9
1955	4.8	12.3	17.8	23.7	41.3	16.4
1950	4.5	12.0	17.4	23.4	42.7	17.3

SOURCES: Compiled from U.S. Bureau of the Census, "Consumer Income 1984," *Current Population Reports*, Series P–60, No. 151, Table 12 (Washington, D.C.: U.S. Government Printing Office, 1985); and Isaac Shapiro and Robert Greenstein, *Selective Prosperity: Increasing Income Disparities Since 1977* (Washington, D.C.: Center on Budget and Policy Priorities, July 1991), p. 4.

recorded by the Census Bureau. This 71 percent stands in sharp contrast to the 14 percent of the national income received by the bottom 40 percent (the lowest ever recorded). The middle fifth of the population received 15.1 percent of the national income, also the lowest since the Census Bureau began collecting income data.[34]

The income data illustrate the problem even better when the top quintile is examined. In 1977 the wealthiest 1 percent of the population earned 9.2 percent of all pre-tax income; by 1988 this had increased to 12.5 percent. The average after-tax income of the richest 1 percent more than doubled from 1977 to 1988, rising 122 percent after adjusting for inflation. This translates into an after-tax income of $451,000 in 1988 (adjusted in 1992 dollars), up from $203,000 in 1977. Thus, the after-tax income of the richest 1 percent in 1988 was almost as great as the combined after-tax income of the bottom 40 percent of Americans. Put more dramatically, *the richest 2.5 million Americans now have almost as much income as the 100 million Americans with the lowest incomes.* This situation stands in

sharp contrast to 1977, when the total after-tax income of the bottom 40 percent of Americans was double the after-tax income of the richest 1 percent.[35]

In 1983 the richest 1 percent of the population held 20 percent of all household wealth. Moreover, more than 75 percent of the wealth of the top 1 percent was held by the top one-half percent, a group whose net worth in 1983 was $2.5 trillion and whose net income was almost $131 billion. In other words, the net worth of the top one-half percent in 1983 was 75 percent of the total net worth of 90 percent of the American population. The wealth of this elite group translates into power, and the richest 1 percent of the population controls 36 percent of all real estate, 58 percent of public stocks, 58 percent of all bonds and trusts, and 51 percent of all business assets.[36]

The income data also suggest that the center of the middle class is eroding, as shown in Figure 6.1. While the rich are getting richer, real earnings for most Americans have either stagnated or fallen during the past decade. From

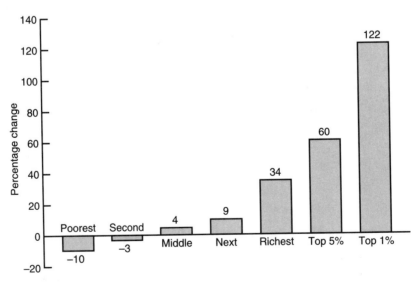

Figure 6.1. Post-Tax Income Gains and Losses for Household Groups, from 1977 to 1988, in Fifths and Percentages. (SOURCE: Center on Budget and Policy Priorities, *Selective Prosperity: Increasing Income Disparities Since 1977* [Washington, D.C.: Center on Budget and Policy Priorities, July 1991], p. 3.)

1977 to 1990 the median income for the wealthiest 5 percent of the population grew by $12,819 (in 1990 dollars); for the wealthiest 10 percent it grew by $9,256. By contrast, median income for the poorest 40 percent of the population was actually $1,088 *lower* (in 1990 dollars) in 1990 than it was in 1977.[37]

Lower-income families with children also fared worse. From 1977 to 1988, average family income for the poorest fifth dropped 10 percent (after adjusting for inflation). For the next poorest fifth it dropped 3 percent. Only families in the wealthiest fifth came out ahead. If we examine these data over a fifteen-year period, the figures are even bleaker. From 1973 to 1988 the incomes of the poorest fifth with children fell 15 percent (after adjusting for inflation).[38] It is estimated that from 1980 to 1984 there was a net transfer of $25 billion in disposable income from poor and middle-income families to the richest fifth of the population.[39]

In 1988, the income of the typical poor family fell further below the poverty line than at any time since the Census Bureau began collecting income data in 1959, as can be seen in Table 6.4. In particular, 38 percent of poor persons were below 50 percent of the poverty line in 1988; another 28 percent were between half and three-quarters of the poverty line. This compares with 32.9 percent of the poor who were under 50 percent of the poverty line in 1979.[40] In effect, this means that a three-person family that fell below 50 percent of the poverty line in 1988 had a combined yearly income of less than $4,528.

An issue closely related to the skewed distribution of incomes is the skewed distribution of assets. In 1988, the average net worth of all households was $35,752. For African-American and Hispanic-American households it was $4,169 and $5,524, respectively. Moreover, while the median net worth for white female householders was $22,099, it was $757 and $736, respectively, for African-American and Hispanic-American female householders. This asset inequity led Washington University's Michael Sherraden to pioneer the concept of "stakeholding," the substitution of assets for income transfers through social policy. Accordingly, Sherraden has proposed the creation of Individual Development Accounts (IDAs) to bolster the assets of the working poor. IDAs would be designated for specific purposes: housing, postsecondary education, self-employment, and retire-

TABLE 6.4. Trends in the Distribution of Income for Families and Children, 1968–1989 (Percentage shares of cash family income to each fifth)

Calendar Year	Lowest Fifth	Second Fifth	Third Fifth	Fourth Fifth	Highest Fifth	Total
1968	7.4	14.8	19.5	24.5	33.8	100
1970	7.2	14.7	19.4	24.7	34.0	100
1972	6.8	14.2	19.5	25.1	34.5	100
1974	6.4	14.3	20.6	25.1	34.6	100
1976	6.4	13.9	19.7	25.3	34.7	100
1978	6.1	13.7	19.5	25.4	35.4	100
1980	5.6	13.3	19.5	25.5	36.1	100
1982	4.9	12.7	19.1	25.9	37.5	100
1989	4.6	10.6	16.5	23.7	44.6	100

SOURCE: Compiled from *The American Profile Poster* by Stephen J. Rose. Copyright 1986 by Social Graphics Co. Reprinted by permission of Pantheon Books, a division of Random House, Inc.; and Lawrence Mishel and David Frankel, *The State of Working America* (Armonk, N.Y.: M. E. Sharpe, Inc., 1991), p. 20.

ment. The heart of the IDA concept is that the federal or state government would match the IDA deposits made by people in qualifying low-income families. The amount of the governmental supplement would vary with the activity—say $5 a in governmental match for $1 saved for housing, or $2 in governmental match for $1 saved for retirement.[41] The IDA concept was incorporated in the 1992 electoral platform of Bill Clinton.

Tax Policy and Incomes

Federal and state tax policies, which have become less progressive over the past 15 years, have played a major role in promoting both income inequality and poverty. In 1986 Congress passed a major tax reform act. Although this bill decreased the tax load on the working poor by bringing it back to 1979 levels, and took back 25 percent of the tax cuts previously awarded to the richest 5 percent of the population, tax cuts for the wealthy still cost the federal treasury $60 billion in 1989. According to Robert McIntyre, director of Citizens for Tax Justice, supply-side tax policy lowered federal taxes for the richest 5 million American families (including their share of corporate tax reductions) by almost $370 billion during the 1981–1988 period, more than double the 1987 budget deficit. Conversely, supply-side tax policies increased the federal tax burden sixfold on poverty-level families of four, from 1.8 percent of their income in 1979 to 10.8 percent in 1986.[42]

The inequalities in taxation are illustrated by examining before- and after-tax rates. For instance, families in the middle fifth of all wage earners pay roughly as much in federal taxes as they did in 1977, but families in the top fifth (and especially in the top 1 percent) pay significantly less. Congressional Budget Office data indicate that in 1993 the richest 1 percent of households would owe an additional $43 billion in federal taxes if they paid the same percentage of taxes as they did in 1977.[43] The wealthiest 1 percent of all households paid 13.6 percent of all federal

taxes in 1977 compared with 18.3 percent in 1992. This rise occurred, however, not because the real level of their taxes went up but because they received a larger share of the national income. Furthermore, from 1977 to 1988 the average *before*-tax income of the middle fifth of households rose by 3.6 percent while their average *after*-tax income rose by 3.9 percent. During that same period, the *before*-tax income of the wealthiest 1 percent of households rose 95 percent while their *after*-tax income rose by 122 percent (see Figure 6.2). These differences were largely a result of changes in federal tax policy.[44]

The tax burden for at least 90 percent of all American families was higher in 1990 than it was in 1977. The combination of federal, state, local, and Social Security taxes equaled about 14 percent of the average family's income in 1960; by 1991 they accounted for 25 percent.[45] If the tax changes since 1977 had not taken place, a middle-class family's income would have been $400 higher in 1990. On the other hand, a family in the richest 1 percent would have paid $40,000 more in 1990.

Although Americans complain about the burden of taxation, it is relatively light when compared with that of other industrialized nations. In 1987 the rate of taxation as a percentage of the gross domestic product (GDP) was lower in the United States (30 percent) than it was in 24 other industrialized nations, including Greece, the United Kingdom, France, Finland, Spain, Canada, and Japan. Moreover, from 1947 to 1989, the total U.S. tax burden rose from 24.6 to 32 percent of the gross national product (GNP), a modest amount. From 1967 to 1987, most industrialized nations experienced a rise in tax revenues of between 10 and 20 percent. During that same period, the United States recorded a 2.7 percent increase.[46]

The poor often experience the unequal burden of taxation through ill-conceived and regressive state and local taxation policies (see Table 6.5). A 1991 study by Citizens for Tax Justice found that in all but six states, the middle

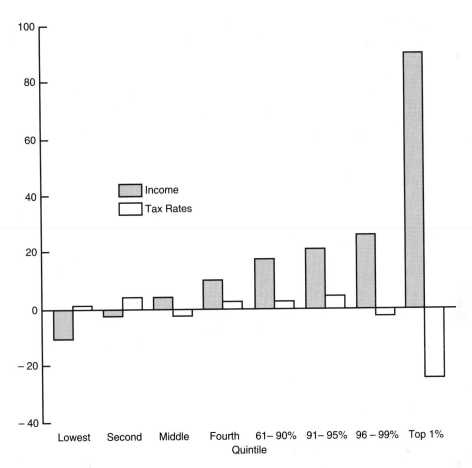

Figure 6.2. Percent Change in Pre-Tax Income and Federal Tax Rates for All Families, 1977 to 1989. (SOURCE: Committee on Ways and Means, U.S. House of Representatives, *Overview of Entitlement Programs, 1992 Green Book* [Washington, D.C.: U.S. Government Printing Office, 1992], p. 1512.)

fifth of families pays a larger proportion in state income taxes than does the richest fifth. Similarly, in all but seven states the poorest fifth pays a larger share of its income in state and local taxes than does the richest fifth.[47] Among the 34 states that raised taxes in 1990, only a few did so in a clearly progressive manner. The majority of these states relied on regressive taxes such as sales taxes.

In 1989, 19 percent of all state tax revenues were collected through individual and corporate income taxes. About 37 percent of state revenues were collected through general and selec-

tive sales taxes. Income and corporate taxes are generally thought to be progressive, because the tax received from the individual or corporation is based on the extent of income or profit. At least theoretically, the rich pay more and the poor less. By contrast, general and selective sales taxes are regressive, being based not on the ability of people to pay but solely on purchases. Therefore, an affluent family that purchases $75 worth of clothing will pay the same amount of sales tax as a poor family, even though that purchase represents a greater share of the poor family's income. For example, a pur-

TABLE 6.5. State Sales Taxes and Exemptions, 1987

		Exemptions		
	Sales Tax Rate*	Consumer Electric and Gas Utilities	Food	Low Income Sales Tax Credit
Alabama	4.0%	no	no	no
Alaska	no sales tax			
Arizona	5.0	no	yes	no
Arkansas	4.0	yes	no	no
California	4.8	yes	yes	no
Colorado	3.0	yes	yes	no
Connecticut	7.5	yes	yes	no
Delaware	no sales tax			
Dist. of Col.	6.0	no	yes	no
Florida	5.0	yes	yes	no
Georgia	3.0	no	no	no
Hawaii	4.0	no	no	yes
Idaho	5.0	yes	no	yes
Illinois	5.0	no	yes	no
Indiana	5.0	no	yes	no
Iowa	4.0	no	yes	no
Kansas	4.0	yes	no	yes
Kentucky	5.0	yes	yes	no
Louisiana	4.0	yes	yes	no
Maine	5.0	yes	yes	no
Maryland	5.0	yes	yes	no
Massachusetts	5.0	yes	yes	no
Michigan	4.0	no	yes	no
Minnesota	6.0	yes	yes	no
Mississippi	6.0	no	no	no
Missouri	4.2	yes	no	no
Montana	no sales tax			
Nebraska	3.5	no	yes	no
Nevada	5.8	yes	yes	no
New Hampshire	no sales tax			
New Jersey	6.0	yes	yes	no
New Mexico	4.8	no	no	yes
New York	4.0	yes	yes	no
North Carolina	3.0	yes	no	no
North Dakota	5.5	yes	yes	no
Ohio	5.0	yes	yes	no
Oklahoma	4.0	yes	no	no
Oregon	no sales tax			
Pennsylvania	6.0	yes	yes	no
Rhode Island	6.0	yes	yes	no

TABLE 6.5. *(continued)*

	Sales Tax Rate*	Exemptions		
		Consumer Electric and Gas Utilities	Food	Low Income Sales Tax Credit
South Carolina	5.0	yes	no	no
South Dakota	5.0	no	no	yes
Tennessee	5.5	yes	no	no
Texas	6.0	yes	yes	no
Utah	5.1	yes	no	no
Vermont	4.0	yes	yes	yes
Virginia	3.5	yes	no	no
Washington	6.5	yes	yes	no
West Virginia	5.0	yes	yes	no
Wisconsin	5.0	yes	yes	no
Wyoming	3.0	no	no	yes
U.S. Median Rate	5.0	–	–	–
Number with Provision	46	32	29	7

* This represents only state sales tax rates. Counties or cities may levy additional sales taxes. (SOURCE: Advisory Commission on Intergovernmental Relations, *Significant Features of Fiscal Federalism, 1987;* National Association of State Budget Officers and National Governors' Association, *Fiscal Survey of the States,* September 1987.)

chase of $75 worth of clothing may represent 1 percent of the monthly income of a wealthy family, whereas it may represent 10 percent of the monthly income of a poor family headed by a minimum-wage worker. As a general rule, the poor—when compared with the wealthy—spend a larger proportion of their income on items subject to sales taxes.

Although the tax burden on the poor can be partially relieved by exempting certain necessary items from a sales tax, of the 46 states that had a general sales tax in 1987, only 29 exempted most grocery purchases, while 32 states exempted utilities.[48] To help rectify this problem, seven states have instituted a tax rebate program that provides poor households with a rebate check (or a credit against income tax liabilities) to defray the cost of sales taxes. For example, in 1991 Vermont increased its refundable sales tax credit to help offset an increase in the sales tax, while Minnesota helped cushion the effects of a sales tax hike by instituting an

earned income tax credit. Despite the attempts of more progressive states to equalize the tax burden, inequities continue to grow at the state level. For example, the average poor family in Alabama spent $363 on sales taxes in 1989 compared with $280 in 1980; in Florida, the poor family's sales tax went up from $183 to $442; in Idaho, from $192 to $452; in Kansas, from $192 to $358; in South Carolina, from $276 to $452; and in Texas, from $183 to $390.[49]

Although income taxes tend to be less regressive than general sales taxes, the majority of states have failed to follow the federal government's lead in eliminating poor families from the tax rolls. For example, in 13 states (Alabama, Arkansas, Hawaii, Illinois, Indiana, Iowa, Kansas, Kentucky, Michigan, Montana, New Jersey, North Carolina, and Pennsylvania), a working four-person family earning more than $10,000 a year paid over $100 in state income tax in 1988. Four of these states (Indiana, Kentucky, North Carolina, and Pennsylvania) required that same family to pay over $200 per year in income tax. Eight states in 1988 required working four-person families to pay taxes on earnings of less than $6,000 a year. Apart from paying state income taxes, some of these same families also had to pay local income, sales, wage, or property taxes. Twenty-eight of the 41 states with income taxes required payment from some four-person working families that had incomes below the poverty line. In nine states (Alabama, Arkansas, Illinois, Indiana, Kansas, Kentucky, New Jersey, North Carolina, and Virginia), working families of four with incomes below *half* of the poverty level paid state income taxes in 1988.[50]

Income distribution is a good indicator of social equity. In the United States, however, it reveals a highly stratified economic system in which the rich are getting richer while the poor get poorer. Given this income disparity, it is not surprising that welfare programs appear to be losing the battle to contain poverty. In some measure, welfare programs release the pressure on the system by subsidizing income to compensate for its skewed distribution. However limited these programs may be, without the redistributive function of welfare the economic stratification in American society would undoubtedly be worse.

WORK AND POVERTY

Labor force participation is a key variable in determining poverty. Over two-thirds of the poor in the United States are children, the aged, or the disabled. Apart from these groups—who for the most part are unable to work—poverty is also widespread within the work force. The number of working individuals (aged 22 to 64) who are poor has escalated sharply, increasing more than 50 percent between 1979 and 1991.[51] Forty-one percent of all poor people now work some time during the year. Moreover, the number of poor people who are employed full-time

on a year-round basis stands at two million, an increase of over two-thirds since 1978.[52]

The rise in the number of the working poor is attributable to several factors, chief among them being the replacement of high-paying industrial jobs with low-paying service jobs. Currently, about 20 percent of jobs will not support a worker and two dependents. In 1986, 35 percent of all people who worked part- or full-time earned less than $8,500 a year. Moreover, according to the Joint Economic Committee, about 44 percent of the new jobs created between 1979 and 1985 paid less than $7,400 a year.[53]

This employment trend reflects a clear movement away from higher-paying manufacturing jobs to low-wage service employment. For example, from the 1950s until the 1970s, businesses added about 1.5 million new manufacturing jobs a decade. By the 1980s, corporations had eliminated 300,000 manufacturing jobs. If this trend continues, 1 million more manufacturing jobs will be eliminated in the 1990s. These statistics, however, grossly underestimate the problem. For example, 33 percent of all workers in the 1950s were employed in primary manufacturing jobs (cars, radios, refrigerators, clothing). Only 17 percent were employed in those industries by 1992, a number that is falling. While manufacturing jobs have declined, retail service jobs have increased by 32.5 percent. Retail-trade workers, whose ranks are growing, earn $204 per week. Manufacturing workers, whose ranks are declining, earn $458 per week.[54]

The freeze in the minimum wage from 1981 to 1990 is yet another factor that has increased the ranks of the working poor. In 1950 the minimum wage brought a worker to 56 percent of the average wage. Throughout the 1950s and 1960s (as can be seen from Table 6.6), the average minimum wage hovered between 44 and 56 percent (the mean being 50 percent) of the average wage. However, by 1980 the minimum wage had fallen to 46.5 percent of the average wage, and in 1988 it dropped even further, to 35.7 per-

TABLE 6.6. Value of the Minimum Wage, Selected Years

Year	Percent of Poverty Line for a Family of Three	Percent of Average Wage
1950	81.3	56.0
1955	73.1	43.9
1960	88.2	47.8
1965	103.4	50.8
1968	120.0	56.1
1970	107.4	49.5
1975	101.7	46.4
1980	98.2	46.5
1985	81.3	39.1
1988	73.6	35.7

SOURCE: Adapted from Isaac Shapiro, *The Minimum Wage and Job Loss* (Washington, D.C.: Center on Budget and Policy Priorities, 1988), p. 3.

cent. Even with a minimum wage of $4.25 an hour in 1991, the minimum wage equaled only about 41 percent of the average wage, bringing a family of three to about 85 percent of the poverty line. This figure is considerably below the 120 percent of the poverty level reached by the minimum wage in 1968.[55] For workers who were stuck with a minimum wage that was frozen from 1981 to 1989, the drop in earnings relative to the median income was significant, especially in light of the 40 percent rise in consumer prices during that period. Even with the current minimum wage of $4.25 an hour, it is $1.00 below its 1981 inflation-adjusted value. Furthermore, the $4.25 minimum wage is lower than the minimum was in every year from 1956 to 1986, after adjusting for inflation.[56] The gulf between the minimum wage and the poverty line is illustrated by Table 6.6.

At the heart of the minimum wage debate is the argument that increasing the minimum wage would cause employment opportunities, particularly for teenagers and young adults, to retract. While liberals counter that job-loss arguments are predicated on outmoded and incorrectly interpreted data,[57] the reality is that many young

and old Americans are working for wages that place them at $2,200 below the poverty line for a family of three. Some 18 million Americans—including 8 million children—live in a household with a working family member whose income remains below the poverty line.[58]

Another major factor determining poverty is under- and unemployment. Between 1981 and 1986, 10.8 million workers lost their jobs because of plant shutdowns, layoffs, or other forms of job termination. Five million of these workers had been at their jobs for at least three years.[59] From 1979 to 1984 the Department of Labor conducted a special study of 5.1 million workers whose jobs were abolished between January 1979 and January 1984. This study reported that in 1984, 40 percent of these workers were still unemployed or out of the work force. Of the remainder, close to half were employed at either part-time jobs or jobs with lower weekly earnings than they had previously received, and the majority experienced significant economic losses for a lengthy time after their jobs were terminated.[60]

Unemployment benefits reflect the nature of a selective recession that is disproportionately felt by the poor and lower-middle classes. Throughout most of the 1970s the majority of unemployed workers received unemployment benefits each month. For example, 75 percent of the jobless received benefits in 1975. By 1986, the percentage of unemployed workers receiving benefits had dropped to the lowest levels in the history of the program, with only 32.9 percent of jobless workers receiving benefits in a given month. Although the number of those covered under unemployment insurance rose slightly to 36.8 percent by 1990, 4.3 million of the 6.9 million unemployed workers were not receiving benefits.[61]

As the coverage has declined, so too have the benefits. In 1986 the total insurance benefits were 59 percent lower than they were in 1976 (after adjusting for inflation). These figures are complicated by the fact that from 1980 to 1986 the number of long-term unemployed (those looking for work for more than a year) rose from 820,000 to 1.2 million. These factors, coupled with federal budget cuts in 1981 that largely eliminated unemployment benefits for those unemployed for more than six months, contributed to the falling rates of unemployment coverage and the subsequent increase in poverty rates for the unemployed.

Above all else, the data suggest that the private sector is not at present creating the kinds of jobs necessary to raise large numbers of low-income workers above the poverty line. In order to remedy this situation, the Progressive Policy Institute has called for a non-poverty working wage that would be sufficient to enable any full-time, year-round worker to support a family above the poverty line. This proposal calls for restructuring the Earned Income Tax Credit (EITC) so that, in combination with Food Stamps, the poor working family will be lifted out of poverty. According to the PPI, this proposal will cost $7.8 billion ($3.8 billion for increased EITC benefits and an additional $4 billion to accommodate more Food Stamp beneficiaries), or slightly over one-half percent of the 1990 federal budget deficit.[62]

SOME THEORETICAL FORMULATIONS ABOUT POVERTY

In a tongue-in-cheek fashion, Herbert Gans lists 13 reasons for the existence of poverty in the United States: (1) The poor are expected to do the menial, dangerous, and dirty work that no one else wants to do; (2) the poor do the kind of work (domestic labor) that allows others to pursue more rewarding activities; (3) poverty creates jobs for the middle class (e.g., social workers, law officers, prison guards; (4) the poor buy old, defective, and used merchandise that no one else wants; (5) the poor are used as an object lesson to teach middle-class values (e.g., the poor are called lazy because the general society values hard work); (6) the poor allow the rest of society to live vicariously (i.e.,

the larger society is able to fantasize about the supposed world of the poor—free sex, drugs, alcoholic behavior), (7) the poor often contribute to unique cultural events such as music and dance; (8) the existence of poverty allows the upper classes to maintain their higher status in society; (9) the poor provide a lucrative market for illegal activities, thereby profiting some of the wealthy who are engaged in those businesses; (10) the poor provide a cause for the affluent who desire to pursue charity; (11) the poor bear the burden of economic growth (e.g., the razing of slums to make way for urban renewal); (12) the poor serve political functions (e.g., without the poor vote the Democratic party would lose much of its power); and (13) the poor function as a target for social criticism, thereby deflecting criticism away from the more affluent.[63]

The Culture of Poverty

A question that has plagued contemporary social scientists is, "Why have African Americans remained consistently poor when other groups, such as the Irish, Jews, and Poles, have been able to climb out of poverty?" The attempts made to answer this question have run the gamut from the alleged genetic deficiency of African Americans to the difficulty of African Americans in assimilating because of their color. Cultural, racial, and family explanations have all been touted as the correct answer at some point over the past 30 years.

One of the most controversial answers to this question was offered by Daniel Patrick Moynihan, now a U.S. senator from New York. In his 1969 book, *Maximum Feasible Misunderstanding*, Moynihan stated his argument:

> At the heart of the deterioration of the fabric of Negro society is the deterioration of the Negro family. It is the fundamental source of weakness for the Negro community at the present time. . . . The white family has achieved a high degree of stability.

By contrast, the family structure of lower class Negroes is highly unstable, and in many centers is approaching a complete breakdown! . . . the circumstances of the Negro community in recent years have been probably getting worse, not better . . . the fundamental problem, in which this is most clearly the case, is that of family structure . . . so long as this structure persists, the cycle of poverty and disadvantage will continue to repeat itself. . . . A national effort is required that will give a unity of purpose to the many activities of the federal government in this area, directed to a new kind of goal: the establishment of a stable Negro family structure.[64]

Moynihan maintained that the African-American family was ruptured both during slavery and at the beginning of the twentieth century, when the large migration of African Americans to the urban areas of the North occurred.[65] Prompted by the intense debate over the Moynihan report, Herbert Guttman demonstrated that the African-American family was not profoundly disrupted either during slavery or urban migration; instead, the problems of the contemporary African-American family were associated with modern forces.[66] In any case, Moynihan's perspective clearly located the problem of poverty within the fabric of African-American family life. For Moynihan, the problem of poverty lay in the matriarchal African-American family: The supposed emasculation of the African-American male by a strong matriarch coupled with the absence of powerful African-American men as role models for youngsters contributed to an identity problem for male teenagers, a problem that would play itself out in terms of crime and violence. Outraged by Moynihan's analysis, African-American leaders launched an attack on his pseudopsychoanalytic explanation of African-American family life. What emerges from the speculation about the causes of African-American poverty is an understanding that its causes are complex and rooted in the social, political, and economic realities of contemporary America. In some measure, Moynihan's theories grew out of an earlier belief that America's urban landscape was dominated by a culture of poverty.

Another group, the culture of poverty (COP) theorists, maintain that poverty and, more specifically, poverty traits are transmitted intergenerationally. These theorists, led by Edward Banfield and Oscar Lewis, argued that poverty is a way of life passed on from generation to generation in a self-perpetuating cycle. The COP, according to this theory, transcends regional, rural/urban, and national differences, and everywhere shows striking similarities in family structure, interpersonal relations, time orientation, value systems, and patterns of spending.[67]

Oscar Lewis maintains that the culture of poverty flourishes in societies where (1) there is a cash economy, wage labor, and production for profit; (2) a high rate of under- and unemployment for unskilled workers exists; (3) low wages are common; (4) there is a failure to provide low-income groups with social, political, and economic organization, either on a voluntary basis or by governmental imposition; (5) a bilateral kinship system rather than a unilateral one exists; and (6) a set of values held by the dominant class stresses the accumulation of wealth and property, the possibility of upward mobility, thrift, and the idea that low economic status results from personal inadequacy.

According to Lewis, this culture is characterized by: (1) hopelessness, indifference, alienation, apathy, and a lack of effective participation in or integration into the social and economic fabric of society; (2) a present-tense time orientation; (3) cynicism toward and mistrust of those in authority; (4) strong feelings of marginality, helplessness, dependence, and inferiority; (5) a high incidence of maternal deprivation, orality, and a weak ego structure; (6) confusion of sexual identification; (7) lack of impulse control and the inability to defer gratification; (8) a sense of resignation and fatalism; (9) a widespread belief in male superiority; (10) a high tolerance for psychological pathology of all kinds; (11) a provincialism coupled with little sense of history; (12) the absence of childhood as a specially protected and prolonged state, and thus early initiation into free sexual unions or consensual marriages; (13) a high incidence in the abandonment of wives and children; (14) a matriarchal family structure containing an emphasis on family solidarity that is never achieved because of sibling rivalry and competition for maternal affection; (15) a proclivity toward authoritarianism; and (16) a minimum level of organization beyond the nuclear or extended family, a low level of community organization, and a strong sense of territoriality.

Adherents of the COP theory believe that simply being poor does not initiate one into the culture of poverty. Banfield and Lewis both believe that most people who experience poverty through the loss of a breadwinner, involuntary unemployment, or illness are able to overcome their impoverishment. The poverty that these people endure is not the squalid, degrading, and self-perpetuating kind found among COP victims. Lewis suggests that only 20 percent of those living under the poverty line are actually ensconced in the culture of poverty. Nevertheless, according to Banfield, those who are in the culture of poverty will be poor regardless of their external circumstances, and improvements in their environment will only superficially affect their poverty.

Some opponents of these beliefs argue that this theoretical orientation diverts attention from the real factors that cause poverty. These critics maintain that an unjust society encourages the attitudes that Lewis and Banfield have observed. Other critics argue that many of Lewis's observations about the COP are also true of the middle and upper classes. For example, the inability to defer gratification underlies many credit card purchases. Free sexual unions and consensual (nonlegal) marriages are a common occurrence among the middle classes and are especially publicized in Hollywood. A lack

of community and provincialism are earmarks of the modern suburb as well as of the slum. The inability to achieve family solidarity, and feelings of indifference, helplessness, alienation, and dependence probably afflict middle-class people as often as they do the slum dweller. Consequently, either a culture of poverty does not exist or it has been usurped by the middle classes in the same way that marijuana and jazz have been. An updated variation on the COP theme has emerged in the formulation of a new American underclass.

The Underclass

The current discussion of the underclass was started in the 1980s by journalist Ken Auletta, who descriptively identified four groups that comprise the underclass: (1) the "passive poor," usually those dependent on welfare; (2) hostile "street predators," often dropouts and addicts; (3) "hustlers," or opportunists, who do not commit violent crimes; and (4) "traumatized" alcoholics, shopping bag ladies, and casualties of deinstitutionalization.[68] In the late 1980s, William Julius Wilson revived the term and defined the underclass as:

> [a] heterogeneous grouping of families and individuals who are outside of the mainstream of the American occupational system. Included . . . are individuals who lack training and skills and either experience long-term unemployment or are not members of the labor force, individuals who are engaged in street crime and other forms of aberrant behavior, and families that experience long-term spells of poverty and/or welfare dependency.[69]

Wilson is currently promoting a definition of the underclass that is based on the work of Martha Van Haitsma, who defines it as "those persons who are weakly connected to the formal labor force and whose social context tends to maintain or further weaken this attachment."[70]

Another definition of the underclass is offered by Erol Ricketts and Isabel Sawhill, who define it as a subpopulation characterized by a cluster of behaviors and attitudes that are considered outside of current middle-class social norms.[71] In *The Black Underclass,* Douglas Glasgow attributed the existence of an underclass to "structural factors found in market dynamics and institutional practices, as well as the legacy of racism, [that] produce and then reinforce the cycle of poverty and, in turn, work as a downward pull toward underclass status."[72] These groups share characteristics that, according to Robert Reischauer of the Brookings Institution, differentiate them from "lower-class" status, with its connotation of merely being further down on the socioeconomic ladder.[73]

The definitions of the underclass fall into two broad categories: those used by the structuralists (Wilson, Van Hatisma) and those used by the behavioralists (Sawhill, Ricketts). The structuralists view the underclass as emerging from broad societal forces that cause neighborhoods to deteriorate and economic opportunities to evaporate. For example, according to Wilson, the emergence of an underclass is related to changing employment opportunities (reduced demand for low-skilled labor), declines in African-American marriage rates, and selective outmigration (the movement of the African-American middle class away from the urban ghettoes). This sociological concept is used as a referent for disadvantaged persons living in Census tracks with abnormally high rates of dysfunctional family and employment conditions. The structuralists argue that those left behind in the ghetto are outside the economic opportunity structure, and as such, structural poverty generates cultural poverty. The behavioralists, on the other hand, focus on individuals and categorize them on the basis of their behaviors.[74]

A more precise definition of the term *underclass* is hard to come by, and this leads to a set of difficult conceptual problems. Specifi-

cally, the absence of a clear operational definition for the underclass results in its taking on an air of subjectivity. In other words, although people may not be able to define the underclass, they believe that they know it when they see it. For example, proponents of the underclass concept point to the "wilding" of New York teenagers who savagely beat and raped a female jogger in Central Park, an event replicated when a gang of Boston youths raped and murdered a young mother.[75] Moreover, they point to gang killings in Los Angeles, which soared 69 percent during the first eight months of 1990.[76] They also point to gang-related murders in the nation's capital, which reached a three-year high, and prompted the police department's spokesperson to quip, "at the rate we're going the next generation is going to be extinct."[77] But while these events make for interesting journalism, the ambiguity of what is meant by the *underclass* produces problems for policymakers trying to operationalize the term in order to develop social programs for this group.

Despite problems in defining the underclass, relevant social science research has shown that this group increased from 1970 to 1980. Moreover, some researchers have estimated that in 1980 between one and two million people could be characterized as members of the underclass. According to Ricketts and Sawhill, who are considered to have done some of the best empirical research on the subject, the definition of underclass applies to 1 percent of the American population, roughly one-thirteenth of all people living under the poverty line. Using Ricketts and Sawhill's guidelines, over 2.4 million people would be classified as an underclass in 1992.[78]

The seriousness of the underclass phenomenon was underscored in research conducted by David Ellwood and Mary Jo Bane. In an examination of the Michigan Panel Study of Income Dynamics, Bane and Ellwood discovered that, although most people are in poverty for short periods of time, a significant number have protracted spells in poverty. Table 6.7 shows the

TABLE 6.7. Spells of Poverty for Nonelderly Persons by Percentage

Spell Length in Years	Persons Beginning a Spell at Any Time during Survey	Persons Observed to be Poor at Any Point during Survey
1	41.1	9.7
2–3	27.7	15.5
4–7	13.2	15.8
8+	18.0	59.1
Total	100.0	100.0
Average (years)	4.2	11.0

SOURCE: Reprinted from Committee on Ways and Means, U.S. House of Representatives, *Children in Poverty* (Washington, D.C.: Government Printing Office, May 22, 1985), p. 46.

experiences of people in poverty for varying lengths of time. Significantly, 18 percent of poverty is long-term, and almost 60 percent of the people who are poor at any given time are experiencing a long-term spell of poverty. When the costs of this poverty are borne by minority families who are disproportionately poor, the consequences are disastrous. Since 1970, poor urban families have been more likely to have poor neighbors, evidence of a continuing deterioration in the socioeconomic condition of poor communities that makes it increasingly difficult to alleviate the pathology of "ghetto culture."[79]

Eugenics and Poverty

Eugenic theories, based on a belief that poverty is grounded in genetic inferiority, have surfaced periodically as plausible explanations for poverty, crime, and disease. In 1877 Richard Dugdale wrote *The Jukes*, a study of the New York penal system which found that crime, pauperism, and disease were transmitted intergenerationally and were closely related to prurient behavior, feeblemindedness, intemperance, and mental disorder.[80] A second major book of the eugenics movement was Henry Goddard's *The Kallikak Family*, an account of a Revolutionary War soldier who had an affair with a feeble-minded servant girl before his marriage to a "respectable woman."[81] As part of his analysis, Goddard meticulously listed the disreputable

descendants of the servant girl and compared them with the respectable achievers who emerged from the wife's descendants. Dugdale's and Goddard's findings were reaffirmed by similar pseudoscientific research that further established poverty as an inherited characteristic. Generations of students were taught the dogma of eugenics.

The eugenics movement went into remission when it became obvious to what extent racial and genetic theories had formed the groundwork for Hitler's genocidal policies. However, the movement reemerged after close to 40 years—albeit in a modified form—with the publication in 1969 of Arthur Jensen's article, "How Much Can We Boost IQ and Scholastic Achievement."[82] Jensen concluded that compensatory education was doomed to failure because 80 percent of intelligence (as measured by intelligence tests) was inherited. He pointed to the fact that the average IQ scores of African Americans were 15 points lower than the scores of their white counterparts, and concluded therefore that money spent on compensatory education was wasted.[83]

Jensen's theories were taken one step further by William Shockley, a Nobel laureate in physics who became interested in genetics in 1974. Shockley advocated paying the "unfit poor" (those who paid no income taxes) $1,000 for each point they fell below an IQ of 100, if they agreed to be sterilized. The money they received would be placed in a trust fund and dispensed to them throughout their lives.[84] To encourage the propagation of brilliant people like himself, Shockley invited other Nobel Laureates to follow his lead and contribute to a sperm bank.[85]

Richard Herrnstein, a Harvard psychologist and a colleague of Shockley and Jensen, claimed that income and wealth are distributed among Americans on the basis of their abilities, which, in the final analysis, are related to their IQ. Herrnstein maintained that America was becoming a "hereditary meritocracy," and thought that the most capable citizens should receive the greatest rewards, which would serve as incentives to them to take the responsibility of leadership.[86]

The theories of Shockley, Jensen, and Herrnstein have been repudiated by dozens of educators, psychologists, sociologists, and anthropologists. Critics claim that IQ scores do not guarantee success in life and that many incarcerated criminals in fact have high IQ scores. Moreover, several studies have shown that compensatory education does significantly raise IQ scores.[87] Finally, a variety of studies have found that IQ tests are biased in favor of middle-class and upper-socioeconomic-level students. In short, assertions about genetic inferiority fail to hold up under scrutiny.

The Radical School and Poverty

Another school of thought takes a radical approach. Radicals define poverty as the result of exploitation by the ruling or dominant class. According to Marxians, one function of poverty is that it provides capitalists with an army of surplus laborers who can be used as a means to depress the wage structure of society. For example, the law of supply and demand as applied to the wage marketplace means that employers can use an oversupply of workers to offer only low wages in the knowledge that there will always be an abundance of takers. Moreover, when there is an oversupply of labor, employers

can more easily threaten recalcitrant workers with dismissal because each worker is aware of the competition for his or her job. The oversupply of workers is inextricably linked to the fabric of poverty and, as such, poverty inadvertently becomes a way of disciplining the labor force and thereby forcing concessions from it that might otherwise not be made.

A second function of poverty is to increase the prestige of the middle class by providing a class directly below it. As long as an underclass exists, the middle class has a group it can feel superior to. The superiority felt by the middle class encourages a bond with the upper class around the issue of social stability because both classes fear the loss of their social position. Inadvertently, the existence of the poor obscures the class tensions between the upper class and the middle class over the issue of resource distribution. In that sense, the best way to defuse a conflict between two potential enemies is to create a third enemy (the poor), one that appears to threaten both parties.

According to David Gil, poverty can also be understood in the light of status and resource allocation and the division of labor.[88] Most developed societies must perform several universal processes. For instance, they must develop resources—symbolic, material, life-sustaining, and life-enhancing goods and services. They must also develop a division of labor, which is usually related to the allocation of statuses, as well as assign individuals or groups to specific tasks related to developing, producing, or distributing the resources of a society. The division of labor is used as the basis for assigning statuses to individuals and groups; that is, the more highly the society prizes the function the individual or group is expected to perform, the higher the status and the reward for it will be. By manipulating the division of labor a society is able to assign individuals to specific statuses within the total array of statuses and functions available. These status allocations involve corresponding roles and prerogatives.

Complementing the assignment of status

roles is the issue of rights distribution. Higher-status roles implicitly demand greater compensation than lower-status roles, and such rewards come by way of the distribution of rights. Higher-status groups are rewarded by a substantial and liberal distribution of specific rights to material and symbolic resources, goods, and services through general entitlements. Conversely, lower-status groups are denied these resources by formal and informal constraints. The entire process is couched in the language of the marketplace. This form of status and goods allocation is rationalized by a belief in the omniscient quality of the marketplace, and, so as to make it appear rational, the market is mystically endowed with an internal sense of logic. The implicit ideology is so well masked that it often appears fail-safe, and its rationality is rarely questioned.

Although it often appears to do so inequitably, society must allocate goods and statuses because all valuable resources are finite, with their worth judged by the available quantity. For example, gold is a valuable commodity because its quantity is limited. In that sense, opportunity is a valuable commodity because it, too, is limited. Harvard is a prestigious institution in part because it accepts only a certain number of students yearly, and its policy of admissions is thought to be stringent. Should Harvard adopt an open-door admissions policy, one might expect its prestige to plummet. High-status occupations or social positions are also a scarce commodity and thus are socially distributed.

The question remains as to how these statuses are distributed and how the division of labor is determined. In American society, both the division of labor and status allocation—and their by-product, the distribution of rights—are differentially determined by sex, race, and social class. In large part, those occupying high-status positions determine their successors and, more often than not, the heirs apparent belong to the same social class.

Poverty is a logical outgrowth of an inequitable system of resource, status, and rights distri-

bution. Those who live in poverty have been assigned specific social tasks and roles, and the status of the group often corresponds to the nature of the task. Through the assignment of status, role, and rights distribution, societies attempt to reproduce themselves and the ideologies that justify them. In the end, the main job of any society is to reproduce itself and, in doing so, it often reproduces the relations of production and power.

Although on the surface this argument appears to explain social inequity, it does not necessarily explain poverty. For example, is it possible for status allocation to be based on the need of a society to reproduce itself, and yet for that society to obviate poverty? Adherents of the radical approach argue that so long as society reproduces itself on the basis of the private ownership of the means of production, poverty will be omnipresent. On the other hand, many radical theorists argue that even though status must be allocated, poverty can still be eliminated through the equitable distribution of goods and resources. But although it may be possible to eradicate poverty and, at the same time, allocate status, most radicals doubt that it can be done under the aegis of capitalism.

According to radical critics, the social function of the poor cannot be altered without a basic rearrangement of the social fabric of American society. In short, poverty is an immutable reality in a society marked by discrimination and the inequitable distribution of resources.

A NOTE ON STRATEGIES DEVELOPED TO COMBAT POVERTY

Social scientists and policy analysts have identified three basic strategies for combating poverty. The first strategy, used by Lyndon Johnson in the War on Poverty and Great Society programs, was an attempt to apply a curative approach to the problems of the poor. The curative strategy aims to end the cycle of poverty by allowing the poor to become self-supporting through bringing about changes in their personal lives as well as in their environment. By breaking the self-perpetuating cycle of poverty, the poor are initiated into the working class and, later, the middle class. The goal of the curative perspective is rehabilitation rather than relief, and its target is the causes of poverty, not the consequences.

The second antipoverty strategy is the alleviative approach. This perspective is best exemplified by public assistance programs that attempt to ease the suffering of the poor rather than ameliorate the causes of poverty.

The third approach is the preventive strategy, best exemplified by the nation's social insurance programs (Social Security). In this approach, people are required to save money to insure their future against accidents, sickness, death, old age, unemployment, and disability. The preventive strategy sees the state as a large insurance company whose umbrella shelters its productive members against the vicissitudes of life.

In 1958 John Kenneth Galbraith, later to become one of John F. Kennedy's principal economic advisers, wrote *The Affluent Society*. In this landmark book, Galbraith identified two kinds of poverty: case poverty and area poverty. According to Galbraith, case poverty was a product of personal deficiency, or deficit in human capital. Area poverty was related to economic problems endemic to a region. "Pockets of poverty" or "depressed areas" resulted from a lack of industrialization in a region or the inability of an area to adjust to technological change. This kind of poverty was a function of the changing nature of the marketplace.[89]

One example of a case poverty approach is the federal government's attempts to encourage education as a means of increasing human capital. Poverty is highly correlated with educational deficits, and adolescent parenthood is strongly associated with low levels of basic skills and high dropout rates. For example, youths with the weakest reading and math skills are eight times as likely to have children out of wedlock and seven times as likely to drop out of high school as are students with above-average skills.[90] To help address the educational deficits of the poor, the federal government instituted the Head Start program that was targeted at poor children aged three to five and their families. The High/Scope Educational Research Foundation's 20-year follow-up study of Head Start (and similar preschool) graduates found that they were more likely to complete high school, receive additional vocational or academic training, be employed, be self-supporting, have fewer problems with the law, have lower instances of teenage pregnancy, and not to become public assistance recipients than were nonparticipants in the preschool programs.[91]

The reality of area poverty becomes obvious when examining the poverty demographics on a state-by-state basis. In 1990 the poverty rate for all persons in the United States was 13.5 percent. Some states, however, had much higher poverty rates, including Louisiana (23.6 percent), the District of Columbia (21.1 percent), West Virginia (18.1 percent), Alabama (19.2 percent), Mississippi (25.7 percent), Arkansas (19.6 percent), Kentucky (17.3 percent), and New Mexico (20.9 percent). By contrast, states such as New Hampshire (6.3 percent), Rhode Island (7.5 percent), Connecticut (6.0 percent), and Delaware (6.9 percent) had poverty rates below the national norm.[92] Depressed states such as Arkansas, Mississippi, Alabama, and West Virginia, among others, traditionally experience a recession regardless of the economic prosperity enjoyed by the rest of the nation.

The three approaches to poverty just discussed are not merely hypothetical formulations; they formed the basis for social welfare policy throughout much of the 1960s and beyond. Between 1965 and 1980, social welfare policies were grounded in the view that public expenditures should be used as a direct means of stimulating opportunities for the poor. As a result, major social welfare legislation was enacted and billions of dollars earmarked for the remediation of poverty. Beginning with the Reagan administration in 1980 (and later with the Bush presidency), there was a move away from reliance on social welfare expenditures to an emphasis on ending poverty through economic growth. Consequently, public expenditures for poverty programs decreased as tax cuts to provide incentives to work and save money increased (i.e., the Earned Income Tax Credit program). The Reagan approach assumed that it would be more in the interests of the poor to wait for gains realized through increased economic activity than to rely on welfare programs. This perspective assumed that the trickle-down effect of economic growth would benefit the poor more than direct economic subsidies would. However, according to analyst Kevin Phillips, "Low-income families, especially the working poor, lost appreciably more by cuts in government services than they gained in tax reductions."[93] Despite the emphasis on eradicating poverty through market incomes, the major factors influencing the general decrease in poverty from the 1960s to the late 1970s were governmental cash and in-kind transfers.[94]

Because poverty is a political as well as a social issue, the policies surrounding it are often less than objective. For example, one can cut the rate of poverty in half simply by redefining the poverty index. Conversely, one can swell the ranks of the poor by moving the poverty line upward, that is, by increasing the income level at which people are defined as poor. Poverty can also be technically eliminated by placing a high dollar value on in-kind benefits such as Food Stamps and Medicaid. Like all social policies, poverty-related policies exist in a context marked by political exigencies, public opinion, the economic health of a society, and the complex mask of ideology.

DISCUSSION QUESTIONS

1. The measurement of poverty is at once both complex and controversial. Nevertheless, the way in which poverty is measured has important implications for the development of social policy in America. Describe some of the potential pitfalls in measuring poverty rates and discuss how the calculation of poverty rates affects the creation of social policy.

2. Economic and social indicators suggest that when compared to similar countries, the United States ranks poorly in terms of overall poverty rates, health indicators, and child welfare. What are the main causes of this low ranking? Can and should the United States concentrate on improving its ranking?

3. Income inequality is often seen as an important causative factor in determining poverty. Is inequality in incomes a cause or a symptom of poverty? What specific policy initiatives can be undertaken to narrow income inequality or to lessen its effects?

4. Working families comprise a growing and important segment of the poor. What are some of the causes of the increase in the numbers of working poor as a percentage of the total population in poverty? What specific policies could be implemented to lessen the numbers of working poor families?

5. A number of theories have been advanced to explain why some individuals and groups of people are poor while others are not. Theorists who have tried to tackle this problem include Daniel Patrick Moynihan, Oscar Lewis, and Edward Banfield, among others. Although all these theories of poverty have intrinsic flaws, which theory (or combination of theories) described in this book or elsewhere do you think best explains the dynamics of poverty?

6. Over the past several years an intense debate has arisen over the existence of an underclass in American society. Some critics claim that there is little real evidence to prove the existence of an underclass as a *distinct* subgroup of people in poverty. These critics argue that what is referred to as an underclass is merely a normal group of very poor people. Others argue that the evidence points to the existence of a distinct subgroup of poor peo-

ple who indeed qualify as an underclass. According to these critics, these people have values and behaviors that are so at odds with those of the mainstream that they qualify as a distinct subgroup of the poor. Is there an underclass in America? If so, what kinds of values and behaviors do they exhibit that qualify them as a special subgroup of the poor?

7. Many strategies have been developed to fight poverty, including the curative approach, the alleviative approach, and the preventive approach. Of these strategies, which is the most effective in fighting poverty and why? What alternative strategies, if any, could be developed that would be more efficacious in combating poverty?

NOTES

1. Blanche Bernstein, "Welfare Dependency," in Lee D. Bawden, ed., *The Social Contract Revisited* (Washington, D.C.: Urban Institute Press, 1984), p. 129.
2. Greg J. Duncan et al., *Years of Poverty, Years of Plenty* (Ann Arbor, Mich.: Institute for Social Research, 1984).
3. William O'Hare, Taynia Mann, Kathryn Porter, and Robert Greenstein, *Real Life Poverty in America: Where the Public Would Set the Poverty Line* (Washington,D.C.: Center on Budget and Policy Priorities, and Families USA Foundation Report, July 1990), p. viii.
4. *Federal Register*, vol. 5, no. 46 (Washington, D.C.: U.S. Government Printing Office, March 20, 1987), p. 9518.
5. Committee on Ways and Means, U.S. House of Representatives, *Overview of Entitlement Programs: 1992 Green Book* (Washington, D.C.: U.S. Government Printing Office, 1992), p. 1272.
6. O'Hare et al., *Real Life Poverty in America*, p. vii.
7. Ibid., p. 6.
8. Ibid., p. 8.
9. Ibid., p. vi.
10. Center on Budget and Policy Priorities, "Number in Poverty Hits 20-Year High as Recession Adds 2 Million More Poor, Analysis Finds" (Washington, D.C.: Center on Budget and Policy Priorities, September 3, 1992), n.p.
11. Isaac Shapiro, *White Poverty in America* (Washington, D.C.: Center on Budget and Policy Priorities, 1992), pp. 8–9.
12. Ibid., p. vii.
13. Ibid., pp. 8–9.
14. Ibid., p. 17.
15. U.S. House of Representatives, *1992 Green Book*, p. 1072.
16. Children's Defense Fund, *The State of America's Children* (Washington, D.C.: Children's Defense Fund, 1991), pp. 23–24.
17. *Congressional Record*, Senate, vol. 133, no. 120 (Washington, D.C.: U.S. Government Printing Office, July 21, 1987), pp. S10400-S10404.
18. Children's Defense Fund, *The State of America's Children*, pp. 23–24.
19. Shapiro, *White Poverty*, pp. 8–9.
20. National Commission on Children, "Poverty, Welfare and America's Families: A Hard Look" (Washington, D.C., National Commission on Children, n.d.), p. 5.
21. Elaine Ciulla Kamarck and William A. Galston, *Putting Children First: A Progressive Family Policy for the 1990s* (Washington, D.C.: The Progressive Policy Institute, September 27, 1990), pp. 22–25.
22. American Association of Retired Persons, "A Profile of Older Americans" (Washington, D.C.: AARP, 1991), n.p.
23. O'Hare et al., *Real Life Poverty in America*, p. 9.
24. Kathryn Porter, *Poverty in Rural America* (Washington, D.C.: Center on Budget and Policy Priorities, 1989), pp. 3–11.
25. Ibid.
26. Letter, September 8, 1992, from J. Larry Brown, director of the Tufts University School of Nutrition, to the Hon. Tony Hall, chairman of the House Select Committee on Hunger, Washington, D.C.
27. Shapiro, *White Poverty*, pp. 10–11.
28. This poverty rate is based on the threshold set by the Luxembourg Income Study. Thus, it does not always *exactly* mirror the official poverty rate used by the Census Bureau.
29. Shapiro, *White Poverty*, pp. 10–11.

30. Children's Defense Fund, *The State of America's Children*, p. 137.

31. Ibid., pp. 137–42.

32. Sheldon Danziger, "Poverty," *Encyclopedia of Social Work,* 18th ed. (Silver Spring, Md.: NASW, 1987), pp. 295, 297.

33. Sheldon Danziger and David Feaster, "Income Transfers and Poverty in the 1980s," in J. Quigley and D. Rubinfeld, eds., *Agenda for Metropolitan America* (Berkeley, Calif.: University of California Press, 1985), p. 126.

34. Isaac Shapiro and Robert Greenstein, *Selective Prosperity: Increasing Income Disparities Since 1977* (Washington, D.C.: Center on Budget and Policy Priorities, July 1991), p. 4.

35. Ibid., pp. vii–viii.

36. U.S. House of Representatives, *1992 Green Book*, p. 1568.

37. Lawrence Mishel and David M. Frankel, *The State of Working America* (Armonk, N.Y.: M. E. Sharpe, Inc., 1991), p. 24.

38. Ibid., p. 22.

39. Center on Budget and Policy Priorities, "Analysis of Poverty in 1987" (Washington, D.C.: Center on Budget and Policy Priorities, 1988), p. 11.

40. Mishel and Frankel, *The State of Working America*, p. 169.

41. See Michael Sherraden, *Stakeholding: A New Direction in Social Policy* (Washington, D.C.: Progressive Policy Institute, 1990); and Michael Sherraden, *Assets and the Poor* (Armonk, N.Y.: M. E. Sharpe, Inc., 1991).

42. Robert S. McIntyre, "The Populist Tax Act of 1986," *The Nation*, April 2, 1988, p. 445.

43. Quoted in Scott Barancik and Isaac Shapiro, *Where Have All the Dollars Gone?* (Washington, D.C: Center on Budget and Policy Priorities, August 1992), p. xvi.

44. Shapiro and Greenstein, *Selective Prosperity*, pp. 18–19.

45. National Commission on Children, "Poverty, Welfare and America's Families," p. 3.

46. Mishel and Frankel, *The State of Working America*, p. 48.

47. Robert S. McIntyre, Michael Ettlinger, Douglas P. Kelly, and Elizabeth A. Fray, *A Cry From Afar* (Washington, D.C.: Citizens for Tax Justice, 1991), p. 18.

48. Isaac Shapiro and Robert Greenstein, *Holes in the Safety Nets* (Washington, D.C.: Center on Budget and Policy Priorities, 1988), pp. 27–28.

49. U.S. House of Representatives, *1992 Green Book*, pp. 1488–90.

50. Ibid., pp. 25–27.

51. Center on Budget and Policy Priorities, "Number in Poverty Hits 20-Year High," p. 4.

52. Mishel and Frankel, *The State of Working America*, p. 183.

53. Michael Harrington, with the assistance of Robert Greenstein and Eleanor Holmes Norton, *Who Are the Poor?* (Washington, D.C.: Justice for All, National Office, 1987), p. 10.

54. Donald L. Bartlett and James B. Steele, *America: What Went Wrong* (Kansas City, Mo.: Andrews and McMeel, 1992), p. 18.

55. Isaac Shapiro, *The Minimum Wage and Job Loss* (Washington, D.C.: Center on Budget and Policy Priorities, 1988).

56. Center on Budget and Policy Priorities, "The Bush Administration's Minimum Wage Proposal" (Washington, D.C., March 31, 1989).

57. Ibid.

58. Center on Budget and Policy Priorities, "Many Black and Hispanic Workers Harmed by Minimum Wage Bill Veto, Analysis Finds" (Washington, D.C.: Center on Budget and Policy Priorities, June 15, 1989).

59. Harrington, *Who Are the Poor?* p. 10.

60. Center on Budget and Policy Priorities, *Smaller Pieces of the Pie* (Washington, D.C.: Center on Budget and Policy Priorities, 1987).

61. Center on Budget and Policy Priorities, *Unemployed and Uninsured* (Washington, D.C.: Center on Budget and Policy Priorities, March 1991), p. 4.

62. Robert J. Shapiro, "An American Working Wage: Ending Poverty in Working Families," *Policy Report*, No. 3. (Washington, D.C.: Progressive Policy Institute, February 1990), p. 1.

63. Herbert J. Gans, "The Uses of Poverty: The Poor Pay All," *Social Policy* 2, no. 2 (July/August 1971): 20–24.

64. Daniel Patrick Moynihan, *Maximum Feasible Misunderstanding* (New York: The Free Press, 1969), p. 61.

65. Daniel Patrick Moynihan, *The Negro Family: The Case for National Action* (Washington, D.C.: Office of Policy Planning and Research, U.S. Department of Labor, 1965).

66. Herbert G. Guttman, *The Black Family in Slavery and Freedom, 1750–1925* (New York: Pantheon, 1976).

67. See Edward C. Banfield, *The Unheavenly City* (Boston: Little, Brown, 1966); and Oscar Lewis, *La Vida* (New York: Harper and Row, 1965).

68. Ken Auletta, *The Underclass,* (New York: Vintage, 1982), p. xvi.

69. William Julius Wilson, *The Truly Disadvantaged* (Chicago: University of Chicago Press, 1987), p. 8.

70. William R. Prosser, "The Underclass: Assessing What We Have Learned," *Focus* 13, no. 2 (Summer 1991): 2.

71. Erol Ricketts and Isabel Sawhill, "Defining and Measuring the Underclass," *Journal of Policy Analysis and Management* 7, no. 2 (Winter 1988): 316–25.

72. Douglas Glasgow, *The Black Underclass* (New York: Vintage, 1981), p. 4.

73. Robert Reischauer, "America's Underclass," *Public Welfare* 45, no. 4, (Fall 1987): 28.

74. See Prosser, "The Underclass," p. 3.

75. "Eight Boston Teenagers Charged in Savage Slaying of Young Mother," *Los Angeles Times,* November 21, 1990, p. A–4.

76. Louis Sahagun, "Gang Killings Increase 69%, Violent Crime Up 20% in L.A. County Areas," *Los Angeles Times,* August 21, 1990, p. B–8.

77. Gabriel Escobar, "Slayings in Washington Hit New High, 436, for 3rd Year," *Los Angeles Times,* November 24, 1990, p. A–26.

78. Kathleen Heffernan Vickland, "Is There an Underclass: No," in Howard Jacob Karger and James Midgley, eds., *Controversial Issues in So-cial Policy* (New York: Allyn and Bacon, forthcoming 1993).

79. Christopher Jencks, "Deadly Neighborhoods," *The New Republic,* June 13, 1988, p. 30.

80. Richard Dugdale, *The Jukes* (New York: G. P. Putnam's Sons, 1910).

81. Henry Goddard, *The Kallikak Family* (New York: Arno Publishers, 1911).

82. Arthur R. Jensen, "How Much Can We Boost IQ and Scholastic Achievement," *Harvard Educational Review* 39 (Winter 1969): 1–23.

83. Winifred Bell, *Contemporary Social Welfare* (New York: Macmillan, 1983), p. 261.

84. William Shockley, "Sterilization: A Thinking Exercise," in Carl Bahema, ed., *Eugenics: Then and Now* (Stroudsburg, Pa.: Doidon, Hutchinson and Ross, 1976).

85. Bell, *Contemporary Social Welfare,* p. 263.

86. Richard Herrnstein, *IQ and the Meritocracy* (Boston: Little, Brown, 1973).

87. Bell, *Contemporary Social Welfare,* p. 264.

88. David Gil, *Unraveling Social Policy* (Boston: Schenkman, 1981).

89. John Kenneth Galbraith, *The Affluent Society* (Boston: Houghton Mifflin, 1958).

90. Harrington, *Who Are the Poor?* p. 17.

91. Ibid., p. 22.

92. Christine M. Ross, "Poverty Rates by State, 1979 and 1985: A Research Note," *Focus* 10, no. 3 (Fall 1987): 1–5.

93. Kevin Phillips, *The Politics of Rich and Poor* (New York: Random House, 1990), p. 87.

94. Danziger, "Poverty," pp. 301–302.

CHAPTER 7

Issues in Social Service Delivery

This chapter assesses current problems in the provision of social services. Inevitably, conflicting goals between professional and organizational responsibilities result in tensions that social workers must reconcile if they are to be effective. Inherent problems in the delivery of social services that affect both clients and social workers have led to calls for major changes in service provision. This chapter evaluates three alternatives for enhancing the delivery of human services: unionization, privatization, and restructuring.

Although many chapters of this text examine macrolevel social policy, most social work practitioners have to reckon with the consequences of broad policy by negotiating microlevel social policies in their workplaces. Often, these organizational policies run counter to what social workers believe to be in the best interests of their clients, coworkers, and the community. Thus, policies within the organizational setting have a significant influence on the experience of social workers and may contribute or not to the overall dilemma of how to fulfill both professional and organizational expectations. The need to accommodate professional responsibilities and organizational commitments may result in an ambiguous situation and a push-pull between these often conflicting

roles. How individual social workers resolve this difficult situation is dependent on the values of the worker and the context in which he or she operates. Because social work ethics are necessarily broad—and often vague—their actual application is usually open to interpretation and in some measure is subjective.

BUREAUCRACY AND THE DELIVERY OF SOCIAL SERVICES

Early social work was a voluntary and philanthropic endeavor characterized by little formal organization. By the 1920s, however, Frederick Taylor and others had introduced into the workplace scientific management, a system that emphasized the most economical use of energy to accomplish a given task. Efficiency became the creed of scientific managers, and each step in the production process was designed to be as efficient as possible. Business leaders who strongly influenced Community Chests—the forerunners of the United Way—attempted to apply these Tayloristic notions to the management of social services. As such, voluntary social services were expected to be efficient enterprises run by professional managers.

Eventually, most private and public social

services came to be operated as bureaucratic structures. In a bureaucratic pyramid, most employees are at the bottom (the widest point); as the pyramid narrows there are fewer employees, and, at the top, only a few managers and a chief executive. According to the principle of horizontal integration, each level of the bureaucracy is responsible for specific tasks and organizational functions, and each level is accountable to the one directly above it. In an efficient bureaucracy, each level is intimately aware of the tasks, goals, and effectiveness of the level beneath it. In social welfare, bureaucracies produce services, and they do this by differentiating units for specific purposes. According to the principle of vertical integration, each division is responsible for specialized activities, and divisions should coordinate their respective functions. The main job of the chief executive is to manage the bureaucracy, chiefly by attending to problems, coordinating horizontal and vertical integration, and maintaining the organization. By controlling what Max Weber called "the means of administration," the executive and his or her lieutenants have a great deal of power. A less predictable responsibility of bureaucratic executives is to maintain constructive relations with external elements in the greater community. Most social service agencies have adopted bureaucratic forms of organization because of the scope, complexity, and size of their operations.

Problems in the Delivery of Social Services

The evolution of social programs in the decades following the passage of the Social Security Act in 1935 led many social welfare professionals to observe a progression in how services were delivered to populations in need. By the 1970s, policy and program officers spoke frequently of "social service delivery systems," noting the steady advance in program coverage as well as in outreach efforts to address outlying populations eligible for benefits. Such frequent usage led Neil Gilbert and Harry Specht to define so-

cial service delivery systems as "the organizational arrangements among distributors and between distributors and consumers of social welfare benefits in the context of the local community."[1]

By the early 1990s, social program advocates were less sanguine about the extent to which social service delivery was "systematic." The Reagan era had taken a punishing toll on social program benefits, including how these were to be delivered. In one noteworthy tactic, the conversion of categorical grants under Title XX of the Social Security Act to the Social Services Block Grant reduced fiscal allocations 22 percent. The devolution of responsibility for programs from the federal government to states, coupled with a tenacious budget deficit, compounded the problems in maintaining the service delivery effort because many states labored under acute fiscal crises of their own. As social programs deteriorated, social service delivery "systems" were plagued by four major problems: (1) fragmentation, (2) discontinuity, (3) unaccountability, and (4) inaccessibility. Gilbert and Specht provide an apt description of these four problems:

A man in an automobile accident is rushed by ambulance to ward "A" where he is examined; he is next taken to ward "B" for medical treatment, and then moved to ward "C" for rest and observation. If wards A and B are in different parts of town, operate on different schedules, and provide overlapping services—that's *fragmentation*. If the ambulance disappears after dropping the patient at ward "A"—that's *discontinuity*. If the distance between the accident and ward "A" is too far, if there is no ambulance, if our patient is not admitted to the ward because of his social class, ethnic affiliation, or the like, or if he is taken to a ward for mental patients—that's *inaccessibility*. When any or all of these circumstances exist and our patient has no viable means of redressing his grievances—the delivery system suffers from *unaccountability*.[2]

A realistic assessment of human services in the United States suggests that many services suffer from all these deficiencies.

As a result, catchwords like "efficiency" and "accountability," which had become part of the administrative vocabulary in human services during the 1970s, were suddenly eclipsed by the decidedly more draconian term *austerity*. Caseloads skyrocketed. In the attempt to maintain the provision of services mandated by law, administrators traded in professional workers for employees who were less credentialed. "Declassification" of social workers proceeded in departments of social services across the nation.[3] MSWs were replaced by BSWs, who in turn were replaced by high school graduates with little training; in many instances unpaid social work interns began to fill in for salaried staff. High caseloads combined with less qualified staff resulted in increasing instances of burnout, and this contributed to an ever more rapid turnover of staff. Not only did staff morale suffer,[4] but the quality of client service plummeted. Staff turnover interrupted the continuity of service, leaving clients wondering who their new caseworker was. Cases were lost, and, tragically, some clients suffered severely. As discussed in Chapter 13, many children who had been reported to Child Protective Services were battered to death. The one agency assigned to protect vulnerable children was unable to provide the service for which it was legally mandated.

When bureaucratic resources fail to ensure the provision of professional-quality services, conflict is a likely result. The implict values of social work—democracy, autonomy, and individualization—are by their nature at odds with the values of bureaucratic rationalization—efficiency, depersonalization, hierarchy, and centralization. Social work in particular places a premium on human interaction and process, is labor-intensive, and has a nonlinear view of the

world. When complex technology is at odds with the actual work duties of social services, social work skills can become devalued, and the professional currency of social workers diminished. Increasing bureaucracy and technology, in combination with decreasing resources for public social services, have created a situation that is ripe for change.

SOCIAL WORKERS AND UNIONS

Public employee unions represent a wide-ranging segment of the public work force, of which social work is only a small part. Unlike teachers, who have such professional associations or unions as the National Education Association and the American Federation of Teachers, social workers in most places do not have unions exclusively made up of social workers.

The unionization of social workers has grown despite a decline in the overall percentage of unionized workers in the labor force. Although the exact number of social workers affiliated with unions is difficult to determine, the four largest public sector unions claim more than 125,000 social work members. These include the American Federation of State, County, and Municipal Employees (AFSCME), 70,000; the Service Employees International Union (SEIU), 40,000; the Communications Workers of America (CWA), 10,000; and the National Union of Hospital and Health Care Employees (NUHHCE), 10,000).[5] This 1987 number represents a significant increase from a decade earlier.[6]

The growth in social work unionization is related to the general decline in the employment security of technical/professional workers in health care and government services. This decline can be seen in the impact of diagnostic related groups (DRGs), the declassification of social work positions in many states, and public welfare layoffs. Another contributing factor has been the passage of more liberal public sector labor laws. For example, AFSCME gained

40,000 new members after Ohio passed new public sector labor statutes. Moreover, such bargaining issues as quality of work life, training and career development, pay equity, stress reduction, day care, and job safety have all served to bolster membership.[7] Yet despite their steady growth, unionization and collective bargaining and their impact on social work have received only sporadic coverage in the social work literature.[8]

Common Goals of Labor and Social Work

Although there appears to be little formal association between the National Association of Social Workers and public sector unions on a national level,[9] they do interact nominally through the Coalition of American Public Employees (CAPE). CAPE, an organization that includes NASW as well as the major public sector unions, lobbies on issues surrounding national public welfare. At the local level, however, there have been several examples of active collaboration between professional social work associations and unions, often around issues of social service cuts and other domestic concerns.[10]

In an attempt to encourage a better relationship with professional social workers, Jerry Wurf, former AFSCME president, made this statement in *NASW News:*

> AFSCME's involvement with . . . [social issues] . . . is part of a larger commitment to improving public services and programs. But more importantly, these vital efforts prove the true mission of a labor organization to be closely linked to that of social work. AFSCME's growth in the last decade was due in large part to its role as a social missionary. This precious pursuit has undoubtedly been enhanced by the growing number of social workers in our ranks.[11]

Although relatively few studies have examined the compatibility of unionism and professional social work, all have found that most un-

ionized social workers perceive little incongruity between their two loyalties.[12] For example, Leslie Alexander and his colleagues studied 84 MSW-degreed union members and found that "they view their work as solidly professional and, for the most part, do not see unionism and professionalism as incompatible."[13] Ernie Lightman reported similar findings when studying 121 randomly chosen professional social workers in Toronto. According to Lightman, "the vast majority saw no incompatibility; indeed, many felt unionization may facilitate service goals, offsetting workplace bureaucracy."[14] And Gary Shaffer, reporting on exploratory research into two child welfare agencies, one in Pennsylvania and the other in Illinois, found that "workers did not find unionism incompatible with their educational or professional goals."[15]

Antiunionism in Social Work

Despite the common goals of public sector unions and social work associations, there is opposition to unionization in several sectors of the profession. In general, opponents maintain that (1) unions cost employees money; (2) strike losses are never retrieved; (3) union members have little voice in union affairs and are often purposely kept ignorant; (4) bureaucratic union hierarchies control the economic destiny of employees; (5) union corruption is rampant; (6) the consistent opposition of unions to increases in productivity arrests organizational growth; (7) union featherbedding results in unneeded employees and unnecessary payroll expenses; (8) union membership campaigns foster conflict rather than collaboration; (9) the right of managers to strive for greater productivity is curtailed by union rules; and (10) unions have little consideration for the effects of wage increases on future employment, inflation, and tax increases.[16] In short, the antiunion bias in social work is tightly focused on issues of professionalism and bureaucracy.

Writing in *Social Work,* Dena Fisher examined a 1984 strike by Local 1199 of the Retail Drug Employees Union. This strike involved more than 50 institutions and virtually all the social work staff in hospitals and nursing homes covered by the union. Fisher concluded that:

> Standards for professional practice conflict with the [NASW] Code of Ethics with regard to behavior during a labor strike when the prescribed behavior includes withholding service, failing to terminate clients properly, and picketing activity directed toward consumers of health care . . . The problem is that participation in a strike is a nonprofessional activity . . . Standards of professional behavior conflict with union membership requirements.[17]

Apart from fears that clients will be endangered by strikes, there is also apprehension that when organized into unions, social workers will become like other organized workers who belong to industrial unions and in this process subordinate their professional concerns to union issues. A belief in the "exceptionalism" of social work has evolved in the debate about professionalism versus unionism. This exceptionalism implies that tasks performed by social workers are more important than those performed by many other workers, especially nonprofessionals, and that normal labor relations principles are therefore not applicable. Proponents of social work exceptionalism must address two questions. First, how is it that other semiprofessionals—teachers and nurses—have reconciled their professional priorities with union activities? Are social service activities to be considered more essential than education or health care? Second, does social work exceptionalism contribute to the powerlessness of social workers? If social work places a big value on the empowerment of clients, why should social workers themselves not also be so empowered? The idea of American social work's exceptionalism was put in bold relief in 1991 when members of Canada's Public Service Alli-

ance—many of whom are social workers—participated in one of the largest strikes in that nation's history, inspired by the government's plan to reduce wage increases.[18] If Canadian human service professionals can reconcile professional and union differences, why is this beyond American social workers?

Social workers have responded to the pressures of organizational life in several ways. Some have opted to leave public service for the greener pastures of private agencies. Others have completely dropped out of social work and chosen totally unrelated employment. Still others have chosen to leave the confines of agency life by entering into private practice.

PRIVATE PRACTICE

As a form of independent practice, private practice is influenced by the policies of the states regulating it, by professional associations, and by the insurance companies that pay clinicians for their services. Private social work practice has been controversial within the social work profession. Despite this, private practice continues to be a popular form of practice.

Private practice has become an attractive vehicle for delivering clinical social services, and there is every indication that it will expand in the future. For some time, many of the health and mental health services have been delivered by physicians and psychologists who work predominantly out of private offices. The upsurge of social workers' interest in private practice is such that today a large portion of students entering graduate programs in social work do so with the expressed intent of establishing a private practice. Professional schools of social work are specifically equipped to prepare graduate students for private practice. "MSW programs appear to offer more to the practitioner bound for private practice than to the social worker who would prefer to work in an agency setting," concluded researchers in a study of private and agency-based social workers.[19]

The current enthusiasm for private practice can be attributed to several factors. Private practitioners often enjoy a prestige and income that set them apart from salaried professionals. A 1986–87 survey of salaries of members of the National Association of Social Workers (NASW) revealed that the mean salary of private practitioners who were self-employed or in partnerships was above that of many practice settings.[20] In a subsequent survey of NASW members, researchers reported that the earnings of privately practicing social workers were significantly higher than those working in social service agencies: "Of those individuals in private practice, 65 percent have an annual income over $35,000, compared to 25.1 percent of those in agency practice."[21] It is not surprising that social workers, who are usually female and underpaid, would see private practice as a way to increase their earnings and status. In fact, women are more likely to engage in private practice than to work in traditional social service agencies; two-thirds of private practitioners are women.[22] Private practitioners also have a degree of autonomy that is not available to professionals who are bound by the personnel policies of traditional agencies. In the study of private and agency-based social workers previously cited, Srinika Jayaratne and her associates found that "whereas 55 percent of the private practitioners report a high level of congruence between their expectations and their activities, only 18.3 percent of the agency practitioners do so."[23] This is important for experienced professionals who find continued supervision unnecessary or intrusive and who require some flexibility in their work schedules to make room for other priorities. Finally, private practice allows professionals to specialize in activities at which they are best instead of having to conform to organizational requirements of the private agency or governmental bureaucracy. Again, 66.5 percent of private practitioners reported that they were able to do those things at which they excelled, while only 22.9 percent of agency practitioners said they could do so.[24]

The image of private practice that has emerged is one of freedom and opportunity, sans rules and regulations. This is somewhat misleading. Although private practice may involve comparatively fewer compliance requirements than does salaried employment, it is anything but unfettered practice. In actuality, private practice involves a number of policies with which practitioners must be familiar if they are to be successful. The policies that affect private practice originate primarily from two sources: the professional community (a private entity) and a government regulatory authority (a public entity). This situation is complicated by the provision of service through the marketplace of a capitalist economy that traditionally discriminates against groups—minorities, women, the aged, the handicapped—that do not participate fully in the labor market. These groups frequently lack the resources to purchase the goods and services provided by private practitioners. For this reason, private practice is not easily reconciled with the traditional values of the human service professions, which emphasize service to the community and to the disadvantaged. Paradoxically, private practice has become a popular, yet controversial, method of social work practice.

The Sociology of Professions

In conventional usage, the term *private practice* is reserved for members of a professional community who are self-employed. Although persons providing technical services who do not belong to professional communities may be self-employed, they are not referred to as private practitioners. As a type of service delivery, private practice exists in several settings: solo practice, formal association, and group practice.[25]

Private practitioners enjoy status by virtue of their association with a profession. As special occupational groups, professions exhibit particular characteristics that, in the aggregate, serve to organize practitioners into a professional community. Historically, occupational groups have had varied bases around which they organized their activities. The classic professions—the military and the clergy—relied on custom, belief, and morality as bases for their occupational specialization. Professions emerging after the Enlightenment, such as medicine, strove to emphasize science as a basis for specialization. Abraham Flexner, who was instrumental in elevating the status of physicians in the United States, stated as much in 1915, when he listed the criteria for the modern professions:

> Professions involve essentially intellectual operations with large individual responsibility; they derive their raw material from science and learning; this material they work up to a practical and definite end; they possess an educationally communicable technique; they tend to self-organization; they are becoming increasingly altruistic in motivation.[26]

With reference to social work, Ernest Greenwood identified five criteria. For social work to attain full professional status, it must have (1) a systematic practice theory; (2) an authority to regulate the activities of professionals; (3) community sanction of professional objectives and practices; (4) an ethical code that informs practitioners and the community of the professionals' standards; and (5) a culture that is articulated and maintained by institutions of professional education and association.[27] Professions, of course, vary in the extent to which they demonstrate these essential elements, and, as a result, they hold different positions in the "professional hierarchy."[28] Thus, the attributes of professionalism represent a continuum, with any single community of experts falling somewhere between full professional and occupational status.

In addition to the conventional components of professionalism just noted, several theorists have added a variable that relates to the form of service delivery. Noting the tendency of the "semiprofessions"—nursing, teaching, and social work—to be salaried, Nina Toren introduced "the degree to which members of different professional groups are independent or salaried workers."[29] In other words, among the new professions, full professional status is positively associated with independent practice; conversely, semiprofessional status is correlated with salaried employment.[30]

Among some observers, the concept of independent practice is inseparable from the concept of professionalism. Medical sociologist Eliot Freidson has gone so far as to state that the capacity of a profession to be "given the right to control its own work" is fundamental to the very idea of professionalism.[31] He argues that professions seek legislated independence in practice, initially through collaborating with societal elites, next by convincing the public that professional services are indispensable, and finally by gaining a legislated monopoly. Freidson terms this condition "organized autonomy." Organized autonomy affords some professions the opportunity to practice independently of the institutional constraints affecting other occupations. With respect to the individual practitioner,

> the autonomy of his status and the individualism encouraged by the demands of his work make it difficult for the clinician to either submit to or participate in the regulatory process that attempts to assure high ethical and scientific standards of performance in the *aggregate* of practitioners. He wants to control the terms and content of his own work and is not inclined to want to lose that control to profession-wide systemic auspices. . . . To the consulting practitioner, his work and its results are seen almost as a form of private property.[32]

In an analysis of social work, Sidney Levenstein uses the concept *auspice* as roughly equivalent to the factors identified by Toren and Freidson that hierarchically order professions.

[Auspice] . . . differentiates between the private provision of a service and the provision of that service by an organization set up by the community at large, either through government or voluntary association, with accountability for, and control over, the service resting with the community at large. Such control and accountability are in contrast to the private control of the contractual relationship mutually exercised by a private practitioner and his client. This distinction is basic to any understanding of the private practice of any profession.[33]

In terms of the sociology of professionalism, private practice is one of several variables that differentiate professional communities. Within human services, private practice has become associated with the more affluent professions, such as medicine and psychology.

The Political Economy of Private Practice

The prevalence of private practice within a professional community is determined by the extent of its professional monopoly and its capacity to be reimbursed through vendorship. "Professional monopoly" refers to a privilege to practice that is reserved for particular groups through enacted legislation. In the United States, the states are responsible for legislation that serves a regulatory function. In other words, states may reserve certain activities to professional groups because those activities are too important to be practiced by just anyone. The mechanism for assuring the public of safe, professional practice is the creation of a governmental authority that licenses professionals to practice within its jurisdiction. But how can the state, which is the creation of the lay public in a democratic polity, effectively oversee a professional community which engages in activities that the public cannot practically appreciate? The solution to this problem has been to empanel a group of professionals, under state

auspices, to regulate the activity of the professional community. "Professions historically are allowed to govern themselves, to control entrance into their ranks, to prescribe required training, and to set their own standards of practice somewhat free of the supervision and control of nonmembers," as two scholars explain.[34] Interestingly, licensing often regulates the use of a professional title, not necessarily any activity per se. For example, all states regulate social workers, many in such a manner that only duly licensed professionals may use the title "social worker." Unlicensed professionals may use methods typical of social workers, but they are in violation of the law only if they begin identifying themselves as social workers.

Consequently, professional groups seek legislation that first establishes, then strengthens, their professional monopoly. The exclusive right to practice enjoyed by professionals carries with it a social obligation to the public, namely, that professionals have the welfare of the community as their ultimate concern. Professional monopoly, then, is inseparable from the commonweal, and this is readily evident in the codes of ethics of professions that specify the provision of care to the indigent. The NASW Code of Ethics, for example, specifies that "the social worker should regard as primary the service obligation of the social work profession." Moreover, "the social worker should promote the general welfare of society" through such activities as preventing discrimination, ensuring access to services, respecting cultural diversity, and advocating social policies that promote social justice.[35] In sum, the justification for professional monopoly rests on the proposition that professions have as their ultimate concern the welfare of the society, and that their techniques should be used only by credentialed practitioners.

The development of private practice is only possible in a market economy. In these conditions, the clinician provides a service, the quality and cost of which are subject to the influences of supply and demand. According to Magali Larson, "Professions were and are means for earning an income on the basis of transacted services." Larson goes on to note that "in a society that has been reorganized around the centrality of the market, the professions could hardly escape the effects of this reorganization. The modern model of profession emerges as a consequence of the necessary response of professional producers to new opportunities for earning an income."[36]

As one of the "new opportunities for earning an income," private practice places the practitioner in the role of "clinical entrepreneur."[37] In this capacity, the practitioner is dependent on the market for his or her livelihood, with economic status being directly related to fees earned. Furthermore, to the extent that professions are able to develop a monopoly over their services—a characteristic of high-status professions—they are assured a captive clientele whenever consumers are convinced that professional services are necessary. In an economic sense, this allows professionals the opportunity to increase fees beyond what they might be in a nonmonopolistic laissez-faire market.[38]

Optimizing fees clearly is an important concern among private practitioners. Professional monopoly does not necessarily assure practitioners of adequate reimbursement for their services if their clientele cannot pay according to the prevailing fee structure. Many clients, regardless of their economic circumstances, have insurance that pays for the cost of their care. As insurance is more widely used, vendorship (the collection of third-party payments) becomes an important issue within the professional community. Exactly which professional groups are eligible for reimbursement and for which practices is a matter determined by the insurance carrier. In some instances, state insurance authorities, which regulate the practices of insurance companies, designate the practitioners who can be reimbursed.

For a variety of reasons, then, it is in the interest of private practitioners to become vendors. Some companies will make payments directly to the practitioner, thus obviating the need of the provider to collect first from the client, who is later reimbursed by the insurance company. In this instance, payment is not only more prompt, but the client may not be directly involved in the fee. Insurance companies ordinarily pay according to the "usual, customary, and reasonable" (UCR) fee of the professional community, an amount that may be above what the client is prepared (or able) to pay. Thus, the practitioner is more likely to realize the value of the service rendered when insurance pays for the cost of care than when the client pays directly. Because of its significance in private practice, the UCR warrants further consideration.

The UCR is defined as the amount charged by the majority of practitioners within a geographic area. When, for example, most social workers charge $50 per 50-minute session of clinical service, the UCR is $50. Because the UCR is the prevailing fee, it has normative features that are important for individual practitioners. Clinicians who charge less, perhaps in order to establish a practice or to make service more accessible to the poor, may be subverting the UCR. Subsequently, the practitioner may receive fewer referrals from colleagues. As a result of this, many private practitioners employ a sliding-fee scale according to which they bill clients who pay cash. Clients who are insured may be billed on the basis of an alternative fee scale, usually higher. Because the UCR represents the normative fee of the professional community, it changes with the billing practices of practitioners. Although the UCR could, logically, be driven down if a large number of clinicians lowered their fees in order to compete for a limited number of clients, this has not been the case. Instead, the UCR has increased steadily. In 1976, the average fee was $28, but a decade later more than half of private practitioners were charging between $51 and $75 per hour.[39]

As fees increased, the number of social workers in private practice grew. But a finite client pool meant that too many clinicians were chasing too few clients, and this resulted in the proliferation of part-time private practice. In 1975, 22.6 percent of social workers identified private practice as a secondary source of employment, but 40.9 percent were to do so a decade later.[40]

Professional monopoly and vendorship contribute to private practice being a positive experience for many human service professionals who enjoy higher status and increased incomes. It follows that private practice can be made that much more lucrative by making the professional monopoly more restrictive and further exploiting vendorship. In fact, these are major objectives of professional associations that promote the interests of the professional community to the public. "The professional associations in social work today," concluded one study of private practice, "are indeed a major driving force behind the privatization of social work."[41] In social work, licensing and vendorship have been central and long-standing concerns of the National Association of Social Workers. However, the ability of professional associations to enhance their status through leveraging the political economy is hampered somewhat by the role of the states in regulating professional activity. While there may be only one association representing social workers, there are 50 state authorities that now regulate social work practice.

Private Practice in Social Work

The private practice of social work is a relatively recent phenomenon and the National Association of Social Workers (NASW) did not officially sanction this form of service delivery for its members until 1964. Prior to that, privately practicing social workers identified themselves as psychotherapists and lay analysts. Typically, they relied on referrals from physicians and psychiatrists,[42] and, after World War II, they began to establish "flourishing and lucrative" practices.[43] By the 1970s, private practice in social

work was developing as an important form of service delivery. While the NASW Manpower Survey noted that less than 3 percent of its members engaged in private practice in the early 1970s, these were members reporting full-time commitments.[44] Of survey respondents, 22.6 percent identified private practice as secondary employment, usually involving ten or fewer hours per week.[45] But by 1985 the number of social workers in private practice had increased substantially—10.9 percent reporting it as their primary employment and 54.6 percent reporting private practice as a secondary employment.[46] Nationwide, as many as 30,000 social workers engage in private practice to some degree.[47]

By 1987, most states regulated social workers,[48] with the majority of these requiring a master's degree in social work (MSW). However, a social work license is not automatically awarded to those holding the MSW degree. Many states require candidates for licensure to have two years of post-MSW experience under the supervision of a Licensed Certified Social Worker (LCSW) and to have passed an examination. Beyond these common requirements, states vary greatly in their regulatory practices. Maryland, for example, has a three-tier system: the LCSW for MSWs who have two years of post-MSW experience and who have passed an examination; the Licensed Graduate Social Worker (LGSW) for newly graduated MSWs; and the Social Work Associate (SWA) for those with baccalaureate degrees in social work. To further complicate matters, new licensing legislation often allows candidates who have practiced professionally to become licensed without first meeting the requirements of the licensing legislation. This practice, called "grandfathering," is characteristic of new licensing legislation and, in that social work licensing is a relatively recent development in many states, there are many LCSWs who would not otherwise meet the technical requirements for a license. Moreover, because some states exempt state employees from licensing requirements, many "social workers" in public welfare do not meet the licensing requirements necessary for the title of social worker. As a result, many social workers are licensed but have not met the requirements with which their colleagues must comply. Consequently, states often establish additional requirements for professionals to be eligible for vendorship. Special registries for clinical social workers may be used to identify LCSWs who are eligible for third-party payments.

Professional associations also designate practitioners who have expertise in particular areas. In social work, the most common distinction is membership in the Academy of Certified Social Workers (ACSW). Requirements for the ACSW are two years of post-MSW experience under the supervision of an ACSW and passage of an examination. These are similar to those for the LCSW, but the two designations should not be confused. Because states have the legal authority to license professions, special distinctions established by professional associations are neither equivalent to nor a substitute for state licensure. Thus, it is common for experienced clinicians to list both LCSW and ACSW after their names as indications of professional competence. Recently, the NASW (which administers the ACSW) developed a "diplomate," which identifies those practitioners with skills above those required for the ACSW. Credentials such as the ACSW serve the function of distinguishing expertise among members of the professional community. Such credentials are determined by policies of the professional community and not by a public authority, as in the case of state licensure.[49]

The private practitioner who holds an LCSW and is eligible for third-party reimbursement stands to do well economically. For the agency-based social worker, private practice can provide an important supplement to what is often a low salary. Assuming a modest fee of $30 per hour, working 10 hours per week, with four weeks off each year, and subtracting 30 percent for overhead, the private practitioner will net $10,080 per year. On the other hand, the clinician willing to take the plunge into full-time private practice may do very well. Assuming a fee of $50 per hour, working 40 hours per week, with four weeks off each year, and subtracting 30 percent for overhead, the social worker will clear $67,200 per year. Many private practitioners will fall between these scenarios, varying the number of hours they work to suit their needs. Because private practitioners can generate more income while working fewer hours than agency-based social workers can, they have more freedom in their work hours. In fact, flexibility in work hours is rated by private practitioners as a significant advantage of working in the setting, ranking second to "professional challenge."[50] In 1978, *Psychotherapy Finances,* a trade journal for private practitioners, reported that half of all social workers in private practice earned $20,000 or more[51]; within five years over half of social workers in private practice reported earnings above $35,000.[52] Given the earning potential of private practice, it is no wonder that social workers have found it attractive, particularly in light of funding reductions for programs of the voluntary and governmental sectors.

Financial gain does not appear to be the sole motivation for social workers to enter private practice, however. In research on the motives of private social work practitioners versus social workers employed in agencies, Jayaratne and his associates concluded that stress reduction played an important part in the decision to go private. "Those in private practice reported fewer psychological and health strains, reported higher levels of performance, and, in general, felt better about their life circumstances," concluded the researchers. "On every measure, those in private practice scored significantly better than those in agency practice."[53]

Despite the popularity of private practice, it has provoked a great deal of controversy within the professional community. There are several aspects to this controversy, not the least of which is that many practitioners who have committed themselves to helping the disadvantaged through working with the voluntary and governmental sectors view the instant popularity of private practice as antithetical to everything that is "social" about social work. The extent to which private practice has grown at the expense of traditional auspices of employment is evident in data from California. A 1990 survey of California members of NASW found that 29.5 percent were employed in private, for-profit settings, compared with 34.5 percent in public social services and 36 percent in private, nonprofit agencies.[54] Given trends evident during the 1980s, social work in private, for-profit agencies will eclipse other auspices of practice at some time during the 1990s.

For professionals who have committed themselves to furthering social justice through careers in the voluntary and governmental sectors, private practice is often viewed with disdain. Donald Feldstein, head of the Federation of Jewish Philanthropies of New York, suggested that private social work practice is similar to private medical practice in that it presents "new opportunities for rip-offs by the privileged." Private practice, he maintained, replaced social decision making with market decision making. According to Feldstein, "Social decision making is preferable to marketing human services like soap . . . the private practice of social work is still against everything that is social about the term social work."[55] Another critic impugned the motives of social workers in private practice:

> Over 15 years ago, when I first had exposure to private practitioners, they were objects of envy, never of nonacceptance. Obviously this envy has continued. For we see more social workers developing private practices. But why all the sham? Let's be honest enough to say it's usually done for the money.[56]

Defenders of private practice emphasize the benefits of the method for practitioners and clients. Why should social workers not enjoy the same professional freedom and responsibility as other professions that use private practice extensively, for instance, law, medicine, and psychiatry? Moreover, "some clients prefer the opportunity to choose their own practitioner and a service they consider more personal and confidential."[57] Concern for the client's perceptions means that practitioners must be concerned about their image. This is evident in one privately practicing social worker's description of her office:

> It is decorated with comfortable chairs, built-in book cases, soft lighting, etc., and is arranged in such a way as to offer several different possibilities for seating. It is commensurate with most of the socio-cultural levels of my client group and provides him or her the opportunity for free expression without being overheard. . . . Dealing with only one socio-cultural client group allows me to provide physical surroundings which facilitate the client's identification with the worker.[58]

On the surface, then, private practice often provokes strong responses from welfare professionals who perceive private practitioners as avoiding efforts by the voluntary and governmental sectors to advance social equity. On the other hand, some believe that private practice offers an opportunity to enhance their status and to provide services to a middle class that the profession has neglected.

Beneath this surface issue, there are more substantial problems raised by private practice. Perhaps the most important of these is "preferential selection," the practice of selecting certain clients for service while rejecting others. In an era of specialization, professionals will refer clients with problems that are inappropriate for their practice to other providers. An important finding of Jayaratne's research was that private practitioners do not perceive their clients in the same way that agency-based social workers do. The latter "were significantly more likely to agree with the statement that 'my personal values and those of my clients differ greatly' than those in private practice.''[59] Preferential selection becomes an issue when private practitioners elect to serve less troubled clients (who are able to pay the full cost of care) while referring multiproblem clients (who are unable to pay the practitioner's fee for service directly or indirectly through insurance) to agencies of the voluntary sector. Such ''creaming'' of the client population places an enormous burden on public agencies, which are left to carry a disproportionate share of the chronically disturbed and indigent clients. In effect, then, the public sector absorbs the losses that would be suffered by private practitioners if they served this population. Preferential selection has become so pronounced that researchers have facetiously identified it as a syndrome. According to Franklin Chu and Sharland Trotter, the commercialization of private practice contributes to the ''YAVIS syndrome''—the tendency of clients of private practitioners to be *young, attractive, verbal, intelligent,* and *successful.* One might add *W* to the syndrome, because the clients also tend to be disproportionately white.[60] Consequently, clients of private practitioners are less likely to be poor, unemployed, old, and uneducated.

The Business of Private Practice

Aside from preferential selection, another set of issues relates directly to the business nature of private practice. Because private practice is a business, economic considerations figure prominently in a professional's activities. Robert Barker, an authority on private social work practice, explains how economic factors shaped a new practice he established with a colleague: ''We hired a good secretary, employed interior decorators to redo our offices and waiting room. We hired an investment counselor and established retirement accounts and insurance programs. Most of all we became more serious about getting our clients to meet their financial obligations.''[61]

The market nature of private practice, coupled with economic entrepreneurship, presents the possibility of questionable accounting practices, such as the creation of ''uncollectible accounts,'' the use of ''deliberate misdiagnosis,'' and the practice of ''signing off.'' These practices involve income derived from third-party sources, usually health insurance. As private practitioners become more dependent on insurance reimbursement, these questionable accounting practices become important for the professional community at large.

Health insurance frequently covers outpatient psychiatric care at a UCR rate that is determined by the insurance companies. The UCR is what the therapist charges, not necessarily what he or she expects to collect from cash-paying clients. The practice of charging a fee higher than what is expected to be collected is termed holding an ''uncollectible account,'' and is frequently used with third-party fee payment arrangements. This practice is encouraged because insurance coverage rarely covers all of the practitioner's fee, but leaves a certain percent to be paid by the client. For example, a social worker may have a UCR of $50 per session while the client may have insurance paying only 50 percent of the UCR, which leaves the client responsible for the remaining $25. If the client is unable to pay $25 per session, but can afford $10, a clinician will bill the insurance company directly, using an assignment of benefits procedure, for $50. Meanwhile, the client pays $10 per session, as opposed to the implied obligatory contractual amount of $25. Although the therapist may collect a total of $35 per session, and not the UCR of $50, it may be economical to prefer that amount over an extended period of treatment or possibly until the client can afford the full amount of the copayment. At question here is a professional practice that is contrary to the implied contractual relationship among the client, the clinician, and the third-party payer. Yet it is in the interest of the clinician to establish this as a regular accounting procedure owing to the dependence on income through fees and the fear that the insurance company may lower the practitioner's UCR if a significant number of billings are below the customary rate, usually 50 percent.

A second example is "deliberate misdiagnosis," an intentional error in client assessment on the part of clinicians. In a survey of clinical social workers, 70 percent of whom had engaged in private practice, Stuart Kirk and Herb Kutchins found that 87 percent of practitioners frequently or occasionally used a less stigmatizing, or "mercy," diagnosis to avoid labeling their patients. On the other hand, clinicians frequently misdiagnose in order to collect insurance payments.

> Seventy-two percent of the respondents are aware of cases where more serious diagnoses are used to qualify for reimbursement. At least 25 percent of the respondents . . . indicated that the practices occurred frequently. Since reimbursement is rarely available for family problems, it is not surprising that 86 percent are aware of instances when diagnoses for individuals are used even though the primary problem is in the family. The majority of respondents said that this occurred frequently.[62]

Of course, such "overdiagnosis" is unethical because it places the economic benefit of the clinician before the service needs of the client. Still, overdiagnosis continues to be a prevalent practice. Kirk and Kutchins suggest that "reimbursement systems, which have become increasingly important for psychiatric treatment for the last decade, are undoubtedly a major factor in encouraging over-diagnosis."[63] The undesirable consequences of a reimbursement-driven diagnosis system are multiple. First, of course, is the possibility that clients will be done harm, particularly if confidentiality is breached and the diagnosis becomes known to others outside the therapeutic relationship. Second, if the prevalence of severe mental disorders is overreported to public officials, they may make errors

in program planning as a result. Third, and perhaps most important, overdiagnosis violates the "professional's obligation to their profession to use their knowledge and skill in an ethical manner."[64] While individual digressions can be reported to professional and governmental bodies for investigation, a greater problem exists for practitioners as a whole. Widespread misdiagnosis violates the social contract between the professional community and the state, and thus threatens to "corrupt the helping professions."[65] For these reasons, ethical problems associated with the relationship between diagnosis and reimbursement are of greater concern to the professional community.[66]

Finally, there is the practice of "signing off." Signing off has become important because some insurance covers services provided only by psychiatrists or psychologists. In other instances, insurance will reimburse at a higher rate when the services are provided by a psychiatrist or psychologist than when they are rendered by a social worker. The sign-off practice is one in which the psychiatrist or psychologist signs the insurance claim, even though the services were provided by a social worker, in order to maximize reimbursement. In some instances, psychiatrists and psychologists may recruit social workers, paying them half the fees charged to insurance companies and pocketing the difference. Signing off is a type of fee splitting and is "unethical because it allows practitioners to refer clients not to the professional most suitable for the client's needs, but to the person who pays the highest fee."[67]

In a community where many private practitioners compete for a limited number of clients, aggressive business practices are likely to exacerbate questions about the ultimate concern of practitioners—whether it is the client's welfare or the clinician's income. Although the question is not ordinarily couched in such crude terms, the behavior of private practitioners may not be lost on the client population. Since clients usually seek services voluntarily, their impressions of practitioners are important; negative perceptions will eventually hurt practitioners as their clients seek services elsewhere. When unfavorable impressions emerge, as a result of the practices described, practitioners would be prudent to take corrective action. While the ethical code of the professional community can be a source for such action, much remains at the discretion of the individual practitioner.

Private practice is literally *private,* and practitioners enjoy "substantial discretion in conducting their activities."[68] Economic and other considerations may encourage private practitioners to engage in unethical or questionable practices. In such instances, other practitioners are obliged to report allegations of violations to the state licensing board or the professional association. Ultimately, it is in the interest of the professional community to address questionable practices of practitioners, and this includes the unethical business practices of private practitioners. When the media report that "routine falsification of insurance billings and other peculiarities of the mental health professions have caused acute anxiety among insurance companies . . . [who] now think they have little control over what they are paying for," more government regulation is probably not far behind.[69] In other instances, the consequences are acutely embarrassing for the professional community, as when a leading proponent of third-party reimbursement for social workers in Kentucky was found guilty of insurance fraud and ordered to return $37,000 to Blue Cross-Blue Shield.[70]

The Future of Private Practice

As support ebbs for the traditional bases of social work practice, the voluntary agency and the governmental bureaucracy, many welfare professionals have turned to private practice as a way of securing their economic and professional objectives. Private practice gives program administrators a chance to maintain their direct service skills, educators the opportunity to continue contact with clients, and clinicians

with parental responsibilities the freedom to combine professional practice and attention to family needs. More important, private practice may prove an adjunct to agency activities. "By fostering part-time practice," researchers have noted, "the profession can keep its main focus on agency services where there is a commitment to serve persons without regard to their ability to pay and where there can be a basis for social action and reform."[71]

Reconciling economic opportunity with social responsibility will continue to be an issue in private practice. In 1985, the *New York Times* reported that 82 percent of clinical social workers earned at least $20,000 per year through private practice, while 15 percent earned over $60,000.[72] These income prospects will continue to attract social workers who are willing to take the risk of going into business for themselves. From another perspective, however, the seduction of private practice is a result of larger social forces. Ellen Dunbar, executive director of the California chapter of NASW, observed that "The major overriding trend that engulfs all others is that social work along with other service professions is becoming more commercial . . . [and] more an integral part of the free enterprise system."[73] In fact, the commercialization of social work attracted wide attention as the profession became more immersed in private practice. "There is concern," reported *Newsweek* magazine, "that too many social workers are turning their backs on their traditional casework among the poor to practice therapy." Quoting a discussion at the 1987 NASW annual meeting, *Newsweek* wondered at the consequences of "an apparent middle-class therapy explosion at the expense of public welfare and grassroots service."[74] How social work will reconcile its commitment to social justice with the new opportunities presented by private practice remains a central question before the professional community.

The continued expansion of private practice has a powerful influence on education in the graduate schools of social work in the United

States. To the extent that the social work profession is defined as clinical activity under commercial auspices—private practice—support for more traditional areas of social work education, particularly social service administration and community organization, diminishes. From the perspective of many social work educators, private practice not only is misdirected in that it tends to give short shrift to the poor, but the preponderant shift to private practice also reduces educational opportunities for those fewer students still interested in the public sphere. During the 1980s, for example, many schools of social work pared back course offerings in community organization and administration because of low student enrollment, and some schools closed down community-related programming altogether. Meanwhile, clinical courses swelled. This transition so irked Professor Karger that one day, after much furious word processing, he produced the following piece, which appeared as a letter in *Social Work:*

Private Practice: The Fast Track to the Shingle

Recently I had a revelation: The huge shopping malls springing up in the United States are modern day equivalents of the great European cathedrals. Now, let me explain this insight. In medieval and renaissance society many people were poor and wanted to get away from the bleakness of their lives. Great cathedrals were a bit of opulence or "flash" for a dreary life. In America, where more people are becoming poor and where the lives of many of its citizens grow bleaker, the need for flash becomes greater. People flock to hermetically sealed malls to experience the glitz and opulence missing from their daily lives. Shopping malls are cathedrals of consumption, a form of worship. Like the great cathedrals of renaissance Europe, malls are protected islands surrounded by decay.

The death of public institutions gives birth to glamorous private institutions. Such is the legacy of the Reagan administration.

What does this insight have to do with private practice in social work? The answer lies in an experience I had teaching a class in community organization. The faces of the students told me of their patience. Although many, if not most, could not see the value of this class, they were reconciled that it was just another obstacle to negotiate. The tacit understanding was that the class was being taught because it had to be. Consequently, the course expectations should be easy because the course was just another requirement. To try to make the class more interesting, I brought up the issue of the minimum wage—a debate about salaries ensued. One well-dressed student stated that she could not understand how people could live on an annual salary of $25,000.

Then came the proverbial argument about private practice. A student argued for it and I against it. It was a heated debate and I was losing, primarily because of the sentiment of the audience. An annual salary of $75,000 was not an unrealistic goal for a social worker in private practice. How could I expect the audience to be opposed to making a good salary?

By the end of the argument my emotions were running wild. I felt angry, ashamed, helpless, and hopeless. I was angry because I let myself get baited into this argument and because of the values that surfaced. Doctors turn away clients who can't afford to pay, so why should social workers be any different? Why should social workers be held to higher standards than other professions? Although not my values, these were salient arguments. Then came the clincher. "Why then did you go into social work," I asked. "Because I didn't want to take the time to complete a Ph.D. in clinical psychology," answered the student. For many students interested in private practice, the bottom line is that social work is the fastest track to the shingle.

This rash of private practice-oriented students has occurred for two reasons. First, students who choose social work as a vehicle for private practice represent the informed consumer. They have shopped around and know that social work is a fast and legitimate avenue to a private practice in psychotherapy. Moreover, they also know enough about their rights as consumers to demand graduate courses that prepare them for a psychotherapy career. If those courses are not provided, they feel a legitimate grievance. If education is an item of consumption, then the consumer should have a say. As service providers we should give the consumers what they want. The second reason for the upsurge in private practice-oriented students is the profession itself. Desperate for students in the enrollment trough of the early 1980s, social work educators were forced to respond to the pressures of the marketplace. Because of the demands of students—most of whom want to practice psychotherapy—we have changed our orientation. For example, many—if not most—of the advertised social work faculty jobs are to teach clinical skills. Social policy, which is a requirement of the Council on Social Work Education (CSWE), is tolerated by many schools of social work. Students reluctantly take these courses and faculty are reluctantly hired to teach these courses. Besides, what use is social policy in developing a private practice in psychotherapy? Wouldn't a course in accounting principles be more relevant? What does the private practice trend mean for those people who work in the outlets that grant psychotherapy degrees? I suppose there are worse outcomes than turning out students who earn large sums of money, even if they don't serve the poor.

The profession of social work is at cross purposes with itself: We argue that we have a historic mission to help the poor, yet we focus our resources and energy in providing a clinical track to train private practice social workers. Fearful of losing a student body, the profession has tried to be all things to all people, thereby being nothing. A 2-year master of social work degree program that encompasses policy, research, and human behavior neither produces good psychotherapy practitioners nor good activists. In trying to meet everyone's needs, social work education has diluted itself so that no one's needs are fully met. If we choose to make psychotherapy a focal point, then let's be honest and discard the rest of the curricula. We could then terminate policy and community organization faculty, thus sparing them more pain in the end. Feeling superfluous is nobody's idea of a good time.

We are clearly at a crossroads. Most students want a strongly clinical curriculum; administrators want to keep students coming, and, as a consequence, happy; the National Association of Social Workers and CSWE appear to want to maintain the veneer of social work as an activist profession; universities want a research-oriented faculty; and the profession has lost its direction. To cave in to the clinical direction demanded by students (and many faculty and administrators) is to redefine social work. To hold the ground is to be stressed out by the mounting pressures. To say the least, this does not make for a happy situation.

Now, to get back to my initial point about shopping malls.

There is nobody to discuss it with. No one seems to care.

Howard Jacob Karger, *School of Social Work, Louisiana State University, Baton Rouge, La.*[75]

While private practice is an important concern in social work, it is only the tip of a still larger issue—the privatization of social services. The following section examines this privatization.

THE PRIVATIZATION OF SOCIAL SERVICES

As a function of public dissatisfaction with governmental social programs, increasing reliance on the private sector to finance and deliver social services has emerged as an important theme in American social welfare. *Privatization,* as this idea has been termed, addresses the problem of the proper relationship between the public and private spheres of the national culture. In this case, privatization has come to refer to "the idea that private is invariably more efficient than public, that government ought to stay out of as many realms as possible, and that government should contract out tasks to private firms or give people vouchers rather than provide them services directly."[76] That government should not hold a monopoly on social welfare is not a novel idea. Even liberal policy analysts have entertained ways in which the private sector could complement governmental welfare initiatives.[77] Liberal proponents of welfare programs are often willing to concede a viable role to the private sector—even an innovative role—but insist that government must be the primary instrument to advance social welfare. Conservatives, of course, see the proper balance as one in which the private sector is the primary source of protection against social and economic calamity, and believe that government activity should be held in reserve. According to conservative doctrine, government can deploy the "safety net" of social programs, but these should provide benefits only as a last resort.

A clear articulation of the conservative vision of reinforcing the role of the private sector in social affairs appeared in the 1988 Report of the President's Commission on Privatization. "In the United States . . . the growth of government has been based on the political and economic design that emerged from the Progressive movement around the turn of this century," noted the *Report.* "The American privatization movement has represented in significant part a reaction against the themes and results of Progressive thought."[78] Specifically, the *Report* targeted government social programs and the professional administrators who manage them as the undesirable consequences of the progressive state of mind, which can be corrected by privatization. The implications of this analysis are broad: Not only should benefits be removed from government and provided by the private sector, but the administration of social programs should also be removed from the public sector and placed under private auspices. Accordingly, the President's Commission on Privatization identified three "techniques for the privatization of service delivery": (1) the selling of government assets; (2) contracting with private firms to provide goods and services previously offered by government; and (3) the use of vouchers, whereby the government would distribute coupons authorizing private providers to receive reimbursement from the government for the goods and services they had provided.[79] While all these methods have been used to restructure welfare programs at one time or another, the *Report* introduces an unprecedented idea into the debate by characterizing the issue as a "zero-sum game," one in which the advantage to one party is at the expense of the other. In this case, proponents of privatization suggest that the private sector should assume more responsibility for welfare, but with government social programs reduced. It is this sacrifice of the government's obligation to ensure the general welfare that makes the current debate on privatization so important.

A new question in the debate on the balance between private and public responsibility for welfare was introduced with the recent emergence of human service corporations. This is: If government is to divest itself of its welfare obligation, can the business community pick up the slack? If the answer is "yes," proponents of privatization have two options for the private provision of social welfare: the nonprofit, voluntary sector, and the for-profit, corporate sector. In the years following President Lyndon Johnson's Great Society programs, government began to experiment with contracting out services through both nonprofit and for-profit providers. The for-profit, corporate sector capitalized on the contracting-out provisions of the Medicare and Medicaid programs. Through the "purchase of service" concept introduced in Title XX, nonprofit agencies became contractors providing a range of social services on behalf of public welfare departments. Unfortunately, studies comparing the performance of these sectors have been few and their findings debatable.[80]

In the absence of definitive studies showing the advantages of one sector over another, the privatization debate has become volatile. Advocates of *voluntarization,* or reliance on the voluntary sector to assume more of the responsibility for welfare, point to its historical contribution to the national culture, the rootedness of its agencies in the community, and the altruistic motive behind its programs. Proponents of *corporatization,* or dependence on the corporate sector to provide welfare, argue that it offers more cost-effective administration, is more responsive to consumer demand, and pays taxes. Whether voluntarists or corporatists prevail in the privatization debate will rest largely on the ability of each party to manipulate the social policy process in its favor. Whatever the outcome, this process is certain to be lengthy and complex, as one might expect with the remaking of an institutional structure that has become as essential as social welfare is in the United States. Whether voluntarization or corporatization defines the future of American social welfare, privatization has already highlighted several important issues.

Commercialization

For welfare professionals the idea of subjecting human need to the economic marketplace is often problematic. It is hard to condone health care advertising, which reached $1 billion in 1986, when the United States is still without a universal program for expectant mothers and infants.[81] When research on the AIDS virus led to a diagnostic test, some private physicians exploited the AIDS panic and charged as much as $300 for each test, whereas the U.S. Army negotiated a test price of 82 cents.[82] As objectionable as these market-induced practices may be, the commercialization of human services is a reality that welfare professionals cannot simply dismiss out of a sense of moral indignation.

In one of the few treatments of the matter, Richard Titmuss's *Gift Relationship* explored the differences in the way nations manage their blood banks. Unlike the practice in the United Kingdom, blood in the United States is "treated in laws as an article of commerce"; as such, rules of the market affect the supply and quality of blood. Titmuss observed the growth of blood and plasma businesses with alarm because they bought blood from a population that was often characterized by poverty and poor health. Quite apart from the health hazard posed by a blood supply derived from such a population—a hazard highlighted by the AIDS pandemic—Titmuss was concerned that the profit motive would disrupt the voluntary impulses of community life. "There is growing disquiet in the United States," he observed, "with expanding blood programs that such programs are driving out the voluntary system."[83] Indeed, by 1976, 63.3 percent of blood banks in the United States were commercial.[84]

The commercialization issue is particularly important for financially strapped nonprofit agencies. Faced with declining revenues, some voluntary sector agencies experimented with commercial activities in order to supplement income derived from traditional sources: contributions, grants, and fees. That nonprofit organizations should be allowed to engage in commercial endeavors without restriction is "unfair competition," according to business operators, who note that nonprofits do not ordinarily pay taxes on their income. Limits on the freedom of nonprofit organizations to engage in commercial activities were highlighted in a celebrated case involving New York University Law School and the Mueller Macaroni Company. Seeking a way to enhance revenues to the law school, enterprising alumni acquired the Mueller Company and reorganized it as a nonprofit organization registered in Delaware. Income from the macaroni company was thus redefined as nontaxable income and diverted to the law school as a charitable contribution. This clever arrangement, however, did not go unnoticed by Mueller's competitors, who recognized the possibility of Mueller being able to use its newly acquired tax-exempt status to cut prices and drive other macaroni companies from the market. Further, they argued, what was to prevent any well-endowed nonprofit institution from acquiring profitable businesses as a way of supplementing its income while dodging its tax obligation? The situation soon proved so embarrassing to the law school that it sent no representatives to the congressional hearings that deliberated on the ethics of the arrangement. Eventually, the tax code was altered, thereafter making income from commercial activities that are not related to the service function of the agency taxable.[85]

Since 1950, revenue obtained by nonprofit organizations from commercial activity has been taxable under the unrelated business income tax (UBIT). While the Mueller case served as an adequate measure against gross breaches of business propriety, subsequent developments raised further questions around the commerce issue. For example, a nonprofit hospital association in Virginia attempted to maintain its competitive edge by acquiring several commercial ventures, including an advertising agency, two health clubs, an interior decorating firm, a pharmacy, and a helicopter ambulance service. These acquisitions were criticized by nearby businesses.[86] Even the YMCA has come under fire. In this case, the 1,100-member International Racquet Sports Association complained that "Ys" held an unfair competitive

advantage over for-profit racquet clubs.[87] These and other conflicts between nonprofit and for-profit organizations were aired during hearings held by the House Ways and Means Committee in 1987.[88]

During the hearings, representatives of the business community complained that nonprofits were engaged in "unfair competition" with for-profit businesses. According to business representatives, this unfair competition occurred in two ways. First, the UBIT failed to distinguish between related and unrelated business activities. For example, a nonprofit hospital's pharmacy is considered related to the hospital's mission and is therefore exempt from paying taxes on profit, but a for-profit hospital's pharmacy is part of the business and its profit is therefore taxable. Second, nonprofit organizations benefit from the "halo effect"—that is, the public's perception that their services are superior because they do not operate from the profit motive. Thus, health spas complain that the philanthropic image of "Ys" is inaccurate because "Ys" use many commercial business practices—such as marketing and advertising—to promote their services. Yet the revenues of the "Ys" are tax-exempt.

Although complaints of unfair competition by nonprofit organizations appear to be academic, the accusations open the possibility of further restricting the revenue base of voluntary sector agencies. For example, some "Ys" have stopped advertising their programs for fear that local authorities may interpret that activity as commercial and thereby attempt to tax income derived from them. This unfair competition issue presents some very disturbing questions for administrators of nonprofit organizations. If a nonprofit family service agency bills a client's insurance company for a "usual, customary, and reasonable" fee that is comparable to what is charged by a private practice group that must pay taxes on such income, should this income remain tax-exempt? Should tax-exempt income be limited to charitable contributions only? Do program outreach and public education activities constitute marketing and advertising and, if so, should they be limited if a nonprofit organization is to retain its tax exemption? Questions like these strike at the heart of the function of the voluntary sector. How these questions are resolved will be of great concern to proponents of nonprofit community service agencies, particularly those organizations faced with dwindling revenues.

Preferential Selection

If privatization has implications for program administrators, as evident in the commercialization of human services, it also has significant implications for clients. The application of market principles to client service introduces strong incentives for providers to differentiate clients according to their effect on organizational performance. Such selection can be at variance with professional standards, which emphasize the client's need for service over organizational considerations. But the marketplace penalizes providers who are imprudent about client selection, at the same time rewarding providers who are more discriminating. The subtle or blatant practice of choosing clients according to criteria of organizational performance—as opposed to client need—is defined as "preferential selection." Under marketplace conditions, providers who do not practice preferential selection are bound to serve a disproportionate number of clients with serious problems and with less ability to pay the cost of care, thereby running deficits. By contrast, providers who select clients with less serious problems and who can cover the cost of care often claim surpluses. Preferential selection could be excused, perhaps, as a benign method through which organizations determine those clients who are likely to be best served—if it were not for the odious practice of client "dumping." Dumping occurs when clients, already being served by an organization, are abruptly transferred to another organization because they represent a drain on institutional resources.

Critics of privatization complain that creaming the client population through preferential selection is unethical and should be prohibited. Simply ruling out the practice is, however, easier said than done. Accusations of preferential selection are not new; private, nonprofit agencies were accused of denying services to welfare recipients well before proprietary firms became established.[89] Yet recent reports of dumping when life-threatening injuries are evident have drawn the ire of many human service professionals. In some instances, private hospitals have transferred indigent patients with traumatic injuries to public facilities without providing proper medical care, thus contributing to the deaths of several patients.

Incidents of dumping are directly related to the patient's ability to pay for service, and transfers of poor patients have increased as Medicaid is cut. For example, the transfer of poor patients to the publicly owned Cook County General Hospital in Chicago increased from between 90 and 125 per month to 560 patients in August 1981, one month after Illinois instituted cuts in its Medicaid program.[90] In another instance, researchers at Highland General Hospital, the public health care facility in Alameda County, California, examined the transfer disposition of 458 patients over a six-month period. The researchers concluded that "the transfer of patients from private to public hospital emergency rooms is common, involves primarily uninsured or government-insured patients, disproportionately affects minority group members, and sometimes places patients in jeopardy."[91] In Denver, where public hospitals have borne heavy deficits for carrying a disproportionate burden of the medically indigent, the problem has become critical. Jane Collins, director of clinical social work for the Denver Department of Health and Hospitals, described public hospitals in the city as having become "social dumps."[92]

Given the market, preferential selection on the part of a large number of providers is likely to be adopted by others who wish to remain in a competitive position. In analyzing the practice in health care, a team of researchers from Harvard University and the American Medical Association noted that, ''in the same way that competition from for-profit providers leads to reduction in access, the more competitive the market for hospital services generally, the more likely are all hospitals in that market to discourage admissions of Medicaid and uninsured patients.''[93] In other words, nonprofit providers—who are exempt from taxes because they contribute to the community's welfare—are compelled to adopt the discriminatory practices of for-profit providers in a competitive market, unless the nonprofits are willing to underwrite the losses that more costly clients represent to for-profit providers. ''When competitive pressures are great,'' researchers from Yale and Harvard universities, have noted, ''the behavior of for-profit and nonprofit institutions often converge.''[94]

Cost-Effectiveness

Proponents of privatization frequently cite the discipline imposed by a competitive environment on organizational performance as a rationale for market reforms in social welfare. A competitive environment provides strong incentives for firms to adopt cost-effective practices that reduce waste. This claim has led to a handful of studies of for-profit versus nonprofit service providers. In 1981, Lewin and Associates compared 53 nonprofit hospitals with a matched set of for-profit hospitals in the South and Southwest. They concluded that investor-owned hospitals were more expensive than nonprofit hospitals, largely due to higher ancillary (laboratory, radiology services) and administrative service costs. Also, investor-owned hospitals used fewer full-time equivalent staff to provide care than did nonprofit hospitals.[95] This last finding is unsettling, because lower staff-to-patient ratios have been associated with higher rates of contagious disease in nursing homes.[96] The Florida Hospital Cost Containment Board

released a 1980 analysis comparing 72 proprietary and 82 nonprofit hospitals in that state. With results similar to the Lewin study, the Board reported a 15 percent higher charge for patient care and an 11 percent higher collection rate by investor-owned hospitals over their nonprofit counterparts.[97]

In an ambitious study, researchers from the Western Consortium for the Health Professions compared 280 private voluntary, public, and investor-owned hospitals. The Western Consortium investigators reached conclusions that were even less supportive of subjecting health care to the marketplace. For example, they suggested that investor-owned hospitals used emergency services and room and board as loss-leaders, funneling patients into pricing situations where higher-cost ancillary services would be used. Investor-owned hospitals cared for the smallest proportion of patients dependent on Medicaid. The researchers concluded that ''the data do not support the claim that investor-owned chains enjoy overall operating efficiencies or economics of scale in administrative or fiscal services.''[98] Data from the Health Care Finance Administration of the Department of Health and Human Services confirm these studies. In 1985, the cost for each short-term hospitalization was calculated according to hospital auspice, as seen in Table 7.1.

Significantly, the higher cost of proprietary hospitals could not be attributed to longer periods of hospitalization, because the average stay at for-profit hospitals, 7.8 days, was (along with government institutions) the lowest of the group.[99] Finally, in the most comprehensive review of the issue, the Institute of Medicine of

TABLE 7.1. Cost for Short-Term Hospital Stay by Auspice, 1985

Auspice Of Hospital	Cost per Stay
Church	$5,453
Other nonprofit	$5,542
Government	$4,429
Proprietary	$5,795

the National Academy of Sciences concluded that there is "no evidence to support the common belief that investor-owned organizations are less costly or more efficient than are not-for-profit organizations."[100]

Although skeptics of market strategies in welfare use such studies to criticize the false economies of the human services market, it appears that the practices of for-profit firms are nevertheless influencing nonprofit human service organizations. Many nonprofits have adopted features of for-profit firms—bulk buying, sophisticated information systems, staff reductions—to enhance organizational efficiency. As noted, when nonprofits compete with for-profit firms in the same market, the adoption of competitive practices is inevitable in order to ensure organizational survival. As a result, competitive practices characteristic of human service corporations may become standard organizational procedure, not because they serve the public interest better but because the rules of the marketplace require their adoption.

The promise of cost containment through privatization has not been borne out, and this presents an enormous problem for the governmental sector. Under a privatized system, government is in a weak position to control the prices charged by contracting agencies unless it is prepared to deploy its own set of public institutions, thereby avoiding the private sector altogether. A good example is provided by the Medicare program through which the government subsidizes health care, most of which is provided by the private sector. In response to runaway Medicare costs, Congress enacted the Diagnosis Related Group (DRG) prospective payment plan in 1983, whereby hospitals are reimbursed fixed amounts for medical procedures. Three years after the DRG system was in place, the Congressional Budget Office reported that hospitals had increased their surplus attributed to Medicare by 15.7 percent during 1985. This surplus occurred despite a reduction in the number of Medicare patients admitted to hospitals.[101]

Proponents of privatization often claim that noncompetitive markets and governmental regulation, as in the case of the DRG prospective payment system, impose additional costs that must be passed on to consumers. Research, however, does not bear this out. In a study of 6,000 hospitals sponsored by the National Center for Health Services Research and Health Care Technology Assessment, a research team found that "hospitals located in areas with 11 or more neighboring facilities within a 15 mile radius—the most competitive type of hospital market—have admission costs and patient day costs that are 26 percent and 15 percent higher, respectively, than corresponding figures for hospitals with no competitors." Significantly, the hospitals were surveyed before 1983, so governmental regulation through the DRG system could not have contributed to increased costs.[102]

Standardization

Privatization induces human service organizations to accept an industrial mode of production in which the accepted measure of success is not necessarily the quality of service rendered but the number of people processed. Organizational surplus, essential for investor-owned facilities, tends to be derived from increasing the intensity of production and lowering labor costs. Because the logic of the market dictates that the goal of production is to process the largest number of people at the lowest possible cost, the standardization of services is an important method for expediting the processing of people.

Such uniformity of care has become an issue in the nursing home industry. Because Medicaid regulations stipulate standards of care, providers deriving a large portion of their revenues from Medicaid are induced to standardize care for all patients. Paradoxically, well-to-do patients are unable to purchase better care from a nursing home even though they have the resources to do so. The standardization of care has became a cause for serious concern among nursing home corporations. Richard Buchanan, professor of business administration at Bowling Green State University, noted the social consequences of standardized care:

> The nursing home industry's identical treatment of everyone creates a one-class social system for all patients. This constitutes a denial of the affluent person's rights to purchase the quality of life that had been his or hers until stricken with illness or infirmity. This phenomenon represents creeping socialism of a major order, and creates an atmosphere ripe for either legal or market reprisal.[103]

That standardization of care within an industry dominated by for-profit firms would be equated with socialism is perhaps the best measure of the acuity of the problem.

Under these circumstances, life care—or the continuing-care retirement community—has emerged as an attractive alternative to the nursing home for the provision of long-term care. Under life care, residents can purchase cottages or apartments in self-contained communities that include a range of human services. In many respects, the life care community provides more affluent residents an opportunity to purchase a higher level of long-term care. One continuing-care facility boasted wall-to-wall carpeting, maid service, and a designer courtyard. "Already, the facility has shown its first in-house movie . . . and soon residents will be soaking up steam in the saunas, relaxing in the Jacuzzi, exercising on the mechanical bicycles, or browsing in the library," noted a visitor.[104] Among the amenities found in the more posh life care communities are a cocktail lounge, billiards room, sports facilities, and elegantly furnished restaurants serving continental cuisine. Amenities such as these "provide a lifestyle of grace and activity for seniors with the ability to pay for it," observed an industry reporter.[105] "We sell a style of life," explained David Steel, vice

president of Retirement Centers of America Inc., a subsidiary of Avon.[106]

Entry into life care communities can be equivalent to purchasing a home. Nationwide, in the early 1980s the average entrance fees were $35,000 for a single person and $39,000 for a couple. Monthly fees for medical care, dining and laundry, recreation, and transportation averaged $600 for a single person and $850 for a couple.[107] In more exclusive communities, one- and two-bedroom units sell for from $100,000 to $170,000.[108] By the mid-1980s, 275 life care communities were housing 100,000 elders.[109] But this was only the tip of a very large iceberg. Robert Ball, former commissioner of Social Security, estimated that perhaps 15 million elders could afford this type of care.[110] Despite the well-publicized bankruptcies of several life care communities, the prospect of a market of this scale has attracted the interest of several corporations.[111] Beverly Enterprises, the largest nursing home corporation, announced plans to build or acquire several life care communities.[112] Subsequently, Marriott Corporation stated its intention to build a number of life care communities serving between 300 and 400 residents each.[113] Despite the recession of the early 1980s, the interest of brokerage houses in continuing care remained high.[114] By the year 2000, 15 million Americans will need some form of long-term care.[115]

The prospect of extensive proprietary involvement in life care troubles some analysts. Lloyd Lewis, director of a nonprofit life care community, fears that "well-funded proprietary interests" will "drain off the more financially able segment of our older population, widening the gap between the 'haves' and the 'have nots.'"[116] To a significant extent this is already occurring. Robert Ball noted that life care communities operating under nonprofit auspices are beyond the means of "the poor, the near poor, or even the low-income elderly."[117]

The accommodation of long-term care facilities to the desire for amenities on the part of affluent residents is likely to produce significant change in how the nation cares for its elderly. In 1982, for example, the *New York Times* reported a nationwide shortage of nursing home beds for those "whose nursing care is financed by the government through Medicaid."[118] As human service corporations divert capital to care for those who represent profit margins, economic and political support diminishes for the care of those less fortunate. "Those who cannot gain admission to [a private] institution will be forced into boarding homes . . . or bootleg boarding homes," commented Milton Jacobs, vice president of American Medical Affiliates. "These boarding homes will be filled with what are literally social rejects. We're reverting back to the way the industry was in the fifties and sixties."[119] Left unchecked, long-term care is likely to divide into two clearly demarcated systems: the affluent enjoying the generous care of completely—some would say excessively—provisioned life care communities, the elderly poor dependent on the squalid institutions willing to accept government payment for their care. To a great extent, dual systems of long-term care will be attributed to the desire of the affluent to escape the standardization of care associated with the economies of privatization.

Oligopolization

The privatization of human services invites the development of oligopolies, or the control of a market by few providers, as organizations seek to reduce competition by acquiring competitors. Within the corporate sector, three waves of acquisition can be identified: acquisitions affecting long-term care, acquisitions affecting hospital management, and acquisitions affecting health maintenance industries. Significantly, virtually all this oligopolization has occurred since the mid-1970s.

Driven by the same competitive pressures, the consolidation of proprietary health providers has encouraged nonprofit providers to form franchises. In terms of number of beds, five of the ten largest hospital systems are nonprofit. Of these, three are operated by religious organizations; one—the New York City Health and Hospital Corporation—is a public conglomerate, while another—Kaiser Foundation Hospital—is a private nonprofit entity. Increasingly, nonprofit health providers are having to join together in order to compete with the aggressive proprietary providers, which has led to oligopolies within the voluntary sector.[120]

Oligopolization of human services presents a daunting specter in that a small number of wealthy and powerful organizations are in a strong position to shape social policy to conform with their interests. Within health care, this development has led Arnold Relman, editor of *The New England Journal of Medicine,* to voice alarm at the growing influence of the "new medical-industrial complex" in defining health policy in the United States.[121] Whether human service corporations at present have enough influence and power to be considered a "human service-industrial complex" is doubtful; but further privatization of social welfare would make such a development a distinct possibility.

THE CHALLENGE OF PRIVATIZATION

It is hard for welfare professionals to be sanguine about privatization. For those committed to increasing government's responsibility for ensuring social and economic equality, privatization is simply a retreat from a century of hard-won gains in social programs. Their case is argued cogently by Pulitzer Prize-winning sociologist Paul Starr:

> A large-scale shift of public services to private providers would contribute to further isolating the least advantaged, since private firms have strong incentives to skim off the best clients and most profitable services. The result would often be a residual, poorer public sector providing services of last resort. Such institutions would be even less attractive as places to work than they are today. And their worsening difficulties would no doubt be cited as confirmation of

the irremediable incompetence of public managers and inferiority of public services. Public institutions already suffer from this vicious circle; most forms of privatization would intensify it.[122]

For defenders of government social programs, the problems attributed to privatization—commercialization, client creaming, inflated costs, standardization, and oligopolization—make it a poor vehicle for advancing social welfare.

Yet reliance on the private sector at a time when public social programs are under assault is a reality that must be faced by those concerned about social welfare. In the absence of an effective Left and the diminishing influence of a progressive labor movement, there appears little chance of launching new government social programs. If the public is unwilling to authorize and pay for new governmental social programs, welfare professionals have little choice but to reconsider privatization as a basis for welfare provision. In some instances, private sector analogues to public services have demonstrated surprising success. Take, for example, job placement of the hard-core unemployed. Traditional public sector approaches to this population include policies realized in the Job Training and Partnership Act and the Family Support Act. Yet in New York and Connecticut an innovative program called America Works has evolved from the private sector:

Each year the company finds jobs for more than 700 of the state's hard-core unemployed, 68 percent of whom are (as a result) permanently weaned from the welfare rolls. The company gets paid only after the former welfare recipient has been working for four months and its $5,000 fee is less than half of what it costs New York State to support an average welfare family of three. All told, America Works is saving taxpayers approximately $4.5 million annually and providing many of the state's hard-core unemployed with meaningful work.[123]

Upon inspection, it could be argued that there are compelling reasons to believe that privatization could be a strategy for promoting social welfare. Through commercial loans and issuance of stock, for-profit organizations have faster access to capital than does the governmental sector (which requires a lengthy public expenditure authorization process) or the voluntary sector (which relies on arduous fund-raising campaigns) for purposes of program expansion. The private sector has also been the source of important innovations in programs and organizational administration, which have often become the exemplars for effective administration.[124] It could be argued further that welfare-conscious administrators have missed opportunities for promoting social welfare by ignoring opportunities for professional practice associated with privatization. In this regard, welfare professionals might wonder if patient abuses in the nursing home industry, chronicled in *Tender Loving Greed*, would have been lessened had socially conscious administrators managed long-term care facilities.[125] After years of lobbying, human service advocates have finally secured a regulation ''requiring nursing homes with more than 120 beds to employ full-time at least one [undergraduate] social worker,'' which is hardly enough to ensure compliance considering past abuses.[126]

Human service professionals will continue to deal with the consequences of privatization in the foreseeable future. The President's Commission on Privatization notes that ''the impact of the privatization movement, broadly understood, is only beginning to be felt. Privatization in this broad sense may well be seen by future historians as one of the most important developments in the American political and economic life of the late 20th century.''[127] How welfare professionals choose to respond to the challenge of privatization—whether by reaction or innovation—will be critical for the future of American social welfare. Privatization may come to be a rallying cry for defenders of established programs that have been discredited as being wasteful, inflexible, and currying the favors of special interests, or privatization may ultimately mean discovering new ways to exploit the social carrying capacity of the private sector. Unfortunately, the American social work community has tended to respond to deficiencies in the public social services by exercising the exit option—private practice. This has left many public agencies populated by fewer experienced and capable professionals who are then obliged to manage larger-than-ever caseloads of more troubled clients. As researchers on private practice note, rather than criticize professionals who have opted for the private sector, the social work community should make it a priority to reform the means of service provision through the public sector. "The goal should be to make agency practice good for the health and well-being of the practitioner, because the ultimate beneficiary would be the client."[128] Stan Taubman, who has held direct practice and administrative positions and now couples county employment with private practice, states the matter succinctly: "Private practice isn't keeping social workers out of public services. Public services are."[129] As David Donnison has suggested, welfare professionals would be wiser to reconsider their aversion to the private sector and to try to find the "progressive potential in privatization."[130]

CONCLUSION

An inventory of the shortcomings as well as of the merits of unionization, private practice, and privatization has led some social policy analysts to consider the restructuring of human services as a strategy for enhancing service delivery. An alternative proposal was made several years ago by one of the authors of this book in which he advanced a model for mental health services—the Family Life Center—based on the logic that generated Employee Stock Ownership Plans and other forms of worker ownership.[131] According to this proposal, workers would own their own agencies and thus the means of service delivery. A service delivery strategy in which social workers manage their own work—similar to a cooperative—would be attractive to many social workers. Professional social workers collectively owning and managing their own social service agency would help address social service delivery problems as well as the value and role conflicts that these problems breed.

There is an urgency about the search for more responsive and efficient methods of social service delivery. Federal and state fiscal gridlock attributed to a massive deficit coupled with the unwillingness of elected officials to raise taxes have led to a predictable result—the rationing of services. In 1992, Oregon attempted to replace its Medicaid program with a universal state health program by rationing health care to the poor. Pushed to their financial limits, public officials have begun to consider "managed care" as a method of rationing services. Under managed care, services are contracted out to private providers, who then use a variety of methods to reduce costs. While some methods, such as assigning case managers to clients, improve the coordination and utilization of services, others, such as arbitrarily limiting the number of counseling sessions regardless of the client's problem, compromise professional discretion. How best to deliver human services promises to be a question that will extend well into the next century.

DISCUSSION QUESTIONS

1. The organizational arrangement of human service providers is often referred to as a "social service delivery system." Map the social welfare provid-ers in your community. What are the systemic elements of this arrangment? What is nonsystemic? Are there plans to make services more integrated?

2. What are the major unions representing social workers in your community? What is the relationship between unions representing social workers and the local chapter of NASW? Do these groups work together cooperatively or antagonistically? Other semi-professionals, such as teachers and nurses, have been willing to strike in order to obtain improved working conditions, pay, and client services. Why haven't social workers used this tactic? What would be issues in your community around which social workers might be willing to organize and strike?

3. Privatization is a hotly debated issue in social welfare. To what extent are some of the major concerns about privatization (e.g., unfair competition between nonprofit agencies and commercial firms, preferential selection and dumping of clients, superior performance of private providers, the emergence of an oligopoly of private providers) evident in your community? Should social workers practice in for-profit firms?

4. In many parts of the United States, health care and education are being "restructured." Should social welfare also be restructured? If restructuring were to occur in your community, how would you ensure that the result was improved working conditions for social workers? How would you ensure that clients obtained professional-quality service? How would you convince the public that it was getting optimal value for tax dollars invested in restructuring? Which interests would support restructuring? Which would oppose it?

5. Private practice continues to be a focus of students in schools of social work. How many of your classmates are planning to become private practitioners? What are their motives? Do faculty members in your social work program who also have private practices serve as role models to students? Is there an opportunity in your studies to discuss the implications of private practice for social work?

6. How does your state regulate the practice of social work? What governmental unit is responsible for regulating social work? How is it constituted? Does your state have reciprocity arrangements with other states, honoring licenses granted in other jurisdictions? Has your state's social work licensing unit expelled professionals for unethical practices?

7. What is the position of your state chapter of the National Association of Social Workers on regulating professional practice? Are licensing and vendorship still high on the state chapter's priority list? If so, which social workers in your state remain concerned about the regulation of professional practice? Why?

8. What are the main concerns within your professional community about private practice—fees, misdiagnosis, licensing, image, competition with other professionals, vendorship? How are disagreements arbitrated, formally or informally?

9. The debate between private practice and agency-based practice continues as a heated issue within social work. What are the advantages and disadvantages of each? Is there a common base of social work practice? Can you foresee some ways to resolve the issue and bring private practitioners and agency-based practitioners together?

NOTES

1. Neil Gilbert and Harry Specht, *Dimensions of Social Welfare Policy* (Englewood Cliffs, N.J.: Prentice-Hall, 1974), p. 119.

2. Ibid., p. 121.

3. On the relationship of declassification to the future of social service, see Peter J. Peccora and Michael J. Austin, "Declassification of Social Service Jobs: Issues and Strategies," *Social Work* 28 (November-December 1983): 421–26; and H. Jacob Karger, "Reclassification: Is There a Future in Public Welfare for Trained Social Workers?" *Social Work* 28 (November-December 1983): 427–34.

4. See, for example, Srinika Jayaratne and Wayne E. Chess, "Job Satisfaction, Burnout, and Turnover: A National Study," *Social Work* 29 (September-October 1984): 442–52; Herbert Freudenberger, "Staff Burnout," *Journal of Social Issues* 30 (Winter 1974): 459–65.

5. Gary Shaffer, "Professional Social Worker Unionization: Current Contract Developments and Implications for Managers," National Association of Social Workers, Annual Conference, *Management Conference* (New Orleans, La., September 12, 1987), p. 1.

6. Ibid., p. 2.

7. Ibid.

8. See Howard J. Karger, *Social Workers and Labor Unions* (Westport, Conn.: Greenwood Press, 1988). See also Milton Tambor and Gary Shaffer, "Social Work Unionization: A Beginning Bibliography," *Catalyst* Nos. 17–18 (November 1985): 132; and Gary L. Shaffer, "Labor Relations and the Unionization of Professional Social Workers: A Neglected Area in Social Work Education," *Journal of Education for Social Work* 15 (Winter 1979): 80–86.

9. The lack of sustained formal contact between NASW and public sector labor unions was affirmed in telephone conversations with Thomas Gauthier, senior staff associate, NASW, on November 10, 1986, and with Albert Russo, Community Services Department, AFSCME, November 12, 1986.

10. Leslie B. Alexander, "Unions: Social Work," *Encyclopedia of Social Work* (Silver Spring, Md.: National Association of Social Workers, 1987), p. 798.

11. Jerry Wurf, "Labor Movement, Social Work Fighting Similar Battles," *NASW News* 25, no. 12 (December 1980): 7.

12. See, for example, Leslie B. Alexander, Philip Lichtenberg, and Dennis Brunn, "Social Workers in Unions: A Survey," *Social Work* 25, (May 1980): 216–23; Gary L. Shaffer and Kathleen Ahearn, "Current Perceptions, Opinions, and Attitudes Held by Professional Social Workers Toward Unionization and the Collective Bargaining Process," unpublished paper, School of Social Work, University of Illinois, Urbana-Champaign, 1982; Ernie S. Lightman, "Professionalization, Bureaucratization, and Unionization in Social Work," *Social Service Review* 56, no. 1 (March 1982): 135; Ernie S. Lightman, "Social Workers, Strikes and Service to Clients," *Social Work* 28 (1983): 142–47; and M. L. Kirzner, *Public Welfare Unions and Public Assistance Policy: A Case Study of the Pennsylvania Social Services Union,* unpublished doctoral dissertation, University of Pennsylvania, 1985.

13. Alexander et al., "Social Workers in Unions," p. 222.

14. Lightman, "Professionalization, Bureaucratization, and Unionization in Social Work," p. 130.

15. Gary L. Shaffer, "Labor Relations and the Unionization of Professional Social Workers," p. 82.

16. See Rene Laliberty and W. I. Christopher, *Health Care Labor Relations: A Guide for the '80s* (Owing Mills, Md.: National Health Publishing, 1986), p. 57.

17. Dena Fisher, "Problems for Social Work in a Strike Situation: Professional, Ethical, and Value Considerations," *Social Work* 32 (May-June 1987): 253–54.

18. "Public Service Workers' Strike Disrupts Life in Canada," *Los Angeles Times,* September 10, 1991, p. A–8.

19. Srinika Jayaratne, Kristine Siefert, and Wayne Chess, "Private and Agency Practitioners: Some Data and Observations," *Social Service Review* 62 (June 1988): 331.

20. National Association of Social Workers, *Salaries in Social Work* (Silver Spring, Md.: NASW, 1987), p. 7.

21. Srinika Jayaratne et al., "Private and Agency Practitioners," pp. 327–28.

22. Ibid., p. 327.

23. Ibid., p. 329.

24. Ibid.

25. Eliot Freidson, *The Profession of Medicine* (New York: Dodd, Mead, 1970), pp. 92–96.

26. Quoted in Ralph Pumphrey and Muriel Pumphrey, *The Heritage of American Social Work* (New York: Columbia University Press, 1961), p. 393.

27. Ernest Greenwood, "Attributes of a Profession," *Social Work* 2 (1957): 45–55.

28. Ibid., p. 54.

29. Nina Toren, *Social Work: The Case of the Semi-Profession* (Beverly Hills, Calif.: Sage, 1972), pp. 38–39.

30. A. M. Carr-Saunders, "Metropolitan Conditions and Traditional Professional Relationships," in R. M. Fisher, ed., *The Metropolis and Modern Life* (New York: Russell Sage, 1967), pp. 279–89.

31. Freidson, *The Profession of Medicine,* p. 71.

32. Ibid., p. 184.

33. Sidney Levenstein, *Private Practice in Social Casework* (New York: Columbia University Press, 1964), p. 4.

34. Stuart Kirk and Herb Kutchins, "Deliberate Misdiagnosis in Mental Health Practice," *Social Service Review* 62 (June 1988): 235.

35. National Association of Social Workers, "Code of Ethics of the National Association of Social Workers," *Encyclopedia of Social Work, 18th Edition* (Silver Spring, Md.: NASW, 1987), pp. 952–56.
36. Magali Larson, *The Rise of Professionalism* (Berkeley: University of California Press, 1977), pp. 9–10.
37. Irving Piliavin, "Restructuring the Provision of Social Services," *Social Work* 13 (1968): 34–41.
38. Larson, *The Rise of Professionalism.*
39. Srinika Jayaratne et al., "Private and Agency Practitioners," p. 328.
40. National Association of Social Workers, *NASW Data Bank* (Silver Spring, Md.: NASW, 1985), p. 3.
41. Srinika Jayaratne et al., "Private and Agency Practitioners," p. 334.
42. M. A. Golton, "Private Practice in Social Work," *Encyclopedia of Social Work* (Silver Spring, Md.: NASW, 1973), p. 949.
43. Walter Trattner, *From Poor Law to Welfare State* (New York: Free Press, 1974), p. 250.
44. National Association of Social Workers, *Manpower Data Bank Frequency Distributions* (Silver Spring, Md.: NASW, 1973 and 1975).
45. Patricia Kelly and Paul Alexander, "Part-Time Private Practice: Practical and Ethical Considerations," *Social Work* 30, no. 3 (May-June 1985): 254.
46. National Association of Social Workers, *NASW Data Bank* (Silver Spring, Md.: NASW, 1985), p. 3
47. Robert Barker, "Private and Proprietary Services," *Encyclopedia of Social Work,* 18th ed. (Silver Spring, Md.: NASW, 1987), p. 326.
48. "Licensure Act Passed," *NASW News* 32, no. 8 (September 1987): 10.
49. For details on state licensure and professional certification, see Robert Barker, "Private and Proprietary Services."
50. Srinika Jayaratne et al., "Private and Agency Practitioners," p. 333.
51. "Special Report," *Psychotherapy Finances,* March 1978, p. 16.
52. Srinika Jayaratne et al., "Private and Agency Practitioners," p. 334.
53. Srinika Jayaratne, Mary Lou Davis Sacks, and Wayne Chess, "Private Practice May Be Good for Your Health and Well-Being," *Social Work* 36 (May 1991): 226–27.
54. Jae-Sung Choi, "Members' Views on the California Licensing System for Social Work Practice" (Sacramento: California Chapter, NASW, 1990), p. 6.
55. Donald Feldstein, "Debate on Private Practice," *Social Work* 22, no. 3 (1977): 3.
56. Ibid., p. 4.
57. Patricia Kelley and Paul Alexander, "Part-Time Private Practice," p. 255.
58. N. T. Edwards, "The Survival of Structure and Function in Private Practice," *Journal of the Otto Rank Association* 13 (1979): 12, 15.
59. Jayaratne et al., "Private Practice," *Social Work* 36 (May 1991): 228–29.
60. Franklin Chu and Sharland Trotter, *The Madness Establishment* (New York: Grossman, 1974), p. 61.
61. Robert Barker, *The Business of Psychotherapy* (New York: Columbia University Press, 1982), p. xi.
62. Stuart Kirk and Herb Kutchins, "Deliberate Misdiagnosis in Mental Health Practice," p. 230.
63. Ibid., p. 234.
64. Ibid., pp. 232, 234–35.
65. Ibid., p. 235.
66. Kimberly Strom, "Reimbursement Demands and Treatment Decisions: A Growing Dilemma for Social Workers," *Social Work* 37 (September 1992): 18.
67. Robert Barker, *Social Work in Private Practice* (Silver Spring, Md.: NASW, 1984), p. 113.
68. Kirk and Kutchins, "Deliberate Misdiagnosis in Mental Health Practice," p. 232.
69. Kathy Sawyer, "Insuring the Bureaucracy's Mental Health," *The Washington Post,* April 10, 1979, p. A–8.
70. "'Signing Off' Fraud Charge Warns Kentucky Clinicians," *NASW News* 32, no. 6 (June 1987): 1.
71. Patricia Kelley and Paul Alexander, "Part-Time Private Practice," p. 254.
72. Daniel Goleman, "Social Workers Vault into a Leading Role in Psychotherapy," *New York Times,* April 3, 1985, C–1.
73. Ellen Dunbar, "Future of Social Work," *NASW California News* 13, no. 18 (May 1987): 3.
74. David Gelman, "Growing Pains for the Shrinks," *Newsweek,* December 14, 1987, p. 71.

75. Reprinted from "Letters," *Social Work* 34 (November 1989): 479.

76. Paul Starr, "The Meaning of Privatization," quoted in American Federation of State, County, and Municipal Employees, *Private Profit, Public Risk: The Contracting Out of Professional Services* (Washington, D.C.: AFSCME, 1986), pp. 4–5.

77. Charles Schultz, *The Public Use of Private Interest* (Washington, D.C.: Brookings Institution, 1977); Donald Fisk, Herbert Kiesling, and Thomas Muller, *Private Provision of Public Service* (Washington, D.C.: Urban Institute, 1978); Harry Hatry, *A Review of Private Approaches for the Delivery of Public Services* (Washington, D.C.: Urban Institute, 1983).

78. *Privatization: Toward More Effective Government* (Washington, D.C.: Report of the President's Commission on Privatization, March 1988), p. 230.

79. Ibid., pp. 1–2.

80. See Lawrence S. Lewin, Robert A. Derzon, and Rhea Margulies, "Investor-Owned and Nonprofits Differ in Economic Performance," *Hospitals*, July 1, 1981, pp. 65–69; Robert V. Pattison and Hallie Katz, "Investor-Owned Hospitals and Not-for-Profit Hospitals," *New England Journal of Medicine*, August 11, 1983, pp. 54–65; Robin Eskoz and K. Michael Peddecord, "The Relationship of Hospital Ownership and Service Composition to Hospital Charges," *Health Care Financing Review*, Spring 1985, pp. 125–32; J. Michael Watt et al., "The Comparative Economic Performance of Investor-Owned Chain and Not-for-Profit Hospitals," *New England Journal of Medicine*, January 9, 1986, pp. 356–60; Bradford Gray and Walter McNerney, "For-Profit Enterprise in Health Care: The Institute of Medicine Study," *New England Journal of Medicine*, June 5, 1986, pp. 560–63; Regina Herzlinger and William Kradker, "Who Profits from Nonprofits?" *Harvard Business Review*, January-February 1987, pp. 554–62.

81. Philip Alper, "Medical Practice in the Competitive Market," *New England Journal of Medicine*, February 5, 1987, pp. 337–38.

82. Patricia Franklin, "The AIDS Business," *Business*, April 1987, p. 44.

83. Richard Titmuss, *The Gift Relationship* (New York: Pantheon, 1971), p. 223.

84. Theodore Marmor, Mark Schlesinger, and Richard Smithey, "A New Look at Nonprofits: Health Care Policy in a Competitive Age," *Yale Journal of Regulation* 3 (Spring 1986): 320.

85. W. Harrison Wellford and Janne Gallagher, *Charity and the Competition Challenge* (Washington, D.C.: National Assembly of National Voluntary Health and Social Welfare Organizations, 1987), pp. 13–15.

86. Michael Abramowitz, "Nonprofit Hospitals Venture into New Lines of Business," *The Washington Post*, February 15, 1987, p. C–5.

87. Todd Gillman, "Health Clubs Hit YMCAs' Tax Breaks," *The Washington Post*, June 30, 1987, p. E–2.

88. Anne Swardson, "Hill Taking New Look at Nonprofits," *The Washington Post*, June 21, 1987, p. F–9.

89. Richard Cloward and Irwin Epstein, "Private Social Welfare's Disengagement from the Poor," in Meyer Zald, ed., *Social Welfare Institutions* (New York: John Wiley, 1965), pp. 628–29.

90. Emily Friedman, "The 'Dumping' Dilemma: The Poor Are Always with Some of Us," *Hospitals*, September 1, 1982, p. 52.

91. David Himmelstein, "Patient Transfers: Medical Practice as Social Triage," *American Journal of Public Health*, May 1984, p. 496.

92. Friedman, "The 'Dumping' Dilemma," p. 54.

93. Mark Schlesinger, "The Privatization of Health Care and Physicians' Perceptions of Access to Hospital Services," *The Milbank Quarterly* 65 (1987): 40.

94. Marmor et al., "A New Look at Nonprofits," p. 344.

95. Lewin et al., "Investor-Owned and Nonprofits Differ in Economic Performance."

96. Jerry Avorn, "Nursing-Home Infections—The Context," *New England Journal of Medicine*, September 24, 1981, p. 759.

97. Reported in Arnold Relman, "Investor-Owned Hospitals and Health Care Costs," *New England Journal of Medicine*, August 11, 1983, pp. 370–71.

98. Pattison and Katz, "Investor-Owned Hospitals and Not-For-Profit Hospitals," p. 61.

99. Michael McMullan, personal correspondence, March 7, 1988; and "Use of Short-Stay Hospital Services by Medicare Hospital Insurance Bene-

ficiaries by State of Provider and Type of Control: 1985" (Baltimore: Health Care Finance Administration, 1985).

100. Gray and McNerney, "For-Profit Enterprise in Health Care," p. 1525.

101. "Hospitals' Medicare Profits Up," *San Diego Union*, March 29, 1987, p. A5.

102. "Competition for Doctors and Patients Increases Hospital Costs," *NCHSR Research Activities* No. 101 (January 1988), p. 3.

103. Richard Buchanan, "Long-Term Care's Pricing Dilemma," *Contemporary Administrator*, February 1981, p. 20.

104. Ann LoLordo, "Life-Care Centers Offer Seniors Worry-Free Living," *The Baltimore Sun*, June 4, 1984, p. D4.

105. Carol Olten, "Communities Offering Seniors a Graceful Life," *The San Diego Union*, March 13, 1988, p. D-5.

106. Anthony Perry, "North County Housing Boom: A Lucrative Shade of Gray," *Los Angeles Times*, March 6, 1988, p. E-5.

107. U.S. Senate Special Committee on Aging, *Discrimination Against the Poor and Disabled in Nursing Homes* (Washington, D.C.: U.S. Government Printing Office, 1984), p. 8.

108. Perry, "North County Housing Boom."

109. U.S. Senate, *Discrimination Against the Poor and Disabled in Nursing Homes*, pp. 6–8.

110. Ibid., p. 36.

111. The most well-known bankruptcy of a life care community was that of Pacific Homes of California in 1979.

112. "Sun City—With an Add-On," *Forbes*, November 23, 1981, p. 84.

113. Jesse Glasgow, "Marriott to Test Life-Care," *The Baltimore Sun*, June 16, 1984, p. C-1.

114. "Merrill-Lynch: Bullish on Health Care," *Contemporary Administrator*, February 1982, p. 16.

115. Anne Somers, "Insurance for Long-Term Care," *New England Journal of Medicine*, July 2, 1987, p. 27.

116. U.S. Senate, *Discrimination Against the Poor and Disabled in Nursing Homes*, p. 25.

117. Ibid., p. 10.

118. Robert Pear, "Lack of Beds Seen in Nursing Homes," *New York Times*, October 17, 1982, p. 1.

119. Quoted in William Spicer, "The Boom in Building," *Contemporary Administrator*, February 1982, p. 16.

120. Donald Light, "Corporate Medicine for Profit," *Scientific American*, December 1986, p. 42.

121. Arnold Relman, "The New Medical-Industrial Complex," *New England Journal of Medicine* 303, no. 17 (1980): 80.

122. Paul Starr, "The Limits of Privatization," in Steve Hanke, *Prospects for Privatization* (New York: Proceedings of the Academy of Political Science, 1987), pp. 82–107.

123. Reason Foundation, *Privatization 1992* (Los Angeles: Reason Foundation, 1992), p. 17.

124. David Stoesz, "Human Service Corporations: New Opportunities in Social Work Administration," *Social Work Administration* 12 (1989): 35–43.

125. Mary Adelaide Mendelson, *Tender Loving Greed* (New York: Knopf, 1974).

126. NASW, "'87 Session of Congress Ends in 11th-Hour Win for NASW," *NASW News*, February 1988, p. 1.

127. Reason Foundation, *Privatization*, p. 251.

128. Srinika Jayaratne, Mary Lou Davis-Sacks, and Wayne Chess, "Private Practice May Be Good for Your Health and Well-Being," *Social Work* 36 (May 1991): 229.

129. Stan Taubman, "Private Practice! Oh No!" *NASW California News*, March 1991, p. 8.

130. David Donnison, "The Progressive Potential of Privatisation," in Julian LeGrand and Ray Robinson, eds., *Privatisation and the Welfare State* (London: George Allen & Unwin, 1984), pp. 211–231.

131. David Stoesz, "The Family Life Center," *Social Work* 26, no. 5 (September 1981): 85–92.

PART TWO

The Voluntary and For-Profit Social Welfare Sector

CHAPTER 8

The Voluntary Sector Today

This chapter describes the voluntary sector, made up of those private, nonprofit organizations that are important on the American social welfare scene. Philanthropic contributions have been an important source of revenues for social service initiatives. Prominent human service agencies, such as the Red Cross, the Family Service Association of America, and the Salvation Army, are identified. In addition, the role of voluntary agencies in advocating social justice is described. Finally, the fiscal crisis of the voluntary sector is discussed, as are the recession and the scandal that shook the United Way during the early 1990s, thus further compounding the funding problems of nonprofit service agencies.

Approaching the twenty-first century, welfare professionals are reassessing the capacity of the voluntary sector to meet the nation's social welfare needs. The primary reason for renewed interest in the voluntary sector is the reluctance of taxpayers and politicians to authorize major new governmental welfare initiatives. As governmental expenditures for social welfare fail to increase in the face of rising demand for human services, the voluntary sector has been called upon to shoulder more of the welfare burden. This was stated explicitly by President Reagan, who appealed to the charitable impulses of Americans as a way of addressing human needs while reducing federal appropriations to social programs, and was restated by George Bush in his now-famous reference to "a thousand points of light" during his 1988 presidential campaign.

While many liberals were skeptical about the sincerity of the Reagan and Bush administrations in this regard, suspecting that it was a ruse to gut governmental social programs, other events conspired to focus attention on the voluntary sector. A wave of conservative populism, most evident in the religious right, stalled the introduction of liberally inspired social legislation. Conservative populists challenged welfare programs on the grounds that they divided the family, eroded the work ethic, and subverted communal norms. A widely distributed monograph by analysts from the American Enterprise Institute criticized social "megastructures," which contributed to alienation among Americans, and called for stronger "mediating structures"— voluntary entities—to empower people.[1] Reacting to these conservative trends, Democrats jettisoned from their party platform traditional welfare planks that called for new federal social programs in favor of more pluralist strategies that included the private sector. Finally, welfare advocates established a new organization, Independent Sector, to promote the interests of voluntary sector organizations. By 1986, six years after its inception, Independent Sector was able to boast more than 650 corporate, foundation, and voluntary organization members.

THE "FORGOTTEN SECTOR"

Despite this flurry of activity, the role of the voluntary sector in American social welfare is neither fully appreciated nor well understood.[2] Following the triumph of the New Deal, leading welfare theoreticians expected government to dominate in the creation and administration of the welfare state. In fact, so complete was the expectation that the government-driven welfare state would dominate social welfare in the United States that references to private voluntary agencies became scant in the professional literature. There was little room within welfare state ideology for a dynamic voluntary sector, and references to private, nonprofit agencies virtually disappeared from discussions of American social welfare. When discussed at all, voluntary agencies were viewed as quaint holdovers from an earlier time. Rediscovered during the 1980s, the voluntary sector quickly attracted converts. Perhaps the most notable of the new adherents to the promise of nonprofits was business guru Peter Drucker. Citing the capacity of the "social sector" to address local problems, Drucker not only recited the virtues of the nonprofit sector in books, such as *The New Realities*,[3] but went so far as to establish the Peter F. Drucker Foundation for Nonprofit Management in 1990.[4]

To the extent that the voluntary sector has been included as a part of the governmental welfare state, it has been considered a subcontractor of social service. This role was made possible through an amendment to the Social Security Act, Title XX, which allowed for the "purchase of service" from private providers. Under purchase-of-service contracts, government could avoid the costs and responsibilities

of administering programs directly. Because of an open-ended funding formula, however, federal costs for Title XX services escalated sharply. Congress later capped Title XX expenditures, initially at $2.5 billion, in order to contain program costs, and later the Reagan administration was successful in having the program placed under a Social Services Block Grant, with further funding restrictions.[5] Consequently, in response to Title XX, many voluntary social service agencies secured purchase-of-service contracts, the funding for which allowed nonprofit agencies to expand programs in the late 1960s and early 1970s. However, when funding was reduced, voluntary sector agencies were heavily penalized. Federal expenditures for Title XX fell from $2.8 billion in 1980 to $2.7 billion in 1992, a significant reduction in that it occurred at a time when demand for service was rising sharply.[6] As a result, voluntary social welfare agencies were hard-pressed to maintain such services as home-based care, child day care and protective services, self-support education, and adoption and family counseling services, among others. Although federal assistance to voluntary sector social service agencies became critically important to them, accounting for up to half of agency funding, purchase of service continued to be a relatively minor portion of governmental welfare expenditures. In 1986, for example, Title XX accounted for only about 2 percent of all federal expenditures for welfare programs benefiting low-income people.[7]

Consequently, when policymakers turned to the voluntary sector in the 1980s to compensate for reductions in the governmental welfare effort, little was known about nonprofit social service agencies. Lester Salamon and Alan Abramson, authorities on the voluntary sector, observed that "despite their importance, these organizations have tended to be ignored in both public policy debates and scholarly research."[8] As government assumed a dominant role in American social welfare, the voluntary sector receded in importance. Now, after half a century of neglect, the "forgotten sector" is being called upon to assume new responsibilities in caring for the needy.

Only in recent times have researchers begun to investigate the scope of the voluntary sector. Their task has not been an easy one. The voluntary sector is composed of tens of thousands of organizations, many of which are not associated with a national umbrella association. The picture that is emerging from these preliminary investigations reveals a sector that, if small by economic standards, is extraordinarily rich socially. Perhaps the most convenient measure of the scale of the voluntary sector is to count those voluntary and philanthropic associations that have received tax-exempt status as social service agencies from the Internal Revenue Service—560,588 in 1987.[9] Despite the large number of voluntary sector organizations, they account for only 5.8 percent of the national income, compared with 78.5 percent attributed to commerce and 15 percent to government.[10] Indeed, the strength of the voluntary sector lies in its incorporation into the social fabric of American life. Some 80 million Americans 18 years or older volunteered an average 4.7 hours per week in 1987.[11] A substantial majority of Americans (88.5 percent in 1987) made charitable contributions to voluntary sector agencies, averaging $793.[12] Contrary to popular assumption, the voluntary sector is not bankrolled by wealthy philanthropists and their foundations.

Foundations and corporations account for only 10 percent of voluntary sector contributions; "about half of all charitable dollars comes from families with incomes under $25,000."[13] Table 8.1. breaks down the sources of funds for the independent sector in five separate years.

In 1987, nonprofit social service agencies accounted for $28.4 billion in revenues,[14] a modest increase from the $27.3 billion budgeted in 1982.[15] Voluntary social service agencies vary considerably in their dependence on various sources of revenue, as can be seen in Table 8.2. These data reveal two developments influencing voluntary social service agencies. First, governmental and private giving account for about 80 percent of revenues. Second, governmental support declined sharply during the early 1980s. The significance of this is addressed later in the chapter. Perhaps most important, fees charged to clients of voluntary social service agencies account for about 12 percent of revenues, which dispels any thought that these organizations as a group could become self-sufficient through the collection of client fees. Although some organizations are able to derive more of their revenues from fees, most social service agencies depend on other revenue sources, as Tables 8.1 and 8.2 illustrate.[16]

Proponents of private, nonprofit organizations contend that economic measures do not adequately represent the significance of the voluntary sector in the national culture. Consistent

TABLE 8.1. Independent Sector: Annual Sources of Funds, 1977, 1982, 1984, and 1987 (In billions of dollars)

Sources of Funds	1977		1982		1984		1987	
	Amount	Percent	Amount	Percent	Amount	Percent	Amount	Percent
Private Sector	$83.8	73.3	$155.3	73.0	$185.3	73.1	$241.8	73.9
Contributions	33.8	29.6	55.8	26.2	68.3	26.9	89.4	27.3
Dues, fees, and charges	41.6	36.4	80.6	37.9	95.7	37.8	126.4	38.6
Other receipts	8.4	7.3	18.9	8.9	21.3	8.4	26.0	7.9
Endowments (investment income)	5.3	4.6	12.6	5.9	14.0	5.5	15.7	4.8
Other	3.1	2.7	6.3	3.0	7.2	2.8	10.3	3.1
Government Sector	30.5	26.7	57.4	27.0	68.2	26.9	85.4	26.1
Total	$114.3	100.0	$212.7	100.0	$253.5	100.0	$327.2	100.0

SOURCE: Virginia Hodgkinson and Murray Weitzman, *Dimensions of the Independent Sector* (Washington, D.C.: Independent Sector, 1989), p. 37. Reprinted with permission.

TABLE 8.2. Agency Funding Sources, 1986 (In percent of contributions)

	Private Support	Government	Fees and Dues	Other*
Boys Clubs	66	7	8	19
Catholic Charities	21	47	12	19
Child Welfare Agency	15	65	6	14
Family Service Agency	28	46	17	9
Goodwill Industries	29	19	19	33
Jewish Community Centers	16	7	54	23
Salvation Army	57	14	10	20
Volunteers of America	13	45	8	34
YMCA, YMCA-YWCA	17	4	67	12
YWCA	29	21	36	14

* Other includes such sources of income as bequests, investment income, sale of capital goods, and sale of merchandise. The relatively high percentage of support in the "other" category for Goodwill Industries, the Salvation Army, and Volunteers of America comes from sales of donated merchandise. (SOURCE: Virginia Hodgkinson and Murray Weitzman, *Dimensions of the Independent Sector* [Washington, D.C.: Independent Sector, 1986], p. 21. Reprinted with permission.)

with the label "voluntary," nonprofit social service agencies attract the commitment of millions of volunteers who see human service organizations as a vehicle for improving the quality of life in their communities. During 1987, volunteers in social service agencies put in enough time to equal 409,000 full-time employees.[17] Significantly, volunteering increased in the mid-1980s, to some extent compensating for reductions in governmental support. Despite this outpouring of support for voluntary social service agencies, a question remains concerning the degree to which nonprofit social service agencies should have to rely on volunteers when nonprofit organizations in education and the arts are more likely to have employees providing services.

ADVANCING SOCIAL JUSTICE

In addition to providing social services, the voluntary sector has been important in American social welfare because it has been the source of events that have advanced the rights of disenfranchised populations. In this respect, the voluntary sector is essential to American culture in that it is a correcting influence to the indifference often shown to minority populations by governmental and corporate bureaucracies. This case has been argued vigorously by John W. Gardner, former secretary of Health, Education, and Welfare, president of the Carnegie Corporation, and now chairperson of the Board of Independent Sector. According to Gardner, the voluntary sector fosters much of the pluralism in American life, taking on those concerns that do not attract the broad spectrum of public support necessary for the legislation that mandates governmental programs or concerns that do not represent the commercial prospects necessary to attract the interests of the business community. In other words, the voluntary sector serves as the best—and, in some cases, the only—vehicle for addressing certain social needs. Indeed, much of what Americans would identify as central to their culture can be attributed to organizations of the voluntary sector: hospitals, schools, religious institutions, welfare agencies, fraternal associations, symphonies, and museums, as a partial list. According to Gardner,

Institutions of the nonprofit sector are in a position to serve as the guardians of intellectual and artistic freedom. Both the commercial and political marketplaces are subject to leveling forces that may threaten standards of excellence. In the non-profit sector, the fiercest champions of excellence may have their say. So may the champions of liberty and justice.[18]

Gardner's last reference here is not merely rhetorical, but has its basis in history. As Alexis de Tocqueville observed over a century ago, Americans have depended on voluntary organizations to solve communal problems. In doing so, the voluntary sector has claimed an impressive list of positive additions to American life. Those seeking solutions to current problems often find inspiration in voluntary sector initiatives of the past. Gardner noted that, "At a time in our history when we are ever in need of new solutions to new problems, the private sector is remarkably free to innovate, create, and engage in controversial experiments." He went on to observe that, "In fact, virtually every far-reaching social change in our history has come up in the private sector: the abolition of slavery, the reforms of populism, child labor laws, the vote for women, civil rights, and so on."[19]

Important social welfare initiatives have also originated in the voluntary sector. The War on Poverty—during which new social programs such as Medicaid, Food Stamps, and the Job Corps were launched—can be traced to the Mobilization for Youth, a voluntary sector poverty program in New York City funded by the Ford Foundation. Two champions of community organization, the late Saul Alinsky and Cesar Chavez of the United Farm Workers Union, were also influenced by the privately run Industrial Areas Foundation in Chicago. More recently, services to battered women, patients with AIDS, and the homeless have been pioneered by voluntary sector organizations. Given public apathy toward these groups for so many years, the voluntary sector was the only source of service for these groups.

That social change begins in the voluntary sector has a particular lesson for human service

professionals: The openness of democratic American culture means that anyone is free to organize for purposes of rectifying past injustices. The building blocks of a voluntary sector initiative are well within the reach of social welfare professionals—recruiting participants, forming a board of directors, filing for tax-exempt status under Internal Revenue Service Code 501(c)(3), soliciting contributions, and applying for grants and contracts. Wendy Kopp's Teach For America (TFA) is a good illustration. Having a vision of a Peace Corps-like program for inner cities and rural areas, 23 year-old Kopp began hustling corporate contributions in 1988 to match idealist professionals to disadvantaged communities. By 1990, TFA boasted a $2.7-million budget and had found its first 500 volunteers.[20] What Wendy Kopp has accomplished in New York City illustrates the promise of the voluntary sector in every American community.

CONTEMPORARY NONPROFIT HUMAN SERVICE ORGANIZATIONS

The voluntary human service sector consists of a large constellation of organizations. The more than 500,000 nonprofit social agencies in 1987 provided a range of services, including individual and family services, job training, child care, residential care, and social services. The best depiction of the voluntary sector is not provided by statistics, however, but by a description of the organizations that are instantly recognizable by most Americans (see Table 8.3).

THE UNITED WAY

Perhaps the best-recognized of voluntary sector organizations is the United Way. Local United Ways, as well as the United Way of America, are nonprofit organizations themselves. The purpose of local United Ways is to raise funds that are then disbursed to nonprofit agencies in the community, most of which are United Way

TABLE 8.3. Nonprofit Human Service Organizations, 1992

Name	Budget ($ Millions)	Affiliates	Services	Current Issues/Goals
American Foundation for the Blind	15.5	5 regional offices	Education, rehabilitation, and socialization of the blind; public education about vision impairment	Enhance services to the multihandicapped; develop special services for the aged blind and blind Native Americans; Braille literacy; enhance services to deaf/blind and handicapped children.
American Red Cross	1.105	2,763 chapters; 277 armed forces stations; 56 regional blood centers	Disaster relief; blood donor program; water safety; first aid training	AIDS education; human tissue banks for transplantation
Arthritis Foundation	65.0	69 chapters and divisions	Health and exercise programs for those with arthritis; biomedical research on the causes and relief of arthritis	Establish a separate association for those with rheumatism; pilot a special program for children.
Association for Retarded Citizens of the United States	5.26*	1,300 local groups; 46 state groups	Research, education, and prevention of retardation and physical handicaps	Bioengineering projects to aid the physically handicapped
Big Brothers/Big Sisters of America	3.8	11 regional groups; 4 district groups	Providing adult guidance for children from single-parent households	Increase minority recruitment.
Boy Scouts of America (1988)	49.7	413 councils	Leadership and citizenship training; drug and child-abuse awareness	Enhance number of scouts and leaders; reduce costs of liability insurance.
Boys Club of America	11.7*	1,100 club units	Leadership education, socialization of poor youth	Outreach to at-risk youth; delinquency prevention
Campfire Boys and Girls	3.5	240 local groups	Personal living skills and leadership development	Internal reorganization; develop enterprise dept.; enhance revenue and membership.
Catholic Charities USA	1.46*	633 affiliates	Counseling; adoption; immigration; emergency support; housing	Economic justice; family life; shelter; hunger; health care
Child Welfare League of America	6.5	5 regional groups	Abused children; adolescent pregnancy; child care; adoption services	Develop child day care; adolescent pregnancy prevention; parenting effectiveness education
Council of Jewish Federations	8.1*	200+ in North America	Services to families and the aged; community organization and planning; Jewish cultural development	Make up for decreased United Way funding; develop worldwide satellite transmissions; strengthen relationship with Israeli and North American Jewry and sense of Jewish identity.
Family Service America	8.9*	200+ community agencies	Counseling and advocacy services to families	Expand services dealing with substance abuse and abuse in the family; internal organizational development
Girl Scouts of the U.S.A.	29.0	335 local groups	Leadership, education, and socialization of girls	Eliminate institutional racism; diversify funding; respond to council and community needs.

TABLE 8.3. *(continued)*

Name	Budget ($ Millions)	Affiliates	Services	Current Issues/Goals
Goodwill Industries of America	6.1*	179 members	Vocational rehabilitation for the disabled	Compensate for cuts in govt. funds; focus on hi-tech skills; respond to competition from retail firms.
National Council on Alcoholism	17.0	186 local groups	Prevention of alcoholism; public education policy analysis	Include drugs other than alcohol in programs.
National Easter Seal Society	301.0	150 affiliates in U.S.; 400 service centers	Home health care for the disabled; public education and advocacy of the disabled	Computer applications to assist the disabled; design to accommodate disabilities
National Mental Health Association	1.76*	550 state groups	Client and public policy advocacy for the emotionally disturbed; direct client support services; public education	Increase mental health services as a national priority.
National Urban League	18.9	113 local groups	Advocating equality for minorities; public education; policy monitoring	Improve behavior of adolescent males; mobilize communities to fight crime.
Planned Parenthood Federation of America	383.0	171 affiliates	Family planning; sex education in schools; abortion rights	Expand reproductive rights to underserved groups; respond to changes in health policy; review bioethical implications of new reproductive technology.
The Salvation Army	5.3*	1,097 community centers	Homelessness; disaster relief; services to children and youth	Balance evangelism and social service.
United Cerebral Palsy	6.5*	180 members	Rehabilitation of those with cerebral palsy and other severe disabilities; medical research on causes of cerebral palsy	Increase public education efforts, fund raising, biomedical research.
USO (United Service Organization)	16.0	3 regional groups; 70 state groups	Fleet and airport centers; family support; cultural and recreational services	Make entertainment programs self-sufficient.
Visiting Nurses Association of America	6.0	150 members	Home health services	Decrease cost of home health care to patients.
Volunteers of America	3.4*	400 programs in 200 communities	Shelter and food for the disabled; employment training; community corrections	Literacy; child day care at-risk youth
Young Men's Christian Association	1,432	2,069 local groups	Personal and social development; child care; community development	Obtain liability insurance; retain tax-exempt status.
Young Women's Christian Association	11.2*	Over 4,000 locations in 400 communities	Developing potential of women; social and support services to women; advocacy of equality and justice	Develop non-partisan political training workshop.

* National office only. (SOURCE: *Encyclopedia of Associations, 1993, 27th Edition.* Annual reports of organizations.)

members. Local United Ways also contribute a small percentage of funds to the national headquarters, the United Way of America, which is located in suburban Washington, D.C. Because the United Way is a confederation of organizations, power resides within the local United Ways. The United Way of America provides support services nationwide, but has no direct authority over local United Ways. The influence of local United Ways over the United Way of America will be highlighted momentarily.

Revenues of the United Way are derived from multiple sources, as shown in Figure 8.1. As is generally true of charitable contributions, most of the funds contributed to the United Way are from employees and small businesses. Corporations account for somewhat less than a fourth of United Way revenues. Financial support that the United Way provides to local agencies is also varied, as indicated in Figure 8.2. Health, family services, and youth services account for the largest categories of expenditures. Of course, the amounts actually allocated in communities vary considerably according to the different priorities of each local United Way.

In order to focus local responses on increasing national problems, the United Way of America has established priorities for the na-

tion. Inaugurating its second century in American social welfare, the United Way identified eight social problems as foci for its affiliates: *illiteracy* (programs to help the 23 million people who are functionally illiterate in the United States), *hunger and homelessness* (services to aid the 3 million homeless and 20 million Americans who go hungry at least two days each month), *AIDS* (initiatives to contend with a 60 percent increase in AIDS in 1987), *teenage pregnancy* (services to reduce the number of teenage girls [more than 1 million] who become pregnant each year), *children in crisis* (efforts to improve the plight of poor and minority children who suffer from a high incidence of child abuse and neglect, suicide, and unstable homes), *alcoholism and drug abuse* (programs to counter the epidemic of substance abuse among teenagers and minorities), *aging population* (efforts to see that the aged have an adequate supply of essential services), and *child care* (efforts to make provisions for the 20 million children who, in 1990, would come home to an empty house because their parents work.[21] Certainly, the extent to which the voluntary sector is able to respond to these and other worthwhile objectives depends on its ability to deploy new programs to address significant social changes.

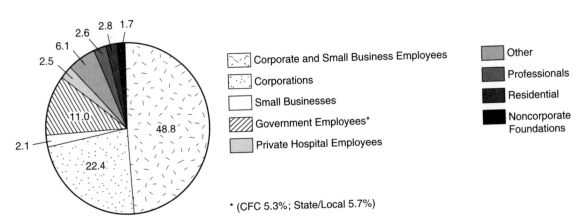

Figure 8.1. Where the Money Comes From, 1992–93: Sources of United Way Campaigns (In percent of contributions). (SOURCE: United Way of America Research Services.)

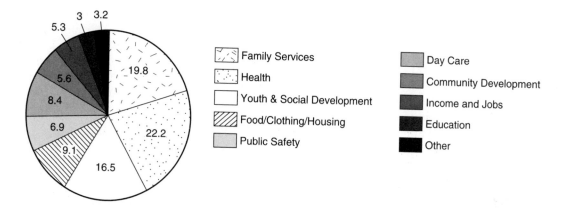

Figure 8.2. Where the Money Goes—1992: United Way Funding to Service Areas (In percent of expenditures). (SOURCE: United Way of America Research Services.)

The Aramony Scandal and Elite Philanthropy

In 1992 the capacity of the nonprofit sector to address mounting social problems was rocked by newspaper reports of financial improprieties by William Aramony, president of the United Way of America. In more than two decades of leadership, Aramony had effectively promoted the United Way of America as the equivalent of a major corporation with hundreds of local franchises. A corporate mentality, evident in modern, spacious offices, was spread throughout local United Ways by the National Academy of Volunteerism, which trained local officials. Opulence of corporate proportions was evident during the centennial celebration of the United Way, when President Reagan spoke before 3,000 guests who had been invited to attend the event at the National Gallery of Art. Mimicking the behavior of corporate executives, who contributed increasing amounts to the United Way of America, Aramony appeared to have vaulted the United Way out of the public relations doldrums associated with social welfare and into a new, dynamic era of human services. To many United Way professionals, William Aramony "walked on water."[22]

The transition was not without its price, however. Muckraking journalists reported that Aramony had supplemented his $390,000 annual salary by authorizing excessive "perks," including a New York penthouse, limousine service, and European trips on the Concorde. Using United Way funds for seed money, Aramony had also authorized the creation of three independent corporations, which later employed his son.[23] Local United Way chiefs recognized that a decadent life-style was utterly inconsistent with their attempt to raise contributions, made more difficult by a nagging recession, and in protest withheld their membership dues to the United Way. Prominent philanthropists called for Aramony's resignation, forcing the issue. To the relief of local United Way officials, Aramony soon resigned from the United Way after 22 years as its head,[24] temporarily replaced by IBM vice president Kenneth Dam.[25] Eventually, Elaine Chao, former director of the Peace Corps, was appointed United Way director at a salary of $195,000, less than half what her predecessor had commanded.[26]

Quickly, the United Way of America moved to ascertain the amount of damage caused by the Aramony scandal. A poll conducted in April 1992 indicated that the number of people who had negative views about the United Way had increased from 14 percent in 1990 to 26 percent in 1992.[27] By July 1992 the Aramony story was more widely known, leaving 49 percent of poll respondents with a more negative view toward the United Way. But the damage seemed to be abating. Although 32 percent of respondents in April 1992 stated that they would give less to the United Way, only 23 percent stated this intention three months later.[28] By the end of 1992 the situation appeared to have subsided. A December 1992 poll indicated that 49 percent of respondents had given the same as usual to the United Way; only 7 percent had reduced their contributions.[29] Yet this could hardly be interpreted as good news. With social needs escalating but the fiscal capacity of voluntary agencies limited by the recession, nonprofit agencies needed a substantial boost in revenues from the United Way. Negative perceptions of the United Way of America undoubtedly diminished how altruistic many Americans were willing to be with their checkbooks. Thus, a final accounting of the Aramony scandal would be translated into the millions of dollars that nonprofit agencies failed to receive in 1992 because of public doubt about the management of the United Way of America.

Perhaps the most intriguing aspect of this debacle was that Aramony had done nothing illegal; he had merely violated norms of propriety informally generated within the philanthropic community. In the aftermath of the scandal, *The Chronicle of Philanthropy* surveyed 117 of the nation's largest nonprofits and determined that one-fourth reported paying chief executives annual salaries of more than $200,000. As examples, Ben Love, chief executive of the Boy Scouts, is paid $223,375; Robert Ross, who heads the Muscular Dystrophy Association, claims $284,808; and Dudley Hafner, executive vice president of the American Heart Association, earns $246,000.[30] Why are nonprofit executives paid so well? Presumably because, in

order to secure charitable contributions, they are expected to associate with the cultural elites who populate American corporations and foundations. To do so requires a substantial enough salary to cover the entertainment, club memberships, and other incidental costs associated with such socialization. Aramony apparently overstepped informally established limits by using United Way funds excessively. Considering the upscale life-style expected of executives of prominent nonprofits, it is easy to understand—if not to condone—how this could occur.

The Aramony scandal has another lesson, and that is the distinction between "elite" and "bourgeois" philanthropy. For purposes of simplification, bourgeois philanthropy supports the relatively modest pursuits of the United Ways that dot the American landscape. Elite philanthropy, on the other hand, has much grander expectations. "Elite American philanthropy serves the interests of the rich to a greater extent than it does the interests of the poor, disadvantaged, or disabled," argues Teresa Odendahl; it "is a system of 'generosity' by which the wealthy exercise social control and help themselves more than they do others."[31] In 1987, for example, Odendahl calculates that $47 billion, about one-half of all gifts itemized on income tax returns, were made by the wealthy.[32] For what purposes do the rich demonstrate such beneficence? They give to institutions that "sustain their culture, their education, their policy formulation, their status—in short, their interests."[33] In other words, wealthy Americans usually use the tax code to maintain institutions of elite culture, such as private schools, museums, the symphony, and the opera, to mention a few. Generosity of sufficient magnitude is often announced to the public by naming an important institution after the benefactor, a tradition that is maintained by cultural elites in major American cities. Using funds, which have been withdrawn from public use by the tax code, in order to reproduce the social institutions of the rich is unacceptable to Odendahl who proposes reforms so that philanthropy will be more truly put to public benefit.

THE DECLINING FISCAL CAPACITY OF THE VOLUNTARY SECTOR

During the early 1980s, the organizations comprising the voluntary sector appeared to make substantial headway in responding to increases in the demand for their services. Funding for nonprofit social service agencies increased comparably to revenue increases for nonprofit activity in education, religion, and the arts. From 1977 to 1987, the total funds for voluntary sector activities increased from $114 billion to $327 billion, more than twofold.[34] Within the voluntary sector, the expenditures for social services increased 152 percent.[35] But this increase obscured deeper problems that have threatened the fiscal stability of nonprofit human service organizations.

Although contributions to social services increased in the early 1980s, social services obtained a smaller portion of all revenues contributed to the voluntary sector. In 1977, social services claimed 10 percent of voluntary sector contributions; in 1984, that proportion dropped to 8.6 percent, then increased slightly to 9.1 percent.[36] In other words, social services struggled to compete with other voluntary sector activities, some of which were new to the nonprofit sector. An example of this can be found in the united giving campaign directed at federal employees, the Combined Federal Campaign, the largest of such fund-raising drives in the United States. Until recently, the United Way claimed about 90 percent of all campaign contributions not specifically designated for other purposes. As a result of challenges brought by agencies as diverse as environmental groups and the National Rifle Association, nondesignated contributions are now apportioned among a larger number of organizations. Consequently, the United Way expected to get approximately 10 percent less than it had in the past from the Combined Federal Campaign.[37]

More discouraging to administrators of nonprofit human service organizations was the precipitous drop in federal governmental funds early in the 1980s. Federal funds to programs in which nonprofit agencies had been active (excluding Medicare and Medicaid) were reduced by about $26 billion each year (about 25 percent) between 1982 and 1984. Yet increased fund-raising efforts to compensate for the loss of governmental funds recovered only 7 percent of the loss.[38] As Table 8.1 shows, throughout the 1980s, government's share of independent sector revenues diminished slightly, but social service agencies were particularly cut. In 1977, government funds accounted for 54.3 percent of the funding for social services provided by nonprofits; in 1987, that amount dropped to 41.4 percent, a reduction of approximately one-fourth.[39]

Unfortunately, the prospect of individual contributors making up for the huge cuts in federal funding is not encouraging. Overall, individuals support the United Way with greater frequency than they do other nonreligious activities,[40] and the majority of United Way contributions, 63.3 percent, come from employees' workplace contributions.[41] Although soliciting higher contributions from employees would seem to be a plausible strategy for increasing voluntary revenues, the decline in wages for middle-income workers in the last several years has left them with less discretionary income to contribute to charitable causes. According to the Economic Policy Institute, family income in 1985 was below that of 1973, the year it peaked.[42] Not only do workers have less discretionary income to donate to charitable causes, but the tax law now provides no incentives for them to make such contributions. The Tax Reform Act of 1986 prohibited individuals from claiming contributions to charitable causes as deductions unless they itemized their income tax returns. Since much of the revenue for the voluntary sector comes from middle-income workers who are less likely to itemize their income tax returns, this tax reform threatened to cut into an important revenue source of nonprofit social service agencies. If the recent past provides little reason to expect increases in workers' giving, the projected future is no more encouraging. In a study of what the American labor force will be like at the turn of the century, the Hudson Institute predicted that workers in the future are more likely to be in lower-paying than in middle- or higher-paying jobs.[43] Not surprisingly, advocates of the voluntary sector have recognized the limits in financial giving that these figures represent. Accordingly, the Independent Sector has asked individuals to contribute time to voluntary organizations if they are unable to contribute money. By 1991, Independent Sector hoped to have brought about wide public exposure to the "fiver" concept—that is, to the idea that individuals should contribute 5 percent of their income or five hours per week to nonprofit organizations.[44]

If individual contributions prove insufficient to mitigate cuts in government funds, other sources of revenue become vital to the ongoing operation of nonprofits. Business accounts for about one-fourth of contributions to the United Way,[45] a figure that had been slowly increasing ever since the late 1970s, when the Filer Commission encouraged greater corporate giving. By 1987, major corporate donors were contributing 1.66 percent of their pre-tax income to charity,[46] although this was still less than Independent Sector's goal of donating "at least 2 percent of pre-tax net income" to voluntary sector organizations.[47] The Conference Board reported that charitable contributions by major service and industrial companies had actually declined about 2 percent in 1986.[48] Another source of revenue to the nonprofits—foundation grants—also shrank. In 1987, foundation gifts were 5.8 percent of foundation assets, down from a high of 8.0 percent in 1981.[49] These trends, the stock market crash of October 19, 1987, and the protracted recession that began in

the early 1990s cast a cloud over the nonprofit sector. Corporations make charitable contributions from discretionary funds, the reserves of which are contingent on past economic performance and the prospects of future growth. Without continuing improvement in the economy, the voluntary sector is not likely to find the business community willing to compensate for cuts in governmental funding.

As a result of diminishing prospects for raising funds from traditional sources, voluntary sector organizations have been forced to consider the entrepreneurial option, that is, of engaging in commercial activities to raise the needed revenues. It is already standard practice for nonprofit service providers to charge fees for service and to bill public and private insurance programs to recoup expenses. Thus, "vendorism" is a common practice of nonprofit social service agencies. But, "entrepreneurialism" is a newer and more significant development. Although it may seem innocuous for financially hard-pressed nonprofit agencies to engage in commercial ventures, some small business operators have complained about the unfair competitive advantage enjoyed by these nonprofits because of their tax-exempt status. (The reaction by the business community to voluntary sector entrepreneurialism is considered in more detail in the discussion of privatization.) Many welfare professionals are also uncomfortable about commercial behavior by nonprofit organizations. Ralph Kramer, an authority on nonprofit social services, has well stated this concern: "In competing with for-profit and other nonprofit organizations for governmental service contracts and for customers for their income producing subsidiaries, it is feared that voluntary agencies can lose their distinctive identity and become more like a commercial organization."[50] Thus, the negative response of the business community and the ambivalence felt by many welfare professionals themselves impose limits on the use of commercial methods to enhance the fiscal capacity of the voluntary sector.

From a broader perspective, it is difficult to be sanguine about the future of the voluntary sector in social welfare. As voluntary sector agencies become more dependent on the communities in which they are located, their success is tied to the affluence of those communities. Compared with those of wealthier communities, agencies in poor communities are unlikely to fare well. For example, the voluntary agencies of Jackson, Mississippi, which depend on government for 66 percent of their revenues, while generating only 7 percent from fees, are less well positioned than those of Flint, Michigan, which depend on government for 33 percent of their funding, but generate fees accounting for 32 percent of revenues.[51] In a pattern all too familiar to many welfare professionals, voluntary agencies in the poorer areas of the United States—rural areas, Appalachia, inner cities, Indian reservations—will again be less able to care for their neighbors in need.

If statistics fail to capture the social significance of many events, the same holds true for recent developments in the voluntary sector. If the voluntary sector possesses a social significance that is larger than its current economic predicament, its advocates should be able to find solace in continuing those peculiarly American activities with which it is associated. But even these activities seem to be in jeopardy. Late in 1987, the Girl Scouts' cookie drive in Fort Collins, Colorado—intended to fund a summer camp—ran into trouble when city officials instituted a sales tax on every box of cookies sold.[52] In another incident, community advocates fought back. When the Marriott Corporation objected to a student bake sale to fund a high school foreign exchange program because it competed with the company's food service contract, students pointed out that Marriott was a $5-billion company, then boycotted the food service until the company dropped its objection to the bake sale.[53] As these instances suggest, advocates of the voluntary sector may claim as their ultimate resource the allegiance of their neighbors.

DISCUSSION QUESTIONS

1. What are the most prominent nonprofit human service agencies in your community? Are they members of the United Way? What do agencies perceive to be the advantages of United Way membership? Do they perceive disadvantages to United Way membership?

2. Has the United Way in your community failed to achieve its goals in contributions in recent years? If so, what are the causes—the recession, the Aramony scandal? Is your local United Way doing anything special to maintain a positive public image?

3. What are the newer nonprofit agencies in your community? What populations do they serve? Are these agencies members of the United Way? If not, how do they attract the necessary resources? What is their perception of the United Way?

4. If there are unmet needs in your community, how would you create a nonprofit agency to meet them? Who would you recruit for your board of directors? Where would you solicit resources, both cash and in-kind? Who would you recruit for staff? What would you name your agency? Would your agency focus on providing services or advancing social change?

5. In response to diminishing resources, many nonprofit social agencies have resorted to entrepreneurial strategies to raise money. What innovative projects have agencies deployed in your community? What entrepreneurial strategies can you think of that might be successful for nonprofit agencies in your community?

NOTES

1. Peter Berger and Richard Neuhaus, *To Empower People: The Role of Mediating Structures in Public Policy* (Washington, D.C.: American Enterprise Institute, 1977).

2. Ralph Kramer, "The Future of Voluntary Organizations in Social Welfare," in *Philanthropy, Voluntary Action, and the Public Good* (Washington, D.C.: Independent Sector/United Way, 1986).

3. Peter Drucker, *The New Realities* (New York: HarperCollins, 1989).

4. Peter Drucker, "It Profits Us to Strengthen Nonprofits," *Wall Street Journal*, December 19, 1991, p. 18.

5. Neil Gilbert, *Capitalism and the Welfare State* (New Haven: Yale University Press, 1983), pp. 6–7; Neil Gilbert and Harry Specht, *Dimensions of Social Welfare Policy*, 2nd ed. (Englewood Cliffs, N.J.: Prentice-Hall, 1989), pp. 46–47.

6. Committee on Ways and Means, U.S. House of Representatives, *Overview of Entitlement Programs, 1992 Green Book* (Washington, D.C.: U.S. Government Printing Office, 1992), p. 830.

7. Ibid.

8. Alan Abramson and Lester Salamon, *The Nonprofit Sector and the New Federal Budget* (Washington, D.C.: Urban Institute, 1986), p. xi. See also Waldemar Nielsen, *The Third Sector: Keystone of a Caring Society* (Washington, D.C.: Independent Sector, 1980).

9. Virginia Hodgkinson and Murray Weitzman, *Dimensions of the Independent Sector* (Washington, D.C.: Independent Sector, 1989), p. 14.

10. Ibid., p. 15.

11. Ibid., p. 10.

12. Ibid., p. 91.

13. Brian O'Connell, *Origins, Dimensions and Impact of America's Voluntary Spirit* (Washington, D.C.: Independent Sector, 1984), p. 2.

14. Hodgkinson and Weitzman, *Dimensions*, p. 22.

15. W. Harrison Wellford and Janne Gallagher, *The Role of Nonprofit Human Service Organizations* (Washington, D.C.: National Assembly of Voluntary Health and Social Welfare Organizations, 1987), Chapter III, p. 15.

16. Ibid., p. 21.

17. Hodgkinson and Weitzman, *Dimensions*, p. 169.

18. Gardner quoted in O'Connell, *Origins, Dimensions and Impact of America's Voluntary Spirit*, p. 6.

19. John W. Gardner, *Keynote Address* (Washington, D.C.: Independent Sector, 1978), p. 13.

20. Irene Lacher, "Teaching America a Lesson," *Los Angeles Times*, November 11, 1990, p. E–1.

21. *Centennial Report* (Alexandria, Va.: United Way of America, 1988), pp. 1–2.

22. Eleanor Brilliant, *The United Way: Dilemmas of Organized Charity* (New York: Columbia University Press, 1990), pp. 278–91.

23. David Lauter, "United Way's Chief Quits in Funds Dispute," *Los Angeles Times*, February 28, 1992, p. A–1.

24. Sara Fritz, "United Way Dues Withheld Over President's Lifestyle," *Los Angeles Times*, February 27, 1992, p. A–1.

25. "Former United Way Chief Still Drawing $390,000 Pay," *Los Angeles Times*, March 7, 1992, p. A–2.

26. Michael Ross, "Peace Corps Director to Head United Way," *Los Angeles Times*, August 27, 1992, p. A–18.

27. United Way of America Research Services, "April 1992 Public Opinion Poll" (Fairfax, Va.: United Way of America, 1992).

28. Ibid.

29. Ibid.

30. Lynn Simross, "When Sharing the Wealth, Let the Donor Beware," *Los Angeles Times*, April 5, 1992.

31. Teresa Odendahl, *Charity Begins at Home* (New York: Basic Books, 1990), pp. 3, 245.

32. Ibid., p. 49.

33. Ibid., p. 232.

34. Hodgkinson and Weitzman, *Dimensions*, p. 6.

35. Ibid.

36. Ibid., p. 12.

37. Judith Havemann, "Federal Charity Drive Opened to More Groups," *Washington Post*, January 2, 1988, p. A–1.

38. Abramson and Salamon, *The Nonprofit Sector and the New Federal Budget*, pp. xvi–xvii.

39. Hodgkinson and Weitzman, *Dimensions*, pp. 180–81.

40. *The Charitable Behavior of Americans* (Washington, D.C.: Independent Sector, 1991), p. 14.

41. *Centennial Report*, p. 1.

42. "Family Incomes in Trouble" (Washington, D.C.: Economic Policy Institute, 1986), p. 1.

43. William Johnston et al., *Workforce 2000* (Washington, D.C.: U.S. Department of Labor, 1987), p. 31.

44. Independent Sector, *Program Plan 1986–1990* (Washington, D.C.: Independent Sector, 1986), p. 26.

45. *Centennial Report*, p. 1.

46. Hodgkinson and Weitzman, *Dimensions*, p. 133.

47. *Program Plan 1986–1990*, p. 27.

48. Cindy Skrzycki, "Pace of Giving by U.S. Firms Slowed in '87," *Washington Post,* January 2, 1988, p. E–6.

49. Hodgkinson and Weitzman, *Dimensions*, p. 121.

50. Kramer, "The Future of Voluntary Organizations in Social Welfare," p. 504.

51. Hodgkinson and Weitzman, *Dimensions,* p. 140.

52. "Girl Scouts View Sales Tax on Cookies as Crummy," *San Diego Tribune,* December 17, 1987, p. C–6.

53. National Public Radio, November 20, 1987.

CHAPTER 9

The Corporate Sector

This chapter considers the role of the business community in American social welfare. Historically, business leaders have made important contributions to the health and welfare of their employees by envisaging utopian work environments and pioneering the provision of benefits to employees. Business leaders were also instrumental in fashioning early governmental welfare policies. More recently, emphasis on the "social responsibility" of corporations has encouraged business leaders to assess the broader implications of corporate activities. Corporations also shape social welfare policy through influencing the political process and subsidizing policy institutes. Human service professionals have become more involved in the corporate sector with the creation of Employee Assistance Plans through which social workers engage in occupational social work. Finally, proprietary human service firms have become well established in several markets: nursing care, hospital management, health maintenance, child care, life/continuing care, and corrections.

The business community in the United States influences social welfare in several important ways. Benefit packages for employees, which are usually available to dependents, pro-

vide important health and welfare benefits to a large segment of the working population. Corporate philanthropy has sponsored important—and, in some cases, controversial—social welfare initiatives. And policy institutes reflecting the priorities of the business community have made substantial changes in American "public philosophy." More recently, the corporate sector has begun to exploit the growing human service markets in long-term care, health maintenance, and corrections. These instances reflect the significant role that the corporate sector has played in American social welfare.

Among welfare theorists, corporate activities have tended to be underappreciated. Many progressive scholars attributed the cause of much social and economic dislocation to industrial capitalism, and therewith implicated its institutional representative, the corporation. Thus, the corporation was not a source of relief, but rather the perpetrator of social and economic hardship. As a result, liberal theorists concluded that the government was the only institution capable of regulating capitalism and compensating the victims of its caprices. Welfare state ideology, as it evolved, left little room for the corporation, viewing it as the source of much suffering and as generally unwilling to pay its share of the tax burden to remediate the problems it had spawned. As an example of this, Citizens for Tax Justice, a liberal advocacy group, reported that between 1981 and 1983, *"128 (or 51%) of the 250 major corporations [studied] paid no federal income taxes or less (i.e., they received rebates of taxes paid in earlier years or sold 'excess' tax benefits) in at least one of the three years, while earning profits of $57.1 billion"* [original emphasis].[1]

Societal abuses committed by the business community have been well chronicled by advocacy groups. These include the disruption, then abandonment, of Love Canal because of improper disposal of toxic waste; the exploitation of Mexican agricultural workers in the Southwest; and the extortion of huge sums from New York City housing officials by landlords who provide single-room occupancy for the homeless. To corporate critics, chief executive officers (CEOs) flaunt their positions by commanding salaries way out of proportion to their productivity. When American automobile executives traveled to Japan to learn more about that nation's superior competitiveness, their average annual salaries of $2 million proved an embarrassment at a time when many were cutting production and laying off tens of thousands of American workers.[2] Such wealth and status are put to effective political use when wealthy executives leave private life and run for public office. "It's no accident that the [U.S.] Senate is a citadel of multi-millionaires," observed one long-time Washington journalist.[3]

Their privileges, power, and wealth notwithstanding, the corporate sector has made contributions to the commonweal, and these are less often recognized. To be sure, most Americans would be able to associate some of the most prominent of American foundations (shown in Table 9.1) with the companies that established them. But what else do they know about corporate involvement in the welfare of the country?

Through a variety of activities, from corpo-

TABLE 9.1. The Ten Largest U.S. Foundations, 1989

Name	Assets ($ billions)
Ford Foundation	5.8
J. Paul Getty Trust	4.5
W. K. Kellogg Foundation	4.2
Lilly Endowment Inc.	3.4
The Pew Charitable Trusts	3.3
MacArthur Foundation	3.2
Johnson Foundation	2.6
The Rockefeller Foundation	2.1
Andrew W. Mellon Foundation	1.8
The Kresge Foundation	1.3
Total	$32.2

SOURCE: Lester Salamon, *America's Nonprofit Sector* (New York: Foundation Center, 1992), p. 19.

rate philanthropy to workers's benefits, corporate executives have made significant improvements in American social welfare. Ironically, many welfare advocates who had leveled blanket indictments of the corporate sector during the 1960s found themselves furtively seeking grants from corporate foundations when government funds for new social programs dried up in the 1980s.

At this point, it would be fair to concede that many welfare theorists are beginning to reexamine the role of the corporate sector in American social welfare. The concept of "the mixed welfare economy" combines the corporate proprietary sector with the governmental and voluntary sectors as primary actors in social welfare.[4] And the issue of "privatization" has provoked a vigorous argument about the proper balance between the public and private (including corporate) welfare sectors.[5] Although Neil Gilbert's *Capitalism and the Welfare State* provides a timely review of the issues posed by "welfare capitalism,"[6] empirical investigations of for-profit human service corporations have only begun.[7] Thus, the role of the corporate sector in American social welfare has yet to be fixed.

HISTORY OF THE CORPORATE SECTOR

For most of the history of the United States, private institutions have been the basis of welfare provision. During the colonial era, the town overseer contracted out the poor to the resident who was willing to provide food and shelter at the lowest bid. Similarly, medical care for the poor was subsidized through purchase of physicians' services. Through the eighteenth and nineteenth centuries this practice contributed to the emergence of private institutions—hospitals and orphanages, among others—that served the needy.[8] Although many of these early welfare institutions were communal efforts and not developed as private businesses, others were precisely that. Thus, many early hospitals in the United States were owned and operated by physicians who became wealthy by providing health care to the community. By 1900, approximately 60 percent of hospitals were privately owned by physicians.[9]

With industrialization, however, the business community took a new interest in the health and welfare of employees. To be sure, certain captains of industry saw employee welfare as a concession to be made as a last resort, sometimes only after violent confrontation with organized workers. Such was not always the case, however. Early in the Industrial Revolution, before government assumed a prominent role in societal affairs, altruistically minded businessmen saw little recourse but to use their business firms as an instrument for their social designs. In some cases, their experiments in worker welfare were nothing less than revolutionary. During the early 1820s, the utopian businessman Robert Owen transformed a bankrupt Scotch mill town, New Lanark, from a wretched backwater populated by paupers into a "marvelously profitable" experiment in social engineering. Owen abolished child labor, provided habitable housing for his workers, and implemented a system to recognize the efforts of individual employees. Soon New Lanark attracted thousands of visitors, who were as awed by the contrast between the squalor of other mill towns and the brilliance of New Lanark as they were by the substantial profits—eventually £60,000—Owen realized from the venture. A humanist, Owen believed that the solution to the problem of poverty lay not in the stringent and punitive English Poor Laws but in "making the poor productive." An irrepressible idealist, Owen later transported his utopian vision to the United States, where he attempted to establish a rural, planned community in New Harmony, Indiana. Ultimately, this American experiment in local socialism failed.[10]

Business leaders in the United States began to acknowledge that industrial production on a grand scale required a healthy and educated work force. Locating such workers was not easy amid the poverty and ignorance that characterized much of the population of the period. To improve the dependability of labor, several large corporations built planned communities for workers. During the early 1880s, the Pullman Company, manufacturer of railroad sleeping cars, "constructed one of the most ambitiously planned communities in the United States—a company town complete with a hotel, markets, landscaped parks, factories, and residences for over 8,000 people."[11] Although some industries later built communities and facilities as a means of controlling and, in some cases, oppressing workers—for example, "the company store" operated by mining companies to keep miners forever in debt—many expressions of corporate interest in employee well-being clearly enhanced the welfare of the community.

In other instances, businesspeople experimented with alternative forms of business ownership. Current "workplace democracy" and "employee ownership" programs can be traced to the Association for the Promotion of Profit Sharing, established in 1892. In 1890, Nelson Olsen Nelson, a founder of this association, set aside a 250-acre tract in Illinois for workers in his company. Naming the village Leclair after a French pioneer of profit sharing, Nelson included in the town plan gardens, walkways, and a school and encouraged employees to build residences in the community. Consistent with his philosophy, Nelson offered employees cash dividends as well as stock in the company; and by 1893, 400 of the 500 employees held stock, thus earning 8 to 10 percent in addition to their wages. Not content with an isolated experiment in industrial socialism, Nelson advanced his ideas in a quarterly journal that promoted profit sharing. Eventually, Nelson went so far as to convert his company into a wholly employee-owned cooperative, but overexpansion and irregular earnings led to his ouster in 1918.[12]

It is important to recognize that such experiments in the social function of the business firm were not solely the work of utopian crackpots, nor were they always the product of peculiar circumstances. Welfare capitalism, "industry's attending to the social needs of workers through an assortment of medical and funeral benefits, as well as provisions for recreational, educational, housing, and social services," was a popular idea among some business leaders prior to World War I.[13] Indeed, concern about the optimal purpose and value of business in the national culture was a frequent subject of discussion among the elite of American commerce. Even a staunch capitalist like John D. Rockefeller took a relatively progressive stance on the corporate role when, in 1918, he asked on behalf of the Chamber of Commerce of the United States:

Shall we cling to the conception of industry as an institution, primarily of private interest, which enables certain individuals to accumulate wealth, too often irrespective of the well-being, the health and happiness of those engaged in its production? Or shall we adopt the modern viewpoint and *regard industry as being a form of social service,* quite as much as a revenue-producing process?. . . . The soundest industrial policy is that which has constantly in mind the welfare of employees as well as the making

of profits, and which, when human considerations demand it, *subordinates profits to welfare.*[14]

As often ill-begotten fortunes accumulated in the hands of the few, some wealthy individuals felt compelled to return a portion of their wealth to the commonweal. "In the latter part of the nineteenth century, men who had great fortunes from the massive industrial growth of the post–Civil War period developed a humanistic concern which was manifested in lavish contributions toward social betterment."[15] Andrew Carnegie, who in 1886 had hired "an army of 300 Pinkerton detectives" to put an end to the violent Haymarket strike,[16] wrote seven years later that massive wealth was a public trust to be put toward the public interest. Eventually, Carnegie donated some $350 million through foundations for this purpose, most visibly for community libraries (often bearing his name) that began to dot towns across the country. For his part, John D. Rockefeller contributed about $530 million.[17]

Although largely based on the guilt associated with the great fortunes won by a handful of individuals in the midst of cruel circumstances for many, philanthropic foundations also fostered enduring contributions to social welfare. The Commonwealth Fund proved instrumental in the execution of a series of child guidance experiments during the 1920s, and these served as prototypes for today's juvenile service departments.[18] The Russell Sage Foundation funded the publication of important works on the development of social welfare, including the classic *Industrial Society and Social Welfare* as well as a series of volumes that were precursors of the *Encyclopedia of Social Work.*[19]

The Rockefeller Foundation took a leading role in providing health care to a Southern African-American population that was neglected by state officials.[20] The active role of the Rockefeller Foundation in the eradication of hookworm warrants particular mention. Shortly after the turn of the century, Charles Wardell Stiles was appointed zoologist of the U.S. Department of Agriculture. Hypothesizing that hookworm was caused by a parasite, Stiles convinced his superiors to fund his trip to the South for the purpose of confirming his theory. Yet the confirmation of his theory notwithstanding, Congress refused to finance an eradication program. So Stiles turned to the Rockefeller Foundation. In 1909 it established the Rockefeller Sanitary Commission for the Eradication of Hookworm Disease, naming Stiles as an officer. Having diagnosed and treated millions of the rural poor—mostly African Americans—shortly before World War I, the commission was well on its way to eradicating the disease that had caused such extensive malaise and listlessness among the poor.[21]

The American business community was also involved in early insurance programs designed to assist injured workers. Although court decisions initially absolved employers of liability for injuries incurred by employees, a swell in jury-awarded settlements to disabled workers convinced corporations of the utility of establishing insurance funds to pool their risk against employee suits. Eventually, companies realized that they would pay lower premiums through state-operated workers' compensation programs than they had been paying through commercial insurance. Consequently, between 1911 and 1920, all 45 states enacted workers' compensation laws.[22] Later, when the Great Depression overtaxed voluntary social welfare agencies, and when labor volatility resulting from high unemployment threatened political stability, it is not surprising that politicians, businessmen, and labor leaders drew on their workers' compensation experience in designing the New Deal. Instrumental in creating federal social programs in the Roosevelt era was Gerald Swope, an executive with the General Electric Company. Having envisaged a "corporate welfare state," including "a national system of unemployment, retirement, life insurance, and disability programs and standards," Swope helped fashion the Social Security program from his po-

sition as chairman of Roosevelt's Business Advisory Council.[23] Moreover, the Social Security program clearly bore the imprint of the business community. As conceived, only workers who had contributed to a trust fund would be able to draw benefits, thus ensuring that no public funds would be required to operate the program.[24] What became known as the "social security concept" illustrated a public pension program that was in fact modeled on programs of the private sector. As such, it "represented the acceptance of approaches to social welfare that private businessmen, not government bureaucrats had created."[25]

The Social Security Act, the crown jewel of the New Deal, meant that the social and economic security of millions of Americans would be underwritten by the state. Although benefits from programs mandated by the Social Security Act became a staple of the American welfare state, the business community continued to make independent decisions regarding the welfare of workers. Major corporations, such as General Electric, General Motors, and IBM, began offering "fringe" benefits as supplements to salaries, and these became important incentives in attracting desirable employees. By the standards of the time, the benefits offered by large corporations were quite generous, including annual vacations, health care, recreation, life insurance, and housing. Business historians Edward Berkowitz and Kim McQuaid have suggested that the conscientiousness with which some corporations cared for their employees was "almost as if these firms were consciously demonstrating that the true American welfare state lay within the large and progressive American corporation."[26] Indeed, the extent to which the business community provided benefits for its workers eclipsed the federal welfare effort. As indicated in Figure 9.1, the assets in private pension funds have exceeded expenditures for all social insurance programs and have, with the exception of a period in the mid-1970s, exceeded total public welfare expenditures.[27] In 1989, 39.2 percent of employees had private

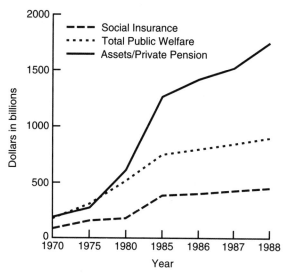

Figure 9.1. Assets in Private Pension Funds and Expenditures for Social Insurance and Public Welfare. (SOURCES: Bureau of the Census, *Statistical Abstract of the United States, 1991* [Washington, D.C.: U.S. Government Printing Office, 1991], p. 356; and *Social Security Bulletin, Annual Statistical Supplement* [Washington, D.C.: U.S. Government Printing Office, 1986], p. 67.)

pension plans, and 53.4 percent were covered by group health insurance.[28]

CORPORATE SOCIAL RESPONSIBILITY

The corporation has also influenced American social welfare as a result of accusations that it has been insensitive to the needs of minorities, the poor, women, and consumers. During the 1960s, criticism of the corporation focused on American business's neglect of minorities and of urban blight. A decade later, issues relating to affirmative action, environmental pollution, and consumer rip-offs were added to the list. These problems contributed to a public relations crisis, as a leading business administration text noted.

> The corporation is being attacked and criticized on various fronts by a great number of political and citizens' organizations. Many

young people accuse the corporation of failing to seek solutions to our varied social problems. Minority groups, and women, contend that many corporations have been guilty of discrimination in hiring and in pay scales.[29]

Melvin Anshen, Paul Garret Professor of Public Policy and Business Responsibility at Columbia University's Graduate School of Business, bemoaned the fact that "profit-oriented private decisions are now often seen as antisocial."[30]

In order to improve their public image, many corporations established policies on social responsibility. Corporations that were reluctant to take the social implications of their operations seriously ran the risk of inviting the surveillance of public interest groups. As an example, the Council on Economic Priorities (CEP), founded in 1969, developed a reputation for investigating the social responsibility of American corporations. In 1986, CEP released *Rating America's Corporate Conscience,* a rating of 125 large corporations based on their standing with respect to seven issues: charitable contributions; representation of women on boards of directors and among top corporate officers; representation of minorities on boards of directors and among top corporate officers; disclosure of social information; involvement in South Africa; conventional weapons-related contracting; and nuclear weapons-related contracting.[31] Social responsibility audits such as this one, provide a guide for consumers to select companies according to their own social consciences and thereby create an incentive for companies to follow socially responsible practices.

Although the facade of public relations frequently glosses over the substantive abuses of business interests, specific corporate social responsibility policies have advanced social welfare. General Electric and IBM instituted strong policies on equal opportunity for and affirmative action toward minorities and women during the late 1960s. Under the title public interest director, Leon Sullivan assumed a position on the

General Motors board of directors, from which he presented six principles governing ethical practices for American corporations doing business in South Africa.[32] According to the "Sullivan principles," American firms with affiliates in South Africa were engaged in ethical practices when they adhered to the following:

1. Nonsegregation of the races in all eating, comfort, and work facilities
2. Equal and fair employment practices for all employees
3. Equal pay for all employees doing equal or comparable work for the same period of time
4. Initiation of and development of training programs that will prepare, in substantial numbers, blacks and other nonwhites for supervisory, administrative, clerical, and technical jobs
5. Increasing the number of blacks and nonwhites in management and supervisory positions
6. Improving the quality of employees' lives outside the work environment in such areas as housing, transportation, schooling, and recreation and health facilities.[33]

In another instance, Control Data Corporation has actually sought out "major unmet social needs, designed means for serving them within the framework of a profit-oriented business enterprise, and brought the needs and the means for serving them together to create markets where none had existed before."[34] These and other initiatives demonstrate that the corporate sector has been willing to undertake significant programs to support troubled communities.[35]

Corporate practices have also been applied directly to social problems. In a venture reminiscent of Robert Owen, developer James Rouse established the Enterprise Foundation in 1981. While technically a foundation that supports charitable projects, what makes it different is that within the foundation is the Enterprise Development Company, a wholly owned taxpaying subsidiary. Profits from the Development Company, projected at $10–$20 million by 1990, are transferred to the foundation to fund projects. By the late 1980s, this fiscally self-sufficient "charity corporation" had developed innovative projects for low-income housing in dozens of cities.[36]

Recognizing the tendency of community institutions in poor areas to become dependent on government or philanthropy for continuing operations, the Ford Foundation sought contributions from corporations for a program to apply business principles to social problems. By 1983, the Local Initiatives Support Corporation (LISC) had developed investment funds in 24 regions supporting 197 community-development projects.[37] LISC projects provided jobs and commodities needed in disadvantaged communities, including a fish processing and freezing plant in Maine, a for-profit construction company in Chicago, and a revolving loan fund to construct low- and moderate-income housing in Philadelphia.[38]

In the light of such ventures, some business leaders have become enthusiastic about the activist response on the part of the corporation toward social problems. David Linowes, a corporate leader, foresaw a new role for business in public affairs.

> Mounting evidence proves that the private sector is uniquely well qualified to fulfill many of the social goals facing us more economically and expeditiously than government working alone. . . . I can visualize a wholesale expansion of existing incentives along with a spate of new reward strategies introduced to America's socio-economic system. Increasingly, I believe, this will help to change the attitude of businessmen regarding social involvement. I look forward to the day, in fact, when competition to engage in government-business programs will be every bit as spirited as competition for the consumer dollar is today.[39]

As chairman of the President's Commission on Privatization, Linowes worked to define ways in which the private sector could complement the responsibilities of government.[40]

CORPORATE INFLUENCE ON SOCIAL WELFARE POLICY

Corporate social responsibility notwithstanding, it would be naive to think that the corporate sector is above self-interest in its orientation toward social welfare. The conservative political economist Irving Kristol stated as much when he wrote that "corporate philanthropy is not obligatory. It is desirable if and only if it serves a corporate purpose. It is expressly and candidly a self-serving activity, and is only legitimate to the degree that it is ancillary to a larger corporate purpose. To put it bluntly: There is nothing noble or even moral about corporate philanthropy."[41]

Corporate influence in social welfare is not exerted simply through myriad corporations acting independently. Special interest organizations, such as the National Association of Manufacturers and the United States Chamber of Commerce, have routinely pressed for public policies that clearly reflected the priorities of the business community. In 1974, Congress passed campaign reform legislation that defined contribution limits to political action committees (PACs). Unfortunately, these attempts to control political influence actually contributed to the proliferation of PACs, particularly those financed by the corporate sector. In 1974, corporations already had 89 PACs, but by 1986 the number had grown to 1,902. That corporate PACs influence the political process in a conservative direction is well known. Labor organizations, which tend to be liberal in inclination, fielded only 418 PACs in 1986, a poor showing compared with the number of corporate PACs. Consequently, corporate PACs favor Republican candidates for office, sometimes overwhelmingly. In 1982, for example, the U.S.

Chamber of Commerce PAC endorsed only Republican candidates.[42]

Corporations exert an indirect influence on social policy by funding public interest organizations, nonprofits engaged in research, policy analysis, and public education. In the past, corporations have been an important source of support for liberal organizations, such as the Brookings Institution, that have advocated governmental policies to help the disadvantaged. More recently, argues conservative scholar Marvin Olasky, corporations have used their contributions to placate "specific vocal minorities."[43] But corporations also give a substantial portion to conservative public policy groups. In 1985, corporations contributed $4.3 billion to nonprofit organizations. In that year, the largest corporate contributors were Exxon ($72,756,000), Chevron ($32,341,000), Atlantic Richfield ($31,846,000), AT&T ($30,974,000), and General Motors ($28,019,000).[44] Table 9.2 illustrates the diversity of contributions from the largest American corporations.

PACs and public interest organizations, however, proved unreliable vehicles for influencing public policy. PACs subsidized the campaigns of individual candidates, of course, but did little to forge consensus around, or propose new directions for, public policy. Public interest organizations, by contrast, represented a wide diversity of thought and were largely independent of the ideological preferences of corporate donors. Subsequently, during the 1970s, the corporate sector turned to the policy institute as a method for influencing social policy. Also known as think tanks, prominent policy institutes favored by the business community were the American Enterprise Institute for Public Policy Research (AEI) and the Heritage Foundation. Established as nonpartisan institutions for the purpose of enhancing the public's understanding of social policy, these policy institutes distanced themselves from the special interest connotations of earlier business advocacy groups. At the same time, conservative think tanks served as vehicles for the business com-

TABLE 9.2. Contributions to Organizations from the Largest American Corporations

Organizational Recipient	Number of Corporations Contributing	1985 Contributions
Urban League	24	$1,586,000
American Enterprise Institute	18	1,133,000
NAACP/NAACP Legal Defense and Education Fund	20	707,000
Urban Institute/Center for Community Change	10	567,000
Independent Sector/Council on Foundations	17	479,000
La Raza and other Hispanic groups	14	418,000
Brookings Institution	16	366,000
Heritage Foundation/Hoover Institution	11	347,000

SOURCE: Marvin Olasky, *Patterns of Corporate Philanthropy* (Washington, D.C.: Capital Research Center, 1987), p. 2.

munity to take a less reactive stance regarding social policy. Conservative policy institutes, then, addressed the complaint voiced by Lawrence Fouraker and Graham Allison of Harvard's Graduate School of Business Administration: "Public policy suffers not simply from a lack of business confidence on issues of major national import, but from a lack of sophisticated and balanced contribution by *both* business and government in the process of policy development."[45]

The American Enterprise Institute (AEI)

Once noted for its slavish adherence to probusiness positions on social issues, AEI, by the early 1980s, had developed an appreciation for American "intellectual politics."[46] With a budget and staff comparable to that of a prestigious college, AEI was able to recruit an impressive number of notable people and scholars and to maintain projects in several domestic policy areas: economics, education, energy, government regulation, finance, taxation, health, jurisprudence, and public opinion. The significance of these activities for social welfare was stated by AEI's then-president, William J. Baroody, Jr.

The public philosophy that has guided American policy for decades is undergoing change. For more than four decades, the

philosophy of Franklin Delano Roosevelt's New Deal prevailed, in essence calling upon government to do whatever individual men and women could not do for themselves.

Today we see growing signs of a new public philosophy, one that still seeks to meet fundamental human needs, but to meet them through a better balance between the public and private sectors of society.

The American Enterprise Institute has been at the forefront of this change. Many of today's policy initiatives are building on intellectual foundations partly laid down by the Institute.[47]

For such an ambitious mission, AEI empaneled a staff of influential and talented personnel. At the height of its influence, from the late 1970s through the mid-1980s, AEI maintained a stable of more than 30 scholars and fellows *in residence* who prepared analyses on the various policy areas.[48] The Institute's senior fellows included the previously mentioned Irving Kristol, Herbert Stein, an economist and chairman of the President's Council of Economic Advisors in the Nixon administration, and Ben Wattenberg, a veteran public opinion analyst. The AEI "distinguished fellow" was Gerald R. Ford, who had served as thirty-eighth president of the United States. Michael Novak, director of AEI's project on democratic capitalism, prepared analyses that focused on social welfare policy.

Instrumental in shaping the social priorities of the Reagan administration, AEI was to become the most important think tank of the period. And AEI's budget ballooned accordingly—from $800,000 in 1970 to $5 million in 1978 and then to $11.7 million in 1982. Forty-three percent of the 1982 budget was derived from large corporate contributors, such as Bethlehem Steel, Exxon, J. C. Penney, and the Chase Manhattan Bank.[49] With a budget so heavily dependent on corporate funding, AEI required a lifeline to the business community, and the Board of Trustees served that function. Of the 24 members of the AEI Board of Trustees in 1984, 21 were chief executives of *Fortune* 500 companies.[50] AEI was also careful to select its staff from government service and to grant leaves to staff members when their services were desired by an administration. Two AEI scholars were former members of the President's Council of Economic Advisors. When Ronald Reagan assumed office, 18 AEI staff joined the new administration, claiming such important offices as director of the Congressional Budget Office and director of the Office of Management and Budget.

This situation ensured that no social policy proposal would receive serious consideration without first passing the review and comment of AEI. By the time a policy proposal had reached the legislative arena, the odds were high that the AEI imprint would be reinforced by testimony from one or more of the highly credentialed scholars in residence, the 77 adjunct scholars, or the 250 professors across the nation who were affiliated with AEI.[51] Influence was sometimes exerted in a subtle manner. In 1982, for example, AEI marked the completion of its project "to determine whether the private sector [could] play a larger role in dealing with a range of problems in our society and in delivering needed human services" by publishing *Meeting Human Needs: Toward a New Public Philosophy*. The first copy was delivered personally to President Reagan by AEI's President William Baroody.[52]

In domestic affairs, AEI established two projects that influenced social welfare policy. In launching the "mediating structures" project, AEI enlisted the services of Peter Berger, a sociologist, and Richard Neuhaus, a theologian. In the major publication of the project, *To Empower People,* Berger and Neuhaus stated that the fundamental social problem of American society was the growth of megastructures, such as big government, big business, big labor, and professional bureaucracies, and the corresponding diminution of the individual. The route to empowering people, then, was to revitalize "mediating structures," among them, the neighborhood, family, church, and voluntary associations.[53] *To Empower People* proved a readable and lucid booklet that served AEI well, and the project's implicit critique of government programs became clearly evident in other studies of "mediating structures." For example, in *Federalizing Meals on Wheels,* Michael Balzano argued that the federal Older Americans Act was wrong because it reduced the voluntary impulses of church and community groups (mediating structures) by subsidizing nutritional programs for the elderly. "In most cases, common sense and the desire to help one's neighbor are all that are necessary." Balzano concluded sarcastically, "One does not need a master's degree in social work or gerontology to dish out chow at a nutrition center."[54]

Following the mediating structures project, AEI's project on democratic capitalism endeavored to elevate the role of the corporation in public life. This necessitated a bit of theoretical hanky-panky in that the mediating structures project had portrayed big business as a megastructure and, therefore, inimical to the vitality of mediating structures, but the problem was disposed of deftly by Michael Novak, a philosopher of religion and director of the project. In *Toward a Theology of the Corporation,* Novak needed no more than a footnote to transfer big business from its designation as a megastructure to that of a mediating structure, and effectively to characterize big government as an institution of cultural and economic oppression against a corporate sector that had been the genius behind the American experience.[55]

Under the direction of Novak, the project on democratic capitalism intended to reform public philosophy by depicting the corporation as a promoter of cultural enlightenment rather than as a perpetrator of inequality. "The social instrument invented by democratic capitalism to achieve social goals is the private corporation," he proselytized. "The corporation . . . is not merely an economic institution. It is also a moral and a political institution. It depends on and generates new political forms. . . . Beyond its economic effects, the corporation changes the ethos and the cultural forms of society."[56]

At the same time, Novak took careful aim at the public sector, explaining, "I advise intelligent, ambitious, and morally serious young Christians and Jews to awaken to the growing danger of statism. They will better serve their souls and serve the Kingdom of God all around by restoring the liberty and power of the private sector than by working for the state."[57]

The Heritage Foundation

In 1986, AEI faltered, and organizational problems led to the resignation of Baroody. With the weakening of AEI, the Heritage Foundation assumed leadership in defining a probusiness and antigovernmental outlook on social policy. Established in 1973 by a $250,000 grant from the Coors family,[58] the Heritage Foundation's 1983 budget of $10.6 million already approximated those of the liberal Brookings Institution and the conservative American Enterprise Institute.[59] Espousing a militantly conservative ideology, Heritage influenced social policy by proposing private alternatives to establishing governmental programs and by slanting its work to the religious right. By breaking new ground while

building mass support for policy initiatives, Heritage complemented the less partisan analyses of AEI. Like AEI, Heritage sustained a group of conservative scholars—over 100—who prepared position statements. Also like AEI, Heritage placed some of its staff—26 full-time and 13 part-time—in government posts during the Reagan administration.[60]

Heritage social policy initiatives emphasize privatization, which, in this case, means transferring activities from government to business. Implicit in this is an unqualified antagonism toward government intrusion in social affairs. Government programs are faulted for breaking down the mutual obligations between groups, for their lack of attention to efficiencies and incentives in the way programs are operated and benefits awarded, for inducing dependency in the beneficiaries of programs, and for the growth of the welfare industry and its special interest groups, particularly professional associations.[61]

This critique served as a basis for the aggressive stance taken by the Heritage Foundation in urban development, income security, and social welfare policies. With regard to urban development, Heritage proposed the Urban Enterprise Zone (UEZ) concept, which would enable economically disadvantaged communities to attract industry by reducing taxes, employee costs, and health and safety regulations.[62] The UEZ concept came to the attention of then-Congressman Jack Kemp, who convinced the Reagan administration to make it the centerpiece of its urban policy, thus replacing the Economic Development Administration and Urban Development Action Grant programs in which government had provided technical assistance and funds for urban development.[63] When UEZ legislation stalled in Congress, Heritage changed tactics and targeted states and localities directly. By late 1984, 30 states and cities had created more than 300 UEZs.[64] As secretary of Housing and Urban Development in the Bush administration, Kemp was well placed to reintroduce the enterprise zone concept as a way of aiding troubled communities, yet this initiative failed to materialize at the federal level.

In the area of income security, the Heritage Foundation—in conjunction with the conservative CATO Institute—prepared an oblique assault on the Social Security program, promoting a parallel system of Individual Retirement Accounts (IRAs). Under "The Family Security Plan," proposed by Peter Ferrara, former senior staff member of the White House Office of Policy Development, the initial IRA provisions of the 1981 Economic Recovery and Tax Act would be expanded to allow individuals "to deduct their annual contributions to . . . IRAs from their Social Security payroll taxes."[65] Although the idea of substituting IRA investments for Social Security contributions was blocked by liberal politicians, Heritage was clearly banking on future support from workers of the baby boom generation. "If today's young workers could use their Social Security taxes to make . . . investments through an IRA," hypothesized Ferrara, "then, assuming a 6 percent real return, most would receive three to six times the retirement benefits promised them under Social Security."[66] According to this calculus, the interaction of demographic and economic variables would lead to increasing numbers of young workers salting away funds for themselves because of high investment returns as well as the fear that Social Security would provide only minimal benefits on retirement. If correct, the result would be a surefire formula for eroding the popular and financial support for Social Security.

Regarding welfare policy, Heritage was instrumental in scouting Charles Murray, whose *Losing Ground* provided much of the rationale for the conservative assault on federal welfare programs. In 1982, a pamphlet Murray had written for Heritage, entitled "Safety Nets and the Truly Needy," came to the attention of the Manhattan Institute, a conservative New York think tank.[67] Traded by Heritage to Manhattan, Murray elaborated his allegation that government social programs during the War on Poverty had actually worsened the conditions of the poor. Murray's wrecking-ball thesis advocated no less than a "zero-transfer system," which consisted of "scrapping the entire federal welfare and income support structure for working-aged persons."[68] Remembering his earlier sponsor, Murray returned to Heritage on December 12, 1984, to promote his book to a standing-room-only audience at a symposium entitled "What's Wrong with Welfare?"

Unlike the more restrained AEI, Heritage has been willing to lend its name to militant conservatives of the religious right, providing intellectual support to "the traditionalist movement." The most comprehensive and sympathetic treatment of the traditionalist movement is found in *Back to Basics*, by Burton Pines, then vice president of Heritage. In this highly readable book, Pines applauds local conservative activists for their challenge to liberal values and chronicles the offensive launched against programs of the welfare state. "Pro-family" traditionalists had disrupted the Carter administration's White House Conference on Families, a grass-roots mobilization that effectively precluded any progressive legislation that might have evolved out of the conference. Traditionalists also engaged proponents of the Domestic Violence Bill in protracted debate, holding up the legislation until a Republican-controlled Senate let it expire. Finally, traditionalists supported the Family Protection Act, a conservative proposal limiting contraception, abortion, children's rights, and sex education and reducing federal support for programs aiding homosexuals and the divorced.[69] Although the Family Protection Act was not passed, it succeeded in diverting the attention of the public away from liberal values, which were considered ruinous and toward traditional values, which were portrayed positively.

Pines noted the pivotal role of conservative think tanks in the traditionalist movement, and was quick to acknowledge his debt to AEI, an organization he described as focusing "primarily on long (sometimes very long) range and fundamental transformation of the climate of opinion.'' Bringing the conservative Hoover Institution of Stanford into the fold, Pines characterized their work as a crusade. "Together," he concluded, "Hoover, AEI and Heritage can today deploy formidable armies on the battlefield of ideas—forces which traditionalist movements previously lacked."[70]

THE FUTURE OF CORPORATE INVOLVEMENT IN SOCIAL WELFARE

Corporations will continue to influence social welfare policy through the remainder of the century, reflecting the preference of business leaders that the corporate sector assume a primary role in activities of both the voluntary and governmental sectors. John Filer, chairman of Carries Life and Casualty and chairman of the 1975 Commission on Private Philanthropy and Public Needs, contended that "the future of corporate America depends critically on our ability to recognize promptly the changing role of the corporation, the changing expectations and demands of the public, and the changing constituencies which we serve."[71] Filer encouraged corporations to increase contributions to philanthropic causes, and from 1975 to 1984 corporate contributions to the voluntary sector increased from $1.2 billion to $3.8 billion.[72] But corporate giving is contingent on corporate performance, and there is little question that the generosity of chief executive officers was dampened suddenly when the Dow Jones Industrial Average plunged 508 points on October 19, 1987. "Everybody is just reeling," the director of planned giving for a major West Coast philanthropy said of the stock market crash. "People are not doing a lot of thinking about giving at this moment."[73] Thus, corporate giving to human service agencies on the part of America's largest corporations dropped from 36.9 percent of all charitable contributions in 1978 to 27 percent in 1987.[74]

The social responsibility of the corporate sector was questioned when a national campaign launched by Trans-Africa in the mid-1980s to pressure American corporations to cease doing business in South Africa brought negative publicity to those firms that refused or were slow to divest. Fewer corporations were willing to adopt the Sullivan principles. During the latter half of 1992, the number of American corporations that had "signed" the Sullivan principles dropped by approximately one-half.[75] Further, the high proportion of employee costs attributed to fringe benefits drove many employers to demand concessions or "give-backs" from employees, thus drawing the wrath of unions. Still, holding corporations to some social standard served as a rationale for advancing social programs. A creative illustration of this appears in the "Decency Principles" proposed by Nancy Amidei, a social worker and syndicated columnist. Noting that the Sullivan principles addressed the responsibilities of firms doing business in South Africa, Amidei wondered about the responsibilities of firms doing business in the United States. Her standards for responsible business practices include:

1. *Equitable wages* (high enough to escape poverty, comparability across lines of race, age, sex, and handicapping conditions);
2. *Employee rights* (to equal opportunity, to organize for collective bargaining, to affordable child care, to safe working conditions, and to health coverage);
3. *Housing* (working for more affordable housing, helping relocated or migrant workers obtain affordable housing);
4. *Environmental* (responsible use of resources, sound handling of dangerous substances, conformance with environmental protection laws).

Amidei suggested that a corporation's adherence to the "Decency Principles" be a basis for government decisions on such matters as providing tax abatements to corporations to attract new industry or awarding government contracts.[76]

Financed by the business community, conservative policy institutes persisted in their efforts to roll back the welfare state. While the Heritage Foundation appeared unable to fashion "a conservative vision of welfare,"[77] AEI reasserted its influence by publishing *The New Consensus on Family and Welfare*. Under the direction of Michael Novak, a group of 20 scholars—including prominent liberal scholars from the Brookings Institution—presented a conservative platform for welfare reform. Suggesting that "existing welfare policy [was] toxic," the group's report judged that initiatives of the states, local jurisdictions, and the voluntary sector were preferable to federal social programs.[78] *The New Consensus* implied that poverty in America was inevitable and concluded that "the nation's goal . . . should not be to 'eliminate' poverty but to reduce it as much as possible by adapting quickly to its ever new forms and unforeseen necessities."[79]

Although business leaders remained antagonistic toward governmental social policies, others adopted a more liberal stance, viewing public policy as an essential component of an internationally competitive economy. As early as 1980 the editors of *Business Week* noted that the nation's attention should be directed less to social needs than to economic revitalization:

> In the U.S. during the past 20 years, policy has emphasized improving the quality of life, particularly attempts to redistribute income to low-income groups and minorities and to create an egalitarian society. Now it is clear that the government cannot achieve such goals, no matter how admirable, without economic growth.[80]

"We have become so concerned with problems of redistributing wealth," echoed Reginald H. Jones, chairman of the General Electric Company, "that we've forgotten about the creation of wealth."[81] This call for governmental intervention to aid the business community was reinforced by an increasingly rapid loss of economic advantage to the economies of Japan and Germany, both of which received substantial assistance from their governments. Governmental aid to business, labeled "industrial policy," was endorsed by liberal economists, such as Lester Thurow, who proposed "the national equivalent of a corporate investment committee" to coordinate economic policy.[82] Subsequent industrialization would provide increased revenues for welfare programs but, more important, create jobs for the unemployed. In the final analysis, further improvement in the economic circumstances of the poor and the unemployed was politically feasible only under conditions of an expanding economy.

The accommodation of social needs to economic requirements was advocated by economist Robert Reich. According to Reich, much of the American industrial malaise was attributable to underinvestment in human capital. However, human capital investments can be wasteful, leading to nonproductive dependency, when not coupled with the needs of industry. "Underlying many of the inadequacies of American social programs, in short, is the fact that they have not been directed in any explicit or coherent way toward the large task of adapting America's labor force."[83] The attachment of social needs to industrial productivity would fundamentally alter social welfare. "Government bureaucracies that now administer these programs to individuals will be supplanted, to a large extent, by companies that administer them to their employees," suggested Reich. "Companies, rather than state and local governments, will be the agents through which such assistance is provided."[84]

Significantly, industrial policy has attracted conservative adherents as well. Influential analyst Kevin Phillips has proposed a more business-directed version of industrial policy. In Phillips's "business-government partnership," labor and business would agree to work cooperatively with government so that the United

States could regain its dominant role in the international economy. For Phillips, however, industrial policy offers less for social welfare:

> Political liberals must accept that there is little support for bringing back federal agencies based on New Deal models to run the U.S. economy, and that much of the new business-government cooperation will back economic development and nationalist (export, trade competition) agendas rather than abstractions like social justice or social welfare.[85]

The primacy of business interests in public policy is not accepted by many social welfare advocates. While "corporatism" may seem plausible to corporate executives, government officials, and labor unions, it offers little to the unemployed and welfare or working poor.[86] In fact, some critics of industrial policy suggest that its very emergence signifies the inability of advanced capitalism to ensure the provision of basic goods and services to the economically disadvantaged through the welfare state.[87] If these critics are correct, industrial policy is an indication of the demise of welfare capitalism rather than a blueprint for enhancing social welfare. Exactly how the relationship among business, labor, and government will be articulated in the future has much to do with the development of public policy. Although the precise nature of such policy must be left to conjecture, the increasing sophistication of the corporate sector in shaping social policy suggests that social welfare policy of the future will show greater congruence with the priorities of American business.

Although many welfare advocates are distrustful of corporate involvement in social welfare, other social welfare professionals have found the corporate sector a desirable context in which to practice clinically. Since the 1970s, social workers have been involved in Employee Assistance Programs (EAPs) that provide a range of services to workers, a population often neglected by traditional welfare programs.[88] By the late 1980s, occupational social welfare had become a popular specialization within social work, with graduate schools offering special curricula on the subject, a national conference inaugurated for specialists in the field, and a special issue of *Social Work* dedicated to it.[89] Although studies of EAPs are scarce,[90] there is evidence that occupational social work is likely to expand, particularly when located within the corporation. In a modest study of 23 "private-sector, management-sponsored" EAPs, Shulamith Straussner found that those located in-house demonstrated notable advantages over those contracted out. For example, EAPs located within the corporation cost one-third that of contracted-out services. In-house EAPs proved adaptable to management priorities, developing "short-term programs to deal with company reorganization or retrenchment, special health concerns . . . [and] other organizational needs." Significantly, union representatives approved in-house EAPs twice as frequently as they did contracted-out programs.[91] These findings suggest that EAPs that are managed by employers are perceived by management and unions as superior to services provided by an external agency. If corporate executives and labor leaders develop personnel policies consistent with these findings, welfare professionals will find the business community a hospitable setting in which to practice. In that event, occupational social work within the corporation may become as prevalent an auspice of practice as the voluntary and governmental sectors are.

HUMAN SERVICE CORPORATIONS

As the postindustrial service sector expands, continued demand for human services has drawn the corporate sector directly into social welfare in the United States. Corporate exploration of the growing human services market has proceeded rapidly while government welfare programs have been held in check. Heavily dependent on government support and the contributions of middle-income Americans who have experienced a continual erosion of their economic position, the voluntary sector has been unable to meet this demand. Relatively unfettered by government regulation and with easy access to capital from commercial sources, the corporate sector has made dramatic inroads into service areas previously reserved for governmental and voluntary sector organizations.

Interestingly, the incentives for corporate entry into human services were initially provided through government social programs. Between 1950 and 1979, government expenditures for social welfare increased from $23.5 billion to $430.6 billion, a factor of 18.[92] Per capita expenditures for welfare increased from $153 to $1,912 during these years, a thirteenfold increase.[93] In addition, health care allocations figured prominently in public welfare expenditures. In 1970, the government spent $27.8 billion on health care; by 1985 that figure had grown to $148.8 billion.[94] The potential profits for corporations entering the social welfare market were unmistakable.

Concomitantly, public policy decisions have encouraged proprietary firms to provide welfare services. This was the case when Medicaid and Medicare were enacted in 1965. By using a market approach to ensure the availability of health care for the medically indigent and the elderly, Medicaid and Medicare avoided the costs of constructing a system of public sector facilities and, in so doing, contributed to the restructuring of American health care. What had been essentially a haphazard collection of mom-and-pop nursing homes and small private hospitals was transformed, in a short period, into a system of corporate franchises, complete with stocks traded on Wall Street. Incentives offered through Medicaid and Medicare to encourage the corporate sector to become involved in hospital care were replicated in the health maintenance industry almost a decade later. The Health Maintenance Organization Act of 1973

stimulated a sluggish health maintenance industry that has since grown at an explosive rate.

Initially dependent on government welfare programs, the corporate sector has developed a life of its own. Exploitation of the nursing home, hospital management, and health maintenance markets has led to corporate interest in other markets. By the 1980s, human service corporations had established prominence in child care, ambulatory health care, substance abuse and psychiatric care, home health care, and life and continuing care.[95] Increasingly, proprietary firms were able to obtain funds for facilities through commercial loans or sales of stock, and to meet ongoing costs by charging fees to individuals, companies, and nongovernmental third parties. Insofar as resources for human service corporations are not financed by the state, firms are free to function relatively independent of government intervention.

The Scope of Human Service Corporations

How big is the corporate sector in American social welfare? By the early 1990s, two of the largest firms—Hospital Corporation of America and National Medical Enterprises—reported annual revenues that were greater than all contributions to the United Way of America.[96] Each of these corporations employed over 50,000 workers, more than the number of state and local workers for public welfare programs in any state in the union.[97] Some of the more salient features of the larger human service corporations are depicted in Table 9.3.

Human service corporations in the United States share several striking features. First, virtually all were incorporated after World War II, the benchmark of the postindustrial era, and the great majority of these were incorporated after 1960. All told, the overwhelming majority of these large firms have been in business for less than 25 years. Second, these corporations have recorded a rapid growth in revenues. Of the 66 human service corporations reporting annual revenues above $10 million in the mid-1980s, 14

TABLE 9.3. Prominent Human Service Corporations, 1992

Firm	Revenues ($ millions)	Markets	Employees
American Medical International	$2,052.4	Acute health, psychiatric care	47,000
Beverly Enterprises	2,300.9	Long-term retirement facilities	93,000
Charter Medical Corporation	1188.3	Psychiatric services	14,700
Community Psychiatric Centers	392.9	Psychiatric services	6,586
Corrections Corporation of America	67.9	Correctional facilities	1,513
Hospital Corporation of America	4,985.4	Acute health care	70,000
Humana	5,865.0	Acute health, psychiatric care	70,500
Kinder-Care Learning Centers	411.0	Child day care	20,500
National Medical Enterprises	3,982.0	Acute health, psychiatric and home health	51,906
PacifiCare	1,232.8	HMOs, managed health care	1,647
United Health care	824.0	HMOs, managed health care	3,200
U.S. Health Care	847.0	HMOs, managed health care	2,538

SOURCE: *Standard and Poor's, 1993.*

had more than doubled their earnings, 17 had more than quadrupled their earnings, and 23 had actually increased their income by a factor greater than 10 since 1980! This is particularly significant because their earnings escalated at a time not particularly favorable to the business community. Nevertheless, human service corporations seemed immune from the recession of the early 1980s and continued to thrive despite attempts by the Carter and Reagan administrations to contain costs for health and human service programs. Although most of the companies focus on health-related services, many diversify into other service areas and, in some instances, other types of corporations acquire human service firms in order to balance their operations. For example, when cigarette sales plummeted, GrandMet USA acquired soft drink and pet food subsidiaries, then diversified further by acquiring Children's World, the second largest franchise of child care centers, and Quality Care, a leading provider of home health care.

While the human service markets were characterized by rapid expansion and consolidation during the 1970s and early 1980s, the late 1980s and early 1990s saw entrepreneurial activity in health and human services skyrocket. In

less than five years the number of firms reporting annual revenues in excess of $10 million increased from 66 to 121 in 1992, as shown in Figure 9.2. Despite a recession and federal measures to contain health care costs, for-profit

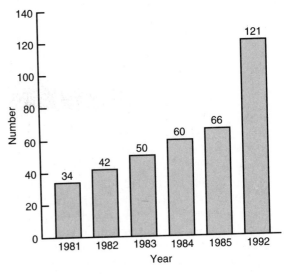

Figure 9.2. Human Service Corporations Reporting Annual Revenues above $10 Million. (SOURCE: *Standard and Poor's, 1993.*)

firms consolidated their holdings and charged aggressively into new markets.

THE NEW HUMAN SERVICE MARKETS

Within social welfare, human service corporations have become prominent, if not dominant, in several areas: nursing homes, hospital management, health maintenance organizations (HMOs), child care, and home care. More recently, proprietary firms have established beachheads in other markets, notably life and continuing care and corrections.

Nursing Homes

Among corporate initiatives in social welfare, expansion into the nursing home industry is unparalleled. Between 1965 and 1978, expenditures for nursing home care increased 16.9 percent *annually*.[98] By the early 1980s, nursing homes had become a $25-billion-a-year industry, and the number of nursing home beds exceeded those in acute care facilities for the first time.[99] At that time, 70 percent of nursing homes were under proprietary management. Market conditions such as these led to the following observation in *Forbes* magazine: "This is a guaranteed opportunity for someone. How the nursing home industry can exploit it is the real question."[100] Under favorable market conditions, nursing home corporations proliferated. David Vaughan, president of a real estate firm specializing in facilities for the elderly, noted:

> The overall affluence of the over fifty-five population makes investments in special care facilities an extremely attractive venture. The need of capital in meeting the housing needs of this segment of the U.S. population has been so great that we have been able to invest in these facilities with only limited competition.[101]

Guaranteed growth of the nursing home market led to the consolidation of proprietary firms and the emergence of an oligopoly. As early as 1981, the following three corporations held more than 10,000 nursing home beds: Beverly Enterprises held 38,488; ARA Services held 31,325; and National Medical Enterprises (NME) held 14,534.[102] Beverly Enterprises attained first ranking by its purchase, in 1979, of Progressive Medical Group, which was the eleventh largest chain of nursing homes. NME attained third ranking in 1979 by purchasing Hillhaven, then the third-largest operation. ARA Services grew 26 percent in 1979, thereby attaining second ranking, by consolidating smaller operations in Indiana, Colorado, and California.[103] Undeterred by the filing of the first antitrust action in the nursing home industry, nursing home firms continued such acquisitions and mergers.[104] In 1984, using its Hillhaven subsidiary, NME acquired Flagg Industries, which held 12 facilities in Idaho, bringing its total holdings to 339 health care facilities with 42,000 beds. Not to be outdone, Beverly Enterprises acquired Beacon Hill America for $60 million, thereby retaining its top ranking. By the mid-1980s, Beverly Enterprises controlled 781 nursing homes with a total of 88,198 beds in 44 states and the District of Columbia.[105] Given this trend, one industry analyst believed that the industry would eventually fall into the hands of "five or six corporations."[106]

Hospital Management

The growth of the nursing home industry is matched by corporate involvement in hospital management. Between 1976 and 1982, the number of investor-owned or investor-managed hospitals increased from 533 to 1,040, accruing gross revenues of approximately $40 billion.[107] Richard Siegrist, Jr., a Wall Street analyst, concluded that the future for the industry looked bright, noting that revenues and bed ownership for the five largest companies had roughly tripled between 1976 and 1981. According to this analyst, in 1978 Humana doubled its size through an unfriendly takeover of American Medicorp (worth $450 million), gaining 39 hospitals and 7,838 beds. Meanwhile, Hospital Corporation of America (HCA) purchased Hospital Affiliates (worth $650 million), gaining 55 hospitals, 8,207 beds, and 102 hospital management contracts; General Care Corporation (worth $78 million) gained eight hospitals with 1,294 beds; and General Health Services (worth $96 million) gained six hospitals with 1,115 beds. At the same time, American Medical International (AMI) acquired Hyatt Medical Enterprises (worth $69 million), with eight hospitals, 907 beds, and 26 hospital management contracts, as well as Brookwood Health Services (worth $156 million), with nine hospitals, 1,271 beds, and five hospital contracts.[108]

AMI's strategy of purchasing financially troubled community hospitals proved so successful that the company reported a 29 percent increase in net income for 1983 as compared with 1982, accomplished a four-for-three stock split in February 1983, and declared a 21 percent dividend per share. Moreover, in 1984, AMI acquired Lifemark's 25 hospitals and three alcoholism treatment centers through a $1-billion stock transfer.[109] Despite such large-scale growth, AMI continued to rank second behind HCA, which owned 393 hospitals having 56,000 beds.[110] But Humana was to hold the trump card in hospital management. Boldly gambling on its offer to implant artificial hearts in 100 heart patients at no cost, Humana captured the public's attention in 1984. Even though the artificial hearts failed to perform as planned, the project reflected a management strategy that pushed Humana to the head of the pack. By 1993, Humana had forged ahead of its competitors to become the largest health and human service corporation in the world.

Health Maintenance Organizations

Pioneered by the nonprofit Kaiser-Permanente in California, the concept of health maintenance organizations (HMOs) was slow to attract the interest of the corporate sector. However, from 1973 to 1981, the Health Maintenance Organization Act of 1973 authorized funds for the establishment of facilities in a large number of favorable marketing areas. This funding, coupled with the growth in the nursing home and hospital management industries, reversed investor apathy. By 1983, 60 HMOs were operating on a proprietary basis.[111]

An early leader in the HMO industry was HealthAmerica, a for-profit HMO begun in 1980. Within a few years HealthAmerica enrolled almost 400,000 members in 17 locations across the nation, becoming the largest proprietary HMO (second in size only to nonprofit Kaiser-Permanente). Seeking capital for further expansion, HealthAmerica offered stock publicly in July 1983 and raised $20 million for 1.5 million shares. One month later, Phillip Bredesen, chairman and president of HealthAmerica, reported that he anticipated "dramatic growth in the HMO segment of the health care business," and that "HealthAmerica [was] well-positioned with the people and systems that this growth [would] represent."[112]

HealthAmerica's growth did not go unnoticed by Fred Wasserman, founder of Maxicare, a proprietary HMO. Wasserman suspected that Bredesen had stretched his company too thin in an ambitious expansion into new market areas. In November 1986, HealthAmerica was purchased by Maxicare for $372 million. Coupled with its earlier acquisition of HealthCare USA for $66 million, the purchase of HealthAmerica enabled Maxicare to claim more than 2 million members nationwide and annual revenues approaching $2 billion. After the HealthAmerica takeover, Wasserman spoke optimistically about overtaking Kaiser-Permanente in pursuit of a health maintenance market[113] expected to consist of 30 million members and $25 billion in revenues by 1990.[114] Wasserman's optimism was misplaced, however. The firm proved unable to manage the debt incurred by its appetite for mergers in the mid-1980s. Maxicare sought protection against creditors, filing for bankruptcy under Chapter 11 in the late 1980s. The collapse of Wasserman's HMO empire was evident in his firm's revenues. Peaking in 1987, Maxicare reported earnings of $1.8 billion; three years later, the firm earned $387 million, less than a fourth of its earlier value. The HMO market surged in the late 1980s as managed care became the method of choice for containing health care costs. As business and labor groups attempted to limit the fiscal drain caused by escalating costs of health care, proprietary firms stepped forward to manage care more efficiently. By the early 1990s, more than a dozen managed care companies were reporting hefty revenues.

Child Care

As a human services market, child care is exploited effectively by proprietary firms. In an important study of child welfare services delivery, Catherine Born showed the influence of for-profit providers relative to that of providers in the voluntary and public sectors. She noted that:

> . . . in the case of residential treatment, among all services purchased, 51 percent was obtained from for-profit firms, 26 percent from voluntary organizations, and 22 percent from other public agencies having contractual agreements with the welfare department. For contracted institutional services, 48 percent was provided by proprietary concerns, 14 percent by voluntary vendors, and 38 percent by other public agencies. The pattern was similar in the case of group home services where 58 percent was proprietarily contracted, 17 percent was obtained from the private, nonprofit sector, and 25 percent was purchased from other public agencies.[115]

The day care market—along with its largest provider, Kinder-Care—has expanded rapidly. Begun in 1969, Kinder-Care has demonstrated

prodigious growth, claiming approximately 825 "learning centers" in 1983, representing $128 million in revenue. The net earnings for Kinder-Care in fiscal year 1983 represented a 68 percent increase over fiscal year 1982. The company executed a five-for-four stock split in November 1982 and a four-for-three stock split in May 1983. Also, during fiscal year 1983, the company entered the market of freestanding immediate medical care by purchasing First Medical Corporation and its 10 facilities for an undisclosed sum.[116] By the second quarter of 1984, Kinder-Care reported that more than 100 new learning centers and 20 new clinics were under construction.[117]

By the early 1990s, Kinder-Care's 1,236 centers and annual revenues of $411 million dominated the market, but new competitors emerged to serve a seemingly infinite need for organized child care. Children's Discovery Centers of America claimed 93 centers and $57.2 million in revenues in 1991; Rocking Horse Child Care Center of America owned 87 preschool and elementary learning centers in 1991 and reported earnings of $34.7 million; Sunrise Preschools—the new kid on the block—earned $10.4 million in 1991 through its 15 preschool programs.

Home Care

Several companies in the home care market have replicated the success of corporations in the nursing home industry. Home Health Care of America, renamed Caremark, began in 1979. A leader in the field, the company has grown particularly quickly. Caremark generated net revenues of $1 million in 1980, $35.8 million in 1983, and $133.2 million in 1986. In 1983, Caremark increased the number of its regional service centers from 10 to 31 and, despite the costs incurred by this expansion, net income for the year increased 129 percent.[118] Growth of this magnitude, characteristic of the home care market, which expanded dramatically during the 1980s, continued into the 1990s. Elsie Griffith, chief executive officer of the Visiting Nurse Service of New York and chair of the board of the National Association for Home Care, observed that home health care "is expanding at a phenomenal rate."[119]

During the early 1990s, home health companies adjusted their services to meet earlier hospital discharges resulting from implementation of Medicare's prospective payment system. As patients went home sooner, the need for a range of specialized in-home health services grew. Quickly, home health companies began to offer a variety of services to patients. In markets where conventional home health companies failed to offer such specialized care, new firms entered the market and expanded rapidly.

Corrections

Among the more ambitious of human service corporations is the Correction Corporation of America (CCA), founded in 1983 by Tom Beasely with the financial backing of Jack Massey, founder of the Hospital Corporation of America. CCA officials noted that many states were unable to contend with overcrowding of facilities and proposed contracting with state and local jurisdictions for the provision of correctional services. As CCA acknowledged in its 1986 annual report, court orders to upgrade facilities, coupled with governmental reluctance to finance improvements, provided strong incentives for jurisdictions to consider contracting out correctional services.

> Government response to . . . [overcrowding] . . . has been hampered by the administrative and budgetary problems traditionally plaguing public sector facilities. Most systems have suffered a lack of long-term leadership due to their ties to the political process, and many jurisdictions have placed a low priority on corrections funding. The outcome has been a proliferation of out-dated facilities with a lack of sufficient capacity to meet constitutional standards.[120]

By 1986, CCA operated nine correctional facilities, totaling 1,646 beds, and was negotiating with the Texas Department of Corrections "to build and manage two minimum security prisons which will provide an additional 1,000 beds."[121]

Most analysts expect that proprietary correctional facilities will grow in popularity as governmental agencies recognize the cost savings of contracting out correctional services. CCA's per diem charge in 1986 was $29.77, about 25 percent less than the cost in public facilities.[122] In the near future, Texas, Oklahoma, and Arkansas are to put 3,000 correctional "beds" out to bid, perhaps signifying the willingness of states to use proprietary firms on a large scale.[123] The most dramatic example of the prospective growth of for-profit corrections almost occurred in 1985, when CCA startled Tennessee state officials by offering to take over the state's entire prison system. Like 30 other states and the District of Columbia, Tennessee's system was characterized by too many prisoners in archaic facilities and was operating under court supervision. When CCA offered the state $250 million for a 99-year contract, state officials were hard-pressed not to give it careful consideration. Ultimately, state officials balked at the idea, primarily because of a conflict of interest between CCA and leaders of state government.[124]

Undaunted, CCA moved steadily ahead, capitalizing on the dire need of local and state governments for greater prison capacity. By 1991, CCA managed 17 facilities and reported annual revenues of $67.9 million. Although these earnings were small when compared with other human service firms, they were astonishing in light of the $7.6 million CCA had earned just six years earlier.

Life and Continuing Care

The graying of the American population has led some corporations to construct special residential communities that include health care as a service. Life care, or continuing care, provides more affluent elders an opportunity to purchase a higher level of long-term care than is ordinarily found in nursing homes. Life care communities usually feature recreational, cultural, and other services in addition to health care. By the mid-1980s, 275 life care communities housed 100,000 elders.[125] Robert Ball, former commissioner of Social Security, estimated that perhaps 15 million elders could afford this type of care.[126]

Despite well-publicized bankruptcies of several life care communities, the prospect of a market of this magnitude has attracted the interest of several corporations. Beverly Enterprises, the largest nursing home operation, declared its intent to build or acquire several such communities.[127] Subsequently, the Marriott Corporation announced plans to have 200 Lifecare Retirement Communities in operation by the year 2000.[128] Despite the recession of the early 1980s, the interest of brokerage houses in life care remained high. Harold Margolin, a vice president of Merrill Lynch, stated that "the financial climate could impact on the growth of the continuing care segment of the health care industry, but only on the timing. It's going to be a very large industry."[129]

As corporate performance in the new human service markets demonstrates, substantial investments are being made in social welfare by the corporate sector. In fact, the number of human service corporations almost doubled in the relatively short period between 1981 and 1985, and almost doubled again between 1985 and 1991, as illustrated in Figure 9.2.

IMPLICATIONS FOR SOCIAL WORKERS

Despite the proliferation of human service corporations, social workers have been slow to adopt the corporate sector as a setting for practice. The number of welfare professionals practicing in the corporate sector is difficult to determine since the largest organization of social workers, the National Association of Social Workers, does not differentiate between private practice (which is proprietary but on a small scale) and the larger corporate providers. Based on data from a survey of California welfare professionals, Elizabeth Ortiz speculates that as few as 1.4 percent consider it primary employment, while 7.7 percent count it as secondary.[130] This level of participation does not correspond with the size of the for-profit sector in human services, suggesting that social workers are underrepresented. Considering that organizations under traditional auspices—the voluntary and governmental sectors—are limited in their capacity to provide services, it is probable that social workers will discover that human service corporations are a suitable location for practice.

Social workers electing to work within the for-profit sector could find it advantageous for several reasons. Proprietary firms may provide access to the capital needed for expanding social services. A primary explanation for the rapid growth of human service corporations is their ability to tap commercial sources of capital. Through loans and the sale of stock, they can quickly obtain the funds necessary for expansion. This has given them an enormous advantage over their competitors in the voluntary sector, which often resort to arduous and painstaking fund-raising campaigns, and competitors in the governmental sector, which must rely on the even more protracted methods of bond sales or tax increases to raise funds. For human service corporations, the cost of commercially derived capital can be reduced by depreciating assets and writing off the interest against income during the first years of operation. This presents obvious advantages for human service administrators who are faced with diminishing revenues derived from charitable or governmental sources. Perhaps the best example of this advantage is the meteoric rise of long-term care corporations, which were almost nonexistent 20 years ago. By convincing commercial lenders and investors that long-term care was viable, for-profit firms eventually gained control over the industry.[131]

In some instances, the corporate sector more readily offers opportunities for program innovation than what is possible under other auspices. Governmental programs must be mandated by a public authority, and this requires a consensus on how to deal with particular concerns. Voluntary sector agencies are ultimately managed by a board of directors that reflects the interests of the community in organizational policy. When human service issues are controversial, welfare professionals can encounter stiff opposition to needed programs. Some of this can be obviated by a corporate organizational form that is not so directly wedded to the status quo. An example of how a human service corporation offers opportunities not possible through traditional human service organizations is the ability of for-profit correctional companies to expand the scope of correctional facilities when government is reluctant to finance new construction and the voluntary sector is unable to raise the necessary capital.

In a related matter, the corporate sector offers greater organizational flexibility than that usually found in governmental agencies and a level of sophistication in managerial innovation not often found in the voluntary sector. To be sure, economic advantages enjoyed by the corporate sector make this possible, but the track record in organizational experimentation by the corporate sector is undeniable. In fact, examples of alternatives that could be of value to traditional welfare organizations are frequently derived from the corporate sector, as such popular books as *In Search of Excellence* and *The Changemasters* attest.[132]

Of course, some human service professionals are skeptical about the assurance of social welfare through human service corporations. According to the critics of proprietary human service delivery, the corporate sector is the organizational manifestation of a capitalist economy that is at the root of much social injustice and human need. For these welfare advocates, professional practice within a corporate context is antithetical to what is "social" about social work. In fact, studies of the organizational practices of human service corporations raise important questions about their suitability for promoting social welfare. Human service corporations are less cost-effective than nonprofit and governmental agencies, engage in a discriminatory selection of clients that penalizes the poor, and attract clients away from voluntary social service agencies. (These practices are considered in greater detail in Chapter 7.) Despite the undesirable attributes of proprietary human service providers, they are likely to continue to play an active role in defining social welfare. The economy of the United States, after all, is capitalistic, and entrepreneurs are free to establish businesses in whatever markets they consider profitable. Unless government strictly regulates—or prohibits—the for-profit provision of human services, human service corporations are likely to continue to influence American social welfare in the future.

DISCUSSION QUESTIONS

1. What are the major corporate philanthropic organizations in your community? What activities have they funded traditionally? To what extent do they incorporate social welfare projects in their funding priorities? Can you determine how priorities and funding decisions are made within these organizations?
2. If you were the director of a nonprofit welfare agency, which sources of philanthropy would you approach in your community to obtain contributions? How would you know which person or persons to approach in the organization? How would you approach them? If a major contribution were secured, how would you recognize the donor?
3. If you were inclined to establish a business providing a human service, what population would you focus on? How would you get capital to start the business? Would you own the business or would you share ownership with stockholders? How

would you market your service? What would you do with the profits—provide stockholders with dividends, enlarge the business, or make contributions to nonprofit agencies? What would be the name of your business?

4. Think tanks exist in Washington, D.C. and most state capitals. Obtain a copy of the annual report of a think tank. Who funds the think tank? Is there a relationship between the funding source and the ideological character of reports that the think tank publishes? What is the think tank's track record in social welfare issues?

NOTES

1. Robert McIntyre and Robert Folen, *Corporate Income Taxes in the Reagan Years* (Washington, D.C.: Citizens for Tax Justice, 1984), p. 5.
2. Jinlay Lewis, "CEOs' Presence in Bush Party Draws Attention to their Pay," *San Diego Union,* January 13, 1992, p. E-3.
3. Fred Barnes, "The Zillionaires Club," *The New Republic,* January 29, 1990, p. 23.
4. Sheila Kamerman, "The New Mixed Economy of Welfare," *Social Work* 28 (January-February 1983): 76.
5. Paul Starr, "The Meaning of Privatization," and Marc Bendick, "Privatizing the Delivery of Social Welfare Service" in *Working Paper 6* (Washington, D.C.: National Conference on Social Welfare, 1985); David Stoesz, "Privatization: Reforming the Welfare State," *Journal of Sociology and Social Welfare* 16 (Summer 1987): 139. Mimi Abramovitz, "The Privatization of the Welfare State," *Social Work* 31, no. 4 (July-August 1986): 257–64.
6. Neil Gilbert, *Capitalism and the Welfare State* (New Haven: Yale University Press, 1983).
7. David Stoesz, "Corporate Welfare," *Social Work* 31, no. 4 (July-August 1986): 86; "Corporate Health Care and Social Welfare," *Health and Social Work,* Summer 1986: 158; and "The Gray Market," *Journal of Gerontological Social Work* 16 (1989): 31.
8. Abramovitz, "The Privatization of the Welfare State," p. 257.
9. Theodore Marmor, Mark Schlesinger, and Richard Smithey, "A New Look at Nonprofits: Health Care Policy in a Competitive Age," *Yale Journal of Regulation* 3, no. 2 (Spring 1986): 322.
10. Robert Heilbroner, *The Worldly Philosophers* (New York: Simon and Schuster, 1967), pp. 98–106.
11. Edward Berkowitz and Kim McQuaid, *Creating the Welfare State* (New York: Praeger, 1980), p. 4.
12. Ibid., pp. 5–10.
13. Gilbert, *Capitalism and the Welfare State,* p. 3.
14. Original emphasis, quoted in Norman Furniss and Timothy Tilton, *The Case for the Welfare State* (Bloomington: Indiana University Press, 1977), p. 156.
15. Murray Levine and Adeline Levine, *A Social History of Helping Services* (New York: Appleton-Century-Crofts, 1970), p. 237.
16. Harold Wilensky and Charles Lebeaux, *Industrial Society and Social Welfare* (New York: Free Press, 1965), p. 88.
17. James Leiby, *A History of Social Welfare and Social Work in the United States* (New York: Columbia University Press, 1978), p. 170.
18. Levine and Levine, *A Social History of Helping Services,* pp. 236–43.
19. Wilensky and Lebeaux, *Industrial Society and Social Welfare,* p. 9; National Association of Social Workers, *Encyclopedia of Social Work,* 18th ed. (Silver Spring, Md.: NASW, 1987), p. 781.
20. James Jones, *Bad Blood* (New York: The Free Press, 1981), p. 34.
21. Thomas DiBacco, "Hookworm's Strange History," *Washington Post,* June 30, 1992, p. 14 (health section).
22. Berkowitz and McQuaid, *Creating the Welfare State,* pp. 33–36.
23. Ibid., p. 83.
24. Michael Boskin, "Social Security and the Economy," in Peter Duignan and Alvin Rabushka, eds., *The United States in the 1980s* (Stanford, Calif.: Hoover Institution, 1980), p. 182.
25. Berkowitz and McQuaid, *Creating the Welfare State,* p. 103.

26. Ibid., p. 136.

27. *Statistical Abstract of the United States* (Washington, D.C.: U.S. Government Printing Office, 1986), p. 369; *Social Security Bulletin, Annual Statistical Supplement* (Washington, D.C.: U.S. Government Printing Office, 1986), p. 67.

28. *Statistical Abstract of the United States, 1990*, p. 419.

29. Michael Misshauk, *Management: Theory and Practice* (Boston: Little, Brown, 1979), p. 6.

30. Melvin Anshen, *Managing the Socially Responsible Corporation* (New York: Macmillan, 1974), p. 5.

31. Steven Lydenberg, *Rating America's Corporate Conscience* (Reading, Mass.: Addison-Wesley, 1986).

32. Theodore Purcell, "Management and the 'Ethical' Investors," in S. Prakash Sethi and Carl Swanson, eds., *Private Enterprise and Public Purpose* (New York: John Wiley, 1981), pp. 296–97.

33. *The [Sullivan] Statement of Principles: Fourth Amplification* (Philadelphia: International Council for Equality of Opportunity Principles, 1984).

34. James Worthy, "Managing the 'Social Markets' Business," in Lance Liebner and Corrine Schelling, eds., *Public-Private Partnership: New Opportunities for Meeting Social Needs* (Cambridge, Mass.: Ballinger, 1978), p. 226.

35. Melanie Lawrence, "Social Responsibility: How Companies Become Involved in Their Communities," *Personnel Journal* 61, no. 7 (July 1982): 381; James Chrisman and Archie Carroll, "SMR Forum: Corporate Responsibility—Reconciling Economic and Social Goals," *Sloan Management Review* 25, no. 2 (Winter 1984): 173.

36. Enterprise Foundation, *Annual Report 1983* (Columbia, Md.: Enterprise Foundation, 1983), p. 1.

37. Brian O'Conell, *Philanthropy in Action* (New York: The Foundation Center, 1987), p. 218.

38. Local Initiatives Support Corporation, *The Local Initiatives Support Corporation* (New York: LISC, 1980); "A Statement of Policy for Programs of the Local Initiatives Support Corporation" (New York: LISC, 1981).

39. David Linowes, *The Corporate Conscience* (New York: Hawthorn Books, 1974), p. 209.

40. *Privatization: Toward More Effective Government* (Washington, D.C.: U.S. Government Printing Office, 1988), pp. 2–3.

41. Irving Kristol, "Charity and Business Shouldn't Mix," *New York Times,* October 17, 1982, p. 18.

42. Hedrick Smith, *The Power Game: How Washington Works* (New York: Random House, 1988), pp. 252–53, 260.

43. Marvin Olasky, *Patterns of Corporate Philanthropy* (Washington, D.C.: Capital Research Center, 1987), p. 2.

44. Ibid., p. 19.

45. Lawrence Fouraker and Graham Allison, "Foreword," in John Dunlop, ed., *Business and Public Policy* (Cambridge, Mass.: Harvard University Press, 1980), p. ix.

46. Peter Steinfels, "Michael Novak and His Ultrasuper Democraticapitalism," *Commonweal,* February 15, 1983, p. 11.

47. William J. Baroody, Jr., "The President's Review," *AEI Annual Report 1981–82* (Washington, D.C.: American Enterprise Institute, 1982), p. 2.

48. Peter Stone, "Businesses Widen Role in Conservatives' 'War on Ideas,'" *Washington Post,* May 12, 1985, p. C–5.

49. Bernard Weinraub, "Institute Plays Key Role in Shaping Reagan Programs," *New York Times,* January 5, 1981, p. D–1.

50. David Stoesz, "Policy Gambit: Conservative Think Tanks Take on the Welfare State," *Journal of Sociology and Social Welfare* 16 (1989): 86–95.

51. Stone, "Businesses Widen Role in Conservatives' 'War on Ideas.'"

52. American Enterprise Institute, *Annual Report 1981–82,* (Washington, D.C.: American Enterprise Institute, 1982).

53. Peter Berger and Richard Neuhaus, *To Empower People* (Washington, D.C.: American Enterprise Institute, 1977).

54. Michael Balzano, *Federalizing Meals on Wheels* (Washington, D.C.: American Enterprise Institute, 1979), p. 37.

55. Michael Novak, *Toward a Theology of the Corporation* (Washington, D.C.: American Enterprise Institute, 1981), p. 5.

56. Ibid., p. 50.

57. Ibid., p. 28.

58. Richard Reeves, "How New Ideas Shape Presidential Politics," *New York Times Magazine,* July 15, 1984, p. 18.

59. Heritage Foundation, *The Heritage Foundation Annual Report* (Washington, D.C.: Heritage Foundation, 1983).

60. Reeves, "How New Ideas Shape Presidential Politics," p. 21.

61. Interview with Stuart Butler, at the Heritage Foundation, Washington, D.C., October 4, 1984.

62. George Sternlieb, "Kemp-Garcia Act," in George Sternlieb and David Listokin, eds., *New Tools for Economic Development* (Piscataway, N.J.: Rutgers University Press, 1981), p. 42.

63. Stuart Butler, "Enterprise Zones," in Sternlieb and Listokin, *New Tools for Economic Development,* pp. 73–94.

64. Gilbert Lewthwaite, "Heritage Foundation Delivers Right Message," *Baltimore Sun,* December 9, 1984, p. 2.

65. Peter Ferrara, *Social Security Reform* (Washington, D.C.: Heritage Foundation, 1982), p. 51.

66. Peter Ferrara, *Rebuilding Social Security* (Washington, D.C.: Heritage Foundation, 1984), p. 7.

67. Chuck Lane, "The Manhattan Project," *The New Republic,* March 25, 1985, p. 34.

68. Charles Murray, *Losing Ground* (New York: Basic Books, 1984), pp. 226, 227.

69. Burton Pines, *Back to Basics* (New York: William Morrow, 1982).

70. Ibid., p. 254.

71. John Filer, "Editorial Notes: Commission on Private Philanthropy and Public Needs," *Social Casework* 23 (May 1976): 342.

72. Virginia Hodgkinson and Murray Weitzman, *Dimensions of the Independent Sector* (Washington, D.C.: Independent Sector, 1986), p. 53.

73. Donald Bauber, "Small Dent Expected in Charitable Giving as a Result of Crash," *San Diego Tribune,* November 1, 1987, p. I–1.

74. Allison Zippay, "Corporate Funding of Human Services Agencies," *Social Work* 37 (May 1992): 210.

75. *Eleventh Report of the Signatory Companies to the Statement of Principles for South Africa* (Cambridge, Mass.: Arthur D. Little, November 5, 1987), p. 3.

76. Nancy Amidei, "How to End Poverty: Next Steps," *Food Monitor* (Winter 1988), p. 52.

77. Stuart Butler, "A Conservative Vision of Welfare," *Policy Review* 10 (Spring 1987): 80.

78. Michael Novak, *The New Consensus on Family and Welfare* (Washington, D.C.: American Enterprise Institute, 1987), pp. xiv, 101–119.

79. Ibid., p. 120.

80. "Government's Role in the Consensus," *Business Week,* June 30, 1980, p. 87.

81. "Expectations That Can No Longer Be Met," *Business Week,* June 30, 1980, p. 84.

82. Lester Thurow, *The Zero-Sum Society* (New York: Basic Books, 1980), p. 95.

83. Robert Reich, *The Next American Frontier* (New York: Times Books, 1983), p. 223.

84. Ibid., pp. 247–48.

85. Kevin Phillips, *Staying on Top: The Business Case for a National Industrial Policy* (New York: Random House, 1984), pp. 5–6.

86. Yeheskel Hasenfeld, "The Changing Context of Human Services Administration," *Social Work* 29, no. 4 (November-December 1984): 524.

87. James O'Connor, *The Fiscal Crisis of the State* (New York: St. Martin's Press, 1973); Ian Gough, *The Political Economy of the Welfare State* (London: Macmillan, 1979).

88. See Sheila Akabas, Paul Kurzman, and Norman Kolben, eds., *Labor and Industrial Settings: Sites for Social Work Practice* (New York: Council on Social Work Education, 1979); Martha Ozawa, "Development of Social Services in Industry: Why and How?" *Social Work* 25 (November 1980): 86–93; and Dale Masi, *Human Services in Industry* (Lexington, Mass.: D. C. Heath, 1982).

89. "Social Work in Industrial Settings," *Social Work* 33 (January-February 1988): 65.

90. But see J. Decker, R. Starrett, and J. Redhorse, "Evaluating the Cost-Effectiveness of Employee Assistance Programs," *Social Work* 31 (September-October 1986): 83.

91. Shulamith Straussner, "Comparison of In-House and Contracted-Out Employee Assistance Programs," *Social Work* 33 (January-February 1988): 53.

92. Social Security Administration, *Social Security Bulletin* 46, no. 8 (August 1983): 10–12.

93. Social Security Administration, *Social Security Bulletin* 44, no. 11 (November 1981): 8.

94. Bureau of the Census, *Statistical Abstract of the United States, 1984* (Washington, D.C.: U.S. Government Printing Office, 1984), p. 103.

95. Life/continuing care refers to residential communities for the elderly that have a complete range of health services available to residents.

Such communities usually require residents to purchase their homes and to pay a monthly fee for a comprehensive range of services, including health care.

96. David Stoesz, "Human Service Corporations and the Welfare State," *Transaction/Society* 16 (1989): 80–91.

97. Bureau of the Census, *Statistical Abstract of the United States, 1986* (Washington, D.C.: U.S. Government Printing Office, 1986).

98. U.S. Department of Commerce, *1982 U.S. Industrial Outlook for 200 Industries with Projections for 1986* (Washington, D.C.: U.S. Government Printing Office, 1982), p. 406.

99. J. Avorn, "Nursing Home Infections—The Context," *New England Journal of Medicine* 305 (September 24, 1981): 759.

100. J. Blyskal, "Gray Gold," *Forbes,* November 23, 1981, p. 84.

101. D. Vaughan, "Health Care Syndications: Investment Tools of the '80s," *Financial Planner,* December 1981, p. 49.

102. Blyskal, "Gray Gold," p. 80.

103. V. DiPaolo, "Tight Money, Higher Interest Rates Slow Nursing Home Systems Growth," *Modern Health Care,* June 1980, p. 84.

104. National Senior Citizens' Law Center, "Federal Antitrust Activity" (Los Angeles: National Senior Citizens' Law Center, 1982), p. 2.

105. "NME Makes More Health Care Acquisitions," *Homecare News,* February 17, 1984, p. 4.

106. Quoted in W. Spicer, "The Boom in Building," *Contemporary Administrator,* February 1982, pp. 13–14.

107. B. Gray, "An Introduction to the New Health Care for Profit," in B. Gray, ed., *The New Health Care for Profit* (Washington, D.C.: National Academy Press, 1983), p. 2.

108. R. Siegrist, Jr., "Wall Street and the For-Profit Hospital Management Companies," in B. Gray, ed., *The New Health Care for Profit,* p. 36.

109. American Medical International, *1983 Annual Report* (Beverly Hills, Calif.: AMI, 1983).

110. "GAO Says Proprietary Hospital Chain Mergers Raise Medicare/Medicaid Costs," *Homecare News,* February 17, 1984, p. 6.

111. National Industry Council for HMO Development, *Ten Year Report 1971–1983* (Washington, D.C., 1983).

112. HealthAmerica, *Company Profile* (Nashville, Tenn.: HealthAmerica, 1983).

113. M. Abramowitz, "Maxicare HMO Soars with Farsighted Founder," *Washington Post,* November 30, 1986, p. 12.

114. National Industry Council, *Ten Year Report,* p. 22.

115. Catherine Born, "Proprietary Firms and Child Welfare Services: Patterns and Implications," *Child Welfare* 62 (March-April 1983): 112.

116. Kinder-Care, *Annual Report 1983* (Montgomery, Ala.: Kinder-Care, 1983).

117. Kinder-Care, *Second Quarter Report* (Montgomery, Ala.: Kinder-Care, March 16, 1984).

118. "Home Health Care of America," *Standard and Poor's Stock Reports* (March 1984), p. 4165.

119. "Interview with Elsie Griffith," *American Journal of Nursing* 18 (March 1984): 341.

120. "Digest of Earnings Reports," *The Wall Street Journal,* August 13, 1987, p. 41.

121. Stephen Boland, "Prisons for Profit," unpublished manuscript, School of Social Work, San Diego State University, 1987, pp. 5–6.

122. Ibid., p. 8.

123. Eric Press, "A Person, Not a Number," *Newsweek,* June 29, 1987, p. 63.

124. D. Vise, "Private Company Asks for Control of Tennessee Prisons," *Washington Post,* September 22, 1985, p. D–2.

125. U.S. Senate Special Committee on Aging, *Discrimination Against the Poor and Disabled in Nursing Homes* (Washington, D.C., U.S. Government Printing Office, 1984), p. 8.

126. Ibid.

127. "Sun City—With an Add-On," *Forbes,* November 23, 1981, p. 84.l

128. Paul Farhi, "Marriott Corp. Caters to America's Rapidly Aging Population," *Washington Post,* January 2, 1989, p. 5.

129. "Merrill Lynch: Bullish on Health Care," *Contemporary Administrator,* February 1982, p. 16.

130. Elizabeth Ortiz, "For-Profit Social Services and Social Work Education: Rapid Change and Slow Response," *Journal of Independent Social Work* 2, no. 1 (Fall 1987): 20–21.

131. D. Stoesz, "The Gray Market," p. 45.

132. Thomas J. Peters and Robert W. Waterman, Jr., *In Search of Excellence* (New York: Harper and Row, 1982); and Rosabeth M. Kanter, *The Changemasters* (New York, Simon and Schuster, 1983).

PART THREE

The Government Sector

CHAPTER 10

Income Maintenance: Social Insurance and Public Assistance Programs

This chapter explores the major social insurance and public assistance programs. First, it examines the main social insurance programs, including Old Age, Survivors, and Disability Insurance (OASDI), Unemployment Compensation (UC), and Workers' Compensation (WC). Second, it examines key public assistance programs, including the Earned Income Tax Credit (EITC), Aid to Families with Dependent Children (AFDC), Emergency Assistance Funds (EAF), Supplemental Security Income (SSI), and General Assistance (GA). Finally, this chapter explores the problems inherent in each of these policy areas.

The American social welfare state is a complex brew of programs, policies, and services. Perhaps few people, including many policymakers, fully appreciate the complexity of the welfare system. One reason is that unlike many European countries, which operate under a comprehensive and integrated welfare plan, the American system of social welfare is a patchwork quilt of programs and policies. Because of the country's historical ambivalence about providing public relief, most welfare legislation has resulted from compromises and adroit political maneuvering rather than from a systematic plan. In short, the U.S. welfare state is not a coordinated, comprehensive, integrated and nonredundant system of social welfare services; instead, it is a helter-skelter mix of programs and policies.

DEFINITION OF SOCIAL INSURANCE

Social insurance is a system whereby people are compelled—through payroll or other taxes—to insure themselves against the possibility of their own indigence resulting from the loss of a job, the death of the family breadwinner, or physical disability. Based on some of the principles used in private insurance, social insurance sets aside a sum of money that is held in trust by the government and earmarked to be used in the event of the death, disability, or the unemployment of the worker. The major goal of social insurance is to maintain income by replacing lost earnings. It is a pay-as-you-go system in which the workers and employers of today pay for those who have retired, are ill, or have lost their jobs. Although originally designed to replicate a private insurance fund, the Social Security program has been broadened to encompass a series of programs that attempt to provide a socially adequate replacement income. Because the benefits for some retired workers exceed their contributions to the system, Social Security has taken

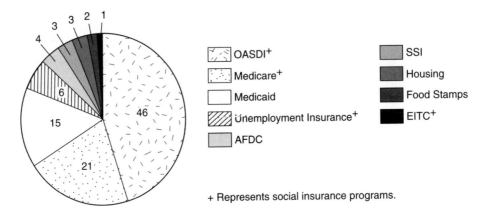

Figure 10.1. Percentage of the Social Welfare Budget Used by Social Insurance and Public Assistance Programs, 1991 (Only programs costing over $3 billion are included). (SOURCE: Compiled from tables in Committee on Ways and Means, U.S. House of Representatives, *Overview of Entitlement Programs, 1992 Green Book* [Washington, D.C.: U.S. GPO, 1992].)

on some of the characteristics of an income redistribution and/or public assistance scheme.

There are substantial differences between social insurance and public assistance programs. First, expenditures for social insurance are far greater than they are for public assistance, as can be seen in Figure 10.1. Second, beneficiaries of social insurance programs are required to make contributions to the system before they can claim any benefits. Third, social insurance is universal; in other words, people receive benefits as legal entitlements regardless of their personal wealth. Table 10.1 illustrates federal spending for major social insurance programs and the number of benficiaries for each. Because the benefit structure is linked to occupationally defined productive work, social insurance programs tend to be less stigmatized or not at all stigmatized.

Public assistance programs, by contrast, are financed out of general tax revenues. They are not occupationally linked and are therefore not based on a previous work record. In addition, public assistance recipients must be determined indigent through a means or income test. Because of this criterion, public assistance recipients are often stigmatized, whereas social insurance beneficiaries are not.

Although some people complain about the costs of public assistance programs, social insurance schemes are financed at a level roughly four times higher than public welfare is. For example, social insurance programs (OASDI, Workers' Compensation, Medicare, and Unem-

TABLE 10.1. Federal Spending for and Beneficiaries of Major Social Insurance Programs, 1975 and 1992 (Beneficiaries in millions, expenditures in billions)

Programs	1975	1992
OASDI	$65.8	$284.7
Beneficiaries	32,084	40,592
Medicare	$14.1	$128.3
Beneficiaries	28,478	31,083
Unemployment Insurance	$8.2	$34.6
Beneficiaries	8,300	10.7
Workers' Compensation	$2.2	$2.9
Beneficiaries	(NA)	(NA)
Total	$90.3	$450.5

SOURCES: Compiled from various tables in U.S. Bureau of the Census, *Statistical Abstract, 1990* (Washington, D.C.: U.S. Government Printing Office, 1990); and Committee on Ways and Means, U.S. House of Representatives, *Overview of Entitlement Programs: 1992 Green Book* (Washington, D.C.: U.S. Government Printing Office, 1992).

ployment Insurance, among others) cost about $450 billion in 1992 compared with about $106 billion for public assistance programs (AFDC, SSI, Food Stamps, WIC, and others). Furthermore, social insurance programs accounted for about 9 percent of the total GNP in 1992, whereas public assistance programs accounted for less than 3 percent. The growth of public assistance programs as a percentage of the GNP has been falling since the 1970s, so that it is now at almost the same level it was in 1965. Finally, the average OASDI beneficiary received $569 a month in 1992 compared with $402 for a mother with two children on AFDC.

THE BACKGROUND OF SOCIAL INSURANCE

The first old age insurance program was introduced in Germany in 1889 by Chancellor Otto von Bismarck. Although originally intended as a means of curbing the growing socialist trend in Germany, by the onset of World War I nearly all European nations had old age assistance programs of one sort or another. In 1920 the U.S. government began its own Federal Employees Retirement program. By 1931, 17 states had enacted their own old age assistance programs, although these often had stringent eligibility requirements. For example, in some cases where relatives were capable of supporting an elderly person, benefits were denied. Often the elderly who applied for assistance had to sign over all their assets to the state when they died. These state-administered welfare programs were restrictive and often punitive.[1] Nevertheless, the concept of governmental responsibility for welfare grew during the early part of the twentieth century and, by 1935, all states—with the exception of Georgia and South Carolina—had programs that provided financial assistance to widows and children.[2]

Spurred on by the Great Depression of the 1930s, and the growing rebellion inspired by a California physician named Francis Townsend

(who advocated a flat $200 per month for each retired worker), President Franklin Roosevelt championed a government assistance program that would cover both unemployed and retired workers.[3] The result of Roosevelt's efforts was the Social Security Act of 1935, through which the federal government established the basic framework for the modern social welfare state.

The current Social Security Act, as amended, now provides for: (1) OASDI; (2) UC programs under joint federal and state partnership; (3) federal assistance to the aged, blind, and disabled under the SSI program; (4) public assistance to families with dependent children under the AFDC program; (5) federal health insurance for the aged (Medicare); and (6) federal and state health assistance for the poor (Medicaid). Although all these programs fit under the rubric of the Social Security Act of 1935, not all are social insurance programs (e.g., Medicaid, AFDC, and SSI). The following section focuses on the social insurance programs covered under the Social Security Act.

The insurance feature of Social Security emerged as the result of an intense debate: Progressives wanted Social Security funded out of general revenue taxes whereas conservatives wanted it funded solely out of employee contributions. The compromise reached was that old age insurance would be financed by employer and employee contributions of 1 percent on a base wage of $3,000, with a maximum cap for worker contributions set at $30 per year. At age 65, single workers would receive $22 per month, while married workers would get $36. In order to allow the trust fund to accumulate reserves, no benefits were paid out until 1940.

The Social Security Act of 1935 has been modified repeatedly, almost always in the direction of increasing its coverage. The original Social Security Act of 1935 afforded retirement and survivor benefits to only about half the labor force; farm and domestic workers, the self-employed, and state and local government employees were excluded. In 1950 farmers and self-employed persons were added, thereby bringing the coverage to more than 90 percent of the labor force. Congress made survivors and dependents of insured workers eligible for benefits in 1939, and in 1956 disability insurance was added to include totally and permanently disabled workers. In 1965, Health Insurance for the Aged (Medicare)—a prepaid health insurance plan—was incorporated into the law. In later years, the act was amended to allow workers to retire as early as age 62, provided they agreed to accept only 80 percent of their benefits. In 1977 an automatic cost-of-living index was affixed to benefit payments. A major attempt to constrict the Social Security program was made, unsuccessfully, by the Reagan administration when it urged that the minimum benefit of $122 per month be retained for present beneficiaries but eliminated for future recipients. Other Reagan-inspired recommendations for Social Security included the elimination of payments for children aged 18 to 21 of deceased, disabled, and retired workers.

KEY SOCIAL INSURANCE PROGRAMS

OASDI

OASDI is a combination of old age and survivors' insurance (OASI) and disability insurance (DI). OASDI, or what most people refer to as Social Security, is currently the largest social program in the nation, covering approximately nine out of every 10 workers. In 1992, about 40 million people received benefits from OASDI, which has a total yearly expenditure of around $285 billion. OASDI is a completely federal program administered by the Social Security Administration, which is part of the Department of Health and Human Services. It is also a stellar example of a program that has worked. For example, the poverty rate for the elderly in 1992 was about the same as it was for the general population, roughly 12.2 percent. As recently as 1969, before the Social Security cost-of-living adjustments (COLAs) took effect, the poverty

rate for the elderly was double that of the general population, 25.3 percent as opposed to 12.1 percent.[4] According to Michael Harrington, the poverty rate for the elderly in 1984 would have been 47.6 percent without Social Security.[5] OASDI operates in the following manner:

1. In 1992 the employer and the employee each paid an OASDI tax equal to 6.20 percent of the first $55,000 in earnings and a Medicare Hospital Insurance (HI) tax equal to 1.45 percent of the first $130,200 of earnings. Self-employed persons paid 15.30 percent. The full Social Security contribution was therefore 15.3 percent. In general, increases in the wage base are automatic and are based on the increase in average wages in the economy each year. The highest Social Security tax a worker could pay in 1987 was $5,328, with a joint employer/employee tax of $10,656. Self-employed persons in 1992 had their taxes computed on a lower base (net earnings from self-employment less 7.65 percent), and half of that tax was deductible for income tax purposes.

2. Based on their age at retirement and the amount earned during their working years, workers receive a monthly benefit payment. Retired workers aged 62 receive a reduction of 5/9 of 1 percent for each month of entitlement before age 65, with a maximum reduction of 20 percent. Benefits are modest, with the average retired worker receiving $629 a month in 1992.[6] The maximum benefit in 1992 for a retired worker at age 65 was $1,088 per month, and for a couple, $1,632.

3. Under the OASI program, a monthly payment is made to an unmarried child or eligible dependent grandchild of a retired worker or a deceased worker who was fully insured at the time of death, if the child or grandchild is: (1) under age 18; (2) a full-time elementary or secondary school student under age 19; and (3) a dependent

or disabled person aged 18 or over whose disability began before age 22. A grandchild is eligible only if the child was adopted by the insured grandparent.

4. A lump sum benefit of $255 is payable to a spouse who was living with an insured worker at the time of his or her death.

5. Under the Disability Insurance Program (DI), monthly cash benefits are paid to disabled workers under age 65 and to their dependents. The purpose of the DI program is to replace lost income when a wage earner is no longer able to work. Monthly cash benefits are paid and computed generally on the same basis as they are in the OASI program; that is, they are calculated on the basis of past earnings. Medicare benefits are provided to disabled workers, widows or widowers, or adult children after they have been entitled to disability benefits for 24 months.

6. Almost all people, whether or not they paid into Social Security, are eligible for Medicare benefits. (Medicare is treated in depth in Chapter 11).

7. Social Security beneficiaries are required to have completed at least 40 quarters of work (10 years) before they are eligible to draw benefits.

Charles Prigmore and Charles Atherton maintain that the Social Security program is guided by several principles: (1) The program should be financed by both employer and employee contributions; (2) benefits should be work-connected and based on earnings; (3) coverage should be universal and participation mandatory; (4) benefits should not be dependent on need; and (5) benefits should move in the direction of social adequacy.[7]

Social Security, especially OASDI, has been a heated topic for much of its relatively short history. Political conservatives and laissez-faire economists are troubled because social security basically socializes a portion of the national income. Other critics claim that Social Security will lead to moral and economic ruin because it discourages savings and causes retired people to become dependent on a supposedly fragile governmental system. On the other hand, the Social Security system is popular with the elderly, who rely on it for much of their income, and with their grown children, for whom it helps to provide peace of mind.

The criticism leveled at the Social Security system was particularly pointed during the 1980s. Adversaries argued that Social Security was depressing private savings (thereby providing less capital for investment), overpaying the elderly, slighting younger workers (who could get a better return if they invested privately), and leading the country to fiscal collapse. Despite these criticisms, the system has held up remarkably well, probably because of its widespread public support.

Merton and Joan Bernstein challenge the criticisms leveled at Social Security. These authors claim that rather than discouraging private savings, Social Security actually stimulates financial planning for retirement and thus encourages savings.[8] Moreover, the overpayment argument is countered by noting that 60 percent of family households over age 65 had total annual incomes of under $30,000 in 1990, while only 16.8 percent had annual incomes exceeding $50,000. Almost 50 percent of elderly nonfamily households (persons living alone or with relatives) had annual incomes below $10,000.[9] These statistics do not suggest an aged population that has become wealthy by exploiting an overly generous Social Security system.

Although OASDI has become an important component of economic security for many of the nation's elderly, there are problems that threaten its future viability. The original strategy of the Social Security Act of 1935 was to create a self-perpetuating insurance fund, with benefits for the elderly being in proportion to their contribution. That scenario did not materialize. For example, in 1992 a single worker retiring at age 65 would have received a *maximum* Social Security (OASDI) benefit of $13,056 per year, plus an additional $1,756 yearly in Medicare reimbursements. If that worker started contributing to the Social Security fund in 1950, and regularly contributed at the maximum level until he retired in 1992, his total contribution would have been about $52,000. Yet in 3.5 years this worker will have received his entire contribution back in benefits. If he survives to age 72 (the average life expectancy for a male), he would have realized a benefit level of more over $51,300 in excess of his contributions. That amount does not include any cost-of-living increases. This situation has led some observers to doubt the long-term viability of Social Security.

Social Security began to show signs of being in trouble by the mid-1970s. Between 1975 and 1981, the Old Age and Survivors Fund suffered a net decrease in funds and a deficit in the reserve of between $790 million and $4.9 billion a year. This imbalance between incoming and outgoing funds threatened to deplete the reserve by 1983. Moreover, the prospects for Social Security seemed bleak in other ways. Whereas the ratio of workers to supported beneficiaries (the dependency ratio) was then three to one, by the end of the century (with the retirement of the baby boom generation) that ratio was expected to be only two to one. In short, the long-term costs of the program would have exceeded its projected revenues. The crisis in Social Security was fueled by demographic changes (a dropping birthrate plus an increase in life expectancy), more liberal benefits paid to retiring workers, high inflation, high unemployment, and the COLAs passed by Congress in the mid-1970s.

Facing these short- and long-term problems, Congress moved quickly to pass P.L. 98–21, the Social Security Amendments of 1983. Among the newly legislated changes were a delay in the cost-of-living adjustments and a stabilizer placed on future COLAs. In other words, if trust funds fall below a certain level, future benefits will be keyed to the consumer price index (CPI) or the average wage increase, whichever is lower. Another change was that

Social Security benefits became taxable if taxable income plus Social Security benefits exceeded $25,000 for an individual or $32,000 for a couple. A third change will increase the retirement age in 2027 to 67 for those wanting to collect full benefits. Although people could still retire at age 62, they would receive only 70 percent of their benefits instead of the current 80 percent. Finally, coverage was extended: New federal employees were covered for the first time, as well as members of Congress, the president and vice president, federal judges, and employees of nonprofit corporations.

Despite these changes, the fiscal viability of the Social Security system continues to remain in question. Unfortunately, no definitive answer is possible. Some analysts suggest that Social Security is on a sound footing. These analysts point to the fact that the reserve in the combined OASDI trust funds is expected to reach $100 billion by 1996. By 2025 that amount is projected to peak at $8 trillion.[10] Proponents maintain that the finances of the system will be in close actuarial balance for the next 75 years, with no more than a 5 percent difference between incoming and outgoing revenues.[11] Other analysts point to the Congressional Budget Office (CBO) projections that by 2015 (when the post-World War II baby boomers retire), OASDI taxes will fall short of expenditures. Beginning in 2015 the government will no longer have Social Security surpluses. Moreover, the OASI trust fund (the largest fund) is expected to be totally exhausted by 2042 (see Figure 10.2). Social Security's disability fund is expected to be depleted by 1997 unless it is restructured.

Other critics complain that the federal government is borrowing from the current Social Security surplus to fund other programs and is thereby hiding the real extent of the deficit. In 1990, $65 billion in Social Security surpluses went for non-Social Security spending. As a result, part of every federal program is paid for by the Social Security payroll tax. In that sense, the *real* budget deficit—and the absence of a *real* Social Security surplus to pay for future

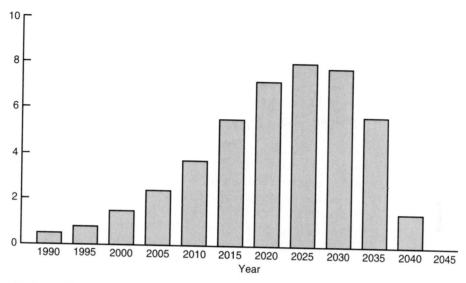

Figure 10.2. Projected Size of Social Security Trust Funds (Dollars in trillions). (SOURCE: Committee on Ways and Means, U.S. House of Representatives, *Overview of Entitlement Programs, 1992 Green Book* [Washington, D.C.: U.S. Government Printing Office, 1992], p. 93.)

benefits—has been hidden from the public.[12] When the Social Security system begins reclaiming its IOUs in the early years of the twenty-first century, the federal government may be forced to raise taxes, cut programs, or default on the Social Security system.

Although the Social Security Amendments of 1983 provided a short-term solution, structural problems continue to plague the system. For example, one problem is the "graying of America." Since 1900 the percentage of Americans 65 years and older has tripled (from 4.1 percent in 1900 to 12.6 percent in 1990), and the absolute number has increased 10 times (from 3.1 million to 31.2 million). Demographic projections suggest that by 2030 the number of persons over age 65 will increase to 65.6 million. In other words, the percentage of elderly is expected to climb from the current rate of 12.6 percent to more than 21 percent by 2030. Furthermore, the elderly are living longer. Between 1900 and 1990 the 75–84-year-old group increased 13 times while the 85-and-over group was 24 times larger.[13] These demographic

trends suggest that the dependency ratio will significantly increase, as will the pressures on the Social Security system. For example, in 1960 the worker/beneficiary ratio was 5 to 1; by 1980 it had dropped to 3.2 to 1. By 2040 the worker/beneficiary is expected to be 2 to 1.[14] Therefore, a question remains as to whether two workers in 2040 will be able to support one retired person, and whether the Social Security system—at least as it is presently structured—can support more than 20 percent of the American population.

Another problem facing Social Security is the increasing tax burden. Social Security taxes on working families grew more rapidly in the 1980s than at any time since the passage of the Social Security Act in 1935. From 1983 to 1990 the Social Security tax rate was raised six times, and the income level subject to the tax almost doubled from 1981 to 1992. As a result, a worker's maximum payroll tax jumped from $1,502 in 1981 to $3,924 in 1992, a 66 percent increase allowing for inflation. Between 1976 and 1992, Social Security taxes increased by over 200 percent, from $895 to $3,924 per year. From 1937 to 1990 the maximum Social Security tax increased 100 times.[15] Social Security taxes now represent the second largest revenue producer for the federal government. The tax burden of Social Security rests on the shoulders of workers and employers and results in a net decrease in both consumption and production.

Projections about the future of Social Security are predicated on the belief that certain economic and demographic factors will be in play for the next 50 years. But, economic and demographic shifts could easily invalidate the most earnest predictions, and Social Security could again go into crisis. For example, stagnant industrial productivity, changing demographic trends, an oil crisis, and major changes in immigration patterns would all have profound consequences for the future of Social Security. However, there is nothing inviolate about the way Social Security is currently funded. An act of Congress could easily eliminate the insurance feature of Social Security and replace it with general revenue taxation. Given the widespread dependence on Social Security, which was recognized by the prompt action taken by Congress on the Social Security crisis in the early 1980s, it seems highly unlikely that policymakers and the public will allow the Social Security system to go bankrupt.

Unemployment Compensation

The Social Security Act of 1935 created the federal/state unemployment compensation system. The objectives of UC are: (1) to provide temporary and partial wage replacement to involuntarily and recently unemployed workers, and (2) to help stabilize the economy during recessions. Although the U.S. Department of Labor oversees the general program, each state administers its own UC program.[16] The current guidelines of the UC program require employers to contribute to a trust fund, which is then activated if an employee loses his or her job. Employers currently pay a federal UC tax that is equal to 0.8 percent of the first $7,000 of an employee's wages.

The UC system consists of two basic parts: (1) regular state-funded benefits that are provided for up to 26 weeks, and (2) a federal/state extended benefits program. The second part provides an additional 13 weeks of benefits to unemployed workers who have used up their regular benefits and are still searching for a job. Extended benefits in the UC system are activated when the level of unemployment insurance claims in a state rises above a specified threshold. The extended benefits program is based on the assumption that when a state's unemployment rate is high, it usually takes longer to find a new job.[17] States pay 50 percent of the benefits provided by the UC extended benefits program.

To be eligible for UC benefits a worker must be ready and willing to work, be unemployed, be registered for work with the state employment service, and have been working in covered employment during a base eligibility period. Conversely, a worker who is fired for misconduct, quits a job without a legally acceptable reason, fails to register with the state employment service, refuses a job equal to or better than the one previously held, or goes on strike is ineligible for unemployment benefits. However, states cannot deny benefits to workers who refuse to be strikebreakers or who refuse to work for less than the prevailing wage rate.[18]

Basic decisions concerning the amount of benefits, eligibility, and length of benefit time are determined by the states. In all states, unemployment benefits are temporary and usually last no more than 39 weeks. Benefits are not equal to previously earned income, and an average unemployed worker in 1991 received benefits totaling around 36 percent of his or her previous wage. Normal state unemployment benefits vary widely, and in 1991 they ranged from a weekly low of $110 in Louisiana to a high of $218 in New Jersey. In 1991 the mean benefit was $155 per week.[19]

The UC program is rife with difficulties and inequities. For one thing, many states in recent years have tightened eligibility requirements. In addition, the UC program often fails to help the states with the most severe unemployment problems. For example, the calculation of unemployment rates is based on a study conducted by the Department of Labor in which 60,000 households (individuals 16 years or older are included in the survey) are interviewed each month. Part-time workers in this study are counted as employed, and discouraged workers who have dropped out of the labor force are not counted at all. Although the UC program includes mechanisms that allow states to receive more federal reimbursement when unemployment rates are unusually high, the official state rate is lowered because many of the unemployed are not counted. The consequence is that this artificially low rate of unemployment may not set off the extended benefits mechanism.[20] Furthermore, states with "pockets of poverty" receive no additional help when the overall state unemployment rate is not high enough to set off the triggers.

Another problem with the UC program involves coverage. In 1967 the unemployment rate stood at 3.8 percent, with 43 percent of all unemployed workers covered under the UC program. By 1975, the unemployment rate had soared to 8.5 percent and a record 75 percent of the unemployed were covered. However, from 1984 to 1989 the share of unemployed workers receiving benefits averaged 33 percent. In five of those six years, the percentage of unemployed persons covered under UC fell to the lowest level ever recorded. While in 1991 the number of unemployed persons covered under UC rose slightly to 42 percent, 750,000 more jobless workers would have received aid had coverage been at the same level it was in 1980. Disaggregating the national data paints an even bleaker picture. In 1991 there were only 14 states in which more than half of the unemployed received benefits. In that same year, 10 states gave benefits to less than one in four un-

employed workers.[21] Table 10.2 gives the unemployment protection picture by state in the years 1980 and 1991.

Equity problems also exist in the UC program. For example, the federal unemployment insurance tax rate has been raised only three times since it was initially set at $3,000 in 1935. In 1940, the taxable wage base encompassed 98 percent of a worker's wages; by 1988 the taxable wage base covered just 32 percent of an employee's wages. But this is not the only inequity that the taxation system for UC incorporates. For instance, an employer pays the same federal unemployment insurance tax on an employee who earns $100,000 a year as for an employee who earns only $7,000. Yet the worker with a higher income is eligible for higher unemployment benefits. This tax and benefit structure effectively discriminates against low wage earners who are at or near the taxable wage base.[22]

Finally, some 3.5 million UC recipients (35 percent) exhausted their regular 13 weeks of benefits in 1991. Although the unemployment rate rose to over 7 percent in 1992, in the early part of that year *no* state had activated its extended benefits program. There are two primary reasons for this phenomenon. First, as mentioned earlier, states pay half the cost of the minimum benefits program. Second, many states believe that extended benefits serve as a disincentive for recipients to actively pursue employment opportunities. Under a contract from the Department of Labor, a study conducted by Mathematica Policy Research, Inc., found that 60 percent of workers who had exhausted their benefits were still unemployed 10 weeks later. The study also found that the work disincentive did not appear to be a dominating factor in explaining the exhaustion of UC benefits.[23]

Workers' Compensation

Workers' Compensation provides cash, medical care, rehabilitation services, and disability and death benefits to persons (or their dependents) who are victims of industrial accidents or occu-

TABLE 10.2. Unemployment Insurance Protection by State, 1980 and 1991

State	Unemployment Rate, 1991	Percent of Unemployed Receiving Benefits, 1980	Percent of Unemployed Receiving Benefits, 1991	Percentage Point Change, 1980–1991
Alabama	7.2	44.4	32.4	−12.0
Alaska	8.5	72.8	70.0	−2.8
Arizona	5.7	31.6	37.0	+5.4
Arkansas	7.3	50.7	40.1	−10.6
California	7.5	50.4	50.4	0.0
Colorado	5.0	28.8	32.1	+3.3
Connecticut	6.7	42.6	54.0	$11.4
Delaware	6.2	42.7	34.8	−7.9
Dist. of Col.	7.7	52.9	56.8	+3.9
Florida	7.3	29.1	27.8	−1.3
Georgia	5.0	36.4	44.1	+7.7
Hawaii	2.8	54.3	55.3	+1.0
Idaho	6.1	53.5	49.0	−4.5
Illinois	7.1	52.9	37.9	−15.0
Indiana	5.9	42.2	29.5	−12.7
Iowa	4.6	47.1	37.0	−10.1
Kansas	4.4	48.7	42.1	−6.6
Kentucky	7.4	52.8	34.1	−18.7
Louisiana	7.1	38.4	27.0	−11.4
Maine	7.5	50.3	60.2	+9.9
Maryland	5.9	38.6	41.6	+3.0
Massachusetts	9.0	54.9	50.8	−4.1
Michigan	9.2	67.5	41.0	−26.5
Minnesota	5.1	45.1	41.9	−3.2
Mississippi	8.6	43.2	29.5	−13.7
Missouri	6.6	54.6	39.8	−14.8
Montana	6.9	57.8	34.3	−23.5
Nebraska	2.7	39.7	40.4	+0.7
Nevada	5.5	46.7	58.3	−11.6
New Hampshire	7.2	36.8	33.5	−3.3
New Jersey	6.6	63.5	53.7	−9.8
New Mexico	6.9	30.2	28.2	−2.0
New York	7.2	50.4	49.3	−1.1
North Carolina	5.8	38.1	40.8	+2.7
North Dakota	4.1	52.7	40.0	−12.7
Ohio	6.4	57.4	40.8	−16.6
Oklahoma	6.7	30.3	21.6	−8.7
Oregon	6.0	54.4	60.0	+5.6
Pennsylvania	6.9	61.8	51.0	−10.8
Rhode Island	8.5	70.9	64.1	−6.8
South Carolina	6.2	43.9	39.6	−4.3

TABLE 10.2. *(continued)*

State	Unemployment Rate, 1991	Percent of Unemployed Receiving Benefits, 1980	Percent of Unemployed Receiving Benefits, 1991	Percentage Point Change, 1980–1991
South Dakota	3.4	30.0	20.8	−9.2
Tennessee	6.6	53.2	40.4	−12.8
Texas	6.6	25.5	26.0	+0.5
Utah	4.9	41.3	29.0	−12.3
Vermont	6.4	55.0	56.0	+1.0
Virginia	5.8	32.4	24.0	−8.4
Washington	6.3	48.6	55.2	+6.6
West Virginia	10.5	50.3	31.1	−19.2
Wisconsin	5.4	62.5	49.2	−13.3
Wyoming	5.1	32.2	32.5	+0.3
Nation	6.7	50.4	41.6	−8.8

SOURCE: Adapted from Isaac Shapiro and Marion Nichols, *Far From Fixed: An Analysis of the Unemployment Insurance System* (Washington, D.C.: Center on Budget and Policy Priorities, March 1992), Tables III and V, pp. 16 and 22.

pational diseases. In 1988, Workers' Compensation laws protected more than 91 million employees. While laws vary from state to state, the basic principle is that employers should assume the costs of occupational disabilities without regard to fault.[24]

The specific laws governing Workers' Compensation vary from state to state. As such, there is little consistency either in benefit levels or in the administration of the programs. For example, some states require employers to carry insurance, other states provide a state-sponsored insurance fund, others allow employers to act as self-insurers, and still others do not require compulsory Workers' Compensation coverage. Many state programs exempt employees of nonprofit, charitable, or religious institutions. Nevertheless, because of the potential for large claims, most employers transfer their responsibility by purchasing insurance from private companies that specialize in Workers' Compensation.

Workers' Compensation programs are problematic in several ways. First, benefit levels are established on the basis of state formulas and are usually calculated as a percentage of weekly earnings (usually about 66.5 percent). As such, each state sets its own annually adjusted benefit level, which varies widely across states. For example, the benefit level in 1988 ranged from $175 a week in Georgia to $1,094 in Alaska, with the median at $340.50. Second, the cost to employers for providing Workers' Compensation insurance has been rising rapidly. Employers paid $43 billion to insure their workers in 1988, a 12.6 percent increase over the 1987 figure of $38.1 billion. The bulk of that money—$28.5 billion—was paid to private insurance carriers.[25] Third, there is great variability among states in the way claims are handled. Workers are often encouraged to settle out of court for an attractive lump sum, even though that amount may not equal their lost wages. Often, benefits are uneven. For example, the price attached to the loss of a body part has been interpreted differently from state to state. Prigmore and Atherton note that in Hawaii the loss of a finger was valued at $5,175 in 1978, more than the courts in the state of Wyoming allowed for the loss of an eye.[26] In addition, there are often long delays between the time an injury occurred and the period in which benefits start. Finally, in some states employers are exempt from the Workers' Compensation tax if they can demonstrate that they are covered by private insurance. Unfortunately, private insurance coverage may prove inadequate after a disability benefit is determined. Even though injured workers or their survivors received $30.8 billion in benefits and medical payments in 1988, Workers' Compensation may not provide adequate protection for many disabled workers.[27]

ISSUES IN SOCIAL INSURANCE

Social insurance programs are replete with both contradictions and difficulties. The scope of these problems is most visible in OASDI, the largest social insurance program. While originally intended to supplement private pension funds and to operate as a pay-as-you-go insurance scheme, OASDI has taken on many of the characteristics of a public welfare program in the past 50 years. For example, some workers receive high benefit levels even though their fiscal contributions to the system have not justified them. Almost all current retirees are realizing benefits far in excess of what they contributed over the course of their working lives in Social Security taxes. (Those retiring in 1993 are the first group of workers who will receive less in benefits than they have paid out in taxes.) The bill for those benefits is being paid by the young workers of today.

Given this scenario, should social insurance be modified so as more clearly to reflect social assistance and income redistribution goals? If the answer is yes, then benefits must be structured to reflect the current needs of retired workers rather than their past contributions. Furthermore, if Social Security is viewed as a public welfare program, then its regressive tax structure should be modified to reflect a more progressive framework. For example, Social Security is the single largest tax paid by a low-

income worker, yet that same worker receives the lowest benefits when he or she retires. Thus, the workers hurt most by the tax receive the fewest benefits. Using that same line of reasoning, if Social Security is designed for social assistance, then should everyone, regardless of income, be eligible? More particularly, should the wealthy be allowed to be beneficiaries? The answers to these questions will obviously be rooted in the values of the inquirer.

Another issue in Social Security involves the comparison between public (compulsory) and private (voluntary) pension plans. Some critics argue that private pension plans are preferable to public schemes because they are based on less dependence on the government and have the potential for yielding higher returns. Private pensions originated as a means of encouraging employee loyalty and as a way of easing out aging workers. However, only about one-third of all workers and one-fourth of current employees are covered under private pension plans. Moreover, only a small fraction of these plans are indexed for inflation.

Critics of private pension plans argue that they are basically unreliable. Employees can switch jobs and thus lose their pension rights, companies may go bankrupt, corporations may attempt to raid pension funds, and corrupt or incompetent managers can wreak havoc on well-endowed pension plans. U.S. pension reserves are currently worth well over one trillion dollars and form a major source for investment capital. Despite federal tax subsidies to private pension plans, totaling more than $64 billion in 1988, coverage under these plans has actually decreased since 1980. Supporters of Social Security argue that unlike the riskier private pension plans, OASDI benefits are portable and indexed for inflation, workers are immediately vested, and benefits are not contingent on the financial condition of the employer.[28]

Social insurance programs, especially OASDI, have become a mainstay of the American social welfare state. Despite the original intent of its architects, Social Security has become a primary source of financial support for America's elderly. Moreover, OASDI is one of the few social programs that has demonstrated the ability not only to arrest the poverty rate for its constituents but actually to reduce it. In short, a majority of Americans have come to view Social Security as a right and to count on its benefits.

PUBLIC ASSISTANCE PROGRAMS

Public assistance programs are one of the most misunderstood facets of the American welfare state. Although expenditures for public assistance programs are far less than they are for social insurance programs, they tend to be more controversial. Unlike social insurance, public assistance programs are based entirely on need and are therefore means-tested. Table 10.3 lists the major benefit programs and the expenditures on each.

The rationale for public assistance programs (offering cash, medical, and other forms of assistance) is grounded in the concept of "safety nets" designed to ensure that citizens receive basic services and that they do not fall below a certain poverty level. Despite the belief in a single safety net, there are actually 51 separate safety nets—one in each state and the District of Columbia. Although federal guidelines help determine the level of aid for the poor, individual states have extensive freedom to fashion their own safety nets. One national study found that the vast majority of states lack an adequate safety net to help the poor and the jobless.[29] Nevertheless, a major component of the safety net consists of programs designed to ensure that families and individuals receive the resources necessary for survival. This section covers public assistance programs, including Earned Income Tax Credits (EITC), Aid to Families with Dependent Children (AFDC), Emergency Assistance Funds (EAF), Supplemental Security Income (SSI), and General Assistance (GA).

The Earned Income Tax Credit

A program that crosses the increasingly vague boundary between social insurance and public assistance is the Earned Income Tax Credit (EITC) program. Specifically, while the EITC is limited to those participating in the work force, it is also means-tested. Because of this means testing, we have included EITC within the public assistance sector.

The EITC can be described as both tax reform and public assistance. It is tax reform in that it moderates the regressive social security tax for low-income workers. And it is a public assistance program in that it supplements the wages of low-income households.[30] Although the EITC was developed prior to the Reagan administration, it fit squarely within his philosophy of substituting tax policy for welfare policy. As a result, the idea of tax expenditures—indirect payments through tax exemptions, credits, or rebates—appeared regularly in social policy discussions throughout the 1980s. In fact, when direct public welfare expenditures for the poor were under assault in the 1980s, indirect payments under EITC actually increased, as Table 10.4 shows.

Created by Congress in 1975, the EITC was designed to provide low-income taxpayers with a rebate. The ostensible goals of the program were to (1) offset the burden of social security payroll taxes on poor working families, (2) supplement low wages, and (3) promote work as a viable alternative to welfare.[31] The EITC is available to working families (including unmarried heads of households) with at least one child and who file a joint return or a "head of household" return. The EITC functions somewhat like a negative income tax. Specifically, a working family receives the full amount of the EITC tax credit even if that credit is greater than the family's tax liability. The amount by which the credit exceeds the taxes owed is paid as a refund. Thus, if a working family has no income tax liability, it receives the full EITC refund.[32]

The original EITC rebate equaled 10 per-

TABLE 10.3. Major Cash and Noncash Benefit Programs for Persons with Limited Income, 1980 and 1991 (Recipients in thousands, expenditures in $ millions)

Program	1980	1991	Program	1980	1991
Aid to Families with Dependent Children (AFDC)			School Lunch Program		
Recipients	$10,587	$ 12,587	Federal Cost	2,111	4,029
Federal Cost	7,198	12,457	State or Local Cost	—	—
State Cost	6,237	10,414	Total Cost	2,111	4,029
Total Cost	13,435	22,871	Head Start		
Supplemental Security Income (SSI)			Recipients	376	583
			Federal Cost	735	2,202
Recipients	4,142	5,118	Total Cost	735	2,202
Federal Cost	5,866	14,765	*Housing Assistance		
State Cost (State Supplements)	2,074	3,769	Recipients	4,007	5,465
			Federal Cost	5,364	16,619
Total Cost	7,940	18,534	State or Local Cost	—	—
General Assistance (GA)			Total Cost	5,364	16,619
Recipients	910	1,332	Low-Income Energy Assistance		
Federal Cost	—	—	Recipients	—	5,798
State or Local Cost	1,386	2,605	Federal Cost	1,539	1,139
Medicaid			Total Cost	1,539	1,139
Recipients	21,605	25,255	†Jobs and Training Programs		
Federal Cost	14,550	53,519	Recipients	1,208	604
State or Local Cost	11,231	40,691	Federal Cost	3,326	1,761
Total Cost	25,781	94,310	Total Cost	3,326	1,761
Food Stamps			Title XX		
Recipients	19,200	22,600	Federal Cost	2,791	2,800
Federal Cost	9,188	19,765	State or Local Cost	863	—
State or Local Cost	375	1,247	Total Cost	2,791	2,800
Total Cost	9,576	13,466	Total	$73,511	$179,856
Women, Infants, and Children (WIC)					
Recipients	411	1,034			
Federal Cost	725	2,125			
State or Local Cost	—	—			
Total Cost	725	2,125			

* Housing assistance includes Section 8, low-rent public housing, rural housing loans, rural rental housing loans, and interest reduction payments.
† Jobs and training programs include employment and training services, the summer youth employment program, the Job Corps, the senior community service employment program, and the work incentive program, among others. (SOURCE: Compiled from various tables in Committee on Ways and Means, U.S. House of Representatives, Overview of Entitlement Programs: 1992 Green Book [Washington, D.C.: U.S. Government Printing Office, 1992].)

cent of the first $4,000 of earned income (a maximum credit of $400). Under the Tax Reform Act of 1986, the maximum tax credit was increased to $800 (14 percent of the first $5,714 of earned income). The EITC was further expanded as part of the 1990 budget agreement (OBRA-90) negotiated by Congress and President George Bush. This OBRA-90 agreement added $18 billion to the EITC from 1990 to 1995. In 1992, families with children who had incomes up to

TABLE 10.4. Total Amount of Earned Income Tax
Credit Rebates, Selected Years

Years to Which Credit Applies	Total Amount (millions)
1975	$ 1,250
1980	1,986
1985	2,088
1990	5,858
1991	8,806
1992	10,697
1993	11,914*

* Projected (SOURCE: Adapted from Committee on Ways and Means, U.S. House of Representatives, *Overview of Entitlement Programs* [Washington, D.C.: U.S. Government Printing Office, 1992], p. 1019.)

$22,370 were eligible for EITC. The EITC has three components: a basic credit, a young child supplement, and a health insurance credit.

1. All eligible families receive a basic credit. Families with earnings between $7,520 and $11,480 receive the maximum tax credit, which was $1,324 in 1992. This maximum credit is slowly reduced as income rises until it vanishes altogether at a yearly income of $22,370.
2. Qualified EITC families with a child under age one are also eligible for a young child supplement, which in 1992 carried a maximum credit of $376.
3. EITC families who pay premiums for a health insurance policy that covers a child can also receive the health insurance credit, which in 1992 carried a maximum value of $451.[33]

Although economists Saul Hoffman and Lawrence Seidman agree with the basic principles of the EITC, they also recognize its limitations. According to Hoffman and Seidman, the EITC program:

> . . . provides benefits to one-third of all poor families and one-quarter of all Afri-

can-American families. The EIC [EITC] population is, however, predominantly white and non-poor. The typical EIC family has a low-to-moderate income that places it above the poverty line. . . . Finally, the average credits were quite low, so the contributions of the EIC program to the economic well-being of low- and moderate income families is certainly quite modest.[34]

It was estimated that the recent expansion of the EITC in 1990 would lift an additional 1.2 million people out of poverty by 1994. However, unless the federal minimum wage is raised substantially, full-time, year-round employment paying the minimum wage plus the maximum 1994 EITC credit ($1,861) will still result in a family of four being several thousand dollars below the poverty line. Moreover, it is difficult to imagine that the EITC program will make a profound difference in the economic lives of the working poor, especially given the *maximum* family credit of $1,324 in 1992. The EITC is also less useful for large families since the credit amount is not adjusted to family size after the second child. Finally, the EITC program is plagued with the problem of nonfilers. In 1990 a family of four who earned less than $13,650 a year would not owe any tax and would therefore not be required to file an income tax return. But without a tax return they would not receive the EITC credit to which they were entitled.[35]

Aid to Families with Dependent Children

AFDC is perhaps the most controversial program in the American welfare system. The ostensible purpose of AFDC is to maintain and strengthen family life by providing financial assistance and care to needy dependent children in their own homes or in the homes of responsible caretakers. Despite these modest goals, the AFDC program and its recipients have often been used as symbols in the ideological struggle between liberals and conservatives. This situation has caused AFDC recipients to be victim-

ELIGIBILITY CRITERIA

ized in two ways: (1) by their own poverty and (2) by ideologically motivated assaults against their character and motives.

AFDC is the largest public assistance program. The requirement for receiving AFDC is deprivation of the parental care of one parent because of death, desertion, separation, or divorce. (In the case of AFDC-Unemployed Parent, it is deprivation of parental economic support through unemployment or illness.) In 1992, AFDC served close to 4.7 million families (about 13.5 million individuals) at a cost of almost $23 billion. Of the 13.5 million recipients about 67 percent, or 9 million, were children. The average AFDC benefit level for a family of three was $372 per month in 1992. The AFDC-UP program assisted 266,000 families (more than 1.1 million recipients) in 1991. In 1992, AFDC recipients equaled about 5 percent of the general population, and about 13 percent of all children in the United States were covered under AFDC. In 1990, about 60 percent of all children in poverty were recipients of AFDC benefits, a significant reduction from the 81 percent of poor children who were covered in 1973.[36]

AFDC Funding and Eligibility Criteria

FUNDING

AFDC is funded jointly by the individual states and the federal government. The federal share of AFDC benefit payments is determined by a matching formula specified for Medicaid in Title XIX of the Social Security Act. (Although some states may choose an alternative formula, none do so.) The federal Medicaid matching rate is inversely related to the per capita income within a state. Thus, federal matching varies from state to state, ranging from 50 percent in states with high per capita incomes to close to 80 percent in low per capita income states, such as Mississippi. The federal government pays 50 percent of the costs of administering the AFDC program in all states. States handle the matching portion in different ways, and some require localities to finance a portion of the nonfederal share of AFDC benefits. On average, the federal government pays about 62 percent of all AFDC costs.[37]

AFDC provides cash benefits to (1) needy children who are deprived of parental support or care because their father or mother is absent from the home continually, or because he or she is incapacitated, deceased, or unemployed; and (2) certain others in the household of such a child. Eligibility for AFDC ends on a child's eighteenth birthday (or, at state option, on the nineteenth birthday). AFDC-UP is designed to offer AFDC benefits to children in two-parent families who are needy because of the unemployment or illness of the principal wage earner. In order to receive benefits under the AFDC-UP program, the principal wage earner must have worked six or more quarters in any 13 calendar quarters and must have received or been eligible for unemployment compensation within one year prior to an application for assistance. All states operate an AFDC and an AFDC-UP program.

AFDC benefits are based on a family's countable income and needs as determined by state law. The concept of "total basic need" is a major criterion for eligibility. AFDC guidelines specify that if a family's total basic need is greater than its countable income, then the family is eligible for AFDC. Countable income was revised by the Family Support Act of 1988, and in 1992 it was capped at $90 per month, with a child care allowance of $175 ($200 for a child under age two). Any rebates paid under EITC are disregarded. Total basic need (the need standard) is determined almost exclusively by the states. Each state establishes a "need standard" (the income the state decides is necessary for basic consumption items) and a "payment standard" (100 percent or less of the need standard). While the federal government requires all states to have a needs standard, it does not compel them to pay that amount to AFDC beneficiaries. Benefits are generally computed by subtracting countable income from the state's payment standard. Because of this formula, maximum AFDC payment schedules differ widely from state to state.

Some Assumptions That Underlie the AFDC Program

American attitudes toward AFDC are characterized by a mixture of indifference, compassion, and hostility. This ambivalence plays out in a series of harsh and often conflicting assumptions about AFDC and its recipients. Moreover, the struggle around AFDC is a symbolic one, reflecting the tension surrounding American ideas about wealth, opportunity, privilege, and the American dream.

The argument goes like this: If privilege in America is something that is earned by application and hard work, then people are poor because they lack the desire to elevate themselves out of poverty. In short, the poor have not applied themselves because they are lazy. Moreover, the refusal of the poor to compete seems a serious character flaw to those driven by the intense competition that marks capitalist society. On the other hand, all that separates the welfare recipient from the average citizen is a few paychecks—thus the compassion. While the dogma of capitalism implies that hard work guarantees success, the reality of people's lives often tells a different story. The tensions and contradictions that characterize contemporary life shade people's views toward both AFDC and the welfare state. The following assumptions, among others, underlie the AFDC program: (1) Generous AFDC benefits create a disincentive to work (therefore recipients must always get fewer benefits than the minimum wage provides); (2) welfare recipients need to be prodded to work because they lack internal motivation; (3) although economic opportunities are available, recipients must be forced to take them; (4) work is the best antipoverty program; (5) AFDC and other public assistance programs must be highly stigmatized, because if they lost their stigma, people would turn to them too readily; and (6) all women receiving AFDC should work and poor children should not have the luxury of being raised by a full-time homemaker. Although middle- and upper-class children should, ideally, be brought up by a full-time homemaker, homemaking is not an acceptable occupation for the mothers of poor children. These assumptions about AFDC—many of which are remarkably similar to those that underlie the Elizabethan Poor Laws—lead to numerous myths and fears, most of which are not borne out by the facts.

Myths about AFDC and Public Assistance

There are a lot of commonly held myths about AFDC. We attempt in this section to discriminate between fact and fiction.

Myth 1. The AFDC rolls are composed of many families containing an able-bodied father who refuses to work.

Fact. The AFDC-UP program (266,000 families) accounted for only 12 percent of the total 4.7 million families on AFDC in 1992. The truth is that 90 percent of AFDC families are headed by one parent—mostly mothers who are either single, divorced, widowed, or separated—with only 10 percent of AFDC households being two-parent families.[38] Ninety percent of AFDC children live with their mothers and 10 percent with their fathers. Sixty-six percent of AFDC recipients are children, the remaining recipients being mothers (18.6 percent) and the aged (15.6 percent). Less than 1 percent of all welfare recipients are able-bodied males. Among children who are AFDC recipients, almost 60 percent have parents who are not married to each other.[39] Forty-one percent of the fathers of AFDC children cannot be found.[40]

Myth 2. Most poor people are on AFDC and the number is growing.

Fact. The percentage of poor people receiving welfare has actually declined since the early 1970s. Although the number of poor people with children rose 50 percent between 1973 and 1989, the number of AFDC families grew by only 20 percent.[41] Moreover, two-thirds of the poor

(21.2 million of the 33.6 million poor people in 1991) receive *no* money from AFDC, and more than a third do not receive Food Stamps or Medicaid.

Myth 3. Recipient mothers have more children in order to collect greater benefits; therefore AFDC families are large and steadily growing in size.

Fact. The average AFDC family is composed of 2.9 persons. Nearly three-quarters of all recipients have two or less children. Forty-two percent of AFDC families have one child; only 10 percent have four or more children.[42] Moreover, the average size of AFDC families has been steadily decreasing, from a high of 4.0 in 1969 to 2.9 by 1990. Furthermore, having additional children to increase an AFDC benefit hardly seems worth the effort. For example, in 1991 the difference in gross AFDC benefits for a family of three and a family of four in Louisiana was $44 per month. As the family size increases, the benefit is lowered; for example, the difference in benefits between a Louisiana family of five and a family of six was $39 per month in 1991.[43] This may explain why mothers on AFDC give birth to only one-fourth the number of babies as nonwelfare mothers do.[44] Finally, some of the lowest benefit states, including Mississippi, Arkansas, Louisiana, and Alabama, have the highest out-of-wedlock birthrates.[45]

Myth 4. Once on welfare always on welfare.

Fact. The truth is that nearly 10 percent of all welfare spells end within two months. An additional 15 percent of welfare spells end within six months. Thus, 25 percent of all AFDC spells end within six months. Moreover, half of all welfare spells last less than one year and more than 60 percent last two years or less. Only 17 percent of those persons beginning a spell will be on welfare for eight or more years.[46] Long-term recipients are obviously those with the fewest market opportunities.

Another myth centers around the dependency created by welfare programs. According to Greg Duncan and Saul Hoffman, the total income package received by welfare families often contains more income from other sources than it does from welfare, with labor income being mixed with welfare income.[47] Moreover, roughly 25 percent of the U.S. population lived in families in which some form of welfare was received between 1969 and 1978, but fewer than 44 percent of those families received income from welfare sources for at least eight of those 10 years.

Myth 5. Welfare dependency is transmitted intergenerationally.

Fact. The question of welfare receipt across generations is complex and not yet fully understood. According to Greg Duncan and Saul Hoffman, only 19 percent of African-American and 26 percent of white women coming from heavily dependent welfare homes were observed to be heavily dependent on welfare themselves. The 19 percent of African-American women heavily dependent on welfare was the same percentage as African-American women heavily dependent on welfare who did not come from heavily dependent welfare households. The authors maintain that African-American men who came from heavily dependent welfare households showed no decrease in the average number of working hours, while white men from heavily dependent welfare homes averaged fewer hours of work per week than did otherwise similar white men.[48]

On the other hand, Peter Gottschalk found a positive intergenerational relationship between the use of welfare by mothers and the use of it by daughters.[49] M. Ann Hill and June O'Neill also found persistence in welfare receipt across generations. Looking at data from the National Longitudinal Survey of Youth (NLSY), the authors found that young white women from welfare families have a 24 percent chance of being on welfare compared with a 2 percent chance for white women coming from nonwelfare families. Comparable figures for African Americans were 42 percent and 15 percent; for Hispanic Americans, 34 percent and 8 percent.[50] In their study of men's earnings, Mary Corcoran, Roger Gordon, Deborah Laren, and Gary Solon found that "One of our strongest results is the large negative association between a son's outcomes and welfare receipt in his family of origin."[51] Although some correlation may exist between welfare receipt and family of origin, the question remains as to whether parental receipt of AFDC is the *cause* of the children's behavior. Because receiving AFDC is a symptom of poverty, it would make more sense to analyze how low-income status is transmitted intergenerationally rather than to focus on intergenerational welfare receipt.

Myth 6. Most welfare recipients are African Americans.

Fact. Close to the same number of whites as African Americans receive AFDC. In 1990 whites constituted 38 percent of recipients, African Americans 39 percent, and Hispanic Americans 16 percent. The remaining 7 percent were composed of Asian Americans, Native Americans, and others.[52]

Myth 7. Fraud and cheating in AFDC and Food Stamps are rampant among welfare recipients.

Fact. There is no available evidence to support the charge that fraud is widespread in either the Food Stamp or the AFDC program. Contrary to popular belief, both individual states and the federal government have quality control systems to monitor the error rate in public assistance programs, including AFDC. In 1990 the national overpayment dollar error rate for AFDC was only 6 percent. States that exceed the national error rate set by the federal government are penalized.[53] According to Elizabeth Huttman, a 1977 study concluded that 51 percent of AFDC errors were made by welfare agencies or social workers. This report noted that 5.3 percent of the 11.2 million AFDC recipients were ineligible, 13 percent were overpaid, and 4.9 percent were underpaid. According to the study, fraud or misrepresentation occurred in less than four-tenths of one percent of the total national caseload.[54] Moreover, according to the *Washington Post*, "USDA officials note that the most costly scams in the Food Stamp program have originated or involved the federal employees assigned to monitor and distribute the coupons, not the people who receive them."[55]

Myth 8. AFDC benefits provide a disincentive to work; people on AFDC either don't want to work or are too lazy to work.

Fact. In 1991 there were only three states in which the AFDC cash benefit for a family of three reached 75 percent of the poverty line. In 45 states, AFDC benefits were below 50 percent of the poverty threshold. Eight states provided a single parent with two children less than $250 per month in AFDC benefits in 1993; five out of those states provided $200 or less. The maximum AFDC benefit level for a family of three in 1992 ranged from a low of 13.5 percent of the poverty line in Mississippi to a high of 77.5 percent in California. In the typical or median state, AFDC benefits in 1992 for a three-person family equaled $372 per month, or 41 percent of the poverty line. Even with the inclusion of Food Stamps, in every state except Alaska the combined benefits fall below the poverty line, and in over half the states the combined benefits of Food Stamps and AFDC do not equal two-thirds of the poverty line.

A recent report by the Congressional Budget Office noted that all growth spurts in the AFDC program occurred around recessions. For example, between 1983 and 1989 the number of AFDC families grew by less than 1 percent a year. In 1988, AFDC caseloads actually declined in 22 states. However, because of the recession that began in 1989 only three states registered such declines in 1990.[56] Most of the poor either work or desire a job, although their employment frequently does not allow them to overcome poverty. In 1990 nearly two out of every three poor families with children (63 percent) included at least one worker; 25 percent of poor people live in families with at least one year-round full-time worker.[57] Compulsory experiments in workfare suggest that AFDC recipients believe they *ought* to work for their checks.[58]

Myth 9. AFDC recipients are doing better than ever.

Fact. The reverse is true. AFDC recipients are actually doing worse than ever. Specifically, benefit levels have not kept pace with inflation, having fallen 43 percent (after adjusting for inflation) in the typical state from 1972 to 1992. This reflected a benefit loss of $279 per month, or more than $3,300 a year in 1992 dollars.[59]

Myth 10. Unmarried mothers constitute the bulk of welfare recipients.

Fact. According to Duncan and Hoffman, the most important causes for beginning welfare spells are (1) divorce or separation (45 percent), (2) an unmarried woman becoming a pregnant household head (30 percent), and (3) a drop in earn-

ings of the female head of the household (12 percent). Conversely, the predominant reasons for terminating welfare spells are (1) remarriage (35 percent), (2) an increase in the earnings of a female householder (21 percent), and (3) children leaving the parental home (11 percent).[60]

Myth 11. It is easy to get on welfare and therefore too many undeserving people are receiving benefits.

Fact. In addition to meeting stringent income and asset guidelines, potential Food Stamp and AFDC recipients must also provide extensive documentation and meet verification requirements. Almost 97 percent of Food Stamp benefits go to households with incomes at or below the poverty line. More than half those benefits go to households with gross incomes at or below *half* of the poverty line.[61] Moreover, 63 percent of all applications for AFDC assistance were denied in 1990.[62]

Myth 12. AFDC recipients migrate to states where benefits are high.

Fact. A Wisconsin study showed that only 10 percent of AFDC recipients who had entered the state within the past year were motivated primarily by the availability of higher benefits.[63] Other studies indicate that poor people migrate for a variety of reasons, including proximity to family and friends, the desire for a better life, and the hope of finding a job. However, research completed by the Wisconsin Policy Research Institute concludes that poor people do migrate across state lines to receive higher benefits.[64] The study fails to show, though, that it is high benefits per se that cause migration. At best, the question about migratory patterns of poor people and welfare receipt remains unresolved.

Myth 13. Welfare spending consumes a large portion of state budgets.

Fact. In 1991, states spent an average of 3.4

percent of their total budgets on AFDC. However, 1.5 percent of that sum came from the federal government. Thus, states spend only 2 percent of their budgets on AFDC.[65]

Myth 14. AFDC benefits influence decisions having to do with family structure (i.e., childbearing, marriage, divorce, and living arrangements) by encouraging women to head their own households.

Fact. Although some empirical studies have found a small correlation between AFDC benefits and the number of women who choose to head households or remarry, most researchers believe that the available evidence does not support the hypothesis that the generosity of the welfare system has been responsible for the trends in illegitimacy or the growth in single female-headed households. For example, although total welfare benefits have declined since 1975, the number of single female-headed households and the illegitimacy rate continued to grow.[66]

EMERGENCY ASSISTANCE FUNDS

Under the AFDC program, states may make additional payments to cover the "special needs" of AFDC recipients. Special needs payments can be used to help prevent families from becoming homeless or from losing vital services such as heat or electricity. Under the special needs allocation program, some states pay for high shelter costs, fuel or utility costs, burial costs, clothing, and expenses that result from natural disasters or eviction.

In addition to making special needs payments, states can operate an Emergency Assistance Funds (EAF) program that is intended to provide short-term cash assistance to families in crisis. Like the special needs funds, these payments can be used for preventing evictions, utility shutoffs, and so on. Like AFDC, the EAF is a joint federal/state program. States can cover all families with needy children or limit their

programs only to families that receive AFDC. The participating states have substantial flexibility in determining what types of emergencies are covered and the amount of aid that will be provided. There are, however, federally established limits on the frequency with which EAF can be provided. Unlike AFDC, the EAF program is based on a fixed matching rate of 50 percent applied equally to all participating states.[67]

Although states can choose whether or not to participate in the EAF program, large numbers of states have chosen not to. In 1992, some 31 states operated EAF programs. In many of these states, EAF money is an important source of assistance for families who are homeless or threatened with homelessness.[68] Nationally, EAF caseloads averaged 65,000 per month in 1991 and total benefit payments were around $324 million.[69]

SUPPLEMENTAL SECURITY INCOME

When President Richard Nixon took office in 1972, he attempted to streamline the welfare system by proposing a Family Assistance Plan (FAP). In this plan Nixon proposed a guaranteed annual income that would replace AFDC, Old Age Assistance (OAA), Aid to the Blind (AB), and Aid to the Permanently and Totally Disabled (APTD). Although the overall plan was rejected by Congress, the OAA, AB, and APTD programs were federalized (P.L. 92–603) in 1972 under a new program called Supplemental Security Income (SSI). Basically, the federal government took the operation of those programs out of the hands of the state governments. No longer would the state governments set eligibility levels, establish minimum payment levels, or administer the programs. In essence, SSI is a program designed to provide cash assistance to the elderly poor and the disabled poor.

In 1992 the SSI program served more than 5.4 million people (1.4 million aged, 85,000 blind, and 3.9 million disabled people) and cost the federal government $20.8 billion. Unlike

OASDI, SSI is a means-tested, federally administered public assistance program funded through general revenue taxes. The basic SSI payment level is set nationally and is adjusted annually for inflation. A portion of the elderly receive SSI in conjunction with Social Security. Age is not an eligibility criterion for SSI, and children may receive benefits under the disabled or blind portion of the Act (in determining benefits, the income of the parents is a factor). Among others, the following people are eligible for SSI: (1) the mentally retarded, (2) the aged who are at least 65 years old and have little or no income, (3) those considered legally blind, (4) adults (at least 18 years old) who qualify as disabled because of a physical or mental impairment expected to last for at least 12 months, (5) visually impaired persons who do not meet the criteria for blindness, (6) drug addicts and alcoholics who enter treatment, and (7) children under 18 who have an impairment of comparable severity with that of an adult.

To qualify for SSI, an applicant's resources must be limited. In 1992, SSI applicants were required to have resources valued at less than $2,000 for an individual and $3,000 for a couple (excluding a house, and a car valued at under $4,500). SSI benefits are not generous, although they are higher in many states than AFDC benefits are. For an individual living alone in 1992 the maximum SSI benefit was $422 per month ($5,064 a year); for a couple it was $633 per month ($7,596 a year). About 30 percent of an SSI payment is deducted if the person lives in the home of someone who is contributing to their support.

A major concern regarding SSI involves the low level of income and the requirements for eligibility. In fact, 27 states (and Washington, D.C.) supplement SSI payments with an additional grant, and some states have opted to let the federal government administer that stipend. States may also choose to set their own requirements for supplementary SSI payments, thereby including only certain beneficiaries or limiting disabilities. In any case, the median state supplement was $36 a month for an elderly individual and $49 a month for an elderly couple in 1991.

It is common for states with SSI supplements to fail to keep those supplements up to the level of inflation. As a result, the purchasing power of SSI supplements has been falling. From 1975 to 1991 the value of the SSI supplement in the typical state fell 53 percent for an elderly individual and 63 percent for an elderly couple.[70] (Because the national SSI benefit is adjusted annually the *total* SSI benefit fell considerably less.)

Under the changeover to SSI, states were not allowed to pay recipients less than they had been granted previously. However, stringent eligibility requirements and complex red tape have kept many people off the SSI rolls. For example, the cases of recipients are reviewed every three years (usually involving a medical review) and "continuing disability reviews" may be required. Some critics believe that the federal government has purposely made entrance and continued maintenance in SSI difficult in order to discourage participation.

GENERAL ASSISTANCE

Although not formally connected to SSI or AFDC, General Assistance (GA) often serves a similar clientele. GA is a term applied to a variety of state and local programs designed to provide cash or in-kind benefits to needy families and individuals who are, generally speaking, not within the eligibility categories for either AFDC or SSI. In short, GA is the program of last resort for people who fall through the cracks in the federally funded safety net. The program commonly serves nonelderly individuals or childless couples, including individuals who are disabled for a year or less and are awaiting determination of their eligibility for SSI. In some cases, GA may be used when AFDC or SSI recipients have benefits that are too low to cover an emergency.[71] GA programs are entirely financed and administered by state, county, or local governmental units (or some combination thereof). No federal funds are used for GA and several states have no such program.

Although 42 states had some form of GA in 1992, that does not mean that there were uniform standards across the state or even that there was any state role in administration. Because no federal standards apply to GA, the total discretion that states or localities have in this area has led to a wide variety of programs, some of which are funded solely by counties or towns, others of which are funded totally or partially by the state. As a result, states and localities have the ability to easily scale back or even eliminate GA programs. Moreover, because no federal funds or federal standards apply to GA, it is difficult to find reliable data or even to draw a national picture as to the extent and comprehensiveness of General Assistance programs.[72]

Seven of the statewide uniform programs and five of the nonuniform statewide programs are "comprehensive" in that they cover all needy families and individuals who do not fit within the categories of persons eligible for AFDC or SSI. The other statewide programs cover only limited groups of people that are ineligible for federally subsidized cash assistance. Some statewide programs provide aid for an extended period if needed, while others limit aid to a fixed period regardless of need. Other states pay only if there is an emergency. And some states treat all eligible individuals the same as far as the type and duration of the benefits are concerned.[73] In many ways, the GA program represents a holdover from the days of county welfare. For example, in San Diego, California, GA is given as a loan that must be repaid.

The overall cost of GA is estimated to be in the vicinity of $4 billion, and in 1991 some 1.4 million households were beneficiaries. GA benefits are often lower than the state's AFDC

benefits, but in a few places they are the same or higher. In the typical state with a statewide GA program, the maximum monthly benefit for an individual was $215 in 1993, or just 36 percent of the federal poverty line for 1992. Overall, GA benefits have been declining since 1982. Between 1982 and 1989, the maximum GA benefit fell (in real dollars) in 28 programs and increased in only seven. In 1992, GA benefits were reduced or eliminated entirely in eight states. This came on the heels of an elimination or reduction of GA benefits in 14 states in 1991. From 1991 to 1993, GA reductions affected more than a half million recipients in 17 of the 28 states that operated statewide GA programs in 1991.[74] In particular, the real value of GA benefits declined in the six states with the largest number of GA recipients: New York (-13%); Pennsylvania (-12%); Ohio (-1%); Michigan (-20%); California (-3%); and Illinois (-17%).[75]

Perhaps the most dramatic example of GA cuts occurred in Michigan where the program was eliminated on October 1, 1991, leaving approximately 82,000 beneficiaries without any federal, state, or local help to face the winter. These people faced a bleak job market in a state with an unemployment rate of 9 percent.[76] A follow-up study done in eight Michigan counties where almost two-thirds (55,000) of the former recipients lived revealed that nearly 20,000, or about 36 percent of the former recipients, had been evicted because they could not pay the rent. At the time of the study, more than 20,000 of the former 55,000 recipients surveyed had no regular place to live.[77] The correlation between homelessness and the unavailability of GA benefits was also shown by Martha Burt, who examined homelessness in 147 cities from 1981 to 1989. Burt found that the highest rates of homelessness were in cities where no GA program existed. The next highest incidence of homelessness was in cities where GA benefits were provided only to the disabled and to families. The lowest rates of homelessness were found in cities where GA benefits were extended to "able-bodied" individuals.[78]

ISSUES IN PUBLIC ASSISTANCE

Welfare Reform and the History of AFDC

Welfare reform has been a heated topic in the United States for several decades. Most presidents since John F. Kennedy have either offered welfare proposals or at least given lip service to the need for reform. It is also a concept that has a relatively narrow meaning in the United States because it is associated primarily with the AFDC program. However, to understand the broader debate around welfare reform, it is important first to examine the history of the AFDC program.

Originally called Aid to Dependent Children (ADC), the AFDC program was part of the Social Security Act of 1935 and was designed to provide support for children through dispensing aid to their mothers. In 1950 the adult caretaker (usually the mother) was made eligible for ADC benefits.[79] Also in the 1950s, medical services, paid in part by the federal government, were made available for ADC recipients. In the late 1950s and early 1960s, some critics began to believe that ADC rules led to the desertion of fathers, since only families without an able-bodied father were eligible for relief. In 1961 a new component was added that allowed families to receive assistance in the event of a father's incapacity or unemployment. The new program, Aid to Families With Dependent Children-Unemployed Parent (AFDC-UP), was not made mandatory for the states, and until the welfare reform act of 1988, only 25 states and the District of Columbia had adopted it. In 1962 the name of the program was changed to AFDC to emphasize the family unit.

By 1962 the focus of the AFDC program had shifted to rehabilitating the poor. Policies were enacted that mandated massive casework and treatment services. To increase the chances for success, the social service amendments of 1962 limited the caseloads of social workers to a maximum of 60. By 1967 the service requirement was transformed into job assistance. Before 1967 all services provided to AFDC recipients were delivered by one worker who was responsible for financial as well as social services. Since 1972, federal policy has dictated that the AFDC program be divided into social services and income maintenance. The new policy separating social services from income maintenance required that one worker be assigned the AFDC paperwork, while the other social worker was responsible for social services.

Despite intensive social services, the number of AFDC recipients grew dramatically throughout the 1960s. The number of AFDC individuals tripled in the 10-year period from 1960 to 1970, from 3 million to 9.6 million. From 1971 to 1981 that figure rose 50 percent, and in 1991 it reached an all-time high of 4.7 million families. While in 1950 the number of AFDC recipients accounted for 1.5 percent of the population, by 1970 that proportion had reached 4 percent. The growth in the AFDC rolls also gave rise to a grass-roots protest organization started by a former chemistry professor, George A. Wiley. Under the leadership of Wiley, by 1967 the National Welfare Rights Organization (NWRO), a direct-action advocacy group of welfare recipients, had grown to encompass more than 100,000 dues-paying members representing some 350 local groups.[80] Although at its height the NWRO had a sizable constituency—and received a grant of $400,000 from the outgoing Johnson administration in 1968—its lasting effects remain unclear.

One of the more egregious chapters in AFDC history involved the man-in-the-house rule. This policy mandated that any woman who had an able-bodied man in the house be cut off from AFDC because, regardless of whether he was the father of her children, it was thought to be his responsibility to support the family. This policy was manifested in "midnight raids," in which social workers made late-night calls to determine if a man was present. Even a piece of male clothing found on the premises could be used as an excuse for cutting off aid. In some states the man-in-the-house rule was extended to include rules on dating. In 1968 the U.S. Supreme Court struck down the rule in Alabama, and later reinforced its decision in a California case.[81]

During President Ronald Reagan's term in office, several changes were made in the AFDC rules that can be summarized as follows: (1) New AFDC rules made it unlikely that a family with a parent working at a low-paying job would receive a supplementary AFDC benefit[82]; (2) children in AFDC families who were not expected to graduate from high school or vocational training programs by age 19 were no longer eligible for benefits (before 1981, over two-thirds of the states provided assistance to students living at home until they reached age 21)[83]; (3) pregnant women with no other children were made ineligible for AFDC benefits until their sixth month of pregnancy[84]—a policy that resulted in many expectant mothers being declared ineligible for Medicaid and thus being denied early access to prenatal care; (4) the income of stepparents was counted in determining a child's eligibility[85]; (5) a limit was placed on how much in child care costs a working AFDC mother could exempt from her maximum benefits[86]; and (6) the efforts of states to collect child-support payments were improved.[87] During the early and mid-1980s, almost 450,000 families were removed from the welfare rolls because of these and other AFDC changes.[88]

The belief that welfare mothers ought to work is a constant theme in AFDC debates. Although conservatives argue that work is the best antipoverty program, some liberals assert that child rearing is also a productive form of work. Moreover, liberal supporters contend that while it is socially acceptable for middle-class mothers to stay at home with young children, when poor mothers try to do the same thing they are often considered lazy and unmotivated. Despite this nagging debate, workfare programs have been a constant feature of the welfare landscape since 1967, when new AFDC amendments were added that pressured recipient mothers into working. As part of those new rules, work re-

quirements became mandatory for unemployed fathers, mothers, and certain teenagers. AFDC recipients who were deemed employable and yet refused to work could be terminated.[89] A work incentive program (WIN) was developed to provide training and employment for all welfare mothers considered employable (recipients with preschool age children were exempt). Day care was made available to facilitate the WIN program. As a further incentive, AFDC recipients were allowed to retain the first $30 of their monthly earnings in addition to having one-third of the remainder exempt from consideration for eligibility assistance. However, owing to a lackluster federal commitment (in 1985 the total federal contribution to WIN was only $258 million), the performance of the program was disappointing. In addition, many states were reluctant to enact mandatory job requirements because they believed that enforcing them would cost more than simply maintaining the families on AFDC. Workfare was again resurrected in 1988, when it formed the backbone of the Family Support Act.

In 1975 the AFDC rules were revised to allow states to track down biological parents and force them to pay child support. In 1984 this law was further strengthened by extending assistance to all families in which the children needed financial support. Under this law, states could (1) withhold a parent's wages if support payments were 30 days overdue, (2) impose liens against the assets of a delinquent parent, and (3) intercept federal and state income tax refunds. Even with stringent enforcement laws, the track record for collecting child support payments was dismal. In 1991 only 10.5 percent of AFDC assistance payments were recovered through child support collections. In effect, this meant that only $1.10 was collected through AFDC support collections for every administrative dollar spent.[90]

Recent Welfare Reform Initiatives

Welfare reform has traditionally had liberal connotations in that reform proposals usually called for major increases in benefits as well as expanding eligibility for welfare programs. Thus, welfare reform tended to mean some form of a guaranteed annual income for the poor—one component of the classic liberal formulation for social welfare reform that also included a national health care program and full employment. By the late 1980s, however, neoconservatism and neoliberalism had made a clear imprint on social welfare policy. In contrast to the ambitious proposals advanced by previous administrations—such as the Family Assistance Plan of the Nixon administration, which proposed a guaranteed annual income, and the Program for Better Jobs and Income of the Carter administration, which proposed a public jobs effort—the welfare reform plans that were to gain serious attention during the late 1980s were comparatively modest. They incorporated a carrot-and-stick approach. Specifically, programs were designed not to expand welfare benefits per se, but to link welfare receipt to issues of reciprocity, productivity, and familial responsibility.

Reciprocity is based on the idea that welfare programs contribute to dependency and dysfunctional behaviors, especially when benefits are not conditional on a standard of conduct expected of recipients. Consequently, a common feature of current welfare reform proposals is that employment—or, in the absence of a job, education or job-finding activities—be a condition for eligibility. Although reciprocity has been advanced as a way to encourage socially desirable behavior on the part of welfare recipients, it also contributes to the public credibility of welfare programs. In introducing his Family Security Act, which included a workfare component, Senator Daniel Patrick Moynihan (D-NY) made this argument:

> Mothers, the custodial parents in most single-parent families, must try to earn income, at least part time to help support their children. The statistics are a stark testament to the need: 72 percent of all mothers with children between 6 and 18 are in the labor force. Over half of all mothers with children under age 3 are in the labor force.
>
> This marks a great change in the position of women in American life. The only women who have not participated in this change are the heads of AFDC families of whom fewer than 5 percent work part-time or full-time. As a nation, we find a 7 percent unemployment rate barely tolerable. What then are we to think of a system that keeps 95 percent of poor mothers unemployed and out of the labor force?[91]

Productivity is based on the idea that all people, including welfare recipients, have an obligation to contribute to the economic health of the nation. There are two ways in which productivity affects welfare reform. First, programs that put to work the employable—women and minorities—stand a better chance of passage than programs that maintain populations not expected to compete in the labor force. Second, allying welfare with economic productivity draws social programs closer to the American economic system, a strategy that is necessary at present to justify greater social welfare expenditures.

Familial responsibility is an important theme in current welfare reform proposals. Specifically, it is based on the belief that the government should abandon its role as the "rescuer of first resort." In keeping with traditional values, this philosophy declares that spouses (usually the father, since the mother is most often the custodial parent) have the ultimate responsibility for supporting their offspring. Perhaps more a principle than a fiscal attempt to gain revenue, this policy reinforces society's belief in the responsibility of the parent to physically provide for the child.

A relatively recent proposal that reflects these values is the Family Support Act (FSA) of 1988, one of the most important pieces of welfare legislation to emerge in the United States since the New Deal. Touted by Thomas Downey, chairman of the House Subcommittee on Public Assistance, as the first "significant change in our welfare system in 53 years,"[92] the welfare reform bill (which cost $3.34 billion over a five-year period) contained several interesting components. For one thing, the bill attempted to change AFDC from an income support to a mandatory work and training program. The stated objective of the bill was to encourage self-sufficiency among welfare recipients. To carry out this goal, the bill required women on welfare with children under age three (at state option, age one) to participate in a work or training program. By 1990 each state was required to enroll at least 7 percent of its recipients in a state basic education program, job training, a work experience program, or a job search program. By 1993 that requirement was to rise to 20 percent. As a further incentive, recipients who became employed were to get 12 months of child care assistance and Medicaid benefits after they terminated AFDC.[93]

Adoption of the AFDC-UP program became mandatory for all states, although they could decide to limit enrollment for two-parent families to 6 out of 12 calendar months in a year. Moreover, one family member of an AFDC-UP household was required to participate at least 16 hours per week in a make-work job in return for benefits. By 1994, 40 percent of AFDC-UP recipients were expected to be in a make-work program, and by 1997 that number was to increase to 70 percent. In addition, the AFDC reform bill called for mandatory child support payments to be automatically deducted from an absent parent's paycheck, even though that payment might not be in arrears. Finally, the bill allowed states to require a welfare recipient under age 18 to live with a parent or in a "supervised environment" to be eligible to receive benefits.[94]

At the time, Dan Rostenkowski, chairman of the House Ways and Means Committee, which oversees most welfare legislation, estimated that an additional 65,000 two-parent families would receive benefits, that 400,000 people

would participate in workfare by 1993, and that 475,000 people would be eligible for transitional Medicaid benefits under provisions of the bill.[95] But the promised savings of workfare soon faded. Two years into the JOBS component part of the FSA, the Congressional Budget Office projected that 10,000 families would be off AFDC by 1991, 20,000 by 1993, and 50,000 by the end of the five years of the program—a 1.3 percent reduction in the number of AFDC families. "The effect of the JOBS program on the number of AFDC recipients or on spending on benefits in welfare programs is thus expected to be modest," concluded the House Ways and Means Committee.[96] In a review of workfare projects, Harvard's David Ellwood calculated increased earnings at between $250 and $750 per year. According to Ellwood, "most work-welfare programs look like decent investments, but no carefully evaluated work-welfare programs have done more than put a tiny dent in the welfare caseloads, even though they have been received with enthusiasm."[97] The same sentiment was expressed by workfare expert Judith Gueron:

> [While] welfare-to-work programs have paid off by increasing the employment and earnings of single mothers and reducing their receipt of public assistance . . . MDRC's research also reveals the limits of past interventions. Whether the targeted group were welfare mothers, low-income youth who dropped out of high school, teenage parents with limited prospects, or unemployed adult men, the programs had little success in boosting people out of poverty. . . . Often, welfare recipients who get jobs join the ranks of the working poor.[98]

One reason for these disappointing results has been the lackluster response to the FSA on the part of many of the states. For one thing, the meager appropriations in the FSA fell far short of the actual implementation costs. Second, many states found it difficult to prepare and implement the work/training strategies required by the bill. Third, many states are faced with fiscal crises and therefore shun programs that might lead to higher expenditures.

The FSA is flawed in another way. In 1992 the unemployment rate exceeded 7 percent nationally; there were almost 8.2 million unemployed workers, of which almost 1 million were long-term unemployed. In addition, there were several million working poor who, even though they were working full-time, did not earn enough to escape poverty. If these people are unable to find work or to earn enough from the work they have, how can welfare recipients be expected to become self-sufficient?

Nevertheless, how much real "reform" was contained in the FSA? The most significant improvements were the extension of child day care and Medicaid for one year after the recipient found employment and the inclusion of two-parent households in the program. These provisions doubtlessly helped parents who were occupationally upwardly mobile; however, the great majority of people on AFDC exhibit job histories in which welfare complements episodic and low-wage employment. Thus, the FSA extends important benefits to the working poor, but it is unlikely by itself to boost people off welfare. Unless wages increase and jobs become steadier, the working poor will continue to need welfare benefits periodically. On the other hand, some provisions of the bill were clearly punitive and are unlikely to enhance the self-sufficiency of AFDC recipients. Requiring one parent of two-parent households to do make-work in exchange for benefits is unlikely to increase economic independence and may actually impede it if beneficiaries are forced to do make-work when they could be seeking work in the labor market. Garnishing wages is unlikely to increase economic independence if a parent's wages are so low that such a requirement creates incentives to quit work instead of paying child support. Mimi Abramovitz observed that for poor men this provision "may be more like squeezing blood from a stone."[99] Finally, the

reliance on states to operate workfare programs that are not adequately funded is likely to result in welfare reform that is uneven; relatively generous states like Massachusetts and California may expand on workfare programs that are already in place, but poorer states, such as Mississippi and New Mexico, will be hard-pressed to deploy programs that are anything other than punitive.

With limited exceptions, welfare reform in 1988 was clearly a conservative triumph. "By replacing liberal tenets of entitlement, self-determination and federal responsibility with more conservative notions of contract, compulsion, and states' rights," observed Mimi Abramovitz, "welfare reform erodes some of the fundamental principles that support the U.S. welfare state."[100] Perhaps the clearest example of how regressive welfare reform has become is found in the way income has been reapportioned from poor families to workfare officials. From 1970 to 1988, the median state's AFDC benefit dropped 35 percent in constant dollars as a result of inflation. In other words, had AFDC benefits simply remained constant with inflation, beneficiaries in 1988 would have received $5.88 billion *more* than what they were getting. The FSA proposed to "reallocate," over a five-year span, only 57 percent of this lost income ($3.34 billion) back to the poor through compulsory workfare.[101] At the same time, AFDC benefits remained below the poverty level for all states except Alaska.[102] For the poor, welfare reform in 1988 represented little more than diverting only a portion of the income supplement lost since 1970 to welfare managers who operated stringent workfare programs. From this perspective, there is little in the FSA that represented a net improvement in the lives of families living in poverty.

A similar approach to the FSA was outlined in President Bill Clinton's pre-election welfare reform package. Specifically, Clinton promised to provide the poor with education, training, job placement assistance, and child care for up to two years. After that time, recipients would be required to work in either the private sector or in community service jobs. Clinton's campaign literature stated: "Bill Clinton has a plan to end welfare as we know it. He'll expand opportunity for welfare recipients, but demand responsibility by requiring those who can work to go to work after two years. . . . And he'll crack down on deadbeat parents who fail to pay their children's support."[103]

The carrot-and-stick approach has also been used in several statewide welfare reform initiatives. One proposal, labeled "wedfare," represents an attempt by states to encourage the marriage of unmarried caretakers who are receiving AFDC benefits. Wedfare proposals are generally aimed at promoting marriage to someone other than the parent of the child or children receiving aid. This idea is predicated on the belief that a person who voluntarily takes on the responsibility of raising someone else's children should be rewarded. It is also predicated on the idea that it is contrary to the American ethic to reward a parent for accepting responsibility for his own biological children. Wedfare proposals cover a broad range of policy options, including the deduction of a stepparent's wages in determining AFDC benefits, and, in more extreme forms, providing a lump sum monetary bonus for a marriage followed by an absence from the AFDC rolls for a given period of time.[104]

Several states have also developed "incentives" to discourage additional pregnancies while the recipients are on AFDC. For example, New Jersey recently enacted the "Family Development Program," which denies grant increases to women who conceive additional children while on AFDC. (At least three other states—California, Maine, and South Carolina—are considering similar proposals.) At the same time, such women are allowed to earn more than they could previously without a loss in benefits. The new work incentives do not apply to AFDC families that do not have an additional child while receiving aid. The New Jersey program also requires all AFDC recipients to participate in education and job-training pro-

grams, raises state-funded benefits for two-parent families that do not qualify for AFDC, and allows participants to keep a larger portion of their grant if they marry someone who is not the natural parent of their child. The program also includes a 20 percent reduction for families who do not comply with certain program rules. In a somewhat similar vein, Connecticut and Michigan require teenage parents who receive AFDC to reside with a responsible adult.[105]

Another statewide welfare initiative under discussion is "learnfare," a label given to various proposals designed to increase the school attendance of children receiving aid or of recipient teenage parents. A form of learnfare is already required in AFDC by virtue of the JOBS program requirement that is part of the 1988 Family Support Act. The learnfare reforms range from increasing the emphasis on the existing federal requirements to the more radical step of linking school attendance to AFDC benefits. For example, Maryland deducts $25 per child from the benefits of an AFDC family whose children fail to attend school for 80 percent of the school term. Other states have proposed a fixed dollar reduction coupled with a fiscal bonus for individuals who cooperate. In addition to New Jersey, Wisconsin and Ohio are already running learnfare projects. The Ohio approach involves only the school attendance of teen parents and uses a flat reduction and bonus approach. The Wisconsin approach targets all teen parents and all teen children and imposes a benefit sanction (i.e., the loss of the child's AFDC benefits) without any bonus. Wisconsin is currently planning to extend the learnfare project to six- to twelve-year-olds. Other states considering similar proposals include California, Connecticut, and New York.[106]

State welfare reform proposals have also been tied to the immunization of children. For example, Georgia passed a law that imposes a penalty on AFDC families who have no proof of the immunization of all dependent children under age seven. Such families could lose up to $45 in monthly benefits for failing to provide proof of immunization. Maryland adopted a similar policy and penalizes AFDC families $25 per child for failing to provide proof of immunization.[107]

Another proposal under consideration is time-limited payments for AFDC and GA. In this approach, payments for AFDC and GA would be limited to a specific period of time, regardless of whether the need persisted. A variation on this theme is a two-tiered approach to aid. In other words, lower benefit payments would come into effect after aid had been received for a certain period of time. Eight states are currently considering the latter proposal.[108]

Finally, some states have begun to enact policies designed to discourage the migration of welfare recipients. California enacted a provision that cuts benefits for AFDC families who are new residents of the state. All AFDC families who have moved to California within the preceding 12 months receive benefits no greater than the maximum benefit they would receive in their state of origin. Both Illinois and Wisconsin have attempted to enact similar provisions.

Current welfare reform proposals do not merely reflect a series of benign policy initiatives; they represent a fundamental shift away from sweeping notions of universal entitlements toward a strongly residual conception of social welfare. Welfare reform ideologies that stress reciprocity, productivity, and familial responsibility reflect a return to the traditional values of self-reliance, independence, and individual responsibility and a belief in the limited role of government. For liberals who have advocated expanding federal social programs, this approach embodies a return to a harsh and punitive world that is incongruent with modern civilization. According to these critics, postindustrial capitalism is marked by an interdependence between individuals and government, with human and market needs being inextricably linked. From this perspective, a conservative ideology of welfare reform is not only out of sync with the requirements of a postindustrial economy but also serves to condemn individu-

als for their own impoverishment, to "blame the victim," and to aggravate social injustice.

Other Issues in Public Assistance

The system of public assistance is also plagued by other serious problems. One of the knottiest problems is the adequacy of AFDC benefit levels. The argument over AFDC benefit levels has three primary dimensions: (1) the adequacy of the poverty index as a determinant of poverty; (2) the adequacy of state-established need levels; and (3) the conformity of states to their own formulated need levels. Because the adequacy of the poverty index has been addressed in Chapter 6, we will focus here on the latter two questions.

The AFDC program is characterized by dramatically different state benefit levels. In 1993 the yearly benefits for an AFDC family of three (one adult and two children) ranged from a low of $1,440 in Mississippi to a high of $11,400 in Alaska. In 1992 the average three-person AFDC family received a yearly benefit of $4,464. As previously noted, AFDC benefits paid to recipients are largely determined by the need standards established by the states, and these standards reflect wide fluctuations. For example, Missouri claimed that a family of three (one adult and two children) had a need standard of $312 per month in 1992. Louisiana, a state with an even lower per capita income, claimed that the need standard for the same hypothetical family was $658 per month. The need standard is important for four reasons: (1) It represents the minimum income necessary to sustain a family in a particular state; (2) as an integral part of the AFDC eligibility and benefit structure, it is used to set a gross income eligibility limit; (3) it determines the maximum amount a family can receive in 15 states; and (4) it determines benefits for children living with stepparents and grandparents in some states. The need standard also has an impact on the fill-the-gap form of AFDC benefit calculation. Specifically, if the maximum benefit a state provides is less than the need standard, the state may allow AFDC recipients to fill the gap between the need standard and the maximum benefit with other income. Without fill-the-gap budgeting, AFDC families can lose a dollar of AFDC benefits for every dollar earned.[109]

Establishing a need standard, however, does not require the state to meet that standard. For example, in 1992 Illinois failed to match its own need standard of $844; instead, it provided AFDC recipients with only $367 per month, or 43 percent of its own established need standard. Despite Louisiana's need standard of $658 per month, the AFDC benefit level was only $190 for a family of three. On the other hand, Delaware was able to fully meet its meager need standard of $338 per month. Table 10.5 shows the need standards set by the states and the degree to which they are able to meet them.

The recently enacted cuts coupled with the historical inadequacy of AFDC benefits have left the poor considerably worse off. Part of this dilemma is related to the worsening fiscal problems experienced by the individual states. Unwilling to raise taxes to increase revenues, many states were forced into enacting deep budget cuts in all areas of public service, including social welfare. Thus, regardless of the states' need standards or their AFDC payment levels, in 1991 there were only three states in which AFDC benefits reached 75 percent of the poverty line; in 45 states the AFDC benefit levels were less than 50 percent of the poverty line. In 1992, the combined benefits of AFDC and Food Stamps lifted the median benefit level for a family of three to $647 per month, or only 72 percent of the poverty line. Moreover, over 3 million needy children and their caretakers—more than a third of the entire AFDC caseload—were plunged deeper into poverty in 1991 by the cuts in AFDC benefit levels enacted in 40 states and the District of Columbia. Their total income loss was more than $400 million. Children suffered losses as five states eliminated benefits given to families with special needs. In 1992, AFDC benefits were reduced more than in any year

since 1981, with 44 states cutting or freezing benefits. Furthermore, these cuts followed a 15-year period in which the numbers of people in poverty grew, AFDC benefit levels and total expenditures fell, and the number of poor children served by AFDC declined. Although the numbers served by AFDC began to grow after 1989, expenditures per recipient in real dollars have continued to shrink.[110]

Unlike federal programs like Social Security and SSI, AFDC benefits in most states (with the exception of Alaska, California, Connecticut, and the District of Columbia) are not automatically adjusted for inflation. Therefore, benefits overall decreased by 42 percent from 1972 to 1991 (see Table 10.6). Moreover, in 12 states AFDC benefits fell more than 50 percent since 1972. For example, AFDC benefits in Illinois (when calculated in 1991 dollars) fell from 87 percent of the poverty line in 1980 to just 38 percent of the poverty line in 1991.

Although Table 10.6 suggests that some states are more generous with regard to AFDC benefits than other states are, on closer observation some of these differences begin to disappear. This is particularly true if the combined AFDC and Food Stamp benefits are measured against the median wage in individual states (a relative and more realistic measure of poverty) rather than against a nationwide poverty threshold. In fact, using this measure of poverty turns some of the data upside down. For example, the combined AFDC and Food Stamp benefits in a "nongenerous" state like South Carolina are actually closer to that state's median wage than the combined welfare benefits in a more "generous" state like Minnesota. The meager AFDC benefit provided by Arkansas brings a welfare recipient there almost to the same level (in relation to the state's median wage) as the considerably higher AFDC benefits offered by Massachusetts (see Table 10.7).

Another issue in public assistance is the redundancy of benefits and programs. While the public assistance component of the American welfare state is composed of four *major* income

TABLE 10.5. AFDC Benefits by State Need Standards and Payments to AFDC Families with No Countable Income, 1992

	AFDC Family Composed of One Adult and Two Children		
State	**Need Standard**	**Maximum Benefit (Monthly)**	**Maximum Benefit Level as Percentage of Need Standard**
Alabama	$ 631	$149	23
Alaska	924	924	100
Arizona	928	334	36
Arkansas	705	202	29
California	694	663	95
Colorado	421	356	84
Connecticut	680	680	100
Delaware	338	338	100
Dist. of Col.	712	409	57
Florida	928	303	33
Georgia	424	280	66
Hawaii	1067	666	62
Idaho	554	315	57
Illinois	844	367	43
Indiana	320	288	90
Iowa	849	426	50
Kansas	422	422	100
Kentucky	526	228	43
Louisiana	658	190	29
Maine	573	453	79
Maryland	522	377	72
Massachusetts	539	539	100
Michigan	551	459	83
Minnesota	532	532	100
Mississippi	368	120	33
Missouri	312	292	94
Montana	478	390	82
Nebraska	364	364	100
Nevada	620	372	60
New Hampshire	516	516	100
New Jersey	424	424	100
New Mexico	324	324	100
New York	577	577	100
North Carolina	544	272	50
North Dakota	401	401	100
Ohio	817	334	41
Oklahoma	471	341	72
Oregon	460	460	100
Pennsylvania	614	421	69
Rhode Island	554	554	100

TABLE 10.5. *(continued)*

	AFDC Family Composed of One Adult and Two Children		
State	Need Standard	Maximum Benefit (Monthly)	Maximum Benefit Level as Percentage of Need Standard
South Carolina	440	210	48
South Dakota	404	404	100
Tennessee	426	185	43
Texas	574	184	32
Utah	537	402	75
Vermont	1112	673	61
Virginia	393	354	90
Washington	1014	531	52
West Virginia	497	249	50
Wisconsin	647	517	80
Wyoming	674	360	53

SOURCE: Adapted from Committee on Ways and Means, U.S. House of Representatives, *Overview of Entitlement Programs: 1992 Green Book* (Washington, D.C.: U.S. Government Printing Office, 1992), p. 642.

support programs (AFDC, SSI, EITC, and Food Stamps), additional income supports are folded into other programs such as the Low-Income Home Energy Assistance Program (LIHEAP), Section 8 housing, and the Women, Infants, and Children Program (WIC), to name only a few. For example, in 1988 an incomeless four-person family in New Jersey who had taken full advantage of their potential benefits could have received the following yearly grants: $8,346 in combined AFDC and Food Stamps, $388 in LIHEAP benefits, $336 a year (the minimum) in WIC benefits, and a Section 8 subsidy of $3,000. Thus, this poverty family could have accrued a yearly income of $12,070, excluding the valuable Medicaid perk for which they would be automatically eligible.[111] A similar family with two minimum-wage earners would have earned $12,864 that year, plus the maximum EITC benefit of $658, thereby realizing $13,522. The difference of $1,452 between the working family and the welfare family would have been made up by the working family's need to purchase health care insurance and day care—costs that would result in far less net income for the working family.[112] In this instance,

public assistance programs may provide some built-in incentives to choose welfare over work.

The redundancy of welfare programs also fosters an inequality among welfare recipients. Those who are skilled at the manipulation of public assistance programs will inevitably do better than novices who assume a passive stance in the search for benefits. The working poor—who qualify for some benefits, including Food Stamps—may be out of the welfare loop and thus may not be aware of the possibilities for welfare receipt. This could partly explain why more than 40 percent of eligible families did not receive Food Stamps in an average month in 1991.[113] Paradoxically, the very complexity of the welfare system sets up a Darwinian scramble for resources that rewards the most assertive recipients at the expense of those less able to compete.

Another major problem in the welfare state is the tangled web of redundant social programs. For example, AFDC and SSI are similar in many respects; that is, both programs serve people who do not fully participate in the labor force. Both programs also benefit the poor: AFDC is targeted at poor families with children; SSI is

TABLE 10.6. Percentage Changes in Maximum AFDC Benefits for a Three-Person Family, 50 States and the District of Columbia, 1972 and 1991 (In 1991 dollars)

State	Maximum Yearly Benefit for a Three-Person Family, 1991	Maximum Benefits as Percent of Three-Person 1991 Poverty Line ($10,419)	Inflation-Adjusted Change in Four-Person Maximum Benefit (1972–1991)
Alabama	$1,488	12	−58
Arizona	4,008	38	−26
Arkansas	2,448	23	−40
California	8,328	80	−21
Colorado	4,272	41	−43
Connecticut	8,160	78	−29
Delaware	4,056	39	−50
Dist. of Col.	4,908	47	−42
Florida	3,528	34	−25
Georgia	3,360	32	−11
Idaho	3,804	37	−61
Illinois	4,404	42	−49
Indiana	3,456	33	−47
Iowa	5,112	49	−47
Kansas	5,064	49	−53
Kentucky	3,456	33	−43
Louisiana	2,280	22	−46
Maine	5,436	52	−25
Maryland	4,872	47	−26
Massachusetts	6,468	62	−40
Michigan	4,932	47	−55
Minnesota	6,384	61	−41
Mississippi	1,440	14	−9
Missouri	3,504	34	−21
Montana	4,680	45	−36
Nebraska	4,368	42	−47
Nevada	3,960	38	−42
New Hampshire	6,192	59	−39
New Jersey	5,088	49	−50
New Mexico	3,888	37	−30
New York	6,924	66	−47
North Carolina	3,264	31	−46
North Dakota	4,812	46	−52
Ohio	4,008	38	−40
Oklahoma	4,092	39	−46
Oregon	5,520	53	−53
Pennsylvania	5,052	48	−51
Rhode Island	6,648	64	−36
South Carolina	2,519	24	−20

TABLE 10.6. *(continued)*

State	Maximum Yearly Benefit for a Three-Person Family, 1991	Maximum Benefits as Percent of Three-Person 1991 Poverty Line ($10,419)	Inflation-Adjusted Change in Four-Person Maximum Benefit (1972–1991)
South Dakota	4,848	47	−50
Tennessee	2,219	21	−41
Texas	2,208	21	−42
Utah	4,824	46	−47
Vermont	8,076	78	−26
Virginia	4,248	40	−52
Washington	6,372	61	−41
West Virginia	2,988	29	−56
Wisconsin	6,204	60	−47
Wyoming	4,320	41	−46
Average			−42

SOURCE: Adapted from U.S. House of Representatives, *Overview of Entitlement Programs: 1992 Green Book* (Washington, D.C.: U.S. Government Printing Office, 1992), pp. 1199–1201.

for the aged, blind, and disabled. Likewise, neither of these public assistance programs require any past history of labor force participation or any prior contribution, and both pay low benefits that may in some instances be supplemented by Food Stamps and housing and utility assistance. Despite the similarities in these programs, they are operated under different auspices and therefore have separate and costly administrative structures. In fact, the administrative costs in 1990 for each AFDC family totaled $776 (a total of $3 billion); for SSI, the figure was $465 (a total of $1 billion); and for Food Stamps, more than $600 per family (a total of $2.5 billion). Taken together, the administrative costs of these programs amounted to $6.5 billion in 1990.[114]

Another debate in public assistance involves the issue of marriage penalties for AFDC recipients. According to a number of studies, no more than a fifth of AFDC mothers leave the program as a result of earnings increases; most exits result from a change in marital status.[115] Yet the AFDC program punishes marriage in two ways: by how it treats a married couple with children in common, and by how it treats families with stepparents. First, a needy two-parent family with children is less likely to be eligible for aid than a one-parent family. Although the nonincapacitated two-parent family can apply for AFDC-UP, the restrictions involving work history and the six-month time limit imposed by many states make the program inaccessible to many poor families. Second, a stepparent has no legal obligation to support the children of his or her spouse in most states. Nevertheless, AFDC cuts or limits benefits when a woman marries by counting much of the stepparent's income when calculating the family's countable income, thus jeopardizing a mother's eligibility status. The net effect of this policy is to reduce or eliminate family benefits even if the stepparent is working at a minimum-wage job.[116] In effect, there is a strong economic incentive for a low-income woman to remain unmarried and to live together with a male who has earnings rather than to face a stiff economic penalty by legally becoming married.

TABLE 10.7. Comparison of Median Family Income of a Four-person Family in Individual States with Combined AFDC and Food Stamp Benefits, 1986

State	Median Family Income	Combined AFDC and Food Stamp Benefits (Yearly Maximum)	AFDC and Food Stamps as Percent of Median Family Income
United States	$34,716	$ 8,904	26
Alabama	29,799	5,328	18
Alaska	41,292	13,392	32
Arizona	33,477	7,512	22
Arkansas	27,157	6,192	22
California	37,655	12,192	32
Colorado	36,026	9,492	26
Connecticut	44,330	10,692	24
Delaware	35,766	7,812	22
Dist. of Col.	35,424	8,760	25
Florida	33,368	7,140	21
Georgia	34,602	7,104	21
Hawaii	36,618	9,564	26
Idaho	27,075	7,320	27
Illinois	36,163	7,512	21
Indiana	32,026	7,368	23
Iowa	30,556	8,796	29
Kansas	32,512	8,424	26
Kentucky	28,464	6,646	23
Louisiana	29,614	6,156	21
Maine	31,297	11,832	38
Maryland	42,250	8,496	20
Massachusetts	42,295	10,692	25
Michigan	36,088	10,044	28
Minnesota	36,746	10,836	29
Mississippi	26,763	8,730	33
Missouri	33,149	7,368	22
Montana	29,130	8,604	30
Nebraska	31,484	8,544	27
Nevada	33,604	7,572	23
New Hampshire	39,503	8,982	23
New Jersey	44,491	9,084	20
New Mexico	27,474	7,080	26
New York	36,796	10,026	27
North Carolina	31,787	6,816	21
North Dakota	29,424	8,844	30
Oklahoma	29,071	7,002	24
Oregon	31,392	9,252	29
Pennsylvania	32,700	8,874	27
Rhode Island	35,837	10,080	28
South Carolina	31,025	9,016	29

TABLE 10.7. *(continued)*

State	Median Family Income	Combined AFDC and Food Stamp Benefits (Yearly Maximum)	AFDC and Food Stamps as Percent of Median Family Income
South Dakota	27,008	8,190	30
Tennessee	29,568	7,236	24
Texas	32,442	6,126	19
Utah	30,635	8,748	29
Vermont	32,490	10,812	33
Virginia	37,885	7,670	20
Washington	35,071	10,332	29
West Virginia	27,094	7,092	26
Wisconsin	33,739	11,202	33
Wyoming	28,742	8,136	28

SOURCE: Adapted from Department of Health and Human Services, *1987 AFDC Recipient Characteristics, Annual Study, 1989* (Washington, D.C.: U.S. Government Printing Office, 1989); and U.S. Bureau of the Census, *Statistical Abstract of the United States, 1989* (Washington, D.C.: U.S. Government Printing Office, 1989).

For many welfare mothers the decision to marry a man who is at, near, or even above the minimum wage may prove to be a poor financial decision. The Congressional Research Service has calculated that an AFDC recipient in Texas (capitalizing on AFDC, Food Stamps, and Medicaid) who marries a man earning $10,000 a year will lose 24 percent of her disposable income; if he earns $15,000 per year, she will lose 25 percent; and if the man earns $20,000, she will lose 29 percent. That same recipient in New York who marries will have her disposable income reduced by 10 percent, 41 percent, and 42 percent, respectively.[117] For example, a poor female-headed four-person family in New Jersey in 1988 who fully capitalized on their potential benefits could have realized $12,070. Thus, the yearly per capita income would have been $3,018. If that same mother married a man earning $15,000 a year, the annual *gross* per capita income of that now five-person family would shrink to $3,000 a year. That gross income would be further diminished by the Social Security tax, the federal income tax, work expenses, and so on. Perhaps more important, the former AFDC mother would lose her extremely valuable Medicaid perk. According to the conservative Heritage Foundation's Robert Rector:

The current welfare system has made marriage economically irrational for most low-income parents. Welfare has converted the low-income working husband from a necessary breadwinner into a net financial handicap. It has transformed marriage from a legal institution designed to protect and nurture children into an institution which financially penalizes nearly all low-income parents who enter into it. Across the nation, the current welfare system has all but destroyed family structure in the inner-city. Welfare establishes strong financial disincentives, effectively blocking the formation of intact, two-parent families.[118]

The AFDC program faces other problems. For example, many recipients complain that they are denied the same rights to privacy as nonrecipients. The finances of AFDC beneficiaries are scrupulously examined, and many are asked highly personal questions as well as given unsolicited advice regarding parenting and other family matters. In short, many AFDC recipients report being treated as second-class citizens by welfare departments. To exacerbate matters, AFDC recipients are forced to negotiate benefits and eligibility criteria that are complex and constantly changing.[119]

The AFDC program has frequently been accused of encouraging the breakup of families. In the past, intact families in the 25 states without AFDC-UP programs had to rely on highly limited state or local general assistance programs. For the most part, children in these non-AFDC-UP states were ineligible for assistance unless the families dissolved, which, unfortunately, many were forced to do. Because the FSA allows states to limit AFDC-UP to six months out of a twelve-month period, many of these intact families will continue to suffer. If all states adopted the AFDC-UP program for the full year, it is estimated that an additional 100,000 families would be eligible for assistance.[120] It would also mean that an additional 100,000 families would be helped to stay intact.

Myths abound about the welfare state, and especially the AFDC program. In a symbolic sense, the debate about AFDC seems to have little to do with the program itself. Instead, the ideological controversy centers around the symbolic values reflected in AFDC.

SUMMARY

Social insurance programs represent a major source of security for both America's elderly and its present group of workers. In the past 50 years, Americans have come to believe that regardless of the ebb and flow of economic life, Social Security embodies a firm societal commitment to care for the elderly. Economic gains made by the elderly since the mid-1960s have validated this belief. Furthermore, because Social Security is linked to past contributions, beneficiaries experience little stigma.

Unfortunately, recipients of public assistance programs do not fare so well. Public assistance programs such as SSI, AFDC, and GA contain a large dose of stigma, with the character of recipients being maligned because of their need. Moreover, the relative success of Social Security in arresting poverty among the elderly has not been replicated in public assistance programs. In fact, the reverse is true; public assistance recipients have endured greater levels of poverty during the 1980s and early 1990s than they did in earlier decades. It remains to be seen whether this trend will reverse itself given the election of the first Democratic president in 12 years.

This is clearly a difficult time for the American welfare state. Even after huge expenditures on social welfare services, according to Richard Estes, the United States ranks only twenty-third internationally in terms of the adequacy of its social provisions.[121] Given the present economic trend in which vast numbers of service jobs are produced—many of which are part-time, have few, if any, benefits, and pay the minimum wage—long-term welfare benefit packages will likely be required for an increasing number of citizens. How much these income benefit packages will contain, and at what cost, will be a matter for future discourse in public policy.

DISCUSSION QUESTIONS

1. The social insurances, especially Social Security, are among the most popular social welfare programs in the nation. Part of the reason for this popularity is that unlike income maintenance programs, the social insurances are not stigmatized. What are other reasons for the popularity of the social insurance programs?

2. There are serious questions about the future of the Social Security system. Some critics argue that Social Security is doomed because the trust funds are expected to be depleted by the middle of the next century. Other observers argue that Social Security is sound because the federal government is backing it. Is the Social Security system cur-

rently on solid ground and can we expect it to be healthy in the future? If so, why? If not, why? What can be done to make the system more stable?

3. The Social Security is currently plagued by a number of problems. What is the most important problem facing the system?

4. The EIC has components of both a social insurance program and an income maintenance program. Nevertheless, it is a relatively popular (if little understood) part of the social welfare state. What are some reasons for the popularity of the EITC program? What elements of the EITC could lead some critics to argue that it is basically an income maintenance program? What components of the EITC could lead other analysts to argue that it is basically a social insurance program?

5. AFDC is arguably the most controversial program in the American welfare state. It is frequently lambasted by critics for encouraging everything from welfare dependency to teenage pregnancy. Supporters argue that it is a poorly funded program that barely allows its recipients to survive. Why is the AFDC program so controversial? What, if anything, can be done to make the AFDC program less controversial?

6. A number of myths have arisen around the AFDC program. In your opinion, what myths have been the most harmful to the program and to AFDC recipients? Why?

7. GA is often the hardest hit when states decide to implement social welfare funding cuts. What accounts for the relative unpopularity of GA? Is the GA budget the most logical place to cut when states are faced with fiscal crises? What, if anything, can be done to strengthen the image of GA?

8. Since the 1970s, most strategies for reforming AFDC have revolved around implementing a mandatory work requirement for recipients. This strategy was evident in the programs of Presidents Carter and Reagan and was the centerpiece of the 1988 Family Support Act. More recently, President Clinton has picked up a similar theme and publicly stated that AFDC benefits should last for only two years, after which a recipient would be required to work. Is establishing a mandatory work requirement a viable strategy for reforming AFDC? If so, why? If not, why not? What would be a better strategy for reforming the AFDC program?

9. AFDC benefit levels vary widely from state to state. This situation exists because the federal government is reluctant to establish a national minimum benefit level. Moreover, there is little federal pressure on states to increase benefit levels and thereby curtail the erosion of AFDC benefits that has taken place since the 1970s. Should the federal government establish a minimum national benefit level for AFDC and compel states to meet that level? If not, why? If you agree, what should that level be?

NOTES

1. Frances Fox Piven and Richard A. Cloward, *Regulating the Poor: The Functions of Public Welfare* (New York: Vintage Books, 1971).

2. David P. Beverly and Edward A. McSweeney, *Social Welfare and Social Justice* (Englewood Cliffs, N.J.: Prentice-Hall, 1987).

3. Piven and Cloward, *Regulating the Poor,* p. 100.

4. Department of the Census, *Current Population Reports, 1981,* Series P-60, No. 125 (Washington, D.C.: U.S. Government Printing Office, 1981).

5. Michael Harrington, with the assistance of Robert Greenstein and Eleanor Holmes Norton, *Who Are the Poor?* (Washington, D.C.: Justice for All, 1987), p. 24.

6. Committee on Ways and Means, U.S. House of Representatives, *Overview of Entitlement Programs: 1992 Green Book* (Washington, D.C.: U.S. Government Printing Office, 1992), p. 4.

7. Charles Prigmore and Charles Atherton, *Social Welfare Policy* (Lexington, Mass.: D. C. Heath, 1979).

8. C. Merton and Joan Broadshaug Bernstein, *Social Security: The System That Works* (New York: Basic Books, 1987).

9. AARP, "A Profile of Older Americans" (Washington, D.C.: American Association of Retired Persons, 1991), pp. 9–10.

10. U.S. House of Representatives, *1992 Green Book*, p. 85.

11. Bernard Gavzer, "How Secure is Your Social Security?" *Parade,* October 18, 1987.

12. Robert J. Shapiro, "The Right Idea for 1990: Cut Social Security Taxes," *Economic Outlook,* no. 4., January 29, 1990, n.p.

13. AARP, "A Profile of Older Americans" (1991), p. 1

14. U.S. House of Representatives, *1992 Green Book,* p. 109.

15. Social Security Administration, *Social Security Bulletin, Annual Statistical Supplement, 1984–85* (Baltimore, Md.: Social Security Administration, April 1986); and Shapiro, "The Right Idea for 1990."

16. U.S. House of Representatives, *1992 Green Book,* p. 485.

17. Isaac Shapiro and Marion Nichols, *Far From Fixed: An Analysis of the Unemployment Insurance System* (Washington, D.C.: Center on Budget and Policy Priorities, March 1992), p. viii.

18. Diana M. DiNitto, *Social Welfare: Politics and Public Policy* (Englewood Cliffs, N.J.: Prentice Hall, 1991), p. 87.

19. U.S. House of Representatives, *1992 Green Book,* pp. 520 and 513–14.

20. Ibid.

21. Shapiro and Nichols, *Far From Fixed,* pp. viii and 16.

22. Isaac Shapiro and Robert Greenstein, *A Painless Recession* (Washington, D.C.: Center on Budget and Policy Priorities, February 1991), p. xiii.

23. Walter Corson and Mark Dynarski, *Unemployment Insurance Recipients and Exhaustees: Findings from a National Survey Summary Report,* MPR Reference No. 7805 (Washington, D.C.: Mathematica Policy Research, Inc., January 1991).

24. U.S. House of Representatives, *1992 Green Book,* pp. 1707–09.

25. Ibid.

26. Prigmore and Atherton, *Social Welfare Policy,* pp. 66–67.

27. W. Joseph Heffernan, *Introduction to Social Welfare Policy* (Itasca, Ill.: F. E. Peacock, 1979), p. 138.

28. Bernstein and Bernstein, *Social Security.*

29. Isaac Shapiro and Robert Greenstein, *Holes in the Safety Nets* (Washington, D.C.: Center on Budget and Policy Priorities, 1988).

30. "The Increasing Role of the Earned Income Tax Credit," *Focus* 13, no. 1 (Spring 1991): 19.

31. Frederick Hutchinson, Iris J. Lav, and Robert Greenstein, *A Hand Up: How State Earned Income Credits Help Working Families Escape Poverty* (Washington, D.C.: Center on Budget and Policy Priorities, April 1992), p. vii.

32. Ibid., p. ix.

33. Ibid.

34. Saul D. Hoffman and Lawrence S. Seidman, *The Earned Income Tax Credit* (Kalamazoo, Mich.: W. E. Upjohn Institute for Employment Research, 1990), p. 34.

35. Ibid., p. 82.

36. U.S. House of Representatives, *1992 Green Book,* pp. 653–87.

37. Ibid., pp. 649–51.

38. Ibid., pp. 669–71.

39. Department of Health, Education, and Welfare, *Aid to Families with Dependent Children* (Washington, D.C.: Social Security Administration, Office of Research and Statistics, 1979), p. 1.

40. Children's Defense Fund, A *Children's Defense Budget* (Washington, D.C.: Children's Defense Fund, 1986), p. 43; and Department of Health, Education, and Welfare, *Welfare Myths and Facts* (Washington, D.C.: Social and Rehabilitation Service, ca. 1972), p. 1.

41. U.S. House of Representatives, Select Committee on Hunger, "Myths and Realities: Food Stamp and AFDC Recipients" (Washington, D.C.: U.S. Government Printing office, April 9, 1992), p. 59.

42. Ibid.

43. League of Women Voters of Louisiana, "1991 Welfare Fact Sheet" (Baton Rouge, La.: League of Women Voters, October 1991), n.p.

44. See Children's Defense Fund, A *Children's Defense Budget, 1986.*

45. Children's Defense Fund, *The State of America's Children, 1991* (Washington, D.C.: Children's Defense Fund, 1991), p. 156.

46. Peter Gottschalk, "Achieving Self-Sufficiency for Welfare Recipients—The Good and Bad News," in Select Committee on Hunger, *Beyond Public Assistance: Where Do We Go From Here?* Serial No. 102–23 (Washington, D.C.: U.S. Government Printing Office, 1992), p. 56.C

47. Greg J. Duncan and Saul D. Hoffman, "Welfare

Dynamics and Welfare Policy,'' unpublished paper, Institute for Social Research, Ann Arbor, Mich., 1985.

48. Ibid.
49. Peter Gottschalk, "Is Intergenerational Correlation in Welfare Participation Across Generations Spurious?" Boston College, November 1990, Conference Papers, 1990 ASPE-JCPES Conference on the Underclass (Washington, D.C.: U.S. Department of Health and Human Services).
50. M. Ann Hill and June O'Neill, "Underclass Behaviors in the United States: Measurement and Analysis of Determinants," City College of New York, March 1990, Conference Papers, 1990 ASPE-JCPES Conference on the Underclass (Washington, D.C.: U.S. Department of Health and Human Services).
51. Mary Corcoran, Roger Gordon, Deborah Laren, and Gary Solon, "Problems of the Underclass: Underclass Neighborhoods and Intergenerational Poverty and Dependency," University of Michigan, 1991, Conference Papers, 1990 ASPE-JCPES Conference on the Underclass (Washington, D.C.: U.S. Department of Health and Human Services).
52. U.S. House of Representatives, *1992 Green Book*, p. 670.
53. Ibid., p. 1597.
54. Elizabeth D. Huttman, *Introduction to Social Policy* (New York: McGraw-Hill, 1981), p. 179.
55. Quoted in Select Committee on Hunger, "Myths and Realities," p. 58.
56. Ibid., p. 59.
57. Ibid.
58. Harrington, *Who Are the Poor?* p. 21.
59. Iris Lav and Steven Gold, *The States and the Poor* (Washington, D.C.: Center on Budget and Policy Priorities, 1993), p. 11.
60. Duncan and Hoffman, "Welfare Dynamics."
61. Select Committee on Hunger, "Myths and Realities," p. 57.
62. U.S. House of Representatives, *1992 Green Book*, p. 1606.
63. Select Committee on Hunger, "Myths and Realities," p. 58.
64. Thomas Corbett, "The Wisconsin Welfare Magnet: What Is an Ordinary Member of the Tribe to Do When the Witch Doctors Disagree?" *Focus* 13, no. 3 (Fall and Winter 1991): pp. 2–4.

65. Select Committee on Hunger, "Myths and Realities," p. 58.
66. Robert Moffitt, "Incentive Effects of the U.S. Welfare System: A Review," *Journal of Economic Literature* 30 (March 1992): 1–61.
67. Center on Social Welfare Policy and Law, "Compilation of Information About 1992 State Cutbacks in AFDC, GA and EAF," Publication No. 167 (Washington, D.C.: March 1992), pp. 3–4.
68. Ibid.
69. Isaac Shapiro, Mark Sheft, Julie Strawn, Laura Summer, Robert Greenstein, and Steven D. Gold, *The States and the Poor: How Budget Decisions in 1991 Affected Low-Income People* (Washington, D.C.: Center on Budget and Policy Priorities, December 1991), p. ix.
70. Ibid., pp. 25–30.
71. Center on Social Welfare Policy and Law, "Compilation of Information About 1992 State Cutbacks in AFDC, GA and EAF," pp. 2–3.
72. Ibid.
73. Ibid.
74. Lav and Gold, *The States and the Poor*, p. 36.
75. Center on Social Welfare Policy and the Law, "1991: The Poor Got Poorer as Welfare Programs Were Slashed," Publication No. 165 (Washington, D.C.: Center on Social Welfare Policy and the Law, February 1992), pp. 5–6.
76. Shapiro et al., *The States and the Poor,* p. 23.
77. Knud Hansen, "The Impact of the Elimination of General Assistance Programs in Michigan, Interim Report," Center for Urban Studies, Wayne State University, August 29, 1992.
78. Martha Burt, "Over the Edge" (Washington, D.C.: The Urban Institute, 1992).
79. Heffernan, *Introduction to Social Welfare Policy*.
80. Piven and Cloward, *Regulating the Poor*.
81. Huttman, *Introduction to Social Policy,* p. 168
82. Children's Defense Fund, A *Children's Defense Budget, 1986*, p. 145.
83. Ibid.
84. Ibid., p. 146.
85. Diana DiNitto and Thomas Dye, *Social Welfare: Politics and Public Policy* (Englewood Cliffs, N.J.: Prentice-Hall, 1987), p. 124.
86. Ibid.
87. Ibid.
88. Children's Defense Fund, *A Children's Defense Budget, 1986,* p. 146.

89. Huttman, *Introduction to Social Policy.*

90. U.S. House of Representatives, *1992 Green Book,* pp. 759 and 763.

91. Daniel Patrick Moynihan, *Congressional Record,* pp. S10401–2.

92. William Eaton, "Major Welfare Reform Compromise Reached," *Los Angeles Times,* September 27, 1988, p. 15.

93. American Public Welfare Association, *Conference Agreement on Welfare Reform* (Washington, D.C.: American Public Welfare Association, September 28, 1988) pp. 1–3.

94. David Stoesz and Howard Karger, "Welfare Reform: From Illusion to Reality," *Social Work,* 35, no. 2, (March 1990): 141–47.

95. Spencer Rich, "Panel Clears Welfare Bill," *The Washington Post,* September 28, 1988.

96. Committee on Ways and Means, U.S. House of Representatives, *Overview of Entitlement Programs, 1990 Green Book* (Washington, D.C.: U.S. Government Printing Office, 1990), p. 618.

97. David Ellwood, *Poor Support: Poverty in the American Family* (New York: Basic Books, 1988), p. 153.

98. Judith M. Gueron, "Statement by the President," *Manpower Demonstration Research Corporation, 1991 Annual Report* (New York: MDRC, 1991), p. 2.

99. Mimi Abramovitz, "Why Welfare Reform Is a Sham," *The Nation,* September 26, 1988, p. 239.

100. Ibid., p. 240.

101. Computations are based on *Background Material and Data on Programs within the Jurisdiction of the Committee on Ways and Means* (Washington, D.C.: U.S. Government Printing Office, 1988), pp. 415, 424.

102. Ibid., pp. 408–410.

103. "The Clinton/Gore Plan: End Welfare as We Know It," campaign flyer, n.d., n.p.

104. Center on Social Welfare Policy and Law, "Compilation of Information About 1992 State Cutbacks in AFDC, GA and EAF," pp. 8–9.

105. Lav and Gold, *The States and the Poor*, pp. 29–30.

106. Center on Social Welfare Policy and Law, "Compilation of Information About 1992 State Cutbacks in AFDC, GA and EAF," pp. 8–9.

107. Lav and Gold, *The States and the Poor*, pp. 30–31.

108. Center on Social Welfare Policy and Law, "Compilation of Information About 1992 State Cutbacks in AFDC, GA and EAF," p. 10.

109. Kathryn A. Larin and Kathryn H. Porter, *Enough to Live On: Setting an Appropriate AFDC Need Standard* (Washington, D.C.: Center on Budget and Policy Priorities, October 1992), p. x.

110. Center on Social Welfare Policy and the Law, "1991: The Poor Got Poorer as Welfare Programs Were Slashed," p. i.

111. This scenario assumes that welfare beneficiaries actually are enrolled in all programs for which they qualify. Yet in 1988, residents of New Jersey had less than a 40-percent chance of receiving subsidized housing, and almost half of WIC eligible women and children were not on the program. See Karger and Stoesz, Committee on Ways and Means, U.S. House of Representatives, *Overview of Entitlement Programs, 1990 Green Book*, p. 1318.

112. Although the bulk of income maintenance benefits are concentrated in the three main programs, the supports found in the smaller programs make it difficult to calculate actual welfare benefits.

113. U.S. House of Representatives, *1992 Green Book*, p. 699.

114. U.S. House of Representatives, *1990 Green Book.*

115. Moffitt, "Incentive Effects of the U.S. Welfare System," p. 30.

116. Mark Greenberg, testimony before the Domestic Task Force, Select Committee on Hunger, U.S. House of Representatives, April 9, 1992, in *Federal Policy Perspectives on Welfare Reform: Rhetoric, Reality and Opportunities*, Serial No. 102–25 (Washington, D.C.: U.S. Government Printing Office, 1992), pp. 52–53.

117. U.S. House of Representatives, *1992 Green Book*, pp. 1216–20.

118. Robert Rector, "Strategies for Welfare Reform," testimony before the Domestic Task Force, Select Committee on Hunger, U.S. House of Representatives, April 9, 1992, in *Federal Policy Perspectives on Welfare Reform: Rhetoric, Reality and Opportunities*, Serial No. 102–25 (Washington, D.C.: U.S. Government Printing Office, 1992), pp. 67–68.

119. Huttman, *Introduction to Social Policy.*

120. Children's Defense Fund, A *Children's Defense Budget, 1986*, p. 143.

121. Richard J. Estes. *The Social Progress of Nations* (New York: Praeger, 1984), p. 109.

CHAPTER 11

The American Health Care System

This chapter examines the American health care system—specifically, the demographics of U.S. health care, the organization of medical services, key governmental health programs such as Medicare and Medicaid, and federal attempts to curb health care costs. In addition, it examines how medical services are organized in Great Britain, Israel, and Canada. Finally, this chapter explores the current crisis in medical care and reviews alternative health care proposals.

Most health care costs in the United States are paid for by private insurers, public plans, and the direct public provision of health care. Only about 25 percent of health care costs are paid for directly by consumers. The dominant form of health care coverage in the United States is private insurance, which covers about 80 percent of the population (with two-thirds being covered by employer-based plans). Eighteen percent are covered by Medicare and Medicaid, and about 14 percent have no health care coverage whatsoever. Many elderly people use private health insurance plans to supplement the coverage given by the public plans.

The landscape of American health care is marked by several contradictions. Although the vast majority of Americans have easy access to a wide variety of medical services through em-ployment-based or public insurance programs, some 36 to 40 million people are totally without coverage. Thus, while these uninsured people *may* be admitted to a hospital emergency room if they are in cardiac arrest (due to legal prohibitions against turning them away), in less life-threatening situations they may not be so lucky. A child with a chronic ear infection may go untreated by a private physician in a rural area that has no free clinics and thus may suffer pain and possibly permanent hearing loss. A pregnant woman may not get prenatal care in a county that lacks a public clinic, and may therefore give birth to a low birth-weight baby. A homeless man may be turned away if he seeks a preventive checkup, or treatment for a cough or other "noncritical" illness. Approximately one million Americans seeking health care are turned away each year because they cannot pay, and millions more forgo preventive services.[1] This situation exists even though every major city has at least one major medical center with an annual budget of $100 to $200 million.[2]

The cost of providing health care has risen dramatically in the past 25 years. In 1960 total health care expenditures came to $120 billion (in 1990 dollars); by 1993 that amount had risen to $912 billion. Put another way, 5.3 percent of the total GNP in 1960 was devoted to medical care;

by 1992 that share was 13.2 percent.[3] In comparison, education was only 7.3 percent of the GNP in 1992 and military spending had actually decreased to below 6 percent.[4] Health care costs have risen faster than the general rate of inflation. From 1975 to 1979, health care expenditures grew at a rate of 13 percent a year. During the early 1980s this rate of growth increased to 15 percent a year.[5] In 1990, when the overall inflation rate was 6 percent, the medical inflation rate was 9.6 percent.[6] In the past decade the share of the GNP spent on health care rose by 1 percent every 35 months.[7] Even if health-related expenditures are held constant, the United States will spend at least 15 percent of its GNP on health care by the year 2000.[8] In other words, without wide-ranging health care reform, health care spending is expected to reach $1 trillion by 1995 and $1.7 trillion by the year 2000.[9] As Table 11.1 suggests, the growth in the health care industry eclipses that of most other American business sectors.

When health care expenditures are broken down (see Figure 11.1), the largest share (almost 50 percent) goes to hospitals; in 1990 hospital care alone cost $256 billion.[10] Increases in the cost of hospital care have been a key factor in driving up health care costs. In 1980 the average daily charge for a hospital room charge was $127; by 1989 this had risen to $262. In 1980 the average cost per day for hospital care was $245; by 1987 the cost had increased to $539. Finally, the average cost per stay in a hospital was $1,851 in 1980; by 1987 it had more than doubled to $3,850.[11] Without serious health care reform, hospital and physician expenditures are expected to grow at a rate of 10 percent a year throughout the 1990s.[12]

The second largest expenditure is for physicians' services, which accounted for over 20 percent of all expenditures and totaled almost $126 billion in 1990.[13] Increases in the incomes of physicians have grown alongside the increases in general medical costs. For example, the income of physicians grew by 11.6 percent annually from 1980 to 1990, with inflation and population growth accounting for only 40 percent of this increase.[14] By 1991 the average medical doctor had a yearly income of $170,600. The gross annual income of specialists was considerably higher than the median income for physicians. In 1987 the gross annual income for office-based psychiatrists was $140,000; for anesthesiologists, $214,000; for OB/GYNs, $290,000; for plastic surgeons, $378,000; for neurosurgeons, $413,000; and for cardiovascular surgeons, $480,000.[15] Physician organizations argue that these high salaries are necessary to repay the high debts accrued by medical students. They point out that the average medical school debt was $55,859 in 1993. The median cost of a four-year private medical school for the class of 1995 is expected to reach $79,160. At public institutions, the total cost of medical education in 1993 was $27,500 for in-state students and $65,572 for out-of-state students.[16] The problem of rising physician salaries is aggravated by the recent growth in the number of high-cost providers. Seventy percent of current

TABLE 11.1. U.S. Gross National Product (GNP) and National Health Care Expenditures for Selected Years, 1960–1990 (in constant 1990 dollars)

Year	Amount (Billions)	National Health Care Expenditures	
		Percentage of GNP	Amount Per Capita
1960	$115	5.3	$ 638
1965	172	5.9	846
1970	232	7.3	1,136
1975	323	8.3	1,438
1980	382	9.2	1,678
1985	513	10.5	2,077
1990	671	12.2	2,604

SOURCES: Compiled from Committee on Ways and Means, U.S. House of Representatives, *Overview of Entitlement Programs: 1992 Green Book* (Washington, D.C.: U.S. Government Printing Office, 1992), Tables 1–4, pp. 287–90; and Henry J. Aaron, *Serious and Unstable Condition* (Washington, D.C.: Brookings Institution, 1990), p. 39.

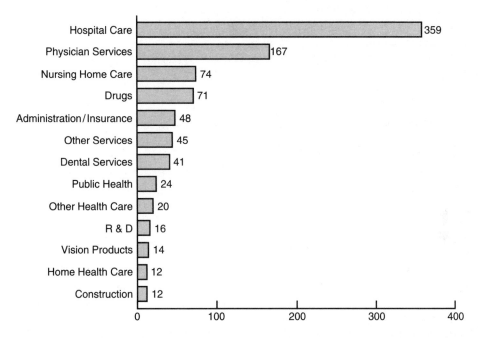

Figure 11.1 Where Health Care Dollars Are Spent, 1993 (In billions of dollars). (SOURCE: Adapted from Stephen Conley, "Dissecting Health-Care Dollars," *USA Today*, May 5, 1993, p. B1).

medical school graduates are specialists (only 30 percent are generalists), which is a reversal of the ratio that existed 30 years ago.[17] Not unexpectedly, the average doctor visit went from $30 in 1986 to $46 in 1992.[18] Moreover, while health care costs more than doubled in the last decade, prescription drug prices increased by a whopping 152 percent.[19]

The huge increases in health care costs have put increasing pressure on the government to subsidize more of the health care budget, as shown in Table 11.2. From 1950 to 1992, the percentage of health care costs paid for by the government rose from 27.2 percent to 41.4 percent. In 1992, the federal government spent approximately $328 billion on health care, of which only $100 billion was raised through Medicare payroll deductions.[20] Moreover, the combined costs of AFDC, the Women, Infants and Children's Program (WIC), Food Stamps, and

the school breakfast programs totalled only about one-fifth of the amount spent on Medicaid and Medicare in 1992. While social service spending generally remained static, the costs of Medicare and Medicaid grew by over 10 percent a year from 1982 to 1992.[21] The Congressional Budget Office estimates that without health care reform, 25 percent of all federal expenditures will be dedicated to Medicaid and Medicare by 2002. This growth would mean an additional allocation of $313 billion, an amount equivalent to the 1993 defense budget.[22] Partly as a result of federal spending, the proportion of personal health care expenditures paid for directly by consumers decreased from 55 percent in 1960 to 28 percent in 1987. By 1987 the government had become the single largest payer of medical bills, paying for some 40 percent of health care expenditures, compared with 31 percent paid for by private insurance companies.[23]

TABLE 11.2. Sources of Payment for Personal Health Care in Selected Years, 1929–1986 (In percentages)

Year	Direct Payment	Private Health Insurance	Philanthropy and Industry	Governmental		
				Total	Federal	State and Local
1929	88.4	NA	2.6	9.0	2.7	6.3
1940	81.3	NA	2.6	16.1	4.1	12.0
1950	65.5	9.1	2.9	22.4	10.4	12.0
1960	54.9	21.1	2.3	21.8	9.3	12.5
1965	51.6	24.2	2.2	22.0	10.1	11.9
1970	40.5	23.4	1.7	34.3	22.2	12.1
1975	32.5	26.7	1.3	39.5	26.8	12.7
1980	28.7	30.7	1.2	39.4	28.4	10.9
1982	27.8	31.4	1.2	39.6	29.3	10.3
1984	28.8	30.7	1.2	39.3	29.5	9.8
1986	28.7	30.4	1.2	39.6	30.2	9.4

SOURCES: U.S. Department of Health and Human Services, *Health, United States–1987.* DHHS Pub. No. (PHS) 88–1232, Table 102 (Washington, D.C.: U.S. Government Printing Office, 1988), p. 158.

The Organization of Medical Services

Before proceeding to a discussion of Medicare and Medicaid, it may be useful to look at the overall organization of medical services in the United States. This organization has five major components: (1) physicians in solo practice; (2) group outpatient settings, including groups of physicians sharing facilities, group health plans and HMOs, physicians in industrial (Employee Assistance Plans) settings, or doctors operating under university auspices (over the past few decades physicians have increasingly worked in group practices or other organized settings, and in 1984 this segment accounted for about half of all patient-physician services);[24] (3) hospitals—private, nonprofit, or public; (4) public health services delivered on the state, local, regional, national, or international level, including health counseling, family planning, prenatal and postnatal care, school health services, disease prevention and control, immunization, referral agencies, sexually transmitted diseases (STD) services, environmental sanitation, health edu-

cation, and maintenance of indexes on births, deaths, and communicable diseases; and (5) sundry and corollary health services, including home health services, physical rehabilitation, group homes, nursing homes, and so forth.

THE MAJOR PUBLIC HEALTH CARE PROGRAMS: MEDICAID AND MEDICARE

Medicaid

Before 1965, medical care for those who could not afford to pay for it was primarily a responsibility of charitable institutions and of state and local governments. In 1950 the federal government authorized states to use federal/state funds under the Social Security Act of 1935 to provide medical care for the indigent. By 1957, the Kerr-Mills Act provided for a federal/state matching program to provide health care for the elderly and the poor. However, Kerr-Mills was not mandatory, and many states chose not to participate. Designed as a compromise to ward off more far-reaching health policies, President Lyndon Johnson signed into law the Medicaid and Medicare programs in 1965.[25] Replacing all previous programs, Medicaid became the largest public assistance program in the nation, covering about 9.7 percent of the population, including more than 15 percent of all children. In 1992, Medicaid served more than 25 million people at a total federal/state cost of $127 billion.

The $127-billion Medicaid budget in 1992 represented a 35 percent increase over 1991. Moreover, this huge increase occurred even though the actual number of Medicaid recipients grew by just over 200,000 (less than 10 percent) in the same period.[26] Although much of this spending rise is attributable to new federal mandates for increased eligibility, part of it is credited to rising health care costs. In fact, health care spending is the second-fastest-growing component of the federal budget, overshadowed only by the growth in the public debt. Overall, health care spending accounts for at least 14 percent of total governmental expenditures at the state and federal levels.[27]

Medicaid is a means-tested public assistance program. Eligible persons receive services from physicians who accept Medicaid patients (in many places a minority of the physicians) and other health care providers. These health care providers are then reimbursed by the federal government on a per-patient basis. Medicaid is also a federal/state program. States determine eligibility within broad federal guidelines. As such, states make many of the key decisions as to where to set income eligibility limits, which groups to cover, which services to cover, and how much to pay for services. In general, Medicaid serves the following groups: (1) all AFDC and AFDC-UP families; (2) first-time pregnant women if they would qualify for AFDC upon the birth of their child; (3) pregnant women in qualifying two-parent families in which the breadwinner is unemployed; (4) children who were born before 1983 and who live in families below the poverty line; and (5) most SSI recipients (see Table 11.3). Thirty-seven states also extend coverage to the medically indigent—those people ineligible for public assistance but who cannot obtain medical care or pay a medical bill. More than half the states extend coverage to families in which the breadwinner is receiving unemployment compensation.

Because Medicaid is funded by federal/state matching funds (states pay on average 50 percent of the costs), states also help to set the benefit levels. While all states are required to provide inpatient and outpatient hospital care, physicians' services, laboratory and X-ray services, skilled nursing home services for adults, home health care, family planning services and supplies, nurse and midwife services, and early periodic screening for children, they also have the option of further extending Medicaid benefits (e.g., to include drugs, eyeglasses, inpatient psychiatric care for individuals under age 21 or over age 65, etc.). In addition, states have broad administrative powers over Medicaid, including the determination of reimbursement rates. As a result, individual states can discourage Medicaid participation by promulgating low reimbursement rates and low state-defined income standards.

States may also restrict the content, scope, and duration of various services. For example, the state of Oregon challenged federal Medicaid guidelines by moving away from the goal of providing all possible health services to a limited number of Medicaid recipients. Instead, Oregon opted to provide coverage to a greater number of persons by establishing a list of medical priorities and then allocating a specified level of dollars according to that priority list. Other care was not to be provided under the Oregon Medicaid plan.[28] Under Oregon's plan, 120,000 more people would be covered under Medicaid (almost everyone under the poverty line), but certain procedures would be disallowed, including specific forms of cancer and AIDS treatment. Although the Bush administration vetoed the proposal, the Clinton administration reversed the veto on March 19, 1993, thus giving Oregon the go-ahead to implement its rationing-based Medicaid plan.

Other states have modified Medicaid by

TABLE 11.3. Medicaid Recipients by Category, 1972–1990 (In thousands)

Year	Total	Age 65 or Older	Blindness	Total Disability	Families with Dependent Children		
					Adults	Children	Other
1972	17,606	3,318	108	1,625	3,137	7,841	1,576
1975	22,013	3,643	106	2,265	4,529	9,598	1,800
1977	22,831	3,636	92	2,710	4,785	9,651	1,959
1980	21,605	3,440	92	2,819	4,877	9,333	1,499
1982	21,603	3,240	84	2,806	5,356	9,563	1,434
1984	21,365	3,165	80	2,870	5,598	9,771	1,185
1990	25,255	3,202	83	3,635	6,010	11,220	990

SOURCES: Social Security Administration, *Social Security Bulletin, Annual Statistical Supplement, 1984–85* (Baltimore, Md.: Social Security Aministration, 1986), pp. 219–22; and Committee on Ways and Means, U.S. House of Representatives, *Overview of Entitlement Programs, 1992 Green Book* (Washington, D.C.: U.S. Government Printing Office, 1992), p. 1653.

placing a limit on the number of days of hospital care a patient can receive or by limiting the number of physician visits covered in a year. States are also free to impose limited copayments for some Medicaid services.[29]

Federal law provides several options for states to provide Medicaid benefits to poor children and pregnant women who are not on AFDC or AFDC-UP. One such option involves the establishment of a Medically Needy component under the state Medicaid program. Under this option, a family whose countable income is greater than the state's Medicaid income eligibility limits but whose medical expenses are so large that the remaining income places the family below the poverty line is eligible for Medicaid. The Medically Needy component allows states to set Medicaid income limits that are up to one-third higher than the state's maximum benefit for AFDC. This option is particularly important for families who were once self-sufficient but who now face a medical catastrophe that will deplete their economic resources. Families whose health insurance limits are exhausted, or who have no insurance, may also be eligible. Thirty-six states had adopted a Medically Needy program by 1988.[30]

Although Medicaid was designed as a federal/state program to pay for health care for low-income and disabled citizens, the greatest outlay of Medicaid funds goes to the elderly. In 1990, 27 percent of all Medicaid funding went toward nursing home care (excluding care for the mentally retarded).[31] As a result, close to three-fifths of all nursing home expenditures are paid for by the federal government. Not surprisingly, the growth of the nursing home industry parallels the creation of Medicaid. From 1965 (the year Medicaid was created) to 1970 the number of nursing home residents rose by 18 percent. From 1970 to 1975 that number rose another 17 percent; from 1975 to 1980, 14 percent; and from 1980 to 1985, about 12 percent. Since four-fifths of nursing homes are for-profit facilities, Medicaid functions as a de facto subsidy for the nursing home industry.

Despite federal guidelines, four important gaps exist in Medicaid coverage: (1) the low eligibility limits set for Medicaid; (2) the refusal of many states to adopt most or all of the Medicaid options; (3) the gaps in coverage for the elderly and disabled; and (4) the general ineligibility of single poor persons and childless couples for Medicaid unless they are elderly or disabled. In addition, the Children's Defense Fund observed no increase in the percentage of pregnant women receiving early prenatal care from 1986 to 1991. The Robert Wood Johnson Foundation noted that Medicaid reached 19 percent fewer poor and near-poor families in 1986 than it did in 1976.[32] According to the Bureau of the Census, only about two-fifths of the nation's poor were covered under Medicaid in 1990.[33] (Close to 25 million people received Medicaid in 1992, considerably less than the 33.5 million in poverty.) Moreover, about 5 million children and 6 of every 10 women of childbearing age below the poverty line are ineligible for Medicaid.[34]

Despite these inadequacies, the Medicaid program has produced significant results. In 1963 only 63 percent of pregnant women received prenatal care; by 1976 that number had increased to 76 percent. Between 1964 and 1975,

the use of physicians' services by poor children increased 74 percent. In part, the increased utilization of medical services resulted in a 49 percent drop in infant mortality between 1965 and 1988. For African-American infants the drop in mortality was even sharper: Infant mortality dropped by only 5 percent in the 15 years before Medicaid, but by 49 percent in the 15 years after the program began. Ongoing preventive care also cut program costs for Medicaid-eligible children by 10 percent.[35] Table 11.4 compares the infant mortality rates in 33 states for the year 1988.

TABLE 11.4. State Infant Mortality Rates by Rank, 1988

Rank	State	Rates per 1,000 Live Births	Rank	State	Rates per 1,000 Live Births
1	District of Columbia	23.2	19	Arizona	9.7
2	Georgia	12.6	20	Colorado	9.6
3	North Carolina	12.5	21	Oklahoma	9.0
4	South Carolina	12.3	21	Washington	9.0
4	Mississippi	12.3	21	West Virginia	9.0
5	Alabama	12.1	21	Nebraska	9.0
6	Delaware	11.8	21	Texas	9.0
7	Alaska	11.6	22	Wyoming	8.9
8	Maryland	11.3	22	Connecticut	8.9
8	Illinois	11.3	23	Idaho	8.8
9	Michigan	11.1	24	Montana	8.7
10	Louisiana	11.0	24	Iowa	8.7
10	Indiana	11.0	25	California	8.6
11	Tennessee	10.8	25	Oregon	8.6
11	New York	10.8	26	Nevada	8.4
12	Arkansas	10.7	26	Wisconsin	8.4
12	Kentucky	10.7	27	New Hampshire	8.3
13	Florida	10.6	28	Rhode Island	8.2
14	North Dakota	10.5	29	Kansas	8.0
15	Virginia	10.4	29	Utah	8.0
16	Missouri	10.1	30	Maine	7.9
16	South Dakota	10.1	30	Massachusetts	7.9
17	New Mexico	10.0	31	Minnesota	7.8
18	Pennsylvania	9.9	32	Hawaii	7.2
18	New Jersey	9.9	33	Vermont	7.2
19	Ohio	9.7	U.S. total		10.0

SOURCE: Children's Defense Fund, *The State of America's Children* (Washington, D.C.: Children's Defense Fund, 1991), p. 155.

Medicaid is one of the most important governmental health programs in the United States. In 1986, Medicaid payments represented 55 cents of every public health dollar spent on children; 26 cents out of every dollar (public or private) spent on hospitalization for children under age six; 30 cents of every dollar spent on delivery services for pregnant teens; and 10 cents out of every dollar spent on ambulatory pediatric services.[36]

Despite these successes, Medicaid has been under constant attack by the Reagan and Bush administrations, Congress, and various state governments. Cuts in federal funds and rule changes has led many states to reduce eligibility and to provide fewer services. For example, roughly 800 Medicaid-related cost containment measures were adopted in the vast majority of states between 1984 and 1988. These measures included limiting the number of hospital days and reimbursable visits to physicians, reducing or freezing Medicaid provider rates, imposing copayments and deductibles, requiring preadmission screening, and mandating second opinions for elective surgery.[37]

Medicare

Medicare, Public Law 89–79, was added to the Social Security Act on July 30, 1965. This program was designed to provide prepaid hospital insurance for the aged, as well as voluntary medical insurance. Medicare is composed of two parts: compulsory Hospital Insurance (HI), known as Part A; and Supplemental Medical Insurance (SMI), known as Part B. Part A is a compulsory hospital insurance plan for the aged, with the premiums coming out of a payroll tax (1.45 percent in 1991) that is part of the Social Security deductions. Most Americans 65 or older are automatically entitled to Part A. Those not eligible may pay the full actuarial coverage ($192 per month in 1992). After two years, those under age 65 who receive disability benefits are eligible for Part B.

SMI, a voluntary supplemental medical insurance plan, pays doctor bills and additional medical expenses. The costs of SMI are paid for by the beneficiary ($31.80 a month in 1992); the remainder is subsidized by general tax revenues. SMI is open to anyone over age 65 willing to pay the premium. The SMI premium is paid by the federal government only if the beneficiary is on public assistance. Medicare coverage includes physicians' services in the home, hospital, or office and all covered services in a participating skilled nursing facility.

In 1988, President Ronald Reagan signed the Catastrophic Health Insurance Act, the most sweeping reform ever attempted. This legislation was designed to provide 33 million elderly and disabled Medicare beneficiaries with protection from catastrophic hospital, doctor, and outpatient drug costs. The catastrophic health insurance bill would also have applied to Medicaid by allowing the noninstitutionalized spouse of a nursing home resident applying for Medicaid to retain a sufficient portion of their combined income to avoid becoming destitute. Moreover, the bill would have required states to provide pregnancy-related services to women with incomes below 75 percent of the poverty line, and full Medicaid benefits to poor children under age one.

The new Medicare benefits were to be financed by two premiums. The first was applicable to all Medicare enrollees and would have been $4 per month in 1989, rising to $10.20 in 1993. (This amount was to be paid in addition to the regular 1988 premium of $24.80 per month.) The second, income-related premium was to be paid each year in conjunction with the federal income taxes paid by the 40 percent of Medicare enrollees with the highest incomes. Even if enrollees chose to forgo the catastrophic benefits, everyone eligible for Medicare hospital benefits would have been required to pay the supplemental premium if their incomes were high enough to meet the taxation threshold.[38] Because of consumer pressure (i.e., the elderly refused to support the self-financing part of the reforms) and the rising deficit, the Catastrophic

Insurance Act was repealed by Congress even before it was implemented.

The Medicare program contains extensive gaps in coverage. For example, Medicare does not cover long-term custodial nursing home care, most dental care, private-duty nurses, eyeglasses, eye exams, most prescription drugs, routine physical exams, and hearing tests and devices. This situation has led many elderly recipients to purchase supplemental private health insurance policies to cover the gaps in the Medicare program.

CUTTING FEDERAL HEALTH CARE COSTS: THE DIAGNOSTIC RELATED GROUPS (DRGs)

In 1993, Medicare served 35 million people and cost over $142 billion, a huge increase from the $14 billion it had cost in 1975. Both the scope and costs of Medicare have grown since its inception: In 1967, Medicare accounted for 2 percent of the federal budget; by 1987 it consumed 7 percent of federal outlays. In addition, hospital care in 1991 accounted for 46.3 percent of personal health care expenditures; the federal government subsidized 75 percent of those costs. From 1966 to 1981 the federal contribution to hospital care rose from 13 to 41 percent.[39] This fiscal burden led the federal government to seek alternative ways to lower hospital costs, including the Diagnostic Related Group system (DRG).

In 1983 Congress enacted the DRG form of medical payment. Although earlier Medicare rules had restricted the fees hospitals could charge, the government generally reimbursed them for the entire bill. This style of reimbursement was called retrospective (after-the-fact) payment. By contrast, DRGs are a form of prospective (before-the-fact) payment; the federal government specifies in advance what it will pay for the treatment of 468 classified illness- or diagnosis-related groups.

Developed by health researchers at the Yale-New Haven Hospital, the DRG system is designed to enforce economy by defining expected lengths of hospital stays. This system provides a treatment and diagnostic classification scheme, using the patient's medical diagnosis, prescribed treatment, and age as a means for categorizing and defining hospital services. In other words, the DRG system determines the length of a typical patient's hospital stay and reimburses hospitals only for that period of time. Additional costs beyond the DRG allotment must be borne by the hospital. Conversely, if a patient requires less hospitalization than the maximum DRG allocation, the difference is kept by the hospital. Hospitals may not charge the patient more than the DRG allotment. Hence, patients not yet ready for discharge (e.g., those patients who do not have appropriate aftercare services available) may be discharged—a situation that can result in patient dumping.

Exceptions to the DRG classification system are made for long hospital stays, certain kinds of hospital facilities (i.e., psychiatric and rehabilitation units), hospitals that are the only facility in a community, and hospitals that serve large numbers of poor people. The DRG classification applies only to the HI part of Medicare.

Proponents of the DRG system argue that hospital costs must be curbed and that there is no painless way to accomplish this goal. Moreover, supporters contend that because DRGs require physicians to be designated as the primary professional responsible for cost containment, they are relieved of some of the financial incentives for ordering unnecessary hospital admissions and longer stays. In addition, there is less incentive for physicians to overuse medical tests, ancillary services, surgery, and so forth. Often removed from the economics of cost containment, physicians are forced to acknowledge that "maximum efficiency leads to maximum reimbursement in the DRG system."[40]

Critics maintain that patient care suffers when it is subordinated to the economies required by the DRG system. Erring on the side of cost containment, doctors often curtail necessary medical tests and ancillary services. Moreover, the DRG system supports the dominance of the medical model in that it emphasizes the physiological causes of disease at the expense of the psychological correlates of health and illness.

Social workers employed in medical settings often experience great stress when they realize that the urgency of discharge planning overrides the psychosocial needs of clients. Patients requiring additional recuperative time must be referred to relatives, rediagnosed, transferred to nursing homes, or simply discharged early. Other observers argue that DRGs fail to take into account regional differences in medical costs. In sum, critics argue that instead of making hospitals more efficient, DRGs only cause more problems for patients and, in the end, increase medical costs. Regardless of the arguments, both sides agree that DRGs are revolutionizing the American hospital system.

OTHER GOVERNMENTAL HEALTH SERVICES

Other government-sponsored health services, to name a few, include the Veterans Administration Hospitals (the largest network of hospitals in America); Community and Migrant Health Centers; services provided under Title V, Maternal and Child Health Block Grant; and the Title X Family Planning Program. The federal government has also supported the development of health maintenance organizations (HMOs).

In 1973 Congress passed the Health Maintenance Organization Act, which offered federal assistance to groups wishing to start an HMO. Typically, HMOs provide comprehensive health care, often prevention-oriented, for enrolled members. Members usually pay a fixed fee and are then entitled to free (or heavily subsidized) physician and hospital care. Under the Health Maintenance Organization Act, an HMO must have four characteristics: (1) an organized system for providing health care in a geographic area, (2) a set of basic and supplemental medical services, (3) a voluntarily enrolled group of people, and (4) a community rating. The 607 HMO plans currently available take two basic forms: group HMOs and Individual Practice Associations (IPAs). A group HMO contracts with one or more medical groups to provide services to members under one roof, except for hospital care. IPA HMOs contract with a physician organization, which in turn contracts with individual physicians. Patients in IPA HMOs generally see physicians in their private offices.[41]

HMOs experienced rapid growth as enrollments rose from 60,000 in 1976 to 312,000 by 1989. Of that number, 180,000 members were in group plans and 132,000 were in IPAs.[42] Most HMO members (180,000) are in plans that enroll 100,000 or more members, the largest being Kaiser-Permanente.[43] Of the currently available HMO plans, 387 are IPA and 220 are group plans. In 1984, seven of the fourteen largest HMOs were investor-owned in 1984, and they accounted for half of all members. Moreover, stock prices of major investor-owned HMOs rose by two to five times between 1983 and 1985.[44]

Advocates of HMOs maintain that the concept encourages more efficient and less expensive medical care and that it stresses prevention over treatment. Because doctors employed by HMOs have little incentive to "overtreat" patients and recommend unnecessary medical care, the system is expected to be more efficient. In some cases, the economic rationalization of the system has been effected by requiring patients to see nurses or physician assistants rather than doctors.

Critics maintain that research studies show no evidence that HMOs provide better-quality services than traditional medical settings.[45] Furthermore, these critics point out that the presumed administrative advantages in HMOs can also lead to greater bureaucratization and impersonality. Finally, some opponents maintain that the lower cost of HMOs is attributable to two factors: (1) The capitation method of reimbursement has removed the financial incentive for physicians to overuse services; and (2) HMOs generally enroll young, healthy, employed, middle-class people who use hospital facilities less often than the general public. Because HMOs are usually linked to employment, they have generally avoided the high users—the disabled and the elderly.[46] Despite these criticisms, HMOs have become a major part of America's medical landscape.

THE HEALTH CARE CRISIS IN AMERICA

Any analysis of the American health care system must first examine whether it works. The following section explores some parameters of that question. Specifically, this section examines the internal effectiveness of the American health care system, the effect of AIDS on health care, and how the American medical care system fares when compared with other health care systems.

In 1989, the United States registered the highest per capita medical care expenditures in the world, as illustrated by Table 11.5. In that same year, the United States spent 11.8 percent of its gross domestic product (GDP)—again, the highest in the world—on health care. Health care in the United States costs 40 percent more than in any other industrialized nation.[47]

Despite the high costs of medical care, the United States offers the least social protection against hospital care costs of all the major industrialized nations. In other words, the United States has the smallest percentage of its population (40 percent compared to the 100 percent covered by most countries) eligible for publicly subsidized hospital care (as shown by Table 11.6). Furthermore, the United States provides the least social protection against ambulatory medical care costs, and it covers only 25 percent of the population for outpatient physician visits

compared with between 90 and 100 percent for most other nations. Finally, social protection against the cost of medical goods (pharmaceuticals) is provided to only 10 percent of the U.S. population, again a low figure when compared with the 90 to 100 percent for other industrialized nations.

Accounting for the enormous costs of the U.S. health care system is problematic. Many health policy analysts attribute these high costs to the strong growth in spending on hospitals and physician services, to the growth of new and expensive medical technology, the increased emphasis on practicing defensive medicine, fraud, the rise in the numbers of elderly (important consumers of medical services), and the dependence on third party payers.[48] The evidence is mixed regarding these claims. For example, only 14.7 percent of the U.S. population was admitted to a hospital (the costliest of health care services) in 1987. This percentage was in the mid-range of hospital admission rates elsewhere—a range that went from 7.5 percent in Japan to 22.6 percent in Finland.[49] Furthermore, the average length of stay in a U.S. hospital in 1989 was only 9.9 days, one of the lowest figures in the industrialized world. On average, Americans consulted doctors nearly six times a year,[50] less than the average for consumers in many other industrialized nations.[51] Finally, Americans used about 4.3 drugs a year in 1977, one of the lowest rates of pharmaceutical consumption among the industrialized nations.

While it is easy to blame rising health care costs on the elderly, the Congressional Budget Office maintains that increases in the aged population accounted for only 5 percent of the increase in per capita health care spending between 1965 and 1990. Increases in the numbers of elderly are expected to add only modestly to the growth of health care spending in the 1990s. Moreover, although spending on HIV and AIDS victims has grown faster than all other health care spending, it is still relatively small. Overall expenditures on HIV-positive individuals are expected to increase from 1.3 to 1.4 percent of

TABLE 11.5. Total Health Expenditures as a Percentage of Gross Domestic Product (GDP), Per Capita Health Spending, and Percent of Health Expenditures Publicly Financed for Selected Calendar Years, 1970–1989

	1970	1975	1980	1985	1989	Per Capita	Public Spending
Australia	4.9%	5.5%	6.5%	7.0%	7.6%	$1,125	70%
Austria	5.4	7.3	7.9	7.6	8.2	1,093	67
Belgium	4.1	5.9	6.3	6.9	7.2	980	89
Canada	7.1	7.2	7.4	8.5	8.7	1,683	75
Denmark	6.1	6.5	6.8	6.3	6.3	912	84
Finland	5.7	6.3	6.5	7.2	7.1	1,067	79
France	5.8	7.0	7.6	8.5	8.7	1,274	75
Germany	5.9	8.2	8.5	8.6	8.2	1,232	72
Greece	4.0	4.1	4.3	4.9	5.1	371	89
Iceland	5.2	6.2	6.5	7.4	8.6	1,353	88
Ireland	5.6	7.6	9.0	8.3	7.3	658	84
Italy	5.2	6.1	6.8	7.0	7.6	1,050	79
Japan	4.4	5.5	6.4	6.5	6.7	1,035	73
Luxembourg	4.1	5.6	6.8	6.8	7.4	1,193	92
Netherlands	6.0	7.7	8.2	8.2	8.3	1,135	73
New Zealand	5.2	6.7	7.2	6.6	7.1	820	85
Norway	5.0	6.7	6.6	6.4	7.6	1,234	95
Portugal	—	6.4	5.9	7.0	6.3	464	62
Spain	3.7	4.8	5.6	5.7	6.3	644	78
Sweden	7.2	7.9	9.5	9.3	8.8	1,361	90
Switzerland	5.2	7.0	7.3	7.6	7.8	1,376	68
Turkey	—	3.5	4.1	—	3.9	175	37
United Kingdom	4.5	5.5	5.8	6.0	5.8	836	87
United States	7.4	8.4	9.3	10.6	11.8	2,354	42
Mean	5.4	6.5	7.1	7.4	7.4	1,059	76

SOURCE: Committee on Ways and Means, U.S. House of Representatives, *Overview of Entitlement Programs, 1992 Green Book* (Washington, D.C.: U.S. Government Printing Office, 1992), p. 330.

the total health care budget between 1992 and 1995.[52]

The Bush administration argued that a major cause of the explosion in health care costs is due to the practice of "defensive medicine." Fearful of malpractice suits, some physicians behave overcautiously and order the use of inappropriate diagnostic and treatment methods. Some policy analysts estimate that as much as 30 percent of current health care expenditures goes toward services that are not needed, much of this under the guise of defensive medicine.[53]

The Congressional Budget Office has put the cost of practicing defensive medicine at 5 percent of total health care spending, while the American Medical Association has estimated that it may account for as much as 14 percent.[54] In 1991, the cost of practicing defensive medicine was conservatively estimated at $25 billion. Moreover, annual malpractice insurance premiums for general surgeons rose from $9,900 in 1982 to $22,500 in 1991. In 1991, malpractice insurance for physicians cost $5.1 billion.[55]

Other factors also influence health care

TABLE 11.6. **Percent of Population Eligible for Hospital Care under a Public Scheme in Selected Industrialized Nations, 1983**

Country	Percent
Australia	100
Austria	99
Belgium	98
Canada	100
Denmark	100
Finland	100
France	100
Germany	95
Greece	98
Iceland	100
Ireland	100
Italy	100
Japan	100
Luxembourg	100
Netherlands	88
New Zealand	100
Norway	100
Portugal	100
Spain	87
Sweden	100
Switzerland	97
United Kingdom	100
United States	40

SOURCE: OECD, *Measuring Health Care, 1960–1983* (Paris: Organization for Economic Cooperation and Development, 1985), p. 68.

costs. For one, rapid advances in medical technology have a significant impact on medical expenditures. Although the United States leads the world in the development of medical technology, many of these advances have come at a high price. Between 1980 and 1991, the number of coronary bypass operations for men increased from 108,000 to 206,000; diagnostic ultrasounds for women rose from 114,000 to 652,000; and the use of CAT scans increased from 306,000 to more than 1.4 million.[56] Moreover, some technologies are introduced before being sufficiently tested to determine cost effec-

tiveness and superiority to existing technologies. Another problem is fraud. The U.S. General Accounting Office estimated that in 1991 fraud cost $70 billion, or 10 percent every health care dollar. Lastly, administrative costs also add to rising expenditures. It is estimated that as much as 25 percent of every health care dollar goes for managing the mountains of paperwork required to run the system.[57]

Despite huge health care expenditures, the net benefit appears questionable. In 1989 the life expectancy for U.S. males was 71.2 years, putting it in the mid-range of industrial nations, but lower than the United Kingdom. For females it was 78.2 years, more than one year longer than it was in the United Kingdom, but less than it was Australia, France, Japan, and other countries (see Table 11.7). Despite high health care costs, Americans are neither healthier nor do they live longer than in other industrial nations where health care spending is lower.[58]

The American medical system is effective for much of the upper-middle and upper classes who are protected by adequate health insurance policies. However, this health care model has resulted in dual system of medical care: A large proportion of Americans receive the best and most advanced health care in the world, while a growing percentage of the population receive little or no medical care. Of the 36 to 40 million people currently without health care coverage (more than 17 percent of the nonelderly population), 39 percent (over 10 million) are children under age 18.[59] In 1992, the vast majority of the uninsured (89 percent) were neither individuals on public assistance nor the disabled; instead, they were low-income working families whose adjusted gross annual income was below $20,000. Moreover, despite increases in Medicaid spending, the number of uninsured individuals increased by five million from 1980 to 1988.[60] Although 80 percent of health insurance coverage occurs through the workplace, more than 30 percent of employers who pay more than half their work force the minimum wage do not provide health insurance. Moreover, the refusal

TABLE 11.7. Life Expectancy at Birth (1980) and Infant Mortality as a Percent of Live Births (1983) in 24 Industrialized Countries

	Life Expectancy at Birth (1980)		Infant Mortality (% of live births, 1983)
	Females	Males	
Australia	78.0	70.9	0.96
Austria	76.1	69.0	1.19
Belgium	75.5	69.8	1.12
Canada	79.0	71.0	0.85
Denmark	77.6	71.4	0.77
Finland	77.6	69.2	0.62
France	78.3	70.1	0.89
Germany	76.5	69.7	1.03
Greece	77.8	73.2	1.46
Iceland	80.5	73.6	0.61
Ireland	75.0	69.5	0.98
Italy	77.4	70.4	1.24
Japan	79.2	73.7	0.62
Luxembourg	75.1	68.0	1.12
Netherlands	79.2	72.5	0.84
New Zealand	76.4	69.7	1.25
Norway	79.0	72.2	0.79
Portugal	75.0	67.0	1.90
Spain	78.0	71.5	0.96
Sweden	78.9	72.6	0.68
Switzerland	79.1	72.4	0.80
Turkey	62.3	58.3	11.0 (1980)
United Kingdom	75.9	70.2	1.02
United States	76.7	69.6	1.09

SOURCES: OECD, *Measuring Health Care, 1960–1983* (Paris: Organization for Economic Cooperation and Development, 1985), p. 131.

of employers to automatically cover families is also a growing problem. In 1980, more than 51 percent of employers who offered health insurance paid the full cost of dependent coverage. By 1988 that number had shrunk to 32 percent. Three-quarters of the 37 million noncovered persons are spouses or children of workers, and one in four workers earning less than a poverty-level income has no health insurance.[61]

The economics of health insurance are particularly problematic for the poor. On the average, purchasing health insurance from an employment-based program costs about $3,500 a year, more than half the yearly income of a minimum wage worker. Almost one in five employers in 1980 contributed nothing toward the coverage of dependents, and from 1980 to 1983, the proportion of employees required to pay part of the premium for family coverage rose from 40 to 50 percent.[62] Only 27 percent of businesses with less than 10 employees offered health insurance in 1990, compared to 98 percent of companies with 100 or more employees.[63] In addition, a 1989 survey found that 46 percent of small businesses in rural areas do not sponsor health insurance, a figure far above the 28 percent of small businesses in urban areas that decline such coverage.[64] In part, these obstacles help to explain why 60 percent of poor working adults in 1988 had some private health insurance coverage, whereas 10.7 million children younger than age 18 went uncovered.

Leaving a large proportion of Americans without any form of health insurance affects all of society. For instance, when the uninsured receive medical care, they may not be able to pay for it; this results in uncompensated care, which includes both bad-debt and charity or free care. Hospitals have traditionally offset the costs of uncompensated care by shifting these costs to patients who had private insurance, Medicare, or Medicaid. The American Hospital Association estimated that 6,438 nonprofit and state and local government hospitals provided a total of $14.6 billion worth of uncompensated care in 1988, a rise from $2.8 billion in 1980.[65] Later estimates suggest that cost shifting was valued at $21 billion in 1991.[66] In addition to cost shifting, some hospitals engage in patient dumping, thereby leaving public hospitals (and those with a historical commitment to serve the poor) with the job of providing health care for those unable to pay. The net result is an increased health risk for the uninsured or underinsured.[67]

Evidence suggests that the overall benefits

of increased health care spending are spurious. For example, although there are an adequate number of health care facilities in the United States, they are maldistributed among and within the 50 states. Some urban areas have a surplus of medical facilities, whereas some rural areas cannot attract a single physician. For example, 111 nonmetropolitan counties in the United States had no physician in 1988. No metropolitan county lacked a physician. In that same year, there were 97 physicians per 100,000 people in nonmetropolitan counties, compared with 225 per 100,000 in metropolitan counties. In 1988, almost 1,500 nonmetropolitan counties lacked an obstetrician and a pediatrician, a figure representing almost two-thirds of all rural counties. From 1981 to 1988 almost 400 community hospitals closed in the United States. About half these hospitals were located in rural areas.[68]

Inadequate care for those relying on the American health care system is exacerbated by gaps in medical coverage even for those who are fully insured. Gaps in private health insurance may include high copayments, limits placed on the length of hospital stays, dollar limits on payments to hospitals and physicians, exclusion of certain laboratory tests, refusal to cover office visits and routine health care, noncoverage for mental health services, declaring ineligible individuals who are found to be in poor health when applying for insurance, refusal to cover preexisting conditions, and a lack of coverage for dental and eye care. Because privately purchased health insurance has become almost unaffordable, the availability of health insurance may be a major factor in an employee's job search or decision to continue in a job. One analyst estimates that "job lock," created when workers are unwilling to leave their current jobs because they fear losing health care benefits due to a preexisting condition or the fear of benefit reductions, results in a $13.6 billion productivity loss each year.[69] Moreover, employers may be reluctant to hire individuals with high-risk conditions because of the negative effect on their

insurance premiums. Lastly, one of the most dramatic gaps is the frequent failure of private health insurance to cover catastrophic medical costs—those costs that could reduce a middle-class family to the status of "medically indigent" within only a few months.

Acquired Immunodeficiency Syndrome (AIDS)

The crisis in U.S. health care is clearly aggravated by the AIDS epidemic, which surfaced during the presidency of Ronald Reagan. A review of public statements and administrative policy indicate that the Reagan administration initially saw the AIDS problem as being of little consequence. Indeed, expressing public concern for the suffering of homosexuals was a political liability, especially since the Republican party was desperately courting the religious right, most of whose leaders, like Jerry Falwell and Pat Robertson, saw AIDS as a divine punishment for the sin of homosexuality. As a result, the Reagan administration did not make an AIDS-related budget request to Congress until FY 1985, by which time 20,000 Americans had already died from the disease. Moreover, this budget request came three years after the alarms had sounded, and after Congress had already allocated $34 million between 1982 and 1983. The approach to AIDS that was to mark both the Reagan and Bush administrations—that is, congressional rather than presidential leadership—was already established by 1983.[70]

The current epidemiological data on AIDS are frightening. Through June 1992, 230,179 AIDS cases had been reported in the United States. Of these 230,179 cases, 4,000 were pediatric AIDS cases (50 percent were directly linked to IV drug use by mothers) and 24,000 were female. More than 152,000 people have died from AIDS in the United States since it was identified in the early 1980s, and some 59 percent of the reported AIDS cases have resulted in death. Although AIDS is quickly spreading within the heterosexual community and among non-IV drug users, the differential impact is still felt the most strongly by the traditionally vulnerable groups. According to the Centers for Disease Control, adult/adolescent AIDS cases break down according to the following risk factors:

Men who have sex with men: 130,822—58 percent

IV drug users: 51,477—23 percent

Men who have sex with men and inject drugs: 14,487—6 percent

Those with hemophilia/coagulation disorder: 1,875—1 percent

Those having heterosexual contacts: 14,045—6 percent

Those undergoing transfusion of blood products: 4,659—2 percent

Other/undetermined factors: 8,916—4 percent[71]

AIDS is maldistributed within racial groupings. Of the 230,179 reported AIDS cases, 120,952 occurred in white males and 65,872 in African-American men. Thus, while African-American males make up about 6 percent of the total U.S. population, they account for almost 25 percent of AIDS victims. This same overrepresentation occurs in pediatric AIDS cases and among women: African-American women and children face twice the risk of contracting AIDS as do white women and white children.[72]

Under the revised definition of AIDS proposed by the Centers for Disease Control, it was possible that there would be more than 400,000 reported AIDS cases by the end of 1992, a number originally projected for mid-1994. AIDS became the second leading cause of death in men aged 25 to 44 in 1992, and one of the top five causes of death in women of the same age group.[73] Middle-range projections suggest that over 5.8 million Americans may be infected by the AIDS virus in 2002.[74] Moreover, 1990 data indicate that AIDS is beginning to spread into smaller cities and rural areas, with an average of 3,000 new cases reported monthly. For exam-

ple, until 1984 five U.S. cities accounted for 63 percent of AIDS cases; by 1990 their share had dropped to 38 percent.[75]

The scope of the AIDS problem extends beyond the borders of the United States. Extraordinary increases in AIDS cases are being reported to the World Health Organization (WHO): AIDS cases in Russia have risen 271 percent since 1988; in Bulgaria, 133 percent; in Poland, 338 percent; and in Romania the number of AIDS cases has increased by an astounding 4,680 percent. Epidemiologists expect the next big explosion in AIDS cases to be in India and East Asia. Asian/Pacific infections were estimated at 500,000 in 1991; by 1992 that estimate had doubled. WHO predicts that by the year 2000 the number of HIV-positive children in sub-Saharan Africa will run in the millions. Moreover, WHO estimates that 10 million people are infected worldwide, a number expected to triple by the year 2000.[76]

The AIDS problem is exacerbated by the inability of the poorer nations to adequately treat PWAs (Persons With AIDS). For example, in 1990 the typical treatment in Tanzania (a country with one physician per 32,000 people) was bed rest and aspirin. The total budget of Zaire's largest hospital was equivalent to the cost of treating 10 AIDS patients in the United States. Moreover, the U.S. military spent $43 million in 1990 to identify 5,890 infected soldiers, a sum greater than Central Africa's total health budget.[77]

The AIDS epidemic is having a dramatic effect on public policy and society at large. For example, at least 10 percent of the U.S. population is somehow affected by AIDS, through contacts with friends, family members, or colleagues. There are also significant costs in treating the AIDS epidemic. Fred Hellinger estimated that in 1991 the average cost of treating a person who was HIV-positive (but without AIDS) was $5,150 per year, and the average cost of treating a PWA was $32,000 per year ($24,000 for inpatient hospital care and an additional $8,000 for other services). The lifetime cost of medical care for a PWA is estimated at $85,333. Although the cost of treating all HIV-infected persons was estimated at $5.8 billion in 1991, Hellinger suggests that this figure will rise to $10.4 billion by 1994.[78] While high, these health care costs are not out of line with the costs of treating other serious traumas. For example, the lifetime health care expenses of someone suffering a major heart attack are $66,837; for cancer of the digestive system, $47,542; and for paraplegia resulting from an auto accident, $68,700.[79]

The AIDS epidemic is costly to American society in other ways. Health care economist Anne Scitovsky estimated that in 1991 the U.S. economy absorbed $55 billion in annual losses in productivity due to illness and premature deaths caused by AIDS.[80] Moreover, the incidence of AIDS is greatest in the group generally thought to be the most productive, the 20- to 44-year-old age group.

AIDS is also having an important impact on health insurance. Private insurers paid $1 billion in AIDS-related health and death claims in 1989, a 71 percent increase over the previous year. AIDS-related insurance payments are expected to reach the $15-billion mark by 1994.[81] As a result, the cost of private health insurance is likely to rise as AIDS-related increases are passed on to employers and policyholders. Some analysts predict that insurance companies may eventually require HIV tests and/or AIDS risk assessments for all potential applicants.

The groups most vulnerable to AIDS are often those least able to afford treatment. For example, IV drug users tend to be disproportionately African American, Hispanic American, and poor. Many, if not most, of these PWAs will gravitate toward Medicaid, thereby further straining a system that is already close to its breaking point. With lifetime health care costs of PWAs estimated at $85,000, if only 100,000 of the projected 400,000 AIDS cases in 1994 occur among the poor, the amount required of Medicaid would be staggering.

AIDS has other important implications for public policy. For one thing, it is likely that the entire health care system will be strained as it tries to meet the enormous medical needs of PWAs, who may live two years or longer with proper care. This tension may be the catalyst for radical health care reforms, such as a universal health care system that is free at point of access or a cap on profits made by medical facilities and pharmaceutical companies. On the other hand, escalating costs may force the adoption of draconian measures such as health care rationing. In the end, the AIDS crisis may force society to decide what and how many resources it will allocate to the care of terminally ill patients. The AIDS epidemic clearly has the potential to shape an important public debate around health care and public priorities.

A COMPARATIVE ANALYSIS: HEALTH CARE IN BRITAIN, ISRAEL, AND CANADA

Often intoxicated by patriotic rhetoric, Americans sometimes overlook what is happening in other parts of the world. The following section briefly explores a continuum of medical systems in three countries: Great Britain (socialized medicine), Israel (an HMO-based system), and Canada (a single-payer system).

The British Health Service

The National Health Service (NHS) is the most enduring pillar of the British Labour party's postwar welfare state. The direct inspiration for the NHS was a 1944 white paper written by Sir William Beveridge for the wartime coalition government. The Beveridge Report maintained that a ''comprehensive system of health care was essential to any scheme for improving living standards.''[82]

The NHS began on July 5, 1948, and, in the words of the act establishing it, the aim was to promote ''the establishment of a comprehensive health service designed to secure improvement in the physical and mental health of the people . . . and the prevention, diagnosis and treatment of illness."[83] The principle of freedom of choice was upheld in that people could either use the NHS or seek outside doctors. Doctors were guaranteed that there would be no interference in their clinical judgment, and they were free to take private patients while participating in the service. The essential goal of the act was to provide free medical services to anyone in need. Moreover, the NHS Act developed a tripartite system: (1) hospital service with specialists; (2) general medical doctors, dentists, and eye doctors, maintained on a contractual basis; and (3) prevention and support systems, provided by local health departments.

The backbone of the NHS is the general practitioner (GP). Patients in Britain are registered with a GP who provides family care. GPs are paid by the NHS on the basis of an annual capitation fee for each registered patient; in 1981 the average list was 2,200 patients. Roughly half of a GP's income comes from capitation payments, with the rest made up by allowances for services such as contraceptive advice and immunization. The role of the GP is to provide primary medical care and they are forbidden to restrict their practice to any special client group. Individuals can register with any GP provided the doctor is willing to accept them. GPs see almost 75 percent of their registered patients at least once a year and, because mobility is low in Britain, many people retain the same GP for a considerable length of time.[84]

The GP has considerable professional latitude and equips his or her own office, hires staff, and may choose to work singly, in pairs, in groups, or in a government health center. Close to 50 percent of all GPs practice in groups of three or more. Health centers, part of the original Health Service Act, mushroomed in the late 1960s and 1970s, and by 1975 there were 600 nationally. Sweeping changes in 1967 gave GPs increased benefits, including a higher capitation rate if they had a patient load of between 2,500 and 3,500. In addition, extra remuneration was provided for each person on their list who was over 65, for night calls, for transients, for maternity care, for family planning services, and for certain preventive measures. GPs also receive partial reimbursement for secretaries, receptionists, and nurses, as well as for the rental costs of their offices. Extra payments are also provided for seniority, postgraduate education, vocational training, for working in groups of three or more, and for practicing in under-doctored areas.[85]

The second tier of the British health care system is the physician specialist. Most patient referrals to specialists—except for accidents and emergency care—are made through GPs. Although employed by the government and under contract to a public hospital, physician specialists are allowed a small private practice. In effect, patients in the community are served by GPs, whereas in the hospital they are under the care of specialists. As in the U.S. health care system, physician specialists are accorded greater prestige and remuneration. Approximately 60 percent of specialists receive extra remuneration in the form of a merit award.[86]

The NHS was reorganized in 1974, and at its head is the Secretary of State for Social Services, the person ultimately responsible to Parliament. The secretary is aided by junior ministers and civil servants in the Department of Health and Social Security (DHSS), a planning and administrative body.[87] In turn, DHSS delegates many of the detailed responsibilities to the next level of administration,[88] the Regional Health Authorities (RHAs).[89] The primary task of the RHAs is to distribute the region's health resources in accordance with national and regional policies. For example, RHAs are responsible for planning hospital and consulting services, appointing hospital staff, and distributing clinical work throughout the regional hospitals.[90] The 14 RHAs delegate activities—retaining primarily planning and supervisory work—by placing the day-to-day activities in the hands of the 192 district health authorities. The district health authorities have the responsibility for studying area health needs, coordinating duties, and providing community health services such as maternal health clinics, district general hospitals, family planning, and various child health programs.[91] The reorganization in 1974 called for the creation of district-level community health councils (CHCs), which are designed to provide citizen participation in a health care system otherwise characterized by professionalized central planning.

The NHS is funded from general taxes, with the proceeds divided among regional health authorities that plan local health services. The regions, in turn, divide their money among districts that pay for hospitals through global prospective budgets.[92] Health services under the NHS are relatively comprehensive, with hospital and primary medical care being free. However, there are significant patient charges for dentistry and eyeglasses and a notational charge for prescriptions (which the elderly do not pay). Drug prices are agreed upon between the health department and the pharmaceutical industry according to a specific pricing formula based on company profits. In addition, the government subsidizes medical education so that the direct cost to the student is low.[93]

Much of the American-based reporting on the NHS has tended to emphasize its flaws. Although some GPs express dissatisfaction with the system, the public continues to use it in large numbers. For example, about 10 percent of Britons have private insurance, but most use it as a supplement rather than as a substitute for the NHS. While some of the insured use private doctors and hospitals, a growing number also use NHS pay-beds and consultants.[94]

The NHS faces serious problems despite its high rate of utilization. For one thing, NHS funding is not based principally on the medical needs of consumers, but rather on how much the British treasury believes it can afford to spend on health care. The result is de facto health care rationing. For example, men over age 55 normally cannot get kidney dialysis through the NHS; consumers complain of long waits in GP offices; and hospital buildings are often in poor shape. Moreover, there are long waiting lists (1 million or more people) for elective surgery. (There is believed to be little wait for urgent surgery.) On the other hand, research has shown that the long waiting lists are misleading in that they often include people who have died, moved, or already had their operations or who have been kept waiting by consultants who want to secure more resources (or more private patients).[95]

Critics also complain that NHS hospital funds are doled out in a haphazard manner. For example, significant funds are spent on health care facilities in fast-emptying city centers rather than in burgeoning population centers. One of the reforms suggested to remedy this problem is the creation of "internal markets," whereby the distribution of money within the NHS would follow patients rather than the other way around. An even more important problem is that hospitals receive nothing extra for efficiently treating more patients at less cost, which results in less incentive to improve efficiency.[96]

Other critics charge that despite government efforts, there are serious shortages of doctors in certain parts of Britain. Furthermore, expenditures and resources under the NHS seem to be slanted toward hospitalization rather than toward primary, first-level care. In addition, critics complain about the lack of accountability of doctors and about strong unions that have supported restrictive practices and fought attempts to privatize support services (e.g., cleaning). Critics of the NHS also charge that except for the capitation fees, money does not flow to doctors in accordance with their work loads.[97] Finally, other critics charge that the inequality in the British health system has resulted in higher disease and mortality rates for lower socioeconomic groups.

Despite these criticisms, the NHS appears to be serving the majority of the British population as well as, and in some ways better than, the American health care system. For example, per capita health care expenditures in Britain are considerably lower than they are in the United States—$836 per capita versus $2,354 per capita. (Much of this lower cost is attributable to the success of GPs in keeping down hospital admission rates and to the relatively low administrative costs of the NHS.) Despite the lower cost of the British health care system, most health indicators (e.g., life expectancy, infant mortality rates) are equivalent to or better than those found in the more expensive U.S. health care system. Enoch Powell, a former health minister, summed up the dilemma of the NHS:

> One of the most striking features of the NHS is the continual, deafening chorus of complaints which rises day and night from every part of it, a chorus only interrupted when someone suggests that a different system altogether might be preferable . . . it presents what must be a unique spectacle of an undertaking that is run down by everyone engaged in it.[98]

The Israeli Health Care System

The Israeli health care system was chosen as an example because it represents a unique blend of private and public health care provision. Specifically, the social organization of Israeli health care functions somewhat like a large governmentally subsidized HMO.

The Israeli health care system is based on voluntary or semivoluntary health insurance in public nonprofit sick funds, known as Kupat Holim. Most of the sick funds have a long-standing political identity or are somehow affiliated with political groups. The largest of these sick funds, the General Kupat Holim, is run by the Histadrut (the General Federation of Labor) and is politically affiliated with the Israeli labor movement. The General Kupat Holim covers nearly 70 percent of the total population. The other, smaller sick funds cover an additional 24 percent. The current arrangement provides

health insurance coverage to about 94 percent of the country's population.[99]

The General Kupat Holim developed at an important juncture in the history of Israel. Specifically, it was a time when most of the population had a low standard of living, when there was an abundant supply of doctors with a relatively weak professional organization, and when the medical profession contained a strong body of opinion that identified with the collective aims of the country. Under these circumstances, the General Kupat Holim and the other sick funds were able to flourish and thus provide their members with a comprehensive range of medical services.

In recent years there has been a significant change in the membership of the various sick funds. In the mid-1980s the General Kupat Holim covered 85 percent of the employee population and about 70 percent of the nonworking population. However, the membership of employees in the General Kupat Holim has declined in recent years, and by 1989 only 76 percent of employees remained while the others moved to smaller sick funds.[100]

The General Kupat Holim system operates in the following manner. Employees who belong to the Histadrut (the labor union) can join the General Kupat Holim, with employers and employees sharing the cost of coverage. Insured individuals and their families receive service through clinics that are scattered throughout the country or from private doctors under contract to the General Kupat Holim system. Most medical care is free at the point of access and throughout the entire process of treatment. In addition, most drugs are subsidized by the Kupat Holim, and in 1992 they cost about $1.00 per prescription. Similar to the NHS, specialist services in the Kupat Holim require a referral through a primary care physician. Hospital care is provided through governmental, for-profit, or private nonprofit hospitals. Finally, all General Kupat Holim doctors have the option of establishing a private practice in their off-hours. Given the relatively low income of Kupat

Holim-employed doctors (about $1,300 per month in 1992), many take advantage of this option. Apart from the General Kupat Holim, there are other smaller HMOs available that do not require labor union or political party affiliation. All Israeli HMOs offer similar coverage.

The Kupat Holim system has experienced several difficulties in the past decade, including (1) increased strains in its relationship with doctors, (2) the growing cost of medical care, (3) the changing attitudes of the Israeli government toward the Kupat Holim system, and (4) the negative impact of increased bureaucratization on its consumer-members. First, the medical profession has become a powerful organization that militantly promotes the interests of its members. As a result, doctors' strikes grew in frequency throughout the 1980s and regularly undermined the delivery of medical care. Second, the cost of medical care in Israel has risen sharply over the last two decades. This increase is attributable to several factors. One is that the rapid growth in the elderly population has led to higher costs. In addition, the effect of the "global medical economy" is being felt in Israel. In particular, the growth of medical technology in the Western world has dramatically raised consumers' expectations of medical care, especially among the middle classes. No longer content with an emphasis on primary care, consumers expect state-of-the-art medical care replete with the newest and most sophisticated technology. This problem is exacerbated as doctors returning from postgraduate training in North America and Western Europe demand that Israeli hospitals and medical schools provide the same level of facilities, laboratories, and medical equipment as the places in which they were trained. Their expectations result in higher medical costs, especially in the areas of hospital and specialist services.

Third, the main sources of income for the sick funds are based on the contributions paid by insured members, a parallel health insurance tax paid by employers, and health care fees paid directly by consumers. While all of these costs have rapidly increased in the past decade, the wages and incomes to which these contributions are linked have remained static. The income of the sick funds has inevitably lagged behind the costs, especially for the General Kupat Holim, which covers most of the low-income population. Finally, the direct contribution of the government to the sick funds decreased sharply during the 1980s. For instance, government contributions fell from 7 percent of the total sick fund expenditure in 1984 to only 2 percent in 1988.[101]

Several proposals to reform the Israeli health care system have surfaced in the past few years. For example, new complementary private health insurance plans are being launched to cover medical services that were intended to be covered by the existing sick fund arrangements. Also, private medical practice is spreading within government-owned and nonprofit health care facilities. Both these measures are basically indirect or hidden forms of privatization, and they have significant effects on access to medical care, especially for weaker population groups.[102]

In general, most Israelis want the Kupat Holim system to continue because it has served them well. This system ensures reasonable access to most medical services at no cost at the point of entry. Experience has shown that private medical care is simply beyond the means of the majority of the people. At the same time, there are widespread feelings about the need to rid the Kupat Holim of some of the cumbersome bureaucratic features it has acquired.[103]

The Canadian Health Care System

The current Canadian health care system began 27 years ago, when a hospital insurance plan in Saskatchewan evolved into a network of plans developed by each of Canada's ten provinces and two territories.[104] Canada's Medicare program is a nationwide, federal/provincial health insurance system that is publicly funded, privately delivered, and free at the point of access.[105] Although the insurance plans of the ten provinces and two territories are unique, all are essentially universal and comprehensive, covering all residents for inpatient and outpatient hospital and physician services. To receive federal funds, the plans must meet national eligibility standards: (1) They must be universal and apply to all residents; (2) they must be portable and cover residents who are temporarily away from home or who move to another province; (3) they must be comprehensive and cover all medically necessary services; and (4) they must be free at point of access and incorporate no financial barriers to care. Each province is responsible for administering its own health care plan.[106]

Unlike the U.S. system, health care in Canada is grounded in the idea of universal entitlement rather than employment. All of Canada's 25 million residents are eligible for provincial health insurance, except for segments covered by other federal programs (e.g., the military). The practices of extra physician billing and hospital user charges were eliminated with the passage of the Canada Health Act of 1984.[107]

General practitioners (GPs) make up the majority of physicians in the system and provide most of Canada's health care. Specialists can be used only if a referral is received from the GP. Although patients may choose their primary-care physician, the choice is contingent upon whether the physician has openings for new patients. Patients also use the hospital in which the physician has admitting privileges. Besides providing free physician and hospital care, most provinces also cover the cost of travel and medical services if the treatment cannot be obtained in the area where the patient resides. While health care is free at the point of access, some services not covered include out-of-hospital drugs, dental services, eyeglasses, physical therapy, and chiropractic care not ordered by a medical doctor.[108]

Contrary to some misconceptions, the Canadian health care system is not based on socialized medicine; instead, it is a social insurance model that mixes public funds with private health care delivery. Canada's single-payer model is based on the provincial governments being single-source payers of health care with a centralized locus of control. As such, Canada's provincial governments reimburse both hospitals and physicians on a prospective budgeting basis. Specifically, private physicians' fees are negotiated between the provincial governments and the medical associations. Reimbursements for physicians are on a fee-for-service basis. The salaries of physicians in Canada are generally 85 percent of those of their American counterparts. However, because of budgetary problems, several provinces have limited the earnings of physicians. In addition, some provinces are currently considering placing a limit on the number of doctors to be licensed and ending the fee-for-service policy.[109]

There are at present 1,250 hospitals in Canada, of which 57 percent are run by religious orders or nonprofit organizations. Hospital reimbursements are made on a global prospective basis. In other words, hospitals operate on a negotiated but fixed yearly budget. As such, they must stay within the budgetary allotment granted by the province regardless of the number of patients seen in a year.[110]

Funding for Canada's Medicare system is based on a mixture of federal and provincial funds. Federal funds are transferred to the provinces through block grants and transfer payments as specified in the Canada Health Act of 1984. Provincial funds to operate the medical system are derived from general revenue taxes, and, in the case of Alberta and British Columbia, from insurance premiums paid for by employers. In provinces where premiums are charged, exemptions or subsidies are provided for the aged, the unemployed, and the indigent.[111]

Critics of the Canadian health care system point to numerous problems facing the system. One of the most important of these is the question of funding. In 1990, the Canadian Parliament passed the Expenditure Restraint Act, which froze all federal support to provincial health plans at the 1990 level. Cutbacks in government spending (from 1981 to 1992 the Canadian government cut transfer payments to the provinces by almost $8 billion), an ongoing recession, increasing demands for services, and the high cost of technology have made controlling costs—estimated at $50 billion in 1990—the number one issue facing the Canadian health care system. As a result, the province of Ontario was expected to lose 3,300 hospital beds and 4,300 full-time equivalent hospital staff in 1992. The "cure" being discussed for these problems is a massive downsizing of the Canadian health care system, particularly the hospital sector.[112]

Some critics charge that the prospective hospital global budgeting system has caused health care rationing. These critics argue that Canadian hospitals have coped with budgetary constraints by closing down hospital wards during certain times of the year, by filling up one-third of hospital beds with long-term elderly patients to keep high-volume (and expensive) traffic down, by using cheaper medical materials, by rushing medical procedures and thus curtailing accuracy, by providing substandard hospital care, by not investing in technology or capital improvements, and by prioritizing illnesses into "urgent," "emergent," and "elective" cases, thereby causing artificial queues for treatment.[113] According to these critics, health care rationing is having a dramatic effect on Canada's medical system: The wait in Canada for a cataract removal is four months; for a coronary bypass it is over five months; and for a hernia repair Canadians wait over five and a half months. It is estimated that about 260,000 Canadians are currently awaiting surgery.[114]

Several health care analysts have suggested that the United States should adopt a health care reform package similar to the Canadian model.[115] They argue that a single-payer system allows for greater control of systemwide health care capacity—that is, supply, distribution, and costs—than a fragmented insurance system in which no party has the overall authority for controlling the production and distribution of medical goods and services. These analysts point to the failure of previous federal attempts to control costs (e.g., DRGs, certificates of need) without directly controlling global reimbursement rates.

Health care analysts also point to the uneven coverage provided to Americans under the present patchwork of private and public health insurance plans. Compared to the universal, comprehensive, and publicly funded health care system that Canadians have, most Americans are forced to purchase employer-based health insurance offering coverage that ranges from minimal to comprehensive, depending on the type of policy. Moreover, a significant number of Americans fall through the cracks in health insurance; they receive no employment-based health insurance and they are ineligible for Medicaid or Medicare. Critics claim that a Canadian-style universal health care policy would ensure all Americans adequate medical care without regard to their ability to pay or the generosity of their employers.

Perhaps the most formidable argument for the United States to adopt a Canadian-style health care system is provided by an examination of leading health indicators and per capita health care spending. Health care analysts point out that before Canada adopted its health care system in 1966, it lagged behind the United States in both infant mortality and life expectancy (two recognized indicators of the health of a nation). Impressive gains now place Canada ahead of the United States on both health indicators. Moreover, in 1989 Canada was able to achieve those gains by spending only 8.7 percent of its GNP on health care, compared with 11.8 percent spent by the United States. Although health care costs have also been rising in Canada, they are doing so at a lower rate than in the United States.[116]

Factors that influence lower health care costs in Canada include lower physician and administrative costs and less concern with malpractice litigation. In 1985 the per capita physician expenditure in Canada was $202 (calculated in U.S. dollars) compared with $347 in the United States. According to the *Journal of the American Medical Association*, the higher per capita expenditure in the United States is explained entirely by higher fees, because the quantity of physician visits per capita is actually lower in the United States than in Canada. Fees for procedures in the United States are more than three times as high as they are in Canada; the difference in fees for evaluation and management services are about 80 percent lower in Canada.[117] Part of the difference in fee structures may be related to the lower rates of malpractice litigation in Canada. For example, fewer malpractice suits may place less pressure on Canadian doctors to practice the defensive (and costlier) medicine that their American counterparts frequently practice.

Because Canadian health care is based on a single-payer system, overhead costs run at about 3 percent, compared with the private U.S. health insurance companies, which operate at 8 percent. In part, this is due to the significant portion of America's health care budget that goes for advertising and billing. Because of prospective billing, the Canadian system does not require advertising.[118] Moreover, the single-payer system also lessens the paperwork load on physicians, thereby freeing them to see more patients. One indicator of the success of Canada's health care system is that the majority of Canadians are generally satisfied with it. In contrast, 89 percent of Americans in a Harvard University poll conducted in the early 1990s thought that the American system needed either fundamental change or a completely different structure.[119]

It is difficult to compare the quality of the British, Israeli, and Canadian health care systems with that in the United States. For affluent or middle-class Americans with good health insurance, the U.S. system of health care may well provide the best medical care in the world. And for complex medical procedures that involve sophisticated medical equipment, the American system is probably unequaled. Moreover, unlike the long waits characteristic of the foreign systems discussed, the waiting period for surgery, tests, and other procedures in the United States is relatively short. Finally, American physicians are probably about the best trained in the world. However, the American emphasis on expensive technology is not without a price. Medical care that emphasizes specific diseases rather than primary care and preventive medicine usually results in good care, but for fewer people. On the other hand, systems that emphasize personal and primary care, accessibility, local control, and free or inexpensive out-of-pocket expenses for consumers often reach more people. Thus the health care systems in Britain, Israel, and Canada appear to more equitably distribute health resources than does the American system.

The examination of health care in other industrialized nations raises important questions for American medicine. What is society's responsibility for providing health care to all its members? How much technological medicine can a society afford? How should medical resources be allocated? What, if any, limitations on personal freedom are permissible in the name of promoting health and preventing disease? These and other questions urgently require answers.

The American health care system is in an acute state of crisis. The cost for business of providing health care coverage is escalating more rapidly than inflation and increased profitability combined.[120] This situation led Harold Poling, chief executive officer of the Ford Motor Company, to acknowledge that Ford spends more money on health insurance than it does on steel. According to Poling, 20 percent of Ford's labor costs are paid out for health insurance premiums.[121] American employers paid 9 to 12 percent more for health insurance in 1993 than in 1992.[122]

Much of America's health care crisis is based on runaway medical costs. In particular, it is grounded in the failure of either the market-place or the federal government to curb health care expenditures, an overreliance on medical technology at the expense of providing primary health care services, the failure of cost containment measures in Medicaid and Medicare, the growth in health care administrative costs, and an upsurge in the number of employed workers and their families who cannot afford any form of health care coverage. Furthermore, huge expenditures on health care in the United States are not reflected in greater longevity, lower rates of infant mortality, or in any other indicator of a healthier nation. This frustration has led some observers to propose alternative schemes for American medicine.

ALTERNATIVE PROPOSALS FOR THE AMERICAN HEALTH CARE SYSTEM

Numerous schemes for health care reform have been put forward on both the national and state levels. For example, there were nearly 50 different health care bills in the U.S. Congress in 1992.[123] In general, proposals to remedy America's health care problems fall into two broad categories: (1) reform of the present system, and (2) a radical restructuring of health care. This section will examine some of these proposals for health care reform.

Most reform-oriented health care proposals can be divided into four categories: (1) employer mandates, (2) the expansion of current arrangements, (3) the use of tax incentives, and (4) the fine-tuning of the health care marketplace. One employer-based health care proposal currently under discussion is the "play-or-pay" option. This proposal would require employers to provide a minimum level of health care coverage to all employees and their dependents. Employers could provide health insurance directly to their employees, thus following governmental guidelines as to the breadth of the insurance coverage and the proportion of the premiums to be paid by the employer. Employers would also have

the option of paying a fixed percentage of their payroll (or a fixed percentage up to a maximum limit per worker) into a pool, whose funds would cover the cost of health insurance for employees and their dependents. This insurance pool could be organized by the public sector and would offer health insurance to those not otherwise covered (e.g., the unemployed and those absent from the labor market). Individuals insured through this arrangement are likely to pay a significant portion of the costs of coverage. Companies with few workers could be exempted from this requirement. The current health care system in Hawaii is an example of play-or-pay in that all employees (but not their dependents) who work 20 or more hours per week are covered. The Medicaid and Medicare programs would remain basically intact under the play-or-pay option.[124]

The second option would permit various persons (i.e., vulnerable populations) to buy into Medicare or Medicaid. Specifically, this group would be composed of Americans who are not poor enough to qualify for Medicaid, but not rich enough to purchase private health insurance—the "working poor." In addition, all pregnant women, infants, young children, disabled persons, and those who retire before age 65 would be given access to one of these public programs. Medicaid and Medicare premiums would be proportional to income.[125]

A third set of proposals would modify current tax incentives around health insurance. The first option in this series of proposals would be a tax subsidy for the purchase of employer-based coverage. By omitting the employer's contribution to health insurance from an employee's income, this scheme would eliminate both payroll and income taxes on this component of compensation. The second tax subsidy would be connected to the federal income tax. Specifically, a person could claim a tax deduction for medical expenditures (including privately paid health insurance premiums) that were greater than 7.5 percent of gross adjusted income. George Bush favored a system of tax incentives and vouchers that would in theory allow all Americans to purchase their own health insurance. In effect, the poor would be given vouchers to purchase health insurance, while the better off would receive progressive tax deductions for the price of their insurance.[126]

One example of a reform-oriented health care bill was the stillborn Massachusetts Health Security Act. Signed by Governor Michael Dukakis in 1988, this bill would have required Massachusetts employers to pay a minimum amount toward each employee's health insurance. By 1992, everyone in Massachusetts was to have been able to purchase health coverage. Premiums were to be adjusted to the purchaser's income and subsidized by the state and employers. The self-employed, workers in large and small businesses, the unemployed, students, mothers, children, and the disabled were to be matched to an insurance offering. Employers with six or more employees would have been required to pay $1,680 per employee for health insurance provided either by the employer or through the state. Employers and hospitals were to pay a small tax to help subsidize the unemployed. The law did not compel anyone to accept or pay for health insurance, and Massachusetts was to have a special hospital fund for the uninsured.[127] The bill was never implemented, however, because of the budget crisis in Massachusetts.

Another variation of health care reform is managed competition, which is an attempt to fine-tune the health care marketplace. Based on neoclassical economic theory, managed competition is grounded in the belief that the health care system should replicate efficient markets. Managed competition assumes that if all health care consumers are cost-conscious and choose their health plan based on cost and quality, the medical services market will respond as any other market. As such, managed competition is based on reforming the economic incentives driving the health care market. It embodies a belief in the substitution of "cost-conscious-

ness" for "cost-unconsciousness," thereby providing a disincentive for overtreatment and an end to the philosophy of open-ended treatment without fiscal limitations. Supporters of managed competition argue that the behavior of consumers and providers must be governed by market consequences.[128]

The idea of managed competition was further expanded upon by an ad hoc group of health care professionals meeting in Jackson Hole, Wyoming. Referred to as the Jackson Hole Group, these professionals reiterated the need for cost consciousness in health care, and the need for substantial investment in outcome and evaluation research. The Jackson Hole Group proposed a plan called the 21st Century American Health System, which would establish a health care system based on universal access (all individuals would have health benefits from some source) and cost consciousness. To achieve these goals the group advocated the establishment of two mechanisms: health insurance purchasing cooperatives (HIPCs) and accountable health partnerships (AHPs).[129]

HIPCs would function as collective purchasing agents for consumers. In effect, they would bring together large numbers of consumers and channel their combined purchasing power to create an economy of scale. HIPCs would be created by states as semiprivate entities, each managed by an elected board of directors. During biannual meetings, enrollees could decide to change providers or benefit packages. States would be divided into regions, with each served by a HIPC. Under the Jackson Hole plan, benefits would consist of a uniform, basic, and universal health benefits package. Individuals wishing more extensive coverage would shoulder the additional cost. Preexisting health conditions would no longer be a barrier to coverage. AHPs would function as providers that integrate the twin functions of health care delivery and insurance, and they would facilitate coordinated care that stresses primary care and prevention. In effect, AHPs would control costs because reimbursement would be capitated (based on a uniform per capita fee), thereby creating an incentive for providers to control the use of technology and to use early (and cheaper) interventive strategies. AHPs would also be required to monitor quality and effectiveness and to report those results to the HIPCs. In summary, HIPCs would create large buying cooperatives, thereby ensuring that all Americans enjoy the benefits of an economy of scale as well as universal coverage. Moreover, HIPCs would purchase services from those AHPs that offer uniform, effective benefit packages subject to quality-based monitoring. The socialization of health care costs would prevent the segmentation of the market into groups of sick versus well individuals.[130]

Although managed competition appears to fit within the American experience, it is also seriously flawed. For one, it may not be far-ranging enough to counter the special interests within the American health care community, especially insurance companies, physician organizations, hospital associations, and so forth. Secondly, without the yoke of a global budgeting system (such as the Canadian model), little incentive exists to keep health care costs under control. Thus, instead of restraining health care expenditures, high costs may simply be passed on to HIPCs and in the end to the consumer and the government. Thirdly, flaws exist in the basic premise of the managed competition model. Specifically, health care cannot replicate a real market because it is an inelastic commodity (i.e., it is not responsive to market forces of supply, price, and demand). For example, after examining issues of price, quality, and technological sophistication, the rational consumer may decide to delay the purchase of a personal computer until prices fall, or to shop unhurriedly to find the best computer at the best price. As a response, dealers and manufacturers may decide to increase quality and drop prices in order to attract more customers. The computer market is therefore in a continual state of adjustment. Companies that are insensitive to consumer preferences, or cannot control costs, are dislodged from the marketplace as they watch

their market share plunge. The well-known struggles of IBM are a case in point. However, consumers facing serious health problems may not be able to shop around for the best quality and the best service at the best price. Moreover, many consumers cannot accurately judge the quality of the health care they receive. A man having undergone heart catheterization may feel that his surgery went well and that he received excellent treatment. However, he may be unaware that his surgery could have been unnecessary in the first place. Attempts to apply quasi free market principles to health care are inevitably fraught with difficulties. The inherent danger in managed competition is also its tendency to encourage the growth of large provider organizations. While these organizations may initially offer consumers better services at lower costs, this system may also lead to provider monopolies that will eventually provide lower quality yet expensive health services.

According to Terri Combs-Orme, a progressive reconstruction of the health care system must be grounded in the following principles:

1. Accessible health care should be a universal right of all Americans, not a privilege to be purchased or earned.

2. The quantity, quality, and accessibility of health care should be equal for all, not dependent on income or categorical status. No health care system should result in differential quantity, quality, or accessibility of care based on income, gender, age, or any other criterion.

3. Health care should not be linked to employment. A majority of Americans purchase health care insurance through their place of employment, but the fear of job loss or other issues not under their control undermines the security of this arrangement and limits their job mobility.

4. The quality, quantity, and accessibility of health care should not vary according to state.

5. A progressive health care system should balance the needs and rights of children and the elderly in a fair and rational way.

6. A comprehensive health care system should include coverage for and accessibility to long-term care for the elderly.[131]

The United States is one of the few industrialized countries in the world that does not have a comprehensive plan for national health insurance or socialized medicine. Moreover, the United States is one of the few industrialized countries where medical expenses can cause poverty. One 1980 study found that although roughly 85 percent of all people had medical coverage (private insurance or public programs), only 29 percent had coverage that protected them from catastrophic or major medical expenses; only 40 percent were covered for outpatient doctor costs; only 44 percent were covered for nursing home care; and less than 20 percent of the population was covered for prescription drugs.[132]

One proposal for radically restructuring the health care system on a single-payer basis is Senate Bill 2817 (The National Health Care Act of 1992). Supported by the National Association of Social Workers and modeled after the Canadian system, this bill calls for a single-payer national health care system. As with the Canadian model, states would have responsibility for ensuring delivery of health services, for paying all providers, and for planning in accordance with federal guidelines. Private health insurance coverage would be discontinued.[133] Supporters of this bill claim that it would immediately reduce health care spending by 18 percent ($150 billion). Moreover, they argue that a ''single-spigot'' would reduce the fraud that is endemic to a multiple payer system.[134]

Another proposal to restructure America's health care system is National Health Insurance (NHI). NHI proposals date back to the turn of the century. According to sociologist Paul Starr, the United States was on the brink of establishing national health insurance a number of times during the twentieth century, but each time factors unique to the political and social institutions of America prevented its adoption.[135] In the 1930s, NHI plans began to proliferate as part of Roosevelt's New Deal, but the idea was abandoned because of the strident opposition of the American Medical Association (AMA)—originally a supporter of NHI—and the fear that its inclusion would jeopardize passage of the Social Security Act. President Harry Truman took up the NHI banner in the days following World War II, but by that time most middle-class and unionized workers were covered by private insurance plans. Moreover, the AMA again set its powerful lobbying machine into motion, this time equating national health insurance with socialized medicine and with Communism, a tactic that proved successful during the ''red hysteria'' of the late 1940s and early 1950s. NHI bills were introduced in Congress every year between 1935 and 1965, and every year they failed.[136]

Of the several national health insurance plans that have been advanced, the most comprehensive one was proposed in the 1970s by Senator Edward Kennedy (and a number of successive coauthors). The Kennedy plan, supported by large segments of organized labor, included a National Health Board that would be appointed by the president to develop policy guidelines, manage the program, and plan and direct the yearly federal health budget. In addition, a national health insurance corporation would be developed to collect tax premiums from workers and disperse them to private insurance companies, which would then process all claims. Under this system every American would have compulsory health insurance: Workers would be insured through their employers, the poor through a special federal insurance fund. Based on its broad coverage, the Kennedy plan would have eliminated the need for Medicare and Medicaid.[137]

Critics of NHI argue that it would modify

payment mechanisms rather than encourage major changes in the health care system. They claim that the nature of private medical practice would remain intact, as would the organization of hospitals and other health institutions. Although NHI schemes would equalize the ability of patients to pay, they would not improve the accessibility or quality of services. Furthermore, most NHI proposals call for coinsurance (copayments), a sum that many poor people would not find affordable.[138] Contrary to what some critics claim, NHI schemes are not socialized medicine: Hospitals would remain private, doctors would continue to be private practitioners, and most plans preserve a major role for private insurance companies. In the end, the general profitability of the health care industry would remain in the hands of those who prosper from the current arrangement, although coverage would be provided to the entire population.

The creation of a National Health Service (NHS) is the most radical proposal for reforming the American health care system. Since the mid-1970s, left-wing health planners have worked with certain members of Congress to draft proposals for a National Health Service. Proposed by Congressman Ronald Dellums (a social worker) in the late 1970s, the National Health Service (NHS) would establish health care as a right of citizenship. Similar to the British model, the NHS would provide free (no fee at the point of access and no indirect payments from third-party vendors) and comprehensive health care, including diagnostic, therapeutic, preventive, rehabilitative, environmental, and occupational health services. Also included would be free dental and eye care, emergency and routine transportation to medical facilities, child care, homemaking, social work, and counseling. To improve the maldistribution of medical services, the NHS would provide free medical education in return for required periods of service in medically underserved areas. In addition, poor communities would receive extra resources for funding, personnel, and equipment needs.[139]

The financing of the NHS would come from progressive taxation on individual and corporate income, supplemented by a gifts and estate tax. The goal of the NHS would be the elimination of private profit in the health care system, and a national commission would be responsible for establishing a formulary of drugs, equipment, and supplies, with regional branches purchasing these goods in their inexpensive generic forms. Although private insurance companies would have no role in the NHS, the Dellums bill is vague as to whether private medical practice would be abolished.[140]

Proponents argue that the nationalization of health care would allow coordination of health services and reduce profiteering by professionals and corporations. Moreover, these planners believe that the experience of other countries shows that strict budgeting, nationalization, and the elimination of the profit motive arrests the escalation of health costs and that, in the end, it may prove less expensive than the present system. Although the NHS appears unlikely to be adopted in the near future, the reality of the present does not always dictate the future. As illustrated by the New Deal programs of the 1930s, Americans can make abrupt changes in a short period of time, and naysayers who predict more of the same are wrong as often as they are right.

Left unchecked and convulsed by wildly escalating costs, health care in America may someday be out of reach for the majority of citizens. Moreover, the increasing share of the GNP and the federal budget currently allocated to health care may soon reach a saturation point, making it unaffordable for all but the most well-off. Although the likely outcome of the American health care crisis is unknown, what is known is that left solely to the caprice of the marketplace the situation will undoubtedly worsen.

DISCUSSION QUESTIONS

1. The American health care system currently costs over $900 billion a year. Moreover, its cost has risen dramatically over the past 25 years in terms of the actual amount spent, the percentage of the GNP used for health care, and the per capita costs of health care. What are the main factors that have driven up health care costs? Can these factors be controlled? If so, how?

2. Some of the most striking increases in health care costs have occurred in the area of Medicaid and Medicare. What are the major factors contributing to the steep rise in Medicaid and Medicare costs? What can be done to stabilize these costs?

3. Some critics charge that Medicare and Medicaid costs cannot be brought under control without radically reforming the entire health care system. They argue that incremental reforms in the Medicare and Medicaid programs will have only a minuscule impact on the steep increase in federal and state expenditures for health care. Are these critics correct? If so, why? If not, why not?

4. Evidence of the effectiveness of the DRGs in curbing federal health care expenditures has been mixed, although generally negative. Critics charge that not only has the DRG system failed to substantially reduce health care costs, but it has also led to a reduced level of patient care. Is the DRG system successful? If so, should it be used as a model for further health care reforms? What changes, if any, should be made in the DRG system in order to make it more cost-effective and more responsive to the health care needs of the populations affected by it?

5. Many critics charge that there is a serious health care crisis in the United States. Describe the main characteristics of that crisis (e.g., health care costs, issues of accessibility and noncovered populations, U.S. health indicators compared with those of other nations).

6. The AIDS epidemic promises to be one of the most important public health issues facing the global community in the coming decades. Some critics insist that more money should be spent on basic AIDS research, outreach, and treatment. Other critics argue that AIDS is only one of many health care problems facing the United States and other countries around the world. They argue that the money spent on AIDS research should be in proportion to the numbers affected by the disease, which are relatively small when compared to those suffering from cancer and heart disease. Is AIDS a significantly more important public health problem than cancer, heart disease, or the effects of drugs, alcohol, and tobacco? Should the federal governmental spend proportionally more on AIDS research than on other diseases? If so, why?

7. Several health care analysts are calling for radical reform in the U.S. health care system. Many of these analysts insist that America's free market system of health care must be replaced by a more cost-effective and comprehensive system of health care. Assuming that these health care analysts are correct, which of the health care systems described in this chapter (the British, Israeli, or Canadian) would be the best model for the United States to emulate and why?

8. Many health care proposals currently exist for reforming the American health care system. Which of these proposals offers the best chance for positively restructuring the U.S. health care system and why?

NOTES

1. Terri Combs-Orme, "Should the Federal Government Finance Health Care for All Americans?: Yes," in Howard Jacob Karger and James Midgley, eds., *Controversial Issues in Social Policy* (New York: Allyn and Bacon, 1993).

2. Irving J. Lewis and Cecil G. Sheps, *The Sick Citadel* (Boston: Oelgeschlager, Gunn, and Hain, 1983), p. 16.

3. Committee on Ways and Means, U.S. House of Representatives, *Overview of Entitlement Programs: 1992 Green Book* (Washington, D.C.: U.S. Government Printing Office, 1992), p. 287; Paul Starr, *The Logic of Health-Care Reform*

(Knoxville, Tenn: Grand Rounds Press, 1992), p. 20.

4. Starr, *The Logic of Health-Care Reform*, p. 45.

5. Victor W. Sidel and Ruth Sidel, *A Healthy State* (New York: Pantheon Books, 1983), p. 89.

6. Michael Clemens, "Rising Costs Reflect Many Influences," *USA Today*, May 5, 1993, p. B2.

7. Barbara L. Wolfe, "Changing the U.S. Health Care System: How Difficult Will it Be?" *Focus* 14, no. 2 (Summer 1992):16.

8. U.S. General Accounting Office, *U.S. Health Care Spending Trends, Contributing Factors, and Proposals for Reform* (GAO/HRD-91–102), (Washington, D.C.: U.S. General Accounting Office, 1991).

9. Clemens, "Rising Costs Reflect Many Influences," p. B2.

10. U.S. House of Representatives, *1992 Green Book*, p. 287.

11. U.S. Department of the Census, *Statistical Abstract of the United States, 1991* (Washington, D.C.: U.S. Government Printing Office, 1991), p. 107.

12. Robert G. Frank, "Health-Care Reform: An Introduction," *American Psychologist*, 48, 3 (March 1993):258–260.

13. U.S. House of Representatives, *1992 Green Book*, p. 287.

14. *Methods of Technology Assessment* (Washington, D.C.: National Academy Press, 1991), p. 32.

15. U.S. House of Representatives, *1992 Green Book*, p. 103.

16. "Doctors Under the Knife," *Newsweek*, April 5, 1993, p. 31.

17. J. M. Colwill, "Where Have all the Primary Care Applicants Gone?" *New England Journal of Medicine* 326 (1992):387–392.

18. Clemens, "Rising Costs Reflect Many Influences," p. B2.

19. "Doctors Under the Knife," p. 31.

20. Bob Kerry and Philip J. Hofschire, "Hidden Problems in Current Health-Care Financing and Potential Changes" *American Psychologist* 48, 3, (March 1993):262.

21. Ibid.

22. Congressional Budget Office, *Economic Implications of Rising Health Costs* (Washington, D.C.: Congressional Budget Office, 1992).

23. John H. Goddeeris and Andrew J. Hogan, "Nature and Dimensions of the Problem," in John H. Goddeeris and Andrew J. Hogan, eds., *Improving Access to Health Care: What Can the States Do?* (Kalamazoo, Mich: W. E. Upjohn Institute for Employment Research, 1992), pp. 14–15.

24. Sumner A. Rosen, David Fanshel, and Mary E. Lutz, eds., *Face of the Nation 1987* (Silver Spring, Md: NASW, 1987), p. 75.

25. For a good historical analysis of the Medicare program, see Theodore R. Marmor, *The Politics of Medicare* (Chicago: Aldine, 1973).

26. U.S. House of Representatives, *1992 Green Book*, p. 1628.

27. Wolfe, "Changing the U.S. Health Care System," p. 16.

28. Ibid., p. 19.

29. Isaac Shapiro, Mark Sheft, Julie Strawn, Laura Summer, and Robert Greenstein, *The States and the Poor* (Washington, D.C.: Center on Budget and Policy Priorities, December 1991), p. 37.

30. Ibid., p. 17.

31. Wolfe, "Changing the U.S. Health Care System," p. 16.

32. Children's Defense Fund, *The State of America's Children* (Washington, D.C.: Children's Defense Fund, 1987), pp. 110–18.

33. U.S. House of Representatives, *1992 Green Book*, p. 1646.

34. Rosen et al., *Face of the Nation*, p. 75.

35. Children's Defense Fund, *A Children's Defense Budget*, p. 109.

36. Ibid., p. 107.

37. Rosen et al., *Face of the Nation*, p. 76.

38. Spencer Rich, "Provisions of 'Catastrophic' Insurance Act," *Washington Post*, July 1, 1988, p. A21.

39. Quoted in Marie A. Caputi and William A. Heiss, "The DRG Revolution," *Health and Social Work*, 3, no. 6 (June 1984):5.

40. Ibid., p. 9.

41. U.S. Department of the Census, *Statistical Abstract of the United States, 1991*, p. 100.

42. Ibid.

43. Rosen et al., *Face of the Nation*, p. 75.

44. Ibid.

45. Howard Waitzkin, *The Second Sickness: Contradictions of Capitalist Health Care* (New York: The Free Press, 1983), p. 220.

46. Thomas H. Ainsworth, *Live or Die* (New York: Macmillan, 1983), p. 89.

47. G.J. Schieber and J.P. Poullier, "International Health Care Spending: Issues and Trends," *Health Affairs*, 10 (1991):110.

48. "Doctors Under the Knife," p. 29.

49. Leon Ginsberg, *Social Work Almanac* (Washington, D.C.: National Association of Social Workers, 1992), p. 123.

50. Clemens, "Rising Costs Reflect Many Influences," p. B2.

51. Ginsberg, *Social Work Almanac*, p. 123.

52. U.S. Congressional Budget Office, *Projections of National Health Care Expenditures* (Washington, D.C.: U.S. Congressional Budget Office, 1992).

53. R. Brook, C. J. Kamberg, and A. Meyer-Okaes, *Appropriateness of Acute Medical Care for the Elderly: Analysis of the Literature* (R3717) (Santa Monica, CA: Rand Corporation, 1989).

54. See U.S. Congressional Budget Office, *Projections of National Health Care Expenditures*. See also American Medical Association, *Trends in Health Care* (Chicago: American Medical Association, 1987).

55. Randolph D. Smoak, "Costs Hurt Doctors, Patients Alike," *USA Today,* May 5, 1993, p. A13.

56. Clemens, "Rising Costs Reflect Many Instances, " p. B2

57. Thomas A. Daschle, Rima J. Cohen, and Charles L. Rice, "Health Care Reform: Single-Payer Models," *American Psychologist* 48, no. 3 (March 1993):265–267.

58. Ibid.

59. Employee Benefit Research Institute, *Sources of Health Insurance and Characteristics of the Uninsured: Analysis of the March 1991 Current Population Survey* (Issue Brief No. 123) (Washington, D.C.: Employment Benefit Research Institute, 1992).

60. Richard Kronick, "Health Insurance, 1979–1989: The Frayed Connection Between Employment and Insurance," *Inquiry*, 28 (1991):313–332.

61. Children's Defense Fund, *The State of America's Children* (Washington, D.C.: Children's Defense Fund, 1988), p. 105.

62. Ibid.

63. Health Insurance Association of America, *Survey of Small Business Insurance Practices* (Washington, D.C.: Health Insurance Association of America, 1990), p. 65.

64. Laura Summer, *Limited Access: Health Care for the Rural Poor* (Washington, D.C.: Center on Budget and Policy Priorities, March 1991), p. xv.

65. John M. Herrick and Joseph Papsidero, "Uncompensated Care: What States are Doing," in Goddeeris and Hogan, eds., *Improving Access to Health Care*, pp. 139–40.

66. D. Moran and J. Shields, *Employer Cost-Shifting Expenditures* (Washington, D.C.: Lewin-ICF, 1991), p. 453.

67. John M. Herrick and Joseph Papsidero, "Uncompensated Care: What States are Doing," in Goddeeris and Hogan, eds., *Improving Access to Health Care*, pp. 139–40.

68. Summer, *Limited Access,* pp. xiv–v.

69. W. Greenberg, "Elimination of Employer-Based Health Insurance," in R. B. Helms, ed., *American Health Policy: Critical Issues for Reform* (Washington, D.C.: AEI Press, October 1992), pp. 1–4.

70. Robert Searles Walker, *AIDS: Today, Tomorrow* (New Jersey: Humanities Press International, 1992), p. 134.

71. U.S. Department of Health and Human Services, *HIV/Surveillance*, 2nd Quarter Edition Atlanta: Centers for Disease Control, National Center for Infectious Diseases, July 1992, p. 3.

72. Ibid., pp. 9–10.

73. Walker, *AIDS*, p. x.

74. Ibid., p. 157.

75. Ibid., p. 158.

76. Ibid., pp. x, 158.

77. Eric Ekholm and Jon Tierney, "AIDS in Africa," *New York Times*, September 16, 1990, p. A1.

78. Fred J. Hellinger, "Forecasting the Medical Care Costs of the HIV Epidemic: 1991–1994," *Inquiry* 28 (Fall 1991):213.

79. Walker, *AIDS*, p. 128.

80. Anne A. Scitovsky, "Estimates of the Direct and Indirect Costs of AIDS in the United States," in Alan F. Fleming, ed., *The Global Impact of AIDS* (New York: Alan R. Liss, 1988), p. 156.

81. Walker, *AIDS*, p. 125.

82. Ruth Levitt, *The Reorganised National Health Service* (London: Croom Helm, 1979), p. 15.

83. Quoted in Levitt, p. 17.
84. Sidel and Sidel, *A Healthy State,* p. 144.
85. Ibid., pp. 144, 157–59.
86. Ibid., p. 172.
87. Levitt, *The Reorganised National Health Service,* p. 27.
88. Ibid.
89. Sidel and Sidel, *A Healthy State,* pp. 161–62.
90. Ibid.
91. Ibid., p. 163.
92. "Nye Bevan's Legacy," *The Economist*, July 6, 1992, p. 12.
93. Sidel and Sidel, *A Healthy State,* p. 172.
94. "Nye Bevan's Legacy," p. 12.
95. Ibid.
96. Ibid.
97. Ibid.
98. Quoted in "Nye Bevan's Legacy," p. 12.
99. Most of this section is drawn from Abraham Doron, "The Future of the Israeli Health Care System." Unpublished paper, the Paul Baerwald School of Social Work, The Hebrew University of Jerusalem, 1992.
100. Ibid.
101. Ibid.
102. Ibid.
103. Ibid.
104. W. Barnhill, "Canadian Health Care: Would it Work Here?" *Arthritis Today* 6, no. 6 (November-December 1992):8.
105. Elaine Vayda and R. B. Deber, "The Canadian Health Care System: An Overview," *Social Science and Medicine*, 18, no. 3 (1984):191–97.
106. I. Callaway, "Canadian Health Care: The Good, the Bad, and the Ugly," *Health Insurance Underwriter* (October 1991), pp. 18–35.
107. Jonathan S. Rakich, "The Canadian and U.S. Health Care Systems: Profiles and Policies," *Hospital and Health Services Administration* 36, no. 1 (Spring 1991), pp. 26–27.
108. Barnhill, "Canadian Health Care," p. 19.
109. Ibid.
110. Ibid.
111. Rakich, "The Canadian and U.S. Health Care Systems," p. 32.
112. Cynthia Crosson, "Canadian Health Care is in Critical Condition," *National Underwriter*, January 20, 1992, p. 12.
113. See Barnhill, "Canadian Health Care"; I. Munro, "How Not to Improve Health Care,"

Reader's Digest, September 1992, p. 21; and B. Gilray, "Standing Up for American Health Care," *Health Insurance Underwriter*, February 1992, p. 10.
114. Robert E. Moffitt, "Should the Federal Government Finance Health Care for All Americans?: No," in Howard Jacob Karger and James Midgley, eds., *Controversial Issues in Social Policy* (New York: Allyn and Bacon, 1993).
115. For example, David Himmelstein and Steffie Woolhandler, "A National Health Care Program for the United States: A Physicians' Proposal," *New England Journal of Medicine* 320 (January 12, 1989):102–108; and Terri Combs-Orme, "Should the Federal Government Finance Health Care for All Americans?"
116. Combs-Orme, "Should the Federal Government Finance Health Care for All Americans?"
117. "How Does Canada Do It?: A Comparison of Expenditures for Physicians' Services in the United States and Canada," *Journal of the American Medical Association* 265, no. 19 (May 15, 1991):2474.
118. Combs-Orme, "Should the Federal Government Finance Health Care for All Americans?"
119. Ibid.
120. Wolfe, "Changing the U.S. Health Care System," p. 16.
121. "Clinton's Economic Summit," *The Advocate*, December 11, 1992, p. 1A.
122. Clemens,"Rising Costs Reflect Many Influences, p. B1.
123. "Health Care Reform Legislative Prospects and Industry Impact," *Forecasts*, February 24, 1992, p. 37.
124. Wolfe, "Changing the U.S. Health Care System," p. 17.
125. Ibid.
126. Ibid.
127. Bruce Spitz and Stephen Crane, "Massachusetts Has You Covered," *Los Angeles Times*, August 30, 1988, p. II7.
128. Alain Enthoven and Richard Kronick, "Universal Health Insurance Through Incentives Reform," *Journal of the American Medical Association*, 265, (1991):2532–36.
129. Alain Enthoven, "A Cure for Health Costs," *World Monitor*, April 1992, pp. 34–39.
130. Jeff Bingaman, Robert G. Frank, and Carrie L. Billy, "Combining a Global Health Budget With

a Market-Driven Delivery System," *American Psychologist* 48, no. 3 (March 1993):271–72.

131. Combs-Orme, "Should the Federal Government Finance Health Care for All Americans?"

132. Quoted in Diane M. DiNitto and Thomas R. Dye, *Social Welfare: Politics and Public Policy* (Englewood Cliffs, NJ: Prentice Hall, 1987), p. 226. See also *Health Policy: The Legislative Agenda* (Washington, D.C.: Congressional Quarterly, 1980), p. 11.

133. "Summary of S. 2817, The National Health Care Act of 1992," *NASW-LA News* 16, no. 5 (September/October 1992):2.

134. Daschle et al., "Health-Care Reform," p. 267.

135. Paul Starr, *The Social Transformation of American Medicine* (New York: Basic Books, 1984).

136. Ibid.

137. Ibid .

138. Waitzkin, *The Second Sickness,* p. 218.

139. Ronald V. Dellums et al., *Health Services Act* (H.R. 2969) (Washington, D.C.: U.S. Government Printing Office, 1979). For a good summary of the act, see Waitzkin, *The Second Sickness,* pp. 222–26.

140. Dellums et al., *Health Services Act.*

CHAPTER **12**

Mental Health and Substance Abuse Policy

This chapter reviews the provision of mental health services to the seriously mentally impaired. Prior to the community mental health movement, states were solely responsible for the care of the mentally disturbed. When the movement to improve mental health services through federal assistance to the states stalled, many who suffered from serious mental illness were left without care. This lack of adequate care was made worse by a series of legal decisions that reinforced the civil rights of mental patients while requiring the states to provide adequate services. As a result of these developments, many former mental patients are now living on the streets or in squalid single-room-occupancy hotels. Added to this mental health crisis, problems associated with alcohol and drug abuse are becoming more prevalent. The failure to adequately support substance abuse prevention and treatment efforts, coupled with the economic collapse of inner-city neighborhoods, has left many urban areas subject to unprecedented levels of street violence and social deterioration.

Throughout the history of American social welfare, states have played a prominent role in mental health services. During the nineteenth century, social problems attributable to immigration, urbanization, and industrialization overwhelmed the local poorhouses established during the colonial era. In the United States, Dorothea Dix championed the humane treatment of the mentally disturbed and, by the 1840s, she was instrumental in convincing many states to construct special institutions to provide asylum to the emotionally deranged. In fact, Dix's leadership was so persuasive that Congress passed legislation authorizing federal aid to the states for mental institutions. However, because President Franklin Pierce thought that the federal government should not interfere with the responsibility of the states to ensure social welfare, he vetoed the legislation in 1854.[1] It would not be until more than a century later that the federal government would assume a central role in determining mental health policy through the Community Mental Health Centers Act.

Consequently, mental health policy in the United States was articulated through the various states that operated their own mental hospitals. Originally, state mental hospitals were intended to be self-sufficient communities offering good air, clean water, nutritious food, and healthful activities consistent with the dictates of "moral treatment." Considering the quality of life experienced by many Americans at that time, such refuges were sorely needed. Conditions in rural America were no less dire than the conditions of urban America in the nineteenth century. Some newspaper clippings from an immigrant community in Wisconsin, circa 1890, reveal social conditions that were truly dispiriting.

> The naked body of the wife of Fritz Armbruster, a woman who had worked in Best's Butcher Shop, was found frozen by the roadside near Albion, 6 miles from Black River Falls. She and her husband had separated, he living in town, she living alone in the house. Although no one had noticed that she had been suffering from any physical or mental disorder, 2 years ago, the loss of a child is said to have affected her very deeply and may have led to her becoming partially demented. The probability is that she rose in a fit of delirium and wandered away. . . .

> Mr. Axel, a farmer living about 6 miles east of Kiel, Manitowoc County, cut his wife's throat a few days ago so that she might not recover and then killed himself. There were various rumors as to the cause of the tragedy such as domestic infelicity etc., but a few who had dealings with Axel of late attributed the act to an aberration of mind. . . .

> Milo L. Nichols, sent to the insane hospital a year or two ago after committing arson on Mrs. Nichols' farm is now at large . . . and was seen near the old place early last week . . . . He has proven himself a revengeful firebug.[2]

In response to these psychological casualties, the state hospital served as a haven for the disturbed as well as protection for the community.

> Admitted July 19, 1893. Town of Black River Falls. Norwegian. Married. Age 29. Seven children. Youngest 8 months. Housewife. Poor. First symptoms were manifested . . . when patient became afraid of everything and particularly of mediums. She is also deranged in religion and thinks everyone is disposed to persecute her and to injure her husband. . . . .

> Admitted January 20th, 1896. Town of Garfield. Age 52. Norwegian. Married. Two children, youngest 19 yrs old. Farmer. Poor. Illness began 10 months ago. Cause said to be his unfortunate pecuniary condition. Deluded on the subject of religion. Is afraid of injury being done to him. Relations say he has tried to hang himself . . . September 29, 1896: Discharged . . . improved . . . Readmitted May 4, 1898: Delusion that he and his family are to be hanged or destroyed.[3]

An adverse social climate, coupled with the absence of welfare programs to cushion people against poverty, joblessness, inadequate housing, and illness, served to swell the population of state hospitals. By the 1920s the state hospital was an asylum in name only, and much of the care amounted to merely warehousing patients. In this milieu, some of the scientifically minded reformers of the Progressive era found in the ideas of the eugenics movement a straightforward and surgically precise solution to the problem of state institutions being inundated by "mental defectives." Proponents of the eugenics movement who believed that the human race could be improved by selective breeding argued that mental patients often suffered from hereditary deficiencies, and that generational patterns of mental impairment should be eliminated by sterilization. In that adherents of eugenics were less concerned about the civil rights of individual mental patients than they were about the future of civilization, the fact that some patients might object was merely an inconvenience. In such instances, eugenicists obtained court permission to sterilize patients involuntarily. Many patients, of course, lacked the mental capacity to comprehend sterilization and had no idea that the surgical procedures to which they were subjected would terminate their reproductive lives. By the 1930s, 30 states had passed laws authorizing involuntary sterilization, and by 1935, 20,000 patients had been sterilized, almost half of them in California. Involuntary sterilization of the feebleminded generated great controversy, eventually culminating in a Supreme Court decision, written by Oliver Wendell Holmes, that validated the practice. Tragically, the case on which the decision was based involved a young woman in Virginia who was sterilized, only to be judged psychologically normal years later. The case record upon which Holmes based his decision had been prepared by a social worker.[4]

MENTAL HEALTH REFORM

More humane efforts to reform state institutions invariably involved the National Association for Mental Health (NAMH). Begun early in the century as an extension of the work of Clifford Beers, who had himself recovered after being hospitalized for mental illness, NAMH became critical of the custodial institutions operated by state governments. The issue of mental health attracted wide public attention during World War II, when approximately one in every four draftees was rejected for military service owing to psychiatric and neurological problems.[5] In response to the public outcry about mental health problems, immediately after the war Congress passed the Mental Health Act, which established the National Institute of Mental Health (NIMH). Accompanying the Mental Health Act of 1946 was an appropriation for an exhaustive examination of the mental health needs of the nation. In 1961, NIMH released *Action for Mental Health,* a report that called for an ambitious national effort to modernize the U.S. system of psychiatric care.[6]

As David Mechanic observed, *Action for Mental Health* was a utopian vision of mental health care, the idealism of which conformed

perfectly with a set of extraordinarily propitious circumstances. First, the postwar economy was booming and, with cutbacks in military expenditures, a surplus existed that could be tapped for domestic programs. Second, a new generation of drugs—psychotropic medication—showed promise of being able to stabilize severely psychotic patients who before had been unmanageable. Third, a literature emerged that was critical of the "total institution" concept of the state hospital and implied that noninstitutional—and presumably community—care was better. Finally, because of his experience with mental retardation as a family problem, President John F. Kennedy was supportive of programs that promised to improve mental health care.[7] These political and social circumstances did not go unnoticed by Dr. Robert H. Felix, a physician who had grown up with the Menninger family in Kansas and had developed a sharp critique of the state mental hospital as an institution for the care of the emotionally disturbed. Felix was later to become director of NIMH. A primary architect of the community mental health movement, Felix was able to draw on his extensive experience in the Mental Hygiene Division of the U.S. Public Health Service as well as on the breadth of professional and political contacts that three decades of public service afforded.[8] Felix's objective was as simple as it was radical. He intended to pick up the banner last advanced by Dorothea Dix and reassert the role of the federal government in the nation's mental health policy. Through the community mental health movement, Felix would use federal legislation to reform the archaic state mental hospitals. The legislation that enabled NIMH to reform mental health care was the Community Mental Health Centers Acts of 1963 and 1965.

THE COMMUNITY MENTAL HEALTH CENTERS ACT

Under the unusually advantageous circumstances of the postwar era, the Community Mental Health Centers (CMHC) Act was passed by Congress and signed by President Kennedy on October 31, 1963. The enactment of CMHC legislation was not, however, without obstacles. To allay the American Medical Association's fears that the act represented socialized medicine, the CMHC Act of 1963 appropriated funds only for construction purposes. It was not until 1965, when the AMA was reeling from governmental proposals to institute federal health care programs for the aged and the poor, that funds were authorized for staffing CMHCs. Advocates of the CMHC acts of 1963 and 1965 maintained that a constant target of the legislation was "to eliminate, within the next generation, the state mental hospital, as it then existed."

The strategy of the mental health leadership and their allies was to "demonopolize" the state role in the provision of mental health services and attempt to establish a triad of federal, state, and local support for mental health services. At this time, federal bureaucrats planned to blanket the whole country with comprehensive community mental health services. Their intention was not to federalize the total program through its financing, but to obtain a degree of control through the resulting federal regulations and standards.[9]

The philosophical basis for transferring mental health care from the state hospital to the community was borrowed from public health, which had developed the concept of prevention. In adopting this formulation, proponents of community mental health presumed that services provided in the community would be superior to the warehousing of patients in state institutions. Prevention, according to the public health model, was of three types. *Primary prevention* efforts were designed to eliminate the onslaught of mental health problems. Certain psychiatric disturbances, such as depression and anxiety disorders, seemed to be caused by stress, which could be reduced by eliminating the source of stress. *Secondary prevention* consisted of early detection and intervention to keep incipient problems from becoming more debilitating. For example, screening school children for attention deficit disorders and providing corrective treatment could enhance a child's educational career and, thereby, enhance development throughout adolescence. *Tertiary prevention* consisted of "limiting the disability associated with a particular disorder, after the disorder had run its course." Typically, tertiary prevention activities sought to stabilize, maintain, and—when possible—rehabilitate those with relatively severe impairments.[10] It was clear to the community mental health activists that the state hospital addressed only tertiary prevention (and then poorly), whereas community mental health offered the prospect of combining primary and secondary intervention with a more adequate effort at tertiary prevention. The structure through which prevention would be operationalized was the community mental health center (CMHC).

According to the CMHC acts, the United States was to be divided into catchment areas, each with a population of from 75,000 to 200,000 persons.[11] Eventually, NIMH planned a CMHC for each catchment area, some 2,000 in all.[12] Programmatically, each CMHC was to provide all essential psychiatric services to the catchment area: inpatient hospitalization, partial hospitalization, outpatient services, 24-hour emergency services, and consultation and education for other service providers in the community. Soon after passage of the CMHC Act, child mental health as well as drug abuse and alcoholism services were added to the array of services provided. To make sure that patients were not lost between programs within the CMHC network, a "case manager" role was defined, whereby every case was assigned to one professional who monitored the patient's progress throughout treatment. Financially, NIMH provided funding to disadvantaged catchment areas through matching grants over an eight-year cycle. At the end of the cycle the catchment area was supposed to assume financial responsibility for the CMHC.[13] With this framework, mental health reformers believed that the CMHC was an effective alternative to the state hospital.

DEINSTITUTIONALIZATION

Enthusiasm for community mental health reform ebbed when a series of circumstances, beyond the control of the CMHC architects, began to subvert the movement. Despite promising growth in the number of CMHCs during Johnson's presidency, the Nixon administration did not look favorably on CMHCs and impounded funds appropriated for mental health programs. Although funds were later released, the Nixon administration had clearly stated its disapproval of governmental mental health initiatives. Subsequent legislation to restore momentum to the flagging CMHC movement was crushed by a veto from President Ford. By the time a more sympathetic Carter administration assumed office, economic problems were so serious that additional appropriations for mental health were constrained.[14] Still, at the end of Carter's term, 691 CMHCs continued to receive federal assistance. With the Omnibus Budget and Reconciliation Act of 1981, however, the Reagan administration collapsed all mental health funding into a block grant available to states for any mental health services they deemed fundable. As a result, the designation of CMHCs in direct receipt of federal funds ceased in 1981.[15]

In the meantime, many states planned to shift responsibility for the mentally ill to the CMHCs. In fact, the community mental health movement had proved a timely blessing for officials in states where the maintenance of archaic state hospitals was an increasing economic burden, as noted in Figure 12.1. As the states discharged patients from state institutions, immediate savings were realized; moreover, "the continuing fall in the numbers of patients to be housed provided state governments with plausible reasons for abandoning expensive schemes of capital investment designed to extend and

(or) renovate their existing state hospital systems."[16] Subsequently, 14 state hospitals were closed between 1970 and 1973. The prospect of substantial cost savings through the "deinstitutionalization" of patients received wide support. As governor of California, Ronald Reagan proposed closing all state hospitals by 1980.[17] Unfortunately, the transfer of patients from state institutions to those in the community was not well planned. Through the mid-1970s, the deinstitutionalization movement was characterized by "severe fragmentation of effort and distribution of activity broadly throughout government with little effective coordination at the state or national level."[18] For purely economic reasons, then, state officials were strongly encouraged to facilitate deinstitutionalization regardless of whether or not alternative forms of care were available for those discharged from state hospitals.

Deinstitutionalization was further confounded by a series of judicial decisions in the mid-1970s that enhanced the civil rights of mental patients while at the same time requiring states to provide them with treatment. In *Wyatt v. Stickney,* Alabama District Court Judge Frank Johnson ruled that the state of Alabama was obliged to provide treatment to patients in state hospitals and ordered Governor Wallace and the state to appropriate millions of dollars for that purpose—a judgment with which the state subsequently failed to comply. Shortly thereafter, in *Donaldson v. O'Connor,* the Supreme Court determined that "the state could not continue to confine a mentally ill person who was not dangerous to himself or others, who was not being treated, and who could survive outside the hospital." Finally, in *Halderman v. Pennhurst,* the Third District Court established that institutionalized patients deserved treatment in the "least restrictive alternative."

As a group, these rulings had a profound effect on institutional care for the mentally impaired. Only persons dangerous to themselves or others could be hospitalized involuntarily. For those hospitalized, involuntarily or other-

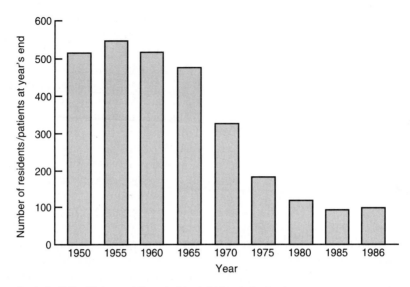

Figure 12.1. Inpatients in U.S., State, and County Mental Hospitals (In thousands). (SOURCE: Elaine Brooks, Maria Zuniga, and Nolan Penn, "The Decline of Public Mental Health," in Charles Willie, Bertram Brown, Bernard Kramer, and Pat Reiker, eds., *Mental Health, Racism, and Sexism* [Pittsburgh: University of Pittsburgh Press, forthcoming 1993].)

wise, states were obliged to provide adequate treatment in a manner that was least restrictive to the patient. These decisions promised to be enormously costly to state officials who were trying to curb mental health expenditures. To comply with the court decisions, states would have to pump millions of dollars into the renovation of institutions that had been slated to be closed. The solution, in many instances, was to use a narrow interpretation of *Donaldson* to keep the emotionally disturbed out of state institutions. Judicial decisions, coupled with the fiscal concerns of state officials, provided a convoluted logic that served as the justification for first emptying state hospitals of seriously disturbed patients and then requiring the manifestation of life-threatening behavior for their rehospitalization. If people were not hospitalized in the first place, the states bore no obligation to provide the adequate, but expensive, treatment demanded by *Wyatt v. Stickney*. The criteria for hospitalization specified the most serious self-destructive behaviors; but, once admitted, pa-

tients were stabilized as quickly as possible, then discharged. As a result, those in greatest need of mental health services, the seriously mentally ill, were often denied the intensive care they needed. The consequences for the mentally ill were substantial. In his interpretation of the legal decisions influencing mental health services, Alan Stone, psychiatrist and professor in the Harvard University School of Law, observed that the true symbol of the Supreme Court *Donaldson* decision was a bag lady.[19] Thus, legal decisions favoring the mentally ill often proved illusory; in the name of enhancing the human rights of the mentally ill—but with no corresponding improvement in services—they offered nothing more than the right to be insane.[20]

THE REVOLVING DOOR

The shortfall of the community mental health movement, state transfers of patients from mental hospitals, judicial decisions assuring patients of their civil rights, and the deinstitutionalization movement in mental health all combined to leave tens of thousands of former mental patients adrift. Although some former mental hospital patients were able to deal with community agencies in order to obtain mental health care, many of the seriously mentally ill were left to themselves.[21] By the late 1970s, some 40,000 poor, chronic mental patients had been "dumped" in New York City. The 7,000 on the Upper West Side represented "the greatest concentration of deinstitutionalized mental patients in the United States."[22] Reporting in *Scientific American,* two mental health researchers described their experiences with deinstitutionalized patients.

> Time and time again we see patients who were released from state hospitals after months or years of custodial care; who then survive precariously on welfare payments for a few months on the fringe of the community, perhaps attending a clinic to receive medication or intermittent counseling; who voluntarily returned to a hospital or were recommitted . . . who were maintained in the hospital on an antipsychotic medication and seemed to improve; who were released again to an isolated "community" life and who, having again become unbearably despondent, disorganized, or violent, either present themselves at the emergency room or are brought to it by a police officer. Then the cycle begins anew.[23]

The high incidence of readmissions for psychiatric patients—the "revolving door"—had become an unavoidable problem in mental health. In 1970 the ratio of readmissions per resident of a mental hospital was 1.4; in 1974 the ratio was 1.74; but by 1981 it had reached 2.83, double that of a decade earlier.[24] Through the mid-1980s, the ratio of admissions per resident continued to edge up so that by 1986 it stood at 2.98.[25]

Meanwhile, resources for state mental hospitals dwindled, leaving patient care uncertain. In an attempt to manage patients more cost-effectively, state mental institutions relied more heavily on psychoactive medication, sometimes with disastrous consequences. In California, for example, a federally funded group that oversees mental health care complained of unnecessary deaths of mental patients who had been left unsupervised after receiving medication:

> The 28-year-old . . . patient died December 26, 1989, while he was locked in his dorm room . . . for 3 and one-half hours, the report charges. In addition to lithium and Valium, he was given Cogentin, which can cause vomiting, and Thorazine, which can suppress the body's natural coughing reflex. He suffocated on his own vomit and a piece of Christmas candy, the report said.
>
> The [other deaths] involved a 24-year-old patient who collapsed and died after he was given five different medications, and a 21-year-old man who had a fatal heart attack after he was given an injection of the psychiatric drug Haldol, the report said.[26]

A coherent mental health policy had ceased to exist in the United States by the 1980s. State hospitals had been divested of much of their responsibility for patients with serious psychiatric problems, but a complete system of CMHCs was not in place to care for many of those who had been deinstitutionalized. As state hospitals converted from long-term custodial care to short-term patient stabilization, psychotropic medication came to be a routine form of treatment. But the psychopharmacological revolution, though consistent with the relatively orderly movement toward deinstitutionalization in the late 1960s, seemed incongruent with the psychiatric chaos of two decades later. Shown to stabilize psychotic patients until interpersonal treatment methods could be employed, the major tranquilizers—Prolixin, Thorazine, Haldol, Stelazine, to name a few—seemed clinically indicated within the controlled environment of the hospital. In a community setting, however, psychotropic medication became problematic. Once stabilized on major tranquilizers, patients frequently found the side effects of the medication—dry mouth, nervousness, torpor, lactation in women, impotence in men—unacceptable and stopped taking the medication.

Yet without medication, such patients frequently decompensated and, without the regular supervision of psychiatric personnel, patients disappeared into inner-city ghettos or rural backwaters, adding to an already growing homeless population. Definitive data on the psychological condition of the homeless are difficult to generate, but a study of the homeless in Fresno, California, revealed that "34 percent were rated severely impaired and urgently in need of [psychiatric] treatment. An additional 33 percent were rated moderately impaired so that treatment would be of substantial benefit."[27] A Baltimore study found that 80 percent of the homeless were mentally ill, and most of these were also abusing illicit drugs and alcohol.[28] In the absence of mental health care, increasingly desperate former mental hospital patients turned to petty crime to gain income, thus clogging local courts. Commenting on the surge in arrests of the mentally ill, one mental health worker became exasperated: "These people are forced to commit crimes to come to the attention of the police and get help."[29]

CMHCs UNDER SIEGE

The discharge of patients from state mental hospitals eventually imposed an enormous burden on the CMHCs. Since the seriously mentally ill were often unable to get care from hospitals, the CMHCs provided the only service these people received. A Philadelphia CMHC reported that 44 percent of its patients were chronically disturbed and that these patients consumed 70 percent of the mental health services provided.[30]

TABLE 12.1. Percent of CMHCs Reporting Changes in Services, 1975–1985

Service	Percent
Community residential services	+75
Services for young chronic adults	+72
Day treatment/partial care services	+68
Case management	+63
Outpatient services	+49
Consultation and education	−57
Prevention	−48
Evaluation	−36

SOURCE: Judith Larsen, "Community Mental Health Services in Transition," *Community Mental Health Journal*, Winter 1987, pp. 19, 20.

CMHCs had to restructure their activities so as to focus on immediate care for the seriously disturbed, with the result that "indirect" services, such as prevention and evaluation, were cut back, as shown in Table 12.1. A study of 94 CMHCs showed that increasing demand for direct services to the seriously mentally disturbed began to skew mental health service delivery.[31] Thus, rather than being a mental health agency that provided a comprehensive range of services to all persons in a catchment area, the CMHC rapidly became an outpost for the seriously mentally disturbed, a population that it was not intended to serve, at least exclusively.

While client demand escalated, CMHCs faced significant cuts in federal funding. As Table 12.2 illustrates, the Reagan years, beginning in 1980, led to dramatic shifts in the sources of mental health funding. As funding from the federal government evaporated, CMHCs became more dependent on the states, which had historically defined mental health care in the United States. CMHCs were able to compensate for federal reductions to some extent by obtaining more funding from government assistance programs. Significantly, nongovernmental sources, such as client fees and private insurance, continued to account for a relatively minor portion of CMHC operating expenses.

TABLE 12.2. CMHC Revenue Sources as Percent of Total Revenues, Selected Years

Sources	1976	1980	1984
Government			
Federal	24	17	2
State	30	39	50
Local	6	11	8
(Subtotal)	(60)	(67)	(60)
Entitlement Programs			
Medicare	1	2	5
Medicaid	9	14	16
Tital XX	—	5	1
(Subtotal)	(10)	(21)	(22)
Nongovernment			
Client fees	3	4	8
Insurance	4	3	3
Other services	22	3	5
All other	1	2	1
(Subtotal)	(30)	(12)	(18)
(Total)	(100)	(100)	(100)

SOURCE: Judith Larsen, "Community Mental Health Services in Transition," *Community Mental Health Journal,* Winter 1987, p. 23.

TABLE 12.3. Types of Staffing Changes in CMHCs, 1982–1984

Type of Staffing Change	Percent of Centers Reporting Change		
	1982	1983	1984
Layoffs, hiring freezes, attrition	25	16	8
Reorganization of clinical assignments	12	11	6
Reassignment of staff	17	7	15
Addition of staff to fill vacancies	18	2	8
Addition of staff for new programs	11	2	0

SOURCE: Judith Larsen, "Community Mental Health Services in Transition," *Community Mental Health Journal,* Winter 1987, p. 22.

Precisely how this reduction in federal assistance affected the CMHC effort varied, of course, with individual programs. CMHCs in wealthier states, for example, were better able to weather the fiscal turmoil than were those in poorer states. Generally, however, CMHCs had to reduce staffing and programming, as Table 12.3 shows.

By the mid-1980s, CMHCs seemed to have made the necessary organizational adjustments to funding changes, but these were at the expense of staffing and programming needs that had been increasing. CMHCs were able to hire some new staff to make up for earlier reductions, but programming had stagnated completely. Eventually, the morale of CMHC staff suffered as mental health professionals could no longer see any relief from their inability to provide even minimal care to the seriously mentally ill. In San Diego, for example, county officials decided to target scarce resources for only the most seriously disturbed, which drew this editorial response from a CMHC staff member:

In the future . . . the community mental health clinics will provide little or no talking therapy to their thousands of clients. Instead, most patients will find their treatment limited to a 15-minute visit with a psychiatrist and a prescription for expensive psychotropic medications—bought, incidentally, at taxpayer expense.[32]

THE FUTURE OF MENTAL HEALTH POLICY

By the early 1990s, governmental mental health policy was in disarray. Deinstitutionalization had contributed to the homelessness problem, with as many as 50 percent of the homeless being former mental hospital patients.[33] When winter threatened the safety of some homeless people in New York City, a team of mental health workers was authorized to pick up those who posed a danger to themselves and to commit them to Bellevue Hospital for a three-week observation period, a policy referred to as "preventive commitment." The first person picked up was Joyce Brown, who "was dirty, malodorous and abusive to passersby and defecated on herself."[34] To the chagrin of then-Mayor Ed

Koch, Brown had been stabilized in Bellevue when attorneys from the American Civil Liberties Union challenged her involuntary commitment. The prospect that pending litigation might cancel the program led one supporter to observe that "for the severely mentally ill, liberty is not just an empty word but a cruel hoax."[35]

Despite initial setbacks in preventive commitment, 26 states and the District of Columbia have laws authorizing the practice. The high number of treatment dropouts from outpatient therapy and the revolving door of hospitalization served to encourage local authorities to find some method for ensuring that the seriously mentally ill would not deteriorate owing to lack of intervention by mental health professionals. Preventive commitment

> provides for commitment of individuals who do not meet the statutory standard for involuntary hospitalization but who, it is asserted, are mentally ill, are unable to voluntarily seek or comply with treatment, and who need treatment in order to prevent deterioration that would predictably result in dangerousness to self or others or grave disability.[36]

A seemingly humane policy, preventive commitment nevertheless presents serious problems when there are inadequate mental health services to see that it is used properly. Without adequate staff resources, preventive commitment can become a form of social control—as opposed to therapy—in which treatment "consists of mandatory medication and little else."[37] One authority on preventive commitment speculated that mental health professionals would have little choice but to use "forced medication" as "the treatment of choice" for those in preventive commitment, and that they would have to "actually track down noncompliant patients at their place of residence or elsewhere and administer medication as part of a mobile outreach team."[38]

For those concerned with the civil rights of the mentally impaired, such an eventuality is nothing less than ghoulish, an exercise in tyranny on the part of the state in the name of social welfare.[39] Even under conditions of adequate staffing, preventive commitment remains problematic. The side effects of psychoactive medication are so pronounced for many patients that they simply refuse to take it, even under duress. Among the contraindications of psychoactive medication is tardive dyskinesia, permanent damage to the central nervous system resulting from long-term use of medications such as Prolixin and Stelazine. Because tardive dyskinesia is irreversible and is manifested by obvious symptoms—"protrusion of tongue, puffing of cheeks, puckering of mouth, chewing movements"[42]—the disorder raises a haunting specter: In an attempt to control psychological disturbances, psychiatry has created a host of physiological aberrations. Because tardive dyskinesia appears after long-term use, and sometimes after medication is discontinued, the number of mental patients with the disorder promises only to grow. In fact, one observer has prophesied that the mental health problem "of the next decade is tardive dyskinesia."[41] Unfortunately, the critics of preventive commitment who cite the danger of tardive dyskinesia offer no alternative for the care of the seriously mentally ill that is economically or politically plausible. As a result, preventive commitment is likely to be a feature—however troublesome—of future mental health policy.

A more comprehensive approach to future mental health policy involves the integration of services and payment through a capitation method. This has been developed in several localities. Under a capitation method of payment, agencies are awarded a predetermined amount per client with which they must provide a range of services. Agencies are funded the capitation amount regardless of the actual cost of serving an individual client. Capitation in mental health care would mimic health maintenance organizations (HMOs), which have a successful track record in providing preventive and primary health care. "Mental health HMOs would centralize financing and delivery system responsibility, create financial incentives to reallocate resources from inpatient to outpatient settings, and reduce system fragmentation, as perceived by patients."[42] Such an arrangement has the advantage of being easy to administer, and it builds into the reimbursement scheme certain incentives that do not exist in other arrangements. Under a capitation reimbursement method, for example, agencies are encouraged to cut down on expensive services, such as hospitalization, since a surplus can be realized when the actual cost of care is below the capitation amount. "Money can be used to develop walk-in crisis centers, step-down units that provide intermediate care after an acute hospitalization, special case management programs for coordinating services and rehabilitation or special housing services."[43] In addition, agencies are penalized for neglecting to serve clients, because every capitated client represents a resource base for the agency.

An example of how a capitation method of payment could be used in mental health service delivery is the integrated mental health (IMH) concept being developed in New York State and Philadelphia. Capitated mental health care under IMH would have three major features. First, current categorical funding—Medicaid, Supplemental Security Income, Food Stamps, local funding—would be aggregated into a common fund from which capitation "premiums" would be paid. Second, a nonprofit planning and coordination agency would be established to oversee mental health care, in so doing negotiating contracts with providers, monitoring performance, and evolving innovative programs. Third, particularly high-usage clients would be targeted for provision of less costly services in order to generate surpluses for less intensive services.[44]

The magnitude of cost savings that can be realized through IMH is illustrated by the deployment of a capitated system in two New York counties. In order to induce CMHCs to participate in the capitation arrangement, payment rates were established for levels of service for three types of patients: "continuous patients" who had been hospitalized for some time, $39,000; "intermittent patients" who generally required intermediate care (two rates), $18,000 and $13,000; and "outpatients" who needed the least intensive care, $5,000. State officials calculated that such payments would realize savings, since state hospital care exceeded $100,000 per patient annually. By 1991–92 the continuous patient rate was reduced to $28,000, the intermittent rate was combined and lowered to $15,600, and the outpatient rate was increased to $11,600. Initial assessment of the program indicated cost savings and improved patient functioning. Participating CMHCs planned to used their revenue surpluses to extend mental health services to children and the elderly.[45]

The idea of integrating services through an arrangement such as the IMH is likely to become an important source of innovation in future mental health policy. Such an eventuality has significant implications for human service professionals, who may miss an important opportunity to shape mental health programs unless they are willing to sharpen their administrative skills. The capitation of mental health services, as might be suspected, places a premium on fiscal analysis, cost accounting, and strategic planning skills. In a policy environment in which capitation is an increasingly prevalent method of ensuring access to service while containing program costs, mental health administrators who are not knowledgeable about fiscal management may well lose control of programs to professionals from business and public administration. Unfortunately, there is a precedent for such a loss of program control. When Medicare and Medicaid subsidized long-term care for the elderly, human service professionals were slow to take advantage of administrative opportunities in the emerging nursing home industry. Eventually, long-term care came under the control of business executives who were not particularly sensitive to the psychological and social problems of patients in nursing homes. Outside the nursing home industry, human service professionals have had to lobby aggressively for the inclusion of advocacy services for the hospitalized elderly, a struggle that continues today. The prospect of a similar development in mental health policy is as troubling as it is plausible. Social workers have been reluctant to become managers in human service corporations,[46] yet case management services for the seriously mentally ill "have enjoyed a rapid increase in prominence within the mental health system."[47] Unless mental health professionals increase their understanding of capitalism, they may find themselves working under the direction of business executives—or outside mental health services altogether. Such a development is unlikely to be in the best interests of the seriously emotionally disturbed.

SUBSTANCE ABUSE

Mental health services are often associated with substance abuse. Human service professionals in direct services are familiar with clients who have chosen to anaesthetize themselves from stress or misery with alcohol and other substances. Individual psychological problems are of course compounded by reliance on such substances, and these problems not only affect the families of substance abusers but also become more severe when addiction is manifested. Ordinarily, addiction is associated with alcohol and drugs, less often with tobacco. Substance abuse has become an important area of public policy not only because of appropriations for treatment programs but also because of the enormous costs that substance abuse extracts from society. As these costs have escalated, substance abuse policy has attained a higher profile in domestic affairs.

The interaction of emotional difficulties, alcoholism, and substance abuse is reflected in social welfare policy and has been institutionalized in the Alcohol, Drug Abuse, and Mental Health Administration (ADAMHA) of the Department of Health and Human Services. ADAMHA oversees the federal Alcohol, Drug Abuse, and Mental Health block grant, which consolidates several separate, or "categorical" programs established earlier, such as the CMHC Act. Since 1981 all mental health expenditures have been in block grants to states. By using a block grant strategy, the federal government removed the power from federal agencies and transferred it to the individual states. The federal ADAMHA budget (see Table 12.4) has increased, but many critics would argue that it is still insufficient to address the mounting demands for substance abuse programs.

A block grant enables states to apportion funds on the basis of what they deem most im-

TABLE 12.4. Expenditures in the Federal Alcohol, Drug Abuse, and Mental Health Administration (In thousands)

Program	Allocations by Year		
	1991*	1992†	1993†
Mental health	622,388	671,264	675,875
Drug abuse	415,964	429,074	440,200
Alcohol abuse	171,085	184,304	193,034
Treatment research	8,129	8,598	8,894
Abuse prevention	271,464	285,082	305,549
Treatment state grants	1,268,505	1,360,000	1,360,000
Treatment programs	158,372	135,530	274,419
Buildings and facilities	8,469	5,247	3,980
Management and support	11,091	12,878	13,909
Total	2,935,467	3,091,977	3,275,860

* Actual allocations; † estimated allocations. (SOURCE: Adapted from *Budget of the U.S. Government, Fiscal Year 1993* [Washington, D.C.: U.S. GPO], pp. 1–505.)

portant. As a result, some states invest more in mental health services, other states prefer to fund drug abuse programs, while still others favor alcoholism programs. Although the block grant method of funding provides states with the flexibility to tailor programs to suit their needs, it also raises the risk of defunding programs that are no longer topical. For example, the recent concern about cocaine use may well lead to increased funding for substance abuse programs that could come at the expense of alcohol and mental health programs unless additional money is budgeted for the ADAMHA block grant. Because increased funding is unlikely, new cocaine treatment programs will probably be developed to the detriment of long-standing alcoholism and mental health programs.

The consolidation of categorical grants into a block grant reflects the preference of many human service professionals for preventive programs that apply generically to all forms of substance abuse. This approach has been argued persuasively by Mathea Falco:

> An estimated 18 million Americans are alcoholics and 55 million are regular smokers, compared to 5.5 million serious drug abusers. Each year alcohol causes 200,000 deaths from disease and accidents, while more than 400,000 Americans die from smoking. By contrast, deaths from all illicit drugs range from 5,000 to 10,000. The costs of health care and lost productivity caused by tobacco-related illnesses are estimated at $60 billion a year, and those attributed to alcoholism exceed $100 billion. For all illegal drugs, the National Institute of Drug Abuse sets the annual bill to society at $40 billion.[48]

What is the logic in having separate preventive programs for tobacco, alcohol, and illegal drugs, when effective prevention programs can be developed for all of them? In the light of diminishing resources for social programs, Falco's book, *The Making of a Drug-Free America: Programs That Work*—a call for integrating prevention efforts—is compelling.

History of Substance Abuse

Although most societies have incorporated addictive substances into their religions or social conventions, their use is ordinarily circumscribed. For historical and demographic reasons, American culture has been accepting of certain substances, ambivalent about some, and phobic about others. Tobacco, a crop the colonists were encouraged to cultivate by their European sponsors, has been a legal commodity since Europeans first settled in North America. Alcoholic beverages appear in most agrarian societies, and these are a fixture in American folklore. Still, the consequences of excessive consumption on family life led some religiously inspired Progressives to call for the prohibition of alcohol. From 1919 to 1933, the Eighteenth Amendment to the Constitution prohibited the manufacture and sale of alcoholic beverages in the United States. Cocaine was a common ingredient in many early patent medicines and popular beverages like Coca-Cola. Concern about quality in production, however, led to the Pure Food and Drug Act of 1906, which required that ingredients be listed on product labels. When the public learned that there was cocaine in some products, local jurisdictions prohibited their sale. Imported with the Chinese laborers who built the western rail system, opium was initially ignored until reports surfaced that women from upright families were frequenting "opium dens." The Hague Opium Convention of 1912, of which the United States was a leader, controlled the production and sale of opium internationally. In the United States, restrictions on the manufacture and sale of cocaine, heroin, and marijuana were first established through the 1914 Harrison Narcotic Act. Marijuana was effectively made illegal through the Marijuana Tax Act of 1937.[49]

Despite this legacy, governmental control of mind-altering substances is anything but consistent. Although the federal government wages a "drug war," some states, for all practical purposes, disregard marijuana possession. The sale and use of cocaine and heroin have become so essential to the economy of many poor, inner-city communities that the police are ineffectual in controlling trade, able at best only to harass users. During the 1980s, cocaine was commonly used by young, urban, professionals (YUPPIES) as the drug of choice and glamorized by Hollywood. Meanwhile, a substantial market emerged in prescription drugs, such as Valium, which were as available as there were corrupt physicians willing to prescribe them.

Public intolerance of drug abuse escalated because of several factors. Continued carnage on the nation's highways because of drunk drivers led to the founding of Mothers Against Drunk Drivers (MADD), a voluntary group that fought aggressively for stiffer penalties for drivers under the influence of alcohol. The deaths of entertainers—Janis Joplin, Jimi Hendrix, and Elvis Presley—were sobering experiences for many young people. When sports stars Len Bias and Don Rogers died from cocaine overdoses, drug abuse took center stage in America. In the meantime, an ominous development served to underscore drug abuse as a public health problem, not simply as an individual moral problem. AIDS, initially associated with male homosexuals, was increasingly prevalent among inner-city intravenous drug users (IDUs). Needle sharing among cocaine and heroin addicts was identified as a primary means of transmitting HIV. Indiscriminate injections by IDUs quickly transmitted AIDS within the African-American and Hispanic communities in major urban centers. When IDUs practiced unsafe sex, AIDS was passed to minority heterosexuals. As women who had contracted AIDS became pregnant, they bore infants who were HIV-positive. By the early 1990s, concerns about substance abuse drew together diverse groups in America. The anguish of white, suburban mothers of MADD was shared by black, inner-city mothers with AIDS.

Alcohol Abuse

Americans steadily increased their consumption of alcohol from the end of World War II until the 1980s, when drinking began to decrease. By 1987, the average American drank a little more than 2.5 gallons of alcoholic beverages a year.[50] However, that amount was not evenly distributed throughout the population. One-third of the population abstains from alcohol consumption; one-third considers its consumption as light; and the remaining third are considered moderate to heavy drinkers. In 1987, the National Institute of Health estimated that approximately 18 million adults in the United States have problems attributable to alcohol use.[51]

These problems are directly related to serious social problems. Forty-eight percent of all convicted offenders used alcohol just prior to committing a crime, and 64 percent of public order offenses are alcohol-related.[52] In 1980, almost 100,000 deaths were related to alcohol consumption.[53] The cost of alcohol abuse and dependence was estimated at $136.3 billion in 1990.[54] Perhaps the most significant adverse consequence of alcohol consumption is highway accidents. Approximately 23,000 people died in 1987 in traffic accidents in which alcohol was implicated. The tragic death toll on American highways provoked the establishment of MADD and cries to increase penalties for drunk drivers as well as public education campaigns to dissuade people from drinking while driving. This combination of motivators seemed to have a positive effect. Between 1982 and 1986 the percent of inebriated drivers involved in fatal accidents dropped, as is shown in Table 12.5.

Among the most pernicious effects of alcohol consumption is fetal alcohol syndrome (FAS), a physiological and mental deformation in infants caused by their mothers' ingestion of alcohol during pregnancy. FAS children exhibit behaviors that make them extraordinarily difficult to manage growing up: limited attention span, slow response to stimuli, and an inability to incorporate a moral code. Because of these

TABLE 12.5. Percent of Drunk Drivers* Involved in Fatal Accidents, 1982 and 1986

Vehicle Type	1982	1986	Change
Motorcycles	40.7	41.0	+1
Passenger cars	36.7	27.5	−25
Light trucks and vans	36.3	30.9	−15
Medium trucks	7.2	6.2	−14
Heavy trucks	4.2	2.6	−38

* Drivers with a blood alcohol content of .10 percent or higher (SOURCE: Adapted from *Alcohol and Health, Seventh Special Report to the U.S. Congress* [Washington, D.C.: U.S. Government Printing Office, 1990], p. 165.)

deficiencies, FAS children tend to have difficulty in the early socialization experiences of elementary school. Children with FAS frequently fail to understand complicated instructions, wander about, and take the property of classmates without understanding the inappropriateness of such behavior. FAS is particularly difficult to diagnose in that its milder form, fetal alcohol effect (FAE), does not cause any physiological abnormality in facial structure. The National Institute of Health estimated that the incidence of FAS among heavy-drinking women was as high as 25 per 1,000 births and that the cost of the disorder was almost one-third of a billion dollars.[55]

Although FAS has been recognized by pediatric researchers since 1973,[56] the syndrome was not widely known to the public until Michael Dorris's account of his adopted son's FAS condition was published in *The Broken Cord.* A novelist and the husband of award-winning author Louise Erdrich, Dorris wrote poignantly about his adoption of Adam, a Native American infant with FAS. Ignorant of Adam's condition, Dorris spent years consulting with teachers, having his son tested by psychologists, and transferring Adam to special schools. It was not until he visited an Indian reservation and a special education bus discharged a group of FAS children for school that Dorris learned about FAS from a friend. Suddenly, Dorris understood that Adam was suffering from a permanent disorder brought about by his birthmother's drinking.

In *The Broken Cord,* Dorris and Erdrich write movingly about the consequences of FAS. Since both are Native Americans themselves, their observations are as acute as they are controversial. Noting that as many as 25 percent of the children born on the Sioux Pine Ridge Reservation suffer from FAS, Dorris contends that alcohol consumption during pregnancy represents genocide among Indian peoples. In order to contain FAS, Dorris suggests that women who have given birth to FAS children and who demonstrate an inability to control their drinking during pregnancy be incarcerated until they give birth. Erdrich concurs, her rationale being that the health of the fetus has primacy over the mother's freedom to consume alcohol:

> Knowing what I know now, I am sure that even when I drank hard, I would rather have been incarcerated for nine months and produce a normal child than bear a human being who would, for the rest of his or her life, be imprisoned by what I had done. And for those so sure, so secure, I say the same thing I say to those who would not allow a poor woman a safe abortion and yet have not themselves gone to adoption agencies and taken in the unplaceable children, the troubled, the unwanted: If you don't agree with me, then please, go and sit beside the alcohol-affected while they try to learn how to add.[57]

The idea of restraining women during pregnancy to prevent fetal damage surged in the popular media. This controversy was fueled by two related issues. First, a rapid increase in the number of infants who tested positive for cocaine at birth raised the specter of a "bio-underclass" consisting of a generation of minority children condemned to disability by maternal substance abuse.[58] Second, arrests of women for exposing their infants to substance abuse in utero enraged feminists who had watched the cutbacks in maternal health and social services during the 1980s. "It has become trendy," columnist Ellen Goodman observed acidly, "to arrest pregnant women for endangering their fetuses."[59] By the early 1990s an unstable truce had evolved between proponents of fetal health and women's rights. Clearly, both camps favored aggressive public education and early treatment for substance abuse before, during, and after pregnancy, but lack of funding made such initiatives unlikely.

As a result, the question of how to manage substance-abusing women during pregnancy has been passed down to program managers and clinical staff. As the number of infants testing positive for substance abuse increased, opposition to social control intervention on the basis that it violated women's rights became less tenable for human service professionals. Indeed, the possibility of compulsory treatment for pregnant drug abusers became an unavoidable issue when drug abuse was associated with the transmission of AIDS.[60] Compulsory treatment, of course, runs contrary to the individual liberties guaranteed by the Constitution because it is possible only through some commitment procedure. Proponents of compulsory treatment and preventive commitment have argued that it is the only way to protect potential victims against the uncontrolled and hazardous behavior of addicts. Critics, on the other hand, insist that effective public education and treatment would make such draconian measures unnecessary.

This dilemma has serious implications for clients of substance abuse programs, as it does also for practitioners. Compulsory treatment is likely to deter some people from seeking treatment for problems that they might have sought voluntarily, though perhaps at a later date. Compulsory treatment also places the practitioner in the role of social control agent, a role not conducive to building a client's trust. Compulsory treatment is likely to drive the problem underground, further exacerbating the very

problem it is intended to remedy. Without adequate investments in education and treatment, the future of substance abuse policy appears likely to be plagued by a series of such negatively reinforcing decisions.

Drug Abuse

By contrast with alcohol abuse, the prevalence of drug abuse is more difficult to ascertain, since the use of controlled substances—the focus of drug abuse—is illegal. It now appears that general drug abuse has begun to decline after peaking during the period 1979–1980. Still, by the late 1980s as many as 30 million Americans used drugs illegally. "During each of the last few years," reported one analyst, "police made about 750,000 arrests for violations of the drug laws."[61] But even while drug abuse was stabilizing, the use of cocaine—or its popular derivative, crack—mushroomed. The sale and use of cocaine among residents of poor urban communities as well as among professionals in middle-income communities had become epidemic by the late 1980s. Between 1976 and 1985, the number of emergency room episodes attributed to cocaine use rose by a factor of 10, to almost 10,000.[62] The cocaine epidemic proved extremely costly for the governmental agencies that bore the primary responsibility for interdiction of controlled substances as well as for the incarceration and treatment of substance abusers. One analyst placed these costs at about $10 billion per year, although this does not include the costs associated with loss of employment or productivity.[63] The National Institute on Drug Abuse pegs the annual cost of drug abuse due to lost productivity at $33 billion.[64] But the rise in cocaine use became of urgent concern to public health officials when it was discovered that as many as 25 percent of the persons who had contracted AIDS were intravenous (IV) drug users.[65] A haunting scenario began to take shape: IV drug users were no longer tortured souls in the slow process of self-destruction; they had become transmitters of an epidemic that promised to be as costly as it was deadly.

The federal response to illicit drug use has been twofold, involving both interdicting the supply of illegal substances and reducing the demand through treatment and public education. Government strategies toward containing drug abuse have oscillated wildly between interdiction and prevention. Before Reagan came to power, federal policy emphasized treatment and public education, assuming that these strategies would diminish demand. During the early 1970s, for example, two-thirds of the federal appropriations for drug abuse were for treatment and education. A decade later, however, supply interdiction had superseded demand reduction as the prime strategy, consuming 80 percent of federal drug funds. Federal funds for law enforcement increased from $800 million in 1981 to $1.9 billion in 1986. Meanwhile, funding for prevention, education, and treatment decreased from $404 million in 1981 to $338 million in 1985, a 40 percent drop when adjusted for inflation.[66] Despite massive infusions of funds for the Drug Enforcement Administration (DEA) and the Coast Guard, by the end of the 1980s most analysts agreed that supply interdiction had failed. Experts contended that emphasizing law enforcement would not solve the nation's drug problem. "It would be naive to assume that this well-meant legislative effort will be an end to our drug dilemma," concluded the late Sidney Cohen, former director of the Division of Narcotic Addiction and Drug Abuse of the National Institute of Mental Health:

> We have not yet come to understand the resolute, determined, amoral nature of the major traffickers or their enormous power. Perhaps we do not even recognize that, for tens of hundreds of thousands of field workers, collecting coca leaves or opium gum is a matter of survival. At the other end of the pipeline is the swarm of sellers who could not possibly earn a fraction of their current income from legitimate pursuits. If they are

arrested, they are out after a short detention. If not, many are waiting to take their place.[67]

If efforts to reduce the propagation of coca in South and Central America proved futile, attempts to reduce street trafficking were similarly unsuccessful. A kilogram of cocaine wholesaled in Miami for $60,000 in 1981; by the late 1980s, the cost had plummeted to $10,000.[68] The price of cocaine was so low that crack houses were able to offer cocaine free to new customers, charging regulars as little as $2.[69]

To compound the problem, the application of interdiction at the street level, where drugs were sold, led to arrests of users and petty distributors, swelling already overcrowded prisons. Between 1980 and 1990 the number of federal prisoners incarcerated for the violation of drug laws increased from 1,945 to 9,804.[70] Thus, the focus on interdiction proved perverse. To contain drug use through law enforcement, thousands of addicts were imprisoned at enormous cost. Meanwhile, funds for prevention and treatment were held in check. Most ironic, drug treatment for incarcerated addicts was virtually nonexistent. With the passage of the Anti-Drug Abuse Act of 1988, the emphasis shifted back to prevention, education, and treatment. Yet under the Bush administration, when appropriations for drug abuse swelled to $12 billion, supply interdiction once again became the focus of policy, consuming 70 percent of federal funding.[71]

Under such circumstances, the development of a coherent system of drug abuse treatment facilities has been problematic. Generally, employees with generous health insurance have been able to gain ready admission to drug abuse treatment programs. The poor, by contrast, have found treatment available irregularly, if at all. In response to the pervasive use of alcohol and drugs, treatment facilities expanded rapidly. From 1978 to 1984, the number of hospital units treating alcohol and drug abusers increased 78 percent (from 465 to 829) and the number of beds in these facilities increased 62 percent (from 16,005 to 25,981). However, inpatient facilities provided only a fraction of treatment services to substance abusers. Of the 540,411 persons in treatment for alcohol and drug abuse in 1984, 8 percent were in an inpatient facility and 10 percent were in residential facilities, but 82 percent were under outpatient care.[72] Treatment is virtually nonexistent for the abusers who are incarcerated. For those in the community, drug abuse programs are too few in number. Perhaps half of the 5.5 million currently using drugs would elect treatment if it were available, but that number is one million more than the number of available treatment slots.[73]

The mismatch between the needs of drug addicts and the eligibility requirements of social programs was captured by journalist Barry Bearak, who followed a group of junkies in New York City. Scavenging what funds he had left, one junkie decided to have himself admitted to a detox program. After a full day's bouncing from one welfare agency to another seeking eligibility to "special" Medicaid, which would pay for the detox services, Georgie, a middle-aged Hispanic, found himself in a line for public assistance only a few minutes before closing time. While Georgie waited, a friend who had come with him also to get into detox was shooting up in the rest room:

> The line moved slowly. Georgie's turn finally came a few minutes before 5 p.m. It was a short discussion. He had been in the wrong spot. He needed to be at the Application Desk, back over by Table Five where he had started.
>
> He hurried across the big room. "Can I ask you a question?" he said to a clerk.
>
> "I'm sorry," she answered, her fingers busy in a file drawer. "I need to get this out of the way."
>
> Georgie spoke up with more urgency: "I want to get into detox."
>
> The woman turned to face him now. "You came too late," she said, shaking her head. "We're not giving out any more appointments."
>
> "We've been getting the runaround all day."
>
> She eyed him more carefully, looking over his sweaty face. She spoke slowly and distinctly for the junkie's benefit. "When you come back in, all they'll give you is an appointment," she said. "You won't get emergency Medicaid. Then, with an appointment, you have to come back in a week or so and see an interviewer. Then, after they have reviewed the case, the client is contacted by mail, and that takes three weeks or a month."
>
> Georgie took this in and was stunned. "So the mumbo jumbo about getting on Medicaid the same day is bull—?" he said without anger, but with resignation.
>
> "That's right. The only way to get on is with HIV [the AIDS virus]." At last, good news. His face brightened. "Well, I'm HIV," he said.
>
> The clerk took a step back from him. "You'd have to be able to prove it with a certified letter from your doctor," she said.
>
> With that, Georgie was beaten. His shoulders sagged. And the clerk knew she could shift her attention back to the end-of-the-day filing.[74]

For human service professionals, the emphasis on treatment over interdiction is a positive development in drug abuse policy; yet resources targeted at prevention have been available only recently. The $500 million for school drug abuse prevention programs through the Drug Free Schools Act was not available until the early 1990s. Applying the prevention trinity used in public health to drug abuse, it is evident that most funding has been directed toward rehabilitating addicts, tertiary prevention, or treatment of abusers, secondary prevention. Limited primary prevention efforts have been field-tested, but these are only now being widely adopted. Falco notes that all have not been equally effective. Life Skills Training (LST) developed in New York City and STAR (Students Taught Awareness and Resistance) deployed in Kansas City have been superior to DARE (Drug Abuse Resistant Education). But the real test of school prevention programs comes in poor neighborhoods where drug abuse is part of the community fabric. Programs such as the Westchester Student Assistance Program in New York, Smart Moves of the Boys and Girls Clubs, and the Seattle Social Development Project show promise; yet, upon evaluation, program graduates tend to report resistance to "soft" drugs—tobacco, alcohol, marijuana—while avoidance of "hard" drugs has not been clearly demonstrated.[75] This inability of prevention programs to produce resistance to hard drugs in high-risk neighborhoods may be due to methodological problems. Those high-risk youth susceptible to hard drug use are probably unlikely to complete a prevention program; nor are they good candidates to report hard drug usage through an outcome instrument. Instead, they are likely to be casualties of the research process for the same reasons they are casualties of substance abuse. For these reasons, some researchers have contended that substance abuse prevention efforts will not be successful until a much more expansive definition of primary prevention—including social, economic, and institutional factors—is adopted.[76]

During the 1980s the combination of reductions in governmental assistance to cities and the prevalence of drug trafficking was to have a pronounced effect on inner-city neighborhoods. Gradually, once squalid but quiet urban neighborhoods began to echo with gunfire as rival gangs fought over turf. By the 1990s, areas in many industrial cities had virtually imploded.[77] The "wilding" of New York City teenagers who savagely beat a female jogger was replicated when a gang of Boston youth raped and murdered a young mother.[78] Gang killings in Los Angeles soared 69 percent during the first eight months of 1990.[79] In 1992, Los Angeles reported more than 800 drug-related homicides for the

year.[80] Gang-related murders in the nation's capital reached a three-year high, leading the police department's spokesperson to quip, "At the rate we're going the next generation is going to be extinct."[81]

Observers of urban poverty described a serious deterioration in inner-city communities of the 1980s contrasted with those of the 1960s. When Claude Brown returned to Harlem 20 years after the publication of his *Manchild in the Promised Land,* he was shocked by the casual viciousness of gang members toward their victims.[82] "In many if not most of our major cities, we are facing something very like social regression," wrote Senator Daniel Patrick Moynihan. "It is defined by extraordinary levels of self-destructive behavior, interpersonal violence, and social class separation intensive in some groups, extensive in others."[83] In the socioeconomic vacuum that had developed in the poorest urban neighborhoods, the sale and consumption of drugs became central to community life. The toll this conversion was to take on young African Americans proved astonishing. As of 1988, 43 percent of those convicted of drug trafficking were African American. In New York, Hispanics and African Americans accounted for 92 percent of arrests for drug offenses in 1989. In 1990, a criminal justice reform organization, the Sentencing Project, reported that one-fourth of all African Americans between the ages of 20 and 29 were incarcerated, on parole, or on probation. Harvard economist Saucy Freeman calculated that 35 percent of all African Americans aged 16 to 35 had been arrested in 1989.[84] Indeed, drugs had become so associated with poor minority neighborhoods that it became a cause célèbre among American intellectuals—evident in Dennis Hopper's movie *Colors*[85] and in Richard Price's book *Clockers.*[86]

Drug-related violence spread throughout inner-city communities, extracting a horrifying toll on minority populations. The effect on African-American family life was depicted poignantly by Alex Kotlowitz, who followed the daily activities of two youngsters, Lafayette and Pharoah Rivers. The boys ventured out of their mother's apartment in one of Chicago's housing projects at risk of being shot by drug dealers.[87] In New York City, a popular elementary school principal, Patrick Daly, was shot to death while walking through a drug-infested neighborhood searching for a nine-year-old who had left school in tears after a fight.[88] During the summer of 1992, drug-related street violence in Baltimore reached the point where the state chapter of the National Association for the Advancement of Colored People formally requested the governor of Maryland to declare a state of civil emergency and call out the National Guard to restore order in the city.

Legalization of Drugs

Seemingly endless retreats in the war on drugs led some analysts to propose legalizing controlled substances.[89] Drug legalization had been a standard demand among libertarians, who argued that individuals should have the freedom to engage in any activity so long as it does not harm others. During the 1980s, a small number of leaders representing law, economics, and politics complemented the libertarian position, calling for the legalization of controlled substances. Noting the massive sums pumped into law enforcement and the meager results demonstrated by interdiction and treatment, proponents of legalization argued that American substance abuse policy was at best naive and at worst counterproductive. Those favoring drug legalization argued that the current policy was little more than a replication of Prohibition, a futile effort to ban alcohol from American culture. A more mature and pragmatic policy would be to admit that certain substances were part of contemporary life-styles and simply to regulate them, much as tobacco and alcohol are regulated. By legalizing drugs, substantial sums would be freed from law enforcement and put toward abuse prevention and treatment programs. Legalization would decriminalize drug abuse, thereby cutting the prison population significantly, and by destigmatizing abusers make it more likely that they would enter treatment. Additional revenues could be raised by government since illegal substances would be available legitimately and taxed accordingly. Advocates of legalization questioned the claims of defenders of the status quo that prevention, treatment, and interdiction were effective strategies that would show positive results in the long run. Legalization of drugs, countered its adherents, could produce substantial results immediately.

Momentum toward legalizing drugs reached its peak during the mid-1980s, then flagged. Public policy scholars raised a number of questions for which there were no ready answers. Should all drugs be legalized, or should legalization be limited to soft drugs, such as marijuana and minor tranquilizers, while restrictions on hard drugs were maintained? Should availability be unlimited, or should age restrictions apply, as they do now with tobacco and alcohol? If there are taxes on drugs and restrictions on their purchase, would not the government still have to fund law enforcement, enforce product safety, and maintain a taxing authority in order to contain an illicit market? If the government were to attempt to counter a black market by supplying drugs directly, it would be in the contradictory position of supplying drugs while also treating abusers of those same drugs.[90]

Further confounding the issue of drug legalization was the firestorm of controversy over crack cocaine. Proponents of legalization visualized drugs as relatively benign substances, similar to tobacco and alcohol. Marijuana, heroin, and many psychedelics could be used discreetly, they contended, without disrupting society or drawing public attention to users. The proliferation of crack cocaine, however, presented a completely different picture. Crack had not only been implicated in violent incidents, but the craving for it by IUD addicts was so intense that many failed to practice the needle hygiene necessary to prevent the transmission of HIV. The prospect of legalizing a substance over which users seemed to have so little control and which, moreover, was connected to homicides, addicted infants, and community destruction seemed inconsistent with the vision implied by drug legalization.

By the 1990s the legalization of drugs had drifted to the margin of the substance abuse debate. Despite obvious contradictions represented by the status of tobacco and alcohol, few suggested that other substances should be legalized. In fact, pressure increased to contain the use of tobacco and alcohol. Municipalities expanded the areas they designated as smoke-free, and stricter standards and fines were established for driving under the influence of alcohol. Increasingly, authorities came to believe that soft drugs served a "gateway" function, introducing young users to more addictive substances. Rather than loosen the regulation of such substances, continued restrictions were called for.[91] Finally, the most limited form of legalization—allowing physicians to prescribe certain substances for addicts—faltered when the country that had pioneered this strategy, Great Britain, halted the practice.[92]

If a consensus began to emerge about not legalizing controlled substances, there was far less unanimity about reclaiming neighborhoods in which drugs had become central to social and economic life. Aggressive action by law enforcement officers appeared to have reached an apex, then degeneralized into a lawless netherworld when, as an example, DEA agents raided the wrong house and critically wounded a San Diego man in a drug bust gone wrong. The practice of handing down severe sentences for even first-time offenders began losing its luster as a strategy when the cost of incarceration proved to far exceed the value of taking small-time drug traffickers off the street. The seizure of property belonging to persons who had been implicated in drug transactions became a small scandal when newspapers reported that innocent people had lost belongings to overzealous law enforcement officers.[93] The promise of paramilitary boot camps for first-time offenders who had been convicted of drug-related crimes, while an appealing solution to a public frustrated by increasing numbers of crime-prone youth, failed to demonstrate any long-term changes in behavior.[94]

In the last decade of the century, many inner-city neighborhoods were more lethal for minority Americans than they had been at any time in the nation's history. Children learned that they could make hundreds of dollars a day carrying crack between dealers, easily eclipsing the income of conventionally employed adults in the community. This made a joke of the work ethic; no one with any self-respect would consider a dead-end job paying the minimum wage. Young men who had little hope of finding a good job traded their future for quick wealth and community notoriety in the drug trade. Many did not expect to live to the age of 30 and impregnated girlfriends as the only way they knew to ensure posterity. Drug-related violence made a mockery of already fragile community institutions. Gang members were shot to death in funeral homes, schools, even hospitals. Most tragically, infants born of crack-addicted mothers writhed and screamed at birth as they experienced withdrawal only to be diagnosed later with HIV. Unwanted, they suffered in group homes and died at an early age.

While academics debated the finer points of drug legalization, the quality of life for the urban poor grew increasingly desperate. What had once been a grim struggle to reconcile meager income with daily living requirements had become a frantic scramble for safety. At best, the drug scourge forced inner-city residents to sharply curtail their expectations. At worst, it abruptly terminated expectations altogether. Eventually, the degradation of life attributed to the proliferation of drugs entered the popular media, clashing with cherished images of America. For too many of the urban poor, the American dream had not just faded from memory; it had been replaced by an image that was perversely antithetical—the American nightmare.

DISCUSSION QUESTIONS

1. In the early 1980s, funding for community mental health centers (CMHCs) was converted to a mental health block grant. To what extent did your community evolve complete community mental health centers? What happened to them during the 1980s? What priorities have been established through the mental health block grant? How has this changed mental health services in your community?

2. The misuse of psychoactive medication has been implicated in several undesirable consequences. Has tardive dyskenisia become a significant problem among mental health patients in your community? If so, what is being done to prevent it? Are more or fewer mental patients going through the "revolving door"?

3. Legalization of drugs has become a heated issue. What are the implications of drug legalization for substance abuse programs? How could drug legalization be structured in your state? How would substances be taxed? How would tax revenues from legalization be allocated?

4. The effect of substance abuse on innocent people presents several difficult policy dilemmas for decision makers. What policies could be put in place to prevent the birth of infants with FAS or AIDS? How could the rights of mothers be protected? What should be the role of human service professionals in such circumstances?

5. In many poor urban communities, drug-related street violence has escalated to unprecedented heights. How has your community balanced resource allocations for supply interdiction versus resources for demand reduction? To what extent is substance abuse treatment available to inmates in local correctional facilities? Have specific neighborhoods in your community organized to contain and reduce drug trafficking? Which agencies have supported such initiatives?

6. As the war on drugs failed to live up to its promise, more attention has been focused on prevention, particularly among children. What models have agencies in your community adopted to prevent substance abuse among kids? How much money has been allocated for prevention programs? What is the track record of the prevention programs adopted in your community?

NOTES

1. Jean Quam, "Dorothea Dix," *Encyclopedia of Social Work,* 18th ed. (Silver Spring, Md.: NASW, 1987), p. 921.

2. Michael Lesy, *Wisconsin Death Trip* (New York: Pantheon, 1973), p. 33.

3. Ibid.

4. Stephen Gould, "Carrie Buck's Daughter," *Natural History,* July 1984, pp. 85–92.

5. Walter Trattner, *From Poor Law to Welfare State* (New York: Free Press, 1974), p. 175.

6. Joint Commission on Mental Illness and Health, *Action for Mental Health* (New York: Basic Books, 1961).

7. David Mechanic, *Mental Health and Social Policy* (Englewood Cliffs, N.J.: Prentice-Hall, 1969), pp. 59–60.

8. Henry Foley, *Community Mental Health Legislation* (Lexington, Mass.: D. C. Heath, 1975), pp. 13–14.

9. Ibid., pp. 39, 40.

10. Bernard Bloom, *Community Mental Health* (Monterey, Calif.: Brooks/Cole, 1977), pp. 74–75.

11. National Institute of Mental Health, *Community Mental Health Center Program Operating Handbook* (Washington, D.C.: U.S. Department of Health, Education, and Welfare, 1971), pp. 2–6.

12. Foley, *Community Mental Health Legislation*, p. 126.

13. The description of CMHCs is derived from the *Community Mental Health Centers Policy and Standards Manual*, 1988; see *Community Mental Health Centers Program Operating Handbook*, 1989.

14. Bloom, *Community Mental Health*, pp. 46–56.

15. *Statistical Abstract of the United States, 108th Edition* (Washington, D.C.: U.S. Government Printing Office, 1987), p. 104.

16. Andrew Scull, *Decarceration* (Englewood Cliffs, N.J.: Prentice-Hall, 1977), p. 71.

17. Ibid., p. 69.

18. Donald Stedman,"Politics, Political Structures, and Advocacy Activities," in James Paul, Donald Stedman, and G. Ronald Neufeld, eds., *Deinstitutionalization* (Syracuse, N.Y.: Syracuse University Press. 1977), p. 57.

19. Alan Stone, *Law, Psychiatry, and Morality* (Washington. D.C.: American Psychiatry Press, 1984), pp. 116, 117.

20. Rael Jean Isaac, "'Right' to Madness: a Cruel Hoax," *Los Angeles Times,* December 14, 1990, p. E–5.

21. Uri Aviram, "Community Care of the Seriously Mentally Ill," *Community Mental Health Journal* 26, no. 1 (February 1990): 23–31.

22. Peter Koenig, "The Problem That Can't Be Tranquilized," *New York Times Magazine,* May 21, 1978, p. 15.

23. Ellen Bassuk and Samuel Gerson, "Deinstitutionalization and Mental Health Services," *Scientific American* 238, no. 2 (February 1978): 18.

24. Steven Segal, "Deinstitutionalization," *Encyclopedia of Social Work, 18th ed.* (Silver Spring, Md.: NASW, 1987), p. 378.

25. Per conversation with Joanne Atay on September 22, 1988. Source: Division of Biometry and Applied Sciences, *Additions and Resident Patients at End of Year, State and County Mental Hospitals, by Diagnosis and State* (Rockville, Md.: National Institute of Mental Health, 1988).

26. "State Blamed for 3 Deaths at Mental Hospitals," *Los Angeles Times,* October 2, 1991, p. A–4.

27. Joseph Sacks, John Phillips, and Gordon Cappelletty, "Characteristics of the Homeless Mentally Disordered Population in Fresno County," *Community Mental Health Journal,* Summer 1987, p. 114.

28. "Survey of Homeless Shows Mental Illness and Addiction," *New York Times,* September 10, 1989, p. 16.

29. Hector Tobar, "Mentally Ill Turn to Crime in a Painful Call for Help," *Los Angeles Times,* August 26, 1991, p. A–1.

30. A. Anthony Arce and Michael Vergare, "Homelessness, the Chronic Mentally Ill and Community Mental Health Centers," *Community Mental Health Journal,* Winter 1987, p. 9.

31. Judith Larsen, "Community Mental Health Services in Transition," *Community Mental Health Journal,* Winter 1987, pp. 19, 20.

32. Donald Woolson, "Policy Makes Short Shrift of Mentally Ill," *Los Angeles Times,* November 2, 1986, p. C–4.

33. Community for Creative Non-violence, *Homelessness in America* (Washington, D.C.: CCNV, 1987).

34. Josh Barbanel, "Homeless Woman to be Released after Being Forcibly Hospitalized," *New York Times,* January 19, 1988, p. 8.

35. Charles Krauthammer, "How to Save the Homeless Mentally Ill," *The New Republic,* February 8, 1988, p. 23.

36. "Developments in Mental Disability Law: 1986," *Clearinghouse Review* 20 January 1987: 1148. Quoted in Ruta Wilk, "Involuntary Outpatient Commitment of the Mentally Ill," *Social Work,* March-April 1988, p. 133.

37. Ibid., p. 133.

38. Ibid., p. 136.

39. See, for example, Thomas Szasz, *The Myth of Mental Illness* (New York: Harper and Row, 1961); David Ingleby, ed., *Critical Psychiatry: The Politics of Mental Health* (New York: Pantheon, 1980).

40. *Physician's Desk Reference* (Oradell, N.J.: Medical Economics Company, 1986), p. 2014.

41. Harris Chaiklin, "The New Homeless and Service Planning on a Professional Campus," 53. Chancellor's Colloquium (Baltimore, Md.: University of Maryland, December 4, 1985), p. 10.

42. Jon Christianson and Muriel Linehan, "Capitated Payments for Mental Health Care: The Rhode Island Programs," *Community Mental Health Journal* 25, no. 2 (Summer 1989): 122.

43. A. P. Schinnar, A. B. Rothbard, and T. R. Hadley, "Opportunities and Risks in Philadelphia's Capitation Financing of Public Psychiatric Services," *Community Mental Health Journal* 25, no. 4 (Winter 1989): 256.

44. Schinnar et al., "Opportunities," pp. 257–58.

45. Phyllis Marshall, "The Mental Health HMO: Capitation Funding for the Chronically Mentally Ill. Why an HMO?" *Community Mental Health Journal* 28, no. 2 (April 1992): 9–14.

46. David Stoesz, "Human Service Corporations: New Opportunities for Administration in Social Work," *Administration in Social Work* (forthcoming 1993).

47. Charles Rapp and Ronna Chamberlain, "Case Management Services for the Chronically Men-

tally Ill,'' *Social Work,* September-October 1985, p. 417.

48. Mathea Falco, *The Making of a Drug-Free America* (New York: Times Books, 1992), p. 24.

49. Mathea Falco, *Winning the Drug War* (New York: Priority Press, 1989), pp. 19–20.

50. U.S. Congress, *Alcohol and Health, Seventh Special Report to the U.S. Congress* (Washington, D.C.: U.S. Government Printing Office, 1990), p. 14.

51. *Alcohol and Health: Sixth Special Report to the U.S. Congress* (Washington, D.C.: Department of Health and Human Services 1987), pp. 2, 12.

52. Ibid., p. 13.

53. Ibid., p. 6.

54. *Alcohol and Health, Seventh Special Report to the U.S. Congress,* p. 163.

55. Ibid., pp. 140, 139.

56. Ibid., p. 139.

57. Louise Erdrich, ''Foreword'' to Michael Dorris, *The Broken Cord* (New York: Harper & Row, 1989), p. xviii.

58. Charles Krauthammer, ''The Horror of Addicted Newborns,'' *San Diego Tribune,* July 31, 1992, p. B–7.

59. Ellen Goodman, ''Community Begs Off, but Prosecutes Mom,'' *Los Angeles Times,* February 9, 1992, p. B–9.

60. Department of Health and Human Services, *Compulsory Treatment of Drug Abuse* (Washington, D.C.: U.S. Government Printing Office, 1989).

61. Ethan Nadelmann, ''The Case for Legalization,'' *The Public Interest,* Summer 1988, p. 14.

62. C. Schuster, ''Initiatives at the National Institute on Drug Abuse,'' in *Problems of Drug Dependence 1987* (Rockville Md.: Department of Health and Human Services, 1987), pp. 1–2.

63. Nadelmann, ''The Case for Legalization,'' pp. 14–16.

64. Falco, *Winning the Drug War,* p. 6.

65. Carl Leukefeld and Frank Tims, ''An Introduction to Compulsory Treatment for Drug Abuse: Clinical Practice and Research,'' in *Compulsory Treatment of Drug Abuse: Research and Clinical Practice* (Rockville Md.: Department of Health and Human Services, 1988), p. 2.

66. Falco, *Winning the Drug War,* pp. 26–27.

67. Sidney Cohen, ''The Drug-Free America Act of 1986,'' *Drug Abuse and Alcoholism Newsletter* (San Diego, Calif.: Vista Hill Foundation, 1987), pp. 1–3.

68. Falco, *Winning the Drug War,* p. 29.

69. Barry Bearak, ''A Room for Heroin and HIV,'' *Los Angeles Times,* September 27, 1992, p. A–18.

70. ''Drug Policy: It's Time to Try Something Very Different,'' *Los Angeles Times,* January 4, 1993, p. B–6.

71. Barry Bearak, ''In War on Drugs, Battle Against AIDS Falls Behind,'' *Los Angeles Times,* September 28, 1992, p. A–16.

72. *Alcohol and Health,* Seventh Special Report, pp. 120–21.

73. Barry Bearak, ''Road to Detox: Do Not Enter,'' *Los Angeles Times,* September 30, 1992, p. A–1.

74. Bearak, ''Road to Detox,'' p. A–18.

75. Falco, *The Making of a Drug-Free America,* Chapters 3 and 4.

76. Derek Mason, Mark Lusk, and Michael Gintzler, ''Beyond Ideology in Drug Policy: The Primary Prevention Model,'' *Journal of Drug Issues* 22, no. 4 (Fall 1992): 81–89.

77. Christopher Jencks, ''Deadly Neighborhoods,'' *The New Republic,* June 13, 1988, p. 18; Juan Williams, ''Hard Times, Harder Hearts,'' *Washington Post,* October 2, 1988, p. C–4.

78. ''Eight Boston Teenagers Charged in Savage Slaying of Young Mother,'' *Los Angeles Times,* November 21, 1990, p. A–4.

79. Louis Sahagun, ''Gang Killings Increase 69%, Violent Crime Up 20% in L.A. County Areas,'' *Los Angeles Times,* August 21, 1990, p. B–8.

80. Jesse Katz, ''County's Yearly Death Toll Reaches 800,'' *Los Angeles Times,* January 19, 1993, p. A–23.

81. Gabriel Escobar, ''Slayings in Washington Hit New High, 436, for 3rd Year,'' *Los Angeles Times,* November 24, 1990, p. A–26.

82. Claude Brown, *Manchild in the Promised Land* (New York: Macmillan, 1965); Claude Brown, ''Manchild in Harlem,'' *New York Times,* September 16, 1984, p. 16.

83. Daniel Patrick Moynihan, *Came the Revolution* (San Diego: Harcourt Brace Jovanovich, 1988), p. 291.

84. Jonathan Marshall, ''Targeting the Drugs, Wounding the Cities,'' *Washington Post Weekly,* May 25–31, 1992, p. 23.

85. Stanley Kaufmann, ''Review of *Colors,*'' *The New Republic,* May 15, 1988, p. 4.

86. Richard Price, *Clockers* (New York: Basic Books, 1992).

87. Alex Kotlowitz, *There Are No Children Here* (New York: Doubleday, 1991).

88. Barry Bearak, "Brooklyn Neighborhood Grieves for Its Mr. Chips," *Los Angeles Times,* December 19, 1992, p. A–6.

89. Nadelmann, "The Case for Legalization."

90. James Jacobs, "Imagining Drug Legalization," *The Public Interest,* No. 101 (Fall 1990): 27–34.

91. Falco, *The Making of a Drug-free America,* p. 100.

92. Jacobs, "Imagining Drug Legalization," p. 30.

93. Jim Newton, "Seizure of Assets Leaves Casualties in War on Drugs," *Los Angeles Times,* October 14, 1992, p. A–1; David Savage, "Drug-Case Forfeitures Will be Reviewed," *Los Angeles Times,* January 16, 1993, p. A–2.

94. David Lamb, "Last Shot to Salvage Their Lives," *Los Angeles Times,* January 17, 1993, p. A–1.

CHAPTER 13

Child Welfare Policy

This chapter examines the evolution of child welfare policy in the United States. Child protective services, foster care, adoption, and Head Start have been the focus of child welfare policy since the 1960s. More recent child welfare issues include day care, teenage pregnancy, and maternal and infant health care. The erosion of basic welfare programs that support American families increases the likelihood that the circumstances of children will worsen and that demands for child welfare will increase in the future.

In American social welfare, the condition of children is inextricably linked to the status of their families. Because the United States has failed to establish a family policy that ensures basic income, employment, and social service supports to parents, they frequently have difficulty in caring for their children. As families are less able to care for their children, the demand for child welfare services escalates. In recent years, the proportion of children living in poverty, the proportion of children in single-parent households, the percentage of mothers in the work force, and the birthrate of women in minority groups have all increased. While an increase in a broad range of family and child welfare services might be expected as a result of these trends, the societal response has been ex-

tremely varied. As Jeanne Giovannoni notes, "at best we have a hodgepodge of funding and regulatory mechanisms, and we rely predominantly on market mechanisms dictating both the amount and variety of care available."[1] A classification of child welfare services completed by the Child Welfare League of America identified nine diverse components: services in the home, day care, a homemaker service, foster care, adoption, group home care, institutional care, protective services, and services to an unmarried parent.[2] Of these, protective services, foster care, and adoption are most frequently identified as being exclusively related to child welfare and, therefore, are the focus here.

Child welfare services are often controversial because they sanction the intervention of human service professionals in family affairs that are ordinarily assumed to be private matters relating to parental rights. This dilemma places extraordinary demands on child welfare professionals, who are mandated to protect the best interests of the child while not intruding on the privacy of the family. Recently, this conundrum has become more pronounced as advocates for child welfare services demand more programs, while traditionalist groups attempt to cut programs which they perceive as designed to subvert the family. Ironically, much of this argument could be defused if the United States adopted a family policy that assisted parents in caring for children more adequately, thus reducing the need for the more intrusive child welfare interventions. For the moment, any family policy is unlikely, and child welfare policy remains among the more controversial in American social welfare.

HISTORY OF CHILD WELFARE POLICY

Although many states established orphanages during the eighteenth century, current child welfare policy has its origins in the 1870s.[3] The large number of child paupers led Charles Loring Brace, founder of New York's Children's Aid Society, to remove thousands of children from deleterious urban conditions in New York City to farm families in the Midwest. Eventually, criticism of Brace's methods, which were divisive of family and community, contributed to more preventive approaches to children's problems.

By the beginning of the twentieth century, most large cities had children's aid societies that practiced the "boarding out" of children (the payment of a fee for child rearing) to a sponsor in the community.[4] The boarding out of children until adoption (or, in the case of children with handicaps, those who were unlikely to be adopted) was the beginning of foster care and adoption programs in the United States.

Protective services for children began with one of the more unusual incidents in American social welfare. In 1874, a New York church worker, Etta Wheeler, discovered that a nine-year-old child, Mary Ellen, was being tied to a bed, whipped, and stabbed with scissors. On investigating what could be done for Mary Ellen, Wheeler spoke with the director of the New York Society for the Prevention of Cruelty to Animals (NYSPCA) on behalf of the indentured child. Although it was subsequently believed that intervention on behalf of Mary Ellen

was predicated on her status as an animal warranting protection, rather than as a child, a careful review of the case indicated that Mary Ellen's case was adjudicated consistently with legal precedents involving abused children.[5] The following year, the New York Society for the Prevention of Cruelty to Children was established.[6] By 1922, 57 societies for the prevention of cruelty to children had been established to protect abused youngsters.[7]

Child welfare proved an effective rallying issue for Progressives, who advocated intervention on the part of the federal government. In 1909, James E. West, a friend of President Theodore Roosevelt and later head of the Boy Scouts of America, convinced Jane Addams and other welfare leaders to attend a two-day meeting on child welfare. This first White House Conference on Children focused attention on the plight of destitute families, agency problems with the boarding out of children, and the importance of home care. The conference proved so successful that it was repeated every 10 years—with the exception of 1981, when the conference was canceled by the Reagan administration. Still, the White House Conference on Children served as a model for legitimating and attracting attention to social welfare needs. One significant product of the White House Conference on Children was the call to establish a federal agency to "collect and exchange ideas and information on child welfare." With an initial appropriation of $25,640, the U.S. Children's Bureau was established in 1912 under the auspices of the Department of Commerce and Labor.[8] Instrumental in the early years of the Children's Bureau were Lillian Wald, of New York's Henry Street Settlement House, and Florence Kelley, an alumna of both the Henry Street Settlement and Hull House. Julia Lathrop, a former resident of Hull House, was the Bureau's first director.[9]

Because of the economic circumstances of poor families, child labor emerged as a primary concern of early child welfare advocates. The absence of public relief meant that families were compelled to work at whatever employment might be available, however wearing and demeaning. Children worked full shifts in coal mines and textile mills; women labored in sweatshops. Neither were protected from dangerous or unhygienic working conditions. Under the guidance of Florence Kelley, the National Consumer League fought for children and women using a dual strategy. First, the League lobbied for reform in the working conditions of women through regulating sweatshops and factories, and for ending the exploitation of children through prohibiting child labor. Second, it advocated ameliorating the grinding poverty of many families by means of a family subsidy that would make such deplorable work less necessary. For Kelley, the family subsidy was a preventive measure with which she was quite familiar; she had successfully lobbied for passage of the Funds for Parents Act in 1911 in Illinois. This act was a precursor of the Aid to Dependent Children program, part of the original Social Security Act of 1935.[10]

Before the Great Depression, welfare advocates could boast of a series of unprecedented initiatives designed to improve the conditions of America's poor families. The Children's Bureau Act of 1912 established a national agency to collect information on children. The Child Labor Act of 1916 prohibited the interstate transportation of goods manufactured by children. The Maternity and Infancy Act of 1921 assisted states in establishing programs that dramatically reduced the nation's infant and maternal mortality rates. Yet these successes, however hardwon, were constantly at risk of being subverted. The Supreme Court ruled the Child Labor Act unconstitutional in 1918, and the Maternity and Infancy Act was terminated in 1929 when Herbert Hoover and Congress refused further appropriations.[11] Child and family welfare initiatives remained unsuccessful until the Social Security Act of 1935 ushered in a complete set of welfare policies.

The Social Security Act addressed child welfare in two of its provisions. Title IV introduced the Aid to Dependent Children program, which provided public relief to needy children through cash grants to their families. Title V reestablished Maternal and Child Welfare Services (which had expired in 1929) and expanded the mandate of the Children's Bureau, whose goal was to oversee a new set of child welfare services "for the protection and care of homeless, dependent, and neglected children, and children in danger of becoming delinquent."[12] Significantly, both family relief and child welfare services were to be administered by the states through public welfare departments. As a result, as of 1935 the provision of child welfare services shifted largely from the private, voluntary sector to the public, governmental sector.

PROTECTIVE SERVICES FOR CHILDREN

Through the Social Security Act, states proceeded to develop services to children independently of one another and within the relatively loose specifications of the act. Free of a centralized authority that would ensure standardized care throughout the United States, child welfare services varied greatly from state to state and even within states. In the two decades following the passage of the Social Security Act, child welfare services had become established within American social welfare, but with a high degree of fragmentation.

By the 1960s, the status quo in child welfare was upset by reports of increasing incidents of child abuse and neglect. A pediatrician, C. Henry Kempe, identified nonaccidental injuries to children as the "battered child syndrome." As more states began to address the problem, child welfare advocates built a compelling case for a national standard for child protective services. This lobbying led to the passage of the Child Abuse Prevention and Treatment Act of 1974, which established the National Center for Child Abuse and Neglect within the Department of Health and Human Services, as well as a model statute for state child protective programs. All 50 states eventually enacted the model statute, which, among its provisions, specified the following:

1. A standard definition of child abuse and neglect
2. Methods for reporting and investigating abuse and neglect
3. Immunity for those reporting suspected injuries to children
4. Prevention and public education efforts to reduce incidents of abuse and neglect

As a result of these national standards, the National Center for Child Abuse and Neglect was able to report—for the first time—trends in child abuse and the need for protective services for children. Alarmingly, the data collected by the National Center revealed a dramatic increase in reports of child abuse, which more than doubled between 1976 and 1986, when reports of child abuse numbered 2 million.[13] In 1991, Chicago's National Committee for the Prevention of Child Abuse reported that 1,383 children died as a result of abuse, 50 percent more than the number reported in 1986.[14] Most troubling was that reports of child abuse continued to climb through the mid-1980s, while at the same time expenditures for child protective services were decreasing.[15]

Increases in child abuse reports and decreases in expenditures led to a crisis in child welfare services. The magnitude of this crisis was mapped by Douglas Besharov, an authority on child welfare policy:

Of the 1,000 children who die under circumstances suggestive of parental maltreatment each year, between 30 and 50 percent were previously reported to child protective agencies. Many thousands of other children suffer serious injuries after their plight becomes known to authorities. . . . *Each year, about 50,000 children with observable injuries severe enough to require*

hospitalization are not reported [original emphasis].[16]

Stories of child abuse fatalities began to appear with greater frequency in the media. Shortly before Thanksgiving of 1987, the report of the beating death of a six-year-old girl under the care of a middle-class couple in Greenwich Village became a feature story in *Newsweek*.[17] Unfortunately, incidents of child abuse were too often associated with child welfare programs mandated to protect children. In Kansas City, 25 percent of the children in foster care were found to have been abused.[18] During the spring of 1988, National Public Radio broadcast a report of two Illinois state "social workers" who had been dismissed for failure to make home visits and falsification of records that were associated with the deaths of two children who had been reported as victims of child abuse.[19] In Baltimore, a group of current and former foster children won a decision in the Fourth District Court of Appeals after charging that 20 administrators and caseworkers of the Baltimore City Department of Social Services had failed "to adequately monitor and protect children in foster care."[20] Such litigation placed child welfare personnel in a double bind: being faced with increasing demands for services, yet not having adequate staff resources to respond effectively. "If you take children out of the home, you're snatching them. If you leave them in the home [and they're abused], you didn't protect them," complained Jim Bell of the Massachusetts Department of Social Services. "We try to deal the best we can in that environment and protect the [case]workers. We don't want them hanging out there all alone."[21]

One consequence of this disintegration of children's services was a volatile debate over the definition of child abuse and neglect. One solution to the widening disparity between resources for children's services and increasing reports of abuse and neglect, of course, would be to redefine the criteria in accordance with which emergency services for children were deployed. If conservatives could promulgate a more restrictive definition of abuse and neglect, they would benefit directly in that such a change would effectively subvert demands for greater funding for children's services and parents would retain wider latitude for their behavior in the home. Contending that confirmed reports of child abuse had consistently declined since implementation of the Child Abuse Prevention and Treatment Act, Besharov argued for a more restrictive definition.[22] Countering this claim, David Finkelhor of the University of New Hampshire's Family Research Laboratory noted that annual data from the American Humane Association indicated fairly steady rates of validated abuse and neglect, from 40 to 43 percent of all reports. Since more specific research on the nature of general abuse and sexual abuse suggested increasing incidence, Finkelhor argued for more resources for child protection.[23]

CONCL FUT

The rapid deterioration of child welfare services led children's advocates to call for more funding of social services. But proposals for increased support for child welfare services did not go unchallenged. Ambiguity in the definition of what constituted child abuse and neglect had contributed to incidents in which child welfare workers appeared to disregard parental rights in their eagerness to protect children. Perhaps the most notorious instance of such overzealousness occurred during the summer of 1984, when social workers from the Vermont Department of Social and Rehabilitation Services and the state police rounded up 112 children from "a radical Christian sect" and detained them for three days to search for indications of abuse. When the American Civil Liberties Union threatened to sue the state on behalf of the religious community, state officials reconsidered, and the children were returned to their parents.[24] Similar but less newsworthy incidents enraged parents who, feeling unjustly accused, formed VOCAL (Victims of Child Abuse Laws) in an attempt to restore traditional parental rights in the face of what they perceived to be

the intrusiveness of the state. The 3,000 members of VOCAL have taken their complaint into the public arena, and, in Arizona, VOCAL held up a $5.4-million appropriation to improve child protective services.[25]

The criticism of child welfare professionals has not been limited to fundamentalists. In *The War Over the Family*, Bridgitte Berger, a sociology professor at Wellesley College, and Peter Berger, a sociology professor at Boston University, argued vociferously that middle-class social workers use the public social services as a method of evangelizing among lower-class clients; they manipulate the concept of children's rights as a way of undermining the family for the purpose of establishing professional hegemony in family affairs. Consequently, the Bergers suggest, in questions of parental versus child rights, it is preferable to "trust parents over against experts."[26] Although the Bergers' analysis undoubtedly lends credibility to groups like VOCAL, it does little to advance solutions to the urgent problem of child abuse. Apart from reducing a complex social issue to a question of rights, the Bergers leave an important question unanswered: If public welfare workers are faulted for being so far removed from the experiences of their poor and troubled clients, how much more distant are professors from prestigious private colleges?

FOSTER CARE FOR CHILDREN

When parents are unable to care for their children, foster care is often used to provide alternative care. As an extension of the practice of boarding out children, most foster care in the United States is at no cost to the parents, and children are placed in the homes of other families. There is an important relationship between child protective services and foster care in American social welfare. Foster care is a primary service for victims of child abuse; over half of children in foster care were placed there by child protective service workers. The second most prevalent reason for child foster care is the "condition or absence of the parent," accounting for about 20 percent of foster care placements.[27]

As in the case of protective services, foster care for children was not coordinated under the provisions of the Social Security Act. States adopted separate policies and, unfortunately, took few measures to monitor children in foster care. During the early 1960s, a series of studies began to document a disturbing development. Rather than being a temporary arrangement for child care, foster care had become a long-term experience for many youngsters: 70 percent of children had been in foster care for more than one year.[28] Not only had states planned poorly for the reunification of children with their original families, but, in many instances, child welfare agencies had lost track of foster care children altogether. During the summer of 1992, the District of Columbia's Department of Human Services (DHS) was rocked by a foster care scandal, when it was reported that the department had literally no idea of the location of one out of every four children it had placed in foster care.[29]

In response to the deterioration of children's services, several demonstration projects were begun that offered intensive services to families in order to prevent their children from being placed in foster care and to effectively reunite children with their biological parents. The demonstrations seemed to be cost-effective. In Virginia, 14 prefoster care placement service projects concluded that family functioning improved in 69 percent of the families receiving intensive support services. Moreover, the cost of support services was $1,214 per child, substantially less than the cost of foster care ($11,173) or residential care ($22,025) for the average length of time (4.6 years) a child was in these more intensive forms of treatment.[30] As a result of these field experiments, "permanency planning" became a central feature of the Adoption Assistance and Child Welfare Act of 1980.

Permanency planning is "the systematic

process of carrying out, within a brief time-limited period, a set of goal-directed activities designed to help children live in families that offer continuity of relationships with nurturing parents or caretakers and the opportunity to establish lifetime relationships."[31] The Child Welfare Act was an ambitious effort, and one expert heralded it as making it "possible to implement at state and local levels a comprehensive service delivery system for children."[32] As a result of permanency planning, the number of children in foster care plummeted. In 1977, 500,000 children were in foster care; by 1983 the number had dropped to 251,000. Welfare workers swiftly removed children from foster care and reunited them with their biological families under the rationale that community support services would assist parents. Early research on family preservation services indicated positive results, but families needed extensive service, as much as $2,600 per family. One study of 367 families found that the average family consumed "67 hours of service (about six hours a week), and more than a third of the service time was spent in the home."[33] Despite evidence of the effectiveness of permanency planning, public agencies struggled to pay for necessary services. An analysis of a model family reunification program found that deficits in agency resources—gaps in service, large caseload and worker turnover, inadequate family preparation, among others—presented problems in more than half of all cases. The researchers were "unaware of any reported successful permanency planning program that has high caseloads as a program component."[34]

Tragically, inadequate resources sometimes created a vicious circle: When biological parents received few support services, they were less able to care for their children, thereby contributing to the need for child protective services. In the absence of intensive support services, permanency planning for many children meant a revolving-door placement in foster care, reunification with the biological parent(s), then a return to foster care. In 1982, 43 percent of children had been in multiple placements, but by 1983, 53.1 percent had been in more than one placement. Of this number, 20.1 percent had been placed twice, 24.2 percent three to five times, and 8.8 percent six or more times.[35] The National Association of Social Workers newsletter reported the instance of a four-year-old New York boy who was placed in 37 different homes in two months, and another who had been placed in 17 homes in 25 days.[36]

In large measure, the permanency planning movement faltered due to lack of support services to families. Not long after passage of the Adoption Assistance and Child Welfare Act of 1980, Ronald Rooney observed prophetically that "if the promise of permanency planning is to be realized, those who allocate funds must provide money for a continuum of services that are delivered from the point of entry into foster care and include programs designed to prevent the removal of children from their homes."[37] Yet in 1981 an important source of family support services, Title XX, was cut 21 percent. For 1992 the Title XX appropriation, $2.8 billion, was $100 million less than the amount funded in 1981, despite a 58 percent increase in reports of child abuse and neglect since that time.[38] Yet gross appropriations for Title XX reveal only a small part of the defunding of the program. Once inflation is factored into the appropriations, it can be seen that between 1977 and 1992, Title XX actually lost $3.2 billion, or 55.4 percent of its funding.[39] A decade after the early permanency planning demonstration projects, Theodore Stein feared that the movement was being subverted by budget cuts and a reliance on crisis services in child welfare.[40]

Limited funding under Title XX for child welfare induced states to become more dependent on other federal sources of revenue. Because it was funded completely by the federal government and did not require any state matching funds, Title XX was the optimal funding source for child welfare program administrators, but it had one important flaw: Revenues were capped. Other federal assistance, such as

Title IV–B of the Social Security Act, allocated a fixed amount of funds for children's services but required a 25 percent state matching contribution. In addition, though Title IV–E of the Social Security Act was not capped, federal funds did require a matching contribution on the part of the state ranging from 25 to 50 percent. Moreover, the two programs that child welfare program administrators looked to under Title IV–E, foster care and adoption assistance, were reserved for poor children who would have been eligible for AFDC had they stayed at home. In other words, beyond Title XX, child welfare administrators could try to address increases in service demand through other federal programs, but Title IV–B funds were capped and required a state match, while open-ended Title IV–E funds were earmarked for AFDC children in addition to requiring a state match.

Under these circumstances, Byzantine patterns of service funding evolved during the 1980s as child welfare officials strove for matching formulae that optimized federal reimbursement. Imaginative program managers from affluent states first matched federal requirements for AFDC children in order to capture Title IV–E funds, then fronted the state match for IV–B funds, to the extent possible reserving Title XX funds for non-AFDC children. Program managers from states unwilling to meet the federal matching requirements had little choice but to use scarce Title XX funds, sometimes for AFDC children. Three sources of federal revenues for children's services are found in Table 13.1. The rapid expansion of funds for foster care of AFDC children under Title IV–E, an open-ended entitlement, contrasts with capped funding under Title IV–B and Title XX, raising the specter that states may be induced to place poor, and disproportionately minority, children in foster care rather than to help them stay at home by funding in-home support services.

To compound the problems faced by foster care workers, quality foster care placements became scarce. A declining standard of living

TABLE 13.1. Federal Funding for Child Welfare*
(In millions of dollars)

Fiscal Year (selected)	Title IV–B Child Welfare	Title IV–E Foster Care	Title IV–E Adoption Assistance
1981	163.6	308.8	0.5
1983	156.3	394.8	12.6
1985	200.0	546.2	41.8
1987	222.5	792.6	73.7
1989	246.7	1,153.1	110.5
1991	273.9	1,762.4	171.5
1993 (estimate)	273.9	2,676.6	181.9

* Title XX is not included because the federal government has no record of how funds are expended. (SOURCE: Committee on Ways and Means, U.S. House of Representatives, *Overview of Entitlement Programs, 1992 Green Book* [Washington, D.C.: U.S. Government Printing Office, 1992], p. 847.)

forced many women into the job market, thus restricting the pool of families with a parent at home to supervise children[41]—a requisite for desirable foster care. Soon the shortage of foster homes became critical. The director of the Illinois Department of Children and Family Services pleaded for 1,000 new foster parents to prevent the collapse of the state's foster care program.[42] In an investigation into the death of one foster care child, a Virginia grand jury cited "the acute shortage of suitable shelter for the 6,000 neglected, abused, and disabled children" in the state as a factor contributing to the child's death.[43] Thus, by the late 1980s, permanency planning was beset with multiple problems, leaving foster care as an unreliable way of serving many of the most troubled children in the United States. In 1986 the National Committee for Prevention of Child Abuse reported that child deaths had increased dramatically due to "the current overload of state child welfare systems." "In the twenty-four states for which data were available, the number of confirmed or suspected child deaths increased 26.7 percent over 1985, from 386 to 489, whereas deaths in those same states had declined by 2 percent between 1984 and 1985."[44]

ADOPTION

From the standpoint of permanency planning, adoption has become an important child welfare service. In the early 1980s, the Children's Bureau noted that 50,000 "hard to adopt" children were waiting for homes. Many of these children were of minority origin, handicapped, or older and had been in foster care for several years.[45] Because such children posed a financial burden for adoptive parents, the Adoption Assistance and Child Welfare Act of 1980 provided subsidies to adoptive parents. In 1983, 6,320 children were being subsidized each month at a cost of $12 million.[46] Providing incentives for parents to adopt hard-to-adopt children clearly supported the concept of permanency planning: "90 percent of subsidized adoptions involve foster parents whom the subsidy has enabled to adopt children with whom they had formed a relationship . . . and most of these are minorities or have special needs."[47] Moreover, subsidized adoption proved cost-effective, costing 37 percent less than foster care.

Still, adoption is not without controversy. Because children come from a variety of racial and cultural groups, the issue of transcultural adoption is raised. Should consideration be given to maintaining the cultural identity of children placed for adoption by finding them homes in their "native" culture? This question is at the heart of the Indian Child Welfare Act of 1978. Native Americans were disturbed that "25 to 35 percent of all American Indian children [were] separated from their families and placed in foster homes, adoptive homes, or institutions."[48] However, the fact that 85 percent of such placements were in non-Indian families and the children "without access to their tribal homes and relationships" raised the specter of cultural genocide.[49] To reinforce the cultural identity of Native American children, the Indian Child Welfare Act established:

Minimal Federal standards for the removal of Indian children from their families and the placement of such children in foster or adoptive homes which will reflect the unique values of Indian culture, and for assistance to Indian tribes in the operation of child and family service programs.[50]

Equally important, the Indian Child Welfare Act established tribes, rather than state courts, as the governing bodies for Indian foster children.

While provisions to reinforce the cultural identity of children are unquestionably valid for a pluralistic society, the circumstances of many racial and cultural minorities leave the implementation of such policies in doubt.[51] Without basic health, education, and employment supports, minority families are likely to have difficulty in considering the adoption of children. For example, the number of African-American children available for adoption far outstrips the number of African-American families recruited to adopt children despite the fact that "black families adopt at a rate 4.5 times greater than white or Hispanic families."[52]

Changes in family composition further cloud the picture. The pool of adoptive families has diminished with the increase in the number of female-headed households. The combination of low wages for women and a shortage of marriageable men means that mothers are encouraged to maintain small families, not to expand them through adoption. Esther Wattenberg of the University of Minnesota Center for Urban and Regional Affairs suspected that:

the remainder of the 1980s and the decade beyond will be dominated by a sorting out of "the best interests of the child" in the extraordinary complex family relationships that develop out of extending family boundaries to stepparents, several sets of grandparents, and an assortment of new siblings from remarried families that join and unjoin family compositions.[53]

This high degree of family reorganization is likely to affect minority families, leaving child welfare workers with a small pool of tradition-ally structured families as potential foster or adoptive parents. To the extent that family reorganization becomes pronounced among minority populations, minority families will be less able to adopt children. At the same time, the comparative economic advantage enjoyed by white families, coupled with the low fertility rate of white women, means that they will continue to adopt, and those adopted will often be minority children. As a result, the issue of transcultural adoption is likely to trouble child welfare professionals in the future.

HEAD START

In response to concerns about the lack of educational preparation of poor children, Head Start was incorporated in the Economic Opportunity Act of 1964. A year later, the first Head Start programs were established in poor communities. Intended to compensate for a range of deficits displayed by poor children, Head Start offered health and dental screening, nutrition, and socialization experiences in addition to preschool academic preparation. Of the War on Poverty programs, Head Start was one of a few that captured the imagination of the nation. Despite wide public support, however, official support of Head Start was somewhat uneven, as Table 13.2 shows.

TABLE 13.2. Head Start: Participation and Federal Funding, Selected Years (Dollars in millions)

Fiscal Year	Enrollment	Budget Authority
1965 (summer only)	561,000	$96.4
1970	477,400	325.7
1975	349,000	403.9
1980	376,300	735.0
1985	452,080	1,075.0
1990	548,470	1,552.0

SOURCE: House Ways and Means Committee, U.S. House of Representatives, *Overview of Entitlement Programs, 1992 Green Book*, pp. 1695–96.

Although funding for Head Start has grown significantly since its founding, current appropriations, when adjusted for inflation, are actually lower than when the program first began. Moreover, the number of children now enrolled is lower than when the program was established twenty-five years earlier; by the early 1990s, only 27 percent of eligible children participated in the program.[54]

During the 1980s, when government assistance to the poor was restrained, many poor families dispatched both parents to the labor market to stabilize family income, and this increased the need for Head Start. Even the Deficit Reduction Act of 1990, which held spending for most social programs in check, provided for modest increases in Head Start.[55] In large measure, this reflected a growing appreciation that Head Start was a proven investment in human capital. Award-winning author Sylvia Ann Hewlett noted that "Head Start ($3,000 a year per child) is much less expensive than prison ($20,000 a year per inmate)."[56] Such agreement notwithstanding, the federal fiscal crisis makes it unlikely that Head Start will increase to its optimal allocation of $7.6 billion for 1994.[57]

EMERGING ISSUES IN CHILD WELFARE

Changes in the economic and social circumstances of American families have broadened the scope of issues that have defined child welfare policy in the past. Of these changes, three are likely to shape child welfare in the future: day care, maternal and child health, and teenage pregnancy. Day care for children has risen in importance as more and more parents with children work. The need for child day care is felt both by middle-income families, in which both parents work in order to meet the income requirements of a middle-class life-style, and by low-income families, in which a parent is encouraged, or required, to participate in an AFDC workfare program. The child care available for these families is often unreliable, expensive, and of questionable quality. Furthermore, available child care does not often conform to the work schedules of parents. A study of New York City families found that half had to patch together day care from multiple providers. Low wages fail to attract the more skilled providers to the field, leading the Children's Defense Fund to observe ruefully that "despite their higher levels of education, child care providers are paid less than animal caretakers, bartenders, or parking lot and amusement park attendants."[58]

The crisis in child day care received nationwide attention in 1986 when two Miami children, unsupervised because their mother had to work and could not locate child care, climbed into a clothes dryer in which they "tumbled and burned to death."[59] This incident was cited in the introductory remarks to the proposed $375-million Child Care Services Improvement Act. An indicator of the severity of the day care crisis was that the legislation was sponsored by Orrin Hatch, a conservative senator noted for his prior opposition to social welfare legislation.[60]

Before 1990, the primary policies assisting parents with child care were the Federal Dependent Care Tax Credit and Title XX, neither of which has expanded child care for low-income families. The Dependent Care Tax Credit allows families to deduct up to 30 percent of $2,400 spent on child day care for a given year. As a "tax expenditure"—a de facto allocation through the Internal Revenue Service by not taxing income spent for a specific purpose—the Dependent Care Tax Credit is the largest form of federal assistance for child care.[61] For 1993 this tax credited is expected to cost the treasury $2.8 billion.[62] Unfortunately, this tax expenditure is "nonrefundable," requiring poor families to pay the out-of-pocket expenses before they receive a partial rebate at a later date. Few poor families can afford this; as a result, the Dependent Care Tax Credit is virtually useless for them. Under Title XX, states were able to purchase day care for poor families, but few appropriated significant funds for that purpose.

As part of the 1990 Deficit Reduction Act, the Child Care and Development Block Grant program was established. The Child Care Block Grant provided $750 million in 1991, $825 million in 1992, and $925 million in 1993 to states through a complicated matching formula based on the number of children below five years of age and the number participating in the federal school lunch program. Of these funds, 75 percent are to be spent on direct assistance to families for child care services, and 25 percent for grants and contracts to child care providers. While the Child Care Block Grant represented a triumph for children's advocates, it contained an important flaw. Because federal allocations were predicated on state matching funds, the poor fiscal situation of many state governments led federal analysts to anticipate that only $715 million will actually be used out of the $1.5 billion made available during the first half of the 1990s for child care through the block grant.[63]

Maternal and child health has emerged as an issue among child welfare advocates as younger poor women give birth to low birth-weight babies for which they have received inadequate prenatal care. Low birth weight is a concern because such infants have a higher incidence of developmental disabilities, some of which are permanent and eventually require institutional care. The relationship between low birth weight and developmental disabilities, long recognized by public health officials, resurfaced in *Hunger in America,* a 1985 report by the Physician Task Force on Hunger in America funded through the Harvard University School of Public Health. In this report, researchers noted that "low birth-weight is the eighth leading cause of death in the United States." Efforts to sustain premature and low birth-weight infants are expensive and, even when successful, the consequence is often "long-term growth and developmental problems." Infants born small and premature suffer 25 percent more major neurological problems and 117 percent more minor neurological problems compared with normal infants.[64] Despite such documentation,

the incidence of low birth weight among infants in the United States is relatively high, as indicated in Table 13.3. Moreover, the percentage of low birth-weight infants born to nonwhite teenagers is alarming, ranging from a low of 15.3 percent in Hawaii to a high of 32.9 percent in Mississippi.[65] Given the relatively high number of teen pregnancies in the nonwhite population, these figures show a disturbing reality: Substantial numbers of nonwhite infants in the United States are born with serious neurological deficits.

The primary federal program to enhance prenatal care for low-income families is WIC, the special supplemental food program for women, infants, and children. Under WIC, poor women who are pregnant and those who are breast-feeding youngsters are eligible for food coupons through which they may obtain especially nutritious foods. While the WIC program would seem a logical method for addressing the low birth-weight problem of infants born to poor women, participation in the WIC program is not at desirable levels. Nationwide, only 40.4 percent of the population financially eligible to participate in WIC did so in 1986. In 44 states, fewer than half of eligible women and children were served through WIC.[66]

The consequences of poor prenatal care are devastating. In 1986, twice as many African-American infants died as did white infants, a disparity that has widened since 1940.[67] This difference is depicted in Figure 13.1. By 1990 the first-year cost of extensive medical care for low birth-weight infants rose to $2.1 billion, most of which could have been saved had the nation promoted maternal and child health more aggressively.[68]

Problems relating to maternal and infant health are exacerbated by the sharp rise in the numbers of adolescent females having children. Out-of-wedlock births became an important family issue in the 1980s when the incidence of unwed motherhood increased rapidly, so that by 1983 half of all nonwhite births were outside of marriage.[69] Most troubling about this develop-

TABLE 13.3. Percentage of Infants Born at Low Birth Weight, Selected Countries, 1990

Rank	Nation	Percent	Rank	Nation	Percent
1	Spain	1	40	Uruguay	8
2	Norway	4	40	Tunisia	8
2	Sweden	4	40	Botswana	8
2	Ireland	4	40	Benin	8
2	Finland	4	40	Colombia	8
6	Kuwait	5	40	Ethiopia	8
6	Jordan	5	40	Cuba	8
6	New Zealand	5	50	Peru	9
6	Switzerland	5	50	Mauritius	9
6	Portugal	5	50	Venezuela	9
6	Japan	5	50	South Korea	9
6	Belgium	5	50	Burundi	9
6	Hong Kong	5	50	Algeria	9
6	Egypt	5	50	Iraq	9
6	Iran	5	50	China	9
6	France	5	58	Maylaysia	10
17	Romania	6	58	Mongolia	10
17	Greece	6	58	Madagascar	10
17	Germany	6	58	Hungary	10
17	Saudi Arabia	6	58	Lebanon	10
17	United Arab Emirates	6	63	Senegal	11
17	Soviet Union	6	63	Syria	11
17	Singapore	6	63	Lesotho	11
17	Bulgaria	6	63	Mauritania	11
17	Austria	6	67	South Africa	12
17	Australia	6	67	Thailand	12
17	Canada	6	67	Bolivia	12
17	Denmark	6	67	Mexico	12
17	Czechoslovakia	6	71	Zaire	13
17	Costa Rica	6	71	Guinea-Bissau	13
31	United Kingdom	7	71	Cameroon	13
31	Turkey	7	74	Guatemala	14
31	Yugoslavia	7	74	Tanzania	14
31	**United States**	**7**	74	Indonesia	14
31	Paraguay	7	74	Côte d'Ivoire	14
31	Chile	7		**U.S. black population**	**14**
31	Albania	7	78	Niger	15
31	Oman	7	78	Sudan	15
31	Israel	7	78	Kenya	15
40	Panama	8	78	Central African Republic	15
40	Jamaica	8	78	El Salvador	15
40	Poland	8	83	Sri Lanka	25

SOURCE: Children's Defense Fund, *The Health of America's Children* (Washington, D.C.: Children's Defense Fund, 1992), Table 7, p. 8.

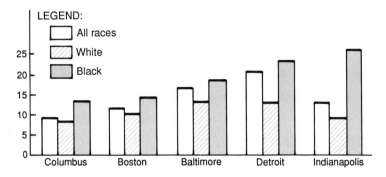

Figure 13.1. Infant Mortality Rates by Race, Selected Cities with 500,000 + Population, 1984. (SOURCE: Children's Defense Fund, *The Health of America's Children* [Washington, D.C.: Children's Defense Fund, 1987], p. 12. Reprinted with permission.)

ment was that the percentage of unmarried teenage mothers was rising so rapidly that by 1984 it was triple what it had been 25 years before.[70] By the mid-1980s, over half of all teenage births were outside of marriage.[71] This increase in very young women having children on their own poses a serious problem for public policy for two basic reasons. First, teenage mothers are more likely to drop out of school and thus fail to gain those skills that would make them self-sufficient. As Figure 13.2 illustrates, adolescent mothers, particularly those who are African-American or Hispanic, are apt to have less command of basic skills. Poor skill development poses a critical problem when these skills are parenting skills. Second, teenage mothers are more likely to have to depend on welfare for assistance, the benefits of which are at levels lower than the actual cost of raising children. This combination of poor skill development and dependence on public welfare programs presents the specter of poor children bearing more poor children in an endless cycle of hopelessness. The consequences are particularly tragic for poor children, who have little prospect of escaping the poverty trap. Reductions in the numbers of working males who are marriageable means that these children have little hope that their mother's marriage will pull them out of poverty, although this is the most prevalent way for mothers to become independent of public welfare.[72] The loss of earning power through the Aid to Families with Dependent Children program means that public assistance will not provide an adequate economic base for poor children.[73] Moreover, the interaction of these factors has devastating implications for African-American children: 30 percent of all African-American children are "persistently poor." Approximately 90 percent of children who are poor for 10 or more years of their childhood are African-American.[74] Unfortunately, the prevalence

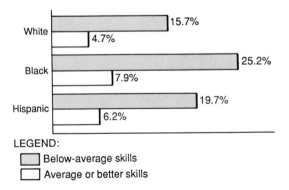

Figure 13.2. Parenthood by Basic Skill Levels, 16–19 Year-Old Women, 1981. (SOURCE: Children's Defense Fund, *A Children's Defense Budget* [Washington, D.C.: Children's Defense Fund, 1988], p. 172. Reprinted with permission.)

of teenage motherhood is likely to worsen the life opportunities of poor children, particularly those who are minorities. For these reasons, Thompson and Peebles-Wilkins reinforce the importance of interventions that incorporate societal supports while distancing friends in order to elevate the self-esteem of African-American adolescent mothers.[75]

THE FUTURE OF CHILD WELFARE

After a half-century of federal legislation, child welfare advocates cannot be hopeful about the care provided to American youngsters. The prospect of using the family as the primary institution for child welfare has diminished because of the absence of economic and social supports to keep the family intact. Without a coherent family policy, families have been less able to care for children, and child welfare services—such as protective services, foster care and adoption—have been deployed to ameliorate the most serious problems experienced by children. During the 1980s, however, even these programs became subject to budget rescissions, further exposing youngsters to economic and social insecurity as well as physical danger. By the 1990s, children's services resembled a tangle of categorical programs more closely connected to vital, but diminishing, funding streams than to the actual troubles that children and their families experienced.

At the national level, child welfare advocates found that the plight of troubled children might prove to be a compelling justification for reassessing the neglect of children's programs. In promoting its welfare reform proposal, the American Public Welfare Association highlighted (in its publication of that title) that "one child in four" was poor in the United States.[76] In May 1991, the National Commission on Children presented its comprehensive report on at-risk children and their families. The report called for an extensive expansion of federal efforts in several areas: income support, health, education, job training, employment, service

collaboration, and moral development. Several suggestions departed from the traditional methods of supporting poor children. First, the Commission recommended that "welfare be reoriented as short-term relief in periods of unanticipated unemployment, disability, or other economic hardship,"[77] as opposed to an indefinite entitlement. Limiting AFDC to a fixed period would, of course, require additional income supports for the poor. The Commission addressed this by suggesting an expansion of the Earned Income Tax Credit (EITC) and the creation of a $1,000 refundable Child Tax Credit. Finally, the Commission recommended the deployment of a demonstration program to test an enhanced child support enforcement and insurance scheme.

A Child Support Enforcement and Assurance (CSEAP) program to replace AFDC had been proposed by Irwin Garfinkel. CSEAP would reform child support in three ways: (1) The amount of child support would be calculated as a percentage of the absent parent's income; (2) support payments would be automatically withheld from paychecks; and (3) a minimum benefit to children would be assured by the federal government.[78] A federal CSEAP initiative with these components, Garfinkel reasoned, could replace most of the highly stigmatized AFDC program. CSEAP is not without its critics, however. Mickey Kaus, for example, opposed the idea because it placed the federal government in the same awkward position it has had with respect to AFDC, namely, subsidizing broken families. For that reason, Kaus favors an enhanced EITC, an increased minimum wage, and a federal jobs program in which any AFDC beneficiary would have to participate after two years, or lose benefits.[79]

Child welfare advocates had much to choose from given the relative neglect of children's issues on the part of the Reagan and Bush administrations. Perhaps the best-positioned among child welfare advocates, the Children's Defense Fund (CDF) had, during the 1980s, brought to the nation's attention a new set of child welfare problems—teen pregnancy, homeless and runaway youth, malnutrition among mothers and infants, and unemployment and school absence among adolescents. Child welfare advocates were particularly pleased when President Clinton selected Donna Shalala to head the Department of Health and Human Services, since Shalala had succeeded Hillary Clinton as chair of the CDF board.[80]

Meanwhile, states were experimenting with various methods for stretching their dollars to do more for children. Gradually, these efforts evolved into a potent critique of the traditional ways in which children's services had been delivered. "What's needed is a complete overhaul of children's services, bringing together public and private organizations to meet the comprehensive needs of children, adolescents, and parents," stated Stanford University's Michael Kirst.[81] Noting that many children from problem families were known to several, separate health and human agencies—none with sufficient resources to substantively help any one child—children's advocate Sid Gardner called for collaborative efforts among service providers: "In fact, we are ultimately failing our children not only because we haven't invested in them, but also because as communities we have failed to work together to hold ourselves accountable for the substantial resources we do invest—and for the outcomes of our most vulnerable residents."[82]

Social worker Bonnie Bernard of the Far West Laboratory for Educational Research and Development observed that, however defined, collaboration or restructuring targets power relations. "True restructuring means the redistribution of policymaking power, not only from the central office administration to the local school," but to professionals and ultimately to consumers and their communities.[83]

The restructuring movement has enormous implications for child welfare. Since the Social Security Act of 1935, child welfare has been integrally connected to federal funding for categorical programs that serve children with specific problems. If categorical programs are consolidated through restructuring, how will services be assured for children who are most at risk—the homeless, the disabled, those with AIDS? Giving parents vouchers to choose their service providers is one way to empower them, but who will see to it that they make prudent choices for their dependent children? And what will happen to the identity of social workers when they are assigned to interdisciplinary teams that include nurses, counselors, and educators? Perhaps most provocatively, does service collaboration around children presage the development of a new, postindustrial profession, the "human service professional," who will effectively replace social work as an activity properly retired with the industrial era?

DISCUSSION QUESTIONS

1. Much of child welfare—protective services, foster care, adoptions—is funded through a complex arrangement of categorical funding. How does your welfare department optimize reimbursement through these funding sources? As a result of this, what are the priorities for children's services? How would you reconcile discrepancies between categorical funding priorities and community needs?

2. Maintaining the cultural identity of minority children who receive foster care and adoption services is a heated issue in child welfare. When

there are too few minority families for the children needing foster care and adoption services, what should the policy of the welfare department be in placing minority children? How consistent is this with current child welfare policy in your community?

3. Providing preschool programs for children is an increasingly important issue as more mothers enter the work force. How adequate are day care provisions in your community? Who is responsible for the oversight of day care? To what extent are the needs of low-income families considered

in planning day care? What percentage of families eligible for Head Start actually participate in this program in your community?

4. Among the health-related child welfare concerns is infant mortality and low birth weight. How do the statistics in your community compare with the state and national incidence of these two important indicators of child welfare? What are the incidences of infant mortality and low birth weight for teenage and minority mothers in your community?

What plans does your community have for improving the health status of infants of minority and low-income families?

5. AFDC is arguably the most unpopular of social programs. What are the advantages and disadvantages of replacing it either by expanding the Earned Income Tax Credit or by a Child Support Enforcement and Assurance program? If you favor one of these, how would you convince the public that it constitutes *real* welfare reform?

NOTES

1. Jeanne Giovannoni, "Children," *Encyclopedia of Social Work,* 18th ed. (Silver Spring, Md.: NASW, 1987), p. 247.
2. Alfred Kadushin, "Child Welfare Services," *Encyclopedia of Social Work,* 18th ed. (Silver Spring, Md.: NASW, 1987), p. 268.
3. Walter Trattner, *From Poor Law to Welfare State* (New York: Free Press, 1974), p. 100.
4. Ibid., pp. 106–107.
5. Sallie Watkins, "The Mary Ellen Myth," *Social Work* 35 (November 1990): 503.
6. Diana DiNitto and Thomas Dye, *Social Welfare* (Englewood Cliffs, N.J.: Prentice-Hall, 1987), p. 153.
7. Kathleen Faller, "Protective Services for Children," *Encyclopedia of Social Work,* 18th ed. (Silver Spring, Md.: NASW, 1987). p. 386.
8. Trattner, *From Poor Law to Welfare State,* pp. 181, 183.
9. James Leiby, *A History of Social Welfare and Social Work in the United States* (New York: Columbia University Press, 1978), pp. 148–49.
10. June Axinn and Herman Levin, *Social Welfare* (New York: Harper and Row, 1982), p. 159.
11. Trattner, *From Poor Law to Welfare State,* p. 186.
12. Axinn and Levin, *Social Welfare,* pp. 224–28.
13. Barbara Kantrowitz et al., "How to Protect Abused Children," *Newsweek,* November 23, 1987, p. 68.
14. Sandra Evans, "Increase in Baby Killings Attributed to Family Stress," *Washington Post,* June 23, 1992, p. A–1.
15. Faller, "Protective Services for Children," pp. 387, 389.
16. Douglas Besharov, "Contending with Over-

blown Expectations," *Public Welfare,* Winter 1987, pp. 7, 8.
17. Kantrowitz et al., "How to Protect Abused Children," p. 68.
18. "Foster Care: Duty v. Legal Vulnerability," *NASW News,* July 1988, p. 3.
19. "Social Workers' Neglect," *All Things Considered* (Washington, D.C.: National Public Radio, April 15, 1988). *NASW News* later reported that the employees cited in this broadcast were not professional social workers but, rather, employees of the state (see n. 18).
20. "High Court Review Urged on Foster Care Liability," *NASW News,* July 1988, p. 3.
21. Ibid.
22. Douglas Besharov, "Right versus Rights: The Dilemma of Child Protection," *Public Welfare* 43 (1985): 19–46.
23. David Finkelhor, "Is Child Abuse Overprotected?" *Public Welfare* 48 (1990): 22–29.
24. Fox Butterfield, "Sect Members Assert They Are Misunderstood," *New York Times,* June 24, 1984, p. 16.
25. Besharov, "Contending with Overblown Expectations," p. 8.
26. Bridgitte Berger and Peter Berger, *The War Over the Family* (Garden City, N.Y.: Anchor, 1983), p. 213.
27. Theodore Stein, "Foster Care for Children," *Encyclopedia of Social Work,* 18th ed. (Silver Spring, Md.: NASW, 1987), pp. 641–42.
28. Ibid., p. 643.
29. Keith Harriston, "D.C. Foster Children Are Missing," *Washington Post,* August 6, 1992, p. C–1.
30. *A Children's Defense Budget* (Washington, D.C.: Children's Defense Fund, 1988), p. 179.

31. A. N. Maluccio and E. Fein, "Permanency Planning: A Redefinition," *Child Welfare*, May-June 1983, p. 197.

32. Duncan Lindsey, "Achievements for Children in Foster Care," *Social Work*, November 1982, p. 495.

33. Marianne Berry, "An Evaluation of Family Preservation Services," *Social Work* 34 (July 1992): 320.

34. Peg Hess, Gail Folaron, and Ann Jefferson, "Effectiveness of Family Reunification Services," *Social Work* 37 (July 1992): 306, 310.

35. Stein, "Foster Care for Children," p. 641.

36. "Foster Care vs. Legal Vulnerability," p. 3.

37. Ronald Rooney, "Permanency Planning for All Children?" *Social Work*, March 1982, p. 157.

38. *A Children's Defense Budget*, p. 54.

39. U.S. House of Representatives, *1992 Green Book* (Washington, D.C.: U.S. Government Printing Office, 1992), p. 830.

40. Stein, "Foster Care for Children," p. 649.

41. Esther Wattenberg, "The Fate of Baby Boomers and Their Children," *Social Work*, January-February 1986, pp. 85–93.

42. Kantrowitz et al., "How to Protect Abused Children," p. 71.

43. Mary Jordan, "Foster Parent Scarcity Causing Crisis in Care," *Washington Post*, July 20, 1986, p. A–9.

44. *A Children's Defense Budget*, p. 55.

45. Elizabeth Cole, "Adoption," *Encyclopedia of Social Work*, 18th ed. (Silver Spring, Md.: NASW, 1987), p. 70.

46. Committee on Ways and Means, U.S. House of Representatives, *Background Material and Data on Programs within the Jurisdiction of the Committee on Ways and Means* (Washington, D.C.: U.S. Government Printing Office, 1985), p. 494.

47. Cole, "Adoption," p. 71.

48. Ronald Fischler, "Protecting American Indian Children," *Social Work*, September 1980, p. 341.

49. Evelyn Lance Blanchard and Russell Lawrence Barsh, "What Is Best for Tribal Children?" *Social Work*, September 1980, p. 350.

50. Fischler, "Protecting American Indian Children," p. 341.

51. Patricia Hogan and Sau-Fong Siu, "Minority Children and the Child Welfare System," *Social Work*, November-December 1988, pp. 312–17.

52. Cole, "Adoption," p. 70.

53. Wattenberg, "The Fate of Baby Boomers and Their Children," p. 24.

54. Children's Defense Fund, *The State of America's Children, 1991* (Washington, D.C.: Children's Defense Fund, 1991), p. 44.

55. Paul Leonard and Robert Greenstein, *One Step Forward: The Deficit Reduction Package of 1990* (Washington, D.C.: Center on Budget and Policy Priorities, 1990), p. 34.

56. Sylvia Ann Hewlett, *When the Bough Breaks* (New York: Harper and Collins, 1992), p. 300.

57. Children's Defense Fund, *The State of America's Children, 1992*, p. 45.

58. Children's Defense Fund, *The State of America's Children, 1988*, p. 207.

59. Ibid., p. 214.

60. Ibid., p. 32; also National Association of Social Workers, "1986 Voting Record" (Silver Spring. Md.: NASW, 1987).

61. U.S. House of Representatives, *1992 Green Book*, p. 948.

62. Ibid., p. 984.

63. Leonard and Greenstein, *One Step Forward*, pp. 33–34.

64. Physician Task Force on Hunger in America, *Hunger in America* (Boston: Harvard University Press, 1985), p. 65.

65. Children's Defense Fund, *The Health of America's Children* (Washington, D.C.: Children's Defense Fund, 1987), p. 72.

66. Ibid., p. 84.

67. Ibid., p. 195.

68. Ibid., p. 25.

69. Michael Novak, ed., *The New Consensus on Family and Welfare* (Washington, D.C.: American Enterprise Institute, 1987), p. 135.

70. Lisbeth Schorr, *Within Our Reach* (New York: Anchor Press, 1988), p. 13.

71. Novak, *The New Consensus on Family and Welfare*, p. 48.

72. William Julius Wilson, "American Social Policy and the Ghetto Underclass," *Dissent*, Winter 1988, pp 80–91.

73. David Ellwood, *Poor Support: Poverty and the American Family* (New York: Basic Books, 1988), p. 58.

74. Committee on Ways and Means, U.S. House of Representatives, *Children in Poverty* (Washington, D.C.: U.S. Government Printing Office, 1985), p. 44.

75. Maxine Seaborn Thompson and Wilma Peebles-Wilkins, "The Impact of Formal, Informal, and Societal Support Networks on the Psychological Well-being of Black Adolescent Mothers," *Social Work* 37 (July 1992): 65–71.

76. American Public Welfare Association, *One Child in Four* (Washington, D.C.: American Public Welfare Association, 1987).

77. National Commission on Children, *Beyond Rhetoric: A New American Agenda for Children and Families (Final Report)* (Washington, D.C.: National Commission on Children, 1991), p. 34.

78. Irwin Garfinkel, "Bringing Fathers Back In: The Child Support Assurance Strategy," *The American Prospect,* Spring 1992, p. 75.

79. Mickey Kaus, *The End of Equality* (New York: Basic Books, 1992).

80. Marlene Cimons, "Shifting toward a Mainstream Approach to Children's Issues," *Los Angeles Times,* December 24, 1992, p. A–5.

81. Michael Kirst, "Improving Children's Services," *Phi Delta Kappan,* April 1991, p. 616.

82. Sid Gardner, "Failure by Fragmentation," *California Tomorrow,* Fall 1989, p. 19.

83. Bonnie Benard, "School Restructuring Can Promote Prevention," *Western Center News,* December 1991, p. 8.

CHAPTER 14

Housing Policies

Problems associated with housing have recently entered the news by way of the national focus on homelessness. Although homelessness is undoubtedly an important social problem, finding and maintaining adequate and affordable housing is also problematic for the working poor as well as for a large section of the middle class. This chapter examines the problems in housing, with particular emphasis on problems related to low-income housing, housing affordability, homelessness, and proposals for housing reform.

THE HISTORY OF HOUSING LEGISLATION

The United States had no national housing policy prior to the Housing Act of 1937. The objective of the act was to:

provide financial assistance to the states and political subdivisions thereof for the elimination of unsafe and unsanitary housing conditions, for the eradication of slums, for the provision of decent, safe and sanitary dwellings for families of low income, and for the reduction of unemployment and the stimulation of business activity, to cre-

ate a United States Housing Authority and for other purposes.[1]

The Housing Act of 1949, which amended the 1937 act, called for federal money for slum clearance and urban redevelopment and for the creation of a public authority charged with building and administering 135,000 low-income housing units annually for six years. In addition, the Housing Act of 1949 included the goal of providing a decent home and a suitable living environment for every American family.[2] Specifically, this bill required each locality to develop a plan for urban redevelopment that contained provisions for "predominantly residential dwellings." The wording of this bill was interpreted by localities to mean that only one-half of new construction was to be devoted to low-income housing. Inadvertently, the federal government created a policy that encouraged urban redevelopment at the expense of existing low-income housing.

The Housing Act of 1949 was amended again in 1954. The term *urban development* was changed to urban renewal, and localities were required to submit a master plan for the removal of urban blight and for overall community development. The new act removed the requirement that new federally subsidized urban construction be "predominantly residential," and thus cleared the way for massive slum clearance projects. In addition, the act allowed localities to more freely lease or sell land and to avoid the construction of public housing. Urban renewal—the eradication of slums through condemnation and bulldozing—led to charges that cities were insensitive to the needs of poor long-term residents. Through renewal projects, localities attempted to revitalize inner cities by attracting middle- and upper-income families at the expense of displaced poor families. From 1949 to 1963, urban renewal projects removed about 243,000 housing units and replaced them with 68,000 units, of which only 20,000 were for low-income families.[3]

The Demonstration Cities and Metropolitan Development Act (Model Cities) was passed in 1966. This aggressive program was part of President Lyndon Johnson's War on Poverty and, in large part, focused on issues of deteriorated housing and blighted neighborhoods. The Model Cities legislation promised to "concentrate public and private resources in a comprehensive five-year attack on social, economic, and physical problems of slums and blighted neighborhoods."[4] In 1974 the Model Cities Act and virtually all neighborhood development acts were superseded by the Housing and Community Development Act of 1974.

In the early 1970s the federal government began to experiment with general revenue sharing. Although this system initially provided more funds, it also shifted major responsibility for the distribution of those funds from the federal government to local government. As funds became heavily controlled by local forces, they also became more vulnerable to the influence of local politics and the power of interest groups. Low-income groups, whose interests were previously protected by the federal government, were now less influential in the play of local political maneuvering.

The Housing and Community Development Act of 1974 was a wide-ranging bill that included provisions for urban renewal, neighborhood de-

velopment, model cities, water and sewer projects, neighborhood and facility grants, public facilities and rehabilitation loans, and urban beautification and historic preservation grants.[5] Although spending priorities were determined at the national level, communities were required to submit a master plan, including specific reference to their low-income housing needs. The amount allocated for fiscal years 1978 to 1980 was almost $11 billion, and more than 1,800 communities received entitlement grants in the first two years of the program.[6]

Two other interesting pieces of legislation emerged in the 1970s: the Home Mortgage Disclosure Act and the Community Reinvestment Act. The Home Mortgage Disclosure Act (HMDA) was concerned with the problem of mortgage redlining. Housing observers had argued that a major cause of community deterioration was a "lending strike," or redlining, by financial institutions. Redlining is defined as "an outright refusal of an insurance company, bank, or other financial institution to provide its services solely on the basis of the location of the property in question. The term is derived from the practice of marking in red the area on a map that is to be avoided by those responsible for the distribution of the services of that institution."[7] As a result of this policy, families seeking to purchase a home in a redlined neighborhood might be denied a mortgage loan, insurance, or other necessary services. In 1976, President Gerald Ford signed the Home Mortgage Disclosure Act, which required virtually every bank or savings and loan association to annually disclose where it made its loans. Although useful for community groups trying to pressure local banks into greater neighborhood involvement, in cities without active community organizations the law was rendered almost useless.

Congress further recognized the problem of mortgage redlining by enacting the Community Reinvestment Act (CRA) in 1977. Significantly broader than the HMDA, the CRA established the principle that each bank and savings institution has an obligation to make loans in every neighborhood of its service area. Virtually all lending institutions are covered under the CRA, and the law requires the federal government to annually evaluate the performance of each lending institution. Primary enforcement involves the control by federal regulatory agencies over new charters, bank growth and mergers, relocations, and acquisitions. Although CRA works well in theory, only a handful of the estimated 250 or more CRA challenges resulted in punitive action against lenders. In the main, the power of the Community Reinvestment Act rests with the ability of community groups to win commitments directly from lending institutions, usually in the form of negotiated settlements. It is estimated that $7.5 billion has been committed by banks and savings associations to low income communities as the result of negotiated CRA agreements.

In 1990, Congress passed the Cranston-Gonzales National Affordable Housing Act, the first new piece of legislation in more than a decade to address the housing needs of low- and moderate-income people. This act authorized a new, indirect approach to housing in the form of block grants to state and local governments. The 1990 act has six specific goals: (1) to decentralize housing policy by allowing states to design and administer their own housing programs; (2) to use nonprofit sponsors to help develop and implement housing services; (3) to link housing assistance more closely with social services; (4) to facilitate home ownership for low- and moderate-income people; (5) to preserve existing federally subsidized housing units; and (6) to initiate cost sharing among federal, state, and local governments and nonprofit organizations.[8]

The 1990 act requires applicants to prepare a comprehensive housing affordability strategy (CHAS), which will outline a state or jurisdiction's housing needs and plans for the subsequent five years. This plan must be updated annually, and will be used to determine whether state and local jurisdictions are utilizing federal housing money to meet the goals set in the CHAS document. Federal housing funds will flow directly to the government agencies that draw up the plans. In addition, the act calls for citizen input into preparation of the CHAS document.[9] The 1990 act also introduced the HOME investment partnerships block grant program, the Homeownership and Opportunity for People Everywhere (HOPE) program, and the national homeownership trust demonstration. (Funds were allocated only to the HOME and HOPE programs in 1992.)

The centerpiece of the National Affordable Housing Act is the HOME program, which is designed to increase the supply of affordable housing for low-income families by providing federal grants to state and local governments. All states and more than 300 local jurisdictions receive HOME funds. Ninety percent of HOME-assisted units must be affordable for families with incomes below 60 percent of the area median, and the remaining units must be affordable for families with incomes at 80 percent of the median. The HOME program allows states and entitlement communities a large measure of flexibility in addressing their local housing needs. Funds under the matching federal/state HOME program can be used for tenant-based rental assistance, property acquisition, or rehabilitation and, in some cases, for new construction. The HOME program also includes an unprecedented opportunity for local innovation. For example, at least 15 percent of HOME funds must be used for projects sponsored by Community Housing Development Organizations (CHDOs) or neighborhood-based nonprofit groups.[10] Although the HOME program was authorized to receive $2 billion in 1992, Congress appropriated only $1.5 billion.

A second major component of the 1990 act is the HOPE program, which is designed to facilitate homeownership by low-income families through the sale of publicly owned or held homes to their current residents or other low-income households. The HOPE program has four components: (1) HOPE I finances the sales of public housing apartments to residents; (2) HOPE II finances the sales of other apartment buildings held by the federal government (such as property acquired from failed savings and loan associations) to low-income persons; (3) HOPE III finances the sale of single-family homes owned by federal, state, or local governments; and (4) HOPE IV represents an effort to combine social services with housing assistance for elderly and disabled households that would otherwise be unable to live independently. Nearly $1 billion was authorized for HOPE I, II, and III in the 1990 act.[11]

Title VI of the 1990 act, the Low Income Housing Preservation and Resident Homeownership Act, is an effort to protect hundreds of thousands of residents in privately owned federally subsidized apartment buildings from displacement through the sale or conversion of their buildings. Under some federal housing programs enacted during the 1960s, private owners received mortgage insurance and subsidies to finance rental housing for low- and moderate-income families. In many cases, the Department of Housing and Urban Development (HUD) offered these owners an option to prepay or pay off their mortgages after 20 years. Upon payment of their mortgages, owners were freed of any obligation to reserve their units for low- and moderate-income residents. The Congressional Budget Office estimated that in 1989 as many as 300,000 rental units would be jeopardized unless Congress acted quickly. Title VI requires HUD to limit the approval of prepayments, and it creates incentives for owners to remain in the program or to sell to new owners who will maintain the project's low-income financial restrictions.[12]

The linkage between housing and social services is further strengthened by the Family Sufficiency program of the 1990 Housing Act. Specifically, this component calls for public housing authorities to offer programs that allow residents access to coordinated social services designed to assist them in gaining employment. Participating families must complete these programs or risk losing their housing assistance. In return, as a participant's income increases, the money normally contributed toward a higher rent (calculated at 30 percent of income) will be set aside in a special escrow account to be used for the purchase of a home. The act also includes modest funds to create "Family Investment Centers" in or near public housing projects, where social services will be provided.[13]

GOVERNMENTAL LOW-INCOME HOUSING PROGRAMS

Housing costs often represent the single largest expenditure in the household budget. It is a fixed cost and is often paid before food, clothing, and health care bills. For many families, the precious little that remains after rent or mortgage payments are made is used to buy necessities for the rest of the month. Despite the importance of housing, governmental assistance for housing has never been provided as an entitlement to all households that qualify for aid. Instead, Congress appropriates funds yearly for a number of new commitments, most of which run for from five to fifty years.

Within the framework of congressional appropriations, the housing needs of lower-income households are addressed by several programs in HUD and the Farmers Home Administration (FmHA). Section 8 is one of the most important of these programs in that it provides subsidized rental payments for more than 2.3 million units. The Section 8 program is based on a voucher system that allows low-income tenants to occupy existing and privately owned housing stock. In effect, the voucher is a subsidy that covers the difference between a fixed percentage of a tenant's income (30 percent) and the fair market rent of a housing unit. The HUD subsidy goes directly to the local public housing authority, which then pays the landlord, provided that the unit meets quality standards. Contract terms for these subsidies last for from five to fifteen years. Apart from direct rental subsidies, Section 8 also provides funds for new construction and for substantial and moderate rehabilitation of existing units.[14]

Another important HUD program is public housing, which is restricted to households whose incomes are too low to afford decent housing on the private market. Public housing is owned—or in some cases leased—by local public housing authorities. In 1992, 1.4 million public housing units were occupied by 3.7 million residents.[15] Still another program is Section 202, Housing for the Elderly and Handicapped, which provides financing to nonprofit organizations wishing to build housing for elderly or handicapped people. In 1974, Section 202 was tied to Section 8, so that instead of providing only low-interest loans to build apartments, it also provides rental subsidies. By 1988, 210,000 units had been produced under Section 202.[16] The Below-Market Interest Rate Program (BMIR) (Section 236) provides developers with low-interest loans in return for construction of moderately priced rental housing. This program was intended to provide housing for people whose incomes were too high to qualify for public housing but too low to meet the rental costs of unsubsidized housing. Finally, Section 235 provides low-income families with subsidized and low-interest mortgages to enable them to purchase a home. In 1988, almost 150,000 units were subsidized under this program; an additional 400,000 units existed where the mortgages were paid off, where the purchasers had graduated to unsubsidized interest rates as their incomes rose, or where the owners had defaulted.[17]

In addition to HUD, the FmHA operates a wide variety of housing programs in small towns and rural areas. The largest FmHA program is Section 502, which makes low-interest loans available for home purchases. A smaller program, Section 504, provides grants or low-interest loans to low-income families for home repairs. By 1985, some 1.6 million rural families had borrowed under the Section 502 program.

In addition, the FmHA operates a rental housing program much like Section 236 and a rural rental assistance program that provides subsidies to tenants. The FmHA also has a number of smaller, special-purpose programs, such as Sections 514 and 515, which provide housing for migrant workers.

ISSUES IN HOUSING POLICY

Deep-seated problems in America's housing market have led some observers to conclude that the United States is facing a serious housing crisis.[18] On first examination, however, the American housing situation has a patina of success. Throughout the 1970s and 1980s home ownership rates remained consistently high. From 1981 to 1991, more than 18 million housing units were started, a number far greater than the 11.6 million units completed between 1960 and 1970. In 1940, 43.6 percent of all dwelling units were owner-occupied; by 1991 that proportion had increased to 64 percent. Moreover, this phenomenon encompassed all sectors of the American population. For example, 23.6 percent of African-American- and minority-occupied units were owner-occupied in 1940; by 1991 that number had increased to 42.4 percent,[19] as shown in Table 14.1. The quality of the housing stock also increased dramatically in the post-World War II period. For example, over 45 percent of

TABLE 14.1. Homeownership by Race, 1960–1991 (In percentages)

Race	1960	1973	1980	1987	1991
White	64.4	67.1	68.7	66.8	67.3
Black	38.4	43.4	43.9	45.4	42.4
Hispanic	NA	43.2	42.4	40.6	39.0

SOURCES: U.S. Bureau of the Census, *Statistical Abstract of the United States, 1989* (Washington, D.C.: U.S. Government Printing Office, 1989), p. 720; and Joint Center for Housing Studies of Harvard University, *The State of the Nation's Housing, 1992* (Boston: Joint Center for Housing Studies of Harvard University, 1992), Exhibit 14, p. 12.

U.S. housing units lacked some or all plumbing facilities in 1940. By 1976 that percentage had declined to 3.4 percent. Moreover, 17.8 percent of all housing units were considered dilapidated or in need of major repairs in 1940; by 1989 that number was reduced to 3.4 percent.[20]

The size and comfort of new owner-occupied homes are a positive development. More than 60 percent of the housing units built in 1988 contained a floor plan greater than 1,600 square feet, three or more bedrooms, two or more bathrooms, and central air-conditioning. In 1991, the median square footage for a new single-family house was 1,890 square feet. Apart from significant regional variations, almost 16 percent of the total U.S. housing stock was constructed after 1970. In the South and West, one out of every five units was constructed between 1970 and 1976. Seven out of ten new housing starts were for single-family housing, underscoring the dramatic shift in home ownership.[21] These statistics can easily lead to the conclusion that the majority of Americans are purchasing good-quality, large, and relatively new homes. The true housing situation emerges only when the veneer of success is rubbed off. From the 1970s on, structural problems have surfaced that call into question the ability of the private market to adequately house the population.

Problems in Homeownership

Beginning in the 1970s, many people were forced to spend a higher percentage of their income on housing than they could reasonably afford. Furthermore, a number of people became so financially overextended that they became vulnerable to mortgage default or eviction, or else they lacked the necessary cash for purchasing other necessities.

Between 1967 and 1991, the median income for homeowners rose slightly (in constant 1989 dollars), from $28,011 to $32,320, while the median home price went from $56,466 to $67,672. During that same period, the total annual cost of homeownership rose from $4,727 to $7,806.

Although this increase is high, it is also geographically sensitive. For example, whereas the annual costs of home ownership rose from $4,502 to $6,545 in the southeastern United States between 1967 and 1991, these costs jumped from $4,549 to $12,686 in the Northeast. In 1967 the median annual mortgage payment was $3,400; by 1991 it had risen to $5,245. Perhaps more important, the total cost of home-ownership as a percentage of income for first-time buyers rose from 17.1 to 31.3 percent between 1967 and 1991.[22]

The increase in the price of single-family homes is even sharper when dollar costs are not adjusted for inflation. In 1970, the average new single-family home sold for $23,400; in 1988 it cost $112,500. For existing single-family homes the price went from $23,200 to $89,300. While in the past the price of new homes was moderated by consumers' ability to purchase existing stock, the relatively low levels of new construction, high rates of new household formation, and increased investment and speculation have caused the median price of a used home to be only slightly lower than that of a new one. The median price of housing also varies widely by city and region. From 1985 to 1989, the median price of an existing single-family home in Los Angeles went from $118,700 to $218,000; in New York and Boston it rose from $134,000 to $186,000; and in Providence, Rhode Island, it rose from $67,500 to $131,000.[23]

Partly because of these increases, 43 percent (1.8 million households) of poor homeowners spent a minimum of 50 percent of their income on housing costs in 1989. More than two-thirds of poor homeowners (2.8 million households) spent 30 percent or more of their income on housing. The median poor homeowner spent 43 percent of his or her income on housing costs in 1989. The housing problems of poor homeowners are also exacerbated by additional housing-related costs. For example, the median expenses for electricity, gas, property insurance, property taxes, and water bills totaled about $160 per month in 1989, an amount that equalled

38 percent of the median income of poor homeowners. Although the effects of the affordable housing shortage are hardest on poor homeowners, moderate-income homeowners also suffer. Almost one-third (32 percent) of moderate-income homeowners spent at least 30 percent of their income on housing in 1989; almost 20 percent spent at least 50 percent.[24]

The effects of the housing crisis are felt acutely by elderly and young households. In 1989, 62 percent of poor elderly households were homeowners. By comparison, only 30 percent of poor nonelderly households owned their own homes. Elderly homeowners are more likely to own their own homes free of mortgage liabilities. Of all elderly homeowners, 82 percent had paid off their mortgages. By comparison, only 29 percent of nonelderly homeowners had no mortgage liability. On the other hand, 68 percent of poor elderly households in 1989 spent at least 30 percent of their income on housing, compared with 23 percent of nonpoor elderly households. Similarly, 41 percent of poor elderly households spent at least 41 percent of their income on housing costs, compared with 8 percent of nonpoor elderly households.[25]

Families in which the householder is under age 25 also experience severe housing problems. The median income of these families is low and has declined since the 1970s. Many of these families face serious housing burdens, and only a small portion own their own homes. Moreover, homeownership rates among young families have been declining since the 1980s. In 1980, almost 50 percent of young families headed by a parent under 30 were homeowners; by 1991 that number had dropped to 33 percent.[26] In 1989, 50 percent of householders under age 25 spent at least 30 percent of their income on housing, thereby exceeding the federal affordability standard.[27]

HUD's guideline that housing costs should not exceed 30 percent of family income is a relative concept. For example, a family earning $100,000 a year and paying 30 percent of its income for mortgage payments will still have $70,000 left over for necessities and other items. By contrast, a family earning $15,000 a year and spending 30 percent of its income on rent or mortgage payments will have only $10,000 left for other necessities. Moreover, HUD's 30 percent rule ignores family size and the fact that a large family must spend more for food and other necessities than a smaller one. For instance, a single person earning $6,000 a year and paying 30 percent of his or her income for rent will have $335 a month left over for other necessities. However, a family of five earning $10,000 a year and paying 30 percent of its income for rent will have only $111 per person left over for food and other necessities. Thus, the relative impact of paying 30 percent of family income for rent or mortgage payments is greater for low income and large families than it is for high- and middle-income families.[28]

A better measure of housing affordability is a "market-based" approach, in which the cost of basic necessities is subtracted from income, with the remainder being earmarked for housing. The amount required for housing expenses can be measured using the Bureau of Labor Statistics' cost-of-living estimates and comparing them with renter incomes. Under this approach, 5.7 million renters (17 percent of all renters) in 1989 could not have afforded anything for housing without sacrificing other basic necessities. The median income of these householders was $4,600 per year.[29]

Factors such as mortgage instruments also have an important impact on housing affordability for poor and moderate-income homeowners. Specifically, many poor, moderate-income, and first-time home buyers lack adequate credit, have a sketchy credit history, or do not have the required down payment or qualifying income necessary for a conventional mortgage. During the high inflation of the late 1970s and early 1980s, a variety of inflation-sensitive mortgage instruments were introduced, including variable or adjustable rate mortgages (ARM). These ARM mortgages often included a low initial interest rate, sometimes two or more percentage points below fixed rates. Although most ARM mortgages were capped, they often fluctuated five or more percentage points above the initial loan rate, depending on the rate of inflation. Thus, a family with an ARM-based home loan may have originated a mortgage at 7 percent, but by the fifth year of an inflationary spiral the interest rate could have climbed to 13 percent, thus resulting in a huge increase in mortgage payments. While this system protected lending institutions against inflation, it made home ownership more tenuous in that the homeowner no longer had the security of predictable fixed payments for the life of the mortgage.

The increase in the cost of housing has led to other alternatives, including "equity participation," whereby the lender shares in any future profits made from selling a mortgaged house. A more common alternative is a "contract for deed," in which the buyer temporarily finances the sale. For example, under a contract for deed a house is sold for $50,000, with a $10,000 down payment. The buyer is then required to pay a monthly fee (including an agreed-upon interest rate) to the seller. In essence, the buyer takes out a "mortgage" directly with the seller, usually for a fixed term of from one to five years. After this period, the buyer is required to pay off the balance of the house's cost. Normally, the buyer will then originate a bank mortgage. Although it initially appears that the major risk is assumed by the seller, in many states if the buyer is more than 30 days overdue on payments the house automatically reverts to the seller, and the down payment is lost. Moreover, if the buyer cannot arrange financing, the home is repossessed by the seller. The buyer is therefore highly vulnerable to default and foreclosure under a contract for deed.

Problems in Finding Affordable Rental Housing

If finding affordable housing has become difficult for poor and moderate-income homeowners, it has reached crisis proportions for low-income renters. There are four major reasons for the affordability gap in rental housing: (1) Real incomes of renter households have been dropping; (2) the number of renter households has been increasing; (3) the number of low-cost unsubsidized rental units has been dropping and governmental housing assistance has not compensated for these losses; and (4) rents have increased.

The median price of a single-family home rose more than 20 percent from 1973 to 1987 (in inflation-adjusted dollars). Rental costs, including utilities, rose by 13 percent. However, median family income rose by a minuscule 0.4 percent during that period. Income for the poorest two-fifths of all families fell by 7 percent; for young families it plunged 24 percent. Thus, the average renter household was almost 13 percent worse off in 1987 than it was in 1973.[30] Moreover, the income limit for the bottom quartile in 1970 (in constant 1991 dollars) was $10,700. By 1989, it had dropped by 30 percent to $7,600.[31] At the same time, the number of poor renter households has been increasing. In 1970, there were 5.6 million bottom-quartile renter households; by 1989, that number had increased to 7.9 million.[32]

Perhaps the most dramatic development in the rental housing market has been the decrease in the number of low-cost unsubsidized rental units. In 1970, there were 6.8 million rental units that cost $250 or less per month. This number was 400,000 *greater* than the number of low-income renters, which stood at 6.4 million. By 1983, there were 5.9 million low-rent units and 9.7 million low-income renters, or a shortage of 3.9 million units. Between 1983 and 1989, the number of low-income renters remained about the same, while the number of low-rent units dipped to 5.5 million. By 1989, there were 9.6 million households with incomes of $10,000 a year or less competing for 6 million units[33] (see Figure 14.1). For example, in 1991 there were 1.9 low-income renters for every low-rent unit in a typical large metropolitan area. In seven metropolitan areas the ratio of low-income ren-

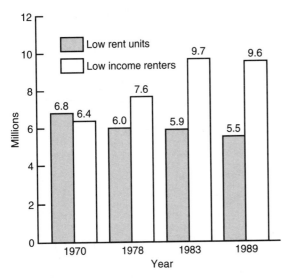

Figure 14.1. Rental Housing Shortage for Households Earning $10,000 per Year or Less, 1970—1989. (SOURCE: U.S. Bureau of the Census, *American Housing Survey, 1989* [Washington, D.C.: U.S. Government Printing Office, 1990], p. 54.)

ters to low-income units available was greater than 2.5 to 1.[34] Moreover, the shortage of affordable housing is not restricted solely to urban centers. In 1970, there were 500,000 more low-cost units in rural areas than there were rural households needing them; by 1985 that ratio was reversed.

Several other factors have converged since the 1970s to further deplete the stock of low-income housing. According to Sternlieb and Hughes, there is evidence that "a new town may be evolving in town."[35] This new town, or "gentrified" neighborhood, is a major component of an urban renaissance taking place in many American cities. Attracted by unique houses amenable to restoration, good transportation facilities, and close proximity to employment and artistic, cultural, and social opportunities, young, professional, white-collar workers have begun to resettle the poor, aging, and usually heavily minority sections of central cities in a process called gentrification.

Although the renovation of central-city areas, such as New York's Soho district, often makes a neighborhood more attractive (and potentially a tourist attraction), the effect on the indigenous—and often poor—population can be devastating. As homes become renovated, the prices of surrounding homes may increase. Although low-income homeowners may be able to command a high resale price for their homes, they may find few other suitable places to move to. Furthermore, as neighborhoods become affluent, property taxes are likely to increase, thus creating a burden on low-income homeowners. Previously affordable rental housing may undergo huge rent increases as neighborhoods become more desirable, thereby driving out older and poorer tenants and precluding the possibility of new low-income residents. Although gentrification has been selective, with the main demographic movement continuing to be suburban, it has had a striking impact on some central-city neighborhoods.

The conversion of apartment buildings into condominiums represents another threat to the poor. As a consequence of tax breaks and income shelters, previously affordable rental housing is rapidly being turned into condominiums. Initiated by either tenants or developers, these condominiums represent a serious depletion of good-quality rental stock. Because apartments in these conversions may cost $50,000 or more, low-income tenants can rarely afford the benefits of condominium living, and although renters are often offered a separation fee when a building undergoes conversion, this amount may barely cover the costs of moving, much less make up for the difference between the current rent and a higher alternative rent.

The commercial renovation of central-city downtown areas is another problem for the poor. The development of new office buildings, large apartment complexes, shopping areas, and parking lots often replace low-income housing bordering on downtown areas. Traditionally affordable (and often rundown) apartment buildings, cheap single-room-occupancy (SRO) hotels, rooming houses, and bed and boards are razed as new office buildings and shopping complexes are erected. Displaced (and often longtime) residents are forced to find housing in more expensive neighborhoods, to double up with family or friends, or, in some cases, to become homeless. According to HUD, demolition, arson, abandonment, condominium conversion, or conversion to nonresidential use removed some 2.8 million rental units between 1970 and 1977. The federal government estimates that 2.8 million families are displaced by private or governmental action each year.[36]

The search for affordable and decent lowincome housing is also hindered by the decrease in housing starts, which, having peaked at more than 2.6 million in 1971, fell to just 1 million by 1991.[37] The 840,000 single-family housing starts in 1991 represent the lowest number of new starts since 1970. Moreover, construction starts for multifamily housing—the units low-income families are most likely able to afford—fell from 1 million units in 1972 to just 174,000 units in 1991, the lowest number since 1967.[38] (See Table 14.2.)

Even with weak economic growth, rents remain close to their highest level in more than 20 years. From 1981 until their peak in 1987, gross rents increased 14 percent faster than the overall rate of inflation. While rents have fallen slightly, this decrease is due largely to lower fuel and utility payments. Although inflation-adjusted rents dropped from $411 to $406 between 1987 and 1991, this decline has not offset the $50 increase that occurred between 1981 and 1987.[39]

Evidence of the crisis in affordable rental housing is illustrated by examining "fair market rent" (FMR)[40] as a ratio of monthly minimum wage income and AFDC benefits. For example, in 10 states the FMR equaled 80 percent or more of the minimum wage; in 14 states it equaled more than 70 percent. In 49 states, the FMR equaled more than 50 percent of the minimum wage. The ratio between the FMR and AFDC benefits is even more striking. In 1991, the FMR exceeded AFDC benefits by more than 100 percent in all but four states; in seven states, the

TABLE 14.2. New Housing Units Started, 1967–1991
(In thousands)

Year	Single-family	Multifamily	Mobile Homes
1967	844	448	240
1968	889	608	318
1969	811	656	413
1970	813	621	401
1971	1,751	901	497
1972	1,309	1,048	576
1973	1,132	913	567
1974	888	450	332
1975	892	268	229
1976	1,162	376	250
1977	1,451	536	258
1978	1,433	587	280
1979	1,194	551	280
1980	852	440	234
1981	705	379	229
1982	663	400	234
1983	1,068	635	278
1984	1,084	665	288
1985	1,072	669	283
1986	1,179	625	256
1987	1,146	474	239
1988	1,081	407	224
1989	1,003	373	203
1990	895	298	195
1991	840	174	174

SOURCE: U.S. Bureau of the Census, *Construction Reports*, Series C–20, Housing Starts (Washington, D.C.: U.S. Government Printing Office, 1992).

FMR exceeded AFDC benefits by more than 200 percent (see Table 14.3). In effect, most AFDC and SSI recipients could not pay FMRs even if they spent their entire grant on rent and utilities. Moreover, the FMR for a one-bedroom apartment in 1991 was beyond the reach of at least 33 percent of all renter households in every single state.[41]

According to the Center on Budget and Policy Priorities, in every one of the 44 major metropolitan areas at least 75 percent of poor renters paid more than 30 percent of their income

TABLE 14.3. Fair Market Rent (FMR) as a Percentage of Monthly Minimum Wage Income and AFDC Benefits

	FMR (2 Bedroom Apartment, January 1992)	FMR as Percentage of Minimum Wage	FMR as Percentage of AFDC Benefit (1991)
Alabama	$332	46.9	314
Alaska	680	85.9	62
Arizona	544	76.8	195
Arkansas	378	53.4	201
California	453	64.0	108
Colorado	482	68.0	135
Connecticut	582	81.8	100
Delaware	622	87.8	175
District of Columbia	830	94.9	171
Florida	363	51.2	177
Georgia	370	52.2	179
Hawaii	851	107.5	111
Idaho	566	79.9	170
Illinois	459	64.8	166
Indiana	377	53.2	156
Iowa	446	57.5	110
Kansas	451	63.7	112
Kentucky	363	51.2	180
Louisiana	389	54.9	247
Maine	512	72.3	130
Maryland	396	55.9	150
Massachusetts	575	81.2	145
Michigan	405	57.2	93
Minnesota	454	64.1	100
Mississippi	388	54.8	358
Missouri	348	49.1	154
Montana	470	66.4	130
Nebraska	446	63.0	121
Nevada	663	93.6	206
New Hampshire	659	93.0	128
New Jersey	521	61.9	153
New Mexico	433	61.1	197
New York	454	64.0	106
North Carolina	365	51.5	154
North Dakota	441	62.3	110
Ohio	383	54.1	132
Oklahoma	382	53.9	129
Oregon	516	65.2	149
Pennsylvania	403	56.9	121
Rhode Island	586	79.0	110
South Carolina	361	51.0	190

TABLE 14.3. *(continued)*

	FMR (2 Bedroom Apartment, January 1992)	FMR as Percentage of Minimum Wage	FMR as Percentage of AFDC Benefit (1991)
South Dakota	413	58.3	112
Tennessee	374	52.8	221
Texas	378	53.4	250
Utah	429	60.6	102
Vermont	670	94.6	94
Virginia	374	52.8	161
Washington	473	66.8	100
West Virginia	396	55.9	181
Wisconsin	418	59.0	91
Wyoming	518	73.1	167

SOURCES: Edward B. Zazere, Paul A. Leonard, Cushing N. Dolbeare, and Barry Zigas, *A Place to Call Home: The Low Income Housing Crisis Continues* (Washington, D.C.: Center on Budget and Policy Priorities and Low Income Housing Information Service, December 1991), p. 39; and Children's Denfese Fund, *The State of America's Children, 1992* (Washington, D.C.: Children's Defense Fund, 1992), p. 37.

for housing, including rent and utilities. In the typical metropolitan area, 84 percent of renters had housing costs that high. In 1989, 81 percent of poor renters nationwide spent more than 30 percent of their income on housing. Moreover, in 35 of the 44 major metropolitan areas more than 60 percent of poor renters paid at least 50 percent of their income for housing; in the median area, 67 percent of renters spent that much. Nationwide, 56 percent of all poor renters spent more than 50 percent of their income on housing.[42] Under federal law, households spending at least half their income on housing are considered to be worst-case housing problems.

African- and Hispanic-American households face particularly severe housing problems. In 1989, some 39 percent of the 10.6 million African-American households and 42 percent of the 6.2 million Hispanic-American households—including poor and nonpoor households—paid at least 30 percent of their income for housing. In contrast, 25 percent of the 76.8 million white households paid that amount. Moreover, 18 percent of African-American and Hispanic-American households paid at least 50 percent of their income for housing, compared with 9 percent of white households. While the housing burdens of minorities are problematic,

they are directly related to the higher levels of poverty among those groups. In fact, the housing burdens faced by poor white households are almost as severe as those faced by minorities.[43]

Deficient and Overcrowded Housing

Another important issue affecting poor households is substandard housing. HUD defines a unit as having "severe" physical problems if it has one or more of the following deficiencies:

- It lacks hot or cold water or a flush toilet or both a bathtub and a shower.
- The heating equipment has broken down at least three times in the previous winter for periods of six hours or more, resulting in the unit being uncomfortably cold for 24 hours or more.
- The unit has no electricity, or it has exposed wiring *and* a room with no working wall outlet *and* it has had three blown fuses or tripped circuit breakers within the past 90 days.
- In public areas such as hallways and staircases, it has no working light fixtures *and* loose or missing steps *and* loose or missing railings *and* no elevator.

• The unit has at least five basic maintenance problems such as water leaks,
holes in the floors or ceilings, peeling
paint or broken plaster, or evidence of
rats during the previous 90 days.[44]

A unit is classified as having "moderate"
physical problems if it has one of the following
deficiencies:

• On at least three occasions in the past
three months, all flush toilets were broken for at least six hours.
• Unvented gas, oil, and kerosene heaters
are the primary heating equipment in the
unit.
• The unit lacks a sink, refrigerator, or
either burners or an oven.
• The unit has three of the four hallway or
staircase problems listed above.
• The unit has at least three of the basic
maintenance problems listed above.[45]

Nineteen percent of poor renter households
(more than 2.2 million households) lived in
housing with moderate or severe physical problems in 1989. By contrast, 7 percent of nonpoor
households lived in those conditions. Poor
homeowners were three times as likely as nonpoor homeowners to live in deficient housing; 16
percent of poor homeowners lived in deficient
homes, compared with 5 percent of nonpoor
homeowners. Although poor households accounted for only 13 percent of all households in
1989, they occupied 24 percent of the units with
severe physical problems, 36 percent of the
units with holes in the floor, 33 percent of the
units with evidence of rats, and 32 percent of the
units lacking kitchen facilities such as a stove or
refrigerator.[46]

Housing is considered overcrowded if it
houses more than one person per room. In 1989,
some 8 percent, or 1 million poor households,
were overcrowded. Five percent of poor homeowners suffered from overcrowding in 1989,
compared with 1.3 percent of nonpoor home-

owners. The problem of overcrowding is particularly acute among Hispanic Americans, where
26 percent of all households lived in overcrowded quarters in 1989. By contrast, 9 percent of poor African-American households and
4 percent of white households lived in such conditions. In 1989, nearly 25 percent of the households living in overcrowded conditions also occupied a physically deficient unit.[47]

Other Factors Affecting Housing

Another problem affecting affordable housing is
property taxes—the heart of local revenue gath-
ering. The escalating costs of providing governmental services have resulted in significant increases in property taxes for homeowners. Renters too are affected by property taxes in that
they are generally passed along by landlords in
the form of higher rents.

In response to this problem, a number of
states have tried to reduce property tax burdens
for low-income households. The most common
form of property tax relief occurs through a
"circuit breaker" program. A typical circuit
breaker program is activated when taxes exceed
a specified proportion of a homeowner's income, and in most programs, low-income
households are sent a yearly benefit check in
which all or part of the property tax is refunded.
Circuit breaker programs for low-income renters operate in a similar manner. Typically, a
portion of the rent paid by a low-income household (usually 15–25 percent) is considered to
represent the property tax passed on by the
landlord and is thus refunded by the state government. Although circuit breaker programs can
provide some relief, they are often restricted to
the elderly or disabled. For example, while 31
states and the District of Columbia have circuit
breaker programs, 21 states restrict eligibility to
elderly and disabled households. Twenty-seven
of these 31 states cover both renters and homeowners; six states restrict eligibility to homeowners. On the other hand, 10 states have broad
circuit breaker programs that cover low-income

families (both renters and homeowners) who are neither elderly nor disabled. Among states with circuit breaker programs, five provided annual benefits of $400 or more in 1989, while 13 states provided average benefits of $200 or less. The remaining states provided average annual benefits of between $200 and $400.[48]

Housing costs are also aggravated by escalating utility rates. In many parts of the country, especially the Northeast and the Midwest, the average family pays thousands of dollars a year in utility bills. According to the National Consumer Law Center, in 1984 families in 21 states had average annual heating bills that exceeded $1,000. In 1986, the average low-income household eligible for energy assistance spent over 15 percent of its income on utility bills, nearly four times the average (3.9 percent) spent by all other U.S. households. Moreover, the cost of home heating oil increased by almost 450 percent between 1972 and 1984, while the cost of heating with natural gas increased fivefold and residential electric rates increased threefold. Increases in home energy bills have disproportionately affected the poor, and, in some cases, have resulted in massive utility shutoffs. For example, it is estimated that in 1984 more than 1.4 million households had their natural gas shut off because of delinquent payments.[49]

In order to mitigate the effects of the federal deregulation of oil prices and the large OPEC oil increases, Congress passed the Low Income Home Energy Assistance Program (LIHEAP) in 1981. This act permits states to offer three types of assistance to low-income households: (1) funds to help eligible households pay their home heating or cooling bills; (2) up to 15 percent of state LIHEAP allotments for low-cost weatherization; and (3) assistance to households during energy-related emergencies. States are required to target LIHEAP benefits to households with the lowest incomes and highest energy costs relative to their income and family size. In addition, states are required to conduct outreach efforts aimed at making elderly and handicapped individuals aware of the program.

Over $2.2 billion was appropriated for LIHEAP in 1992, and it served almost 6 million households.[50]

Housing discrimination is yet another barrier facing the poor. This discrimination takes two forms: racial discrimination and discrimination against families with children. Although illegal, racially based discrimination in housing is still prevalent. In addition, many landlords and real estate agents refuse to rent to families with children. Often, these families are required to pay higher rents, make exorbitant security deposits, or meet qualifications not required of renters without children. According to a 1980 study, 26 percent of housing units totally barred families; another 50 percent instituted restrictions based on the number, age, or gender of the children.[51] Although Congress banned housing discrimination against families with children in 1988, illegal practices continue, and more than 12,000 families have filed housing discrimination complaints with the federal government since the law took effect in 1989.[52]

The Federal Government and Housing

Federally funded housing programs represent the major form of rental assistance to the poor. Overall, there are two primary forms of federal housing assistance: publicly owned housing, and rental subsidies for low-income families living in private housing. Residents in both these categories pay 30 percent of their income in rent. Unlike income-maintenance programs such as SSI and AFDC, housing programs are not entitlement-based, and benefits are not automatically provided to all eligible applicants. Congress allocates a fixed sum toward low-income housing, and because funding levels are usually low, only a portion of eligible applicants actually receive assistance.

This funding situation has resulted in waiting lists for public housing and rent subsidies that are years long. The Council of Large Public Housing estimates that, nationwide, waiting lists for public housing include 2 million parents and children, many of whom will wait two or more years before getting a unit. For example, a qualified family could wait more than twenty years before getting a housing unit in New York; in Baltimore, it could wait from two to ten years; in San Antonio, a family seeking privately owned subsidized housing typically waits two to three years before receiving assistance; and in St. Louis, a family could wait from five months to three years before receiving a housing unit. On average, the wait for public housing lasts from eighteen months to two years, although in some areas the wait is much longer. The typical wait for privately owned subsidized housing is eighteen months.[53] As a result, the U.S. Conference of Mayors found that of the 27 cities surveyed in 1989, 18 had closed their waiting lists because they were already so long.[54] Overall, only 36 percent of poor households received housing assistance in 1989.[55]

Despite the overwhelming need for housing assistance, federal housing programs were cut back sharply in the 1980s. From 1977 to 1980, HUD made commitments to provide rental assistance to 290,000 additional low-income households a year. However, that number dropped to 76,000 a year between 1981 and 1992 (see Figure 14.2). This drop represented a decline of nearly three-fourths in the number of additional households assisted each year. If the number of additional low-income-assisted households had remained at the same level it was in the late 1970s, there would currently be 2.4 million more households assisted each year.[56] Moreover, appropriations for HUD's subsidized housing programs fell from a peak of $32.2 billion in 1978 to $11.7 billion in 1991. After adjusting for inflation, this cut constituted a real decline of 81 percent. Funding for FmHA's direct loan and rental assistance programs dropped from $3.7 billion in 1978 to $2 billion in 1991, a real decline of 72 percent after adjusting for inflation.[57] Despite a HUD report that found that 5.1 million renters had worst-case housing problems in 1991, Congress and the Bush administration provided funds to make

commitments to only 129,000 additional households that year.[58]

Despite the severity of housing problems for poor families, most federal housing subsidies continue to benefit the upper and middle classes. These housing subsidies provide billions of dollars in benefits each year to homeowners through mortgage interest and property tax deductions. Moreover, these subsidies to those who are better off far outstrip assistance provided to the poor. For example, federal spending on low-income housing was $18.3 billion in 1990, whereas subsidies to the middle and upper classes totaled $78.4 billion, an amount more than four times higher than what was spent for low-income families. Furthermore, some 81 percent of the $37 billion in tax benefits from home mortgage deductions in 1991 went to the 20 percent of households with annual incomes above $50,000. This amounted to a subsidy of $2,077 for each household in the top fifth of income earners who claimed this deduction. In addition, the wealthiest 5 percent of households (the 4.3 million households with annual incomes above $100,000) received 31 percent of the benefits of this deduction in 1991. By contrast, only 769,000 of the 47.5 million households with incomes below $20,000 claimed the home mortgage deduction on their tax returns in that year. The average 1991 benefit for these households was $420. Finally, 90 percent of the tax benefits from state and local property deductions went to the top fifth of households in 1991. At the same time, less than two-tenths of 1 percent of those tax benefits went to the 42 percent of households with annual incomes under $20,000. Cushing Dolbeare sums up the problem: "Benefits from federal programs are so skewed that *the total of all the assisted housing payments ever made under all HUD assisted housing programs, from the inception of public housing in 1937 through 1980, was less than the costs to the federal government of housing-related tax expenditures in 1980 alone* [original emphasis]."[59]

The cost/income squeeze in housing has

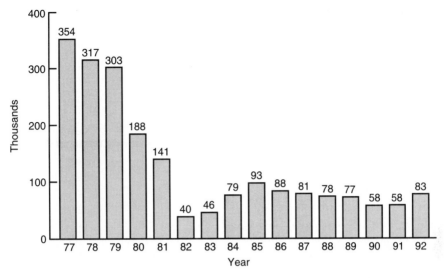

Figure 14.2. New HUD Low-Income Housing Unit Commitments, 1977–1992. (SOURCE: Paul A. Leonard and Edward A. Lazere, *A Place to Call Home: The Low Income Housing Crisis in 44 Metropolitan Cities* [Washington, D.C.: Center on Budget and Policy Priorities, 1992], Figure 6, p. 37.)

proved to be problematic for both middle- and lower-income groups. As a result, many middle-class families are forced to become two-wage-earner families. In some cases the second wage is used entirely to pay for the costs of home ownership. This situation is intensified for the poor, because two wage earners making the minimum wage or slightly above may not have a sufficient combined income to cover the costs of adequate housing. The crisis in housing generates serious problems, including homelessness.

HOMELESSNESS

Homelessness can be defined simply as a lack of housing. Homeless people include those living in streets, parks, transportation terminals, abandoned buildings, automobiles, and campgrounds. It also includes people whose primary nighttime residence is a public or private shelter or an emergency housing placement (such as those used by welfare departments). Less visi-

ble are the homeless who move from one temporary setting to another, doubling up with friends and relatives and using emergency shelters only when necessary. For most people, the major causes of homelessness are a lack of affordable housing, insufficient income, and a decade of inadequate governmental support for housing and income-maintenance programs.

Homelessness represents both a simple and a complex problem. Specifically, homeless people are not a homogeneous group. For some, homelessness is a life choice, the freedom to roam without being tied down to one place. For others, particularly the mentally ill and chronic alcoholics, homelessness reflects the deterioration of an overburdened public mental health system. This breakdown in the mental health system is aggravated by an influx of previously healthy people who, when forced into economic deprivation and homelessness, develop symptoms of mental disturbance. For other people, homelessness is rooted in cuts in federally subsidized housing programs and the cost-income squeeze of the housing market. Finally, large numbers of people experience homelessness as a result of the inability of AFDC benefits to keep pace with the cost of living, especially in the area of housing and utilities. Despite the variety of causes, almost all forms of homelessness are tied to poverty. In that sense, homelessness is simply a manifestation of poverty.

Although homelessness has been a long-standing problem in most large urban areas, it has recently been propelled onto center stage by media images of "bag ladies," the mentally ill, chronic alcoholics, "street people," and uprooted families. While these images make for interesting copy, popular stereotypes obscure the extent of homelessness and the true nature of the problem.

The actual number of homeless persons in the United States is unknown. Some advocacy organizations claim that 1.3 to 2 million people are homeless. Other advocacy organizations estimate that there are about 500,000 homeless people on any given night, and probably twice that number are homeless in the course of a year. Since about 20 percent of the homeless are children, about 100,000 children are without homes nightly, more than the total number of children in Pittsburgh or the entire population of Ann Arbor, Michigan, or Eugene, Oregon.[60] Fearful that an irate public will demand more services if the actual extent of homelessness is acknowledged, financially strapped federal, state, and local authorities often try to downplay the true number of homeless people.

Although the exact number of homeless people is unknown, the population appears to be growing rapidly. Moreover, families constitute the fastest-growing sector of homeless people. In 1978, 21 percent of the homeless people in shelters were families; by 1988 that number had risen to 40 percent. A study by the U.S. Conference of Mayors reported that in the 27 large cities surveyed, requests for shelter by homeless families with children increased by almost 30 percent between 1988 and 1989. Between 1989 and 1990, family requests for shelters increased again, this time by 17 percent.

Only one of the 27 cities surveyed did not expect increases in shelter requests for 1991.[61]

Although it was once believed that the average homeless person was a skid-row drunk, it is now apparent that a wide variety of people lack permanent shelter. The homeless include retired people on small fixed incomes, many of whom lost their cheap SRO hotel rooms to gentrification; runaway teenagers; school dropouts; drug addicts; disabled and mentally ill people lost in a maze of outpatient services; unemployed people who have worn out their welcome with family or friends; young mothers on welfare who remain on long waiting lists for public housing; families who lost their overcrowded quarters; and "street people."

A 1987 study by the Urban Institute of 1,704 homeless people found that 77 percent of the homeless were single, 15 percent were children, and 8 percent were adults in families. Of the homeless adults, 81 percent were men, 54 percent were nonwhite, and 51 percent were between the ages of 31 and 50. Seventy-nine percent of the sample had been homeless for over three months, and 19 percent had been homeless for over two years. Almost half the sample had not graduated from high school. Moreover, only 5 percent had any income from AFDC, only 12 percent from General Assistance, only 4 percent from SSI, and only 18 percent received Food Stamps. In addition, only 25 percent of the sample ate more than twice daily, and 36 percent went one day or more per week with nothing to eat. Seventeen percent had no food for two days a week. About one-third of the homeless had been patients in a detoxification or alcohol/drug treatment center, almost half needed treatment for psychological distress, and 19 percent had attempted suicide.[62]

According to Ellen Bassuk, children living in Boston shelters experience acute effects from homelessness: 47 percent of the children showed at least one developmental lag on the Denver Developmental Screening Test; one-third had difficulty with language skills, fine and gross motor coordination, and social and personal development; almost half the school-age children were depressed and anxious, with one-third showing signs of clinical depression; 43 percent had failed a grade, 24 percent were in special education classes, and nearly half were failing or doing below-average work in school.[63] Many of Bassuk's findings are corroborated by a study done by the Health Care for the Homeless Coalition of Greater St. Louis. Reporting for the period August 1985 to March 1987, the coalition found that among the 360 homeless children given an on-site physical examination in a shelter, over 32 percent suffered from upper respiratory infections, 25 percent had incomplete immunizations, more than 14 percent suffered from infestation and skin disorders, and almost 9 percent had poor dentition.[64]

Proposals for Ending Homelessness

On July 22, 1987, President Ronald Reagan signed into law the Stewart B. McKinney Homeless Assistance Act, one of the few pieces of legislation in the 1980s to authorize new and expanded social service programs. The McKinney Act encompasses more than 20 separate programs and provides funds for the prevention of homelessness, emergency food and shelter, health care, transitional housing, mental health services, and education and job training. In 1990, Congress amended the act to remove barriers that were keeping homeless children from attending school, including proof of immunization, former school records, and proof of residency. The federal government spent more than $1 billion in 1992 on programs to help the homeless.[65]

Apart from the McKinney Act, several broader proposals have emerged for alleviating the problem of homelessness. The "Federal Plan to Help End the Tragedy of Homelessness," prepared under the auspices of the Interagency Council for the Homeless, provides a set of objectives to reduce homelessness.

Increase the participation of homeless families and individuals in mainstream programs that provide income support, so-cial services, health care, education, employment, and housing. In addition, these programs should be monitored to gauge their impact on homelessness.

Improve the efficiency and effectiveness of homelessness-targeted programs in addressing the multiple needs of homeless persons.

Increase the availability of support services in combination with appropriate housing.

Improve access to quality, affordable, and permanent housing for homeless families and individuals.

Develop strategies for preventing homelessness by improving the methods for identifying families and individuals at risk of imminent homelessness, change current policies that may contribute to homelessness, and propose other initiatives to prevent people from becoming homeless.[66]

Chester Hartman proposes a nine-point solution for ending homelessness: (1) Massively increase the number of new and rehabilitated units offered to lower-income households; (2) lower the required rent/income ratio in government housing from 30 to 25 percent; (3) arrest the depletion of low-income housing that is occurring through neglect, abandonment, conversion, and sale; (4) preserve the SRO hotels; (5) establish a national "right to shelter"; (6) require local governments to make available properties that can be used as shelters and second-stage housing; (7) create legislation that gives tenants reasonable protection from eviction; (8) provide governmental assistance to homeowners facing foreclosure; and (9) provide suitable residential alternatives for mentally ill people.[67] A proposal by Kim Hopper and Maria Foscarinis calls for the government to: (1) provide outreach to homeless persons eligible for Food Stamps and SSI benefits; (2) allow homeless people to use Food Stamps to purchase prepared meals; (3) provide health and maternal benefits to homeless people; (4) end permanent address requirements for the receipt of welfare benefits; and (5) increase Section 8 and public housing units.[68] Joel Blau would like to see the formation of a wide-ranging coalition to deal with the basic needs for housing, health care, employment, and adequate income. He has a vision of a "caring human community."[69]

Homelessness cannot be eradicated unless basic changes are made in federal housing, income support, social services, health care, education, and employment programs. Benefit levels for these programs must be made more adequate, the erosion of welfare benefits must be stopped, residency and other requirements that exclude homeless persons must be changed, and programs (including outreach) must be made freely available to the homeless and the potentially homeless. Moreover, a real solution to the homeless problem must involve the provision of permanent housing for those who are currently or potentially homeless. Federal programs and legislation must be coordinated and expanded to provide decent, affordable housing, coupled with needed services for *all* poor families. Finally, both the states and the federal government must intervene directly in the housing market by controlling rents, increasing the overall housing stock, and limiting speculation.

Americans paid little attention to poverty for much of the 1970s and 1980s. It was only when private despair turned into public homelessness that people were shocked into responding to the problems of poverty. Perhaps it was the realization that parts of America were beginning to resemble the Third World. Pictures of New Delhi were becoming the pictures of New York, Chicago, and Los Angeles. Whatever the reason, homelessness captured the attention of the public.

HOUSING REFORM

The housing crisis faced by low-income people has led to numerous proposals for housing reform. Some conservative critics argue that low-

income housing assistance should be abolished, thus allowing the law of supply and demand to regulate rents and, eventually, to drive down prices. Free market philosophy suggests that as rents increase, demand slackens, and that eventually rents will drop. Other critics contend that government intervention in housing should occur only through the supply side. In other words, the government should stimulate production in rental housing by offering financial incentives such as tax breaks to builders, entrepreneurs, and investors. If rental housing is made more profitable, more units will be built, and the increase in the housing stock will lower prices.

Some liberal critics contend that because housing is a necessity, and the demand is relatively inelastic, marketplace laws should not be allowed to dominate. For example, the National Low Income Housing Coalition has called for: (1) the establishment of housing as a human right (i.e., federal housing policy must guarantee every American the opportunity to live in decent and affordable housing); (2) the provision of housing assistance to all low-income households who require it; (3) an increase in the stock of affordable housing units by 750,000 units a year throughout the 1990s; and (4) a ban on involuntary displacements from existing federally assisted housing units.[70] Other critics argue for the imposition of federal credit and price controls to dampen speculation and encourage socially useful investment.[71] Still others argue that housing should be "decommodified"[72] through social rather than profit-oriented ownership and production. This sweeping policy would include comprehensive public financing of all housing, public control of land use, local control of neighborhoods, and public guarantees of housing choice.[73]

CONCLUSION

The housing crisis is grounded in issues of availability and affordability. At bottom, it is a structural problem that is based on the failure of incomes to keep pace with housing costs; an over-dependence on credit to build and buy houses; a profit-making system that drives homeownership, development, and management; and the failure of states and the federal government to actively intervene in the housing market through higher subsidies or stricter regulation. Driven by speculation, the profit motive has forced up the price of rental and residential property faster than income growth can keep pace. As a profit is made by each succeeding link in the housing chain (real estate developers, lenders, builders, materials producers, investors, speculators, landlords, and homeowners), renters and homeowners are forced to pay the costs. In that sense, the cost of every rental unit or home reflects the speculative gains made by all the parties who directly and indirectly came into contact with the property.

The challenge of acquiring adequate low- and moderate-income housing is a serious one facing modern society. The poor have difficulty finding decent and affordable housing, while the middle classes, caught in the classic cost/income squeeze, are having an increasingly difficult time buying and holding onto their homes. This "affordability squeeze" will likely result in increased mortgage foreclosures, higher rates of property tax and delinquency defaults, more evictions and homelessness, more overcrowding and doubling up of families, decreases in the consumption of other important necessities, deteriorating neighborhoods, increased business failures, higher rates of unemployment in the building trades, and the collapse of some financial institutions, especially the already shaky savings and loan associations.

Past and current government programs have had only a minimal impact on the crisis in affordable housing. Current housing programs are seriously underfunded, fragmentary, and without clear and focused goals. Because the federal government has often been viewed as an arbiter of last resort, some critics contend that the government has the responsibility to ensure that adequate housing becomes a right rather than a privilege, and that healthy, sound, and safe neighborhoods become a reality.

DISCUSSION QUESTIONS

1. From 1937 until the present, the history of federal housing policy has been marked by evolving priorities and programmatic shifts. Describe the dominant trends in federal housing policy since 1937 and show how those trends led to the creation of current housing policies. Specifically, what, if any, ideas and programs in current housing policies have their roots in earlier federal policies? In what direction has federal housing policy evolved? What is the current emphasis in federal housing policy?

2. According to some critics, federal low-income housing policy is marked by severe inadequacies. Describe the more serious shortcomings in federal low-income housing policy and discuss alternative policies to rectify those shortcomings.

3. Homeownership is an important variable in American society because it is equated with the growth of assets. For example, a poor family has nothing to show after paying rent for 30 years except its rental receipts. By contrast, another poor family will at least have its home as a major asset after paying off a 30-year mortgage. What are some of the more serious obstacles standing in the way of homeownership for poor people? What policies can be developed to help poor families overcome these barriers?

4. There are serious barriers to finding affordable and decent rental housing. What are some of the most significant problems facing poor people in finding affordable and decent-quality rental housing? What federal or state policies could be implemented to assist poor families in finding such housing?

5. HUD has created a series of guidelines by which to evaluate whether a particular housing unit has "severe" or "moderate" physical deficiencies. Are HUD's criteria for determining physical deficiencies in housing adequate? If not, what other criteria should be added to HUD's guidelines?

6. Homelessness has been described by some commentators as just another housing problem. Others argue that homelessness is simply another manifestation of poverty. Still others contend that homelessness has deeper psychological roots and should be seen as a human service problem. Where do you stand on the issue? Will the homeless problem be solved essentially if people are simply given adequate shelter and decent jobs? Or is homelessness for many a manifestation of deeper psychosocial problems? If so, what programs, if any, should be developed for the homeless?

7. Several proposals have been offered to eradicate the problem of homelessness. Which of these programs (or combination of programs) has the best chance of eradicating homelessness?

8. Many experts argue that the housing situation for low-income renters and homeowners has reached crisis proportions. Do you agree? If so, why? Moreover, what kinds of housing policies are needed to defuse this crisis and stabilize the housing market for low-income families? Should housing be considered a right and as such be removed from the caprice of the marketplace?

NOTES

1. Quoted in Charles S. Prigmore and Charles R. Atherton, *Social Welfare Policy: Analysis and Formulation (Lexington, Mass.: D. C. Heath and Company, 1979), pp. 146–47.*

2. *Robert Morris, Social Policy of the American Welfare State,* 2nd ed. (New York: Longman, 1985), p. 131.

3. Ibid., p. 132.

4. Barbara Habenstreit, *The Making of America* (New York: Julian Messner, 1971), p. 46.

5. Richard Geruson and Dennis McGrath, *Cities and Urbanization* (New York: Praeger, 1977), pp. 6–7.

6. Ibid., p. 40.

7. National Training and Information Center, *Insurance Redlining: Profits v. Policyholders* (Chicago: NTIC, 1973), p. 1.

8. Edward B. Lazere, Paul A. Leonard, Cushing N. Dolbeare, and Barry Zigas, *A Place to Call Home: The Low Income Housing Crisis Continues* (Center on Budget and Policy Priorities and Low-Income Housing Information Service: Washington, D.C.: December 1991), pp. 45–47.

9. Ibid., pp. 48–50.

10. Ibid.

11. Ibid.

12. Ibid., pp. 51–52.

13. Ibid., pp. 52–53.

14. Paul A. Leonard, Cushing N. Dolbeare, and Edward B. Lazere, *A Place to Call Home: The Crisis in Housing for the Poor* (Center on Budget and Policy Priorities and Low-Income Housing Information Service: Washington, D.C.: April 1989), pp. 76–80.

15. Ibid.

16. Ibid.

17. Ibid.

18. See, for example, Chester Hartman, ed., *America's Housing Crisis* (Boston: Routledge & Kegan Paul, 1983).

19. See George Sternlieb and James W. Hughes, "Housing in the United States: An Overview," in George Sternlieb, James W. Hughes, Robert W. Burchell, Stephen C. Casey, Robert W. Lake, and David Listokin, eds., *America's Housing* (New Brunswick. N.J.: Rutgers University, Center for Urban Policy Research, 1980), pp. 5–7; and Sumner M. Rosen, David Fanshel, and Mary E. Lutz, eds., *Face of the Nation, 1987* (Silver Spring, Md.: NASW, 1987), p. 68; and Joint Center for Housing Studies of Harvard University, *The State of the Nation's Housing, 1992* (Boston: Joint Center for Housing Studies of Harvard University, 1992), p. 12.

20. Sternlieb and Hughes, "Housing in the United States," pp. 5–7; and Cushing N. Dolbeare, *The Widening Gap* (Washington, D.C.: Low Income Housing Information Service, June 1992), p. 14.

21. Ibid; and U.S. Bureau of the Census, *Statistical Abstract of the United States, 1991* (Washington, D.C.: U.S. Government Printing Office, 1991), p. 715.

22. Joint Center for Housing Studies of Harvard University, *The State of the Nation's Housing, 1992,* pp. 28–31.

23. U.S. Bureau of the Census, *Statistical Abstract of the United States, 1991,* pp. 715–17.

24. Lazere et al., *A Place to Call Home: The Low Income Housing Crisis Continues*, pp. 9–12.
25. Ibid., pp. 69–72.
26. Children's Defense Fund, *The State of America's Children, 1992* (Washington, D.C.: Children's Defense Fund, 1992), p. 35.
27. Lazere et al., *A Place to Call Home: The Low Income Housing Crisis Continues*, pp. 72–73.
28. Cushing N. Dolbeare, *Out of Reach: Why Everyday People Can't Find Affordable Housing* (Washington, D.C.: Low Income Housing Information Service, September 1991), pp. 1–2.
29. Ibid.
30. Children's Defense Fund, *The State of America's Children, 1992*, p. 35.
31. Dolbeare, *Out of Reach*, p. 2.
32. Ibid.
33. Lazere et al., *A Place to Call Home: The Low Income Housing Crisis Continues*, p. xii.
34. Paul A. Leonard and Edward A. Lazere, *A Place to Call Home: The Low Income Housing Crisis in 44 Metropolitan Areas* (Washington, D.C.: Center on Budget and Policy Priorities, 1992), p. xiii.
35. George Sternlieb and James W. Hughes, "Back to the Central City: Myths and Realities," in Sternlieb et al., *America's Housing*, p. 173.
36. Children's Defense Fund, *The State of America's Children, 1989* (Washington, D.C.: Children's Defense Fund, 1989), p. 196.
37. Joint Center for Housing Studies of Harvard University, *The State of the Nation's Housing, 1992*, p. 30.
38. Children's Defense Fund, *The State of America's Children, 1992*, p. 196.
39. Joint Center for Housing Studies of Harvard University, *The State of the Nation's Housing, 1992*, p. 2.
40. Fair market rent (FMR) is a HUD designation. It is the amount equal to or more than what is paid for rent by 45 percent of recent movers.
41. Dolbeare, *Out of Reach*, p. 3.
42. Leonard and Lazere, *A Place to Call Home: The Low Income Housing Crisis in 44 Metropolitan Areas*, p. xii.
43. Lazere et al., *A Place to Call Home: The Low Income Housing Crisis Continues*, p. 63.
44. Ibid., p. 22.
45. Ibid.
46. Ibid., p. 23.
47. Ibid., p. 24.
48. Ibid., pp. 43–44.
49. Center on Budget and Policy Priorities, *Smaller Slices of the Pie* (Washington, D.C.: Center on Budget and Policy Priorities, November 1985), p. 33.
50. Committee on Ways and Means, U.S. House of Representatives, *Overview of Entitlement Programs: 1992 Green Book* (Washington, D.C.: U.S. Government Printing Office, 1992), pp. 1697–1702.
51. Ibid.
52. Children's Defense Fund, *The State of America's Children, 1992*, p. 38.
53. Lazere et al., *A Place to Call Home: The Low Income Housing Crisis Continues*, pp. 28–30.
54. Children's Defense Fund, *The State of America's Children, 1991* (Washington, D.C.: Children's Defense Fund, 1991), p. 113.
55. Lazere et al., *A Place to Call Home: The Low Income Housing Crisis Continues*, p. 27.
56. Leonard and Lazere, *A Place to Call Home: The Low Income Housing Crisis in 44 Metropolitan Areas*, p. 36
57. Committee on Ways and Means, U.S. House of Representatives, *Overview of Entitlement Programs: 1991 Green Book* (Washington, D.C.: U.S. Government Printing Office, 1992), p. 1445.
58. Lazere et al., *A Place to Call Home: The Low Income Housing Crisis Continues*, p. 32.
59. Ibid., p. 69.
60. Children's Defense Fund, *The State of America's Children, 1991*, pp. 109–110.
61. Ibid.
62. Urban Institute, *America's Homeless* (Washington, D.C.: Urban Institute, 1990).
63. Ellen Bassuk, "Homeless Families: Single Mothers and Their Families in Boston Shelters," in Ellen Bassuk, ed., *The Mental Health Needs of Homeless Persons* (San Francisco: Jossey-Bass, 1987).
64. Health Care for the Homeless Coalition of Greater St. Louis, "Progress Report" (St. Louis, Missouri, 1987).
65. National Low Income Housing Coalition, *1992 Advocate's Resource Book* (Washington, D.C.: National Low Income Housing Coalition, 1992), p. 11.
66. Ibid., p. 10.

67. Chester Hartman, "The Housing Part of the Homelessness Problem," in Boston Foundation, *Homelessness: Critical Issues for Policy and Practice* (Boston: Boston Foundation, 1987), pp. 17–19.

68. Kim Hopper and Maria Foscarinis, "Model Legislation: The Homeless Persons' Survival Act of 1986," in Boston Foundation, *Homelessness,* pp. 59–61.

69. Joel Blau, *The Visible Poor: Homelessness in the United States* (New York: Oxford University Press, 1992), p. 181.

70. National Low Income Housing Coalition, *1992 Advocate's Resource Book,* p. 44.

71. Michael E. Stone, "Housing and the Economic Crisis: An Analysis and Emergency Program," in Chester Hartman, *America's Housing Crisis,* pp.136–37.

72. Decommodification is a term used by Claus Offe, *Contradictions of the Welfare State* (Cambridge, Mass.: The MIT Press, 1984). Offe defines decommodification as the transformation of a need or resource that was previously satisfied in the marketplace into a nonmarket commodity. For example, socialized medicine takes health care from the private marketplace and makes it an entitlement.

73. Emily Paradise Achtenberg and Peter Marcuse, "Toward the Decommodification of Housing: A Political Analysis and a Progressive Program," in Chester Hartman, *America's Housing Crisis,* pp. 220–26.

CHAPTER 15

Food Policy and Politics

This chapter examines the federal response to hunger and the subsequent attempts to distribute foodstuffs to the poor. As part of that examination, this chapter explores Food Stamps, WIC and other food programs, U.S. farm policy, and the overall problems of food production and distribution.

GOVERNMENTAL FOOD PROGRAMS

The politics of food—or the way food is distributed in American society—is a complex phenomenon. Like all resources in a capitalist society, food is a commodity that is bought and sold. In a pure market sense, those who cannot afford to purchase food are unable to consume it. Left to the caprice of the marketplace, many poor people would face malnutrition or even starvation. This problem is particularly acute in an urban society, where many people lack the necessary gardening skills and have little access to land. Providing the poor with access to food is a redistributive function of the welfare state. The obligation of the government to provide food to the poor is similar to that of providing economic opportunity: When both are unavailable in adequate quantities, it is the responsibility of the welfare state to respond.

The federal government's response to hunger and malnutrition has consisted of several major programs: (1) Food Stamps, (2) the Commodity Distribution program, (3) the National School Lunch and Breakfast programs, (4) the Special Milk program, (5) the Special Supplemental Nutrition Program for Women, Infants, and Children (WIC), (6) the Child Care Food program, (7) the Summer Food program, and (8) the Meals on Wheels and Congregate Dining programs.

A Short History of Food Stamps and a Description of the Program

In 1933, Congress established the Federal Surplus Relief Corporation, an agency designed to distribute surplus commodity foods, as well as coal, mattresses, and blankets. In 1939, Congress established the Food Stamp program. This was terminated in 1943, at which time a commodity food distribution program was reestablished. A pilot Food Stamp program began during the presidency of John F. Kennedy, and in 1964 the current Food Stamp Act (FS) was passed.

Although the Food Stamp program is a federal program administered by the United States Department of Agriculture (USDA), it is state and local welfare agencies that qualify applicants and provide them with stamps. Recipients are given an allotment of stamps based on family size and income, with eligibility requirements and benefits determined at the federal level. Food Stamp eligibility is based on a means test. Recipients originally had to pay a set price (depending on family size and income) for their stamps, with the amount to be paid always being less than the face value of the stamps. This enabled some people to purchase $75 worth of Food Stamps for $35. The difference between the amount paid and the face value of the stamps was called a "bonus." However, this system proved unwieldy because many poor people could not afford to purchase any stamps. In 1977, purchase requirements were dropped and, not surprisingly, national participation rates rose by 30 percent.

Several major changes in the FS program were enacted during the Reagan administration: (1) Income deductions were tightened so that only people on or near the poverty level could qualify for FS; (2) family income was calculated in part on the basis of past income rather than only on current income; (3) state FS programs were more closely monitored to reduce fraud and error; (4) benefits were cut by 1 percent; and (5) adjustments for inflation were delayed. Early revisions of the 1990 Food, Agriculture, Conservation, and Trade Acts would have liberalized FS eligibility and benefit rules, but budget constraints dictated minimal expansions.

Food Stamps: Who Is in the Program and What Does It Cost?

Some 22 million people, or about 9 percent of the total U.S. population were on Food Stamps in 1991. Of that number, 46 percent were white, 33 percent were African-American, and 17 percent were Hispanic American.[1] Virtually all FS benefits (92 percent) go to households with incomes at or below the poverty line, and 82 percent of the benefits go to families with children.[2]

AFDC families are automatically eligible

for FS. Eligibility is determined by gross income, which cannot exceed 130 percent of the federal poverty line, and by net income (after subtracting taxes, work expenses, and a part of the rent and utility bills), which must fall below the poverty line. Total assets generally cannot exceed $1,500 dollars. Families with children are particularly hurt by the FS rules for calculating benefits. For example, although elderly and disabled households can disregard that portion of their income used to pay housing and heating bills in excess of half their net income, other families—including those with children—have their housing and heating benefits capped at unrealistically low levels. FS benefits are also reduced for every dollar of child support received by a family, thus diminishing the incentive for families to cooperate in efforts at child support enforcement.[3]

FS program costs tend to be relatively high because of heavy utilization. In 1965 the FS program cost $32 million; by 1970 the costs had risen to $473 million; and by 1980, FS expenditures had jumped to $9.5 billion. In 1991 the total cost of operating the FS program stood at $21 billion[4] (see Table 15.1). The maximum FS allotment for a four-person family in 1991 was $370 a month, and each additional family member received $63.90 in benefits.[5]

Special Supplemental Nutrition Program for Women, Infants, and Children (WIC)

The WIC program was enacted on September 26, 1972. This program originally began as a two-year pilot program to provide nutritional counseling and supplemental foods to pregnant and breast-feeding women, infants, and young children at nutritional risk. The goal of the program was to address areas of child development that were most affected by poor health and inadequate nutrition, including impaired learning.[6]

WIC is administered through the Food and Nutrition Service of the USDA, in conjunction with 1,500 local agencies (mainly health departments). Each state receives cash grants and is

TABLE 15.1. Food Stamps Statistics: Total Federal Expenditures for FS, Participation Rates, Percent of Population Using FS Benefits, and Average Monthly Benefits, 1975–1991 (Participants and dollars in millions)

Year	Cost	Number of FS Participants	Percent of Population	Average Monthly Benefits (per person)
1975	$4,624	16.3	7.6	$21.40
1976	5,692	17.0	7.9	23.90
1977	5,469	15.6	7.2	24.70
1978	5,573	14.4	6.5	26.80
1979	7,383	15.9	7.1	30.60
1980	9,563	19.2	8.4	34.40
1981	11,812	20.6	9.0	39.50
1982	11,674	20.4	8.8	39.20
1983	13,345	21.6	9.2	43.00
1984	13,275	20.9	8.8	42.70
1985	13,470	19.9	8.3	45.00
1986	13,463	19.4	8.0	45.50
1987	13,535	19.1	7.8	45.80
1988	14,369	18.7	7.6	49.80
1989	14,916	18.8	7.6	51.90
1990	17,686	20.0	8.0	59.00
1991	21,012	22.6	9.0	63.90

SOURCE: Compiled from various tables in Committee on Ways and Means, U.S. House of Representatives, *Overview of Entitlement Programs, 1992 Green Book* (Washington, D.C.: U.S. Government Printing Office, 1992), Table 4., p. 1616; Table 9., p. 1629; and Table 12., p. 1639.

responsible for developing, implementing, and monitoring its WIC program.[7] Eligibility is limited to low-income pregnant women, mothers who breast-feed their infants, and children up to age five. Qualified beneficiaries receive supplemental foods each month in the form of actual food items or, more often, are given vouchers for the purchase of specific items in retail stores. Items that may be included in a food package include milk, cheese, eggs, infant formula, cereals, and fruits and vegetables. The USDA requires food packages that provide specific types and amounts of food appropriate for six categories of participants: (1) infants from birth to three months; (2) infants from four to twelve months; (3) women and children with special dietary needs; (4) children from one to five years of age; (5) pregnant and nursing mothers; and (6) postpartum nursing mothers. In addition to food benefits, WIC participants must also receive nutritional counseling.[8] In 1991, the national average cost of a WIC food package was $31.67 a month for each participant. About $2.1 billion was spent on WIC in 1990 and the program served over 4.5 million women and children.

Other Food Programs

Although FS is the largest food program in the United States, it is by no means the only program. For example, the federal government also provides cash assistance and food commodities to participating public and private schools and nonprofit residential institutions that serve meals to children. In 1946 the National School Lunch Act was passed. This provided school-age children with hot lunches at reduced rates, or with free lunches if their parents were unable to pay. After research studies found a positive correlation between poor school performance and the failure of school-age children to have eaten a nutritious breakfast, the federal government instituted the School Breakfast Program. Each program has a three-tiered reimbursement system that allows children from households with incomes at or below 130 percent of the poverty line to receive free meals, permits children from households with incomes between 130 and 185 percent of the poverty line to receive meals at a reduced price, and provides a small subsidy for children whose family income does not qualify them for free or reduced meals.[9]

The National School Lunch Program (NSLP) provides subsidized lunches to students in most schools. In 1991 the average daily participation rate was 24.2 million students, and just over 4 billion meals were served at a total federal cost of $4.1 billion. Roughly half the subsidized NSLP meals go to children from lower-income families, and 90 percent of federal funding is used for these children. In 1991, 42 percent of the children who received NSLP meals received free lunches, 8 percent received reduced-price lunches, and the remaining 50 percent paid full price for their meals. Overall, 52 percent of U.S. students in 92,200 schools benefited from the school lunch program.[10]

Smaller than the NSLP, the School Breakfast Program (SBP) serves only about 15 percent of those served by the School Lunch program. In 1991 the SBP served 4.4 million students at a cost of $677 million. In that same year, the SBP operated in 46,100 schools, or about half the schools participating in the NSLP. Of the 22 million children enrolled in these schools, only 20 percent participated in this program. The SBP differs from the NSLP in that most of the participating schools are in low-income areas, and the children who participate are mainly from low- or moderate-income families.[11]

Although some of the low-income elderly receive Food Stamps, they can also be served by Meals on Wheels and the Congregate Meal Dining program. Meals on Wheels was begun in 1972 and was designed to improve nutrition for the elderly. Various community agencies arrange the daily delivery of meals to elderly persons living at home, and aged persons who receive FS can use them to purchase the meals (for others a donation is requested). The Congregate Meal Dining program provides meals at such places as senior citizen centers.

Other federal food programs include the emergency food and shelter program, which provides funds to local agencies through a national board of charitable organizations. This national charitable board, in part consisting of the United Way, the Salvation Army, and Catholic Charities, distributes funds to local charities, soup kitchens, shelters, and other organizations that deal with hunger and homelessness. The federal government also provides funding to help subsidize emergency food agencies and to help pay for the storage and distribution of federal surplus food commodities.

Have the Food Programs Worked?

Evidence on the effectiveness of federal food policies is inconclusive. For example, the American Dietary Association found little hard evidence that the WIC program was effective.[12] A report by the General Accounting Office (GAO) to the Committee on Agriculture, Nutrition, and Forestry, stated that "no group of studies provided the kind of evidence to refute or confirm the claims that WIC is effective."[13] The GAO report did affirm, however, that the WIC program was responsible for decreasing the proportion of low birth-weight babies of eligible mothers by 16 to 20 percent.[14] Moreover, WIC's effect on mean birth weights also appears to be positive. The report tentatively concluded that African-American and teenage mothers who participated in WIC had better birth outcomes than comparable women. According to Michael Harrington et al., studies by the USDA and others show that WIC has: (1) improved the diets of low-income women, infants, and children; (2) increased the proportion of low-income pregnant women who utilize prenatal care; and (3) reduced anemia among WIC recipients. Harrington also maintains that research conducted at the Harvard School of Public Health demonstrated that every $1 spent on the prenatal portion of WIC saved $3 in short-term hospital costs.[15]

WIC was one of the few programs that escaped major budgetary cuts between 1980 and 1987. However, WIC serves only a minority of eligible women and children. According to the USDA, only 46 percent of all women and children eligible for WIC were served in 1986. In 1991, the Congressional Budget Office (CBO) revised and updated the USDA's findings and estimated that WIC served 56 percent of those eligible.[16] More than 100 counties have no WIC program, and many counties turn away people or have long waiting lists.[17] Although states may provide additional funds for WIC, in early 1988 only 11 states or jurisdictions (District of Columbia, Illinois, Indiana, Massachusetts, Michigan, Minnesota, New York, Pennsylvania, Texas, Washington, and Wisconsin) supplemented the program, and in two of those states (Michigan and Washington), the additional funds were used solely to cover administrative costs.[18]

Because of red tape and inadequate outreach services, the Food Stamp program fails to reach millions of eligible people. A USDA study estimated that only 66 percent of eligible individuals and 60 percent of eligible families participated in FS in 1984. A CBO study estimated that between 50 and 66 percent of the 30.4 million people eligible for FS in 1984 participated in the program. In addition, participation rates differed among subgroups. For example, eligible elderly households had a participation rate of between 34 and 44 percent; eligible households without children or elderly members had participation rates of from 24 to 39 percent.[19] Although the causes for nonparticipation are complex, one University of Michigan study found that more than half of all eligible persons who fail to participate either mistakenly believe they are ineligible or don't know of their eligibility.[20] Modest government efforts to alleviate this problem were hindered when Congress required a 50 percent state match for outreach efforts. Nevertheless, even the most conservative estimates reveal that at least one-third of those eligible for FS receive no benefits from the program.

The late Michael Harrington maintained that USDA surveys indicated that FS had been effective in improving the nutrition of millions of Americans.[21] However, the Harvard School of Public Health estimated that in 1985 some 20 million Americans were hungry. Vincent Breglio updated that estimate and argued that some 30 million Americans experienced hunger in 1992. In 1985, the Physicians' Task Force on Hunger identified 150 "hunger counties," or counties in which substantial numbers of poor people were undernourished and not receiving Food Stamps. The Task Force report recommended: (1) giving recipients cash or credit cards to reduce the stigma associated with FS coupons, (2) improving outreach efforts to nonparticipants, and (3) simplifying the FS application process. In general, estimates of hunger in America range from a low of 22.1 million to a high of 41.2 million.[22]

Food Stamp benefits are not overly generous, the average 1992 benefit being about 69 cents per meal per person. Studies by the USDA reveal that most families whose food expenditures equal the maximum FS benefit lack adequate diets, and only one-tenth of those families receive adequate nutrition.[23] The problem in food assistance was exacerbated by the deep cuts in food programs enacted during the early Reagan years, of which the funding was only partially restored by Congress in the late 1980s. Because most USDA food programs function as a form of indirect income support for farmers, the relationship among food prices, governmental supports, and food subsidization forms a complex web involving both consumers and producers.

FARMING IN AMERICA

The 1980s were a tumultuous time for American farmers, and in many places they faced a crisis rivaling that of the 1930s.[24] Agricultural members of the American Bankers Association estimated that 3.8 percent of all farmers had filed for bankruptcy in 1985 alone.[25] A 1985 USDA study of 1.7 million farms indicated that 214,000 were in serious financial difficulty, with 38,000 classified as technically insolvent.[26] In the mid-1980s, Secretary of Agriculture Bob Bergland identified 700,000 family or commercial farms, and noted that 220,000 of them would not survive financially.[27]

Other farm indicators were equally bleak. In 1981, the total asset value of U.S. agriculture was $1 trillion; by 1985 it had shrunk to $692 billion, a 30 percent drop and the steepest fall since the Great Depression. Moreover, while the prices of U.S. farmland peaked at an average of $823 per acre in 1982, they plunged to $599 per acre over the next five years (a loss of one-third of the value of the nation's farmland). Some states even experienced steeper declines. For example, the total value of farmland (including buildings) in Iowa fell from $67.4 billion in 1981 to only $25.1 billion in 1987. In at least five other states, the total value of farmland was more than halved in that six-year period. Although U.S. farms had declined in number by a modest 16,000 between 1978 and 1982, from 1982 until 1987 they declined by 151,000, or at a rate of about 30,000 annually. Moreover, while the United States exported 163 million tons of farm products in 1980, by 1986 that number was reduced to only 110 million.[28] By 1987, some commentators had already prepared eloquent eulogies to commemorate the death of American farming.

In spite of these dire predictions, U.S. farmers made a relative comeback in the late 1980s. This comeback was due in part to the 1987/88 worldwide drought, which depleted the grain reserves of many nations. Nevertheless, by early 1990, farmland prices in the United States had risen to $693 per acre, and farm exports increased to 148.5 million tons. Real net cash farm income went up from $48.5 billion in 1987 to about the same level as had prevailed in the mid-1970s. Moreover, farm assets rose from $691 billion in 1981 to $1.29 trillion in 1990 (in constant 1982 dollars). More important, the farm debt stabilized.[29] These improvements resulted from the reversal of several factors that had contributed to the farm crisis in the mid-1980s: (1) declining cash income relative to asset values; (2) an increase in the debt-to-asset ratio as farm debt rose faster than asset levels; and (3) an increasing proportion of available cash being paid out as interest to lenders.[30] As these factors reversed themselves, farming conditions became more stable.

Despite this improvement, American farmers are by no means out of danger. Although positive farm income was reported by 89 percent of farms in 1989 (up from 64 percent in 1988), economists warn that the future prospects for a healthy farm income are shaky at best. Moreover, the farming sector has not fully recovered from the crisis of the mid-1980s, and the growth in farm equity is still trailing the 3 to 4 percent rate of general inflation.[31]

The Farming Crisis of the 1980s

The causes of both the current problems in farming and the crisis of the mid-1980s are complex. Historically, American agriculture has never been a stable enterprise. Since the nineteenth century, farmers have ridden an economic roller coaster of good and bad times, with much of this instability attributable to variables outside their control, such as the weather, international trade and monetary policy, and government farming policies.

American agriculture was heavily influenced by large-scale operations from the early days of European colonization. Early agriculture was characterized by the slave plantations of the South, the Spanish haciendas of the Southwest, and the large wheat and cattle farms of the West. Much of agricultural production was in the hands of wealthy individuals or foreign investors.

By the mid-1800s, federal government policies began to encourage the growth of small family farms. The development of small-scale agriculture was aided by the defeat of slavery, the institution of the Homestead Acts, and the general movement westward. Despite the new agricultural opportunities, farmers found themselves caught in the classic cost/price squeeze. High prices for seeds, credit, and transportation (costs) often exceeded the crop prices offered by the large grain monopolies. This situation resulted in a series of rural depressions in the late nineteenth and early twentieth centuries.[32]

Angry farmers responded to these injustices by demanding protection from the railroads, banks, and grain monopolies. Through political organizing they created the Farmers Alliance, the Populist Party, the Greenback Party, and the Non-Partisan League.[33] Although the World War I period brought some relief, it was quickly followed by a major farming disaster almost a decade before the Great Depression of the 1930s.

Coupled with severe droughts, the depression of the 1930s seriously crippled rural America. Outraged by years of poor farming and inadequate or nonexistent governmental policies, farmers began to engage in direct action. In the plains states, farmers barricaded highways to stop foreclosures, insisted that local lenders exercise leniency, called farm strikes, and, in some instances, rioted.[34] Legislatures in farm states tried to curb this insurgency by enacting moratoriums on foreclosures, while the federal government moved to set prices at parity levels (the ratio between farm prices and input/output costs).[35] Congress in the 1930s passed the Farm Parity Program, an innovative piece of legislation that contained three central features:

1. The Commodity Credit Corporation (CCC) was established to set a minimum floor under farm prices. The CCC was de-

signed to make loans to farmers whenever the prices offered by the grain companies were lower than the cost of production. Crops were to be used as collateral, and when prices returned to normal, farmers were to repay the loans with interest.
2. Farm production was managed in order to maintain a balance between supply and demand and thus to prevent surpluses. Managing supply and demand would also reduce the government's responsibility for storing and purchasing surpluses.
3. A national grain reserve was created to stabilize consumer prices in the event of droughts or natural disasters.[36]

In 1942, Congress established the price support levels at 90 percent of parity. From 1942 to 1953, the average prices paid to farmers were at 90 to 100 percent of parity, thereby raising market prices, ensuring a secure income for farmers, reducing the need for excessive debt, and encouraging stabilization in the price of grain.

By the end of World War II, however, powerful corporations, academics, "free traders," and others had begun waging war on the Farm Parity Program. Soil conservation, supply management, and parity were characterized as socialist programs that interfered with a free market economy. Grain companies called for lower prices in order to sell abroad, arguing that expanded exports and food-aid programs would compensate farmers for lower commodity prices. Industrialists maintained that lower food prices would translate into cheaper labor costs, and agribusiness believed that lowered commodity prices would result in more production, thereby increasing the use of their products. The small farmer inevitably lost to this powerful coalition, and President Eisenhower and his Secretary of Agriculture, Ezra Taft Benson, helped defeat the Farm Parity Program in 1953.

The optimism of the corporate sector proved ill-founded, at least with respect to the small farmer. The purchasing power of net farm income decreased even as exports rose. Held constant in 1967 dollars, the purchasing power of net farm income dropped from an annual average of $25 billion from 1942 to 1952 (the years of farm parity) to an average of $13.3 billion from 1953 to 1972. In 1952, net farm income was greater than total farm debt; by 1983 net farm income was less than farm interest payments.[37]

The farming crisis of the mid-1980s did not affect all farmers equally. For example, almost one-sixth of all U.S. farming households suffered net income losses in 1984, whereas a ninth had total incomes of more than $60,000.[38] Farmers with middle-sized operations (in the 80- to 500-acre range) were being forced to abandon farming, while large farms appeared to be growing, as were also small farms. For example, more than two-fifths of all U.S. farms in 1984 had total annual sales of less than $10,000, accounting for only 2 percent of all farm sales. These farms experienced an overall net loss of income, and farm households with sales of less than $100,000 per year earned most of their income from nonfarm employment. By contrast, farm households with sales exceeding $500,000 a year earned an average income of $219,000. Three-fifths of the total income of farming families (a figure that is growing) came from nonfarm employment in 1984.[39]

Unfortunately, statistics do not tell the human side of the farming story. A 1985 article in the Sioux Falls, South Dakota, *Argus Leader,* lets us see the tragic dimension:

Out in the fields, in the countryside beyond the small-town street lights, the harvest continues. But it's not corn being plucked from the snow cover. It's men and women, farmers and farm wives.

A gunshot explodes in rural Pipestone; a farmer is dead.

Four graves are dug in Hills, Iowa, after a distraught farmer kills a banker, a neighbor, his wife and himself.

And the tears falling on the kitchen table in southwest Aurora County are only ripples in a growing sea of agricultural anguish.[40]

Family farming embodies many of America's most cherished traditional values—hard work, independence, strong family life, close-knit communities, and democratic institutions. Farming for many rural families is not a vocation but a way of life. The connection to the land, often a legacy from parents or grandparents, creates a commitment to a specific place and to the family heritage.[41] This psychological connection to farming means that many farmers see themselves as farmer-caretakers, and without that identity the sense of self becomes emptied. Financial failure may therefore leave farmers not only with a sense of personal failure but with feelings of shame and disgrace for having failed both their families and their heritage. This situation can result in emotional disturbances ranging from stress and depression to self-destructive or aggressive behavior.[42] The Reverend Paul Tidemann, a Lutheran minister who studied the farm crisis of the 1980s, reported that "The loss of a farm . . . is not the same as a loss of a job. It signals the loss of a personal and family connection to the land. It prompts a sense of betrayal, in many cases, of generations of farmers, past, present, and future."[43]

Although the hemorrhage in farm foreclosures had slowed somewhat by the late 1980s, a decline in family farms continues to plague the agricultural sector. Most troubling is that the largest decline in new entries into farming has occurred among the youngest farmers. Specifically, entries into farming fell 50 percent for those under age 25, and 35 percent for those 25 to 34. This problem has concerned rural communities and farm advocates who worry about the "graying" of America's rural communities.[44]

Experts attribute the farm crisis of the 1980s to several factors: (1) excessive debt; (2) high interest rates; (3) poor advice from the federal government; (4) the machinations of grain traders, agribusiness, and commodity trading; (5) the slowing down of foreign export markets; (6) the strong dollar of the early and mid-1980s; (7) falling farmland prices and lower inflation; (8) the effect of the free trade ideology; and (9) U.S. foreign policy initiatives that affected agriculture. According to Bruce Bullock, "The agricultural sector financed its trip to the current situation on borrowed capital. Unfortunately, for a large part of the agricultural debt expansion over the past 10 years, the capacity to repay from farm earnings never existed."[45]

The almost frantic borrowing of large amounts of capital by farmers had several causes. One was that in the early and mid-1970s, USDA and farm extension experts advised farmers to plant "fencerow to fencerow" in order to take advantage of export markets and the high rate of inflation. Moreover, these experts were advising farmers that either they would have to "get big or get out." Heeding this advice, and developing a high-production mentality, farmers were forced to raise their input costs by upgrading their farming operation through buying or renting more land, purchasing modern equipment, and relying more heavily on chemical means for increasing production.

The capital for this expansion was raised by borrowing money on the "paper value" of inflated farmland. Although farmers kept losing money on their crops and livestock, eager private, cooperative, and government lenders offered loans based on their belief that farmland prices would continue to rise. The increase in production and the softening of foreign markets (sometimes based on foreign policy, as when President Carter banned grain exports to the Soviet Union) created huge surpluses. The slowing down of inflation, coupled with the high interest rates of the Reagan years, began to force down land prices.[46] As a result, vulnerable farmers were thrust into bankruptcy, and as their land and machinery went to auction, farm values for all farmers were forced down. A downward spiral of falling values led to insolvency for farmers and bankers nationally. In the end, farmers who went into substantial debt for capital and operating loans (using their inflated land as collateral) found themselves with high debt/asset ratios. This situation, coupled with the strong dollar of the mid-1980s (making food and other American exports expensive) and adverse weather conditions in many parts of the farm belt, caused farmers to become unable to repay their debts.

Some critics maintain that traders and the grain monopolies lay at the heart of the problem. For example, whereas farm exports increased by 143 percent from 1973 to 1983, net farm income dropped by 40 percent.[47] On the other hand, grain traders profited from the renewed price instability, which allowed them to reap enormous profits through speculation, and therefore, to increase their control over agricultural, transportation, and food processing industries.[48] The ideological tool used by these large multinational corporations was the concept of free trade. While the tenets of free trade suggest that the market will regulate price and demand, in reality, free trade worked to the advantage of powerful multinational corporations. Moreover, the ideology of free trade was problematic because it encouraged high-volume production at lower profit margins, thereby making it difficult to use sound soil, water, and conservation practices.[49]

The U.S. commodities trade is dominated by a few large corporations such as Cargill, Louis Dreyfus, Bunge and Born, Mutsui/Cook, and Andre/Garnac. These corporations handle 96 percent of all U.S. wheat exports, 95 percent of corn and 80 percent of oats and sorghum. According to critics, these corporations lobbied for lower price supports, further exposing farmers to a predatory marketplace stacked against them. When farm debt rose, multinationals argued that the solution lay in increased exports, a move that required cutting price support levels even further. Thus, instead of ushering in prosperity, the export expansionists brought the farming community a 1930s style depression.[50]

The effects of the farm crisis extended beyond the farming community. As farmers went bankrupt, other agriculturally linked systems experienced the ripples. Agricultural and rural banks—often overextended—felt the economic stress of bankrupt farmers, and many went under. Agricultural implement and feed dealers were also severely affected by the inability of farmers to purchase new goods or repay their debts. Rural churches reported declines in membership and paltry collections as farm families were forced to move away or declined to attend because of their inability to contribute. Counties faced eroded tax bases as land values deteriorated and out-migration occurred. Most observers agreed that the farm crisis had profound consequences for the entire farm-to-market chain as well as for the whole fabric of rural life.

The farm crisis also had secondary economic effects. For example, almost 21 percent of the work force is linked to agriculture, including 55,000 jobs in steel mills. When a farm is sold and its equipment auctioned off, an oversupply of used machinery occurs, thereby creating a disincentive for the purchase of new machinery. Every liquidated farm means the loss of five to seven jobs; every three bankrupt farms destroy another rural business.[51] On the other hand, each dollar earned by a farmer creates an additional five dollars in goods and services.[52]

Although the worst of the 1980s farm crisis may have passed—at least temporarily—many of the structural problems that originally led to the crisis continue. For example, 70 percent of farmers live on small "hobby farms," which account for less than 10 percent of total farm receipts. Moreover, over one-third of farm produce comes from the 1.4 percent of large superfarms whose sales total $500,000 or more a year. Crunched between the "hobby farms" and the superfarms, the mid-sized family farms are being squeezed out. In 1992, one in three farmworkers was a hired employee who earned an average wage of $5.36 an hour.[53]

The concentration of agricultural production into the hands of a few large farmers has profound consequences for many rural communities. A 1986 congressional study of counties dominated by superfarms found that they were populated by a few wealthy elites, a large majority of poor laborers, and virtually no middle class. This trend in agricultural concentration is being driven by a federal farm policy that targets large subsidies—estimated at $13 billion in 1992—toward the nations's largest farms. According to Osha Davidson, 73 cents of every federal farm program dollar ends up with 15 percent of the nation's superfarms.[54]

U.S. Farm Policy

In recent years, the federal government has made several attempts to reduce the agricultural surplus resulting from overproduction. One such attempt was the 1983 Payment-in-Kind (PIK) program. To encourage farmers to participate in this set-aside program, the Secretary of Agriculture offered to compensate them by offering a partial payment in the form of grain stored in government stockpiles. The intent of the PIK program was to avoid cash payments to farmers while at the same time reducing the cost of maintaining a large government inventory of grain. A major drought occurred simultaneously with the PIK program, which, in effect, raised market prices by reducing production. Without the effects of the drought, the release of government grain stocks under the PIK program would have further depressed market prices. In any event, the PIK program was developed only as a short-term measure.[55]

After years of debate among farm, agribusiness, corporate, and commodity groups, President Reagan signed into effect the Food and Security Act of 1985. This legislation was distinctive in three ways: (1) It was the most complicated farm bill ever passed; (2) it cost the federal government more than previous farm bills had (about $80 billion from 1986 to 1990); and (3) the price supports, at least in terms of parity, were lower than they had been in previous bills.[56] The 1985 farm bill operated in the following manner. A target price was set by Congress and the Secretary of Agriculture, and if prices fell below that level, participating farmers received a deficiency payment from the government. This system was directly connected to the loan rates set by the Commodity Credit Corporation (CCC). For example, in 1986 the CCC loan rate for a bushel of corn was $1.92, while the target price was $3.03. Because the market price was roughly the CCC loan rate, the federal government made up the deficiency of $1.10 per bushel of corn. On 7 billion bushels of corn, this required almost $8 billion in subsidies. Despite this, the 1986 target price of $3.03 per bushel of corn was, according to USDA estimates, 17 cents less a bushel than it actually cost to raise corn.[57] This meant that farmers were losing money on every bushel harvested, forcing them to borrow more money to cover their losses. Grain corporations and foreign buyers were thus allowed to purchase grain at prices more than $1.00 below the cost of production. In other words, federal policy was subsidizing the grain corporations at the expense of farmers, taxpayers, and the general public.

An alternative proposal to the 1985 farm bill was the Farm Act of 1987, sponsored by Tom Harkin (D-Iowa) and Richard Gephardt (D-Missouri). This bill would have established price supports at 70 percent of the government-calculated parity price for each commodity. In each year of the program the parity price would have been increased by 1 percent until, in the eleventh year, 80 percent of parity was reached. In addition to price increases, there would have been mandatory production controls (subject to approval by a farmer referendum) limiting agricultural commodity production to meet both domestic consumption demands and export, humanitarian, and strategic reserve needs. Excess production would have been stored and applied toward the following year's quota. In addition, components of the bill would have discouraged the sale of farmland to other than working farm families.[58] Despite strong support from farm lobbies, the Harkin-Gephardt bill was defeated.

In 1990, Congress passed a five-year farm bill that made important changes in policies af-

fecting farmers, consumers, and the environment. Specifically, the 1990 farm bill cut down on the number of acres for which farmers could receive deficiency payments, permitted planting flexibility, and maintained the market-oriented loan rates contained in the 1985 farm bill. In addition, the bill had features to improve the cleanliness and quality of U.S. grain, continue the protection of fragile wetlands, create new incentives to help farmers prevent contamination of ground and surface water on 10 million acres, create incentives to help farmers use fewer pesticides and require farmers licensed to use hazardous chemicals to keep records of their use, protect farmland by helping farmers to stay in farming, help farmers to meet environmental laws, establish the first-ever national "organically grown" label, and provide a significant rural development aid package.[59] Moreover, this bill was estimated to cost $40 billion over five years as opposed to the $80 billion price tag on the 1985 farm bill.

In 1993, Osha Davidson challenged Secretary of Agriculture Mike Espy to acknowledge that the world has changed dramatically since the original farm policies were introduced over 50 years ago. Davidson argued that "U.S. farm policies are hopelessly outdated, exorbitantly expensive and environmentally devastating. But they endure, thanks to the lobbying efforts of agribusinesses that are able to make hay from society's devotion to the fast-disappearing icon, the family farmer."[60]

RURAL POVERTY

The problems in farming have helped to create a widespread rural dilemma. Contrary to popular misconceptions, poverty rates are higher in rural areas than they are in metropolitan centers. In fact, over 9 million poor American (25 percent of all poor people) live in rural areas. Moreover, in 1987, 16.9 percent of the nonmetropolitan population had incomes below the poverty level compared with 12.5 percent of the metropolitan population. In addition, a person living in a nonmetropolitan area is almost as likely to be poor as an inner-city resident of a metropolitan area. Contrary to popular stereotypes, only 10 percent of the rural poor live on farms.[61]

Rural poverty has a great affect on traditionally vulnerable groups. More than two-fifths (44.1 percent) of rural African Americans were poor in 1987. By contrast, only one-third (33 percent) of urban African Americans were poor. Among other traditionally low-income groups (e.g., Hispanic Americans, the elderly, and single female-headed families) rural poverty rates were as high as in central cities. Poverty rates for whites were also as high in rural areas as they were in central cities.[62]

Rural poverty is in large measure geographically determined. Although 17 Southern states contain slightly more than 33 percent of the total U.S. population (and four out of ten rural residents), they encompass 53.6 percent of the rural poor. Of the remaining rural poor, some 25.3 percent live in the Midwest, 14.5 percent in the West, and 14.5 percent in the Northeast. According to a USDA study, all but 18 of the 206 persistently low-income counties (those counties that consistently ranked in the bottom fifth of all rural counties in terms of per capita income) were in the South. Almost half those counties were located in just three states—Kentucky, Mississippi, and Tennessee.[63]

The economic problems experienced by rural communities also translate into a widening rural-urban income gap. For example, only 11 percent of rural households in 1987 had incomes that placed them in the top fifth of American households. By contrast, 23 percent of urban households had incomes that high. On the other hand, 26 percent of all rural households had incomes placing them among the poorest fifth of U.S. households, while 18 percent of urban households had incomes that low. And this income disparity between rural and urban settings is increasing. Data from the Bureau of Economic Analysis show that between 1979 and 1987 per capita income in rural areas fell from 77 to 73 percent of per capita income in urban areas.[64]

Contemporary rural life has been shaped in large part by the absence of economic opportunity and social mobility. In particular, the lack of good-paying jobs has resulted in the migration of rural families to urban areas, especially when the primary breadwinner possesses substantial skills and education. For younger workers, the possibility of better-paying jobs in urban areas is a powerful enticement. The college graduate from a rural area may find it almost impossible to return home given the dearth of economic opportunities that characterize many nonurban areas. In essence, the lure of economic opportunities creates a brain drain from rural to urban areas. As the pool of skilled and intellectual workers in rural areas begins to evaporate, fewer industries are attracted to the area and, in general, the economic conditions further deteriorate. Moreover, as rural counties begin to experience the same social and economic desperation as impoverished urban areas, similar manifestations of poverty begin to appear. Drug and alcohol abuse, theft, and high rates of school dropouts, teenage pregnancies, and other social problems are beginning to become more common in rural areas. The increased need for mental health and economic development services creates a fertile ground for rural social work activities.

CONCLUSION

The production, distribution, and consumption of food have traditionally been political issues. Thus, the federal government must respond to the needs of diverse groups that have an interest in food—farmers, consumers, the poor or their advocates, food distributors, grain traders, Third World countries that depend on America for food, and wealthier nations that purchase U.S. food (and occasionally compete for foreign food markets).

The federal government has responded to these interests by creating a patchwork of policies and programs. One of the most important of these is the Food Stamp program, an ingenious approach that helps keep food affordable for low-income consumers, helps stabilize farm prices, slows down agricultural surpluses by subsidizing consumption, and allows food merchants and distributors to increase their profits by ensuring a volume of subsidized consumers.

America's food problems are indeed serious for many poor people and farmers. For others, including the very poor and marginal farmers, it has reached crisis proportions. Tragically, many farmers now profit from Food Stamps not because the program helps control the surplus of farm goods, but because it provides them direct benefits as recipients. It is truly ironic when the producers of food are unable to purchase what they grow.

DISCUSSION QUESTIONS

1. The Food Stamps (FS) program is currently the single most important federal program for combating hunger. Nevertheless, there are serious questions as to why close to 40 percent of those eligible for FS are not enrolled. Why has the federal government not been more aggressive in promoting FS? What changes, if any, could be made in the FS program to make it more accessible to greater numbers of eligible people?
2. The WIC and FS programs are similar in many respects. What are the specific differences between these programs? Is it necessary for WIC to be a distinct program? If so, why?
3. There are serious questions as to the effectiveness of U.S. food programs for the poor. What alterna-

tives, if any, are there to the matrix of food programs that currently make up the nutritional safety net?
4. The farming situation in America has historically been an economic roller coaster. In recent times, farming was reasonably good in the 1970s, after which it spun into a depression during the early and mid-1980s. By the late 1980s, however, it had recovered somewhat. What programs and policies, if any, should be implemented to stabilize the situation in farming?
5. Poverty continues to be a persistent part of America's rural landscape. Describe the most important causes of rural poverty. What, if anything, can be done to lower the rates of rural poverty?

NOTES

1. Committee on Ways and Means, U.S. House of Representatives, *Overview of Entitlement Programs, 1992 Green Book* (Washington, D.C.: U.S. Government Printing Office, 1992), pp. 1636, 1639; and Isaac Shapiro, *White Poverty in America* (Washington, D.C.: Center on Budget and Policy Priorities, October 1992), p. 35.
2. U.S. House of Representatives, *1992 Green Book*, p. 1627.
3. Children's Defense Fund, *The State of America's Children, 1991* (Washington, D.C.: Children's Defense Fund, 1991), p. 27.
4. U.S. House of Representatives, *1992 Green Book*, p. 1616.
5. Ibid., p. 1639.
6. Illa Tennison, "WIC Policy Analysis," unpublished paper, School of Social Work, University of Missouri-Columbia, 1987, p. 5.
7. Ibid.
8. U.S. House of Representatives, *1992 Green Book*, p. 1687.
9. Ibid., p. 1683.
10. Ibid.
11. Ibid.
12. Tennison, "WIC Policy Analysis," p. 12.
13. Quoted in ibid.
14. Ibid., p. 13.
15. Michael Harrington, with the assistance of Robert Greenstein and Eleanor Holmes Norton, *Who Are the Poor?* (Washington, D.C.: Justice for All National Office, 1987), p. 15.

16. U.S. House of Representatives, *1992 Green Book*, p. 1688.
17. Children's Defense Fund, *The State of America's Children, 1988* (Washington, D.C.: Children's Defense Fund, 1988), p. 186.
18. Isaac Shapiro and Robert Greenstein, *Holes in the Safety Nets* (Washington, D.C.: Center on Budget and Policy Priorities, 1988), pp. 33–34.
19. U.S. House of Representatives, *1992 Green Book*, p. 1628.
20. Shapiro and Greenstein, *Holes in the Safety Nets*, pp. 33–34.
21. Harrington et al., *Who Are the Poor?* p. 26.
22. Letter, September 8, 1992, from J. Larry Brown, director, Tufts University School of Nutrition to the Hon. Tony Hall, chairman, House Select Committee on Hunger, Washington, D.C.
23. Harrington et al., *Who Are the Poor?* p. 26.
24. M. Drabenstott and M. Duncan, "Another Troubled Year for U.S. Agriculture," *Journal of the American Society of Farm Managers and Rural Appraisers* 49, no. 1 (1985): 58–66.
25. Cited in Joanne Mermelstein, "Criteria of Rural Mental Health Directors in Adopting Farm Crisis Programming Innovation," unpublished Ph.D. dissertation, Public Policy Analysis and Administration, St. Louis University, 1986, p. 3.
26. Ibid.
27. Ibid., pp. 3–4.
28. "U.S. Farm Sector, In Annual Checkup, Shows Strong Pulse," *Farmline,* December-January 1991, p. 2.
29. Ibid., pp. 4–5.
30. Jim Ryan and Ken Erickson, "Balance Sheet Stable in 1992," *Agricultural Outlook* 46 (January-February 1992): 29–30.
31. Ibid., p. 29.
32. G. Kaye Kellogg, "The Crisis of the Family Farm in America Today," unpublished paper, School of Social Work, University of Missouri-Columbia, 1987, p. 3.
33. Howard Jacob Karger, *The Sentinels of Order: A Case Study of the Minneapolis Settlement House Movement, 1915–1950* (Lanham, Md.: University Press of America, 1987).
34. Everett E. Luoma, *The Farmer Takes a Holiday: The Story of the National Farmer's Holiday Association and the Farmers' Strike of 1932–33* (New York: Exposition Press, 1967).
35. United States Department of Agriculture, "History of Agricultural Price Support and Adjustment Programs, 1933–84," *Bulletin* No. 485 (Washington, D.C.: Economic Research Service, 1984), pp. 8–9.
36. Kellogg, "The Crisis of the Family Farm," p. 4.
37. Steve Little, "Parity: Survival of the Family Farm," unpublished paper, School of Social Work, University of Missouri-Columbia, 1986, pp. 8–9.
38. Mary Ahearn, "Financial Well-Being of Farm Operators and Their Households," United States Department of Agriculture, *Report* No. 563, (Washington, D.C.: Economic Research Service, September 1986), p. iii.
39. Ibid.
40. Steve Young, *Argus Leader,* December 25, 1985, quoted in Joanne Mermelstein and Paul Sundet, guest eds., *Human Services in the Rural Environment* 10, no. 1 (April 1986): 2.
41. Mermelstein, "Criteria of Rural Mental Health Directors," pp. 5–6.
42. Ibid., p. 7.
43. Quoted in John M. Herrick, "Farmers' Revolt! Contemporary Farmers' Protests in Historical Perspective: Implications for Social Work Practice," *Human Services in the Rural Environment* 10, no. 1 (April 1986): 9.
44. Fred Gale, "What's Behind the Declining Farm Count?" *Agricultural Outlook,* June 1992, p. 26.
45. J. Bruce Bullock, "The Farm Credit Situation: Implications for Agricultural Policy," *Human Services in the Rural Environment* 10, no. 1 (April 1986): 12.
46. Mermelstein, "Criteria of Rural Mental Health Directors," pp. 2–3.
47. Little, "Parity," p. 9.
48. Ibid.
49. United States Department of Agriculture, "Economic Indicators of the Farm Sector," *Farm Sector Review, ERS, ECIFS* 4–3 (Washington, D.C., 1984), pp. 4, 16.
50. Little, "Parity," pp. 10–11.
51. Doug Wertish, "The Effects of Losing 10 Percent of the Faribault Area Farmers" (Faribault, Minn.: Faribault Area Vo-Tech Institute, 1985).
52. Kellogg, "The Crisis of the Family Farm," p. 9.
53. Osha Gray Davidson, "Rise of America's Rural Ghetto," *The San Diego Union Tribune,* January 27, 1993, p. B–6.
54. Ibid.

55. Little, "Parity," p. 12.

56. Ibid.

57. Kellogg, "The Crisis of the Family Farm," pp. 9–10.

58. League of Rural Voters, "The Family Farm Act of 1987 (Harkin-Gephardt Bill)" (Washington, D.C., February 26, 1987).

59. U.S. Government, "Conference Committee Approves Five-year Farm Bill," News Release, Washington, D.C., October 16, 1990, n.p.

60. Davidson, "Rise of America's Rural Ghetto," p. B–9.

61. Kathryn Porter, *Poverty in Rural America: A National Overview* (Washington, D.C.: Center on Budget and Policy Priorities, April 1989), pp. 3–4.

62. Ibid., pp. 7–11.

63. Ibid.

64. Scott Barancik, *The Rural Disadvantage: Growing Income Disparities Between Rural and Urban Areas* (Washington, D.C.: Center on Budget and Policy Priorities, April 1990), pp. ix–x.

CHAPTER 16

Employment Policies

This chapter examines the relationship between employment policy and social welfare. The absence of adequate employment contributes to a variety of psychological and physiological problems; therefore, a range of social programs has been deployed to aid Americans who are unemployed or underemployed. The history of employment policy in the United States shows a gradual expansion of programs until the policies of the Reagan administration reduced them sharply. Employment policy has become increasingly important for social welfare, as the popularity of AFDC workfare programs demonstrates. At the same time, the lack of employment opportunity contributes to a growing American underclass.

In a market economy, most people are expected to meet their needs by participating in the labor market. Work provides them income with which to purchase goods and services as well as benefits that provide some security against the costs of health care, sickness, and old age. The labor market in capitalist economies, however, is not well synchronized, thus resulting in the failure of employment to provide the basic needs of all people. As a consequence, many people who could work must depend on social welfare programs for economic support. A little over half—56 percent—of the poor peo-

ple in the United States are adults of working age.[1]

The failure of the labor market to meet the economic needs of the population has been the source of important distinctions in employment policy. One set of distinctions focuses on the experiences of workers. People over 16 looking for work are counted by the Department of Labor as unemployed. But the unemployment rate does not assess the adequacy of employment. For example, part-time workers who wish to work full-time are counted as employed, and workers holding jobs below their skill levels are not identified, even though such workers are underemployed. Finally, discouraged workers who simply give up and stop looking for work, relying on other methods to support themselves, do not appear in the unemployment statistics because they are not actively looking for work.

A second set of distinctions relates to economic performance. In a robust economy, businesses start up and close down in significant numbers, leaving workers temporarily out of work until they find other jobs. Such frictional unemployment is considered unavoidable and the cost of a constantly changing economy. Structural unemployment "refers to deeper and longer-lasting maladjustments in the labor market," such as changes in the technical skills required for new forms of production.[2] Because of swings in economic performance, unemployment may be cyclical, as when recessions pitch the rate upward. And because certain groups of workers in certain regions have persistent difficulty finding work owing to an absence of jobs, unemployment is sometimes chronic. Michael Sherraden has examined how these components vary in the composition of the unemployment rate and concludes that structural and frictional factors account for about one-third, the cyclical factor for about one-fourth, and chronic unemployment for about one-half.[3]

These distinctions are important because social welfare is connected directly to the employment experience of Americans. When people are out of work, they frequently rely on welfare benefits to tide them over. Thus, welfare programs are often designed to complement the labor market. This has led some observers to refer to welfare as a "social wage," or, in other words, the amount paid workers by the government through welfare programs when they are not able to participate in the labor market. Logically, much of welfare could be eliminated if well-paying jobs were plentiful, but such has not been the case in the United States. Policymakers have tacitly accepted an unemployment rate

of 7 percent, which means that at any given time between 7.5 and 8 million workers are not employed.[4] Yet in 1978, Congress enacted the Humphrey-Hawkins Full Employment Act, which set an unemployment rate of 3 percent—equivalent to frictional unemployment—as a national goal. Since then, many government programs to aid the unemployed, underemployed, and discouraged workers have been reduced or eliminated, leaving many Americans dependent on welfare programs for support.

Moreover, absence of employment opportunity contributes to other social dysfunctions. Research by Dr. M. Harvey Brenner shows that a seemingly small increase in the unemployment rate is associated with an increase in several social problems. For example, during the 1973–74 recession the unemployment rate increased by 14.3 percent and was associated with the pathologies shown in Table 16.1. Brenner calculated that the combination of the 1973–74 increase in the unemployment rate, the decrease in real per capita income, and an increase in the business failure rate was related to "an overall increase of more than 165,000 deaths [from cardiovascular disease] over a ten-year period (the greatest proportion of which occurs within three

TABLE 16.1. Consequences of Increases in Unemployment

Pathological Indicator	Percentage Increase due to Rise in Unemployment	Increase in Incidence of Pathology
Total mortality	2.3	45,936
Cardiovascular mortality	2.8	28,510
Cirrhosis mortality	1.4	430
Suicide	1.0	270
Population in mental hospitals	6.0	8,416
Total arrests	6.0	577,477
Arrests for fraud and embezzlement	4.8	11,552
Assaults reported to police	1.1	7,035
Homicide	1.7	403

SOURCE: Reprinted from M. Harvey Brenner, *Estimating the Effects of Economic Change on National Health and Social Well-Being* (Washington, D.C.: U.S. Government Printing Office, 1984), p. 2.

years)." Overall, the total economic, social, and health care costs of this seemingly slight increase in unemployment came to $24 billion.[5]

HISTORY OF EMPLOYMENT POLICY

The most significant developments in American employment policy occurred during the New Deal. Faced with an unemployment rate of 25 percent and increasing militancy among the unemployed, President Roosevelt initiated the Federal Emergency Relief Administration (FERA) and recruited as its head Harry Hopkins, a social worker who had administered a work relief program for Roosevelt when he was governor of New York. Hopkins quickly conceived a series of work relief programs to get the unemployed back to work. The result was an alphabet soup of programs: the Civilian Conservation Corps (CCC), the Civil Works Administration (CWA), the Public Works Administration (PWA), and the Works Progress Administration (WPA). The flurry of work relief programs served to defuse a volatile labor problem, but—short of some conspicuous public construction projects—did little to remedy the social and economic consequences of the depression. "The sums expended on public works and relief were never enough (even allowing for a generous 'multiplier' effect) to support more than a fraction of the vast numbers of jobless and destitute at anything but a minimum level," concluded a scholar on the fiftieth anniversary of the New Deal.[6] The unemployment problem precipitated by the Great Depression was not to be fully resolved until the entry of the United States into World War II, when the armed services recruited young men in the millions for the war effort.

The legacy of the New Deal for employment policy appears in three programs: the United States Employment Service (USES), which was established under the Wagner-Peyser Act of 1933; the Unemployment Compensation provision of the Social Security Act of 1935; and

the Fair Labor Standards Act of 1938, which established the minimum wage. The USES consists of 2,400 offices nationwide where employers can list job openings. Funded by federal unemployment insurance taxes, the USES offices are operated by state agencies and provide services at no charge to either employers or prospective employees.[7] Although the USES claims to place about 5 million people a year, it is hampered by two problems. First, other welfare programs, such as Unemployment Compensation and Food Stamps, require workers to file with their local USES in order to obtain benefits, which results in unnecessary paperwork for the USES. Second, a system of private employment agencies, such as Manpower-Temporary Services and Kelly (Girl) Services, provides private sector employers with a means of selecting more desirable workers. As a result of this "creaming" of the labor pool, the USES is left with a disproportionate number of less skilled and lower-wage job seekers.

As an insurance program, Unemployment Compensation provides benefits to workers whose employers have contributed to a fund for a minimum number of work quarters. Workers wishing to receive benefits must (1) demonstrate that they are unemployed through no fault of their own, (2) appear in person at a state employment office to register for work, and (3) demonstrate continuing efforts to locate employment. Because the Unemployment Compensation fund is derived from compulsory contributions by employers, and because the amount that employers pay varies in accordance with their history of laying off workers, it is in the interest of employers to challenge claims by former workers seeking benefits, since fewer claims will decrease their contribution rate. In other instances, the Unemployment Compensation obligations of employers are folded into operating costs. This is common practice among defense contractors and within the construction industry, where relatively high-wage workers are able to draw unemployment compensation between contracts or during the off-season.

When the unemployment rate exceeds the national rate, localities are automatically eligible for a 15-week extension of the normal benefit period. Altogether, 91 percent of employed workers are covered by the Unemployment Compensation program.[8] Unemployment Compensation does not adequately address the needs of those at the margins of the labor force. For example, only 42 percent of unemployed workers actually received unemployment compensation benefits in 1991.[9]

The minimum wage ($4.25 per hour in 1992) covers about 90 percent of all nonsupervisory workers. Despite its extensive coverage, the minimum wage has been criticized by both conservatives and liberals. Looking at the persistently high unemployment rate among younger workers—about 35 percent of African-American teenagers[10]—some conservatives have argued that the minimum wage deters employers from hiring unproven workers. Lowering (or eliminating) the minimum wage would encourage employers to make more jobs available to the disadvantaged. On the other hand, liberals have contended that the minimum wage is far from adequate. At its present level, a worker employed 40 hours per week would earn approximately $8,500 per year, far below the 1990 poverty line of $13,359 for a family of four. The controversy surrounding the minimum wage is compounded by the fact that a portion of the service industry—notably convenience stores and fast food franchises—have taken advantage of the large number of younger workers available to hire them on a part-time basis for limited periods of time in order to avoid the expenses of paying benefits associated with full-time employment. In this instance, an industry has clearly profited from the use—or abuse—of young workers who rely on the minimum wage.[11]

JOB TRAINING PROGRAMS

The failure of the labor market to provide adequate employment opportunities to large numbers of workers led to a series of governmental efforts to better prepare the unemployed and underemployed. The first of these was the Manpower Development and Training Act (MDTA) of 1962. Intended as a program to assist workers displaced by technological and economic change, MDTA was also expected to serve the disadvantaged when the Office of Economic Opportunity was established in 1964. As one of the primary weapons in the newly declared War on Poverty, the MDTA grew rapidly, from $93 million in 1964 to $358 million in 1973. In 1973, 119,600 people were enrolled in MDTA. Still, the program was only one of several War on Poverty job programs to aid the disadvantaged, including the Neighborhood Youth Corps (for high school students), the Job Corps (for young adults), and the Work Incentive Program (for AFDC recipients).[12]

By the mid-1970s the proliferation and cost of job training programs prompted the Nixon administration and Congress to consolidate MDTA and other job training programs under the Comprehensive Employment and Training Act (CETA) of 1973. In addition to consolidating federal job training programs, CETA also decentralized program responsibilities for local governments. By 1978, CETA was budgeted at $11.2 billion and enrolled 3.9 million persons[13] (by comparison, the unemployed numbered 6.2 million in 1978).[14] Yet the nation's most ambitious program for contending with joblessness soon became the center of controversy. The recession of the 1970s placed financial burdens on local government, and budget-limiting acts, such as California's Proposition 13 (1978), capped the fiscal capacity of local government. Consequently, strong incentives were created for local governments to use the CETA program to fill civil service positions left vacant because of the retrenchment by local government. Because many of these jobs required work experience, CETA became a means by which a local government could subsidize its personnel budget—often by hiring relatively skilled persons and neglecting the chronically unemployed. This inflamed white-collar labor organizations, which saw civil service rosters being decimated while state and municipal employees were replaced by CETA workers. Moreover, Ronald Reagan, governor of California during the Proposition 13 revolt, was angry that the federal government would subsidize local government activities that the taxpayers had determined to be excessive. As president, Reagan would move quickly to clip the CETA program. Finally, many critics—both conservatives and liberals—charged that the chronically unemployed were often given dead-end, make-work jobs that failed to integrate them fully into the private sector.

Superseding CETA, the Job Training and Partnership Act (JTPA) of 1982 attempted to focus training on the hard-core unemployed in order to make them economically self-sufficient through private sector employment. Approximately 600 Private Industry Councils were created locally to synchronize training and job opportunities. Initially, the Reagan administration allocated $2.8 billion for the first year of JTPA, approximately three-quarters of what had been spent on CETA in 1980.[15] But appropriations were reduced in later years even though the unemployment rate rose above 7 percent. In 1992, appropriations for JTPA were approximately

$1.7 billion. During 1990, 565,200 enrollees were terminated from JTPA; of these, 55 percent found private employment at an average hourly wage of $5.54,[16] on an annual basis considerably below the poverty level for a family of four. The relationship between the funding of JTPA and the unemployment rate is depicted in Figure 16.1.

DUAL LABOR MARKETS

Despite the large enrollments in government employment programs and the substantial expenditures of public funds, the difficulty of elevating people out of poverty through job training programs led several scholars to examine the nature of the work that participants are expected to find. Labor market analysts such as Peter Doeringer, Michael Piore, and David Gordon found that "a group of low-wage, and often marginal, enterprises and a set of casual, unstructured job opportunities where workers with employment disadvantages tend to find work" characterized job seekers and employers participating in job training programs.[17] These researchers reasoned that the segmentation of the labor market—into better jobs versus disad-

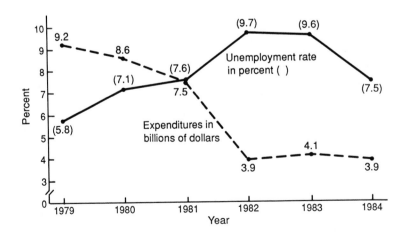

Figure 16.1. Federal Expenditures for Employment Services Compared with the Unemployment Rate, 1979–1984.

vantaged jobs—explained much of the problem at the root of government employment programs.

According to Piore, the labor market can be divided into two segments, or "dual labor markets"—a primary labor market and a secondary labor market:

> the primary market offers jobs which possess several of the following traits: high wages, good working conditions, employment stability and job security, equity and due process in the administration of work rules, and chances for advancement. The other, secondary sector, has jobs which, relative to those in the primary sector, are decidedly less attractive. They tend to involve low wages, poor working conditions, considerable variability in employment, harsh and often arbitrary discipline, and little opportunity to advance. The poor are confined to the secondary labor market.[18]

Piore noted that to the extent that employment is expected to solve the poverty problem, the trick is to see that the poor "gain access to primary employment."[19]

The magnitude of the secondary labor market has been explored by researchers who calculated that 36.2 percent of workers in 1970 fell into the secondary labor market, a modest increase over the number in 1950, 35 percent.[20] By the 1980s, however, two factors increased the proportion of workers in the secondary labor market. First, membership in labor unions—the best security for nonprofessional workers—fell from 30.8 percent of nonagricultural workers in 1970 to 25.2 percent in 1980, leaving millions of workers vulnerable to the employment insecurity typical of the secondary labor market.[21] Second, a higher proportion of the new jobs created were in the service sector of the economy, which consists largely of secondary labor market jobs. Between 1979 and 1985, 44 percent of new jobs paid less than $7,400 per year.[22]

For workers in the secondary labor market, social welfare is an important source of support, whether this is in the form of income payments, such as AFDC, or in-kind benefits, such as Medicaid and Food Stamps. Yet the relationship between public assistance and the secondary labor market is a poor fit. With the exception of Alaska, no state provides benefits above the poverty level, even when the cash equivalent of Food Stamps is added to the AFDC benefit.[23] Consequently, most families have strong incentives to work in order to supplement their meager welfare benefits. The relatively punitive treatment of earnings under AFDC encourages families to underreport their income from work. Piore concluded that "The public assistance system discourages full-time work . . . and forces those on welfare into jobs that are either part-time or which pay cash which will not be reported to the social worker or can be quickly dropped or delayed when the social worker discovers them or seems in danger of doing so."[24] Not surprisingly, public assistance is fraught with inaccurate payments because clients conceal income from the irregular employment that they are, for all practical purposes, obliged to seek in order to compensate for inadequate welfare benefits. The circularity of the dilemma is as frustrating for administrators of public assistance programs as it is for public assistance beneficiaries, especially those with children, who often resort to deception for purposes of survival. In an investigation of income sources of AFDC recipients, Kathryn Edin and Christopher Jencks found that low AFDC benefits produced a perverse consequence: Virtually every recipient supplemented AFDC with other income sources, but only one in four reported any portion of this to welfare authorities.[25]

WORKFARE

The question of assisting workers from the secondary labor market to become economically self-sufficient was investigated by the Manpower Development Research Corporation

(MDRC) in a series of five-year experiments. At 21 sites nationwide, more than 6,500 hard-core unemployed subjects were provided with special benefits and training. According to the summary of the MDRC report,

> the guiding principle of the supported work experiment is that by participating in the program, a significant number of people who were severely handicapped for employment may be able to join the labor force and do productive work, cease engaging in socially destructive or dependent behavior, and become self-supporting members of society.[26]

The goals of the supported work experiment were ambitious considering the four groups MDRC elected to train: women who had been on AFDC for several years, ex-addicts, ex-offenders, and young high school dropouts who were often delinquents. Including the cost of antisocial behavior with that of job training, MDRC figured that an investment of $5,000 to $8,000 per trainee was justifiable.[27] In *The Underclass,* Ken Auletta followed one group of trainees through the supported work program, confirming the mixed results reported by MDRC: "after five years, the MDRC found that for only two of the four target groups—ex-addicts and mothers receiving AFDC payments—'the benefits exceed the costs.'" All told, only one-third of all the trainees who enrolled in the year-long supported work experiment went on to "unsubsidized jobs or returned to public school."[28]

Still, the relative success of the AFDC group proved noteworthy, especially in light of the Reagan administration's attempts to reform welfare by emphasizing work in exchange for benefits ("workfare"). Under the Omnibus Budget Reconciliation Act (OBRA) of 1981, which reordered many social welfare programs, states were free "to design their own work-related programs for AFDC applicants and recipients."[29] Almost overnight, the supported work

experiments—a marginal success at best—became the basis for welfare reform; and, once again, MDRC was instrumental in designing a training program for welfare beneficiaries.

During the early 1980s, MDRC conducted a series of "work/welfare" demonstrations in 11 states, which evaluated several strategies to enhance the employability of AFDC recipients under the Community Work Experience Program (CWEP). As reported by Judith Gueron, president of MDRC, the interim findings of CWEP were generally positive. Of five states reporting, MDRC found that, while jobs were often entry-level and did not provide much skill development, neither were they make-work jobs. Moreover, "a high proportion of participants interviewed were satisfied with their work sites, felt positive about coming to work, believed that they were making a useful contribution, and felt that they were treated as part of the regular work force."[30] However, Gueron could not be sanguine about the CWEP demonstrations at the conclusion of the experiments. Generally, program costs were more than offset by the economic benefits of the employment-related activities expected of AFDC recipients. Unfortunately, the gains won by program participants were usually insufficient to make them financially independent of welfare. Furthermore, the CWEP experiment suggested that even these modest gains were predicated on "an accessible pool of regular jobs," a condition that did not exist in West Virginia, which reported no fiscal savings from CWEP.

MDRC later reinterpreted the data from five workfare experiments to determine if some groups of welfare recipients benefited more than others from variously designed programs. Workfare participants were classified into three groups based on their earnings in the year prior to going on AFDC and the length of time they had been on AFDC, resulting in a three-tier ladder of dependency. According to their performance in workfare programs, the top tier—those with earnings of more than $3,000—showed the least program savings, primarily because this group was able to leave AFDC without having to rely on the workfare program. Of the other two groups, the most welfare-dependent—those with no earnings and who had been on AFDC for more than two years—"attained below-average earnings" in comparison with the other two groups. Yet because the most dependent group represented such high program costs, their participation in workfare resulted in greater program savings. Nevertheless, the report suggested that workfare administrators were likely to realize increased earnings by workfare participants by focusing on the second tier, the mid-dependency group. The conclusions from this MDRC study suggested that workfare programs could claim greater earnings by AFDC recipients by focusing on the middle tier of workfare participants, but yield greater welfare program savings by focusing on the lowest tier.[31] These conclusions are important because they point to different directions for workfare programs. If welfare officials are under pressure to report lower program costs, they should ration workfare resources and reserve them for the most welfare-dependent. On the other hand, if the objective of workfare is to boost recipients off AFDC, workfare should be reserved for the mid-dependent group. Because workfare programs are unlikely to be funded generously, there will be strong incentives for workfare administrators to conserve resources by focusing on the most dependent; yet this strategy may be self-defeating in that it is the one least likely to increase the earnings of workfare participants sufficiently to get them off AFDC. Thus, workfare may prove effective at containing AFDC program costs, but ineffective at helping those on AFDC to become economically self-sufficient.

By 1991, MDRC, on the basis of summaries of field experiments across the nation, was continuing to suggest that workfare could produce modest savings in AFDC. Data on two programs—a mandatory workfare program (SWIM) operated in San Diego, and a voluntary National Supported Work Demonstration

(NSWD)—warranted particular attention.[32] In the best of all possible worlds of workfare evaluation, an optimal program will result in two outcomes: increased earnings by AFDC beneficiaries, and lower program expenditures. Indeed, both the SWIM and NSWD programs evidence higher earnings by AFDC participants coupled with savings in AFDC program costs. Beyond these factors, the ideal workfare program will also return savings greater than the initial costs of its establishment. Here, both SWIM and NSWD become problematic. In SWIM, the first-year start-up costs were $919 per participant, more than the combined increase in earnings by AFDC recipients and program savings. It is not until the second year that increases in AFDC earnings and program savings exceed the initial investment, and then not by much. Thus, the best that SWIM can promise is a greater return on workfare investment some years into the future. In this regard, NSWD is even more problematic. Excluding wage subsidies, the cost per participant was $9,447, an amount that was not recovered until the second year of operation, as was the case with SWIM. Yet once the wage supplement paid to participants—a legitimate program expense—is included, the cost per participant skyrockets to $17,981, an amount that would not be recouped for many years, given current fiscal projections. Other MDRC field demonstrations show similar patterns.

For these reasons, on the eve of several welfare reform proposals put before the 100th Congress, Gueron cautiously summarized MDRC's conclusions on workfare by saying that "the results do not point to a uniform program structure that merits national replication . . . while it is worthwhile to operate these programs, they will not move substantial numbers of people out of poverty."[33] Subsequently, the *Washington Post* editorialized to federal policymakers that, based on an MDRC demonstration in Chicago, the work program "was not successful in speeding people off the [welfare] rolls."[34] Such statements were reinforced by

David Ellwood, professor of public policy at Harvard's John F. Kennedy School of Government, who noted that the enthusiasm with which workfare programs had been received far exceeded their benefits as measured by either increased earned income or program savings. Ellwood concluded that "work-welfare programs alone are not likely to solve the welfare 'problem,' in spite of the grand claims by some proponents."[35] Two years into the JOBS program, the Congressional Budget Office projected that 10,000 families would be off AFDC by 1991, 20,000 by 1993, and 50,000 by the end of the five years of the program—only a 1.3-percent reduction in the total number of AFDC families. "The effect of the JOBS program on the number of AFDC recipients or on spending on benefits in welfare programs is thus expected to be modest," concluded the House Ways and Means Committee.[36] Despite the analysis of one of its more important committees, Congress persevered in including workfare in welfare reform legislation. Although a work requirement may satisfy adherents of the work ethic, the realities of the hard-core unemployed and the secondary labor market make it highly unlikely that a workfare program—even a relatively generously funded one—will reduce either the number of dependents or the costs of welfare programs.

THE UNDERCLASS

A decade of MDRC-sponsored work experiments served to reinforce a suspicion among social policy analysts that, associated with the deterioration of employment opportunities, an underclass was emerging in the United States. That the life circumstances of the minority poor were being severely attenuated was evident as early as the 1970s. Census tract data indicated that ghettoization was increasing significantly, further isolating poor urban minorities from the American mainstream (see Table 16.2). Moreover, while poverty continued to affect poor neighborhoods (census tracts with 20 percent poor), it considerably worsened the conditions of still poorer neighborhoods (census tracts with 40 percent poor).

Compounding the erosion of income and assets, urban minority communities were further disadvantaged by the exodus of middle-income African Americans to the suburbs and by the replacement of better-paying, manufacturing jobs with low-wage service jobs. The interaction of middle-class flight and technological transformation proved devastating for the minorities residing in older industrial cities. For example, the plight of young African Americans is immediately apparent if the unemployment rate is combined with the labor force nonparticipation rate, as shown in Table 16.3. During the 1980s, to be young, African American, and out of school was bad enough; the prospects were even worse for those who lived in the Northeast, particularly as compared with those living in the West. In 1985, 68.0 percent of young blacks living in the Northeast were unemployed, not in school, or not working, compared with 38.9 percent who lived in the West.

Under these circumstances, it is not surprising that the social and economic status of the minority poor plummeted. In 1983 the median worth of nonwhite and Hispanic families was only $6,900, 12.7 percent of that of white families; but by 1989 that had fallen to $4,000, 6.8 percent of white families.[37] By the late 1980s, the poverty rate of African Americans was three times that of whites.[38] But financial data provided only a statistical portrait of a social tragedy that was evolving. In 1990, a criminal justice reform organization, the Sentencing Project, reported that one-fourth of all African Americans between the ages of 20 and 29 were incarcerated, on parole, or on probation. Incredibly, Harvard economist Richard Freeman calculated that 35 percent of all African Americans aged 16 to 35 had been arrested in 1989.[39] Predictably, all this reached the flash point with the 1992 Los Angeles riot.

Of the few proposals advanced to reduce the underclass, most emphasize employment.

TABLE 16.2. Trends in Social Conditions in Large Central Cities, 1970–1980 (In percentages)

Indicator	Census Tracts with 20 Percent Poor			Census Tracts with 40 Percent Poor		
	1970	1980	Change	1970	1980	Change
Employment rate						
Males, age 16+	63.3	56.0	−13	56.5	46.0	−22
AFDC families	19.8	28.0	+40	30.2	42.0	+40
Black persons	27.2	26.5	−3	6.3	8.3	+32
Poor blacks	28.3	30.5	+8	9.4	13.1	+40

SOURCE: Adapted from Sara McLanahan, Irwin Garfinkel, and Dorothy Watson, "Family Structure, Poverty, and the Underclass," in M. McGeary and L. Lynn, eds., *Urban Change and Poverty* (Washington, D.C.: National Academy Press, 1988), p. 130.

New Deal-type job programs were proposed in works that received wide circulation, such as Nicholas Lemann's article "The Origins of the Underclass" in the *Atlantic Monthly*[40] (later expanded in *The Promised Land*)[41] and Mickey Kaus's article "The Work-Ethic State" in *The New Republic*[42] (later rewritten as *The End of Equality*).[43] According to William Julius Wilson, increasing job opportunities for employable members of the underclass would have several related payoffs. For example, much welfare dependency among female heads of households can be attributed to the fact that large numbers of young men in poor neighborhoods are not good candidates for marriage because of their poor education, engagement in illicit activities, and unemployment. According to Wilson, employment programs that would make young men more marriageable would not only reduce the social costs of their current status but also those of the women with children who are dependent on welfare.[44]

It remains to be seen if the Clinton administration will be able to marshal the resources, not to mention the vision, to reverse the dramatically worsening conditions of the urban poor. Experience with employment training programs over the past two decades suggests that the proposition advanced at the beginning of this chapter—that a substantial portion of the welfare problem could be solved if people on welfare found adequate employment—is not likely to be achieved solely through workfare. Although workfare programs may enhance the sense of self-worth of welfare beneficiaries, make for good public relations, and assuage irate taxpayers, these programs—whether coercive or voluntary—have achieved only marginal results in terms of their ability to get welfare beneficiaries into jobs that can make them economically self-sufficient. Given the experience of the MDRC demonstrations, to say nothing of the growing underclass, a more effective strategy would be a national labor policy directed at the secondary labor market. Such a policy

TABLE 16.3. Unemployment Rates and Proportion of Male Central-City Residents Age 16–24 Who Are Not in School and Not in the Labor Force, by Race and Region, 1985

Region and Race	Percentage Not in School and Not in Labor Force	Unemployment Rate
All regions		
White	13.7	6.1
Black	37.1	14.1
Northeast		
White	16.7	9.4
Black	43.5	24.5
West		
White	11.3	5.5
Black	29.6	9.3

SOURCE: Adapted from John Kasarda, "Jobs, Migration, and Emerging Urban Mismatches," in M. McGeary and L. Lynn, eds., *Urban Change and Poverty* (Washington, D.C.: National Academy Press, 1988), p. 187.

would include raising or supplementing the minimum wage or developing a benefit package to complement the minimum wage. In addition, tight labor market policies or the certification of completion of tough government training programs would make the disadvantaged more desirable workers to employers. Without a national labor market strategy that addresses the secondary labor market—and therefore the plight of the unemployed, underemployed, and discouraged workers—workfare is likely to be punitive and the underclass is likely to grow.

DISCUSSION QUESTIONS

1. Progressives have traditionally argued that jobs are preferable to welfare and that the lack of employment opportunity results in increasing needs for social welfare. Is this dynamic relationship evident in your community? What is your evidence?
2. A commonly held belief is that government make-work jobs are inferior to private sector employment, yet many New Deal jobs programs have significantly contributed to the infrastructure of the nation's cities. What New Deal projects are evident in your community? What were the resources used for these projects? If a new governmental jobs program were initiated, what community needs might it address?
3. Both the Job Training and Partnership Act and the Family Support Act have attempted to enhance opportunities for workers in the secondary labor market. What has been the track record of these programs in your community? Has one been more successful than the other? How would you change these programs to more adequately address the needs of the poor in your community?
4. The idea of an American "underclass" has been debated by scholars for more than a decade. To what extent can an underclass be said to exist in your community? What are its demographic characteristics? How might employment policy be changed to better integrate the long-term poor into the labor market?

NOTES

1. Michael Novak, ed., *The New Consensus on Family and Welfare* (Washington, D.C.: American Enterprise Institute, 1987), p. 58.
2. Michael Sherraden. "Chronic Unemployment: A Social Work Perspective," *Social Work,* September-October 1985, p. 403.
3. Ibid., pp. 404–406.
4. As Sherraden notes, the common understanding that an unemployment rate of 7 percent is "normal" is not supported by economists who calculate that structural and frictional unemployment can be reduced to 3 percent through propitious social policies.
5. M. Harvey Brenner, *Estimating the Effects of Economic Change on National Health and Social Well-Being* (Washington, D.C.: U.S. Government Printing Office, 1984), pp. 2–4.
6. Bradford Lee, "The Welfare State Reconsidered," *Wilson Quarterly* 6 (Spring 1982): 69–70.
7. Diana M. DiNitto and Thomas Dye, *Social Welfare: Politics and Public Policy,* 2nd ed. (Englewood Cliffs, N.J.: Prentice-Hall, 1987), p. 200.
8. Committee on Ways and Means, U.S. House of Representatives, *Background Material and Data on Programs within the Jurisdiction of the Committee on Ways and Means* (Washington, D.C.: U.S. Government Printing Office, 1985), p. 279.
9. Committee on Ways and Means, U.S. House of Representatives, *Overview of Entitlement Programs, 1992 Green Book* (Washington, D.C.: U.S. Government Printing Office, 1992), p. 503.
10. Michael Novak, *The New Consensus on Family and Welfare,* p. 32.
11. Amitai Etzioni, "The Fast-Food Factories: McJobs Are Bad for Kids," *Washington Post,* August 24, 1986, p. 6.
12. Sar A. Levitan and Joyce Zickler, *The Quest for a Federal Manpower Partnership* (Cambridge, Mass.: Harvard University Press, 1974), pp. 1–6.

13. Lawrence Mead, *Beyond Entitlement* (New York: Free Press, 1986), p. 27.
14. U.S. Bureau of the Census, *Statistical Abstract of the United States 1982–83* (Washington, D.C.: U.S. Government Printing Office, 1983), p. 391.
15. David Rosenbaum, "Federal Job Program Aids the More Able, According to Critics," *New York Times,* July 22, 1984, p. 9.
16. U.S. House of Representatives, *1992 Green Book,* pp. 1690–92.
17. Peter B. Doeringer and Michael Piore, *Internal Labor Markets and Manpower Analysis* (Armonk, N.Y.: M. E. Sharpe, 1985), p. 163.
18. Michael Piore, "The Dual Labor Market," in David Gordon, ed., *Problems in Political Economy* (Lexington, Mass.: D. C. Heath, 1977), p. 94.
19. Ibid.
20. David Gordon, Richard Edwards, and Michael Reich, *Segmented Work, Divided Workers* (New York: Cambridge University Press, 1982), p. 211.
21. U.S. Bureau of the Census, *Statistical Abstract of the United States 1982–83,* p. 409.
22. Michael Harrington, *Who Are the Poor?* (Washington, D.C.: Justice for All, 1987), p. 10.
23. National Conference on Social Welfare, *To Form a More Perfect Union* (Washington, D.C.: National Conference on Social Welfare, 1985).
24. Michael Piore, "The Dual Labor Market," p. 95.
25. Kathryn Edin and Christopher Jencks, "Reforming Welfare," in Christopher Jencks, *Rethinking Social Policy* (Cambridge, Mass.: Harvard University Press, 1992), chap. 6.
26. Board of Directors, Manpower Research and Development Corporation, *Summary and Findings of the National Supported Work Demonstration* (Cambridge, Mass.: Ballinger Publishing, 1980), pp. 1–2.
27. Ibid.
28. Ken Auletta, *The Underclass* (New York: Random House, 1982), pp. 221, 222.
29. Judith Gueron, "Working for People on Welfare," *Public Welfare* 44, no. 1 (Winter 1986): 7.
30. Ibid., p. 10.
31. Daniel Friedlander, *Subgroup Impacts and Performance Indicators for Selected Welfare Employment Programs* (New York: MDRC, 1988), pp. 7–15.
32. Judith Gueron and Edward Pauly, *From Welfare to Work (Summary)* (New York: Russell Sage Foundation, 1991), pp. 17, 19.
33. Judith Gueron, "Reforming Welfare with Work," *Public Welfare* 45, no. 4 (Fall 1987): 23.
34. "Warning on Welfare Reform," *Washington Post,* January 19, 1988, p. A–14.
35. David Ellwood, *Poor Support: Poverty in the American Family* (New York: Basic Books, 1988), p. 153.
36. U.S. House of Representatives, *1992 Green Book,* p. 618.
37. Ibid., p. 1449.
38. Lawrence Mishel and David Frankel, *The State of Working America* (Armonk, N.Y.: M. E. Sharpe, 1991), p. 171.
39. Jonathan Marshall, "Targeting the Drugs, Wounding the Cities," *Washington Post Weekly,* May 25–31, 1992, p. 23.
40. Nicholas Lemann, "The Origins of the Underclass," *Atlantic Monthly,* June and July 1986.
41. Nicholas Lemann, *The Promised Land* (New York: Knopf, 1991).
42. Mickey Kaus, "The Work-Ethic State," *The New Republic,* July 7, 1986, p. 8.
43. Mickey Kaus, *The End of Equality* (New York: Basic Books, 1992).
44. William Julius Wilson, "American Social Policy and the Ghetto Underclass," *Dissent,* Winter 1988, pp. 84–91.

PART FOUR

The American Welfare State in Perspective

CHAPTER 17

The American Welfare State in International Perspective

James Midgley

As closer links have been forged in communications, travel, trade, and international cooperation, the nations of the world have become much more interdependent. People are better informed of developments in other countries and they now have a better appreciation of the cultures of other societies. Increased world trade has also resulted in greater global economic integration. Today, many Americans wear clothes, drive cars, consume foods, and use electronic appliances that were produced in other countries. This has direct implications for the domestic economy. The export of capital by American businesses, and the loss of jobs resulting from cheaper imports, has become a major political issue.

As the lives of ordinary people are increasingly affected by international events, they need to be prepared to cope with new demands. They need to be more familiar with events in other parts of the world, learn about other cultures and religions, and even acquire skills in different languages. Those who are best equipped to adapt to the realities of increased international collaboration are the most likely to be successful in tomorrow's increasingly interdependent world.

Those working in the social welfare field have also been affected by developments in other societies. International professional associations such as the International Federation of Social Workers and the International Association of Schools of Social Work are encouraging social workers to exchange ideas and experiences.[1] It is very likely that social workers will make greater use of practice innovations from other countries in the future.[2] Internationalists within the social work profession encourage schools of social work to incorporate more international content into their curricula.[3] Developments in social policy are also being informed by events in other parts of the world. Many governments have entered into international agreements on the provision of health, social security, and other services, and attempts to formulate new social policies will rely much more extensively on developments in other countries.

Those undertaking social policy research in the United States can benefit from knowing more about the welfare systems of other countries. A knowledge of social policy in other societies is not only useful in its own right but can promote an understanding of the origins, roles, and functioning of social policy in the United States. By comparing recent events in the

United States with trends in a other countries, better insights may be gained.

THE IMPORTANCE OF COMPARATIVE SOCIAL WELFARE RESEARCH

Research into social policy in the United States has been preoccupied with domestic issues, and comparisons between the United States and other countries are seldom made. However, there are small numbers of American social policy investigators who are interested in other countries and who have made comparative studies of their human services and welfare policies.[4] Unfortunately, their work is often regarded as an exotic intellectual exercise which, although interesting, has little relevance to mainstream social welfare research.

Fortunately, this attitude is changing and many social workers and policymakers now recognize the benefits of international collaboration. Indeed, there are good reasons why American social welfare investigators should relate their own research to international trends. First, it is useful to know how social policy in the United States compares with the policies of other nations. Do other countries spend more on welfare or less? Do their social provisions differ significantly from those in America? What historical factors gave rise to the welfare state in other parts of the world, and how do these factors compare with developments in the United states? Answers to these questions are important and can promote knowledge and understanding.

Second, information about social policy in other nations can help to test theoretical propositions. Often, social scientists reach conclusions about the role and functions of social welfare on the basis of data collected in just one country. While these propositions may indeed explain local events, they can only claim to be truly scientific if they have general validity. This requires that propositions be tested in a wider field and that social welfare in many different societies be analyzed.

Third, comparative research can help to test normative claims about the welfare state.[5] For example, it has often been said that the United States spends too much on social welfare and that high social expenditures are a primary cause of the nation's economic problems. However, comparative research reveals that the United States spends less on social programs than other industrial countries do and that many other industrial countries have a better economic record.[6] By examining claims about welfare policies in the international context, it is possible to muster effective arguments for or against particular normative propositions.

Finally, comparative social policy research can help advance the process of social policy formulation and evaluation. It is useful for social policymakers to be able to apply the experiences of other countries when seeking to introduce new social policies or programs. Programs can be developed and implemented more effectively, and costly mistakes avoided, when policymakers learn from other countries. In addition, it is useful to be able to assess the effectiveness of social policies with reference to performance trends in other nations. If other countries have found that a particular policy approach does not meet its stated objective, this information can help American social administrators in evaluating their own policy outcomes.

Methodological Questions

As the benefits of comparing American social welfare policy with developments in other countries are increasingly recognized, more social policy investigators will relate their findings to events in other nations. However, the task of linking research into social welfare in the United States with research undertaken in other societies is not an easy one. First, it is difficult to obtain accurate data about social needs and social policies in other nations and to use such findings for purposes of comparison. For example, a major study of poverty and income inequality that was undertaken for the World Bank in the 1970s reached many interesting conclusions, but it was based on research data that were of dubious reliability, out of date, and difficult to compare.[7] Fortunately, as information sources in many parts of the world become more reliable, this problem may eventually be overcome.

Another problem is how to define the policies or programs to be compared and how to select countries for comparison. In the United States, the term *Social Security* is used to refer to the federal government's old age, retirement, disability, and survivor's program. In many European countries, however, the term refers to all income maintenance programs, including social assistance and family allowances. Apart from the fact that the United States does not have family allowances, Americans frequently use the term *welfare* to refer negatively to public assistance, whereas in other countries the term is used in a more positive way to describe the sum total of the nation's social policies and programs. In Latin America, social security includes the provision of medical care, and in many developing countries the term is used as a synonym for social welfare as a whole. Clearly, these different uses need to be understood, and their different meanings standardized, before useful comparative research can be undertaken.

It is also difficult to decide which countries should be compared with the United States. Some experts contend that useful comparisons can be made only with countries that have similar social, economic, and political characteristics. There is no point, they claim, in comparing social welfare in the United States with social welfare in an African or Asian country. However, others disagree, arguing that the purpose of the comparison is more important than the countries selected for comparison. For example, if an investigator wants to compare antipoverty programs in the United States with those in an African country, this comparison is legitimate if the comparison is made within the con-

text of particular research objectives. The investigator may also want to make policy recommendations and show that antipoverty programs that have been effective in the African country can be useful in reducing poverty in America.[8]

These and other methodological problems must be taken into account when comparing the social policies of the United States with those of other countries. Thus, while methodological problems pose difficulties, they are not insurmountable and do not prevent international studies from reaching useful conclusions. Used with caution, comparative studies can inform research into American social policy and help investigators to better understand its many features.

COMPARATIVE PERSPECTIVES ON THE AMERICAN WELFARE STATE

The term *welfare state* is now widely used to denote the extensive involvement of government in social welfare. This involvement includes a great variety of social programs, including social assistance, health care, public housing, social security, education, and other human services. Although definitions vary, government's role in these activities and its explicit intention to affect human welfare through diverse programs and policies is regarded as the central characteristic of the welfare state. *A welfare state, therefore, is a country in which the government intervenes extensively to provide social services and promote social well-being.*

The United States is often described as a welfare state. Usually, the core programs of the American welfare state are identified with federal programs such as Social Security, Medicaid and Medicare, AFDC, SSI, Food Stamps, housing assistance, educational grants, Head Start, veteran's benefits, and various job training programs. These programs coexist with state and local programs (which are often subsidized by the federal government) such as public education; social services for children, the mentally ill, the elderly, and other needy groups; General Assistance; Workers' Compensation; and correctional programs.

In addition to these services, a great variety of tax provisions, legislative enactments, and other measures also have an impact on human welfare. These include, for example, federal tax incentives that encourage savings for retirement, legislative prohibitions on discrimination against minorities and the physically disabled, and economic policies that foster investment and the creation of employment. Of course, different experts place more emphasis on some of these programs than on others and, in some cases, only a few of these programs are regarded as forming part of the welfare state. However, most agree that Social Security and major income-tested programs such as AFDC, Food Stamps, and housing assistance form the core components of the American welfare state.

It is these key elements that are most frequently compared with the social provisions of other societies, and, generally, most investigators believe that the American welfare state is not as comprehensive or as extensive as other welfare states. Many have pointed out that whereas Europe and other industrial countries have governmental medical insurance programs that cover the whole population, the United States depends largely on a private system of medical care, with government involvement being limited to assisting the elderly and the poorest groups. Similarly, many experts have pointed out that the United States lacks a comprehensive system of family allowances by which cash benefits are paid to families with children. Like medical care, programs of this kind form a major part of European welfare systems.

In addition to having fewer social programs, comparative studies have concluded that American welfare programs are more fragmented and less coordinated than those in Europe. They also claim that American social welfare is dependent on an incremental style of policymaking that responds haphazardly to political pressures. In Europe, on the other hand, social policy is said to be the result of systematic social planing. European welfare states are also more activist in that they seek to manage the economy more aggressively and to maintain high levels of employment. In the United States, private initiative and a reliance on the private market with minimal government intervention is believed to be the best method of fostering human well-being. In addition, it is claimed that American social policy is more residualist than in Europe. In the United States, the primary function of social policy is to provide a minimal safety net for the poorest sections of the population rather than to cater to the population as a whole. In Europe, by contrast, governments seek to provide a variety of social programs for the whole population and to combine economic and social objectives in an effort to enhance the welfare of all.

These findings have led many social policy analysts to conclude that unlike European nations, America is a reluctant welfare state—a laggard in social policy and human service provision. Harold Wilensky, a leading scholar in the field of comparative social welfare, summed up this idea when he wrote:

> The United States is more reluctant than any rich democratic country to make a welfare effort appropriate to its affluence. Our support for national welfare programs is halting; our administration of services for the less privileged is mean. We move toward the welfare state but we do it with ill-grace, carping and complaining all the way.[9]

Many other social policy experts have reached the same conclusion, some going so far as to claim that the American and European welfare states constitute distinctive types. This has led some analysts to construct abstract models of social welfare that highlight these differences. For example, in 1971 Richard Titmuss constructed a typology of the *residual* versus the *institutional* welfare state, which, he argued, respectively typified the United States and Great Britain. He also added a third category, the *industrial-performance* model, which he argued was typified by the Soviet Union and other Eastern European countries.[10]

American Welfare Exceptionalism

Many social scientists use the term *welfare exceptionalism* to describe America's apparent unwillingness to emphasize social welfare, and they explain this difference[11] by the racial, ethnic, and religious diversity of the United States, which has prevented the emergence of a comprehensive welfare state. Unlike most European nation-states, where people are more homogenous and have a stronger sense of civic responsibility, the conflicting or competing interests of a great number of different groups militates against the emergence of a single, national system of provision that caters to all.

It has also been argued that the high degree of political decentralization in the United States impedes the emergence of strong central institutions. This, combined with the high degree of diversity, effectively prevents the development of a comprehensive and activist welfare state. It has also been noted that the United States does not have a long tradition of bureaucratic government on which centralized state programs can be established. This, some have claimed, is because of the absence of a feudal tradition. Developing this idea, others have pointed to the unique role of the courts in American policymaking, to the separation of the executive and legislative branches, and to the role of powerful political interest groups, all of which impede the emergence of a strong, centralized welfare state.

Some writers have stressed the role of America's uniquely individualistic culture, pointing out that the ideology of individualism is far stronger in the United States than it is in Europe and that it is fundamentally antithetical to state welfare. It has also been argued that trade unions are weaker in the United States than in Europe and that the radical political left, which has played a major role in the emergence of the European welfare state, has not been as strong in the United States.

Although the notion of welfare exceptionalism offers interesting insights into social policy in the United States, it can also be criticized. For example, many early international studies compared the United States with Britain and the Scandinavian countries, which have strong centralized and comprehensive welfare systems. Often, these classifications were marked by strong personal biases. For example, a strong pro-British bias pervades Titmuss's writings. He has been criticized for this and also for presenting his arguments in a way that ensures the moral superiority of the institutional welfare state model.[12] In recent times, as more research has become available, it has become apparent that the different European countries have very divergent welfare systems and that not all welfare states are highly centralized, comprehensive, or highly activist. Studies of welfare policies in other parts of the world have shown the American welfare state in more favorable terms. For example, unlike the United States, Australia does not have a universal social security system and it relies extensively on means-tested programs.[13]

The idea that the United States is a welfare laggard is based largely on a comparison of particular social programs such as government health insurance and family allowances. The absence of these programs is usually emphasized by those claiming that the United States does not have a comprehensive welfare system. While it is true that government health care and family programs are poorly developed in the United States, the role of indirect support for families through tax relief and tax deductions for medical expenses is often ignored, as is the significance of Medicare, Medicaid, and state and local health care programs.

In addition, the United States has excelled in other social fields. During the nineteenth century, it led the world in the development of public education and it still compares favorably with many other countries in terms of access to education, particularly at the tertiary level. Similarly, the United States is a pioneer in environmental protection and although this is not always regarded as an integral part of social policy, the impact of the environment on human well-being should not be underestimated.[14] Comparative studies have also shown that when particular social programs, such as pensions, are compared, the United States fares quite well.[15] In addition, recent historical research reveals that the United States was ahead of other Western countries in the late nineteenth century in developing income maintenance programs for veterans and for women with children. At the turn of the century, no other industrializing country had introduced mothers' pensions, and none came as close to creating a "maternal" rather than a "paternal" welfare state as did the United States.[16]

While these arguments are valid, it is difficult to reach the conclusion that the United States is one of the world's welfare leaders. Despite its extensive educational and social security provisions, the country does not compare favorably with the other industrial democracies in the extent, comprehensiveness, or coverage of its welfare system. In fact, its position even deteriorated in recent years with the retrenchment of social programs under the Reagan and Bush administrations. Public expenditure data from the Organization for Economic Cooperation and Development (OECD), which is made up of the major industrial nations, show that social expenditures in the United States amounted to 20.8 percent of GDP in 1980 and were considerably lower than the OECD average of 25.6 percent. In 1985, social expenditures decreased to 18.2 percent, placing the United States seventeenth in a ranking of 21 OECD states.[17]

Welfare States and Welfare Societies

Although many social policy investigators have bemoaned the country's comparatively low level of welfare provision, others are not disturbed by

these findings. They claim that unfavorable comparisons of government social expenditures between the United States and other countries are based on the idea that state involvement in social welfare is a good thing. These welfare pluralists, as they are known, argue that people's welfare needs can be met in many different ways. Instead of relying only on the state for social welfare, people can enhance their well-being through their own efforts or through the help of neighbors or family members, by purchasing services on the market, or by obtaining help from voluntary organizations when they are in need.[18] They point out that in the United States people make effective use of nongovernmental agencies and that a proper comparison of welfare between countries should not just cover public provision. They also point out that while the United States may lag behind in welfare provision, people enjoy exceptionally high standards of living and unequaled opportunities. That is why the country remains a magnet for immigrants from all over the world who do not want to receive government handouts but to share in the American dream.

Apart from its bias toward government provision, the welfare state concept is difficult to define and also misleading. Arguing that it should be abandoned, critics point out that international studies should compare all the welfare institutions that operate in society. In other words, they should focus not on the welfare state but on the welfare society.

Although this idea has not been accepted by all social policy investigators, it suggests that comparative research that focuses exclusively on government social provision can be misleading. It also casts doubts on the usefulness of the concept of the welfare state. The notion of the institutional welfare state is an abstract construct that has not been properly defined for purposes of comparative research. It is also a normative ideal type that has no counterpart in the real world. Critics contend that instead of trying to relate different countries to an abstract ideal type, it would be better to study what actually exists. This can be facilitated by categorizing different countries in terms of their dominant approach to social policy, the importance they place on state provision, and the way social policies address human problems.

Several attempts have been made to develop typologies based on these criteria, but because they have continued to emphasize the role of government in the provision of welfare, they remain typologies of welfare states. However, the early residual versus institutional welfare state typology has been transcended by new models that recognize the diversity of welfare policies and programs in the modern world.[19]

Norman Furniss and Timothy Tilton were among the first to attempt a broader classification of welfare states by identifying a threefold typology encompassing what they called the "positive state," the "social security state," and the "social welfare state." The United States exemplified the former, Britain the second, and Sweden the third.[20] While Ramesh Mishra retained the essential elements of the residual-institutional model, he stressed the efforts of some countries to forge strong corporatist alliances among government, labor, and business in order to reach a consensus on social welfare issues, and this led him to identify a new type called the "integrated," or social corporatist, welfare state. Locating Britain and the United States within the noncorporatist (or differentiated) welfare state category, he identified Sweden, Austria, and Australia with the corporatist, or integrated, model.[21] Esping-Andersen's typology also recognized the corporatist type, but it classified countries differently. In addition to the corporatist category (Italy, Japan, France, and Switzerland), Esping-Andersen identified two other types—the liberal welfare state (Australia, Britain, and the United States) and the social democratic welfare state (Austria, the Netherlands, and the Scandinavian countries).[22] More recently, Norman Ginsburg has constructed a fourfold typology made up of the social democratic welfare state (Sweden), the social market welfare state (Germany), the corporate market welfare state (United States), and the liberal collectivist welfare state (Britain).[23]

As may be seen, the United States is included in each of these typologies. Although the typologies differ from each other, many use similar criteria when categorizing the United States. These typologies need to be developed further, and a wider conception of social welfare that transcends governmental provision also ought to be formulated. In this way, more useful comparisons between social welfare in the United States and other countries can be made.

DYNAMICS OF THE AMERICAN WELFARE STATE

Most books about social policy in the United States are descriptive, seeking to depict current social policies and programs in factual terms. Few use theoretical concepts to explain the underlying dynamics that account for the changes and shifts in emphasis which have taken place over the past 100 years. The steady growth of government involvement in welfare has not happened automatically but is the result of complex forces that need to be analyzed. Similarly, recent events, which many have viewed as a major assault on the American welfare state, require interpretation.

The dynamics of social welfare require theoretical analysis rather than description. Although theoretical research into social policy is still underdeveloped, it has generated important propositions and provided useful insights. The findings of these studies need to be examined with reference to developments in other countries. Through comparative analysis, it may be possible to uncover the basic processes that account for the origins and functions of social policy in modern societies.

The Origins and Functions of Social Policy

Many descriptive-historical accounts of the emergence of social welfare in the United States have been published. In an attempt to make the material more manageable, these studies usually identify different chronological periods in the development of social welfare. For example, they often distinguish the colonial phase, the time of the Civil War, the period of rapid industrialization, the Progressive era, the New Deal, and the later expansion of the welfare state. Usually, the periods are linked together to form a longer evolutionary model showing that government becomes increasingly responsible for social welfare and that this results in the creation of the welfare state. Although many welfare historians regard the process as a slow evolutionary one in which more and more governmental programs are added, others view the welfare state as having come into existence suddenly as the result of major social upheavals.[24] However, although they may disagree about the timing of the inception of the welfare state, most scholars believe that the modern welfare state represents the culmination of an inevitable and desirable process of social welfare evolution.

There can be no doubt that the development of social welfare in the United States has involved a massive increase in government intervention. Over the past 100 years, many more federal and state programs have been added, and expenditures on social services have increased significantly. Charles Prigmore and Charles Atherton have shown that public expenditures on human services amounted to about 3 percent of GNP at the turn of the century; by 1980, they had reached 17 percent.[25]

While many accounts of the origins of the American welfare state have described its stages, others have provided generalized explanations that emphasize the role of wider social, economic, and other forces in the dynamics of welfare. These accounts are important because they allow social scientists to grasp the fundamental causal processes that account for the emergence of the welfare state and permit a comprehension of the functions of social welfare. If social scientists can discover the underlying forces that create welfare states, they can also obtain insights into the role that social welfare plays in modern society.

One popular explanation of the origins and functions of the American welfare state can be called the *humanitarian impulse hypothesis.* This explanation contends that the modern welfare state is the result of the inborn altruistic concern that human beings have for others. Proponents of this hypothesis believe that human beings are a social species, and that they have an instinctive need to help each other.

Many social welfare textbooks describe the humanitarian activities of the ancient Jews and Greeks, early Christians, medieval communities, and others in some detail in an attempt to show that caring has been an integral part of human society since early times.[26] Some scholars also use contemporary anthropological evidence to show that traditional communities in the Third World are highly integrated and interdependent and that they have strong reciprocal helping traditions.[27] This emphasis on communitarianism fits with the humanitarian impulse hypothesis and suggests that modern societies can solve their problems if they re-create close, integrated communities in which people know each other and provide mutual aid and support.

Proponents of the social impulse hypothesis argue that the process of industrialization undermines natural humanitarian instincts. Urbanization, individualism, and competitiveness all weaken people's natural desire to help others. However, because social needs must be met, the government is compelled to intervene. In industrial society, therefore, the state represents the collective humanitarian instincts of its citizens. As Prigmore and Atherton argue, the growth of the modern welfare state is a return to the institutional arrangements that characterized preindustrial societies.[28]

A second explanation, the *industrialization-welfare hypothesis*, also stresses the role of industrialization in the development of the welfare state, but in this explanation humanitarian motives are not believed to be very important. Instead, this approach argues that industrialization undermines preindustrial welfare institutions and places political pressure on government to intervene. The traditional welfare functions of families and communities are replaced by government welfare programs not because government has strong humanitarian motives or represents the collective social impulse, but rather because government has no option. With the disintegration of traditional welfare institutions, poverty, deprivation, and social needs increase and, as a result, government intervenes to establish a variety of social programs designed to substitute for the traditional welfare system.[29]

A third approach can be called the *maintenance of capitalism hypothesis*. This approach also contends that industrialization is relevant to the creation of modern welfare states, but it emphasizes the role of capitalist industrialization in the genesis of the welfare state. It contends that the welfare state emerges and functions to promote the interests of capitalism. A popular exposition of this point of view is provided by Frances Fox Piven and Richard Cloward, whose historical study of public welfare programs in the United States concluded that the government creates social programs to control the labor force.[30] During times of economic depression and civic unrest, the government makes its social programs generous in order to minimize unrest and to placate the working class. During times of economic growth, on the other hand, it uses welfare punitively to compel workers to seek jobs and to work hard. Those who cannot or do not work, and seek welfare instead, are given little help and subjected to harsh treatment in order to deter them from using the welfare system. In this way the welfare system also serves to discourage those in employment from becoming dependent on the state.

A variation of Piven and Cloward's theory is provided by Mimi Abramovitz, who argues that welfare programs are used by government to control women. Examining the history of social policy in the United States, she argues that social programs have been designed to reward women who fulfill roles defined by men, such as childbearing and homemaking. Similarly, these programs seek to punish those who do not to conform to patriarchal values.[31]

A more complicated explanation of the relationship between government welfare and industrial capitalism is provided by James O'Connor, who argues that Western governments create welfare programs to ensure that capital accumulation takes place and that people accept the capitalist system.[32] These "accumulation" and "legitimation" functions, as he calls them, are essential if capitalism is to survive. To help capitalist accumulation, government introduces social programs that create an efficient labor force and reduce the costs of labor. Public education, health care, and similar programs all help to make workers more efficient and productive. Similarly, since governments rather than capitalist businesses are responsible for meeting social needs, they reduce the costs of labor and make businesses more profitable. Governments also try to legitimate the capitalist system by creating social programs that do not necessarily promote capitalism but do enhance social contentment. These "social expenses" include social security for the retired, services for the disabled, welfare payments, and other provisions, all of which foster contentment and prevent civic unrest.

O'Connor also argues that the accumulation and legitimation functions of welfare capitalism are contradictory and that, sooner or later, the state's ability to provide services that maintain the system will be exhausted. A crisis will then emerge. As will be shown, these ideas have direct implications for studies of the problems that have faced the welfare state in recent years.

The International Evidence

Although several other accounts of the origins and functions of welfare have been formulated, the three theories just discussed are the best developed explanations of the dynamics of welfare in the United States. All have supporters and all have a degree of plausibility. These theories have been subjected to critical analysis by American scholars and some of their weaknesses have been exposed. They have also been tested internationally to determine whether they apply to other Western countries and whether they offer generally valid interpretations of the dynamics of welfare.

The international evidence does not provide a great deal of support for any of these theories. First, despite the claims of the humanitarian impulse theorists, there is not much evidence to show that governments around the world function to give expression to the humanitarian instincts of their citizens. Indeed, many governments are brutal, oppressive, and quite uninterested in welfare. This is true not only of countries that are at an early stage of industrialization, when, it is claimed, humanitarian tendencies are weak, but of nations that have achieved a high degree of industrialization. The idea that the Soviet Union and other Eastern European countries created extensive social programs because of their humanitarianism is countered even by studies that are sympathetic to the social policies in these countries.[33] While there are, of course, examples of governments that have enacted social legislation and introduced social programs that bring real benefits to citizens, it is unrealistic to characterize all governments as representing the collective humanitarian impulse of society.

The idea that industrialization has an internal logic that creates social welfare programs has been verified by extensive statistical studies. Comparing 64 countries, Wilensky claimed that industrialization is the primary causative factor in the genesis of welfare and that other factors are of little relevance.[34] However, when this hypothesis is examined with reference to historical trends in other countries, problems emerge. For example, state welfare programs were introduced in Europe long after industrialization was well advanced. In addition, despite its high level of industrialization, the United States has been a welfare laggard and created

less extensive welfare programs than have other countries with a similar level of industrial development. If industrialization gives rise to state welfare, why did similar welfare programs not emerge in all societies with a similar degree of industrialization? Ann Orloff and Theda Skocpol have examined this question by comparing welfare and industrialization in Massachusetts and England. Although these regions had similar levels of industrialization at the turn of the century, state welfare programs emerged in Britain but not in Massachusetts.[35] Another study by James Midgley compared industrialization and welfare in Korea, Hong Kong, Singapore, and Taiwan (the "four little tigers," or newly industrializing countries of East Asia). The point of this study was to test the relationship between industrialization and welfare provision. Midgley concluded that there was no clear pattern in the way government welfare programs emerged in these countries and little evidence that they were directly linked to industrial development.[36]

The capitalist maintenance hypothesis also encounters difficulties when examined in the international context. Some scholars claim that international evidence supports this theory, but others disagree. Many have pointed out that the first social insurance programs were introduced in Germany by Chancellor Otto von Bismarck, specifically to undermine the labor movement and to placate workers. However, they fail to mention that this was achieved after a fierce struggle against the opposition of German aristocrats and business elites who did not share Bismarck's political foresight and skill.[37] In other countries, capitalist interests have frequently opposed the introduction of the welfare state, and this hardly lends support to the idea that welfare programs are introduced at the behest of capitalists to serve their interests. As the Reagan and Thatcher administrations proved, capitalist interest groups will try to abolish government welfare provision if they have the political prospect of doing so.[38]

There is also a good deal of international

evidence to show that welfare programs are not introduced by capitalists but are the result of the political struggles of working-class people and their political representatives. In Britain and Sweden, working-class movements, unions, and left-wing intellectuals were able to forge coalitions with political elites and bureaucrats that resulted in the introduction of extensive social programs.[39] This research suggests not only that business interests were generally hostile to the expansion of government provision but that they played a limited role in the creation of the modern welfare state. Far from acting as the promoter of capitalist interests, the state functioned autonomously, introducing welfare programs either at its own volition or under pressure from working-class organizations.

The international evidence suggests that current theories of the origins and functions of the American welfare state are still of limited explanatory usefulness. Many rely on a single-cause interpretation and oversimplify what are very complex historical and political processes. Future research is more likely to offer cautious explanations in which a variety of causal factors are identified. It is also likely that more emphasis will be placed on the actual political process, on the ways different interest groups bring pressure to bear on governments, and on the role of beliefs and ideologies in social welfare. Current explanations are excessively deterministic and suffer from reifying commonplace processes. While it is true that wider social forces located within the structure of society do impinge on social welfare, they need to be translated into actual processes and behaviors that affect political action and the dynamics of welfare in different societies.

THE CRISIS OF THE WELFARE STATE

The idea that government should intervene to enhance the welfare of the population was widely accepted in the years after World War

II. Political leaders, intellectuals, and ordinary citizens alike regarded the welfare state as a positive development. While government welfare had some detractors, they were in a small minority and the "liberal welfare consensus," as it became known, dominated American life for many years. In addition, many people accepted the idea that government should assume even larger responsibilities for welfare. When the Johnson administration's War on Poverty programs were created, they were generally well received.

By the 1970s, however, it became apparent that the welfare consensus was under strain. During the late 1960s, the negative rather than the positive aspects of welfare state programs were emphasized by critics from both the political left and right. Government programs were frequently attacked for being punitive, meager, and supportive of the status quo. Piven and Cloward's study of public welfare led many scholars to believe that the welfare state was really a mechanism of capitalist manipulation and oppression. O'Connor's analysis of the functions of the welfare state also attracted widespread attention. O'Connor believed that the welfare state could not indefinitely fulfill its twin functions of accumulation and legitimation. Not only was capitalism inherently unstable, experiencing frequent periods of recession and crisis, but the attempt to use welfare as a means of holding the system together was unworkable. As people demanded more and more social programs, the accumulation function would be impeded, and the state would be unable to provide generous legitimation through social benefits. This contradiction in the system would eventually lead to a major fiscal crisis of the state and cause the system to break down.

Thinkers on the political right also attacked the welfare state. Milton Friedman, a long-standing opponent of the welfare state, became a media figure well known for his frequent assaults on government intervention and, during the 1970s, the idea that the welfare state was damaging the economy gained currency. This idea was articulated by the Harvard economist Martin Feldstein, whose statistical studies concluded that Social Security was having a negative impact on savings and economic investment.[40] In addition, many argued that as social expenditures continued to rise, the tax burden would reach unacceptable levels. Apart from the negative economic effects of high taxation, it was argued that the continued expansion of government would eventually transform America into a socialist state.

The idea that the continued growth of the welfare state would increase the power of government and foster its unwelcome intrusion into the lives of ordinary people comported with a long-standing aversion to state centralism in American culture. It was fueled by Friedman's claim that the growth of the welfare state posed a greater threat to America's security than the Soviet Union. In an interview with *Newsweek* in 1983, he argued that America's huge tax burden, caused by the welfare state, was reducing the country's diplomatic and military effectiveness and would relegate it to a position of little importance in the modern world.[41]

These ideas echoed Friedman's earlier claim that the welfare state was creating a huge central bureaucracy, which would use its growing arbitrary powers to curtail individual liberty. A similar argument was made by members of the Public Choice School, who claimed that the welfare state did not function primarily to serve the needs of ordinary citizens but rather to perpetuate the interests of civil servants and politicians. Others argued that the welfare state was effectively impeding government's ability to act in ways that promoted the public interest. Highly organized groups of beneficiaries had managed to obstruct government's efforts to deal with urgent problems and had perpetuated the status quo at the expense of others. The welfare state had not only created an economic crisis; it had become ungovernable.[42] Critics also claimed that the welfare state was having a negative effect on the attitudes and work habits of ordinary people. The increase in the numbers

of people receiving AFDC during the 1960s and 1970s was linked to the country's declining economic performance, falling productivity, and labor unrest. Many citizens came to believe that government programs were undermining beliefs about hard work and ambition and that they were sapping the country's vitality. Hardworking taxpayers would have to support a growing mass of lazy, irresponsible individuals living comfortably on welfare. Unless curtailed, welfare would eventually turn the American dream into a nightmare.

These events were accompanied by severe economic difficulties during the 1970s. Attempts by governments to use Keynesian demand management techniques seemed to be unsuccessful. Although Maynard Keynes's ideas appeared to work during the 1930s, they did not have the required effect during the 1970s, when inflation emerged as a major problem. Government spending designed to surmount recessionary trends not only failed to stimulate higher economic growth but appeared to fuel inflation. This resulted in *stagflation*, a new economic problem that government policy seemed powerless to counteract. In addition, in 1974 and again in 1979, the world economy experienced major oil shocks that dramatically increased energy costs and had harmful economic effects.

Although the welfare state could not be held responsible for the energy crisis, many attributed economic difficulties, the growth of bureaucracy, social discontent, and other problems to government social programs. The welfare state was widely believed to be in crisis, and instead of looking to government for solutions, many believed that government was the cause of the underlying economic and social problems. The Watergate scandal, America's weakened international influence, and the low popularity of Presidents Ford and Carter further undermined confidence in government. The stage was set for a new dispensation in which a strong leader would emerge to bring new ideas and policies to solve the nation's problems.

Ronald Reagan fulfilled this role. During his

administration, social programs were singled out and severely retrenched. By the end of his first term, unemployment insurance had been reduced by 17 percent, child nutritional programs by 28 percent, Food Stamp expenditures by 14 percent, AFDC by 14 percent, and the Community Service Block Grant program by 37 percent.[43] Tax concessions to the wealthy and the rapid increases in the federal deficit also weakened the welfare state. David Stockman, the president's budget director, approved of the deficit, claiming that it would put an effective brake on future government social spending.

However, apart from cutting back on means-tested programs, the Reagan administration was not able to destroy the welfare state. In particular, it was not able to abolish the major universal entitlement programs that are the cornerstones of the welfare state. Although the Reagan administration launched a concerted attack on Social Security, it became apparent that this move was highly unpopular with the electorate. Overnight the president reversed his position and declared his staunch support for the program. During the 1984 presidential campaign, when Walter Mondale accused the Reagan administration of trying to abolish Social Security, the president again reiterated his commitment to the program.

The Reagan attack on the welfare state was also impeded by the rapid rise of unemployment in the early 1980s. After Friedman's monetarist prescriptions had been adopted in an attempt to reduce inflation, high interest rates caused a dramatic slump in economic production. In 1982 alone, the economic growth rate fell by 3.2 percent, causing unemployment to rise by 4.5 million.[44] The perpetuation of high unemployment rates was politically risky, and, accordingly, monetarist controls were relaxed. In addition, to provide support for the unemployed, expenditures on unemployment compensation increased. The return of a Democratic majority in Congress contributed further to the slowdown in the implementation of the administration's antiwelfare agenda.

Although the welfare state survived the Reagan era, it did not do so unscathed. Indeed, as a result of budget cuts, many government programs have been weakened, staff morale has fallen, and the effectiveness of services has been impeded. The budget deficit has reached unprecedented proportions with serious long-term economic and social implications. In addition, the incidence of poverty, homelessness, crime, infant malnutrition, drug use, inner-city violence, and other social problems has increased significantly. Accordingly, many believe that the crisis of the American welfare state has not been resolved.

The Welfare Crisis in International Context

During the 1980s, some social scientists compared the crisis of the American welfare state with developments in other countries and concluded that other welfare states were experiencing similar problems. This was particularly true of Britain, a country that had frequently been compared with the United States by American social policy investigators. Britain had also experienced economic problems and widespread social discontent during the 1970s, and although the trade unions were more frequently singled out as a cause of these difficulties than in the United States, stagflation, popular discontent, and rising social expenditures were also attributed to government social programs. As in the United States, the ideas of Milton Friedman and other radical right-wing thinkers were widely accepted. In other intellectual circles, the work of O'Connor as well as of British Marxists such as Ian Gough were believed to offer useful explanations of the crisis.[45] Paradoxically, few realized at the time that the writings of O'Connor and Friedman shared many similarities. Both attributed economic problems to the welfare state, and, in their different ways, both regarded social programs as inimical to sustained economic growth.

While comparisons between Britain and the

United States suggested that welfare capitalism was everywhere in crisis, more careful comparisons of other countries reached different conclusions. Mishra found, for example, that countries such as Austria and Sweden, which had created social-corporatist welfare states (in which government, business, and labor work together to resolve conflicts and forge a policy consensus), coped reasonably well with economic adversity.[46] Although they too faced economic difficulties, resistance to high taxes, and other problems, they kept unemployment low, maintained reasonably good rates of economic growth, and did not experience the high levels of poverty, homelessness, and other social problems that continue to plague Britain and the United States.

Comparative research has also demonstrated that many of the explanations of the welfare crisis, as well as arguments made against the welfare state by American critics, do not hold up when examined with reference to other societies. For example, the argument that high social expenditures are responsible for the economic problems facing the United States cannot be sustained when it is realized that the United States spends less on social welfare than most other industrial countries. Many countries that have higher rates of economic growth than the United States has also spend more on welfare. Marmor, Mashaw, and Harvey showed, for example, that Canada, France, Ireland, and Norway all had higher social expenditures *and* higher rates of economic growth than the United States during the 1970s. Social expenditure in Japan, which had the highest rate of economic growth of all the industrial countries, was only slightly lower than in the United States.[47]

Similarly, the idea that the welfare state diminishes individual freedom is hard to support when other countries are studied. Despite its comprehensive welfare state, Sweden is a highly democratic society with strong traditions of local government. As Charles Andrian points out: "Local government in Sweden remains powerful. County and city governments retain fiscal independence [and] locally raised taxes finance health and educational programs."[48]

The finding that other countries have reasonably successful welfare states has important implications for the American welfare state. If other industrial countries can manage to provide adequate social services to their people without severely retarding economic development, if they can contain the incidence of poverty, homelessness, and crime, and if they can improve the quality of life for the population as a whole, surely the United States, which has abundant human and natural resources, can do the same.

Although countries do not always learn from each other, a better knowledge of social policy in countries that are successful welfare states can help to solve domestic problems. By being more aware of developments in other parts of the world, U.S. policymakers may find more effective solutions to domestic problems. Of course, this is not just a matter of transferring expertise. The introduction of social policies that will make a significant difference in the current crisis in welfare depends on a host of factors, including effective political leadership, popular support for government initiatives, and the ability of the nation's leaders to cooperate more closely and to take a wider, more inclusive view of the general welfare. This, in turn, requires a widening of the social and political ethos and a greater commitment to the common good.

DISCUSSION QUESTIONS

1. Is comparative research important for social work and social policy? If so, why?
2. Examine the international evidence concerning the "crisis of the welfare state" and say whether you think this evidence supports or refutes the idea of an international welfare crisis.

3. Describe one or more typologies of the welfare state. How useful are typologies for comparative social policy research?
4. Discuss the major methodological problems facing social policy investigators who wish to undertake comparative research.
5. Arguments for or against the American welfare state can be examined with reference to other countries. Give some examples of common criticisms of the American welfare state that can be refuted when reviewed in an international context.

6. What do you understand by the term *American welfare exceptionalism?* Do you think this term accurately describes social welfare in the United States relative to other countries?
7. Discuss theories of the origins and functions of the welfare state with which you are familiar. Which of these theories do you think most accurately describes the emergence of social welfare in the United States?

NOTES

1. A recent book by Hokenstad, Khinduka, and Midgley contains accounts of social work from many different countries showing that social work is now well established as a profession in different parts of the world. The book urges social workers to share their ideas and practice experiences and to enhance the international exchange of information. See M. C. Hokenstad, Shanti K. Khinduka, and James Midgley, *Profiles in International Social Work* (Washington, D.C.: National Association of Social Workers, 1992).
2. James Midgley, "International Social Work: Learning from the Third World," *Social Work* 35 (1990): 295–301, has argued that social workers in the industrial countries have much to learn from their colleagues in the Third World.
3. The International Committee of the Council on Social Work Education has actively promoted the inclusion of international content in the curricula of schools of social work. For a discussion of how this may be achieved, see Lynne M. Healy, *Introducing International Development Content in the Social Work Curriculum* (Washington, D.C.: National Association of Social Workers, ca. 1991).
4. The terms *international* and *comparative* will be used interchangeably in this chapter.
5. The term *normative* refers to statements that relate to values and beliefs about social policy and that assess policies as being either being "good" or "bad" for society.
6. Organization for Economic Cooperation and Development (OECD), *Social Expenditures, 1960–1990* (Paris, OECD, 1985).

7. Hollis Chenery, Montek Ahluwahlia, C. L. G. Bell, John H. Duloy, and Richard Jolly, *Redistribution with Growth* (Oxford: Oxford University Press, 1974).
8. James Midgley and Peter Simbi, in "Promoting a Developmental Focus in the Community Organization Curriculum: Relevance of the African Experience," *Journal of Social Work Education* (forthcoming 1993), argue that African community development can inform social workers trying to organize community-based antipoverty programs in the United States.
9. Harold L. Wilensky, "Introduction," in Harold L. Wilensky and Charles M. Lebeaux, *Industrial Society and Social Welfare* (New York: Free Press, 1965), pp. xvi–xvii. See also Harold L. Wilensky, *The Welfare State and Equality* (Berkeley: University of California Press, 1975); Theodor R. Marmor, Jerry L. Mashaw, and Philip L. Harvey, *America's Misunderstood Welfare State* (New York: Basic Books, 1990); Bruce Janssen, *The Reluctant Welfare State: A History of American Social Welfare Policies* (Pacific Grove, Calif.: Brookes/Cole Publishing Co., 1993); Theda Skocpol, "America's Incomplete Welfare State: The Limits of New Deal Reforms and Origins of the Present Crisis," in Martin Rein, Gosta Esping-Andersen, and Lee Rainwater, eds., *Stagnation and Renewal in Social Policy* (Armonk, N.Y.: M. E. Sharpe, 1987), pp. 35–58.
10. Richard M. Titmuss, *Social Policy: An Introduction* (London: Allen and Unwin, 1971).
11. Edwin Amenta and Theda Skocpol, "Taking Exception: Explaining the Distinctiveness of Ameri-

can Public Policies During the Last Century," in Francis C. Castles, ed., *The Comparative History of Public Policy* (New York: Oxford University Press, 1989), pp. 292–333; Arnold J. Heidenheimer, Hugh Heclo, and Carolyn Teich Adams, *Comparative Public Policy* (New York: St. Martin's Press, 1975), pp. 258–59; Janssen, *The Reluctant Welfare State*, pp. 316–39.

12. By Robert Pinker, *The Idea of Welfare* (London: Heinemann, 1979).

13. M. A. Jones, *The Australian Welfare State: Growth Crisis and Change* (Sydney: Allen and Unwin, 1980).

14. Wilensky's comparative analysis of 64 countries rates the United States high in education and environmental protection but suggests that this may be at the expense of traditional social programs. See Wilensky, *The Welfare State and Equality;* also Heidenheimer, Heclo, and Adams, *Comparative Public Policy*, p. 258.

15. In 1975, Wilensky, *The Welfare State and Equality*, p. 105, noted that the United States "allocates a larger fraction of its total welfare spending to pensions than any of the twenty-two richest nations [in the world]." However, more recent expenditure data from the OECD show that while pension expenditures remain comparatively high, the United States is by no means a world leader.

16. Theda Skocpol, *Protecting Soldiers and Mothers: The Political Origins of Social Policy in the United States* (Cambridge, Mass.: Harvard University Press, 1992).

17. OECD, *Social Expenditures, 1960–1990.*

18. See Martin Rein and Lee Rainwater, eds., *Public/Private Interplay in Social Protection* (Armonk, N.Y.: M. E. Sharpe, 1986). See also Sheila Kamerman, "The Mixed Economy of Welfare," *Social Work* 29 (1983): 5–11; and David Stoesz, "A Theory of Social Welfare," *Social Work* 34 (1989): 101–107.

19. These typologies break the dichotomous division of welfare states into just two categories and are based on the idea that welfare states are variants of a larger category known as welfare capitalism. They also differ from the developing countries of the Third World and other noncapitalist societies. Comprehensive typologies that include the developing countries and others outside the category of welfare capitalism still need to be con-

structed. Attempts to do so are still preliminary. See James Midgley, "Models of Welfare and Social Planning in Third World Countries," in Brij Mohan, ed., *New Horizons in Social Welfare and Policy* (Cambridge, Mass.: Schenkman, 1985), pp. 89–108; and Stewart MacPherson and James Midgley, *Comparative Social Policy and the Third World* (New York: St. Martin's Press, 1987).

20. See Norman Furniss and Timothy Tilton, *The Case for the Welfare State* (Bloomington: Indiana University Press, 1977).

21. Ramesh Mishra, *The Welfare State in Crisis* (Brighton, England: Wheatsheaf Books, 1984).

22. Gosta Esping-Andersen, *Three Worlds of Welfare Capitalism* (Cambridge: Polity Press, 1990).

23. Norman Ginsburg, *Divisions of Welfare: A Critical Introduction to Comparative Social Policy* (London: Sage, 1992).

24. An example of the former approach is Hugh Heclo, *Modern Social Policies in Britain and Sweden* (New Haven, Conn.: Yale University Press, 1974). An example of the latter approach is Christopher Leman, "Patterns of Policy Development: Social Security in the United States and Canada," *Public Policy* 25, (1987): 261–91. See also Theda Skocpol, "America's Incomplete Welfare State: The Limits of New Deal Reforms and Origins of the Present Crisis," in Rein, Esping-Andersen, and Rainwater, eds., *Stagnation and Renewal in Social Policy*, pp. 35–58.

25. Charles S. Prigmore and Charles R. Atherton, *Social Welfare Policy: Analysis and Formulation* (Lexington, Mass.: D. C. Heath, 1979).

26. Ibid; also Robert Morris, *Rethinking Social Welfare: Why Care for the Stranger* (New York: Longman, 1986); and Frank R. Breul and Steven J. Diner, eds., *Compassion and Responsibility: Readings in the History of Social Welfare Policy in the United States* (Chicago: University of Chicago Press, 1980).

27. Prigmore and Atherton, *Social Welfare Policy*, p. 18.

28. Ibid., p. 11.

29. See Wilensky and Lebeaux, *Industrial Society and Social Welfare*; Wilensky, *The Welfare State and Equality*; and Gaston V. Rimlinger, *Welfare Policy and Industrialization in Europe, America and Russia* (New York: Wiley, 1971).

30. Frances Fox Piven and Richard Cloward, *Regulating the Poor* (New York: Pantheon, 1971).

31. Mimi Abramovitz, *Regulating the Lives of Women* (Boston: South End Press, 1989).

32. James O'Connor, *The Fiscal Crisis of the State* (New York: St. Martin's Press, 1973).

33. See Victor George and Nick Manning, *Socialism, Social Welfare and the Soviet Union* (London: Routledge and Kegan Paul, 1980); Bob Deacon, *Social Policy and Socialism: The Struggle for Socialist Relations of Welfare* (London: Pluto Press, 1983); and Bob Deacon, ed., *The New Eastern Europe: Social Policy Past, Present and Future* (London: Sage, 1992).

34. Wilensky, *The Welfare State and Equality*.

35. Ann Shula Orloff and Theda Skocpol, "Why Not Equal Protection: Explaining the Politics of Public Social Spending in Britain, 1900–1911, and the United States, 1880s–1920," *American Sociological Review* 49 (1988): 732–44.

36. James Midgley, "Industrialization and Welfare: The Case of the Four Little Tigers," *Social Policy and Administration* 20 (1988): 225–38. A different perspective of the role of industrialization in the development of social programs in developing countries is provided by Christine Cockburn, "The Role of Social Security in Development," *International Social Security Review* 33 (1986): 337–58.

37. Rimlinger, *Welfare Policy and Industrialization in Europe, America and Russia*.

38. Howard Glennerster and James Midgley, eds., *The Radical Right and the Welfare State: An International Assessment* (Savage, Md.: Barnes and Noble, 1991).

39. Walter Korpi, *The Democratic Class Struggle* (London: Routledge, 1983); John Stephens, *The Transition from Capitalism to Socialism* (London: Macmillan, 1979).

40. Martin Feldstein, "Social Security, Induced Retirement and Aggregate Accumulation," *Journal of Political Economy* 82 (1974): 905–26. Other studies have questioned Feldstein's conclusions. See, for instance, Henry Aaron and Lawrence W. Thompson, "Social Security and the Economists," in Edward D. Berkowitz, ed., *Social Security After 50: Successes and Failures* (Westport, Conn.: Greenwood, 1987), pp. 79–100.

41. Cited in Charles F. Andrian, *Social Policies in Western Industrial Societies* (Berkeley, Calif.: Institute for International Studies, 1985), p. 204.

42. Marmor, Mashaw, and Harvey, *America's Misunderstood Welfare State*, p. 18.

43. James Midgley, "Society, Social Policy and the Ideology of Reaganism," *Journal of Sociology and Social Welfare* 19 (1992): 13–28.

44. Ibid., p. 25.

45. Ian Gough, *The Political Economy of the Welfare State* (London: Macmillan, 1979)

46. Ramesh Mishra, *The Welfare State in Crisis*; and Ramesh Mishra, *The Welfare State in Capitalist Society* (Hemel Hempstead, England: Harvester Wheatsheaf, 1990).

47. Marmor, Mashaw, and Harvey, *America's Misunderstood Welfare State*, pp. 62–64.

48. Andrian, *Social Policies in Western Industrial Societies*, p. 24.

CHAPTER 18

Reconceptualizing the American Welfare State

This chapter examines the need to restructure the American welfare state so that it can better respond to the changing political, economic, and social forces facing the United States. First, we situate the American welfare state within a broad continuum of welfare states. Second, we examine the crisis faced by the welfare state in terms of today's global economy. Third, we propose five principles necessary for real welfare reform—greater economic productivity, strengthening the family, increased social cohesion, the strengthening of community, and greater social choice. Finally, we present programs designed to make the welfare state more responsive to the real needs of both the working and the nonworking poor and, at the same time, more congruent with the new economic realities of the United States.

Although this chapter includes concrete proposals for restructuring the American welfare state, it does not represent a finished product. Much of the framework presented here is derived from earlier work we have done. Moreover, some of the ideas in this chapter (e.g., the restructuring of AFDC through a work requirement and the establishment of a national service corps) have recently been promoted by President Clinton. As such, the ideas in this chapter are offered not as a "complete" proposal for welfare reform but rather as a useful starting point for a discussion and debate on the future of the American welfare state.

THE AMERICAN WELFARE STATE WITHIN A CONTINUUM

T. H. Marshall argues that social citizenship forms the core idea of a welfare state.[1] As such, the key principles involved in social citizenship must include the granting of social rights (i.e., elevating citizens' rights above the value of the free market), the replacement of class position with the status of citizen, and giving government the authority to arbitrate among the often contradictory needs of the family, the state, and the market. In other words, a true welfare state must mediate between the market and the individual. Moreover, the more developed a welfare state is, the more it will remove the satisfaction of individual needs (i.e., for food, clothing, shelter, education, health, and employment) from the vicissitudes of the marketplace.

Gosta Esping-Andersen argues that workers traditionally depend on cash transactions as the basis for their welfare.[2] But the granting of social rights in a welfare state entails "decommodification," in other words, giving citizens an alternative means of survival to that of the market. Decommodification may refer to the service rendered or to the status of the person. In both instances, it is based on the degree to which the distribution of goods, resources, or opportunities are detached from the mechanisms of the market. Moreover, simply providing welfare benefits does not automatically bring about decommodification unless it significantly releases people from their dependence on the market. Thus, if benefits are stigmatized and meager, only the most desperate will choose to receive them. Esping-Andersen claims that in a highly decommodified welfare state "citizens can freely, and without potential loss of jobs, income, or general welfare, opt out of work under conditions when they, themselves, consider it necessary for reasons of health, family, age, or even educational self-improvement; when, in short, they deem it necessary for participating adequately in the social community."[3] The American welfare state, however, was designed to minimize decommodification and thus to ensure maximum participation in the labor market.

Esping-Andersen classifies modern welfare states according to three categories. The first category, the "liberal" welfare state, is characterized by its major programs being means-tested. The liberal welfare state also includes modest income transfer and modest social insurance programs. Liberal welfare states, such as the United States, Canada, and Australia, serve mainly working-class people who are dependent on the state. The benefits provided are usually sparse, entitlement rules are generally strict, and the means-tested programs are almost always stigmatized. The decommodifying effect of the liberal welfare state is minimal and poverty is usually widespread. Furthermore, the liberal welfare state is characteristic of a society in which social reform has been severely limited by a heavy reliance on the free market to meet individual and familial needs.

Esping-Andersen's second category is the "corporatist" welfare state, embodied by such countries as France, Germany, Austria, and Italy. In this model the liberal preoccupation with free market efficiency and commodification was never dominant, and the granting of social rights came easily. However, status differentials are prominent, and rights are attached to class and status. The emphasis on maintaining status differentials means that the redistributive impact of this welfare state is minimal. Finally, the strong historical connection between these states and the church (often the Roman Catholic church) means that welfare programs are strongly committed to the preservation of traditional family structures. For example, social insurance typically excludes nonworking wives, and family benefits encourage motherhood.[4]

The third and smallest category includes those countries (Sweden, Norway, and, to a lesser degree, Denmark and Finland) in which universalism, decommodification, and social rights are granted to the middle classes. These social democratic countries pursue social policies designed to produce a high level of social equality. In effect, services and benefits are designed to meet the discriminating tastes of the new middle class. Also implicit is a leveling of distinctions, opportunities, and wage differentials among all strata of society. This model promotes a strong sense of solidarity and loyalty to the welfare state because it crowds out the market. In short, everyone is a beneficiary of the welfare state and therefore everyone feels obligated to pay his or her share.

While Esping-Andersen argues that welfare states cluster, he also acknowledges that no single case is pure.[5] Even in the "liberal" welfare state of the United States, Social Security is not purely contributory, because benefits far exceed the contributions paid by most workers. Although Esping-Andersen's categorization is rife with inconsistencies, it nevertheless helps situate the American welfare state within a context, especially when used in conjunction with Titmuss's classical distinction between residual and institutional welfare states.[6] On the other hand, Esping-Andersen does not explain *why* the American welfare state developed as it did.

Several theories have surfaced as to why the American welfare state is less generous than its Western European counterparts. Katzenstein and Cameron both argue that welfare states emerge more readily in small, open economies that are vulnerable to international markets.[7] Their argument is based on the idea that governments are more inclined to regulate class differences when both labor and business are held captive by forces beyond domestic control. Dich argues that early democratic nations, such as the United States, were primarily agrarian and dominated by small property holders who used their influence to reduce rather than raise taxes. In contrast, ruling classes in authoritarian nations were in a better position to impose high taxes on a subjugated population, a precedent that dampened the impact of the higher taxes employed by the subsequent welfare states.[8] Other theorists, including Esping-Andersen, suggest that progressive welfare states emerged in countries where strong working-class movements were able to forge viable political alliances with farmers, something absent in the political history of the United States. Moreover, the dominance of the conservative American Federation of Labor (AFL) in the pre-World War II period was also a major impediment to the development of a progressive welfare state.[9] On the other hand, Christopher Pierson suggests that the American welfare state may not be a laggard. In fact, the U.S. welfare state may be the forerunner of a new and more constricted model of welfare, a direction in which the European welfare states are increasingly moving.[10] Whatever the reasons, the American welfare state was based on fiscal welfare. In other words, instead of developing broad-based and inclusive welfare programs, the government relied on low rates of taxation to subsidize private sector welfare services. As such, American social policy has historically discouraged decommodification in favor of a free market solution.

THE GLOBAL ECONOMY AND THE AMERICAN WELFARE STATE

Welfare states grew steadily during the relatively stable economic period of the 1950s to the early 1970s. By the mid-1970s, however, most industrial economies began to experience high inflation, high rates of unemployment, sluggish economic growth, and unacceptably high levels of taxation. During this difficult period, Western governments were forced to reassess their overall economic strategies, including the resources allocated to welfare activities. Hence, beginning in the early 1970s, most Western governments either cut welfare programs or arrested their growth.[11]

All Western nations are experiencing a crisis rooted in the need to compete in a new global economy.[12] According to conservative policy analysts, national survival in the new economic order can be achieved only if government cuts costs and becomes more efficient. In addition, they argue for the creation of government policies that encourage the accumulation of the capital necessary for investment, industrial modernization, and corporate growth. Conservatives maintain that this precondition for economic survival occurs only when government freezes or lowers personal and corporate tax rates. The subsequent loss of tax revenue, however, often results in heavy governmental debt, cuts in all services (including social services), a deterioration of the infrastructure, and myriad social problems.

The general emphasis on efficiency and profitability also leads to industrial reorganization, which in turn leads to rapidly changing production technologies that displace workers and result in widespread plant closures. These policy changes are exacerbated as cuts in governmental services coincide with the increased demand for social services by victims of the global-based economic changes. Hence, Western industrial nations face a two-pronged assault on the welfare state: (1) the impact of the global economy on government spending, and (2) an increase in the use of social services by workers dislocated by global economic changes.

Most Western industrialized nations pursued liberal social policies after World War II.[13] In the United States, most presidents since Franklin D. Roosevelt tolerated—and in some cases even promoted—a liberal social welfare agenda. Although the general belief in the United States was that people should adjust to the market rather than the other way around, the social consensus also dictated that human capital should be strengthened in order to make people more economically competitive.[14] Thus, social welfare programs were developed to increase human capital in education, employment, health, and housing. The belief was that as human capital increased, the dependent person (or at least his or her children) would eventually compete in a free market. For those who could not compete because of serious deficits (handicaps, old age), a system of social insurance or public assistance was developed to ensure a minimum level of subsistence. Thus, the dual focus of the welfare state was (1) to create programs to increase human capital and (2) to create programs to subsidize people unable to participate in the work force. Even conservative presidents, like Richard Nixon, conceded to this welfare consensus.

A more conservative welfare consensus emerged by the mid-1980s. This new consensus called for: (1) minimal welfare benefits; (2) the abolition of universal social welfare benefits in favor of rigid means-tested programs; (3) a no-growth approach to the welfare state while retaining (albeit curtailed) fundamental programs that affect the elderly and the employed; (4) a retreat from governmental social welfare obligations in the belief that primary welfare functions should revert back to the family; (5) the privatization of social services; (6) a continuation of governmental funding for services combined with contracting out to the private sector the responsibility for delivering those services; and (7) an emphasis on economically rationalizing

social services. In effect, New Right ideologues argued that the liberal welfare state was a failed social experiment.[15]

In order to combat this conservative position it is necessary to develop welfare programs that increase rather than restrict economic productivity. Despite the difficulty in creating such programs, social policies must be developed that address the new economic realities and the shifting consensus around welfare issues. In order to accomplish these aims, new principles must be developed to guide social policy.

FIVE PRINCIPLES FOR WELFARE REFORM

Radical pragmatism provides the philosophical basis for developing a social policy that is relevant to America's postindustrial needs. Such a social policy should focus on five principles: (1) increasing economic productivity, (2) strengthening the family, (3) increasing social cohesion, (4) strengthening the community, and (5) greater social choice. By reconstructing social programs around these values, the American welfare state can be made more congruent both with domestic demands and with international developments.

The American welfare state was predicated on the twin premises of economic growth and low unemployment—a situation that existed until the mid-1970s. However, recent developments in the global economy suggest that the current foundations of the welfare state must undergo significant modification. American goods and corporations no longer dominate the world market. Because U.S. control of the world marketplace can no longer be taken for granted, welfare programs must be designed that reflect the new realities of limited economic growth, fewer chances for upward mobility, and higher levels of unemployment.

Policymakers must start by making a more realistic assessment of the ability of the labor market to produce enough high-paying jobs to move everyone out of poverty. For example, the number of working individuals (ages 22 to 64) who are poor has escalated sharply, increasing more than 60 percent since 1978. Forty-nine percent of all poor people heading families now work for some of the time during the year. This rise in the number of the working poor is attributable to several factors, chief among them being the replacement of high-paying industrial jobs by low-paying service jobs. According to the Joint Economic Committee, about 44 percent of the new jobs created between 1979 and 1985 paid less than $7,400 a year.[16] The dwindling value of the minimum wage is also related to the increase in poverty rates among the working poor. Since 1981 the minimum wage has increased only slightly, whereas the cost of living has increased 27 percent.[17] Another factor contributing to poverty is under- and unemployment. Between 1981 and 1986, 10.8 million workers lost their jobs because of plant shutdowns, layoffs, or other forms of job termination. It is thus clear that the marketplace alone cannot produce the jobs necessary to lift everyone into a secure middle-class life-style. Government must therefore create ongoing income/benefit packages that are flexible and long-term rather than rigid and short-term.

A post–New Deal welfare strategy must also demythologize socially held beliefs about human nature and welfare. For example, many liberals believe that if given a chance all poor people will choose to work. Some liberals also argue that the underclass has the same values as the middle class, except that they are poor. These notions are too simplistic to be a sound basis for social policy. Those in poverty differ as much as nonwelfare populations; some of the poor will eagerly exploit opportunities to raise themselves out of poverty, while others will not. Any welfare initiative that establishes a single policy for *all* poor people will inevitably prove unsuccessful. Therefore, welfare policies must be developed that consider the differences in human nature and, where appropriate, provide positive incentives. In short, a post–New Deal welfare philosophy must incorporate a realistic

assessment of the capacity of the labor market to provide a sufficient number of high-paying jobs and, at the same time, deal in a more sophisticated manner with the idea of human nature. As part of that reexamination, realistic expectations about the welfare state must be developed, as well as valid benchmarks for measuring the success of welfare state programs.

Increasing Economic Productivity

To reestablish the legitimacy of the welfare state it is necessary to demonstrate how social programs can contribute positively to the nation's productivity. In the early decades of the post–World War II period, the federal government grew dramatically, making it a significant player in the national economy. However, government receipts as a percentage of the gross national product have slowed to zero during the past two decades.[18] Continued demands for benefits and services guaranteed through social entitlement programs have outstripped the fiscal capacity of the government to provide them. Thus, government borrows heavily in competition with private corporations. As a result, government social programs are portrayed as stifling private investment and draining the economy of new capital.

Social advocates have recognized that the expansion of social programs requires a robust economy, but they have yet to integrate these programs fully with the nation's economic requirements. After decades of aversion to reciprocal welfare arrangements, social planners must go well beyond workfare in reconstructing social welfare. While the Family Support Act of 1988 broke new ground by including "transitional benefits"—child care, Medicaid, transportation allowances—for a year after a welfare mother gains employment, the question remained as to why poor women should have to be on AFDC in order to obtain benefits that most people in the work force take for granted. Assuring the working poor of basic benefits should be a priority of social welfare policy. For example, the implementation of a "minimum benefit package" to complement the minimum wage would demonstrate how social programs are investments in the nation's productivity. Universalizing benefits such as health care and child care for all those who participate in the labor market is not only justifiable; it also shows middle-income workers that social programs enhance the nation's economic standing.

Although America's high productivity in the 1950s and 1960s allowed it to subsidize a large portion of its work force, this keen technological edge has been reduced, and with it the capacity of the economy to subsidize a large number of nonproductive citizens. To reassert the legitimacy of the welfare state, policymakers must create welfare programs that encourage productivity rather than dependency. Moreover, the resentment of hardworking and financially strapped citizens toward welfare can be overcome only when recipients are seen as contributing to the economy.

Strengthening the Family

The American family is undergoing profound stress as a result of changing economic and social conditions. For example, two incomes are generally necessary to ensure a family middle-class status, yet at the same time, good-quality day care is difficult to find. Fears that their children will fall victim to drug or alcohol abuse or to teenage pregnancy or that they will drop out of school add to the difficulties experienced by many American families. But when vulnerable families turn to social programs, the essential benefits are absent.

Social welfare policy must support the American family rather than tear it apart. Since its inception in the Social Security Act of 1935, AFDC has become a primary means of support for single-parent families.[19] At the same time, some liberals and conservatives alike argue that AFDC contributes to family disintegration. The percentage of unmarried teenage mothers has

risen so rapidly that by 1984 it was triple what it had been 25 years before.[20] Tragically, the relationship between public assistance and family breakup is seen most clearly in minority communities, where single-parent households are the norm and welfare has replaced a wage earner as the source of family income.

In the past, liberals have had difficulty establishing a national family policy because of the conservative fear that it would lead to governmental intrusion in family life.[21] Moreover, problems in the very definition of "family" have plagued liberal attempts to develop a family policy, as evidenced by the political fiasco of President Jimmy Carter's call for a White House Conference on the Family. In a dramatically changing social landscape, an exact configuration of family policy is hard to come by. Richard Louv has provided a useful perspective on this dilemma. For Louv, family policy should seek to support the "web" that keeps families from falling into the safety net of government welfare programs. Some of these family supports would be more generous maternity and sick leave, an increase in high-quality and affordable day care, full medical coverage for all families, an increase in after-school and latchkey programs, and adequate Unemployment Insurance benefits.[22] By carefully enforcing profamily policies in the workplace, the schools, and the community, much can be done for families without relying on onerous welfare programs.[23]

For intact families, basic needs such as shelter can no longer be ignored. Home-ownership is becoming a dim prospect for millions of American families as skyrocketing prices outpace income (see Chapter 14). For poor families unable to purchase or rent a home, the prospect is even bleaker. The Congressional Budget Office reported that 84 percent of low-income renter families in 1988—more than 11 million households—complained of problems of high-cost, substandard, or overcrowded housing.[24] It comes as no surprise, then, that an increasing number of the homeless are not single aberrant men and women but intact families with children. Clearly, basic supports for vulnerable families must be a priority of any social policy.

Increasing Social Cohesion

The interaction between social classes that occurred during the late 1960s has diminished since the ebbing of the civil rights movement and the abolition of the military draft. Moreover, the belief in a collective social entity, in which groups accept their interdependence on each other and on society, has also weakened. In effect, the narcissistic pursuit of self-interest that characterized the Reagan and Bush years has come to symbolize the loss of national direction in a highly material, consumer-driven culture. Secretary of Labor Robert Reich has gone so far as to suggest that technically well trained and affluent professionals are "seceding" from their economic, political, and social obligations to American society.[25] The lack of social integration and the increased separation of the classes clearly contributes to the reemergence of racism as a potent force in American political life.

Any new conception of social policy must expand on the idea of social obligation between social classes to include those who are better off. Upper- and middle-income groups should be encouraged, through economic incentives or appeals to altruism, to fulfill their social obligation toward the less fortunate in ways more meaningful than simply paying taxes. Traditionally, the "progressive" part of progressivism has referred to the expectation that the wealthy would be better able to pay for public services than those less well off (hence the origin of progressive taxation). But leaving the obligation at taxes alone is insufficient, particularly when the rich dodge their responsibility to pay their fair share. Even if the wealthy paid a greater portion of their income in taxes, that would address only the economic disparities in society. Public policy must also reinforce social integration. The civic-mindedness of both the poor and the well-to-do is essential for both democratic govern-

ment and a free society. Recent Congressional approval of a voluntary national service program reflects the concern of many that social obligation is not a responsibility of the poor alone.[26]

Strengthening the Community

The deterioration of America's inner-city communities is obvious even to the casual observer. The decay in physical infrastructures such as schools, roads, housing, and communications is reaching crisis proportions in many American cities. This disintegration in the physical infrastructure corresponds with a decay in the human capital of inner-city communities. High crime rates (involving increasingly younger professional criminals), epidemic rates of drug and alcohol abuse, the proliferation of crack houses, the high incidence of teenage pregnancies, and a dramatic growth in the number of long-term unemployables characterize much of America's urban landscape. These problems have resulted in many inner-city areas becoming a no-man's-land, where even the police are afraid to patrol. Not surprisingly, the communities hit hardest by these problems are the ones with the least resources to combat them.

Many states and cities have attempted to compensate for the absence of federal leadership in community development by establishing their own programs, often with the assistance of nonprofit groups.[27] Unfortunately, these preliminary excursions into community development are inadequately supported because of the social and economic characteristics of many disadvantaged communities. The deterioration of poor communities has been so profound that the term *underclass* is employed with increasing frequency by social commentators. A consensus is also emerging around the realization that efforts to combat chronic unemployment, welfare dependency, family disintegration, and social disorganization will be ineffectual without a comprehensive approach that reinforces community institutions.[28] The restoration of social institutions in poor communities must be a priority of future social policy. Moreover, social policy must incorporate nonprofit voluntary agencies to restore the institutional base of poor communities.

Greater Social Choice

Since World War II, there has been a slow progression in the choices available to welfare recipients in the United States. The GI Bill offered returning veterans a choice of educational providers. Significantly, African Americans used their GI benefits to a greater extent than other groups.[29] Medicaid, enacted during the War on Poverty, provided poor people with access to health care they had previously lacked.[30] By the 1980s, Medicaid recipients were using health services at the same rate as their middle-class counterparts. And Section 8 of the 1974 Housing and Community Development Act offered thousands of poor people the opportunity to escape the ghettos of public housing.[31]

Citing benefits such as cost-effectiveness, social integration, and geographic mobility, the President's Commission on Privatization concluded that ''vouchers are a workable and preferable means of assisting low-income households to obtain housing.''[32] Vouchers have also been advanced as a way of making public education more responsive to the needs of disadvantaged children,[33] with Wisconsin initiating a demonstration program for poor Milwaukee children in 1990. Yet, despite these applications, the promise of vouchers in social services has not been realized, and less than 10 percent of cities and counties have used vouchers for this purpose.[34]

If the nation is to mainstream its poor, it is essential to give them a range of choices similar to those available to better-off citizens. Too often, the poor are given no choice but to rely on a governmental monopoly of services—one that is often characterized by red tape, inferior service, and unresponsiveness to client needs. Any government monopoly of service in a democratic-capitalist society operates on the as-sumption that clients are unable to make wise decisions about their needs. While such paternalism may be warranted in select cases, it is unwarranted when applied to all the poor, many of whom are just as capable of making sound decisions as their fellow middle-income citizens.

Creatively developed, these strategies for promoting productivity, family integration, social cohesion, community intrastructure, and social choice could serve as the basis on which to reorganize the American welfare state. Although some of these ideas may seem conservative—indeed, conservatives have frequently invoked these categories to disavow public policy—there is no reason that they cannot be used to achieve progressive ends. The challenge to welfare advocates is to integrate these values into public policy so that the public itself can appreciate how social programs contribute to the overall well-being of the United States.

RESTRUCTURING THE AMERICAN WELFARE STATE

Full-time work in the United States does not guarantee a family economic security. Thirty percent of the jobs performed by Americans in 1990 were in-person service jobs (i.e., jobs that require little education and training and usually offer low wages and scanty benefits), and their numbers were rapidly growing. As a consequence, more than half the 32.5 million Americans whose incomes fell below the poverty line lived in households with at least one worker. Two-parent families with one full-time worker fell further below the poverty line than any other type of family, including single-parent families on welfare.[35]

Social policy toward families of the working poor has been haphazard at best. Too often, social programs fail to reinforce the integrity of workers and their families. In many states, benefits are denied workers simply because they persist in working, although their wages are so low that they are entitled to public assistance. Until recently, roughly half of all state AFDC programs contributed to family disintegration by, requiring one parent to leave home in order for the children to be eligible for benefits. Under the Family Support Act of 1988, states must provide AFDC grants to two-parent families, but they can limit benefits to six months a year.[36] The idea that social policy could require a parent to move in and out of the home at six-month intervals so that the children can receive necessary income and health benefits does little to advance the notion that social policy is, in some minimal sense, rational.

Productivity, family stability, social cohesion, community strength, and social choice are benchmarks around which future thinking about American social welfare can be organized. In tandem with these principles, we are proposing a "civic welfare state" composed of three main programs: (1) a family conservation program, (2) a community revitalization initiative, and (3) a national service program. These three social programs illustrate how the above five principles just discussed can be used to reconstruct the American welfare state.

A Family Conservation Program

Any social policy initiative that purports to preserve, stabilize, and strengthen the American family must be composed of both preventive and remedial components. The basic axiom for social policy is similar to that for medicine: It is far easier and less costly to *prevent* social dysfunction than to *treat* it. Thus, the preventive component in any family preservation program must establish social conditions that encourage working families to conduct their lives with a minimal use of income maintenance programs. The preventive approach would consist of eight core programs designed to encourage family preservation: (1) the stabilization of Unemployment Insurance (UI); (2) the establishment of a minimum wage that is annually adjusted in proportion to the regional average wage; (3) the cre-

ation of a minimum benefits package; (4) the development of high-quality and affordable day care; (5) the establishment of individual development accounts (IDAs); (6) the creation of progressive individual retirement accounts (IRAs); (7) national health care; and (8) a universal maternal and child health program. The remedial component of a family conservation program would consist of a stable incomes program (SIP), a comprehensive income maintenance program designed to incorporate the principles of reciprocity, productivity, and social choice in a viable and cost-effective income maintenance structure.

Preventive Approaches to Poverty: Firming Up the Income Floor

Any preventive strategy to curb poverty must include the creation of a firm income floor for America's poor working families (i.e., those who are poor but not in immediate need of direct governmental welfare). Creating a firm income floor requires a three-pronged approach: stabilizing the unemployment insurance program, stabilizing family income by establishing a minimum wage that is keyed to the average wage, and establishing a national minimum benefits package. This system of minimum income/benefits security must be complemented by an increase in the availability of quality and affordable day care.

Stabilizing the Unemployment Insurance Program. Secretary of Labor Robert Reich has argued that the global economy is forcing Americans into an increasingly stratified job market, one that is composed of routine production services (traditional production jobs), in-person services (person-to-person service jobs), and symbolic/analytic services (jobs characterized by problem solving, problem identifying, and strategic brokering activities). According to Reich, those in the first two job categories will experience difficult economic times as high-paying manufacturing jobs become scarcer and as the competition for in-person jobs become greater and the wage and benefit levels lower. Workers in the third category, by contrast, may experience greater prosperity. Reich argues that the American economy will be characterized by several economic boats, each one growing more economically independent of the other.[37] If Reich's argument is correct, it only reinforces the urgency of protecting vulnerable economic groups from a capricious global marketplace in which they have little economic influence.

Workers facing job losses brought on by changes in the global economy usually turn first to the government's primary line of defense: the Unemployment Insurance program (UI). Initially designed to cushion the effects of employer layoffs for both individual workers and local economies, the UI program contracted sharply in the 1980s because of changes in federal and state laws.

Low levels of unemployment coverage contribute to high rates of poverty, especially in a recession. Jobless workers without UI benefits, especially the long-term unemployed, are more likely to fall into poverty. However, Byzantine state and federal eligibility guidelines prevent or discourage many jobless workers from using the UI system. The result is that many poor working-class families are sent spiraling into poverty by the loss of one or two paychecks. In order to inhibit this cycle, straightforward eligibility guidelines for UI should be promulgated on a national level. The UI system should also be administered by the federal government in order to ensure uniformity across all states. The compensation for lost income is too important to be left to the whims of individual state legislatures. Moreover, UI benefits should be linked to regional differences in the cost of living.

A Minimum Wage Program. The minimum wage brought a worker to 56 percent of the average wage in 1950. Throughout the 1950s and 1960s, the minimum wage hovered between 44 and 56 percent of the average wage. However, by 1991 it had dropped to 41 percent of the aver-

age wage, bringing a family of three to about 85 percent of the poverty line. This figure compares unfavorably with the 120 percent of the poverty level reached by the minimum wage in 1968.[38]

In order to stabilize the income floor for working families, the minimum wage should be based on a fixed percentage of the average wage. Specifically, a benchmark year could be chosen by which to calibrate present and future minimum wage increases. For instance, since the minimum wage hovered between 44 and 56 percent of the average wage throughout the 1950s and 1960s, we propose that the minimum wage be 50 percent of the average yearly adjusted wage. Moreover, because the average wage differs regionally (supposedly reflecting differences in regional costs of living), the minimum wage should be adjusted to the regional average wage.

This formula would have several benefits. First, a firm income floor would assure all working-class families of a minimum wage that would not fall below a certain percentage of the average wage of their fellow citizens. Second, this formula would help stem the growing disparity between the income brackets. By having a stable income floor adjusted to the average wage, even if working-class Americans did not do better, they would at least not be doing worse in relative terms. Third, the establishment of a stable income floor would also prevent a decrease in wages (at least as a percentage of the average wage) from providing a disincentive for labor market participation. Finally, the creation of an automatically adjusted minimum wage would help still the shrill congressional battles that break out every time there is an attempt to raise the minimum wage.

A Minimum Benefits Package. Any progressive minimum wage legislation must also include a minimum benefits package. Many of the poor currently work without benefits in part-time or seasonal jobs. Various service industries (e.g., convenience stores and fast food franchises) avoid paying benefits to employees by limiting their hours of work. Through a minimum benefits package, employees working 20 hours a week or more would be assured of health care benefits, child day care, and family leave through portable benefits accounts that would follow them from one job to another.

Revenues for the minimum benefits package could be derived from several sources. Current appropriations for workfare under the Family Support Act—$3.5 billion over a five-year period—could establish a fund for the minimum benefits plan, which would be maintained by nominal mandatory contributions from employers and employees. In order to discourage employers from further reducing an employee's hours in order to dodge participation in the program, a "McTax" could be levied against employers who hire workers for less than 20 hours per week. To keep employee and employer payroll tax levels low (so as to avoid interfering with job creation), the minimum benefits fund could be supplemented by eliminating the deduction allowed businesses for meal and entertainment expenses. The Congressional Budget Office calculated that $4 billion in revenues would be lost in 1991 because of deductions for two-martini lunches, greens fees, and Las Vegas junkets.[39]

Day Care. Most mothers work because of financial need, and about 25 percent are the primary wage earners for their children. Many two-parent families also require dual incomes to meet their basic necessities. In 1987, almost 50 percent of all children under age five with mothers in the work force were cared for either in family day care or in organized child care facilities. Despite this large number, the federal government has not been actively involved in setting day care standards, instead leaving this responsibility to the individual states. Even with state regulations (often spotty at best), about 43 percent of all children spend their days in out-of-home child care facilities this are exempt from minimal health and safety standards.[40]

High-quality private day care is unafford-able for most poor working-class families. Moreover, nonpublic institutional child care is also becoming unaffordable for much of the middle class. If the United States is to marshal its productive capacity more effectively, it must ensure that high-quality, affordable, and accessible day care is available for all families. Moreover, if family preservation is a major national goal, then it is critical to ensure that poor working-class families are provided with opportunities to participate fully in the labor force. A minimum wage program and a minimum benefits package must be complemented by universal day care services. Much of the physical and human infrastructure needed to establish a comprehensive day care system can be realized through a community revitalization program, an initiative discussed more fully later in this chapter.

Preventive Approaches to Poverty: Building Economic Security

A viable policy for family preservation requires that policymakers take into account the relationship between strong families and economic security. Economically unstable families are at greater risk for dysfunctional behavior and for becoming welfare recipients. In American society, assets provide the basis for much of the political, social, and economic power enjoyed by the middle class. To ensure that poor working-class Americans enter the economic mainstream, it is necessary to ensure that they possess assets.

Individual Development Accounts. The concept of "stakeholding"—the substitution of assets for income transfers through social policy—has recently entered the social policy debate. Pioneered by Michael Sherraden of Washington University's George Warren Brown School of Social Work, stakeholding is advocated in response to the realization that the distribution of assets is even more skewed than is income, and that the poor can gain directly from benefits that encourage "savings, investment, and asset accumulation rather than income, spending, and income." Accordingly, Sherraden has proposed the creation of individual development accounts (IDAs) to bolster assets for the working poor. IDAs would be designated for specific purposes: housing, postsecondary education, self-employment, and retirement. The federal government would simply match IDA deposits made by people in qualifying low-income families.[41] Through IDAs the federal government could reinforce activities that strengthen families. One such strategy—the Human Investment Policy for Oregon—is now in a planning phase, having been approved by that state's legislature and governor.[42] Since the IDA concept focuses on the essentials of family life for the lowest-wage workers, the fairest way to fund it would be to levy a national sales tax on *nonessential* goods purchased by the more affluent. For example, a 5 percent national sales tax (which would exempt food, housing, and medical care) could have netted more than $52 billion in 1992.[43]

Progressive Individual Retirement Accounts. The IDA concept could also advance retirement security for older Americans. Despite the extensive coverage of Social Security, millions of the nation's elderly remain in poverty. In order to encourage workers to plan ahead for their retirement, younger employees should be given clear incentives to supplement their contributions to Social Security. A viable way to do this is by calibrating individual retirement accounts (IRAs) so that tax deferments granted to poorer workers are greater than those given to the well-off. In 1985, when IRAs were available to all taxpayers according to a regressive formula, more than 15 percent of the tax returns of those individuals who earned less than a $30,000 yearly adjusted gross income contributed to IRAs, with their total IRA contributions exceeding $10 billion.[44]

The working poor underutilize IRAs for several reasons. First, the effective income tax on their wages is relatively low, thereby providing little incentive to use the tax-saving feature of IRAs. Second, many workers believe that Social Security will take care of them when they retire. Third, the working poor have little disposable income and have pressing needs for immediate cash. If progressive IRAs are to have an effect, they will need to provide more attractive incentives for the working poor to invest. Moreover, it must be made clear that Social Security alone is not sufficient to provide a comfortable life-style after retirement. With an aggressive education campaign directed at low-wage workers combined with a more favorable contribution formula, the working poor can be expected to do much more toward planning for their retirement income needs.

The current Social Security program can be enhanced by other relatively minor changes. While an expansion of income security is desirable and should be shared equally among workers, contributions should be assessed by a more progressive method than is currently used. The easiest method to increase Social Security revenues is to remove the present cap on taxable earned income so that the wealthy will contribute their fair share. If the ceiling were lifted so that all income were taxed, more than $18.5 billion would be added to the Social Security coffers.[45] On the other hand, the Social Security payroll tax cannot be increased indefinitely without risking a decline in economic growth or even intergenerational reprisal. Virtually ignored has been the possibility of increasing the supply of workers who contribute to Social Security. This is particularly significant since the ratio of workers to beneficiaries will have plummeted from 5 to 1 in 1960 to 2 to 1 in the year 2040.[46] Unless the supply of workers is dramatically increased, major adjustments will have to be made to maintain current benefit levels, including a doubling of the payroll tax.

A straightforward approach for increasing the supply of workers is to integrate immigration policy with income security policy. Approximately 7 million undocumented workers are currently in the United States, and every year hundreds of thousands enter the country illegally in search of employment.[47] The most recent initiative to address the influx of undocumented workers—the Immigration Reform and Control Act of 1986—offered a one-year window during which persons who had been in the United States since January 1, 1982, could apply for "amnesty." Because only 2 million people took advantage of this provision, the great majority of undocumented workers continue to work illegally without basic wage and workplace protections. Unfortunately, tens of thousands of these workers are contributing to a Social Security program from which they will never collect benefits.[48] Instead of a one-year period during which established workers could apply for legal residency status, immigration policy should incorporate a rolling amnesty date; workers and their families who have been in the United States for five years, say, could apply for legal residency status. In addition, education, health, and social service benefits should be available to qualifying workers to encourage their participation in the labor force. A more humane amnesty provision for undocumented workers would go a long way toward assuring the baby boomers that they will be supported in the manner to which they have become accustomed; and it would also ensure that undocumented workers are not exploited for their contribution to the nation.[49]

Preventive Approaches to Poverty: Health Care

Any meaningful proposal for preserving the American family must include a national health care plan. Despite the massive and uncontrollable infusions of funds, the United States fails to ensure even minimal health care to 37 million citizens. Our deregulated and disorganized method of health care provision is unnecessarily costly, especially when compared to the systems of other industrial nations. The influence of high health care costs on competitiveness was

noted by Lee Iacocca, who in 1989 observed that health care costs added $700 to the price of each Chrysler built in the United States, but only $223 if the same car were built in Canada.[50] While U.S. government-sponsored health care for the poor is being rationed because of government funding rescissions,[51] American health care has come under increasing commercial pressure from large corporate health care providers and insurance companies that continue to profit from skyrocketing health care costs.[52]

National Health Care.   Three options have been suggested for restructuring American health care: (1) a national health insurance plan modeled after Canada's; (2) a national health service similar to that of the United Kingdom; and (3) a mandatory contribution plan through which employers would insure workers not covered under other plans.[53] The best candidate for a U.S. national health program is the first option, drawn from the Canadian national health program.[54] A national health service, such as the Veterans Administration operated by the federal government, is unlikely to respond adequately to market influences and consumer choices, while a mandatory contribution scheme funded by employers simply adds one more piece to an already chaotic and unnecessarily costly *non*system of health care.

A plausible health care program for the United States has been outlined by Harvard University's David Himmelstein and Steffie Woolhandler. Under their "national health program," commercial health care would be gradually phased out in favor of a public insurance system that would cover all health costs for all citizens. Enrollees would be free to choose their provider, yet hospitals and physicians would be limited in the fees they could charge either by a binding fee schedule, a global budget allocated to institutions from which all costs would be paid, or a capitation arrangement. Costs would be negotiated annually between providers and the government, which would be the sole source of payments.[55] The fiscal core of a national health insurance program would be derived from current appropriations for the major governmental health care programs—Medicare, Medicaid, and those of the Veterans Administration.

Much of the costs for extending health care coverage to those now uninsured or subinsured would be obtained from increased efficiencies in program management. For example, a national health insurance program would have saved $29.2 billion in 1983 had it been in place.[56] Supplemental revenues could be derived simply by making the payroll tax allocated for Medicare hospital insurance more progressive. By removing the cap on taxable income, an additional $3.5 billion would have been added to Medicare for 1991.[57] Another financing method to broaden revenue sources might involve a tax on commercial health care providers to create a pool from which care for the publicly insured would be paid. A modest 5 percent tax on occupied rooms in for-profit hospitals, similar to the hotel tax, could defray some of the health care costs for the poor. When health care becomes a commercial activity, it should be taxed as such. Thus, much of the costs for a national health program would be met simply by constructing a system out of the present fragmentation that characterizes health care in the United States. Under a national health insurance plan, private providers would be honored, yet all Americans would be entitled to their choice of providers.

A Universal Maternal and Child Health Program. To make family preservation a primary focus of social policy, a commitment must be made to ensure that all infants receive the best nutritional and health care possible. The absence of a universal maternal and child health program is a national embarrassment whose consequences are predictable. The Women, Infants, and Children Supplemental Food Program (WIC) provides health and nutritional benefits to poor women, but only 40 percent of those who are eligible participate.[58] The social and psychological costs of fetal alcohol syndrome have been brought to public attention by Michael Dorris's award-winning book *The Broken Cord*.[59] Increasingly, delivery room personnel are confronted with infants who were exposed to illegal drugs in utero. The Department of Health and Human Services predicts that 4 million infants and children who have been exposed to cocaine will require billions of dollars of care during the next 10 years.[60] In California, some 72,000 infants are born each year with prenatal exposure to alcohol and illegal drugs.[61] It follows that a universal maternal and child health program is justifiable not only because of concern for the life opportunities of at-risk infants but also because the nation cannot afford to shoulder the costs of care for long-term disabilities. An American maternal and child health program could be created by consolidating the present Maternal and Child Health Care Block Grant, the WIC program, and relevant components of the Medicaid program. Funding to make the program universal, so that all mothers and children are able to participate, could be derived from increased excise taxes on cigarettes and alcohol. The indexing of modest increases in taxes on cigarettes and alcohol in 1991 would have generated $10.1 billion,[62] which could have been earmarked as a special supplement to national health insurance for a universal maternal and child health program.

Taken together, these preventive programs can protect America's most vulnerable workers from those events most likely to make them poor. Ensuring America's working-class families a stable income floor, the prospects of economic mobility, and optimal health care means that the need for governmental income maintenance programs will be reduced. Moreover, these investments in human capital will contribute to a more highly productive labor force better able to compete in a volatile international economy. By improving the productivity of American workers, social welfare programs thus improve the overall economic well-being of American society. Furthermore, greater social equality has the potential to translate into greater social stability. In the absence of such preventive programs, it is only a matter of time before the violence currently erupting in America's poorest communities will spill over, with a fierceness, into the country's more affluent communities. If, as Robert Reich suggests, we are not all in the same economic boat, we certainly all inhabit the same sea.

Combating Poverty: A Stable Incomes Program

The profound economic changes under way will require that many Americans, including many who participate fully in the work force, receive remedial economic help. A stable incomes program (SIP) is intended as a starting point for examining alternatives to the current income maintenance programs.

When people attempt to understand the American welfare system, they are struck by the redundancy of welfare programs, the lack of consistent and integrated social programs, the gaps in coverage, and the often arcane criteria for eligibility. On closer examination, one finds many welfare departments staffed by untrained workers who labor under nearly impossible conditions of low pay, poor supervision, and immense client caseloads. Baffling state and federal manuals that outline eligibility criteria and procedures can occupy a full shelf of office space. It is not surprising, then, that clients often receive different assessments of their eligibility depending on which welfare worker they happen to speak to on a given day. This situation is further complicated by the lack of follow-up and client tracking. At best, most welfare departments have become financial dispensaries rather than purveyors of *social* services. Indeed, the public welfare department has disintegrated to such a point that Alvin Schorr, a longtime supporter of public welfare, admits that "many human service departments cannot manage to answer the telephone, let alone conduct a civilized interview."[63]

The American welfare state is out of control. With multiple, overlapping programs replete with complex eligibility criteria, few people—including many welfare administrators—fully understand the tangle of welfare services. This tangle is understood least of all by clients trying to make their way through an incomprehensible maze of programs. Apart from their complexity, welfare programs include administrative structures that can devour 10 percent or more of the potential benefits earmarked for clients. In that sense, the complexity of the welfare state itself represents a significant expenditure.

Despite this confusion, some social activists continue to believe that the American welfare state embodies a rational approach to rectifying the financial and social distress of clients. On some level, welfare professionals want to believe that the present welfare structure represents a logical and systematic form of organization. However, far from reflecting a well-thought-out and integrated series of social programs, the American welfare state is a patchwork system cobbled together by last-minute negotiations, adroit political maneuvering, and political concessions. Although most welfare programs, when viewed separately, embody good intentions and seem to be well thought out, taken as a whole, the welfare system reflects a jumble of redundant social programs. In that sense, the whole is less than the sum of its parts. It is to this redundancy that we will now turn.

The income maintenance component of the American welfare state is composed of three major programs[64]: AFDC, SSI, and the EITC program. In addition, income supports are folded into other programs such as Food Stamps, the Low-Income Home Energy Assistance Program (LIHEAP), Section 8 housing, and the program for Women, Infants, and Children (WIC), to name a few.

Separating out the EITC program, which is targeted at the working poor, we are left with two programs, AFDC and SSI, that are similar in many respects. For example, both SSI and AFDC mainly serve people who do not fully participate in the labor force. Both programs also benefit the poor: AFDC is targeted at poor families with children; SSI serves the aged, blind, and disabled who are also poor. Likewise, neither of these income maintenance programs require any past history of labor force participation or prior contribution, and both pay low benefits that may in some instances be complemented by Food Stamps, housing assistance, and utility assistance.

AFDC and SSI suffer from important structural problems. For starters, the federal benefits under SSI are so low that 16 states have opted to supplement them. While SSI benefits are standardized nationally and adjusted for inflation, they fail to respect regional cost-of-living differences. In many ways, the AFDC program is even more problematic. With 50 separate state-run programs, AFDC has only limited standardization in terms of service provision and benefits. Because benefits are not standardized, AFDC payments fluctuate widely from state to state, going from a low of $118 per month for a family of three in Alabama to a high of $846 per month for the same family in Alaska. The EITC program is equally problematic. It was enacted in 1975 as a means of providing tax relief to working low-income taxpayers with children, providing relief from Social Security payroll taxes, and improving the incentive to work, yet the average EITC credits are so low that they contribute little to the economic well-being of low- and moderate-income families. Moreover, the EITC program is plagued by the problem of nonfilers.

Given the similarities between AFDC, SSI, and EITC and the problems connected with each, it is difficult to justify the overlapping and expensive duplication of program administration and personnel. Fragmented welfare programs lead to a fragmented welfare state. To rectify the problem of program duplication and inequitable welfare benefits, redundant welfare programs should be integrated into one administrative unit, and geographically sensitive welfare benefits should be developed. Specifically,

to restructure social welfare programs more rationally, AFDC, SSI, and EITC could all be collapsed into one income maintenance program—a stable incomes program (SIP)—which would necessitate only one administrative unit. In addition, all social programs—including Food Stamps, WIC, LIHEAP, and Section 8[65]—should be scoured for their income support features, which could then be incorporated within the SIP structure. In effect, we are calling for a single income maintenance program to replace the tangled web of social programs that currently provide income assistance to the poor.

Restructuring social programs would also require restructuring the delivery of social services. Instead of collecting piecemeal benefits from AFDC, SSI, EITC, Food Stamps, and other programs, each client would receive a single income/benefits package developed with the assistance of a case manager. This income/benefits package would combine market wages with a supplemental cash grant that would bring the working and nonworking poor to a poverty threshold based on the median family income in a target region. This cash grant could be transferred from the IRS to the welfare department in the form of a per capita payment for each recipient, and could be distributed directly to clients or case managers through a quasi-public multiservice agency (MSA). Case managers in the MSAs would determine whether SIP benefits should be awarded in the form of a yearly grant or in monthly installments. The specific details of the SIP program are discussed more fully in the following sections.

Redefining Poverty. By allocating benefits indexed to the median family income in a target region, the SIP program would eliminate the current poverty classification. The official poverty line currently provides a set of income cutoffs adjusted for the size of the household, the number of children, and the age of the household head. The poverty threshold is adjusted yearly using the consumer price index (CPI).

The current poverty line contributes nothing to an understanding of poverty. For one thing, the cost of living differs so dramatically from state to state and between cities and rural areas that a single, national poverty line is rendered almost meaningless. A more accurate, fair, and geographically sensitive measure of poverty would be based on a percentage of the median family income (which is influenced by differences in regional price levels) in a specific geographic area. In other words, the country would be divided into target areas based on metropolitan and rural areas. Within each target area, the poverty line would be based on a percentage of the median family income for that region. Specifically, benefits would be set nationwide to equal 40 percent of the median family income in a regional area. This benefit level would correspond to 1.5 times the minimum wage; or, put another way, it would equal the wages of 1.5 full-time minimum wage earners. A regionally adjusted poverty line would result in SIP benefits for eligible families fluctuating nationally, since they would be keyed to regional rather than national median family incomes.[66]

Because the SIP program would include a mandatory work requirement for *all* recipients judged capable of labor force participation, there would be no incentive to choose welfare over work, thus ending the inherent competition between minimum wage employment and welfare receipt. Looking at benefits on a national level, a welfare family now claiming all its benefits and receiving about $12,000 a year would accrue about the same amount under this formula. However, a single female householder with a four-person family who earns a minimum wage of $4.25 an hour (a yearly salary of $8,160) would now "earn" $12,240 under this formula. Because median family income does not vary widely with the size of the family (most American families have about two children), there will also be no incentive to increase family size in order to gain greater benefits. Finally, eligibility for the SIP program would be capped at 40 percent of the regional median family income. Re-

defining the poverty threshold in this manner would eliminate the need to readjust the poverty line yearly for inflation, and would ensure a fairer and geographically more sensitive measure of poverty. In addition, a work requirement would positively influence the labor supply, thereby increasing the pool of Social Security contributors.

Operationalizing SIP. The organizational auspices for the SIP program would be a community-based multiservice agency (MSA). This agency would be a quasi-governmental entity in the form of a nonprofit agency with a board of directors or a privately held human service collective. Individualized services would be provided by case managers who are human service professionals specially trained in personal finance and domestic problems. Social workers would be logical candidates to provide case management services, since the SIP program would customize benefits to the social economy of eligible individuals. Eligibility for SIP would require that a client's income fall below 40 percent of the regional median family income, with assets limited to $30,000.

Case managers would classify SIP beneficiaries into four employability categories: (1) clients who cannot realistically be expected to participate in the labor force (e.g., the totally disabled); (2) clients who can participate in the labor force within a protected environment (e.g., handicapped or mentally ill clients requiring sheltered workshops); (3) clients who can participate in the labor force on a part-time basis (e.g., mothers with infants); and (4) clients for whom labor force participation on a full-time basis is possible. Clients who cannot participate in the labor force will be required to substantiate their disability by undergoing thorough medical examinations and periodic case reviews. Firm criteria would be established to rate handicaps in terms of percentage of disability. In addition, state welfare departments would monitor clients judged unemployable by the local MSAs through the use of intensive case reviews. Any

MSA found to be consistently classifying employable clients as totally disabled would risk closure.

All SIP clients would work with case managers to develop an individualized plan designed to maximize their welfare benefits, increase their human capital (i.e., through further education or job training), and optimize their personal assets. Clients falling within each of the four employability categories would be provided with a plan to maximize their life opportunities, particularly with reference to IDAs. Totally and partially disabled clients would receive a plan that helped them to maximize welfare and support service benefits. Because employment (either in the private labor market or in a community development agency) would be mandatory for all able-bodied recipients, there would be no incentive to provide lower benefits for those who could not participate in the labor force. In effect, nonemployable people would receive the same benefit levels as those employed in the labor force. Those people for whom limited or full-time labor force participation was possible would have SIP plans that reflected job training and educational opportunities. Full-time workers whose current earnings placed them below the SIP eligibility threshold would be provided with a package that combined labor market income with supplemental welfare funds, thus allowing them to be at 40 percent of the regional median income. Moreover, those in the work force would be provided with plans containing incentives that encouraged deriving a greater share of their income from labor market sources. These plans might include job retraining opportunities, career counseling, or further education. Finally, clients who fully met the objectives of their plan, yet still earned less than 40 percent of the regional median family income, would receive a small supplemental benefit. (A mainstay of SIP would be to reward rather than punish initiative.)

Apart from formulating economic plans, case managers would also be responsible for helping clients to budget their money. In instances where clients were judged incapable of managing their resources, the case manager would function as a broker, dispensing income on a monthly basis. Case managers would also function as a constant point of contact for clients during their participation in the SIP program. Social service referrals and client tracking would be a major responsibility of the case manager. Apart from determining eligibility, case managers would also function as client advocates, ensuring that clients received the full benefits to which they were entitled. In effect, the case manager would be responsible for individual clients from their point of entry into the SIP program until their termination.

Social Service Vouchers. If independent providers are to supply the bulk of human services in postindustrial America, it is essential to devise a mechanism through which social objectives can be achieved while allowing professionals autonomy and clients the freedom to choose the person or agency they deem best suited to help with their problem. The dispensing of social service vouchers is one method for providing a wide range of services to the poor in a manner that is both responsive and cost-effective. Under the SIP program, eligible clients could choose the multiservice agency (MSA) from which to seek services. For those seeking social services, vouchers would be provided that allowed them to choose from a range of service providers who would be reimbursed through the MSA. Service providers from the private sector would be required to meet the standards established by the government for reimbursement purposes. While many of the existing private nonprofit agencies would participate, a voucher system would also open participation to the approximately 20,000 social workers in private practice who could also affiliate with the MSAs.[67]

Each MSA would be responsible for maintaining a client information center, which would update a roster of eligible service providers as well as their performance as evaluated by former clients. Jurisdictions would provide those services now assured through Title XX: home-based care, day care for children, protective and emergency services for adults and children, as well as employment, education, and training services. Because the kinds of services needed by the poor vary widely, an inclusive "service provision inventory" would be developed, similar to those already used in the provision of psychiatric and health care.[68] Reimbursement would be related to the type of care provided, and rates would be negotiated annually between providers and the government.

Because the SIP program and the use of vouchers would effectively make the public welfare department a regulatory agency, a substantial reduction in personnel would occur, and direct service employees of the welfare department would be encouraged to affiliate with MSAs. The most desirable outcome would be the formation of MSAs that are privately held, community-based social service collectives.[69] The funding for social service vouchers could be derived from the $2.7 billion appropriated for Title XX, although states and localities would be free to supplement this for special needs. In applying market principles to the delivery of social services, the use of vouchers can be expected not only to replicate successes in other areas of service delivery, but also to provide low-income beneficiaries the same measure of choice enjoyed by their more affluent compatriots.

Released from their role as providers of direct services, welfare departments would function as financial and administrative conduits, regulators, and evaluators. Specifically, welfare departments would certify individual MSAs and their professional affiliates. The welfare department would subsequently be responsible for regulating, monitoring, and investigating the services provided. This would occur in the same way that state agencies are responsible for monitoring the services provided by group homes for the mentally ill or mentally retarded. For example, welfare departments could make un-announced visits in order to evaluate the progress of individual clients and the quality of services provided. Released from the role of being the funder, provider, and monitor of their own social services, welfare departments would be free to concentrate on ensuring that clients received effective income maintenance and social services. Moreover, welfare departments would shield themselves from charges of encouraging client dependency by helping to ensure that recipients moved in the direction of greater economic independence.

Funding SIP   The initial funding for SIP would come from reallocating funds from AFDC, SSI, EITC, Food Stamps, WIC, and the income support features contained in other social programs. These funds would then be transferred to a specially modified coffer in the Internal Revenue Service. Through the SIP program, these funds would supplement the wages of those in the work force and provide benefits for those outside the labor force.

Specific funding for the SIP program would come from reallocating the $6 billion refunded by EITC, the $18 billion spent on AFDC, the $15 billion spent on SSI, and the $13 billion spent on Food Stamps—a total of $52 billion. The SIP program would also receive additional funds from absorbing the income maintenance features of other social programs, including the WIC program ($2 billion), LIHEAP ($2.3 billion), Section 8 housing, and so forth.[70] Collateral funding for MSAs and case managers would come from reallocating the sizable administrative costs associated with AFDC, SSI, and Food Stamps. For example, administrative costs in 1990 for each AFDC family totaled $776 (a total of $3 billion); for SSI, it was $465 (a total of $1 billion); and for Food Stamps, it was more than $600 per family (a total of $2.5 billion). Taken together, the administrative savings from collapsing these programs would amount to $6.5 billion.[71]

MSAs would be reimbursed on a capitation basis under the SIP program. In other words, they would be given a specific sum for each client enrolled in a particular MSA. Seed money for start-up costs and for administering the MSAs would come from the substantial savings realized by collapsing the administrations of SSI, AFDC, and Food Stamps. Part of this money could then be lent to MSAs at low interest for the purposes of establishing the organization. The loan would then be repaid as part of the capitation formula.

The SIP program would offer several advantages over traditional welfare programs. For one thing, the SIP program would target help directly on clients through intensive case management services. By developing individualized plans, clients would be deterred from becoming totally dependent on welfare programs (as currently happens in most welfare departments) and thus have a better chance of getting their real needs met. Furthermore, since help would be linked to work requirements, the SIP program would encourage rather than discourage labor force participation. Because a work requirement is a key component in the SIP program, there would no longer be a need to peg welfare benefits below the minimum wage so as to discourage a preference for welfare receipt over work. As a consequence, tendencies toward intergenerational welfare dependency would be reduced as recipients accumulated job skills in the public sector and translated them into private sector employment.

The SIP program would also address the administrative confusion caused by redundant welfare structures. A streamlined administrative structure with minimal overlap would result in more money being available for client programs, more cost-effective social programs, and more effective client programming. The SIP program would also decentralize welfare services and thus offer clients greater freedom in choosing their service providers. A standardized welfare program coupled with a geographically sensitive poverty threshold could result in less client migration to states with higher welfare benefits.

Perhaps the most important advantage of the SIP program is that it would reestablish the idea of an interdependent society. By building a more solid income floor under poverty, the poor would have a shorter distance to climb to reach the median wage. As the economic distance between the poor and the middle class was shortened, those in poverty might experience more hope (and thus more motivation) to raise themselves to middle-class levels of economic security.

Community Revitalization

Any serious proposal for welfare reform must address the social deterioration of American communities. During the past two decades there has been a marked slowdown in public investment in the nation's infrastructure, including schools, public buildings, highways, bridges, airports, and public utilities. According to Robert Kuttner, nonmilitary public capital expenditures grew at an average annual rate of 4.1 percent from 1948 to 1969 (greater than the rate of economic growth). However, from 1969 to 1977, those same expenditures grew at a rate of only 1.6 percent; and during the Reagan years, they plummeted to 0.9 percent per year, or less than half the rate of overall growth.[72] This cut in public spending had a differential impact on communities. While affluent communities built new schools, roads, and public utilities during the 1980s, poor inner-city neighborhoods became more desolate as their infrastructures (both physical and human) rotted from a lack of attention and the quality of life in many American communities dropped precipitously. When Claude Brown returned to Harlem 20 years after the publication of his *Manchild in the Promised Land*, he was shocked by the casual viciousness of gang members toward their victims.[73] Daniel Patrick Moynihan observed that "In many if not most of our major cities, we are facing something very like social regression. . . . It is defined by extraordinary levels of self-destructive behavior, interpersonal violence, and social class separation intensive in some groups, extensive in others."[74] The social pathology attributed to economic dislocation was exacerbated by the policies of the Reagan and Bush administrations. Failing to institute a coherent community development policy, these administrations had to rely on economic growth as a vehicle for benefiting lower-income workers; but the trickle-down effect has been mere seepage.

Community Enterprise Zones. A Community Enterprise Zone (CEZ) program should be created to strengthen poor communities. This CEZ would provide technical assistance and time-limited grants for the purpose of generating basic commodities, such as jobs and housing. The geographic basis of a CEZ would be an economic catchment area of from 4,000 to 50,000 people, thereby accommodating both rural and urban environments. Eligibility for community development grants would depend on the social and economic conditions of the catchment area, which are determined by specific socioeconomic indicators such as the incidence of poverty, unemployment, and business closings. Catchment areas would be eligible for benefits when the rates for two of these three indicators exceeded one standard deviation above the national average.

Two types of community aid would be provided. For communities in which the infrastructure had deteriorated substantially, CEZ benefits would consist of technical assistance and development grants. Rather than provide assistance directly, government would contract for services from existing organizations that had established a successful track record in economic development, such as the Enterprise Foundation or the Local Initiatives Support Corporation. For communities experiencing acute dislocation, a system of incentives—including tax credits—would be instituted to retain and promote entrepreneurial activity.

Funding for the CEZ program would be derived from a Community Enterprise Zone Fund created by combining Community Development Block Grants ($3.1 billion for 1991) and Economic Development Administration appropriations ($210 million for 1991), supplemented by nominal limits on mortgage interest deductions and a tax on capital gains from home sales in excess of $125,000 (a figure that totaled $900 million in 1991).[75] The resulting $4.21 billion could be doubled by imposing a modest 1 percent tax on new construction in the United States,[76] yielding a total fund of more than $8 billion. In addition, much of the $1.75 billion allocated in 1990 to the Job Training Partnership Act could be transferred to the CEZ program. In effect, CEZ funding would insure communities against economic dislocation by providing a safety net for all communities in economic distress.

A Community Revitalization Program. During the past decade, a series of community work experience programs administered by the Manpower Demonstration Research Corporation (MDRC) have shown that workfare could prove an effective strategy for reducing welfare costs, depending on the presence of supports for job training and employment. Although initial assessments of the workfare demonstrations were cautious,[77] later studies revealed an unexpected finding: While the most dependent AFDC recipients consumed the most program resources, they also represented the greatest program savings once they were participating in workfare.[78] Studies such as these provided the justification for incorporating workfare in the Family Support Act of 1988. Unfortunately, a serious deficiency in the Family Support Act's workfare component is that aside from supporting job-seeking activity, the legislation says nothing about *which* employment is considered desirable. Charles Moskos argues that "In structuring jobs programs, policymakers have paid insufficient attention to the types of service performed. . . . Only when training programs involve young adults in the delivery of vital services to the community can they hope to inculcate the values that make for good citizenship.''[79]

Incorporating civic content into workfare could be accomplished by connecting the SIP program to a community revitalization program through which public assistance beneficiaries would contribute to the neighborhoods in which they live. Under a community revitalization program, public assistance beneficiaries who were deemed employable, but who were not working or engaged in education/training activities, would be referred by their case manager to a community development agency to which their benefits would be assigned. In order to collect benefits, those on welfare would have to engage in joblike tasks identified by the community development agency. Community development entities would be nonprofit organizations meeting standards of the state department of social services relating to personnel and benefit management, but would otherwise be free to define community development projects and to assign beneficiaries to them.

Instead of developing the dependency associated with public welfare, beneficiaries would be treated like employees of the community development agency. Although still receiving public assistance, they could develop a track record that would be of use in the private labor market. In effect, this benefit assignment strategy addresses a major flaw in the AFDC program. According to William Raspberry, ''You cannot get good at welfare. . . . It does no good for a welfare mother to impress her caseworker with her quick grasp of her sense of responsibility or her willingness to take on an extra task. There is no way for a welfare client to distinguish himself, in any economically useful way, from any other welfare client. There are no promotions on welfare.''[80]

In order to encourage the responsiveness of community development agencies toward beneficiaries, welfare recipients would choose a community development agency in which to enroll. Once enrolled, beneficiaries could transfer to another community development agency—or to other employment—much as employees change jobs in the labor market. Such an arrangement would ensure a measure of social responsibility on the part of welfare beneficiaries in a way that directly benefits the communities in which they live. Moreover, this arrangement would allow the reciprocity goals of the SIP program to be realized, even for the difficult to employ. In effect, those judged employable by their case manager (but not in other job-related programs) would be referred to a community development agency in which they would be required to contribute their labor in exchange for social welfare benefits.

Apart from helping clients to develop positive work attitudes and job skills, community development agencies could also help to rebuild the decaying physical and social infrastructure of poor communities. In this capacity, work teams under the auspices of community agencies could be used to demolish or renovate abandoned buildings (places that are often used as crack houses and gang headquarters) and to rebuild roads, bridges, schools, and other public buildings. In addition, such teams could be used to build new community institutions, including day-care centers, parks, schools, shopping areas, and industrial parks.

Rebuilding a poor community's physical infrastructure must also include rebuilding its *social* infrastructure. As part of their commitment to community revitalization, community development agencies must develop low-cost day-care centers that allow poor families the opportunity to fully participate in the labor force. They must also develop effective preschool and child health and immunization programs. Finally, community development agencies can provide the economic and social leadership that will help communities to compete effectively in a complex economy. This could be done by establishing building-trade cooperatives and personnel agencies and by creating economic incentives that would encourage small and medium-size industries to relocate in inner-city communities. As part of these economic incentives, the community must be able to provide protection from bodily and property crimes to both its inhabitants and the potential industries. This goal could be accomplished by creating local security teams that work in conjunction with the police department to patrol neighborhoods and, where appropriate, to make arrests.

A revitalized community infrastructure can accomplish several goals. Above all, it can lead to a renewed sense of local self-initiative. This goal is particularly important in that a fiscally paralyzed federal government cannot be expected to develop the innovative programs necessary to restore economic and social vibrancy to poor neighborhoods. A revitalized infrastructure may also succeed in attracting back a portion of the black middle class that fled inner-city areas during the past three decades, thus restoring some of the social and economic leadership that has been lost.[81] Finally, vital communities can better capture and exploit the human capital that is wasted by abject poverty, poor education, drug and alcohol abuse, and criminal activities. Recapturing human capital will help not only the poor communities but also the larger society that must effectively marshal its human capital to compete successfully in an expanded economic theater.

Social Intervention Teams.   Public confidence in social programs has diminished in proportion to their inability to deal effectively with people identified as being harmful to themselves or capable of doing harm to others. While the individual consequences of self-destructive behavior are often recognized and subject to legal sanction, the aggregate consequences are not. When the number of individuals harmful to themselves and others proliferates and is concentrated in one community, the result is not simply an arithmetical increase in the number of destructive persons; it also destroys the very competence of the community. The community is no longer able to maintain its essential functions, one of which is to ensure the safety of its residents.

Unavoidably, human service professionals are held responsible by the public when people known to public agencies engage in life-threatening behavior. Two current problems illustrate this: homelessness and child abuse. As a result of deinstitutionalization, thousands of psychiatric patients were discharged from state hospitals in the 1970s and 1980s to often nonexistent community programs. Unable to maintain themselves independently, ex-patients often became homeless street people and are now a prominent part of the urban landscape. The social control issue also contributes to what has become a crisis in the various child protective services (CPS). Douglas Besharov, a social worker and fellow of the American Enterprise Institute, noted that "of the 1,000 children who die under circumstances suggestive of parental maltreatment, between 35 and 50 percent were previously reported to child protective agencies."[82] New York acknowledged that half the deaths in the city due to child abuse and neglect "occurred in families already reported to the public child welfare agency."[83] Larry Brown, author of the American Humane Association's standards for CPS, has observed that "the biggest indictment of [CPS] today is that there are plenty of children in the system whose victimization is not treated appropriately."[84] By 1988, the CPS situation had degenerated to the point where the Supreme Court agreed to determine if state governments were liable for the failure of CPS workers to properly discharge their duties.[85]

A more realistic approach to both these social control issues is simply to consider life-threatening behavior a public safety problem rather than a human service problem. Accordingly, child and adult protective service workers should be reassigned to local police departments, where they would work with police officers in social intervention teams.[86] Social service studies of and field experiments with police street patrols suggest that police/social work teams can be established and that they can effectively manage a wide range of problems that social service departments alone are not prepared to handle.[87] In order to bridge the different orientations to human problems of these two groups, special training programs would be established as part of a national police corps. As part of this program, an undergraduate student aid program could supply public safety departments with officers trained to help communities manage social control problems.[88] Funding for college grants could be derived from targeting Pell grants and consolidating portions of the existing training programs in mental health and social services. Much of the funding for maintaining social intervention teams could come from combining the existing appropriations for police and protective service personnel.

A National Service Program

Postindustrial America has witnessed both the unparalleled success of some of its citizens and a serious deterioration in standard of living for many more. Moreover, many of those who have benefited from the expansion of the service sector have been those very professionals who, despite their pledge to promote the common welfare, have failed to provide services to their fellow citizens. In a development that would have seemed implausible a generation ago, the corporate sector has exploited the rapidly emerging markets in human services such as hospital management, health maintenance, nursing care, and even corrections. These developments speak to the commercialization of compassion and the subordination of goodwill to market forces (the very dynamics that too often generated the need for services in the first place). To the extent that commercialization has dampened the nation's voluntary spirit, it is necessary to bolster America's service ethic.

A National Service Corps.   In 1960, John F. Kennedy sparked the idealism of young Americans by giving them the opportunity to help others through a short-term commitment to living and working in disadvantaged countries. The Peace Corps, and later VISTA, provided many poor communities in the United States and abroad with technical assistance they could not otherwise have afforded, and it provided young people with an exposure to people they would otherwise never have encountered. Recently, six states have followed up on this idea by creating conservation services, the best known being the California Conservation Corps.[89] The popular support these programs enjoy indicate that a range of income groups would participate in a national service program. Indeed, the creation of a national service program figured prominently in the campaign platform of President Bill Clinton.

According to a proposal fielded by Charles Moskos, a national service corps would allow volunteers to elect one-year stints in a nationwide program for which they would be paid $100 per week plus benefits and would, upon completion of their service, be eligible for "generous postservice educational and job training benefits." Enrolling approximately 600,000 youth (excluding those enlisting in the military), a national service corps could make a substantial contribution toward reconstructing distressed communities. Volunteers could engage in such activities as establishing tutorial programs for schoolchildren, helping residents in slums rehabilitate housing, assisting the frail elderly, and organizing child care services, among others. Approximately half the $7 billion budget of the Moskos proposal could be derived from consolidating current job and training programs,[90] with the remainder coming from CEZ appropriations. A promising start for a national service corps was enacted with the National and Community Service Act of 1990, which set aside $56 million in 1991 for demonstration projects in five states.[91]

A national service corps is appealing for several reasons. To start with, it would make available to hard-pressed communities personnel they would not otherwise attract. Significantly, national service would expose affluent volunteers to the circumstances of their less well-off fellow citizens, and it would demonstrate to less advantaged Americans that others are not indifferent to their plight. Perhaps most significantly, a national service corps would perform an essential democratizing function by "increasing the variety of class mixing situations."[92] Moskos noted that "With our tradition of voluntary organizations, coupled with comprehensive national service, we could set our country on an entirely new course of effective yet affordable delivery of human services."[93] In 1993 Congress passed a watered-down version of Moskos's proposal.

Volunteer Tax Credit. The institutional origins of social welfare in the United States are reflected in the myriad nonprofit agencies of the voluntary sector. Organizations such as the Red Cross, Boys' and Girls' Clubs, Boy Scouts and Girl Scouts, the "Ys," and various sectarian agencies have contributed incalculable benefits to American communities. More recent innovations of the voluntary sector have found solutions to a variety of new problems besetting the United States: the first sale of a federally subsidized housing project in Washington, D.C., to its tenants, engineered by Kimi Gray; the construction of a model facility for the homeless in San Diego by Father Joe Carroll; the establishment of a school for inner-city African-American children in Chicago by Marva Collins; the development of a youth development program for delinquency-prone minority adolescents in Philadelphia by Sister Falakah Fattah; and the organization of an international homeownership program for low-income families—Habitat for Humanity—by Millard Fuller. Nonprofit social agencies embody virtues that strike a chord with most Americans: local control, neighborliness, and community well-being.

Yet these organizations are besieged by increased demands for service while governmental support has ebbed. Between 1977 and 1984, government funding of nonprofit social service agencies dropped from 53.5 to 43.9 percent of their revenues.[94] For each of the years from 1982 to 1984, federal aid to nonprofits that pro-

vided nonhealth-related services dropped $26 billion. (Increased efforts at fund-raising in 1985 recouped only one-eighth of that amount).[95] The voluntary sector has traditionally relied on individual and corporate contributions to balance governmental aid, but neither of these sources promises to offset the loss of governmental revenues. Moreover, individual contributions are unlikely to increase substantially because half of all charitable giving to nonprofits comes from families making less than $25,000 per year[96]—families whose incomes have stagnated since the mid-1970s. Furthermore, corporate contributions flagged after the October 1987 stock market crash.[97] Facing a recession after many years of economic expansion, few corporate directors are willing to risk capital reserves to bail out the nonprofit sector.

An important way of revitalizing the voluntary sector would be to give incentives to people to contribute to their local nonprofit social service agencies. The most immediate way to do this would be to restore the deduction allowed for charitable contributions by nonitemizing taxpayers, which was withdrawn by the Tax Reform Act of 1986. However, if voluntary agencies are to fill the void left by government cuts in social expenditures, it will be necessary to raise more revenues than deducted contributions would produce; thus the individual deductions should be changed to a partial tax credit. Furthermore, the relationship between altruistic citizens and nonprofit social service agencies could be strengthened by rewarding those who commited substantial time as volunteers. For all practical purposes, these volunteers become quasi-employees, often assuming a function that cannot be provided by a salaried employee because of inadequate agency funding. Therefore, persons committing more than 30 hours per month to a tax-exempt social service agency should be able to establish volunteer tax credits that would allow them to deduct a portion of the economic equivalent of their volunteering against their tax liability. The amount that this tax expenditure would represent as a loss to the

U.S. Treasury would be negligible compared to the value of investment it would encourage in community institutions.

Nondiscrimination in Service Provision. To the extent that the private sector continues to provide a major portion of human services, it is essential to ensure that people have the right of access to these services. In the past, for-profit health and human service firms have discriminated against people with complex problems who are dependent on government insurance. Instances of preferential selection (when providers skim more treatable, less costly clients for care) and dumping (when indigent clients are capriciously transferred to public facilities without the provision of necessary care) have been documented.[98] Even voluntary sector agencies have been criticized for avoiding multiproblem clients.[99]

Severe penalties should be levied against *all* private sector service providers who discriminate against clients with public sponsorship. This would be a fair price to charge proprietary firms that are profiting from human misfortune. A modest regulation that worked to spread the obligation to serve high-cost clients among all providers could correct market incentives that now tend to disadvantage providers willing to serve a disproportionate number of difficult clients. A nondiscriminatory requirement would also be important for voluntary sector agencies that profess primary concern for community welfare in order to become tax-exempt. In short, nonprofits and for-profits that demonstrate a pattern of discrimination would run the risk of losing their tax-exempt status.

As a related measure, a nondiscriminatory clause should be included in professional licensing standards. The state grants members of professions the exclusive right to practice their particular skills—and thereby to establish a professional monopoly—in exchange for the assurance that service to the community will be a priority in the application of their skills. For some time, the community's welfare has suf-fered as some professionals have used the freedom to practice as a license for personal aggrandizement. Flagrant disregard of the interests of the broader community are no less than a violation of the social contract between a profession and the state. When human service professions cease to function in the interest of society, the state reserves the authority to oblige them to do so as a condition of their exclusive right to practice. Accordingly, if a state licensing authority determines that a human service professional has shown a pattern of discriminatory practice against certain people seeking care, then the provider's license or the agency's mandate to practice should be revoked. Penalties already exist that punish discrimination restricting access to education, housing, and employment; human services should also be included. The public costs of ensuring access to services through the regulation of human service professionals should be borne by providers through increases in licensing fees.

CONCLUSION

The social policy initiatives described in this chapter—stable incomes, community revitalization, and national service—can serve as the basis for reorganizing welfare programs in a manner that is more consistent with the American experience. These strategies recognize the influence of capitalism on the labor force and on the human service professions. These proposals also enhance the altruistic capacity of a voluntary sector that has always played a prominent role in American culture. And these proposals acknowledge the deterioration of families and institutions, particularly in poor communities. However, instead of relying on the federal government for redress, these proposals encourage local communities to seek solutions to their own problems. Whenever possible, the revenues for these policy initiatives should be derived from restructuring existing programs and from reasonable and modest taxes on activities that are related to particular objectives. In some instances, social objectives can be achieved without increased revenues, by simply clarifying the social contract among involved parties. The result is an arrangement that is peculiarly American.

Oddly enough, this arrangement for social welfare policy may also serve as a prototype for social policy in the more established welfare states of Europe. In a provocative analysis, Scott Lash and John Urry have proposed that postmodern "disorganized" capitalism, such as that evident in the postindustrial era, requires a different form of social policy than that characteristic of the fully articulated welfare states of Northern Europe. According to Lash and Urry, the nature of future social welfare will be "less bureaucratized, more decentralized and in cases more privatized . . . as the welfare state of organized capitalism makes way for a much more varied and less centrally organized form of welfare provision in disorganized capitalism."[100] If Lash and Urry are correct, the American welfare state may not be an institutional laggard but, instead, a model for future social welfare policy among the industrial nations.[101]

DISCUSSION QUESTIONS

1. Is the welfare state in harmony with the realities of the changing political, social, and economic forces facing the United States? What is the greatest single problem facing the American welfare state. Why?

2. Where is the U.S. welfare state situated within the international and philosophical continuum of welfare states. Why?

3. Describe several broad goals that the American welfare state must move toward to ensure its future viability. What new philosophical approaches, if any, should policymakers adopt in order to make the welfare state more compatible with the current realities facing the United States?

4. Of the five welfare reform principles proposed by the authors—greater productivity, strengthening of the family, increased social cohesion, community revitalization, and social choice—which, if any, are the most important and why? Are the authors' five welfare reform principles congruent with the values and ethics of professional social work practice? If not, why?

5. Which of the general welfare reform programs proposed by the authors is the most viable and why? Is significant welfare reform feasible? Why?

6. In your opinion, what programs, principles, or policies would constitute *real* welfare reform?

NOTES

1. T. H. Marshall, *Citizenship and Social Class* (Cambridge: Cambridge University Press, 1950).
2. Gosta Esping-Andersen, "The Three Political Economies of the Welfare State," *International Journal of Sociology* 20 (Fall 1990): 93–123.
3. Ibid., p. 107.
4. Ibid.
5. Ibid.
6. See Richard Titmuss, *Commitment to Welfare* (New York Pantheon, 1968).
7. See P. Katzenstein, *Small States in World Markets* (New York: Cornell University Press, 1985); and D. Cameron, "The Expansion of the Public Economy: A Comparative Analysis," *American Political Science Review* 72 (1978): 1243–61.
8. J. Dich, *Den Herskende Klasse* (Copenhagen: Borgen, 1978).
9. Howard Jacob Karger, *Social Workers and Labor Unions* (New York: Greenwood Press, 1988).
10. Christopher Pierson, "The 'Exceptional' United States: First New Nation or Last Welfare State?" *Social Policy and Administration* 23, (November 1990): 15–21

11. Howard Glennester and James Midgley, eds., *The Radical Right and the Welfare State* (London: Wheatsheaf Books, 1991).

12. See Barry Bluestone and Bennett Harrison, *The Deindustrialization of America* (New York: Basic Books, 1982); Samuel Bowles, David Gordon, and Thomas E. Weisskopf, *Beyond the Wasteland* (Garden City, N.Y.: Anchor Press, 1983); Bennett Harrison and Barry Bluestone, *The Great U-Turn* (New York: Basic Books, 1988); Robert Reich, *Tales of a New America* (New York: Times Books, 1987); and Lester C. Thurow, *The Zero-Sum Solution* (New York: Simon and Schuster, 1985).

13. See Charles Atherton, "The Welfare State: Still on Solid Ground," *Social Service Review* 63 (Fall 1989): 167–79; and Joel Blau, "Theories of the Welfare State," *Social Service Review* 63 (March 1989): 226–37.

14. Ibid.

15. Martin Anderson, "Welfare Reform," in Peter Duignan and Alvin Rabushka, eds., *The United States in the 1980s* (Stanford: Hoover Institution, 1980), pp. 145–64; George Gilder, *Wealth and Poverty* (New York: Basic Books, 1981); Lawrence Mead, *Beyond Entitlement* (New York: Free Press, 1986); and Charles Murray, *Losing Ground* (New York: Basic Books, 1984).

16. Michael Harrington, Robert Greenstein, and Eleanor Holmes Norton, *Who Are the Poor?* (Washington, D.C.: Justice for All, 1987).

17. Ibid.

18. J. Kirlin and D. Marshall, "The New Politics of Entrepreneurship," in L. Lynn, ed., *Urban Change and Poverty* (Washington, D.C.: National Academy Press, 1988).

19. Michael Novak, ed., *The New Consensus on Family and Welfare* (Washington, D.C.: American Enterprise Institute, 1987).

20. Lisabeth Schorr, *Within Our Reach* (New York: Anchor Press, 1988).

21. Bridgitte Berger and Peter Berger, *The War Over the Family* (New York: Anchor Press, 1983).

22. Richard Louv, *Childhood's Future* (Boston: Houghton Mifflin, 1990).

23. Ibid.

24. Congressional Budget Office, *Current Housing Problems and Possible Federal Responses* (Washington, D.C.: United States Government Printing Office, 1988).

25. Robert Reich, *The Work of Nations* (New York: Alfred A. Knopf, 1991).

26. See Charles Moskos, *A Call to National Service* (New York: Free Press, 1988); and Timothy Noah, "We Need You: National Service, An Idea Whose Time Has Come," *Washington Monthly*, November 1986, pp. 7–10.

27. David Osborne, *Laboratories of Democracy* (Boston: Harvard Business School Press, 1988).

28. John McKnight, "Do No Harm: Policy Options that Meet Human Needs," *Social Policy* 20 (Summer 1989): 3–10.

29. D. O'Neill, "Voucher Funding of Training Programs: Evidence from the GI Bill," *Journal of Human Resources* 12 (Fall 1977): 46–51.

30. D. Rogers, R. Blendon, and T. Maloney, "Who Needs Medicaid?" *New England Journal of Medicine* 24 (July 1, 1982): 106–115.

31. Committee on Ways and Means, U.S. House of Representatives, *Overview of Entitlement Programs, 1992 Green Book* (Washington, D.C.: U.S. Government Printing Office, 1990).

32. David Linowes, *Privatization: Toward More Effective Government* (Washington, D.C.: United States Government Printing Office, 1988), p. 15.

33. J. Chubb and T. Moe, "Choice *is* a Panacea," *The Brookings Review*, Summer 1990, pp. 4–12.

34. E. Morley, "Patterns in the Use of Alternative Service Delivery Approaches," in *Municipal Year Book* (Washington, D.C.: International City Management Organization, 1989), pp. 23–42.

35. David Ellwood, *Poor Support: Poverty in the American Family* (New York: Basic Books, 1988), p. 99.

36. Committee on Ways and Means, U.S. House of Representatives, *Overview of Entitlement Programs, 1990 Green Book* (Washington, D.C.: U.S. Government Printing Office, 1990), p. 546.

37. Reich, *The Work of Nations.*

38. Isaac Shapiro, *The Minimum Wage and Job Loss* (Washington, D.C.: Center on Budget and Policy Priorities, 1988), p. 13.

39. Congressional Budget Office, *Reducing the Deficit: Spending and Revenue Options* (Washington, D.C: U.S. Government Printing Office, 1990), p. 410.

40. Ibid.

41. See Michael Sherraden, *Stakeholding: A New Direction in Social Policy* (Washington, D.C.:

Progressive Policy Institute, 1990); and Michael Sherraden, *Assets and the Poor* (Armonk, N.Y.: M. E. Sharpe, 1991), p. 16.

42. Congressional Summary, Oregon House of Representatives, "Oregonians Investing in Oregonians," Salem, 1991.

43. Congressional Budget Office, *Reducing the Deficit*, p. 417.

44. U.S. House of Representatives, *1990 Green Book*, p. 821.

45. Figures used are from Congressional Budget Office, *Reducing the Deficit*.

46. Committee on Ways and Means, U.S. House of Representatives, *Background Material and Data on Programs within the Jurisdiction of the Committee on Ways and Means, 1985 Edition* (Washington, D.C.: U.S. Government Printing Office, 1985), p. 261.

47. Sam Fulwood III, "Uncountable Problem at the Border," *Los Angeles Times,* May 17, 1990.

48. Ted Conover, *Coyotes* (New York: Vintage, 1987), p. 207.

49. The need to revise immigration policy to account more adequately for undocumented workers is underlined by two developments: the proliferation of *maquiladora* plants along the U.S.-Mexico border; and the recent interest in a North American trade treaty, among the United States, Canada, and Mexico, in response to the consolidation of the European Economic Community in 1992.

50. Lee Iacocca, "The Competitive Pull to National Health Care," *Los Angeles Times,* April 16, 1989, p. V–5.

51. See Melinda Beck, "Not Enough for All," *Newsweek,* May 14, 1990; and Victor Cohn, "Rationing Our Medical Care," *Washington Post Weekly,* August 13–19, 1990.

52. David Stoesz, "Corporate Health Care and Social Welfare," *Health and Social Work,* Summer 1986; Eli Ginzberg, "For-profit Medicine," *New England Journal of Medicine* 319, no. 12 (September 22, 1988).

53. Alain Enthoven and Richard Kronick, "A Consumer-Choice Health Plan for the 1990s," *New England Journal of Medicine* 320, no. 1 (January 5, 1989).

54. Theodor Marmor and Jerry Mashaw, "Canada's Health Insurance and Ours: The Real Lessons, the Big Choices," *American Prospect* 3 (1990): 18–29.

55. David Himmelstein and Steffie Woolhandler, "A National Health Program for the United States," *New England Journal of Medicine* 320, no. 2 (January 12, 1989).

56. David Himmelstein and Steffie Woolhandler, "Cost without Benefit: Administrative Waste in U.S. Healthcare," *New England Journal of Medicine* 314, no. 7 (February 13, 1986): 442.

57. Congressional Budget Office, *Reducing the Deficit*, p. 399.

58. Dana Hughes, *The Health of America's Children* (Washington, D.C.: Children's Defense Fund, 1987), p. 84.

59. Michael Dorris, *The Broken Cord* (New York: Harper and Row, 1989).

60. Denise Hamilton, "Crack's Children Grow Up," *Los Angeles Times,* August 24, 1990, p. D–7.

61. "Drug-exposed Births Exceed 72,000 a Year," *San Diego Union,* July 14, 1990, p. A–6.

62. Congressional Budget Office, *Reducing the Deficit*, p. 429.

63. Quoted in Howard Jacob Karger and David Stoesz, "Welfare Reform: Maximum Feasible Exaggeration?" *Tikkun,* No. 4 (March/April 1989): 121.

64. We have separated the Social Security program from the means tested public welfare programs for several reasons. First, unlike means-tested public assistance programs, Social Security benefits correspond to individual contributions made to the system. Second, Social Security is a nonstigmatized program. By contrast, SSI and AFDC are highly stigmatized income-maintenance programs that require no contribution or past labor force participation. Although the EITC program requires current labor force participation, its benefits are not based on actual contributions to the system, so that in that sense it is not a social insurance program. Third, despite some theoretical proximity, Social Security is viewed by the public as being as removed from AFDC and SSI as are apples from oranges.

65. Although the Food Stamp program is generally not considered to be an income maintenance program, it does nevertheless provide income support for working and nonworking poor families.

66. While it would be possible to obtain accurate median incomes in most regions of the United

States, we recognize that certain geographical areas will have skewed incomes that will require specific adjustments to be made in the benefit formula.

67. Telephone interview with Donna DeAngeles, National Association of Social Workers, September 27, 1990.

68. The *Diagnostic and Statistical Manual III* (DSM III), used by mental health professionals, and the Diagnosis Related Group system developed by Medicare are prototypes.

69. Privately held, community-based collectives have demonstrated their superiority to governmental and corporate forms of service provision. See David Stoesz, "The Family Life Center," *Social Work* 26 (September 1981): 166–70; Jonathan Rowe, "Up from the Bedside," *American Prospect,* Summer 1990, pp. 10–14.

70. These figures were compiled from U.S. House of Representatives, *1990 Green Book.*

71. Ibid.

72. Robert Kuttner, *The End of Laissez-faire* (New York: Alfred A. Knopf, 1991), p. 275.

73. Claude Brown, *Manchild in the Promised Land* (New York: Macmillan, 1965); Claude Brown, "Manchild in Harlem," *New York Times,* September 16, 1984, p. F–5.

74. Daniel Patrick Moynihan, *Came the Revolution* (San Diego: Harcourt Brace Jovanovich, 1988), p. 291.

75. Congressional Budget Office, *Reducing the Deficit,* pp. 279–81.

76. Computations based on U.S. Bureau of the Census, *Statistical Abstract of the United States, 1990* (Washington, D.C.: U.S. Government Printing Office, 1990), p. 711.

77. For instance, Judith Gueron, "Work for People on Welfare," *Public Welfare,* Winter 1986, pp. 30–41.

78. Daniel Friedlander, *Subgroup Impacts and Performance Indicators for Selected Welfare Employment Programs* (New York: Manpower Demonstration and Research Corporation, 1988).

79. Charles Moskos, *A Call to Civic Service* (New York: Free Press, 1988), p. 90.

80. William Raspberry, "Welfare's Limits," *Washington Post,* April 11, 1988, p. A–15.

81. For a discussion of black flight from inner cities, see William Julius Wilson, *The Truly Disadvantaged* (Chicago: University of Chicago Press, 1987).

82. Douglas Besharov, "Contending with Overblown Expectations," *Public Welfare,* Winter 1987, p. 7.

83. Leroy Pelton, "Resolving the Crisis in Child Welfare," *Public Welfare,* Spring 1988, p. 20.

84. Larry Brown, "Questions and Answers," *Public Welfare,* Winter 1987, p. 21.

85. National Association of Social Workers, "High Court Review Urged on Foster Care Liability," *NASW News,* July 1988, p. 10.

86. Pelton, "Resolving the Crisis," makes this recommendation with regard to child protective services.

87. Harley Treger, *The Police-Social Work Team* (Chicago: Jane Addams School of Social Work, 1975).

88. Progressive Policy Institute, *The Police Corps and Community Policing* (Washington, D.C.: Progressive Policy Institute, 1990).

89. Moskos, *Call to Civic Service.*

90. Ibid., pp. 155–60.

91. U.S. House of Representatives, "National and Community Service Act of 1990," Report 101–893, December 31, 1990.

92. Timothy Noah, "We Need You," p. 38.

93. Moskos, *Call to Civic Service,* p. 154.

94. V. A. Hodgkinson and M. S. Weitzman, *Dimensions of the Independent Sector* (Washington, D.C.: Independent Sector, 1986), pp. 119–20.

95. Ibid., p. 2.

96. Brian O'Connell, *Origins, Dimensions, and Impact of America's Voluntary Spirit* (Washington, D.C.: Independent Sector, 1984), p. 2.

97. C. Skrzycki, "Pace of Giving by U.S. Firms Slowed in 1987," *Washington Post,* January 2, 1988.

98. Stoesz, "Corporate Health Care and Social Welfare."

99. Richard Cloward and Irwin Epstein, "Private Social Welfare's Disengagement from the Poor," in Meyer Zald, ed., *Social Welfare Institutions* (New York: Wiley, 1965).

100. Scott Lash and John Urry, *The End of Organized Capitalism* (Oxford, England: Basil Blackwell, 1987), p. 231.

101. Pierson, "The 'Exceptional' United States."

Glossary

Absolute Poverty. A measurement and classification of poverty that is based on the minimal standard of living (including food, shelter, and clothing) necessary for survival.

Affirmative Action. Programs designed to redress past or present discrimination against minorities (including women) through criteria for employment, promotion, and educational opportunities that give these groups preferential access to such resources or opportunities.

Ageism. Age-based discrimination against elderly persons.

Alleviative Approach to Poverty. Strategies designed to ease the suffering of the poor rather than to eliminate the causes of poverty. Examples include AFDC, SSI, and Food Stamps.

All-Payer System. The imposition of uniform prices on medical services, regardless of the payee.

Almshouse. A historic institution that was used to maintain the poor. Almshouses, or poor houses, as they were sometimes called, were in common use in Great Britain and the United States from the seventeenth through the nineteenth centuries.

Area Poverty. Geographic regions that are economically depressed.

Block Grant. A method of funding social programs by which the federal government makes monies available to states for a wide range of service needs, including social services.

Brown v. Board of Education of Topeka, Kansas. A 1954 landmark U.S. Supreme Court decision ruling that "separate but equal" facilities in education were inherently unequal.

Bureaucratic Disentitlement. The denial of benefits to eligible recipients by agents of public agencies.

Bureaucratic Rationality. The ordering of social affairs by governmental agencies.

Capitalism. An economic system in which most of the production and distribution of goods and services occurs under private auspices.

Capitation. A method of financing services whereby a fixed amount (i.e., the total amount available for care divided by the number of beneficiaries) is payable to the provider. In the health care system, a physician is paid a certain amount to care for a patient over a given period of time. Health care providers do not receive extra payment if costs exceed the amount allocated.

Categorical Grant. A method of funding social services through which the federal government makes available to the states monies that must be spent for very narrowly specified service needs.

Charity Organization Society (COS). A voluntary organization active in the late nineteenth and early twentieth centuries that attempted to coordinate private charities and promote a scientific approach to philanthropy.

Chronic Unemployment. The rate of unemployment attributable to persons who have persistent trouble finding work because of an absence of low-skilled jobs or because they have severe deficiencies in basic social and work skills.

Circuit Breaker Programs. Tax rebate programs designed to relieve the low-income, elderly, or disabled homeowner or renter from the burden of property or utility taxes.

Clinical Entrepreneurs. An interest group within American social welfare that is associated with private practice and the provision of social welfare in the private marketplace.

Commercialization. The consequence of subjecting social welfare to the marketplace, including advertising for services, marketing services, and pricing services.

Commodification. Term describing a governmental policy that takes social needs formerly met in the public sector (e.g., health care, counseling services) and places them within the private market sector.

Commonweal. The general good, or the public welfare.

Comparable Worth. The idea that workers should be paid equally when they do different types of work that require the same level of skill, education, knowledge, training, responsibility, and effort.

Conservatism. An American ideology emphasizing the role of the marketplace and the private sector in meeting both human and social welfare needs.

Corporate Sector. That part of the mixed welfare economy consisting of large, for-profit human service corporations.

Corporate Social Responsibility. The concept that corporations should be held accountable for practices and decisions that adversely affect those communities in which they do business. In addition, corporate social responsibility refers to the responsibility of corporations to promote the general well-being of society.

Cost-of-Living Adjustments (COLAs). Adjustments designed to keep income maintenance and social insurance benefits in line with inflation. COLAs affect Food Stamps, Social Security, and SSI benefits.

Culture of Poverty. Term used by a theoretical school which maintains that poverty is transmitted intergenerationally and that certain of its traits are found in diverse cultures and societies.

Curative Approach to Poverty. An approach designed to rehabilitate the poor through attacking the causes of poverty, for example, illiteracy, poor nutrition, or lack of employment.

Cyclical Unemployment. A type of unemployment attributable to swings in economic performance, such as recessions.

Decommodification. A welfare state which, through generous social programs, allows people to opt out of the labor force without a significant loss of income, jobs, or general welfare. Decommodification can also be used to categorize social programs that take needs formerly met through the marketplace (e.g., health care or personal social services) and turn them into public utilities (i.e., needs met by the public sector).

De Facto Segregation. Racial segregation that is not legally mandated by the state but that characterizes school systems and residential housing patterns.

Deinstitutionalization. Term used to describe the removal, in the late 1960s, of many mentally ill or mentally retarded patients from state institutions and their placement in community settings.

Deliberate Misdiagnosis. The intentional distortion of a diagnosis in order to avoid labeling a client or for the purpose of collecting insurance payments.

Democratic Capitalism. The type of political-economy characteristic of the United States, with a democratic polity and a capitalist economy.

Dependency Ratio. The number of workers required to pay into the Social Security system to support one retired worker living on Social Security.

Diagnostic Related Groups (DRGs). A prospective form of payment for Medicare-incurred charges. Specifically, DRGs are a classification scheme whereby hospitals are reimbursed only for the maximum number of days an illness or surgical procedure is designated to take.

Discouraged Workers. Those who have stopped seeking work out of frustration with their poor employment prospects.

Donaldson v. O'Connor. The court decision ruling that mental patients could not be confined unless they were dangerous to themselves or others, and also that they should not be confined unless they are being treated and cannot survive without hospitalization.

Dual Labor Market. A labor market divided into two classes of workers. See primary labor market and secondary labor market.

Emergency Assistance Funds. Special needs payments that can be made under the AFDC program for extraordinary needs such as homelessness prevention, fuel or utility bills, and burial.

Emergency Assistance Program. A program that operates under AFDC and is intended to provide short-term cash assistance to families in crisis.

Employee Assistance Programs. Social services provided by companies for their employees in recognition that many personal problems are either directly related to, or have impact upon, the workplace.

Entitlements. Governmental resources (cash or in-kind) to which certain groups are entitled, based on their ability to meet the established criteria.

Equal Rights Amendment (ERA). An act which if passed would give women the same rights under the law as men.

Fee for Service. A form of payment in which patients pay doctors and hospitals for each service rendered.

Feminization of Poverty. A social trend marked by the increasing frequency of poverty among women. It is thought to be related to the high incidence of women relying on governmental aid, the low wages that characterize traditional female employment, occupational segregation, and family decomposition (divorce, desertion, or death).

Fill-the-Gap. An AFDC benefit method used by some states in which countable income (i.e., labor market income) does not result in a dollar-for-dollar reduction in the AFDC payment a family receives.

Freedmen's Bureau. An agency set up by the U.S. government after the Civil War to ease the transition of African Americans from slavery to freedom. Formally called the Bureau of Refugees, Freedmen and Abandoned Lands.

Frictional Unemployment. The rate of unemployment, usually about 3 percent, considered inevitable for a viable economy.

Functional Welfare. A social welfare-related concept that holds that social service benefits should be justified in relation to productivity. Usually a standard of conforming conduct is required on the part of recipients in exchange for benefits.

FY (Fiscal Year). A term used by government and social service agencies in reference to a budgetary rather than a normal year. Fiscal years often begin on July 1 rather than January 1.

GDP (Gross Domestic Product). A measure of the total output of goods and services produced by a country's economy.

General Assistance. State or locally run programs designed to provide basic benefits to low-income people who are ineligible for federally funded public assistance programs.

Gentrification. Resettlement of existing low-income neighborhoods by middle- and upper-class homeowners or investors. This development can result in forcing poor and indigenous residents out of their neighborhoods.

Global Budget. Refers to a cap on both private and public health care spending.

GNP (Gross National Product). A measure of the total domestic and foreign output claimed by residents of a country. It is made up of the GDP and of incomes accruing to foreign residents.

Governmental Sector. That part of the mixed welfare economy consisting of social programs administered by government, particularly the federal government.

Great Society. Formerly called the War on Poverty, the Great Society comprehended a series of social welfare programs (including community development, training and employment, health and legal services) enacted between 1963 and 1968 during the administration of President Lyndon Baines Johnson.

Halderman v. Pennhurst. The court decision ruling that institutionalized patients were entitled to treatment in the least restrictive environment.

Health Maintenance Organizations (HMOs). Membership organizations that typically provide comprehensive health care. Members usually pay a regular fee and are thus entitled to free (or minimal-cost) hospital care and physicians' services.

Homework. An economic system of production in common use during the late nineteenth and early twentieth centuries in which workers were paid on a piecework basis for work done at home. This system was frequently used in the garment trades.

Homophobia. The fear of (and subsequent discrimination against) homosexuals on the basis of their sexual preference.

Housing Starts. Number of new houses begun in a given period.

Housing Stock. The number of currently available houses.

Human Capital. Productive investments that are embodied in humans. These include education, training, skills, experience, knowledge, and health. Increases in human capital result from expenditures on education, job training, and medical care.

Human Service Executives. An interest group within American social welfare that is associated with human service corporations and advocates the provision of social welfare through large-scale for-profit programs.

Human Services. A recent concept equivalent to social welfare.

Iatrogenic Diseases. Diseases that are directly caused by medical intervention.

Ideological State Apparatus. The means (i.e., education, the print media, the family, television, and tradition) by which the primary ideology of a society is promulgated and maintained.

Ideology. A set of socially sanctioned assumptions, usually unexamined, explaining how the world works and encompassing a society's general methods for addressing social problems.

Income Distribution. The pattern of how income is distributed among the various socioeconomic classes in a society.

Income Inequality. The unequal distribution of income across socioeconomic classes.

Income Maintenance Programs. Social welfare programs designed to contribute to or supplement the income of an individual or family. These programs are usually means-tested and thus based on need.

Indian Child Welfare Act of 1978. Legislation that restored child-placement decisions to the individual tribes.

Indoor Relief. A historic term used to designate relief services offered in an institutional setting.

In-Kind. Noncash goods or services provided by the government that function as a proxy for cash, for example, Food Stamps, Section 8 housing vouchers, Medicare, and so forth.

Institutional Welfare. A conception of welfare holding that governmental social programs that assure citizens of their basic needs (for food, housing, education, income, employment, and health) are essential to an advanced economy. Such programs are considered a right of citizenship.

Keynesian Economics. An economic school that proposes government intervention in the economy, through such activities as social welfare programs, to stimulate and regulate economic growth.

Liberalism. A primary American ideology that advocates government intervention in the market in order to ensure the provision of basic goods, services, and rights to disenfranchised populations who are otherwise unable to obtain them.

Liberation Theology. A theological school, most often associated with Roman Catholicism, that argues for a stronger connection between religious dogma and social justice. Liberation theology has been especially successful in developing countries in South and Central America and in Africa.

Libertarians. A small but influential group that advocates more individual responsibility and a very limited role for government in social and economic affairs.

Licensed Certified Social Worker. A social worker holding the Master of Social Work degree who has practiced for two years under supervision and who has passed an examination. Twenty-nine states license social workers.

Managed Care. A term for organizing networks of health care providers (e.g., doctors and hospitals) into a system of managed competition.

Managed Competition. A hybrid health care system based on free-market forces and governmental regulation in which health care is organized to encourage competition among health care providers. Specifically, employers and other consumers form large purchasing networks that accept bids for health care from HMOs or other health plans. The competition among health care providers for contracts is intended to foster quality and lower costs.

Market Rationality. The ordering of human affairs by corporate institutions within the marketplace.

Means Test. Income and asset tests designed to determine whether an individual or household meets the economic criteria necessary for receiving governmental cash transfers or in-kind services.

Milford Conference Report. An important report issued in 1923 that addressed professional social work issues.

Milliken v. Brady. A 1974 U.S. Supreme Court decision which ruled that school busing across city-suburban boundaries to achieve integration was not required unless the segregation had resulted from official action.

Mixed Welfare Economy. An economy in which governmental, private nonprofit, and private for-profit providers of social welfare coexist within the same society.

National Association of Social Workers (NASW). The major national organization of professional social workers.

National Health Insurance. Various insurance-based proposals that incorporate comprehensive health coverage for the entire nation.

Neoconservatism. A recent American ideology, based on conservatism, that recognizes the necessity for social welfare but designs social programs so that they are compatible with the requirements of a market economy and traditional values.

Neoliberalism. A recent American ideology, based on liberalism, which assumes that universal social programs, such as those advanced by liberals, are implausible because of current social, political, and economic limitations. Neoliberals opt for more modest changes in social welfare programs.

New Deal. The name given to the massive depression-era social and economic programs initiated under the presidency of Franklin Delano Roosevelt.

NGO. A nongovernmental organization (private or voluntary) that plans, delivers, or funds social services.

Occupational Segregation. The domination of low-wage sectors of the labor market by a minority group. For example, women are thought to be occupationally segregated in "pink-collar" jobs, as secretaries, receptionists, typists, and so forth.

Office of Economic Opportunity (OEO). The federal agency that was charged with the responsibility for designing and implementing the Great Society programs.

Oligopolization. The process through which a small number of organizations effectively control a market.

Omnibus Budget Acts. Inclusive budgets passed by Congress.

Outdoor Relief. A historic term used to designate relief services offered in the home of a client.

Pay-go. A system for determining federal budgetary allocations that emerged out of the 1991 Omnibus Budget Reconciliation Act. In short, funding for any new program (or enhanced funding for an existing program) must come from reallocating existing money.

Per Capita Income. A determination of income based on dividing the total household income by the number of family members.

Permanency Planning. A strategy for helping foster children to live in families that offer continuity of relationships and the opportunity to establish lifetime relationships.

Personal Social Services. A term most often used by the British to denote social services that are delivered on a face-to-face basis (e.g., counseling and rehabilitation services).

Play-or-Pay. A proposed health insurance plan in which employers would either provide their employees with *private* health insurance or be forced to pay into a government pool whose funds would be used to provide health coverage for otherwise noncovered citizens.

Plessy v. Ferguson. The 1896 U.S. Supreme Court decision that formally established the "separate but equal" doctrine in race relations.

Pluralism. The character, climate, or practices of a heterogeneous society in which many competing interest groups help to shape social policies.

Policy Framework. A systematic process for examining a specific policy or a set of policies.

Political Action Committees (PACs). Organizations, usually associated with special interest groups, that divert campaign contributions to candidates running for public office in order to influence their later decisions on public policy.

Political Economy. The blending of economic analysis with practical politics. In effect, political economy views economic activity within a political context.

Political Practice. A method of social work practice by which social workers advance their priorities either by assisting those in political office or by running for office themselves.

Poverty Line. A yearly cash income threshold (based on family size) set by the federal government to determine if an individual or household can be classified as poor. Sometimes called the poverty threshold or poverty index.

Policy Institute. A private organization, funded by contributions and government contracts, that researches social problems and proposes social policies.

Post-Transfer Poor. The individuals or families who remain under the poverty line even after receipt of public assistance.

Preferential Selection. The selection of clients for treatment according to the organizational needs of the provider as opposed to the needs of the client; usually used to describe the practice of private providers who prefer insured clients with less severe problems.

Pre-Transfer Poor. Individuals or households who are under the poverty line *before* receiving public assistance funds.

Preventive Approach to Poverty. Social welfare strategies (e.g., social insurance programs) designed to prevent people from becoming poor.

Preventive Commitment. The institutionalization of persons who do not meet the requirements for involuntary hospitalization but who are likely to deteriorate without inpatient care.

Primary Labor Market. The full-time jobs that provide workers with an adequate salary, a career track, and benefits.

Primary Prevention. Efforts designed to eliminate the causes of social problems.

Private Practice. The provision of clinical services through the marketplace by individual practitioners or small groups of practitioners.

Privatization. The ownership or management of social services by the private sector, either nonprofit agencies or proprietary corporations.

Professional Monopoly. The right to exclusive practice granted an occupational group in exchange for its promise to hold the welfare of the entire community as its ultimate concern.

Progressive Movement. A social movement popular in the United States from the late 1800s to World War I. Progressives stressed the need for morality, ethics, and honesty in all social, political, and economic affairs. This movement advocated numerous progressive reforms. It was also successful in establishing progressive legislation, including the progressive income tax.

Proprietary. A social welfare organization that provides services on a for-profit basis.

Public Choice School. A school of political-economy which suggests that because interest group demands inevitably lead to budget deficits, government should therefore limit concessions to these groups as much as possible.

Public Policy. Policies designed by government that contain a goal, a purpose, and an objective. Public policy may also incorporate a standing plan of action toward a specific goal.

Public Transfer Programs. Programs such as AFDC, SSI, and Social Security, that transfer money from the governmental sector to families or individuals who are either entitled to it or who have earned it.

Quangos. Quasi-governmental organizations that have some affiliation with government but that are predominately private.

Racism. Discrimination against or prejudicial treatment of a racially different group.

Radical Social Work. Adherents believe that the political-economy is incapable of incremental reform and that the system must be challenged through various means to advance social justice.

Rationalization. Measures designed to make an organization or agency as efficient and cost-effective as possible.

Redlining. In the area of housing, the refusal of mortgage or insurance companies to provide services in selected neighborhoods thought to be high-risk areas for defaults or excessive claims.

Reciprocity. The requirement that a specific activity or standard of conduct be demonstrated in order for a client to obtain welfare benefits.

Relative Poverty. A measurement and classification of poverty that is based on and related to the standard of living enjoyed by other members of a society.

Repressive State Apparatus. The set of societal institutions—the police, courts, jails—which intervene to control dissidents when they threaten social stability.

Residual Welfare. A conception of welfare holding that the family and the market are the individual's primary sources of assistance, but that governmental "safety net" programs may provide temporary help.

Secondary Labor Market. Jobs that are characterized by irregular, seasonal, or part-time employment and that pay relatively low hourly wages, provide no benefits, and offer no career track.

Secondary Prevention. Early detection and intervention to keep incipient problems from becoming more debilitating.

Self-Reliance School. A relatively new school of political-economy advocating low-technology and local solutions to social problems.

Settlement Houses. Organizations that began in the late nineteenth century as an attempt to bridge the class differences marking American society. Based on the residence of middle-class volunteers in immigrant neighborhoods, settlement houses emphasized the provision of social services as well as reform activities.

Sexism. Discrimination against women based solely on their gender.

Single-payer System. A centralized system of health care payment in which the government assumes the costs for health services rendered. People choose their doctor and hospital and the government pays the bill according to a fixed-fee schedule. Coverage is often universal and is rights-based rather than employment-based. Canada is the best-known example of a single-payer system.

Single Spigot. Synonymous with a single-payer system in which one governmental authority is responsible for reimbursing health care providers.

Social Darwinism. The application of Charles Darwin's theories on the laws of nature (i.e., the survival of the fittest) to thinking about human society. Two of its main proponents were Herbert Spencer and William Graham Sumner.

Social Gospel Movement. A progressive movement in late nineteenth- and early twentieth-century America that attempted to merge Christianity with a concern for social justice.

Social Insurance. A system that compels individuals to insure themselves against the possibility of indigence. Similar to private insurance, social insurance programs set aside a sum of money that is held in trust by the government to be used in the event of a worker's death, retirement, disability, or unemployment. Individuals are entitled to social insurance benefits on the basis of their previous contributions to the system.

Socialism. A school of political-economy that attributes the need for social welfare to the social problems caused by capitalism. Socialists advocate restructuring the political-economy—in the American case, capitalism—as the most direct way of promoting social welfare.

Social Justice. Connotes equity and fairness in all areas of social, political, and economic life, as well as the provision of basic necessities to all without regard to their participation in the market, an objective of liberals and progressives.

Social Services. Programs designed to increase human capital by ameliorating problems in psychosocial functioning, providing necessary goods and services outside normal market mechanisms, and providing cash supplements for the lack of market income.

Social Stratification. The vertical segmentation of the population according to income, occupation, and status.

Social Wage. A term used to refer to the additional "wage" a worker receives as part of the universal benefits paid out by a welfare state (e.g., health care coverage or housing loans).

Social Welfare Policy. The regulation of the provision of benefits to people who require assistance in meeting their basic life needs, such as for employment, income, food, health care, and relationships.

Sociopolitical Planning. Methods for anticipating program needs that are interactive, involving groups likely to be affected by a program.

Spells of Poverty. Periods of time (often limited) in which individuals or families fall below the poverty line.

Standardization. The reduction of services to a common denominator in order to lower provider costs.

Structural Unemployment. The rate of unemployment attributable to long-lasting and deep maladjustments in the labor market.

Supply-Side Economics. A school of political-economy that proposes reductions in social programs so that tax dollars can be reinvested in the private sector to capitalize economic growth.

Swann v. Charlotte-Mecklenburg Board of Education. A 1971 U.S. Supreme Court ruling that approved court-ordered busing to achieve racial integration in school districts with a history of discrimination.

Tardive Dyskinesia. Permanent damage to the central nervous system, evidenced by involuntary movements, caused by psychotropic medication.

Technomethodological Planning. Methods of anticipating program requirements using data bases from which projections of future program needs can be derived.

Tertiary Prevention. Efforts to limit the effects of a disorder after it has become manifest.

Think Tank. Popular name for a policy institute.

Traditionalism. A social movement that gained increased strength during the 1970s. Traditionalists seek to make social policy conform with their conservative social and religious values.

Traditional Providers. An interest group within American social welfare associated with voluntary nonprofit agencies that promotes local institutions as a preferred method of solving social problems.

Usual, Customary, and Reasonable (UCR). That fee established by a majority of practitioners in a given community for a given procedure. The UCR is defined by insurance companies to determine the proper level of payment for covered procedures.

Underclass. The lowest socioeconomic group in society, characterized by chronic poverty; that is, its members are poor regardless of the economic circumstances in the society at large.

Underemployed. Individuals who are working at jobs in which their skills are far above those required for the position. It may also refer to those who are employed part-time when their desire is to be employed full-time.

Unemployment. The condition of individuals over 16 years of age who are looking for work.

Voluntary Sector. That part of the mixed welfare economy consisting of private, nonprofit agencies.

Vouchers. A system of government-issued coupons that allows lower income consumers to choose freely between various services, often including education, social services, and other benefits.

War on Poverty. See Great Society.

Welfare Bureaucrats. Interest groups within American social welfare associated with governmental social programs that advocate the provision of social welfare through large-scale public social programs.

Welfare Capitalism. An advanced system of social welfare existing in progressive capitalist countries.

Welfare Dependency. The economic dependence of a family or individual on the provision of governmental welfare services, especially cash grants.

Welfare State. The government social programs that assure citizens of basic protection against poverty, sickness, homelessness, unemployment, and malnutrition. The American welfare state has its roots in the Social Security Act of 1935.

Welfare State Exceptionalism. A term often used to characterize the U.S. welfare system and the differences between it and other welfare states, especially those of Western Europe.

Workfare. A system begun in the late 1960s whereby AFDC or AFDC-UP recipients are required either to work or to receive work training (sometimes in the form of higher education). The concept of workfare underlies the welfare reform bill passed in 1988.

Working Poor. Those families or individuals who are in the work force (full- or part-time) but who are still at or below the poverty line.

Worthy Poor. A term sometimes used in reference to groups of people who are poor through no fault of their own—for instance, the handicapped, children, and widows—and are thus thought deserving of charity. Conversely, the unworthy poor are those people who are able-bodied—vagrants, the idle, drunkards—but who refuse to work. This classification formed part of the basis of the English Poor Laws of 1601, and can still be seen in modern social policies.

Wyatt v. Stickney. The court decision requiring states to provide adequate levels of treatment to hospitalized mental patients.

YAVIS Syndrome. The tendency of clinicians to prefer clients who are Young, Attractive, Verbal, Intelligent, and Successful.

Index

Abbott, Edith, 58, 68
Abbott, Grace, 58, 68
Abortion, 114–115
Abramovitz, Mimi, 264, 417
Abramson, Alan, 194
Absolute poverty, 130, 457
Academy of Certified Social
　　Workers (ACSW), 168
Accountable health partnerships
　　(AHPs), 304–305
Accounting practices, 170–172
Acquired immunodeficiency
　　syndrome (AIDS)
　　among intravenous drug users,
　　　326, 328–329, 332
　　effect on health care system,
　　　293–295
　　homophobic attitudes resulting
　　　from, 117
　　impact of, 118
　　voluntary groups assisting
　　　patients with, 4
Act for the Punishment of Sturdy
　　Vagabonds and Beggars
　　(England), 49–50
Addams, Jane, 57, 59, 61, 62,
　　67–68, 112, 339
Adjustable rate mortgages (ARM),
　　362–363
Adolescent Pregnancy Prevention
　　project, 32
Adoption, 345–346
Adoption Assistance and Child
　　Welfare Act of 1980, 343, 345
Adorno, Theodore, 123
Adrian, Charles, 422
Advocacy groups. *See also* Political
　　action committees (PACs)
　　function of, 31–33

as research sources, 46
role in advancing legislation,
　　82–84
Affirmative action
　　explanation of, 104, 457
　　during Reagan administration, 84
　　resistance to, 104
　　social problems addressed by, 7
African Americans
　　available for adoption, 346
　　crime committed by, 331–332
　　discrimination against, 92, 122,
　　　124
　　effect of affirmative action on,
　　　105
　　establishment of associations for,
　　　58–59, 68
　　explanations for poverty of,
　　　146–147
　　housing for, 93–94, 367
　　infant mortality for, 285, 348, 350
　　nineteenth-century studies of
　　　urban, 58
　　out-of-wedlock children born to
　　　adolescent, 348, 350–351
　　poverty of, 93–94, 97, 133–136,
　　　402
　　profile of, 92–98
　　socioeconomic status of, 92–94
　　transition from slavery to freedom
　　　for, 52
　　urban exodus of middle-income,
　　　402
　　voter registration of, 89
　　as welfare bureaucrats, 25
　　WIC participation and, 382
AFSCME, 160–161
Age Discrimination in Employment
　　Act (ADEA) of 1967, 119

Ageism, 118–120, 457
Agriculture. *See* Farming
AIDS. *See* Acquired immuno-
　　deficiency syndrome (AIDS)
Aid to Dependent Children (ADC),
　　260, 340. *See also* Aid to
　　Families with Dependent
　　Children (AFDC)
Aid to Families with Dependent
　　Children (AFDC)
　　African Americans receiving, 98
　　assumptions regarding, 252–253,
　　　253–257
　　benefits from, 266–273, 344, 350,
　　　399
　　during Bush administration, 67,
　　　264
　　description of, 251–252, 431
　　eligibility criteria for, 252, 420,
　　　434
　　fair market rent and, 365–367
　　recipient privacy issues and, 273
　　reciprocity incorporated into, 26
　　reform proposals affecting,
　　　264–266, 271, 273
　　social welfare policy and, 4–5, 88
　　structural problems with, 440–441
　　welfare reform and history of,
　　　260–261, 263
　　workfare and, 400–402
Aid to Families With Dependent
　　Children-Unemployed Parent
　　(AFDC-UP), 260, 263, 274,
　　283. *See also* Aid to Families
　　with Dependent Children
　　(AFDC)
Aid to the Blind (AB), 257
Aid to the Permanently and Totally
　　Disabled (APTD), 257

465